worked with Wallace and me as informants, and of their hope that this book would provide their children and grand-children with a true and accurate record of the old-time ways. More fervently even than in 1952, I hope that this function is being fulfilled.

E. ADAMSON HOEBEL

The Comanches
Lords of the South Plains

The Civilization of the American Indian Series

THE Comanches
Lords of the South Plains

by ERNEST WALLACE &

E. ADAMSON HOEBEL

UNIVERSITY OF OKLAHOMA PRESS

NORMAN AND LONDON

To Sue Ellen Barton

and Ralph Linton

Library of Congress Catalog Card Number: 52–11087
International Standard Book Number: 0–8061–2040–1

The Comanches: Lords of the South Plains is Volume 34 in *The Civilization of the American Indian Series.*

12   13   14   15   16   17   18   19   20   21   22   23   24   25   26   27   28

Preface to the Ninth Printing

THREE and a half decades ago, when *The Comanches* was first published, Professor Wallace and I stated our purpose as follows: "to present in a single piece the salient facts of Comanche history and culture in a way that will satisfy the interests and curiosity of the general reader and also the anthropologist and historian." That the book has continued to be reprinted is gratifying evidence that this intent apparently has been, at least in part, achieved. Ernest Wallace, now deceased, would, I know, share my satisfaction that our work still continues to be used.

The idea for *The Comanches* was born in the creative mind of Savoie Lottinville, then director of the University of Oklahoma Press. He approached me in the early 1950's about collaborating with Ernest Wallace, who was already working on a history of the Comanche tribe. Because my first fieldwork and subsequent Columbia University dissertation concerned Comanche tribal law and government, Mr. Lottinville asked me to provide the anthropological content. Although I was then studying the law-ways of the Rio Grande Pueblos, I was happy to return to the Comanches, and the coauthorship was arranged. It was a congenial and productive arrangement. The project moved smoothly to completion with virtually no problems of organization, content, or style. And yet, we two authors never met! Nor did we even have a telephone conversation. All was accomplished through correspondence. (Those were different days, indeed!)

I greatly regret not having had in-person knowledge of Ernest Wallace. My feeling of comradeship and appreciation for his part in our joint undertaking is very much alive, and I can freely state that without him the book would not have been written.

Many changes have occurred among the Comanches since 1952.

To begin with, they are steadily increasing in numbers. In 1933 when, as part of the Santa Fe Laboratory of Anthropology Field Research Party, I first met the tribe, there were 2,200 registered Comanches. Today there are an estimated 6,500. Only about half of these live in the vicinity of their one-time reservation, while some 500, or more, have moved into the Greater Los Angeles Area in search of new opportunities. The Comanche spirit of nomadism and long-noted adaptability remain strong.

Within the heartland of the old reservation, the remaining Comanches, however, are still settled for the most part in their former band neighborhoods. Descendants of the Honey-eaters (Wasp) still live south of Lawton, Oklahoma. They have intermarried widely with American and Spanish-American neighbors, and they constitute the more progressive, liberal, and assimilated Comanches. The Yap-eater, Antelope and Meat-eater bands live more to the west of Lawton. They identify the southerners as *honitaiβo,* "corn (eating) whitemen." The northerners, among whom peyotism is strong, are more conservative and traditionalist than the southerners, who are more committed to Christianity and "white ways," including intermarriage. Finally, the northern bands have adapted themselves to the Comanche-Kiowa-Apache administrative identity established by the Bureau of Indian Affairs early in this century. It was the southerners who pushed for the establishment of a separate Comanche tribal constitution and the northerners who resisted it. However, in 1966 a tribal constitution and by-laws establishing an elected Business Committee of seven members were adopted, and an annual tribal meeting, with a quorum of 250, is held at the Fort Sill Indian School, Lawton, Oklahoma, on the third Saturday of each April.

In 1957, Quanah Parker and his mother, Cynthia Ann, were reburied with military honors in the cemetery at Fort Sill, the Mennonite Mission and cemetery in which they were previously interred having been absorbed into the Fort Sill Military Reservation in order to provide more room for the testing of ground missiles. Thus, as the Atomic Age impinges upon the Comanches along with the rest of us, I think of the fine Comanche friends who

Preface to the First Printing

THE Comanches were one of the great tribes of the American West. For a century and a half they successfully defended the High Plains and prairie country south of the Arkansas River against all intruders, both red and white. Their superb nomadic horsemanship, their dauntless military prowess, enabled them to guard well the vast, semiarid land they had won and claimed as their own. They made life unsafe for their enemies who dared to live near the periphery of the Comanchería.

Throughout the Southwest their name has become a synonym for wildness, fierceness, and savagery. They stopped the Spanish expansion from south and west. They blocked French plans for trade and held up the Anglo-American advance for half a century. The effect of the Comanche conflict upon the life and history of the Southwest was significant and dramatic.

Yet, for a variety of reasons, the story of the Comanches and their way of life has remained unwritten. No attempt at a comprehensive anthropological study of this people was made until they were visited by the 1933 Ethnological Field Study Group of the Santa Fé Laboratory of Anthropology. Subsequently, they were further studied by Miss Jeannette Mirsky in 1935 and again in 1940 by a group of linguistic specialists from the Department of Anthropology under the direction of Professor George Herzog.

In the notes and records of nineteenth-century military men, government agents, travelers and captive whites are many scattered pieces of information on the Comanches, yet they have not been previously drawn together.

Professor R. N. Richardson has published an excellent account of the historical relations of the Comanches in their conflicts with the whites throughout the nineteenth century in his book, *The Comanche*

Barrier to South Plains Settlement. His work, however, makes no serious attempt to describe and analyze their society and culture or to tell their whole story.

Anthropologists have written a few limited and specialized accounts of several aspects of the Comanche way of life, but no more than the historian have they attempted to round out the picture.

The writing of this book was undertaken to present in a single piece the salient facts of Comanche history and culture in a way that will satisfy the interests and curiosity of the general reader and also the anthropologist and the historian. This means that although we have endeavored to hold fast to the highest canons of historical and scientific accuracy, we definitely have not undertaken to write an ethnographic monograph. We have striven to give meaning to the story of the Comanches, but we have avoided inclusion of the kind of technical discussion that interests only the professional social scientist. Such considerations are best left for presentation in the professional journals.

Our sources, as will become evident in the reading of this book, exist in direct field work among the Comanches on the part of both authors, in published and unpublished data recorded by other scientific investigators, and in published and unpublished historical documents.

Ernest Wallace did most of the archival research and in the summer of 1945 interviewed a number of Comanches. E. Adamson Hoebel did field work among the Comanches as a member of The Santa Fé Laboratory of Anthropology party in 1933. Professor Ralph Linton of Yale University, as director of the Santa Fé Laboratory project, has given us generous permission to draw on all the field notes of this expedition. They contain much information on the Comanches that has been hitherto unpublished. Professor Linton's keen insight in Comanche culture has furnished us with many valuable leads that have made our work much easier and greatly enhanced its significance.

Although in earlier days the Comanches were thought to be recalcitrant and unfriendly to whites, we have enjoyed nothing but happy relations with them. They are good friends and co-operative collaborators. They evinced a strong sense of the historical values of our studies. It was their urgent desire that the record of their story and their ways should be true and adequate. They want their children and grandchildren to be able to read this book when they are gone. The memories of the old ways are to survive in print.

The chief informants used by Mr. Wallace were Wiley Yellow-fish, *Paƙawa* (Kills Something), John *Padoponi* (See How Deep the Water Is), *Pohawe* (Medicine Woman), and *Tawaƙa*. When these Comanches are cited, it means that the data in question were recorded from them by him in the summer of 1945.

The chief informants used by the Santa Fé Laboratory of Anthropology group were Post Oak Jim, *Nayia* (Slope), *Tasuɾa* (That's It), *Quasia* (Eagle Tail Feather), *Tɛnəβ3ƙə* (Gets to Be a Middle-aged Man), Frank *Chiƙoβa* (Breaks Something), *N3m3ɾuiβɛtsə* (She Invites Her Relatives), *H3ƙiyani* (Carrying Her Sunshade), George *Kɔwino,* and Howard White Wolf. When these Comanches are cited, it means that the data were recorded from them by Mr. Hoebel or by other members of the Laboratory of Anthropology group in 1933.

The Reverend Robert Chaat served as interpreter and informant for Mr. Wallace in his work. Mr. Herman *Asenap* (Greyfoot) and Mr. Norton *Teƙwitchi* (Skinny and Wrinkled) were the indispensable interpreters and go-betweens for the Laboratory field party.

We are also indebted to many other persons who aided one or the other of the authors in their work. Among these are Professors Walter Prescott Webb and J. G. McAllister of the University of Texas, Mr. Martin Taylor and Mr. Max Penrod, educators to the Comanches, Professor R. N. Richardson of Hardin-Simmons University, Mr. and Mrs. W. C. Holden, Mr. O. A. Kinchen, and Mrs. Ida Vernon of Texas Technological College, and Mrs. Ernesteen Barton. A fond salute is given to the members of the Santa Fé Laboratory of Anthropology Comanche field party: Gustav G. Carlson, J. Nixon Hadley, Claiborne Lockett, Waldo R. Wedel, and F. Gore Hoebel (an ex-officio member). Mr. Joseph Casagrande generously made the manuscript of his unpublished dissertation on "Linguistic Accommodation to Acculturation in Comanche" available to us.

Illustrations and materials to be used in illustration for this book were kindly provided by the Bureau of American Ethnology, the United States National Museum, the Denver Art Museum, the University of Texas Anthropological Museum, and Texas Technological

College. Their aid has done much toward making this book more valuable and attractive.

Without the direct aid in subvention of research by the Allocations Committee of Texas Technological College and the Santa Fé Laboratory of Anthropology, it is unlikely that this book could ever have been written.

Like any married authors who are members of university faculties we have been sustained, aided, and abetted by our knowing and indispensable wives.

To all these—our sincere thanks!

ERNEST WALLACE
E. ADAMSON HOEBEL

Contents

Illustrations

Linguistic Note

IN THIS BOOK the alphabet of the International Phonetics System has been utilized for Comanche words and names. This method may, at the outset, present a minor difficulty for the person not trained in reading the symbols conventionally used in the system. However, we feel certain that all readers will appreciate the more accurate pronunciation of Comanche that can be conveyed through a scientific linguistic system.

Conventional vowel symbols are pronounced in the continental manner (i.e., *a* = *ah, e* = *ay, i* = *ee, o* = *oh, u* = *u,* as in *you*). Variant Comanche vowels are written and pronounced in the following wise:

ɔ = *aw,* ɜ = *e,* as in *er* (pronounced very broad, without sounding the *r*), ɛ = *eh,* as in g*e*t, ə = *uh,* as in *a*lone, ʌ = *u,* as in sh*u*t. A colon (:) after a vowel signifies that it is prolonged and drawn out. A single quotation mark (') represents a glottal stop.

All Comanche consonants are written and pronounced as in everyday English, except the following:

β = the bilabial fricative, i.e., like a *v* except that the lips are held closed together instead of putting the upper teeth over the lower lip. (Try it!)

ɾ = a "flapped" *r,* one in which the tongue is first placed against the roof of the mouth and quickly let drop while forming an *r*.

t̪ = a dental *t,* formed by placing the tongue against the upper teeth instead of the fore-palate.

The Comanches

Lords of the South Plains

I
Comanchería

ON a sultry summer day in June, 1875, a small band of starving Comanche Indians straggled in to Fort Sill, near the Wichita Mountains in what is now the southwestern part of the state of Oklahoma. There they surrendered to the military authorities.

So ended the reign of the Comanches on the Southwestern frontier. Their horses had been captured and destroyed; the buffalo were gone; most of their tipis had been burned. They had held out to the end, but the end was now upon them. They had come in to submit.

For a good 150 years, since first they had come down from the north, at first alone and later with the aid of their Kiowa allies, the Comanches had been the lords of the Southern Plains. They had decimated the pueblo of Pecos, within thirty miles of Santa Fé, New Mexico, so that in 1838 a pitiful surviving handful of this once-great pueblo abandoned it entirely. The Spanish frontier settlements of New Mexico had long been happy enough to let raiding Comanches pass without hindrance to carry their terrorizing forays into Old Mexico, a thousand miles down to Durango. They had fought the Texans, made off with their cattle, burned their homes, and effectively made their own lands unsafe for the white intruder. They had joyously fought and whipped at one time and another the Utes, Pawnees, Osages, Tonkawas, Apaches, and Navahos.

These were the "Spartans of the Prairies," of whom Thomas J. Farnham had written seven decades before, "their incomparable horsemanship, their terrible charge, the unequalled rapidity with which they load and discharge their fire-arms, and their insatiable hatred make the enmity of these Indians more dreadful than that of any other tribe of aborigines."[1]

These are the people of whom this book is written.

To themselves the Comanches are "The People." They call themselves *nɜmɜnə*, from the root *nɜm*, meaning "human beings." It is not that they failed to recognize other peoples as human, too (they had no racist dogmas), but other tribes were less than Comanches, and *they* were "The People."

The English language had no word for them originally, of course. Nor did the Spanish. But the Spaniards of New Mexico enjoyed first contact with the Comanches and gave the tribe the name by which they were later to be known by Spaniard and American alike.

Early French explorers and the few Americans who penetrated the Great Plains early in the eighteenth century knew the Comanches under their Siouan name, Padouca. But Lewis and Clark, in 1804, knew them only by hearsay and older records. They mentioned the great Padouca nation, "who occupied the country between the upper parts of the river Platte and the river Kanzas," and who "were visited by Bourgemont, in 1724, and then lived on the Kanzas river. The seats, which he describes as their residence, are now occupied by the Kanzas nation; and of the Padoucas there does not now exist even the name."[2] The Padouca had dropped out of existence for the Americans until they were met again as Comanches far to the south a generation later.

It was the Spaniard who taught us to know the Comanches as Comanches. For many years the meaning of the new tribal name was obscure; for it had no roots in the Spanish tongue. Then, nine years ago, Marvin K. Opler unlocked the door to the mystery with a simple key. "Comanche" means "enemy"—not in Spanish but in Ute. In Ute, the word is more exactly rendered *Komántcia,* which in a fuller sense means "anyone who wants to fight me all the time." Generically the Utes applied this term to the Comanches, Arapahos, Cheyennes,

[1] J. T. Farnham, *Travels in the Great Western Prairies (1839)* (vol. XXVIII of R. G. Thwaites [ed.], *Early Western Travels*), I, 149.

[2] M. Lewis and W. Clark, *A History of the Expedition of Captains Lewis and Clark,* I, 36–37.

and Kiowas—all of whom they fought. After 1726, however, the Comanches became the special enemies of the Utes, who fixed the word *Komántcia* on them. The Spaniards picked up the word from the Utes, and the Americans from the Spaniards.[3]

In the sign language of the plains, the Comanches are known as the Snakes. The term is still in general use by older members of the tribe. The gesture is made by placing the right hand palm downward, with forearm across the front of the body, and moving it to the right with a wiggling motion. There are two known oral traditions purporting to explain the origin of this term. One, as reported by Quanah Parker, the last Comanche war chief to surrender to the Americans, attributes it to a band of Comanches who were migrating across the mountains to the northwest in search of better hunting grounds. After several days' journey a number of the people became dissatisfied, principally because of the colder climate. The leader called a council to calm their fear, but a part of the group could not be persuaded. In a fit of anger the leader compared his followers to a snake backing up in its tracks. From that day the universal sign language for Comanche has been "snake going backwards."[4]

The other version relates that when a wolf howled in front of a band of Comanches traveling south, part of the group considered it a warning to go no farther. They turned back. The rest selected a new leader and continued their southward migration. Afterwards the southern group referred to those who turned back as "Snakes," the term soon being broadened to include all who remained in the northland, Utes and Shoshones alike.[5]

[3] Equivalent spellings, frequently occurring in earlier literature, are *Comantz, Camanche, Cammanche,* and *Commanche.* For additional information pertaining to Comanche names, see M. K. Opler, "The Origin of Comanche and Ute," *American Anthropologist,* Vol. XLV (1943), 155–58; James Mooney, "The Ghost Dance Religion and the Sioux Outbreak of 1890," Bureau of American Ethnology (hereafter cited as B. A. E.) *Fourteenth Annual Report,* Part II, 1043; Robert S. Neighbors, "The Naüni or Comanches of Texas," in Henry R. Schoolcraft (ed.), *Information Respecting the History, Conditions, and Prospects of the Indian Tribes of the United States,* II, 126; J. Lee Humfreville, *Twenty Years among Our Hostile Indians,* 174; F. W. Hodge (ed.), *Handbook of American Indians North of Mexico,* B. A. E. *Bulletin No. 30* (hereafter cited as Hodge, *Handbook*), Part I, 327, 594.

[4] Dick Banks to Bessie L. Thomas (investigator), March 29, 1938, Indian–Pioneer Papers (MS collection, University of Oklahoma Library), Vol. V, 61–62. Banks lived for a year with Chief Quanah Parker.

[5] R. B. Thomas, "Kiowa-Comanche Experiences," Indian–Pioneer Papers (MS collection, University of Oklahoma Library), Vol. CX, 155.

The Comanches were relatively late arrivals in the South Plains. It has been suggested that they were encountered by Coronado and that previously they had made inroads on the Pueblo Indians of New Mexico, but the evidence is thin.[6] When first definitely identified by the whites, they were so closely associated with the Shoshones culturally and linguistically that it was impossible to distinguish between the two. At that time the "Shoshones" covered a vast area, including most of Wyoming, the entire central and southern parts of Idaho except for a portion occupied by the Bannock, northeastern Nevada, a small strip of Utah west of Great Salt Lake, the headwaters of the Snake and Green rivers, the upper Platte down to the vicinity of the junction of the North and South forks, part of western Kansas, and the Missouri River from the headwaters eastward for some distance. Lewis and Clark in 1805 found bands of Shoshones on the headwaters of the Missouri in what is now western Montana. They had been driven from their eastern home along the Missouri by the hostile Atsinas and Siksikas, who had by that time obtained firearms from traders to the east.[7]

The language and culture of the Comanches point directly to a Shoshonean origin for the tribe. History also substantiates an origin in Shoshone country. According to Crow tradition, the Comanches once inhabited the Snake River region. Omaha tradition places them on the Middle Loup River probably until the beginning of the nineteenth century.[8] By 1700, a noticeable shift toward the south had begun to take place. La Sever's map (1701) places the Comanches near the headwaters of the Arkansas, principally on the north side, at about its closest point to the *Grande Rivière Cansez* (Kansas River).[9] Étienne Veniard de Bourgemond in 1724 found Comanche villages on the upper Kansas River along the route that later became the Santa Fé

[6] G. P. Winship, "The Coronado Expedition," B. A. E. *Fourteenth Annual Report*, Part I, 523–24; J. P. Harrington, "The Ethnogeography of the Tewa Indians," B. A. E. *Twenty-ninth Annual Report*, 477–78.

[7] Thomas Jefferson, *Message from the President of the United States Communicating Discoveries Made in Exploring the Missouri, Red River and Washita by Captains Lewis and Clark, Doctor Sibley, and Mr. Dunbar*, 60; Farnham, *op. cit.*, I, 261.

[8] J. W. Powell, "Indian Linguistic Families of America North of Mexico," B. A. E. *Seventh Annual Report*, 109.

[9] Waldo R. Wedel, "An Introduction to Pawnee Archeology," B. A. E. *Bulletin No. 112*, p. 4, map 4. The map is reproduced from a copy in the South Dakota Collection, I, 49.

The Comanche Country

Trail, and located the tribe as occupying the territory between the headwaters of the Platte and the Kansas rivers.[10]

According to their own accounts, the Comanches came from the Rocky Mountain country north of the headwaters of the Arkansas to the valley of that stream in what is now eastern Colorado and western Kansas about 1700, having previously occupied the more northern region with the Shoshones. Their account is fairly well substantiated by historical records, and they were unquestionably identified in New Mexico in 1705.[11] So devastating were their incursions into New Mexico in the following years that a punitive expedition was sent against them into Colorado in 1719. No Comanches were found, but rumors were heard of French traders who were active among them to the northeast. Consequently, in the following year the Villasur expedition was dispatched to check the French. The venture met disaster on the Platte, and before the Spaniards could recover, the Comanches had moved into the territory of present eastern Colorado, southern Kansas, western Oklahoma, and northwestern Texas. For control of this territory the Comanches waged a long but successful triangular war with the Jumano allies of the French on their east, the Spaniards and their Indian allies in New Mexico, and the Apaches to the south. The Jumanos were never very formidable; Spanish power in the north was on the decline, and the Spanish system of control was not adequate to the Great Plains. The Apaches, after fierce resistance, were defeated. They retreated, leaving much of their Texas territory to the Comanches. Although Governor Don Juan Bautista de Anza of New Mexico as late as 1786 still held the opinion that the Comanche stronghold was in what is now the state of Colorado, north of the Napestle (Arkansas) River, the Comanches, two decades before that time, had established their supremacy as far south as the San Saba country of Texas. Soon after the turn of the century, American explorers reported them between the Arkansas and the Río Grande,

10 Henri Folmer, "Etienne Veniard De Bourgmond in the Missouri Country," *Missouri Historical Review,* Vol. XXXVI (April, 1942), 290–94; Powell, "Indian Linguistic Families of America North of Mexico," *loc. cit.,* 109; James Mooney, "Calendar History of the Kiowa Indians," B. A. E. *Seventeenth Annual Report,* Part I, 161.

11 Ralph E. Twitchell, *Spanish Archives of New Mexico,* II, 301; Alfred B. Thomas, *Forgotten Frontiers: A Study of the Spanish Indian Policy of Don Juan Bautista de Anza, 1777–1778,* 57.

8

extending from the headwaters of the latter eastward into the Great Plains.[12]

The backbone formed by the Rocky Mountain chain was apparently the shielded route used by most of the Comanches in their movement toward the South Plains, for Pike, Lalande, Pursely, Chouteau and DeMun, James, and others mention the Comanches' and Snakes' using trails along the edge of the mountains on their frequent journeys from the Platte to the Arkansas River and to New Mexico. Bandelier recorded that in 1744 thirty-three Frenchmen visited a Comanche village near Taos on a tributary stream near the head of the Canadian and traded the inhabitants guns, but a few years later the stronghold of the latter was to the east in what is now Oklahoma and Texas.

Any attempt to explain why the Comanches and the Shoshones separated is largely inferential. But if we may accept one Comanche tradition, the split occurred as the result of a dispute over the distribution of a bear which the Comanches had killed. The misunderstanding is supposed to have occurred on Fountain Creek north of Pueblo, Colorado, in the edge of the mountains.[13] Unable to reconcile their differences, the Comanches drifted southward while the Shoshones gradually shifted to the north and west.

A somewhat more plausible legendary account was given to the Santa Fé Laboratory of Anthropology group in 1933 by Post Oak Jim, then aged sixty-four. It is as follows:

« « « Two bands were living together in a large camp. One band was on the east side; the other on the west. Each had its own chief.

Every night the young boys were out playing games—racing, and so forth. They were having a kicking game; they kicked each other. One boy kicked another over the stomach so hard that he died from it. That boy who was killed was from the West camp. He was the son of a chief.

When this thing happened, the West camp cried all night. In

[12] Jefferson, *op. cit.*, I, 78.

[13] G. B. Grinnell, "Who Were the Padoucas?" *American Anthropologist*, Vol. XXII (1920), 260.

the East camp it was silent. Next day, they buried that boy.

The boy's father, the chief, had his crier go around announcing that there would be a big fight to see which camp was best so as to settle the question of his son's death. There was big excitement. Both sides had good warriors. The East camp ran to its horses. "If they really mean what they say, they will kill us," they cried.

The two sides lined up, and the chiefs met in the center. Then an old man from the East camp came up into the center. He wept and told them it wasn't right for them to fight among themselves like that. They took pity on him. Then other old men came out and gathered with him. "You have plenty of enemies to fight," they cried. "These were just boys playing a game. Don't take this thing so seriously. You are setting a bad example for the children. Whatever this chief wants to keep the peace, we'll do it."

That chief called it off. He said he did not realize what he was doing. So the East camp brought them horses and other things.

After that the chief had his announcer tell the people it was time to move camp. "We have had bad luck here. There has been hard feeling." While they were still there, smallpox broke out.

Then they broke up. One group went north; those are the Shoshones. The other group went west. » » »

Simple legendary explanations never tell the whole story, however, for many factors are at work when a people is on the move. It is most probable that the Comanche migration to the South Plains was in part forced by the incursion of more powerful tribes equipped with muskets coming from the northeast. Quarrels may have given no more than the impetus to split the groups.

It was an aggressive southward movement of the Blackfeet and a western advance by the Crows and other eastern tribes that forced the peoples occupying the western fringe of the plains between latitudes forty-three and fifty-two to retire toward the south, west and northwest. According to Flathead tradition, shortly after this eastern impact the Shoshone-Comanches disappeared from the vicinity of the Missouri.[14]

14 James A. Teit, "The Salishan Tribes of the Western Plateau: The Flathead Group," B. A. E. *Forty-fourth Annual Report,* 304, 318.

However, the southward migration cannot be explained altogether as the result of superior enemy pressure alone. The Comanches had obtained the horse, being among the first tribes of the plains to do so, and the desire for a more abundant supply of horses was certainly an important motive for moving closer to the source of supply: the Southwest.

Of the Shoshones, starving and pitiful, whom Lewis and Clark finally found in the mountains of Idaho, the captains observed, "Within their own recollection they formerly lived in the plains, but they have been driven into the mountains by the Pawkees, or the roving Indians of the Sascatchawain, and are now obliged to visit occasionally, and by stealth, the country of their ancestors."[15] And in explanation of this state of affairs, "they [the Shoshones] complain that the Spaniards refuse to let them have firearms. . . . In the meantime, say the Shoshonees, we are left to the mercy of the Minnetarees, who, having firearms, plunder them of their horses and put them to death without mercy."

The gun was the crucial factor, as was clearly recognized by the headman, Cameahwait, who declared fiercely, "But this should not be, if we had guns; instead of hiding ourselves in the mountains and living like bears on roots and berries, we would then go down and live in the buffaloe country in spite of our enemies, whom we never fear when we meet them on equal terms."[16]

The Comanches escaped this pressure by drifting southward into relatively unoccupied areas, where they finally consolidated their position against all comers. Furthermore, once they had horses, they could really launch forth on a buffalo-based economy, and the buffalo was ever present to the south. Thus, "I do not believe the Comanches were driven into the country," declares Professor R. N. Richardson. "On the contrary, it seems that they visited it, found that it was well suited to their mode of existence, and proceeded to fight for it and take it."[17] While taking the more desirable country, they abandoned the less desirable northern territory, and they were better off because of this action.

[15] Lewis and Clark, *op. cit.*, I, 445.
[16] *Ibid.*, 450.
[17] R. N. Richardson, *The Comanche Barrier to South Plains Settlement*, 19.

By 1836 the Comanches claimed and occupied all the country from the Arkansas River on the north to the Mexican settlements on the south, and from the Grand Cordillera on the west to the Cross Timbers on the east, according to the report of the United States Indian agent for the Osages.[18] Actually, however, the territory occupied was hardly that extensive. Comanchería, the land of the Comanches, may reasonably be said to have been in the mid-nineteenth century the vast South Plains area bounded on the north by the Arkansas River, on the west by a line extending from the headwaters of the Arkansas River southward near the Mexican settlements of Taos and Santa Fé, on the southwest by the Pecos River, on the southeast by the white settlements in the vicinity of San Antonio, Fredericksburg, and Austin, and on the east by the Cross Timbers, or approximately along a line slightly west of the ninety-eighth meridian: an area more than six hundred miles from north to south and four hundred miles from east to west. Although they shared parts of this vast country with the Kiowas and the Wichitas, it was theirs to have and to hold. Outsiders, red or white, who entered it did so at their peril.

What was the country like? It is generally level. The eastern portion is slightly rolling with an occasional range of rugged hills. And in the east-central section the solid masses of the Wichita Mountains, geologically one of the oldest exposed land masses in the United States, rise sharply from the plains. The western part is the level tableland of the *Llano Estacado* or Staked Plains. A number of rivers cut southeastward across Comanchería, but even so the distances between them are relatively great. From north to south, the Arkansas, Cimarron, Canadian, Washita, Red, Pease, Brazos, Colorado, and Pecos constitute the major streams. They are low-banked, sand-filled, and sinuous; and because of the gypsum and other minerals contained in their waters, they are not satisfactory for drinking. In the areas contiguous to the headwaters of the streams are escarpments, arroyos, buttes, and canyons. These "breaks" are generally barren and desolate, but contain small running streams and springs that provide an occasional oasis with drinking water, grass, and cottonwood. They give

18 P. L. Chouteau, agent for the Osages, to Governor M. Stokes and General M. Arbuckle, April 25, 1836 (MS copy in National Archives, Western Superintendency file, Office of Indian Affairs, Washington).

excellent protection from the winter blizzards that frequently sweep across the open plains, and horses could always forage on cotton-wood bark.

Growing in the sandy soil along the larger streams were extensive thickets of plum bushes and grapevines; and in much of the eastern portion, pecans, walnuts, haws, and persimmons contributed to the food supply of the Comanches. The mesquite, the tree most commonly found, provided wood for fires and its beans were valuable food for both people and horses. The rocky hills and sides of canyons were covered with scrubby cedar. Other trees found here and there were the ash, elm, redbud, oak, willow, bois d'arc, hackberry, chinaberry, cottonwood, and chaparral.

During the hot, dry summers, the area appeared to be a desert, but shortly after a spring or summer rain, its wide expanse became a sea of nutritious grass. Its warm, salubrious climate, the abundance of edible plant products, and the millions of wild animals which provided food, clothing, and shelter made the area a paradise for nomads who lived by hunting. The Comanche was well off and rarely haunted by the spectre of starvation.

To the west were the Spanish and Pueblo settlements of New Mexico, within striking distance of a Comanche raiding party, or near enough for trade, but sufficiently removed to leave the raider safe from any punitive force that might attempt to pursue him through the adjacent mountainous terrain and across the wide, level expanse of the intervening *Llano Estacado*. The watering places and land-marks were so few as to make any expedition into the region extremely hazardous except for those thoroughly acquainted with the routes.

To the south lay a great expanse of wild waste in the Big Bend country; through this ran a network of Indian trails, by way of water holes, from the central homeland of the Comanches into northern Mexico. Beyond the Río Grande the settlements of northern Mexico were isolated and poorly defended. Striking across this wasteland, the Comanches raided settlements far south of the river, returning with many captives and thousands of horses. The great desert expanse prevented pursuit by forces sufficiently formidable either to punish the marauders or to recapture the plunder, and the Comanches prospered as plunderers.

The streams which led southeastward became highways for Comanche parties raiding the scattered and undefended Anglo-American settlements of Texas. The hills and breaks made it easy for them to strike and to escape with little danger of being apprehended from this quarter.

The Cross Timbers provided a sort of natural boundary on the east which the Comanches seldom passed. Along the margin, numerous weak, semi-sedentary groups of Indians for a time formed a barrier of sorts against white encroachment on the Comanche hunting grounds. From these tribes the Comanches obtained some vegetable products. North of the Red River the Five Civilized Tribes stood between the Comanches and the whites.

The Cheyennes and the Arapahos ranged the country north of the Arkansas River, making Comanchería fairly safe against white aggression from that direction. Moreover, white expansion was generally westward, not southward.

Such was Comanchería—a land ideally suited for a nomadic warrior people. And the Comanches were true warrior nomads. To them a sedentary existence was intolerable. Although a band normally confined its headquarters within a general area, within this area it was always on the move, and its principal encampment might be many miles from its location during the previous or the following year.

Before moving from one area to another, the camp or band headman (or war leader, if a raiding party) usually selected a familiar location which scouts had reported satisfactory. They understood how to select a site well-suited to their needs. The choice of a camp ground, even for a night, involved many factors. Primarily there were five considerations: food, shelter, safety, convenience, and forage for the horses. Colonel Richard I. Dodge relates that he once followed a Comanche raiding party for thirty days before he found a single camp site which he could have approached without discovery.[19]

Among the Plains Indians there is evidence of some tribal differences in preferences for camp sites. The Sioux, who had a mortal dread of ambuscade, preferred to camp near water but away from all timber; the Cheyennes and Arapahos, on the open prairie but near timber; the Osages, Omahas, and Shawnees, in a dense thicket. The

[19] Richard I. Dodge, *Our Wild Indians*, 239.

14

Meeting of the Dragoons and Comanches in 1834
From George Catlin, *North American Indians* (1857)

A Comanche camp
From George Catlin, *North American Indians* (1857)

His-oo-sán-chees (The Little Spaniard)
From a painting by Catlin
Courtesy Bureau of American Ethnology

Comanches and their Kiowa allies preferred to camp near a running stream in open timber. Along meandering creek valleys toward the headwaters of larger streams, where there were adequate canyons, arroyos, and breaks for protection, abundant grass for the large horse herds, ample buffalo and antelope for food, wood for the campfires, and sweet water for drinking, were to be found the Comanche villages. A large camp sometimes extended several miles along a stream or forest edge. A Comanche village which lay east of the Wichita Mountains in 1834 is reported to have extended along Cache Creek from Medicine Bluff north to Chandler Creek and southward to Wolf Creek, a distance of fifteen miles.[20]

Within the camp itself there appears to have been no required plan. If the terrain was favorable, the lodges might be grouped in a rough circular fashion about the lodge of the chief. In another village, the lodges might appear to follow a rectangular plan. There were usually as many groups of lodges as there were leaders, the lodges of the most important men being located nearest that of the leader.[21] There was no privacy in the camp, for neighbors entered and left a tipi at will. While busy wives performed their daily tasks of preparing food, tanning hides, and making tipis and clothes, the men spent their time discussing matters of general import, raiding, hunting, making weapons, or simply idling the hours away at sleep or play, and the children shouted at play or assisted their mothers with their work. In the evenings or on any unusual occasion, the whole camp gave vent to joy or sorrow, anger or enthusiasm, by positive, and at times noisy and colorful, demonstrations. Innumerable lanky, ferocious dogs greeted the approaching stranger by day or gave forth in unison to warn their masters of danger by night.

But what had been a noisy camp could become within a few minutes a lonely prairie with little evidence of previous habitation. On the day before the move, the camp crier rode through the camp making the announcement and describing the new location. The next morning the women were in a hurry to pack and be on their way, for those who were first might obtain choice sites in the new camp. One end

[20] W. S. Nye, *Carbine and Lance: The Story of Old Fort Sill*, 7.
[21] T. A. ("Dot") Babb, *In the Bosom of the Comanches*, 106–107; Nelson Lee, *Three Years among the Camanches*, 127–28; George Catlin, *North American Indians*, II, 72; C. C. Rister, *Border Captives*, 16.

of a tipi pole was tied on each side of a horse or a mule and the other end allowed to drag. This formed the travois on which the family belongings were piled until it was hardly possible to see the back of the animal bearing the burden. Children too large to be carried on their mothers' backs but too small to ride alone were tied on some old horse to be led or herded along with the procession. As an improvised ambulance for the wounded or ill, a buffalo skin was stretched between the poles of the travois, forming a sort of bed upon which the invalid was fastened for the journey. It frequently happened that some of the pack animals became frightened and scattered their burdens for miles over the prairie. Men and boys divided their time along the route between hunting and driving the remuda as they moved across a land they claimed as their own—Comanchería.

II

The People

THE artist George Catlin wrote of the Comanches, "In their movements they are heavy and ungraceful; and on their feet one of the most unattractive and slovenly-looking races of Indians I have ever seen; but the moment they mount their horses, they seem at once metamorphosed, and surprise the spectator with the ease and grace of their movements."[1]

Colonel Richard Irving Dodge, who spent many years with the United States Army on the plains, also thought them a poor thing on the ground but something special on a horse. "In stature," he wrote, "they are rather low, and in person often approach corpulency. . . . The men are short and stout, with bright copper faces and long hair which they ornament with glass beads and silver gewgaws. On foot they are slow and awkward, but on horseback graceful."[2] Captain Marcy saw more of detail and paints a richer picture. "The men are about medium stature, with bright, copper-colored complexions and intelligent countenances, in many instances with aquiline noses, thin lips, black eyes and hair, with but little beard. They never cut the hair, but wear it of very great length, and ornament it upon state occasions with silver and beads."[3] Compared to the usual run of Plains Indians (Cheyenne, Crow, Blackfoot, and Kiowa, for example) the Comanche *is* short, squat, and heavy. Actually, the Comanches

[1] Catlin, *op. cit.*, II, 74–75.
[2] Richard I. Dodge, *The Plains of the Great West*, p. *xxv*.
[3] R. B. Marcy, *Adventure on Red River*, 161.

17

are medium in stature. Goldstein reported an average height of five feet, six inches for Comanche men and five feet for women.[4] This makes them slightly taller than their Ute and Shoshone relatives. The men are robust and well proportioned, but the idle and well-fed among them are inclined to be fat and paunchy. Their chests are wide and fairly deep, and they carry themselves erect and with unassuming dignity. Possibly because of their hard life, the women age somewhat prematurely.

The skin color of the Comanche varies from light brown to a reddish brown or copper, depending to some degree on the amount of exposure to weather and sunlight. The females tend toward somewhat lighter pigmentation than do the males. Like that of any Indians, the hair of a Comanche is black and straight and medium in texture. Among the females there is a greater tendency toward coarseness. It is a rare Comanche who has cause to worry over baldness or graying in old age. Such facial hair as a Comanche naturally grows is sparse and light, but until recently even this feeble growth had little chance, for it was the style to pluck it out, roots and all—eyebrows included.

On their heavy bodies the average Comanches carry relatively large, round heads with a cephalic index of eighty-three. This gives them a somewhat greater relative head breadth than neighboring Plains tribes and the Shoshones, too. The shift from the Shoshone norm may quite possibly be the result of extensive admixture with Mexican Indian captives. The forehead is broad, and the supraorbital ridges vary from slight among the females to moderate in the cases of males.

Eye color varies from medium brown to black like that of all Mongoloids. The eyes of the children are a much clearer, richer brown than those of adults. The sclera of adults is commonly bloodshot, and, contrary to popular notions about sharp-eyed Indians, the vision ap-

[4] Marcus S. Goldstein, "Anthropometry of the Comanches," *American Journal of Physical Anthropology*, Vol. XIX, (1934–35), 289–313. Goldstein's study is the best account of the physical appearance of the Comanches. It was made in 1931 and comprised thirty-five "unmixed" males, twenty-five "unmixed" females, and twenty-five hybrid individuals representing every surviving important band. The numerical figures and comparisons used in this description are taken from Goldstein's study. Otherwise, the description is based on field notes taken by Ernest Wallace in 1945.

pears to be weak. The eyes of about one-half of those studied by Goldstein appear to be slanted slightly to moderately. In most cases the outer canthi are inclined upward, but a few were observed with a downward slant. The so-called Mongolian fold is common among children, but disappears in most cases by the time adulthood is reached.

The Comanche face is broad, even for an Indian people. Goldstein asserts that "In this respect the Comanches are probably exceeded by few or no other tribe." On this wide visage is a broad, high, and long nose with an index of 69.4 as compared to 67.5 for old American whites. In breadth it exceeds that of the Sioux and the Indians of the Southwest, but is practically the same as that of the Shoshones. The depression of the root of the nose is shallow to medium in depth, and the bridge is straight to moderate. The mouth is moderately wide, and the lips are thin. The lower jaw appears to be moderately developed; the chin firm and of medium prominence. All in all, the Comanche exhibits not a "finely sculptured" visage, but rather a heavy face with fairly massive features. In form as well as in personality he is a rugged individual.

Since their arrival in the South Plains, the Comanches have incorporated great numbers of Mexican captives into their tribe, and Mexican infiltration continues today at a rapid pace. Mixture with the Negro seems to have occurred with extreme rarity, if at all. Clark Wissler found that only 62.9 per cent of the Comanches were "fullblood" in 1910, as compared to 96.9 per cent of the Wichitas and 24.2 of the Iowas, the two tribes having respectively the greatest and least amount of alien admixture.[5] That this admixture has continued at an accelerated pace is shown by Marcus S. Goldstein, who believed in 1931 that not more than 10 per cent of the adults could, with any assurance, be considered fullblood.[6]

The Comanches are members of the Uto-Aztekan language family in the sense that English-speaking peoples are Indo-European. The Uto-Aztekan family, which is one of the truly great linguistic stocks of ancient North America, has three major branches: Shoshonean, Sonoran, and Nahuatlan. The Shoshonean peoples, whose home is centered in the Great Basin region of what is now western United

[5] Clark Wissler, *North American Indians of the Plains*, 148.
[6] Goldstein, "Anthropometry of the Comanches," *loc. cit.*, 290.

States, may in turn be subdivided into three linguistic groups speaking mutually unintelligible languages differing both phonetically and morphologically. First, the Mono-Bannock group includes the Monos, the Northern Paiutes (Paviotso), the Snakes of eastern Oregon, and the Bannocks. These are the northernmost representatives of the Uto-Aztekan family. The second group is composed of tribes speaking the mutually intelligible Ute-Chemehuevi dialects of the region where Colorado, Utah, New Mexico, and Arizona meet, there being also fragments in California. In this group are the Southern Paiutes, the Utes of western Colorado and eastern Utah, the Kawaiisus of south-central California, and the Chemehuevis along the Colorado River in southeastern California. The third group is the Shoshone-Comanche-Koso (Panamint), which includes the Shoshones proper, the Comanches, the Gosiutes in the vicinity of Salt Lake, and the Shikaviyams of California.

The area occupied by the Shoshonean linguistic group was exceeded in North America by that of only two other families, the Algonquian and the Athabascan. In the north the Shoshonean area extended far into Oregon, meeting Shahaptian territory at about forty-four degrees north latitude. It included southwestern Montana and southern Idaho and may have extended into Alberta, Canada. The eastern limits of Shoshonean territory are unknown. Tradition declares that when the Blackfeet entered the Great Plains, they found the country occupied by the Snakes (Shoshone-Comanches). Lewis and Clark reported that the Shoshone bands encountered upon the headwaters of the Columbia had within their recollection lived upon the plains east of the Rocky Mountains and had been driven into their western mountain retreats by tribes who had obtained firearms. Western Kansas, western and central Wyoming, western and central Colorado, northern and eastern New Mexico, and northwestern Texas were at one time Shoshonean territory. The family reached west across the Sierras into California, holding a narrow strip of that state in the northeast, with the western boundary extending in a southwesterly direction to the Pacific between the thirty-third and thirty-fourth parallels.[7]

[7] Edward Sapir, "Southern Paiute, a Shoshonean Language," *American Academy of Arts and Sciences Proceedings,* Vol. LXV, 5–6; R. M. Zingg, *A Reconstruction of Uto-*

Although most people of this vast area spoke kindred languages, there was otherwise a wide variation of cultural patterns. The Shoshoneans to the west of the Rocky Mountains differed in culture from their kinsmen east of the mountains. The inhospitable nature of their country compelled those west of the mountains to accept a less adventurous and humbler mode of life. The most western representatives of the family subsisted chiefly on fish caught in coarse grass-nets, on rabbits, snakes, rats, grasshoppers, seeds, and roots. Yet southward a few hundred miles lived the Puebloan Hopi of northeastern Arizona, who differed so widely that they have little in common but linguistic affinity. They lived in villages of adobe and stone houses, were skillful potters and weavers, and derived their subsistence mainly from gardening. On the north and along the entire eastern border of the territory were the Bannock, Ute, Shoshone, and Comanche divisions. None of the latter cultivated the soil, and all derived the greater part of their subsistence from the pursuit of large game. Only the Comanches, however, were dependent almost entirely on the buffalo herds for a livelihood.

The linguistic relation of the Comanches to the Northern Shoshones is so close that it was patent to early observers, and it was on this basis that the derivation of the Comanches from Shoshonean roots was first posited. The two languages are mutually intelligible, and the differences that exist rest in slight phonetic shifts, not in grammatical structure or form. When one of the authors[8] was doing field work with the Seed-eater Shoshones in Idaho, his Shoshone acquaintances were convinced that he and his wife could speak Shoshone because they could bandy some Comanche words. The fact that they could also phonetically record Shoshone and read it back was the clincher. Susie Lipps, one morning before starting work, said, "At breakfast my husband said, 'Our friends can talk Shoshone. Last night I dreamed and they talked to me in our tongue.'" Her reply was, "Of course they can. They can even write it down

Aztekan History, 1–4; R. H. Lowie, "The Northern Shoshone," American Museum of Natural History *Anthropological Papers*, XX (1924), 190–313; Hodge, *Handbook*, II, 555–56; C. F. and E. W. Voegelin, "Map of North American Indian Languages," American Ethnological Society *Publication No. 20*. Powell also regarded the Shoshonean-speaking peoples as constituting a distinct linguistic family.

[8] E. A. Hoebel.

and read it back. They can talk our language, but they just don't want to!" The Comanche language became the lingua franca of the South Plains, and at Indian gatherings the proceedings usually took place through the medium of the Comanche tongue. This may explain why the Comanches were reported not to be so proficient in the use of the sign language as the other Plains tribes.

"Tribe" when applied to the Comanches is a word of sociological but not political significance. The Comanches had a strong consciousness of kind. A Comanche, whatever his band, was a Comanche. He could say, "I am of the Nɜmɜnə: *I am of The People.* By dress, by speech, by thoughts and actions the Comanches held a common bond of identity and affinity that set them off from all other Indians— from all the rest of the world. In this sense, the tribe had meaning. The tribe consisted of a people who had a common way of life. But that way of life did not include political institutions or social mechanisms by which they could act as a tribal unit. There was, in the old days, no ceremonial occasion or economic enterprise that pulled all the far-flung bands together for a spell, be it ever so brief. There was no chieftain or group of chieftains to act for the tribe as a whole. There was no tribal council.

The first time the bands with all their men, women, and children came together was in the dying moments of the old, free culture at the time of the first Comanche Sun Dance in 1874.

The Comanches were organized in family groups and bands. The bands were autonomous units, each loosely organized and each centering its activities in a vaguely defined territory within the Comanche country. But, on the other hand, there were no distinct boundaries between the several band territories, and any Comanche or family was free and welcome to settle, or hunt, or move through the regions of other bands, whatever his own affiliation might be. Although warriors of the Wasp band joined with the United States Army as scouts in the final campaigns against their kinsmen, Comanche bands never warred with each other, but rather co-operated on the friendliest terms whenever happenstance drew them together.

The Comanche band was strikingly similar in organization to the aboriginal Shoshonean groups of the Great Basin in the days preceding white contact. It ranged in size from a single family camping

22

alone to the small camp of related individuals forming a composite extended family to a large group of several hundred people. But the band was not organized around a family group, nor was it the basis for the regulation of marriage. Clan organization was wholly absent. In the large groups, more often than not marriage took place within the band so that a couple belonged customarily to the same band as both their parents. But in cases of interband marriage, residence tended to be virilocal, for a band did not want to lose its fighting strength to another, and in personal disputes a man had to count on the support of his brothers, wherefore brothers stuck together in their parental band. This being so, and a son-in-law being expected to furnish food to his wife's parents, they, in giving consent to marriage, preferred their daughters to take a husband from their own band. Yet the kinship principle was weak, even within the extended family band; for although groups of relatives tended to camp together, the linkage of the person to the band was on the basis of free association. Any person could withdraw from one band and join another at will.[9] There were no restrictions to prevent a change of residence from one band to another at any time, and no formal ceremony was required. With a great deal of interband visiting going on, temporary changes of band membership were frequent. A newcomer simply moved in, and no permission was necessary.

Likewise, groups of individuals under their own leaders sometimes separated from the main band, possibly to reunite later or to join some other band. Such divisions sometimes gave rise to new bands if these cessionists stayed off on their own. In several known instances, smaller or weaker bands merged with larger bands and lost their identity.

In the large band, relatives tended to camp together. Thus the camp pattern retained a degree of regularity. And when the band was subdivided, as was often the case, there is reason to believe that the break-up tended to be into the smaller groups of relatives joined by the families of friends drawn within the orbit of the group.

The family headmen—and there was at least one for each group—

[9] David G. Burnet, "American Aborigines, Indians of Texas," *The Cincinnati Literary Gazette,* Vol. I (May 15, 1824), 154; E. A. Hoebel, "Comanche and Hekandika Shoshone Relationship Systems," *American Anthropologist,* Vol. XLI (1939), 440–57, has a similar analysis of the Comanche band.

were the peace, or civil, chiefs. When the large band was functioning as a unit, it contained several peace chiefs, one of whom was recognized as the head chief of the band. The rest formed an advisory council to the leader and at the same time maintained their positions as family headmen.

Although the various bands had cultures so similar that it was extremely difficult for the uninitiated to differentiate among them, each band had certain peculiarities which served to identify its members in any company. Each had its favorite dance.[10] One band habitually made clothing from antelope skins, although the others preferred deer skins. One made no pemmican, another made it without berries, and a third always added berries.[11] The southern groups were thought to prefer darker clothing than their northern kinsmen.[12] There were also slight differences in speech. For instance, the Wasp band members (Southern Comanche) pronounced their words more slowly than the Antelope band of the Staked Plains.[13] Bands also differed in a number of cultural aspects less easily recognized, such as magical techniques, sexual attitudes, and character traits. Cultural differences persisted, although it was mandatory upon an individual to follow the customs of the group with which he lived in order to be socially accepted by his new associates, and this despite the frequent exchange of band allegiance and the interband marriages. The extent of cultural differences at present corresponds somewhat to that in the United States between North and South or East and West. All the older Comanche informants were as conscious of the differences as a Texan in Boston. "That was —— [name of band] way" was a very common reply of informants to questions or comments. Notwithstanding these and other slight differences that may have existed, there was, on the whole, little gross variation in habits, customs, and institutions.

Only the larger bands received permanent recognition and a name. Before the close of the eighteenth century, the Spaniards in New

[10] R. H. Lowie, "Dances and Societies of the Plains Shoshone," American Museum of Natural History *Anthropological Papers*, XI, Part 10 (1916), 809–12.

[11] Ralph Linton, *The Study of Man*, 221.

[12] W. B. Parker, *Notes Taken During the Expedition Commanded by Captain R. B. Marcy Through Unexplored Texas, in the Summer and Fall of 1854*, 202.

[13] Richardson, *The Comanche Barrier to South Plains Settlement*, 17–18.

Mexico spoke of three major bands. For a time, the Anglo-Americans designated three divisions—Northern, Middle, and Southern—but as they came to know the Comanches better, the practice was replaced by the use of definite band names. Robert S. Neighbors, in 1860, was able to identify eight bands. James Mooney listed thirteen, but Robert H. Lowie, in 1912, recorded only four. R. B. Thomas, who lived with the Comanches for many years during the early reservation period, knew of twelve bands, six of which had already been absorbed or exterminated;[14] and at the time of the work of the Santa Fé Laboratory Field Study Group in 1933, living Comanches still remembered thirteen.[15] Multiple names are usually recorded for a band, and in some instances it is impossible to determine whether two names refer to the same or different bands. Regardless of how many bands there may have been, during the nineteenth century there were five outstanding divisions, the others being small or transitory groupings.

The largest and best-known divisions of all the Comanches was the *Pɛnatɜkɜ*, or Honey-Eaters. Other names by which the band was known include *Teyuwit* (Hospitable), *Tekapwai* (No Meat), *Kuβaɾatpat* (Steep Climbers), *Pɛnanɜ* (Wasp or Quick-stinger, i.e., Raiders), and *Ho'is* (Timber People). This band led in the southward migration and lived adjacent to the Spanish and Texas settlements in the vicinity of the Cross Timbers belt and along the headwaters of the central Texas rivers. A map of the country between the frontiers of Arkansas and New Mexico, based on the expeditions of Captain Marcy from 1849 to 1852, locates the Southern Comanches, or Wasps, between the Pecos River and Fort Phantom Hill.[16] Their residence in the timber belt explains some of the various names by which they were called. They lived near the settlements and associated more with the Caddos, Wichitas, and whites in historic times than with their western and northern kinsmen. Early references by the whites to the Comanches pertain largely to this band. According to their own traditional accounts, the Wasps had moved so far away that for a long time they had no contact with other Comanche groups. They were

[14] R. B. Thomas, "Kiowa-Comanche Experiences," *loc. cit.,* 153.

[15] E. A. Hoebel, *The Political Organization and Law-Ways of the Comanche Indians,* 12–13.

[16] Annie H. Abel (ed.), *The Official Correspondence of James S. Calhoun,* map (unattached).

rediscovered by the Yap-eaters (*Yamparikə*) and Antelope bands (*Kwзharɛnə*), who went far southward into Mexico on a raiding expedition. The relationship was restored, and thereafter they maintained a loose alliance with their western and northern kinsmen.[17] But still they were distinct enough to help the United States troops against other Comanches—a fact remembered with bitterness by members of other bands to this very day.

Another Comanche band which the Anglo-Americans came to know well, though unfavorably, was the Those Who Move Often (*Nɔyɛḳa*), or *Nɔḳoni* (Those Who Turn Back). Although all Comanches were nomadic, these were the real gypsies of the tribe. "They always turned back before they got to where they were going," said Eagle Tail Feather; but it is more likely that they were just drifting about, not going any place in particular. After the death of a chief who bore the same name as his band (*Nɔḳoni*), because of the tabu forbidding the speaking of a dead person's name, the band became known as *Dзtsanɔyɛḳa* (Wanderers Who Make Bad Camps); they moved so much that they were slovenly in their camp habits.

In 1786, Governor Don Juan Bautista de Anza of New Mexico stated that most of the Wanderers were located between the Arkansas and the Red rivers, but that their camps were to be found across Texas as far south as the banks of the Pecos. During the nineteenth century the Wanderers generally ranged immediately north of the Wasps. Together with some of their neighbors, the *Tenawa* and the *Tanima* (Liver-eaters), they composed the group referred to as the Middle Comanches. The map based on the expeditions and accounts of Captain Marcy, 1849–52, shows the Middle Comanches along the headwaters of the Red River for about one hundred miles southward to the headwaters of the Brazos (Main, Double Mountain, Clear Fork, Salt Fork, and Middle Fork) River in the region between Fort Phantom Hill and Fort Belknap.[18] Their favorite retreat and stronghold was in the breaks of the Pease River country where they found protection from the blizzards and safety from pursuing enemies.

Another powerful band was that of the Buffalo-eaters (*Kutsuɛḳa*),

[17] Agent E. L. Clark to Commissioner of Indian Affairs, "Report," May 18, 1881 (Oklahoma Historical Society Library, correspondence file K–13).

[18] Abel, *The Official Correspondence of James S. Calhoun*, map.

so named because they always had plenty of buffalo meat. Buffalo meat was the principal food of all Comanches, but this particular division, whose favorite haunt during the nineteenth century was the Canadian River valley, may well have been more dependent upon that animal, since they were in a favorite rendezvous of the buffalo herds. They established relations with the Spaniards in New Mexico early in the eighteenth century, and after peace was established in 1786, *Comancheros* (traders from New Mexico settlements) visited them frequently and called them *Cuchaneo* or *Cuchantica*. The eastern and southern members of this group likewise came to be well known to the Spaniards in Texas; in fact, they are commonly referred to in the documents of the Bexar archives as Texas or Eastern Comanches. They were noted as a band which was ever out on a raid. An emissary, Francisco Xavier Ortiz, whom Governor de Anza sent in 1786 to visit them, reported that in an area about one hundred miles square between the Pecos and Red rivers, he found eight *rancherías;* that the smallest had thirty tents; all eight together had about seven hundred. He further reported that there were three to four warriors to the tent, which would give an estimated population of between six and seven thousand; on the basis of what we know about the Comanches, this was an exaggeration, although his claim that they owned nine hundred horses and mules is quite credible.[19]

The northernmost part of the Comanche country was occupied by the populous and important band of "Yap-eaters," *Yapainɘ,* or *Yampaɾikɘ,* eaters of a potato-like root called *Yɛp* by the Shoshones, but *Yap'* by the Comanches. As the band closest to the Shoshones, and as the band that clung to Shoshone food-getting habits, digging for roots, they were probably the last of the Comanche bands to break off. Indeed, the Fort Hall Shoshones, in Idaho (who still think *they* are the people—*nɜm*) call all Comanches *Yamparika.* In earlier times this band had been called *Widyu* (Awl), according to Mooney, but because the use of the word became tabu, as in the case of the *Nokoni,* it was changed to *Ditsakana* (Sewers), which conveys the same idea.[20]

[19] A. B. Thomas, *Forgotten Frontiers,* 73, 290–91.

[20] Apparently also spelled *Titchakenah* (Those Who Make Bags While Moving). It is maintained on good authority that the *Titchakenah* was once a separate band who before the reservation days had become a portion of the *Yamparika* band. See Agent Clark to Commissioner of Indian Affairs, "Report," May 18, 1881, *loc. cit.*

According to their own accounts, they came around 1700 from the Rocky Mountain country, north of the headwaters of the Arkansas River, to the valley of that stream in what is now eastern Colorado and western Kansas. Previously they had inhabited the country with the Shoshones. Governor Anza in 1786 located them as ranging across present northern Colorado and south to the Arkansas River. The accounts indicate, however, that the Yap-eaters felt at home south of that stream also. During the nineteenth century they camped generally on the south side of the Arkansas River and along the Canadian, the Arkansas being considered the northern boundary of their territory. They raided, however, far north of that stream across Kansas and Nebraska.

Another populous band, although little known until towards the close of the pre-reservation period, is the Antelope or *Kwᴣharɛnə*. The name of the band is indicative of its life on the open plains where antelope were plentiful. And because they lived and traveled on the glaring, treeless plains, these Comanches carried on their backs a square of rawhide that could be held over the head as a sunshade. Hence they were also nicknamed *Kwahihᴣkɛnə*, "Sunshades on Their Backs." William Clark called them Qua-he-hu-ke, which he said meant "back-shade," because in their treeless country the only way to shade the face was to turn one's back to the sun, but we doubt the correctness of this interpretation.[21] Before the Comanches migrated to the South Plains country, the Antelope band was located just south of the Yap-eaters. The two bands probably drifted south about the same time, and then the Antelopes made the *Llano Estacado* their home and challenged all intruders. Within the wild depths of the Tule and Palo Duro canyons they found protection from the winter blizzards of the uplands and safety from their enemies until Colonel MacKenzie bearded them in their stronghold on September 27, 1874. They harried the frontier of Texas as much, perhaps, as any other Comanche band, and they were the last of the Comanches to submit to the efforts of the United States to bring them under control. For years they scoffed at their beef-eating kinsmen on the reservation, and did not submit until they had been drubbed repeatedly by superior military forces. It has been argued that present-day Comanche

21 W. P. Clark, *Indian Sign Language*, 119.

28

dialects, traditions, and customs are largely Antelope.[22] To what extent this is true is impossible to judge, but even a casual student of Comanche culture cannot fail to note that the influence of the Antelope band is strong. These people are reluctant to accept innovations to this day, a few still preferring the tipi and the arbor to the modern house.

In addition to the above-mentioned major groups, there were a great many bands of less importance. Some of these are difficult to distinguish because of similarity of band names and variations in spelling the same name, and also because some bands had become extinct or had merged with others before becoming known to whites.

The *Tanima* (Liver-eaters), mentioned by James Mooney, were so called because they are reputed to have eaten the liver of their game in its raw state. Although Mooney found only one survivor at the time of his visit, Agent E. L. Clark reported several survivors living with other bands in 1881,[23] and Goldstein was able to identify the band in 1931. The Liver-eaters were neighbors of the Wanderers and with them composed a part of the group known as Middle Comanches.

A third band which lived in the same region as the Wanderers and the Liver-eaters was the *Tenawa* or *Tenawit* (Down Stream), also noted by Mooney. The *Tenawa* and *Tanima* were frequently confused by the whites, partly because of the similarity of the sound of the names and partly because they inhabited the same geographic region. So confused are the accounts of the two that it is often impossible to determine to which band the name refers.[24] The Down Streams were practically exterminated in a battle with the Mexicans about 1845, and the band did not exist when the Comanches went on the reservation in 1869, or else they had been absorbed by other bands. R. N. Richardson believes that the Yupes or Jupes listed by Governor Anza as one of three major divisions known to the Spaniards in New Mexico in 1786 were the *Tenawa*.[25] The Liver-eaters

[22] R. B. Thomas, "Kiowa-Comanche Experiences," *loc. cit.*
[23] Agent Clark to Commissioner of Indian Affairs, "Report," May 18, 1881, *loc. cit.*
[24] Richardson, *The Comanche Barrier to South Plains Settlement*, 21, lists the following variations of the two words and states that it is an incomplete list: Te-na-wish, Ta-ne-wa, Te-ne-wah, Te-na-wa, Tan-nee-wish, Ten-en-e-ree, Te-ne-mes, and De-na-vi.
[25] *Ibid.*, 20–22.

and Down Streams often camped with the Wasps and were probably strongly influenced by them.

The *Itɛta'o* habitually put up more pemmican than they could eat in a winter. They threw the surplus out in the spring, and other Comanches, seeing their dumps of dried, black meat along the trails, dubbed them *Itɛta'o*, "Burnt Meat."

The *Wɔ'ai* carried a name meaning "Wormy," but more inelegantly, according to That's It, the full name means "Maggots on the Penis." They are supposed to have married incestuously, and hence they were also scornfully called *Namaɜ'ɜnə*, "Something together" or "Intercourse." Mooney reported them to be extinct at the time of the reservation period, but the Santa Fé Laboratory Field Group was able to record evidence of them in 1933. There were a few living in the vicinity of Geronimo, Oklahoma, in 1945, and only a few of the older tribal informants had no knowledge of this band.

The *Mutsanɜ* (Undercut Bank) were so called because their favorite camp site was underneath an overhanging cliff. According to Mooney, who called them *Mot-sai,* they were annihilated in a battle with the Mexicans sometime around 1845, presumably suffering the same fate as the Down Stream band. Mooney also identified a group which he called *Pagatsu* (Head of the Stream), probably the same band as that recorded by the Santa Fé Laboratory group as *Panaixtɜ* (Those Who Live Upstream).

A band famous among the Comanches but little known to whites was the Water Horse (*Pahuraix*). According to That's It, who was a member of this band, these people were taller and slimmer than most other Comanches. They were reputedly great runners who excelled at lacrosse. They bet prodigiously on their prowess, and like the Lamarkian giraffe they are supposed to have gotten their height by stretching—they piled their bets so high! In time, on account of their propensity for huge stakes and their unbeatable skill at lacrosse, other bands refused to play them. Robert S. Neighbors says that they were called *Par-ƙee-na-um* (Water People) because they usually camped near lakes and streams.

The *Wia'nɜ* (Hill Wearing Away) was a very small band of six or seven families which camped in a gap between a large hill and a rapidly eroding smaller one.

30

Mooney and Neighbors both listed a few Comanche bands that were not noted by any other reporters. Mooney's *Pohoi* (Wild Sage) were nothing more than some Wind River Shoshones who joined with the Comanches. Neighbors mentions a *No-na-um* band, who he said "live in the high prairie where there is no timber or running water, and never leave that kind of country." He also notes an *It-chit-a-bud-ah* (Cold People) band and a *Hai-ne-na-une* (Corn-eaters). All of these later groups were of little importance or had by mid-nineteenth century been absorbed or otherwise become extinct.

How many people all these bands added up to is hard to say. At best the Comanche tribe was never very large. Mooney estimated its population to be 7,000 in 1690.[26] Governor Anza of New Mexico reported that Comanches visiting Santa Fé and Pecos Pueblo in the first half of the year of 1786 included twenty-three chiefs representing 593 lodges or around 6,000 persons. In the same year Anza's emissary, Francisco Xavier Ortiz, reported that he visited an area about one hundred miles square north and east of the Pecos River where he found eight villages of "Kotsoteka," containing a population of 6,000 to 7,000.[27] The figure given by Ortiz is quite likely exaggerated, but if it is approximately correct, then the tribe at that time could have numbered as many as 20,000 to 30,000.

It was several years after the United States acquired the Louisiana Territory that government agents learned much about the Comanches. One of the first reliable estimates of their military strength was by P. L. Chouteau, agent for the Osages. He wrote in 1836, "The numerical military forces of the Comanches (which includes all males old enough and not too old to bear arms) is estimated, and always has been, by the Mexican Government at 8,000, but from my personal observation, I have been induced to calculate the number of Comanche warriors at 4,500."[28] In the following year United States military authorities estimated the number of warriors at about 5,400.[29] Based upon the figures given by Chouteau and Bonville, the population of

[26] James Mooney, "The Aboriginal Population of America North of Mexico," *Smithsonian Miscellaneous Collections,* Vol. LXXX, No. 7, 13.

[27] A. B. Thomas, *Forgotten Frontiers,* 290–91, 325, 327.

[28] Agent Chouteau to Stokes and Arbuckle, April 25, 1836, *loc. cit.*

[29] B. L. E. Bonville, captain, Seventh Infantry, to Commissioner, General Roger Jones, January 24, 1837 (MS copy, Oklahoma Historical Society Library, Archives, I).

the entire tribe must have been between 15,000 and 20,000 in the eighteen thirties. This would be in accordance with Mooney's estimate of 19,200 for the period 1841–45 and Neighbors' *Report* of 1849 which places the population at 20,000, with 4,000 warriors as "a careful estimate." A more conservative estimate made by Charles Bent, who was well informed, placed the number of lodges at 2,500, or 12,000 people, in 1846. This would approximate W. B. Parker's 1854 calculation of 20,000 for both the Comanches and Kiowas.[30] Twenty thousand is the population of only a small-sized city in America today. But a rough, tough, roving tribe of warrior-plunderers who with their women and children numbered 20,000 on the Southwestern Plains a hundred years ago was then a formidable group.

It could be that all the early estimates were somewhat high in the light of later knowledge of the Comanches, but they may not be unduly so, for all evidence substantiates the conclusion that the population was declining rapidly in the middle decades of the nineteenth century. A low birth rate, disease, and constant warfare on all sides were cutting down "The People." The decline continued until after the turn of the century. In 1866 the Comanches were estimated at 4,700.[31] By 1884 the population had dwindled to a pitiful 1,382,[32] and in 1910 there were only 1,171 survivors. By comparison, the total population in 1910 for all Plains Indians was estimated at 50,208 by Clark Wissler, and he doubts that their combined population at any time ever exceeded 100,000.[33]

30 Charles Bent to Hon. Wm. Medill, Commissioner of Indian Affairs, November 10, 1846 (from Santa Fé), Abel, *The Official Correspondence of James S. Calhoun*, 6–9; Parker, *op. cit.*, 231.

31 Charles Bogy and W. B. Irwin, special agents, to Commissioner of Indian Affairs, December 21, 1866 (National Archives, Treaties, Talks, and Councils file, Office of Indian Affairs, Washington).

32 Agent P. B. Hunt, *Annual Report*, 1884, 79.

33 Wissler, *North American Indians of the Plains*, 44, 48.

III

The Horse
and the Buffalo

THE dominating characteristics
of the "typical" nineteenth century Plains Indian culture, ac-
cording to Clark Wissler, were the use of the horse, the buffalo, the
tipi, the soldier band, and the Sun Dance. Although Wissler tagged
them as a "typical" Plains tribe, the Comanches never developed the
soldier bands beyond a weak, incipient imitation, and it is unlikely
that the Sun Dance acquired any meaning for them, since the only
one they held was a prelude to disaster. The warfare pattern of the
Plains they could readily adopt, for that was an individualistic game.
The military societies, however, called for a kind of internal organization which was foreign to their Shoshonean traditions, and since
there was no notable functional advantage to be derived from such
societies (as there was from warfare), they sensed no need to develop
the military clubs to any great extent. The Sun Dance functioned as
a tribal integrator for most Plains tribes and as a focal point of
Nativistic revivalism for the peripheral Shoshones at the beginning
of the twentieth century, but in the case of the Comanches, again
with Shoshonean atomism in mind, it appears that there was no
interest in tribal integration until sudden disintegration faced them
in the eighteen seventies. Then their interest in the Sun Dance as a
tribal catalyst produced for them nothing but disaster and the destruction of the old culture.

If, then, the Comanches lacked the typical military societies and
the Sun Dance, what was there that made them typical Plains In-

33

dians? Above all, it was the horse-buffalo-tipi complex, in which they equaled or surpassed all other Indians. In horses they were the richest of all tribes; in fact *they* introduced the horse into the plains and they were the medium through which most other Indians received their mounts (at the expense of the Texans and Mexicans). If the horse was the critical factor in later Plains culture, then the Comanches, although they were in other aspects imitators, were in this one very significant aspect the great innovators. Of buffalo they had a plethora and were more richly supplied than the tribes farther north. In warfare no one surpassed them. They were, indeed, typical enough, even without warrior societies and the Sun Dance.

Just prior to the introduction of the horse there were very few nomadic Indians out on the plains proper. In the moist millenia immediately following the retreat of the fourth (Wisconsin) glaciation, a thin veneer of paleolithic hunters, called the Paleo-Indians, spread out across the plains from the eastern slopes of the Rockies. Their epoch lasted from perhaps 20,000 B.C. to around 10,000, during which the archaeological cultures of Folsom and Yuma dominated the scene. From 10,000 B.C. to A.D. 1,000 a series of transitory cultures of nomadic, pre-pottery, pre-gardening societies, called collectively *lithic,* vacillated back and forth as wet periods and alternating Dust Bowl climates made habitation of the plains possible or nearly untenable. Beginning about A.D. 500 emigrants from the Woodlands of the Mississippi Valley and east brought gardening to the river bottoms of the Missouri and its tributaries. These people and their protohistoric successors lived in settled villages of earth lodges or grass-domed houses, growing corn, squash, maize, and tobacco. When they traveled, they went afoot. They hunted the buffalo and the antelope, but always near home and apparently by driving them into funnel-shaped corrals that opened on a bluff over which the stampeding animals would tumble to their deaths. The buffalo was important to their economy, but not critically so. They also fought, but war was stylized and formal and not a central interest.[1]

The coming of the horse from the Southwest and the westward displacement of tribes by the pressures of Eastern Indians armed with guns changed all this, beginning in the seventeenth century.

[1] J. D. Jennings, *Plainsmen of the Past: A Review of the Prehistory of the Plains.*

These forces brought about an immediate and sweeping change in the life of the Comanches that was even more drastic than in the case of most other Indians. Walter Prescott Webb does not exaggerate in his claim that "Steam, electricity, and gasoline have wrought no greater changes in our culture than did horses in the culture of the Plains Indians."[2] With the horse, the Comanche achieved incomparably greater mobility; he mastered the buffalo; he had an exchangeable asset that made him a greater trader; he was transformed from an impotent infantryman into a fierce cavalryman—a dangerous warrior and insatiable raider. As a beast of burden and as a means of personal transportation, the horse had a fundamental value to the Comanche. It enabled the hunter to provide plenty of food, clothing, and shelter for his dependents, the raider to take more plunder, and the warrior to take more enemy scalps with less danger to himself. His life became exuberant, his culture efflorescent.

The Comanche had not been devoid entirely of a beast of burden for use in transportation previous to the acquisition of the horse. He had used the dog to draw his travois, as we have already seen. But his movable goods when toted by dogs were meager and his household poorly furnished. After obtaining the larger animal, he merely enlarged his dog harness, lengthened the travois poles, and "as an indication of appreciation of the boon which had been conferred upon him, named the horse the God-dog."[3] But the difference in the load that could be moved and the distance that could be covered as a result of the change increased considerably the area from which the Comanche could draw sustenance and the load of household appurtenances he could move about in his wanderings.

The horse had other practical advantages over the dog. It could eat grass and even the bark of trees. In the lush plains of the past it was easier to feed in large numbers than was the dog. Furthermore, its flesh could be eaten in times of food scarcity, while the dog, although nutritious, could not be eaten because of the coyote tabu. The skin of the horse provided shelter, robes, saddles, and rawhide thongs. The mane and tail were converted into ropes and bridles. The Comanche hunter was no longer compelled to stalk his game on foot.

[2] W. P. Webb, *The Texas Rangers: A Conflict of Civilization*, 13.
[3] *Ibid*.

He could run down and kill the buffalo on the open plains and afterwards carry it farther and save more of it than had been possible before.

It is difficult to overestimate the military value of the horse to the Comanche. It provided both the means and the incentive for more extended raids. Forays could be made more often and deeper into enemy territory, and the possibility of escaping safely with more plunder was greater with its use. It was primarily the horse that enabled the Comanches to extend their power southward, to beat the Spaniards and the Mexicans for more than a century, to make the Texas frontier unsafe for white settlement until they were restricted to a reservation, and to contend for a time successfully with the military forces of the United States from the Mexican border to north of the Arkansas River.

Horses constituted the most important type of property and the staple form of wealth. Because taking them under difficult conditions had a sociopsychological value, the acquisition of a large herd added greatly to the prestige of the owner. The owner of a large herd could make more munificent gifts to a prospective wife and members of her family and to other members of the tribe. Horses served also as an informal medium of exchange. They could be presented as gifts in reciprocity for services rendered and as fees to medicine men. When they were used in the settlement of controversies between individuals—as they generally were among the Comanches—they had legal as well as monetary significance.

Comanche esteem of horses knew no bounds. Each man had at least one favorite horse, although his personal string might run to dozens, or even hundreds, of animals. His favorite horse was kept picketed close to his tipi at night while the remuda grazed on the open plains. He tended it, petted it, and adored it. "Some men loved their horses more than they loved their wives," said Post Oak Jim. To this, others added, "Or child, or any other any human being." And in seeking legal settlements, whatever else the prosecuting man and his friends might demand of the offending culprit, they were sure to insist on the favorite horse.

In his own experience with a damage suit, Breaks Something had to deal with this problem.

« « « I turned to those two men and asked what Mexican (a personal name) wanted in claim.

They answered that he wanted a certain horse I had got from a dead friend, another horse, a saddle, and a Winchester.

I told them I would not part with that first horse. It was dear to me. I told them I would give them another horse just as good.

Atsaci answered, "We want that horse or none."

I tried three times to try to get them to agree on another horse, but they refused. Finally, I told them, "All right, if you take that horse, you get nothing but that horse. It is enough." I had something else to say, too, and I told Atsaci I wanted to tell him something after we finished.

"What?" he said.

I told him not to forget that he was married to two of my "daughters" (they were daughters of my brother). In these words I spoke to him. "If I accept these terms, and you insist on that horse, you can have it. But if you do, you will lose your two wives. I will take my daughters back from you. You are my son-in-law, and yet you are not caring what you say; you are trying to get the horse I love." » » »

With that Breaks Something won his point.

Killing another man's favorite horse was akin to murder, and in two Comanche cases people were killed in revenge.[4] Favorite horses were emotional objects, like people.

Just how and when the Comanches first obtained horses is not known, but within a short time after they migrated to the South Plains they possessed them in great numbers, and, henceforth, a considerable portion of the male's working hours were spent astride a horse. The first modern horses on the plains were brought by Coronado and De Soto, but those escaping from these expeditions could not possibly have been the progenitors of all the herds of a later date.[5] The Spaniards of northern Mexico possessed a great many horses,

[4] Hoebel, *The Political Organization and Law-Ways of the Comanche Indians,* 68–70.

[5] For this point of view, see Francis Haines, "The Northward Spread of Horses among the Plains Indians," *American Anthropologist,* Vol. XL (1938), 429–30.

some of which escaped and became truly wild. Others were stolen. Most of the horses to reach the plains at an early date probably came by way of New Mexico.

Available evidence indicates that the Plains Indians began using horses some time after 1600. None of the tribes could be classed as having a horse culture before 1630, and probably not until after 1650.[6] Once the Indians of the South came to use horses, the spread northward was rapid. By 1659 Indians to the northwest of the Spanish settlements in New Mexico were raiding the ranch stock, and within another five years raiding was common practice. A significant number of horses, no doubt, were captured by the Indians in the revolt of 1680 in New Mexico, and it is likely that many of these fell into the hands of Plains Indians either as a result of trade or of plunder. In 1675 Fernando del Bosque found no trace of horses or horse-using Indians while exploring along the Río Grande from the mouth of the Conchos to the Pecos River and eastward. The Mendoza-López expedition eight years later likewise found the banks of the Río Grande still barren, but as it progressed northeastward, it encountered Indians with a few horses. The Spanish expedition into East Texas in 1690 found a few horses near the mouth of the Colorado River, and in the same year it was reported that about thirty were seen near the Arkansas-Texas boundary and that the Caddo to the west had four or five per lodge.[7]

All the tribes west of the Missouri had horses when first encountered by the French and English. The Pawnees and other tribes along the Missouri had horses as early as 1680. Du Tisne in 1719 reported that two villages of Pawnees in Oklahoma near the Arkansas River had three hundred horses, which were highly valued and not for sale. By 1724 the edge of the horse belt had reached the neighborhood of the junction of the Kansas and Missouri rivers. By 1754 the Blackfeet had horses in general use both for pack and for riding, having obtained their supply from the Shoshones or Comanches. By 1770 the dispersion had reached its northern limit except for a small extension

6 Francis Haines, "Where Did the Plains Indians Get Their Horses," *American Anthropologist*, Vol. XL (1938), 112–17.

7 Haines, "The Northward Spread of Horses among the Plains Indians," *loc. cit.*, 429–32.

into the timbered area. The Shoshones of Idaho had obtained their horses by the route west of the continental divide about 1690 to 1700, or approximately twenty years before horses had reached the junction of the Kansas and Missouri rivers.

Ponca tradition credits the Comanches with having the first horses seen by the people of their tribe. According to it, the Comanches at the time fought on horseback, using the long-handled stone battle-axe as their principal weapon. Furthermore, the Poncas claim that the Comanches had thick covers of overlapping pieces of rawhide to protect the breasts and sides of their animals. The Comanches taught the Poncas how to ride and to use the horse as a beast of burden. Soon afterwards they left the country, and the Poncas knew not where they went.[8]

The Comanches probably acquired horses as early as, or before, the Shoshones. They certainly had them by the time they moved into the South Plains. They were raiding in New Mexico in 1705. The next year, the Apaches in the northeastern part of that province suffered from Comanche horse-raiding expeditions. Comanche raiding in New Mexico apparently became progressively more frequent, for in 1719 the governor of the province sent a punitive expedition against the Comanches in an attempt to check the forays.

How many horses the Comanches accumulated is impossible to estimate with any degree of accuracy. Probably no Indians were more richly supplied than they. Clinton Smith reported that his band had about 6,000 head, about one-half of which were the property of the chief; and that sometimes within a single night horses by the thousands were captured or stolen.[9] Captain Marcy estimated that the most successful warriors owned from fifty to two hundred animals each. By comparison, a Sioux considered himself wealthy if he owned thirty to forty.[10] The Antelope band, with a population of less than two thousand, had about 15,000 horses and 300 to 400 head of mules in 1867. Modern Comanches say that A Big Fall By Tripping owned 1,500 horses at the time of his death, although he was so fat he could

[8] Alice C. Fletcher and Frances La Flesche, "The Omaha Tribe," B. A. E. *Bulletin* No. 27, 79–80.

[9] Clinton and Jeff D. Smith, *The Boy Captives*, 50–51.

[10] Maximilian, Prince of Wied, *Travels in the Interior of America* (vol. I of Thwaites, *Early Western Travels*), 160.

not ride a single one, but had to travel sitting on a travois. In comparison, the entire Pawnee tribe had 1,400, the Osage 1,200, and the Omaha 1,200. The greater the distance from Texas and Mexico, the fewer the horses found.

The number of horses possessed by the South Plains Indians decreased rapidly in the last half of the nineteenth century. The Antelope band surrendered only 1,500 head to the United States at the time of their capitulation at Fort Sill, Oklahoma, on June 2, 1875.[11] The Comanche, Kiowa, Apache, and Delaware tribes had 14,810 head in 1874, but three years later they possessed only 4,194. Subsequent to just one engagement, on the morning of September 28, 1874, the day after he had destroyed the Comanche-Kiowa-Cheyenne camp in Palo Duro Canyon, Colonel MacKenzie's troop shot and killed some 1,400 Indian horses.[12] Such attrition devastated the great herds.

The Comanches obtained their supply of horses by gift and trade, by breeding, by capturing wild ones, and by raiding.

It was considered a gracious gesture to give a favorite horse to a friend. And although it was general practice to kill a warrior's personal riding string on his grave, many a man before his death willed his favorite horse to his best friend. Even the poorest had at least one horse, for the public approved the rich man who celebrated an important occasion by giving a horse to some poor old fellow who could not rustle one for himself.

In intertribal trading the Comanches exchanged horses for goods, but by 1850 they had so many horses themselves that they never bothered to trade for them. In the great peace-making in 1840 between the Cheyennes on the one side and the Comanches, Kiowas, and Kiowa-Apaches on the other, the Cheyennes gave guns, blankets, calico, beads, and brass kettles, while the Kiowas, Comanches, and Apaches offered horses. Mountain, the Kiowa spokesman, had said, "We all of us have many horses; as many as we need; we do not wish to accept any horses as presents, but we shall be glad to accept any other gifts. We, the Kiowas, Comanches, and Apaches, have made a road to give many horses to you when we come here." They were as good as his word; every Cheyenne man, woman, and child

11 Commissioner of Indian Affairs, *Annual Report,* 1875, 273.
12 Nye, *Carbine and Lance,* 223.

40

received at least one horse. Some unimportant people got as many as five or six, and the Cheyenne chiefs many more.[13]

The numerous wild herds which roamed the Southern Plains afforded an ever ready supply to any Comanches who could take them—frequently a difficult task. The mustang, which played an important part in Comanche culture, was peculiarly fitted for its role. Small, agile, and tough, it was capable of surprising speed and possessed of great endurance. Its small, pointed, alert ears and quick, wicked eyes often signalled approaching danger before the rider himself was aware of it. The mustang was also a good forager and could obtain his own food even in the winter, when he was forced to live on bark and twigs. His life was in a way as hard and unadorned as that of the Indians. The frugal, wiry little creature became the fitting symbol of the equally frugal cultures of the Plains Indians.

The Comanches resorted to several methods of capturing wild mustangs. One necessitated building a corral, usually near or around a water hole, with diverging wings. The unsuspecting animals were driven between the wings until they entered the pen and were trapped. The Kiowas used this method extensively; the Comanches only occasionally. The Spaniards also used the plan, but it was so similar to the old Indian method of impounding antelope that it is probably an Indian adaptation of an old way to a new situation. In 1852 the Comanches were using "corrals into which four hundred or five hundred head could be driven."[14] Fortunately, a good description of such a corral in use before 1836 has survived. The corral was situated in an opening in blackjack timber. It was oval in shape, the opening being at one end. The fence was a stockade formed of blackjack posts set close together on end with brush and limbs of trees piled against the outside of the fence. The wings, made of brush, were heaped up high and wide, so that a horse could neither see through nor jump over them.[15] Once inside the pen, the mustangs were prisoners.

After the introduction of firearms, wild horses were often captured by "creasing"—a delicate task requiring expert marksmanship. To crease a horse was to shoot it through the muscular part of the

---

[13] G. B. Grinnell, *The Fighting Cheyennes*, 63–66.

[14] Anon., "Reminiscences of Service among the Comanches," *Frank Leslie's Popular Monthly*, June, 1882, 662–63.

[15] G. B. Grinnell, *The Cheyenne Indians*, I, 292.

neck above the vertebrae. If the marksman could hit it there and not fracture the spine, the animal dropped to the ground paralyzed for two or three minutes. A neat trick! This gave the hunter time to rope and tie the mustang before it knew what was happening. It would soon recover, however, and when the wound healed, be as good as ever.

Young horses that had been driven from the herds by stallions were often found on the prairie in considerable numbers. When such a herd was discovered in a convenient location, the Indians would drive out a few gentle, old mares as lures. The young horses would mingle with the mares, and after a time some of them could be taken.

Lassoing was a popular Comanche method of capturing wild horses, even though relatively few animals were taken in this manner. It was an art in which the Comanche was often an expert. The skill required and the danger involved in lassoing a wild horse gave young men a real chance to show off and gain prestige while enjoying an exciting sport. It would seem natural that, other things being equal, a horse running free could not be overtaken by one carrying a rider and that the best of the wild horses would get away. The Comanches were wily enough to see to it that other things were not always equal.

In the wintertime or early spring, cold weather and lack of food sometimes made the wild horses thin and weak. At such times a chaser mounted on a fast horse that had received good care could readily overtake the mares that were thin from suckling colts or those that were heavy with foal—and even some of the stallions. In the summer, according to Post Oak Jim, wild horses became so fat that they were sluggish on their feet. Then it was possible to run them down on a good horse that had been kept in trim. In any event, by ganging up on a wild herd, a group of riders spread over a wide area could drive the herd toward a second group of riders hidden in a clump of underbrush or behind a hill. As the herd came near, the concealed Indians would dash suddenly into their midst and do their roping before the wild beasts had recovered from their surprise.

If there was no convenient hiding place, as often there was not on the open plains, the chasers sometimes undertook to surround the herd. In their efforts to break through the circle, the wild horses were forced to pass close enough to some of the riders that they could drop a noose over them.

Of all the techniques of taking mustangs, one of the easiest was to ambush them at the water hole. It was the habit of the wild horses to feed as much as ten or more miles out on the prairie from the nearest water. They would munch on the grass until thirsty. Then they would run the whole distance to the nearest hole. Hot and thirsty, they guzzled their bellies full. The Comanche, mounted on a good, rested horse, could dart from his ambush and quickly take a water-logged mustang which he could not even have approached a few minutes earlier.[16]

In capturing the hard-to-take stallions, however, the best way was to stalk them with a team of co-operating hunters. Each herd tended to move about within a limited range of territory; when flushed, it was likely to travel in a circle, returning eventually to or near the spot where it was originally found. To accomplish this end, one or more horsemen kept the herd continuously on the move without allowing it either to eat or to drink. This was not too difficult, for the stalkers, by remaining on the inside of the circle, traveled a much shorter distance than the herd. When their own mounts wearied, the riders were replaced by others or were supplied with fresh mounts. This procedure was continued without let-up for two or three days or until the herd became exhausted, when a number of riders on fresh mounts rode in and lassoed their pick of the wild horses.

To catch a wild horse is only half the job—if a man intends to ride him. There is yet the breaking to be done. The mustang was choked into exhaustion, thrown to the ground, and subjected to having the breath of the captor blown into its nostrils. The "wild" hairs were pulled from around its eyes. A headstall or hackamore, a loop of rope about the under jaw brought up and tied about the neck with a knot that would not slip, was put on the animal.[17] The captive was usually tied to a gentle mare in such a way as to keep it from injuring the mare during its first efforts to escape. While the horse was still tied to the mare, the owner handled it enough to make it gentle. After a few days it was set free, and thereafter followed the mare wherever she went. When the time came to ride his wild mustang,

[16] Noah Smithwick, *The Evolution of a State*, 187.

[17] C. and J. D. Smith, *op. cit.*, 67; Baldwin Möllhausen, *Diary of a Journey from the Mississippi to the Pacific with a United States Government Expedition*, I, 186–87.

43

the Comanche usually took it into a sand-bottomed creek or into deep water for his first mountings. This precaution took the bounce out of the bucking and made for softer landing.

Capturing wild horses had its points, but to the Comanche stealing them was better. And the Comanche was the top horse thief of them all. When he went raiding, it was sometimes for scalps, but usually he was more interested in plunder and horses than in killing.

Acquisition of horses by plunder appealed to a Comanche, for it enhanced his prestige. Taking horses under difficult conditions provided opportunity for valor and cleverness, and it was in its own right a form of coup: stealing horses from enemies was a distinguished mark of honor, and those most successful in this enterprise were highly respected. Captain Marcy reported that Is-sa-keep, a chief of one of the Northern Comanche bands, said that he was the father of four sons who were a great source of comfort to him in his old age for they could steal more horses than any other men in his band.[18] Some, like Rhoda Greyfoot's father and his two brothers, made it a point of honor never to return from a raid without horses.

The Comanche taking a guarded horse was a ghost. There are instances on record of Comanches' stealing hobbled and guarded mounts of soldiers. Colonel Dodge says that a Comanche could crawl into a "bivouac where a dozen men were sleeping, each with a horse tied to his wrist by the lariat, cut a rope within six feet of the sleeper, and get away with the horse without waking a soul." The Colonel also cites an instance of two Comanche raiders entering a stable under apparently impossible circumstances and making off with two of the best horses. The stable was built of heavy timbers set on end surmounted by a heavy plate doweled into place. The stable yard was enclosed by a heavy picket fence with similar dowel construction. Both yard and stable were guarded by sentries. Yet one stormy night the two Indians cut the dowels, removed enough timbers to permit a horse to go through, and made away with the two best animals without alarming either sentry. They were some sixty miles away before they were overtaken.[19]

[18] Marcy, *Adventure on Red River*, 159.
[19] R. I. Dodge, *The Plains of the Great West*, 401–402.

Northern Mexico afforded a golden harvest of horses with little danger to the Comanche raiders. Padre Jacob Sadelmeyer wrote in 1744 that the Comanches were raiding the Río Grande frontier for horses. Long years of internal strife and revolution after revolution had impoverished the Spanish borderlands, and the poor inhabitants were without adequate means of defense. Spanish and Mexican authorities, fearing revolution, resolutely sought to deprive the people of arms. The fierce Comanche raiders struck the defenseless towns, haciendas, and ranches like a whirlwind, capturing thousands of horses, mules, and cattle, and many Mexican children. They swept south to Durango, within five hundred miles of Mexico City, and over Zacatecas, Chihuahua, Tamaulipas, Coahuila, San Luis, and Nuevo León. "For days together," said one traveler who passed through the country from Mexico City to Santa Fé in 1846, "I traversed a country completely deserted on this account, passing through ruined villages untrodden for years by the foot of man." The same authority stated that from the fall of 1845 until the time of his visit in September, 1846, on the northern frontier of Mexico "upwards of ten thousand head of horses and mules have already been carried off, and scarcely has a hacienda or rancho on the frontier been unvisited and everywhere the people have been killed or captured.[20]

When "Dot" Babb, for many years a captive and later an adopted warrior-member of the Comanche tribe, expressed the view that the Comanches had a limited vocabulary,[21] he was reflecting the view of earlier centuries that primitives are incapable of abstract thought—an incapacity reflected in paucity of language. Of course, it is perfectly true that primitive peoples, whose simpler cultures have fewer objects to identify and fewer abstract concepts demanding expression, do have need for fewer words. But this is no indication of any inability to refine a vocabulary. Boas pointed out long ago that Eskimos, to whom the condition of snow is a life and death matter, have more than a score of words for snow in various degrees of temperature, crystallization, moisture, and compactness. LaBarre, in his recent work among the Aymara Indians of Bolivia, who made potatoes their mainstay in prehistoric times, recorded more than two hundred words

[20] George F. Ruxton, *Adventures in Mexico and the Rocky Mountains*, 112.
[21] Babb, *op. cit.*, 144.

for "potato," each word indicating minutely determined combinations of potato qualities.[22]

Considering that 250 years ago the Comanches did not even know what a horse was, they very quickly built up a vocabulary for describing a horse on the basis of color. A horse was a brown (*dupsikᵘma*), a light bay (*ohaieka*), a reddish brown (*εkakoma*), a black (*duukᵘma*), a white (*tɔsa*), a blue (*epixṭuesi*), a dun (*maana*), a sorrel (*ɔtεkᵘma*), or a roan, either red (*ekaesi*) or yellow (*ohaesi*). Then there was the *dunnia,* a yellow horse with black mane and tail. Pintos were red (*εkasənaco*), sorrel (*ɔdutsənaɾo*), or black (*duu:-tsənaɾo*). And finally there were the red (*εkanaki*), yellow (*ohanaki*), and black (*duunaki*) ears.

Most war ponies and race horses had personal names, while the ruck of a man's herd did not. A Comanche warrior would never be caught riding a mare if he could help it—they were for women and children—and under no circumstances would he ride a mare into battle. And while teen-agers might ride mares, a boy or girl dressed up for "show off" considered mares déclassé; only a sharp horse would do.

Riding horses were almost always gelded, for the Comanches became real pastoralists who knew how to breed up their stock. This drew from T. A. Dodge, U.S.A., the following comment: "In one particular the Comanche is noteworthy. He knows more about horses and horse-breeding than any other Indian. He is particularly wedded to and apt to ride a pinto ('painted' or piebald) horse, and never keeps any but a pinto stallion. He chooses his ponies well, and shows more good sense in breeding than one would give him credit for. The corollary to this is that the Comanche is far less cruel to his beasts, and though he begins to use them as yearlings, the ponies often last through many years."[23]

Only a few choice stallions were permitted to breed the mares. All others were castrated when about two years of age. The Comanche technique was to rope the forelegs, throw the stallion, and tie his front

[22] W. La Barre, "Potato Taxonomy of the Aymara Indians of Bolivia," *Acta Americana,* Vol. V (1947), 83–102.

[23] T. A. Dodge, "Some American Riders," *Harper's New Monthly Magazine,* May, 1891, 862.

feet to a post. Two men grabbed the hind legs, and the operator sat between the legs to do his cutting.[24]

Comanche horses were not ordinarily shod, but a man's favorite horse, if tenderfooted, was fitted with a rawhide boot soaked in water and tied over the sore hoofs.[25] Other riding horses had their hoofs toughened by walking them slowly back and forth near the heat and smoke of a fire.[26]

Among the Comanches, horses were private property. Each member of a family who was large enough to ride had one or more mounts of his own. The young child was usually given an old, gentle mare. The women had their riding mounts as well as mules and gentle horses for packing. Large numbers of mules were frequently found in the Comanche camps around the middle of the nineteenth century. Captives, before they were adopted into the tribe, were also forced to ride mules to lessen the danger of a break for freedom.

Josiah Gregg was of the opinion that the Comanches had a universal custom of marking their animals by a slit in the tip of each ear.[27] Contemporary Comanches deny this, however, saying that any Comanche could distinguish one horse from another by looks just as easily as he could tell one person from another. After all, the Comanches lived with their horses.

Most accounts by early explorers on the plains agree that the Comanches were among the best horsemen the world has produced. Baldwin Möllhausen, a German scientist and traveler who crossed the Southern Plains in 1853, observed that from earliest childhood to the last days of his life the Comanche was continually on horseback. "Indeed, he makes but an awkward figure enough on foot, though he is no sooner mounted than he is transformed; and when with no other aid than that of the rein and heavy whip he makes his horse perform the most incredible feats," which gave him a feeling of independence and superiority.[28] Marcy stated that it was while the Co-

[24] Informant: Post Oak Jim.
[25] Informant: Slope.
[26] H. H. Bancroft, *The Native Races,* I, 518, n.136; Parker, *op cit.,* 203.
[27] Josiah Gregg, *Commerce of the Prairies,* 433.
[28] Möllhausen, *op. cit.,* I, 184.

manche was mounted that he exhibited himself to best advantage. "Here he is at home and his skill . . . is truly astonishing."[29]

One of the first things a Comanche child learned was to ride. He started riding in a pack on his mother's back long before he could walk. Next he was strapped to her saddle on a gentle mare. By the time he was four or five he was off on a pony of his own. Both boys and girls were taught to ride with or without a saddle. Girls were taught to ride astride and became almost as much at home on horseback as boys. But it was not enough for the Comanche boy merely to learn to ride. He had to be a trick rider. Day after day, month after month, he practiced in drill. He learned to pick up objects from the ground while his mount was traveling at full speed. At first, small and light objects were selected, but as the boy grew older and more proficient, heavier and more bulky objects were exchanged for the lighter ones, until at last, unassisted and at full speed, he might be able to pick up from the ground and swing across his horse the body of the heaviest man. To rescue a fallen comrade was the highest obligation of any Comanche warrior. To leave a comrade on the field to be stripped, mutilated, and scalped by desecrating enemies was a disgrace to The People. Every man was expected to be able to meet the challenge when the need arose—and he had to be able to do it alone. Generally, however, rescues were made by two men working together. Rushing neck by neck on either side of the prostrate person, both riders stooped at the same instant and swung the body in front of one of the riders. This stunt was practiced over and over on all kinds of ground until riders and ponies could do it without a hitch.

In attack, the Comanche, like other horse Indians, made his mount a mobile shield between himself and his enemy. How many a trooper or pioneer within his defensive corral of wagons has cursed at the scudding Indian whirling about him, loosing arrows from beneath his horse's neck, with nothing showing but a leg hooked over the horse's backbone! The key to this fancy trick was a loop of rope attached to the cantle or, if the rider was bareback, plaited into his steed's mane. With the loop slipped over his head and under his outside arm, a trained rider (and what Comanche was not?) clung to

29 R. B. Marcy, *Exploration of the Red River of Louisiana in the Year 1852*, 32 Cong., 2 sess., *Sen. Exec. Doc. 54*, 103.

48

the side of his horse with both hands free for shooting or picking up heavy objects while riding hell bent for leather.[30]

Thus it was that Homer Thrall imaginatively saw the Comanche as "the Arab of the Prairie—the model of the fabled Thessalian 'Centaur,' half horse, half man, so closely joined and so dexterously managed that it appears but one animal, fleet and furious."[31]

Long before they got horses, the Comanches, like their Shoshone cousins, liked to put a good bet on a stick game or an arrow-throwing contest. Small wonder that in later years they took to horse racing with gusto and mighty bets.

In one popular race the contestants started from a line and rushed full speed toward a tree, the one touching it first being the winner. In another they rushed at a pole resting horizontally about six feet from the ground. If a rider stopped his horse a moment too soon, he failed to touch the pole; if a moment too late, the horse passed under the pole, possibly leaving the rider dangling to the pole or thrown to the ground. In still another contest, two strips of buffalo hide were stretched across the track about six to ten feet apart. The starting point was about two hundred yards from the strips. The contestants jumped their mounts over the first strip, reversed their direction, and raced back to the starting point. The horse which failed to get beyond the first strip with all four feet or which went beyond the second lost the race regardless.

Most Comanche racers were "doctored" for a race. An owner had a medicine man chew up some unidentified medicine which he spit in the horse's mouth or ear. Whatever its specific effect, it was power in the Comanche view. No woman could come near a racer when it had had medicine made for it, and after racing, both horse and rider went into a creek to wash off the effects of the medicine.

In many instances horse racing proved to be really profitable business for the Comanches—who were not the least loath to fleece a sucker. Colonel Dodge has left a story of a race which the officers at Fort Chadburne, Texas, to their regret arranged with some Comanches. After the first bets had been laid, the Comanches innocently

[30] R. I. Dodge, *The Plains of the Great West,* 331; Marcy, *Exploration of the Red River of Louisiana in the Year 1852,* 103.

[31] H. S. Thrall, *A Pictorial History of Texas,* 445.

brought forth a miserable-looking pony with a three-inch coat of thick hair and a general appearance of neglect and suffering. Its rider "looked big enough to carry the poor beast on his shoulders" and was armed with a club with which he belabored the animal from starting line to the finish. Yet, to the surprise of the whites the Indian pony managed to win by a neck. Within an hour the officers bit again and lost by a nose. Then they suggested a third race and brought out a magnificent Kentucky racing mare. In a frenzy of excitement the Indians bet everything that the whites would take. With the starting signal the Indian rider threw away his club, gave a whoop, and his little mount "went away like the wind." That Kentucky mare was soon so far behind that for the last fifty yards the Comanche sat backwards on his pony beckoning to the white rider to come on. The whites afterwards learned that the shaggy pony was a celebrated racer, and that the Comanches had just come back from fleecing the Kickapoos to the tune of six hundred ponies with that same little horse.[32]

Straight-run relay races from a standing start for a distance "ten times the distance you can shoot an arrow," or a good two miles, made a favorite run. Shorter obstacle races put both speed and control to a rigorous test.

To the Comanche, then, the horse was an intimate household friend, a beast of burden, a counter in the great prestige game of the warriors, a "gamer," and an occasional source of food. But it was to the buffalo that he turned for his economic mainstay.

The buffalo was as indispensable to the Comanche as the horse. No part of the slaughtered animal was wasted except the rump, spine, and skull. Hair, skin, flesh, blood, bones, entrails, horns, sinews, kidneys, liver, paunch, and the dried excrement were all utilized. The Indian ate its flesh, the marrow of its bones, the contents of the gall bladder on raw liver, and even at times its entrails—a habit left over from Shoshone days. Of the edible parts, only the heart was unconsumed; it was left for magical perpetuation of the herds.

When the Comanche was thirsty and water was not available, there was the blood of the buffalo. Its paunch, after the inner lining was removed, was used as a water bag and also as a container in which

[32] R. I. Dodge, *The Plains of the Great West*, 329–30.

to cook stone-boiled soup. The dried excrement (chips) of the buffalo burned slowly and made a hot and lasting fire for both warmth and cooking; it was sometimes used ceremoniously as a support to keep some sacred object from touching the ground, and it was so endowed with power that scouts swore their oaths of veracity on a pile of buffalo chips. The bones, hoofs, and horns of the buffalo were fashioned into cups, spoons, and ornaments; and the horns were occasionally fashioned into bows or worn on headdresses on special occasions. Sinews from the back made bow strings and thread. Ropes were made from the twisted hair. The hide was used to manufacture clothing, lodge coverings, thongs, saddles, bridles, and bags. When properly finished with the fine coat of wool and the hair left on it, it provided an unusually warm robe. Freed from the hair and dressed, it constituted a summer blanket. A green hide served for a pot before the white traders brought kettles, and braided strands of rawhide provided an excellent rope.

There was a time, according to Comanche legend, when the Indians did not have access to the buffalo. In the version recorded fifty years ago by H. H. St.Clair, Coyote effected their release by a ruse.[33] In a hitherto unpublished version given by That's It in 1933 it was *Ka:wus,* the Culture Hero, who turned the trick.

《 《 《 Our knowledge only goes to the point where man and the earth were already here.

The People were out playing three kinds of games one day—the wheel game, throwing arrows, and shooting with the bow. A strange man came amongst them. He talked to no one. Just stood there looking on with a quiver over his shoulder.

After a while he said, "I'll go over there to defecate." He laid down his quiver and jumped in a creek. While he was down there, a young man went up and looked in his bag. There was a nice piece of fat in it. He took it up and showed it to the other Indians. They all wondered where that old man came from. "He certainly has plenty of meat," they all said.

Then they all plotted to stop playing at meal time. They left the

[33] H. H. St. Clair, "Shoshone and Comanche Tales," *Journal of American Folk-Lore,* No. 85 (July–September, 1909), 280–81.

old man all alone on the field. He just kept walking back and forth until, at last, he jumped back into the draw. The People kept looking. Then they saw him come out of the draw as a bird flying up and over the mountain.

Now The People wondered how they could get over the mountain to see. At last they thought of two birds. One was Owl. He flys quietly. The other was Quail. He walks quietly.

These two went over the top of the mountain, and there they saw a single tipi facing east. At sunset they landed near it.

After dark Owl said, "That's what we're here for. I'm going."

As he lit on the tipi pole, the old man inside said, "Uh, there's an Indian."

Owl flew back to Quail and told him, "He knew I landed, and when I flew away, he said, 'Uh, the Indian is gone.'"

Then Owl and Quail went up close together. They could hear someone talking. Then there was no sound for a long time, so Owl told Quail to go up to the tipi. Quail went up and peeked. Three times he looked. Then he went back to Owl. "There are three people there," he said, "an old man, his wife and daughter."

They waited a long time, this time—until midnight.

Then the daughter spoke. "Mother," she said, "let's have something to eat."

Owl said, "There they go. They've got plenty of meat."

Then they waited another long time, and again they heard the girl ask for something to eat. But her mother warned her, "Sh-h-h, don't talk like that. You can't tell how those Indians travel."

Owl nudged Quail, "She means us."

This happened three times when finally the old man said they should eat. So the woman opened a parfleche and took out lots of meat. When they were through eating, she just swept the suet and loose chunks to the back of the tipi.

Then they went to sleep. Quail went up and snitched some pieces. "Here's your meal," he said to Owl. Then they flew back to The People with some meat in their claws.

They exclaimed, "My, they have lots of meat, we shall have to go around the mountain to get at that stuff." So they moved camp. They packed all their stuff on ten horses, representing each band.

52

The old man saw them coming. "What do you want?" he asked them.

"Oh, we're just here for a visit."

He was suspicious, nevertheless, and he drew a line from a tree to a stump, telling them to camp on the other side and not to cross the line. For three successive days he visited them, but he always kept them from coming to his camp. Every time he would say, "I don't know where we can get any meat to eat at all."

Ka:wus was there with The People. He could turn himself into any form. "It's up to you," The People told him. "You have to figure out how to get meat. He isn't ever going to give us any."

"There is only one way," *Ka:wus* replied. "Just leave it to me. Now you people break camp and move away." Then he changed himself into a puppy.

The old man followed after The People to see where they went. After a while, the daughter came to see if she could find anything in their old camp. Just that little puppy was there.

"Oh, you poor little puppy," she cried out. "You're mine." But the pup backed off like it was shy.

"Don't be afraid," she coaxed it. "From now on you are never going to be hungry. I'll prove it to you now. Come on!"

With that she opened the door to the tipi, and *Ka:wus* went in. There was a hole in the floor, and down there he saw a hundred thousand buffaloes!

Just then the old man came back. "Take that dog out," he ordered. "You can see from the look in its eyes that it is a human being. Take it out, or I will kill it."

The old man followed his daughter outside the tipi as she did what she was told. She put the puppy down, and then her father went away again to see if The People were coming back. As soon as he was out of sight, she picked the puppy up and took him right back in the tipi.

"You'll never get hungry," she kept consoling him, and she showed him all those buffaloes.

Then he began to act like he was getting nervous, and he jumped right out of her arms. He jumped around and shouted just like a human being, stampeding the buffaloes. They smashed down the door, and out they poured.

53

That dog was still in there. The girl grabbed a club to brain him, but he turned back to his human form. Hanging on to the side of a buffalo, he rode out without her getting him. He made straight for the hills, and there he saw that mess of buffaloes.

With that he went straight back to his people.

"How did you make out? What happened?" They wanted to know.

He told them, "Tomorrow at sunrise those buffaloes will be right at our door," he said.

After that they always had plenty of buffalo to eat. That is how they got them.   »   »   »

The American bison, or "buffalo," as it is commonly called, is not really a buffalo at all. It is a gregarious bovine ruminant, one of the largest members of the family *Bovidae* that also includes cattle, sheep, goats, and antelope. It is a close relative of the bison of Europe, although quite different in appearance in many respects. It is of rather early origin. Recently discovered fossil remains are said by geologists to belong to the middle Pleistocene age, to be not less than four hundred thousand years old.

The first buffalo seen by Europeans was in 1521 by Cortez in the menagerie of Montezuma. Núñez Cabeza de Vaca was the first European to report seeing buffalo in Texas. Pedro de Castañeda, the chronicler of the Coronado expedition, recorded that there were so many of them he did not know what to compare them to except the fish in the sea; they were so thick that many times his party was unable to go through them.

The buffalo were found on the whole of the Great Plains. The eastern limit of the buffalo land followed roughly from the north along the ninetieth meridian to the northeastern corner of Iowa. Then it bore slightly to the southwest, crossing the Red River about the ninety-eighth meridian, ran south in Texas to about the thirty-first degree of latitude, entered the southern part of New Mexico about the one hundredth and fourth meridian, and roughly followed the eastern slope of the Rocky Mountains to the north. Thus the entire Comanchería fell well within the buffalo range.

Within this area the vast herds drifted back and forth in seasonal migrations. In the fall they moved south from two hundred to four hundred miles to winter in a more favorable climate, drifting north again with the coming of spring. In spring and summer the herds shifted away from the mountains; in winter, toward them.

The number of buffalo on the plains before commercial slaughter began reached a figure that staggers the imagination. In Kansas alone, it has been estimated that the bones of thirty-one million head were gathered and sold for fertilizer between 1868 and 1881.[34] A vast herd comprising considerably more than four million animals was seen by competent witnesses in 1871 on the Arkansas River between Fort Zarah and Fort Larned. The main herd was fifty miles deep and twenty-five miles wide—and this was only one of the many herds in existence at the time. On one occasion when the Great Herd moved north, it extended more than one hundred miles in width and was of unknown length, and it was estimated conservatively that the herd contained over one hundred million head.[35] Small wonder that the Comanches forgot to a great extent the starvation fears that beset the poor Shoshones!

Buffalo hunting for the Comanche followed fairly closely a regular pattern. At certain seasons, when the animals were fat, the hunt became a tribal affair and the slaughter of the great beasts took the shape of a co-operative venture. The great communal hunts occurred during the summer months after the seasonal moulting was done and the hides were in their prime, and during November and December when the hides, covered with a dark, seal-brown coat of fur, were best for winter robes. Preparation for the great fall hunt began in October, and the time was determined in democratic assembly at which everyone was welcome to listen, but in which the war leaders made the important decisions.

Having decided upon an approximate time and location for the hunt, the entire camp became alive with activity. Runners were sent to seek a location for the temporary hunting camp. It must be near water and timber. Scaffolds must be erected for drying the meat. When all was ready, the young and able-bodied men, women, and

[34] Henry Inman, *The Old Santa Fé Trail,* 203.
[35] Martin S. Garretson, *The American Bison,* 44–64. The estimate was made by General Philip H. Sheridan, Major Henry Inman, and Robert M. Wright who lived for fifty years in the heart of the buffalo country.

older children left the main camp for the operating base. Mules and pack horses were used to transport the hunting tents, which consisted simply of one or more undercoated skins thrown over a pole resting on crossed stakes. They were also to bring back to the main camp the many hides and quantities of meat that would be taken. Only weapons, tools, and supplies that seemed necessary for the occasion were carried.

There was plenty of hard work for all concerned, but it was work spiced by anticipation of the excitement of great feasts and sharpened by gay social activity. This was really the "Harvest Season." On at least one and possibly for several evenings before the hunting party left the main camp, the people gathered for the Hunting Dance at the central meeting place of the village just as lengthening shadows faded into darkness. The hunting party itself often continued to dance for one or more nights after they had left the main camp. There was no spiritual significance attached to the dance; each Comanche informant insists that the people danced because they "were glad they were going on a hunt." Why not? For the dance a fire was built, unless a bright autumn moon provided sufficient light. There were two, four, or more drummers and singers, always an even number. The drummers and singers were men who had good voices, but for such strictly social dances no medicine powers were essential. Men and women lined up facing each other, and when the music began, the women crossed over and selected a partner. The dancers joined at intervals in the singing. They wore their everyday clothes, for no special ceremonial dress was necessary on this occasion. During the dance one man took care of the fire, but the wood was gathered by any of the enthusiastic dancers who wished to help. About midnight the dance ended and the people scattered to their lodges for sleep.[36]

The regulation of communal buffalo hunts under the strict surveillance of military police was one of the outstanding features of the cultures of practically all the Plains tribes. But of this the Comanches had nothing. They had, of course, no military fraternities such as those which did the policing for the other tribes, and in spite of their fierce individualism they seem not to have had the need for police

[36] Informants: Face Wrinkling Like Getting Old; Kills Something.

when it came to hunting. Here the unruly Comanche behaved himself very well. Group discipline prevailed, and all worked for the common good. The rules of the game were known and respected.

Each hunt had a hunt leader who was the director for the occasion. He was a respected warrior and a man of good judgment, that we know. But whether he was appointed to the position or merely assumed it by common consent cannot be said. He gave general directions for the conduct of the hunt, and his was the power to signal the attack—for all the hunters charged simultaneously.

In the execution of the hunt the exact location of the herd was first determined by scouts. Then the hunters were out before the dawn of day. A narrow valley with many lateral ravines was considered to be very favorable. Moving up into position against the wind in a great semicircle, the band of hunters remained quietly on horseback out of sight of the buffalo. Buffalo have a keen sense of smell, but their wool partially obscures their sight and their sense of hearing is not acute. As they approached the buffalo, the hunters gradually spread until the herd was encircled except on the windward side. Everything ready, the leader gave the signal, the gap was rapidly closed, and the whole circle closed in. The Indians ran their ponies around the herd, forming it into a compact mass. The bulls would force the cows and calves to the center of the pack, and would then run around and around the margin, presenting themselves broadside to the hunters. In the surround, the buffalo often became bewildered and ceased to run. Killing them was then easy. Outer guards were in a position to turn back or kill any animals which escaped the hunters on the inside of the circle, but escaping buffalo were not pursued if other herds were in the vicinity.

At other times, particularly if the topography of the land was unfavorable for making a close surround, the hunters stalked the herd against the wind to get as near as possible without being detected. Then they lined up to get an even start, and at a given signal all charged the animals. The main function of the simultaneous charge was to prevent the scattering of the herd by a few individuals, but equally important was the need to kill as many buffalo as quickly as possible, for the meat would spoil before it could be cured if the animal when slain was overheated from long running.

It was necessary to have well-trained horses, for the time of the slaughter was short. The first step in training a horse for buffalo running was to make him rope shy. This was done by twisting one end of a rawhide rope around the lower jaw, allowing the free end to trail. The trainer then mounted another pony and proceeded to prod the horse with whip, lance, or switch. For a short time, the horse, stepping on the halter rope, found it difficult to run. A few falls and hard jerks, however, were usually sufficient, and afterwards the horse very skillfully avoided stepping on any rope. Horses were trained also to run without bridle or rope of any kind, being guided by knee pressure.

Buffalo hunting, although hard work and dangerous, was truly exciting. When chasing buffalo, the Comanches, like other Indians, usually discarded all clothing except the breechclout. They rode bareback, although occasionally a small pad was used. Frequently a rope was wound in loose coils around the horse's body, just back of the forelegs; by thrusting his knees under the rope, the rider maintained a firm seat while in action. Each hunter rode upon the buffalo from the rear, coming in close on its right side and shooting at the soft spot between the protruding hip bone and the last rib. This was the only way to reach the vitals. The heart of the animal hung low, and since the rider was slightly behind and above the buffalo, the arrow slanted into the soft spot behind the short rib and ranged forward and downward. Driven with terrific force at such close range, the shaft often completely buried itself or passed all the way through the animal, even on occasion bringing down a second animal running alongside. A hunter sometimes pulled the arrow from the victim while the animal was still running. As soon as he heard the twang of the bow string, a good buffalo-running horse swerved away from its victim in order to be well out of harm's way when the wounded beast turned and charged. Unfortunately, the horse was not always quick enough to prevent being gored, and frequently a mount stepped in a prairie-dog hole, breaking its leg and throwing its rider. Many a hunter received broken limbs as a result of such accidents, and some were killed, but it was a risk taken with joy.[37]

[37] C. C. Rister, "Indians as Buffalo Hunters," *Frontier Times,* Vol. V (April, 1928), 456; Gregg, *op. cit.,* 361–62.

When the hunt was over, each dead buffalo was the property of the man who killed it. Public-spirited men of consequence gave some of their kill to old men or widows or to families who had no hunters to provide for them. A hunter had no extreme difficulty in identifying the buffalo which he had killed. He might be able to recall the location of the animals, their appearance, the position of the wounds, and he easily could recognize his own marked arrows. If arrows of different men were found in the same dead buffalo, ownership was determined by the position of the arrows. If each arrow had inflicted a mortal wound, the buffalo might be divided, or more likely it was set aside as a portion of the charity fund. The hunter leader usually made the decision in case of argument.

Another and early method of killing the buffalo, and one which remained popular among the Comanches until the last, was with the lance. Josiah Gregg says that the Comanche often charged the buffalo with a long-handled spear or lance, which, if the horse was well trained, was much more effective than the bow and arrow or the American pistol.[38] In using the lance, the rider approached the buffalo from behind and held the lance across his body, the opposite hand from the buffalo being the higher. When the buffalo was slightly ahead of the horse, the hunter, using both hands, thrust his lance downward and forward, aiming for the heart, although some hunters thrust downward for the kidneys, hoping to break down and cripple the animal. When the buffalo felt the prick of the lance, it usually ran faster. When it attempted to turn and charge, the hunter pressed the lance firmly into its side until the buffalo gave way and ran on, or until it fell.

Although relatively few buffalo were taken in modern times by any other than the above methods, other means were occasionally employed. One was to drive the buffalo over a precipice or into a river. Fortunately an excellent description of this method has survived.

This mode of hunting was to select one of the most active and fleet young men, who, disguised with a buffalo skin fastened about his body, with the horns and ears so secured as to deceive the buffalo, placed himself at a convenient distance between the herd

38 Gregg, *op. cit.*, 363.

of buffalo and some of the river precipices, which sometimes extend for miles. His companions, in the meantime, get in the rear and along the flanks of the herd and, showing themselves at a given signal, advance upon the herd. The herd, thus alarmed, runs from the hunters toward the river. The Indian, who thus acts as a decoy, when the precipice is reached, suddenly secures himself in some crevice of the cliff previously selected, leaving the herd on the brink. It is then impossible for the foremost of the herd to retreat or to turn aside, being pressed on by those behind, and they tumble headlong off the cliff, strewing the shore with their bodies.[39]

The hunters rushed up to take a heavy toll of those failing to make a quick escape. This, of course, was a survival of the favored buffalo drive of prehistoric Indians on the plains.

The individual hunter sometimes employed a still more unique method. He wrapped himself with the hide of a wolf or a buffalo and on "all-fours" crept within shooting distance of the unsuspecting animals. Care had to be taken to approach toward the wind always. It was then possible for the hunter with bow and arrow to kill a number of animals before the unwary herd realized the source of its danger.[40]

Among many Plains tribes the women took over as soon as the men had shot the buffalo down. According to Comanche informants[41] the heavy work of skinning and butchering was done by the men. Cows were left lying on their sides, but bulls were heaved over to set on their bellies with all fours spread. They were then ready for butchering. The brisket was first slashed across at the neck and folded back so the forequarters could be removed at the joint. Then the hide was sliced down the middle of the spine in such a way as not to cut the sinews, which were removed intact. After the hide was peeled back toward both sides, the hind quarters were disjointed, leaving the rump with the back. The flank was next cut up toward the stomach and removed in one piece with the brisket—the whole thin

[39] J. A. Allen, "History of the American Bison," United States Geological and Geographical Survey, *Annual Report*, IX (1875), 574–75.

[40] Rister, "Indians as Buffalo Hunters," *loc. cit.*, 456.

[41] Informants: Post Oak Jim; Slope.

chunk being made up into one roll of meat. Now the butcher cut up through the ventral to remove the entrails, separating the ribs from the sternum. Slicing between the middle ribs, he next took their free ends in both hands and pulled up and outward to break the rib steaks off from the spine. At last, the bare spine with rump and head was all that remained; the tail had been skinned out with the hide. The meat was bagged in the hides, loaded on the pack horses, and all was ready to be toted back to the main camp for further processing.

Comanche hunters who were out butchering alone had their buffalo horses trained to stand by as sentinels. Butchering in a hurry is an intense business and a man cannot very well keep a close lookout for danger. But he could give a quick glance to his horse's ears. His horse had learned to "wave" his ears alternately if another buffalo or coyote was close. If it was a man, he pitched both ears forward. "Thus many lives were saved," says White Wolf.

Back in the camp, the men's work was done for the time being. While the women turned to, the bucks relaxed in feasting and recounting their exploits. The women were slicing the meat into very thin filets which were hung over the racks for a quick sun-drying. Hides were pegged out on the ground, flesh side up, so that they could be fleshed and scraped for later tanning.

As soon as the women caught up with their work, another kill was made. This procedure continued until enough meat and skins were obtained and cold weather drove the Indians to their winter camp, or until there were no more buffalo.

Buffalo were so plentiful in the Southern Plains that the Comanches rarely bothered to fortify themselves for the communal hunt by making medicine. There were times, nevertheless, when the wandering herds could not be found. Then the "chief," or hunt leader, went with his pipe to a medicine man who had power. Offering his smoke, he asked that the hunt ritual be performed. His wish would be granted, but unfortunately we do not have the details of the kind of medicine that was made. Presumably it was similar to the magic antelope surround described in the next chapter.

The horned toad was also believed to be a help in locating the buffalo, for when asked the question, "he will always run in the direction of buffalo." That is why he is called *kusɛtɛmini,* "asking about the buffalo." Ravens also were buffalo pointers in Comanche belief. They like to eat carrion and were always following the herds to eat the bugs on their hides. When a raven circled over the camp four times, dipping his head and cawing, "he was telling The People where the herd is; he will fly off and show the way."[42]

Toward the end of or soon after the hunt, a man and wife of respectable family who were noted for their goodness and purity were likely to give a Buffalo Tongue Dance or feast. Men, women, and the older unmarried adolescents who had participated in the hunt were encouraged to attend. The ceremony began early in the morning and ended with the meal at midday. A fire was built outside the tipi and the buffalo tongues were roasted over the coals. When the meat was done, the men were asked to seat themselves in a semicircle about the fire. The women took a position about twenty steps from the opening of the circle. The host or a leading medicine man lighted the pipe. He blew the first puff of smoke toward the sun, the second toward the earth, and one in each of the four directions. The pipe was then passed to the other men who smoked likewise. This was an oath by which the smoker bound himself to speak truthfully.

After all had smoked, a woman was called upon to come forward and serve the tongue. Any man who had had illicit sexual relations with her called out, "no, no," and she returned to her place. If everyone remained quiet, she came forward and served the tongue to the assembled group amid much applause and shrill cries of "li-li-li-li" from all the women present. No dancing or singing accompanied the ceremony.[43]

This little act was lifted bodily from the Sun Dance complex of other Plains Indians. A Cheyenne Sun Dance giver must collect hundreds of buffalo tongues to distribute to the Sun Dance officers and participants. The Crow ritual called for an "absolutely virtuous woman to serve as Tree-notcher, one who had been purchased in marriage and had been scrupulously chaste."[44] Virtue was tested in a manner similar to that just described. Among Indians like the Crows

[42] Informant: Post Oak Jim.

[43] Informants: Kills Something; Face Wrinkling Like Getting Old. Other informants were aware of this ceremony.

[44] R. H. Lowie, *The Crow Indians,* 312.

and Comanches, who really did not expect much in the way of marital fidelity, the stunt seems to be a little meaningless. Among the Cheyennes, however, who originally built up the Sun Dance complex,[45] family virtue was actually adhered to, and every military society had four virginal maidens as essential ritual assistants. As an adjunct of Comanche buffalo tongue banquets, ritual chastity had no place, but as a chance for good-humored teasing it seems to have appealed to the Comanche sense of a good thing.

Had the Comanches and other Plains Indians been left undisturbed by intruders, the buffalo might have supplied their needs indefinitely. But the white man pushed ever relentlessly westward, and intruding Indian bands along the border of the Comanche country began to trespass upon the Comanche hunting grounds. The effects of these encroachments on the country soon began to be felt in a vital way—in the diminishing supply of buffalo. The period between 1830 and 1860 witnessed such destruction that the hunters found it increasingly difficult to sustain their families by hunting.

During the colonial period in Texas, buffalo were seen as far south as the vicinity of the present city of Houston. As early as 1833 explorers and adventurers in the region of the Arkansas and Canadian rivers had begun to observe that the eastern edge of the buffalo range was retreating westward rapidly. The Osage agent wrote in 1841 that his Indians had to extend their hunting operations each year farther and farther into the plains to obtain even a scant supply, and that it would soon be necessary for them to learn to farm.[46] In 1846 it was estimated that one hundred thousand buffalo cow hides annually reached the Canadian and American markets. The bull hides were then regarded as worthless for commercial purposes. At the same time Torrey's Trading House was getting three dollars each for ordinary, and eight dollars for choice, hides.[47] It is difficult to determine how extensively professional white hunters operated during the period be-

[45] L. Spier, "The Sun Dance of the Plains Indians," American Museum of Natural History Anthropological Papers, XVI, Part 7 (1921).

[46] Agent Wm. Armstrong, Annual Report, 1841, 27 Cong., 2 sess., House Exec. Doc. 2, No. 34, 316–17.

[47] C. C. Rister, "The Significance of the Destruction of the Buffalo in the Southwest," The Southwestern Historical Quarterly, Vol. XXXIII (1929), 34–39. Torrey's was the official company of the Republic of Texas for trading with the Indians.

fore the Civil War, but it appears that several trading concerns employed men who combined hunting with trading. There were very few buffalo left by 1852 in the vicinity of Fort Phantom Hill, Texas.[48] A few years later, however, there were great numbers of buffalo in the same vicinity. In 1855, John W. Whitfield, Indian agent, wrote that the Comanches, Kiowas, Kiowa-Apaches, Arapahos, and Cheyennes were then confined to a district from which the buffalo had almost entirely disappeared, and that they were feeding upon their horses and mules until the number of those animals had fallen below their necessary supply. He recommended that the government furnish them subsistence until they could be taught to support themselves.[49] The Arapahos in 1857 were on the verge of starvation, and their chief told the agent that his people must learn either to work or starve.[50] The Commissioner of Indian Affairs reported in that same year that the game had diminished to the point that many of the Indians were compelled to live by plunder.[51] The Comanches, although feeling the pinch of the diminishing supply, were faring better than their neighbors. The Civil War interrupted temporarily the encroachments on the Plains Indians' hunting grounds, but when the war was over, the slaughter soon was resumed in such proportions as to make that of the earlier period seem child's play.

By 1870 the original great buffalo range had become permanently divided into two sections. The northern herd ranged from about forty-three degrees north latitude through the Powder River country to the British possessions. The southern herd ranged from North Texas to about forty-one and one-half degrees north latitude. This southern buffalo range corresponded almost entirely with the territory held by the Comanches with the exception of the feeding grounds between the South Platte and the Arkansas. In the winter of that year an eastern company experimented successfully with buffalo hides

[48] Clarksville, Texas, *Standard*, May 28, 1853; A. B. Hasson, Post Surgeon at Fort Phantom Hill, "Report," 1852, West Texas Historical Association *Year Book* (1924), I, 75.

[49] Agent J. W. Whitfield to Commissioner of Indian Affairs, September 4, 1855, 34 Cong., 1 sess., *Sen. Exec. Doc. 1*, No. 46, 437.

[50] Robert Miller, agent for the Cheyennes, "Report," October 14, 1857, 35 Cong., 1 sess., *Sen. Exec. Doc. 11*, No. 60, 432.

[51] Commissioner of Indian Affairs, *Annual Report*, 1857, 35 Cong., 1 sess., *Sen. Exec. Doc. 11*, 296.

for making leather. By 1872 it became generally known that buffalo hides were marketable, the price being about $3.75 per hide. The railroad lines leading into the plains soon swarmed with "would-be hunters" from the East, excited by the prospect of having a buffalo hunt that would yield a monetary return. By rail, wagon, horseback, and afoot, the hunters poured in, and the slaughter was on.

A number of hunting outfits operating from Dodge City crossed into the northern Panhandle of Texas in the autumn of 1873 in violation of the Medicine Lodge Treaty, made in 1867 between the Federal government and the Indians, reserving the region between the Arkansas and Canadian rivers for an Indian hunting ground. The buffalo hunters, refusing to respect the treaty, established a trading post at Adobe Walls, which action instigated the Comanches to resume the warpath. After a short cessation of activities, the hunters shifted to the southern part of the range. By the fall of 1874 some professional hunting was being done in the southern part of the range, and by 1875 the slaughter was definitely under way in an organized and systematic manner. The slaughter abated during the hot summer months, but as soon as the first cold of autumn started the buffalo south, it was renewed. Destruction of the herds went on at an increasing rate throughout 1876 and 1877. The greatest slaughter came in the winter of 1877–78. More than one hundred thousand hides were taken in the months of December and January on the Texas range.[52] J. N. Atkinson claimed that in Fort Griffin at one time there was a stack of buffalo hides as long as a city block, "as high as a man could reach throwing hides out of a wagon, and so wide that it must have been made by driving wagons down both sides of the pile in stacking."[53] Only a few small herds located in the Yellowhouse, Blanco, and Palo Duro canyons, in the valley of the Canadian River, and along other water courses traversing the Southern Plains were to be found in the winter of 1878–79, and by the end of another year the buffalo were gone.

The buffalo slaughter became an important issue with the public. Opponents fought it for sentimental reasons, or cited the great waste and the renewal of the Indian wars in support of their position. On

[52] W. C. Holden, *Alkali Trails*, 13.
[53] Mary J. Atkinson *The Texas Indians*, 331.

the other hand, the buffalo hunters, supported by a strong public opinion, insisted that they were rendering a great service in removing the buffalo from the Great Plains. Their position was summed up by General Philip H. Sheridan, in command of the Southwestern Department, before a joint meeting of the Texas Senate and House of Representatives in 1875. Sheridan argued that it would be a sentimental mistake to attempt to stop the slaughter of the buffalo. Instead of stopping the hunters, he said, the legislature should give them a hearty, unanimous vote of thanks and appropriate money to present to each hunter a medal of bronze with a dead buffalo on one side and a discouraged Indian on the other. He continued in words which reveal clearly the Comanche dependence upon the buffalo:

Those men have done more in the last two years and will do more in the next year to settle the vexed Indian [Comanche particularly] question than the entire regular army has done in the last 30 years. *They are destroying the Indians' commissary* [italics ours]; and it is a well known fact that an army losing its base of supplies is placed at a great disadvantage. Send them powder and lead, if you will, and for the sake of lasting peace, let them kill, skin, and sell until they have exterminated the buffalo. Then your prairies will be covered with speckled cattle and the festive cowboy, who follows the hunter as a second forerunner of civilization.[54]

The general knew whereof he talked.

[54] John R. Cook, *The Border and the Buffalo*, 113.

66

Food, Clothing, and Dwellings

ALTHOUGH the subsistence activities of the Comanches centered around the buffalo, theirs was not a one-crop economy. Elk were plentiful in the brushy regions bordering the rivers and their tributaries. The black bear, found in the Cross Timbers, was hunted largely for its oil, which was used in the preparation of hides. The Comanches considered bear meat less tasty than either buffalo or deer. Principally within the region of the High Plains, in the heart of the buffalo country, roamed herds of antelope in great numbers. A herd of about two thousand was once seen at Fort Dodge.[1]

Food was usually plentiful enough that the Comanches no longer bothered, as did the horseless Shoshones, to run down antelope until the frightened and exhausted animals dropped. But they did retain from their Shoshonean background the magical antelope surround that was so widely used by the Indians of the Great Basin.

It was used among the Comanches only when the whole camp was out of food. Then the camp leaders would go to a medicine man or a medicine woman who had antelope power. They would smoke and tell him the trouble. According to Slope's account, the medicine man called for an antelope dance lasting several days to work up his power and to draw in the antelope. He selected two men to whom he gave some of his power for what they had to do. When all was

[1] Garretson, *op. cit.*, 64.

ready, the people arranged themselves in two parallel lines facing east, the antelope medicine man at the center with the two warriors mounted on either side of him. Everyone else was afoot. In his hands the conjurer held his medicine sticks—two antelope hoofs, each on a piece of wood. Crossing his arms halfway below the elbow, a stick in each hand, he "blocked" the antelope. They could not run away. Then, giving one medicine stick to each of the warriors, he bade them ride off. One went northeast; the other southeast. Circling wide, they met and passed each other a mile or so to the east. They were drawing a magical barrier. Against its power the hapless antelope would be helpless. Each rider returned along the path laid by the other; the circle was closed. Now the two files of people—men, women, and children—followed out along the trails of the horsemen until they were standing in a huge circle, all singing antelope songs.

The antelope were now inside the circle, and the people closed in on them, shouting. The animals were in the corral. They dashed wildly about, but they could not cross the line. At last, when they were exhausted, the medicine man pointed one of his hoofs at an antelope who had one horn down. He would fall dead. "The people then pile in and kill them all."

The skeptic may say that it was the circle of shouting beaters who bunched the animals. But not the Comanche. He was convinced that without the medicine charm they would break through the circle and escape. The medicine hunt was not used often, but Comanches say it worked.

There is some disagreement about how fond the Comanches were of horse meat, but when game was not available, it was eaten and relished. Raiding parties normally carried few rations with them, and when the supply was exhausted, they simply killed and cooked a spare horse on the spot. Thomas C. Battey, who was one of the first white teachers among the Comanches, states that buffalo, antelope, or deer were preferred, but if not obtainable, a pony or a mule was the next choice. Modern Comanches agree with him. We have already called the Comanches "pastoralists," but they were not strictly so in that they did not rely to any great extent on their horse herds for food, and they never killed their mares. Around the middle of the nineteenth century they had plenty of horses to eat, yet the values that had been built up when horses were rare were such that horses remained almost wholly prestige tokens and transport bearers.

Great numbers of cattle obtained from raids on Mexican and Texas settlements were also eaten, especially in later years. The majority were butchered and consumed by the raiders wherever they were found, or as soon as the raider felt himself at a distance safe from attack by the whites. The Comanches made no attempt to herd them. Many head of stolen cattle were not butchered, but went to New Mexican traders in return for ornaments, arrows, kettles, and other articles. Although the Comanches thought beef was poor eating when buffalo was to be had, nowadays an old Comanche likes to sink his teeth into mediocre beef with plenty of fat as the nearest thing to the buffalo he loved.

Dog meat was regarded as an almost sacred dish by the Sioux, and to the Cheyennes "A nice fat, boiled puppy is just like a turkey on Thanksgiving to you white people."[2] But the Comanches did not eat dog meat. Medicine Woman says it is because "Once, when the people moved, they left an old, old lady in camp with a dog. Several weeks later when the people returned to the site, they found that the dog had killed the woman and had consumed most of her body. Henceforth the Comanches refused dog meat, since dogs ate human flesh."[3] There is a deeper reason, however. Dog is Coyote's cousin, and Coyote is tabu. He is the Trickster of Comanche and Shoshone mythology—a demi-god. Although coyotes were occasionally hunted for their furs, they were never eaten or wantonly killed. Post Oak Jim shot one for the fun of it once when out on a cattle raid. Came a cyclone, and Jim thought his horse was spinning on its head; it rained all night, and in the morning it was so cold they nearly froze. "That coyote's mother probably made medicine," said Jim. "Coyote has medicine. If we harm one, it will get back on us some way."

The same with dogs. Post Oak Jim killed a dog once, and ever after he thinks he had bad luck with his children. They all got sick and died. In 1933 Howard White Wolf had a dozen curs on his place. He did not dare to kill them himself, but he asked a member of the Santa Fé Laboratory of Anthropology group to do it for him. White

[2] E. A. Hoebel, Cheyenne Field Notes (unpublished).
[3] Informant: Medicine Woman.

men are immune to dog medicine—or at least White Wolf was willing to let a white chance it! As they feel thus about dogs, it is hardly surprising that the Comanches will not eat them.

Although wild fowl and fish were plentiful, they were not eaten except when food was very scarce, for fish were tabu, and it was common belief that those who ate the turkey would become cowardly and run from their enemies just as the turkey flees from his pursuers. Frogs and swine were also tabu; frogs because, like fish, they were water animals, and swine because they were associated with mud and water. The Comanches, if they knew it, would eat nothing cooked with hog lard.

The Comanches did not eat human flesh. The neighboring Tonkawas, whom the Comanches found in Texas, were loathed and detested because of their cannibalistic practices. The fact of cannibalism is the chief rationalization used by the Comanches in explaining their implacable enmity for the Tonkawas. Like many moral excuses for war, this one, too, seems to come after the fact, since prior to the nineteenth century, when the Tonkawas were busy fighting the Apaches, the Comanches got on well enough with them.[4] It is quite probable that the Comanches themselves were not at all unused to the idea of cannibalism in the early days of their southward migration. That some people will turn cannibal in starvation times is accepted by the Shoshones, although cannibals were reputedly hanged because once having tasted human flesh they acquired an insatiable appetite.[5] Among the Comanches, however, the very idea that one of them might under stress eat another person was vigorously repulsed.

In late winter food sometimes became scarce; neither buffalo, deer, antelope, nor elk could be obtained. The shortages were more likely to occur in February and March, the season designated by a term meaning "when the babies cry for food."[6] When food became scarce, a Comanche ate almost anything—the tabued fish and fowl, rabbits, terrapins, turtles, snakes, skunks, rats, lizards, grasshoppers, meats which were no longer fresh, roots, and bark.

In the preparation of food, meat was generally cooked by holding

[4] H. E. Bolton, "Tonkawa," in Hodge, *Handbook*, II, 783.
[5] Hoebel, *The Political Organization and Law-Ways of the Comanche Indians*, Appendix A, 141.
[6] Informant: Medicine Woman.

it on a stick over a fire. Sometimes it was roasted on hot coals and the burned portion removed before eating. It was served on the flesh side of a dried skin, or sometimes the stick was brought into the tent and the handle end stuck into the ground with a long piece of meat dangling from the other end. The women got copper or iron pots as soon as possible from the traders and thereafter boiled or stewed most of their meat. They had always stewed some meat in the buffalo paunch, heating it by immersing hot stones in the water, since a fire could not be built directly under the paunch. After they obtained metal pots, the large kettle was placed over a fire and all sorts of meats and cuts dumped into it. The contents were stirred at intervals with the broad rib of a buffalo. Hunks of meat were fished from the sloppy stew with the stirring stick, knife, or the hands. The iron pot released women from a lot of labor, but it certainly added nothing to the flavor, sanitation, or dignity of the meal. During the later period a few people dipped their meat into a salt brine as they ate it. Generally, however, no salt was used on the meat, either for curing or when eating.[7] A sauce made from honey, water, and tallow was frequently used over roasted meat. The Comanches were fond of tripe. When it was not consumed raw, the usual method was to clean it and then roast it over hot coals.[8] Terrapins and turtles were collected in sacks and thrown while alive into a crackling fire. Those which sought to escape were thrown back until they roasted, when they were raked from the fire, their shells broken open, and the contents eaten with a horn spoon.[9]

Captain R. G. Carter, whose military life brought him into contact with the Comanches, described their cooking of fish and turkey:

In cooking fish, they enclose them in clay or mud after they have been "drawn" and cleaned, to a depth of several inches, rolling them over, and the hot coals scraped on top. When cooked the hard baked clay is knocked off with the casing, and the fish eaten with salt.

A wild turkey was bled, dressed or "drawn," a few feathers

[7] *Ibid.*

[8] *Ibid.*; Smithwick, *op. cit.*, 178–79; Parker, *op. cit.*, 196.

[9] C. and J. D. Smith, *op. cit.*, 66; Thomas C. Battey, *The Life and Adventures of a Quaker among the Indians*, 95, 323; Rister, *Border Captives*, 18–19.

plucked out and it was flung into the fire or red coals. When one would suppose that there was nothing left to the bird, the burnt, black mess was raked out, left to partially cool, then with dexterous movement of the knife the skin is peeled or stripped from the neck downwards taking the burned feathers, revealing a white and tempting morsel to a hungry man. It was then cut and torn apart.[10]

Even when game was plentiful, the Comanche taste for certain foods would not appeal to us. When a buffalo, beef, deer, antelope, or elk was killed, it was not uncommon for a hunter and his family to gather about, open its veins, and drink the warm blood. Raw brains and the marrow from the leg bones were stirred together on the flesh side of the hide or in a dish made by cutting out a section of the slaughtered animal's ribs, and were consumed without further preparation. The fresh, warm liver covered with the contents of the gall bladder was considered one of the finest delicacies. Children crowded around the butcher and begged for it. Liver cooked on coals and spread with rich marrow also formed a choice dish. Entrails stripped of their contents by drawing them between two fingers, kidneys, paunch, loin tallow, and the tallow around the kidneys were all eaten raw while still warm and without washing. A Comanche would cut into the udder of an animal and, placing his mouth on the gash, suck the warm mixture of milk and blood with the greatest of pleasure. The curdled milk from the stomach of a suckling fawn or calf was a delicacy indeed. Herman Lehmann also refers to their having eaten the heart, but this appears to have been unusual, for it was generally left within the skeleton,[11] probably a ceremonial gesture to propitiate the animal spirit. These appetites may have been indelicate from our point of view, but they provided an effective way to get vitamins and iron in large quantities. The Comanche would have had the hearty approval of the modern dietitian.

Although buffalo meat was their dietary mainstay, the Comanches did not suffer the unrelieved monotony of boiled stew and jerked

10 R. G. Carter, *On the Border with MacKenzie*, 279.

11 Herman Lehmann, *Nine Years among the Indians*, 115, 116; Smithwick, *op. cit.*, 180.

meat. They raised no vegetables of their own, yet they came from a background of food gatherers and did not forget their heritage. They utilized a large number of vegetables and fruits. Women did most of the seeking for plants, but even the men knew what was growing about them and how to use it. G. G. Carlson and V. H. Jones have given the expert judgment that "the average Comanche has a very good knowledge of his plant environment and particularly of those plants which are or have been of value to his tribe."[12] Fifty-two wild plants with their uses as given by Comanche informants in the work of the Santa Fé Laboratory group are listed by Carlson and Jones. Of these, twenty-seven different plants were used as food. It would seem that this number would compare rather favorably with the variety of fruits and vegetables eaten by most Americans today. Twenty-two of the listed plants were used for medicinal effect in the Comanche native pharmacology.

The facts, when marshaled, simply do not support the statement of Captains R. B. Marcy and G. B. McClellan that fresh meat was the only food of the Comanches "with the exception of a few wild plants which they find on the prairies."[13]

Among the fruits, the persimmon, mulberry, "haws," wild plums, grapes and currants, juniper berries, hackberries, prickly pear cactus, and sumac were gathered. Persimmons were eaten fresh and also dehydrated and stored. For storing, the persimmon was beaten to a pulp, the seeds removed, and the paste sun-dried in cakes. The cakes were later soaked in water and used in a variety of ways. Plums were eaten fresh or stored for winter use in a similar manner, as were also grapes. Prickly pears were sun-dried for winter use, and hackberries were pulped, mixed with fat, and roasted in balls on the end of a stick.

Pecan nuts were an obvious delicacy for any Indians living in Texas or Oklahoma, and if times were hard, the Comanches shelled and boiled the acorn of the blackjack oak.

For starchy substance all Comanche bands dug and ate the tuberous roots of Indian potato, either raw or boiled—and one band, remember, was even called the Yɛp-eaters. Four or five other root plants,

[12] G. G. Carlson and V. H. Jones, "Some Notes on Uses of Plants by the Comanche Indians," *Papers* of the Michigan Academy of Science, Arts, and Letters, Vol. XXV (1940), 518.

[13] Marcy, *Exploration of the Red River of Louisiana in the year 1852*, 111.

like wild onions, radishes, and Jerusalem artichoke were also exploited—nor was the bulb of the sego lily overlooked.

A truly favorite sweet dish for the Comanche was a mush made of buffalo marrow mixed with crushed mesquite beans, which are very high in sugar content.

Dried pumpkins, pumpkin seeds, and corn were obtained in trade from the Kiowas, Wichitas, and other tribes to the east. Corn was not really used very much, although the Comanches did like to make a drink of boiled corn meal sweetened with mesquite. If they had let this concoction ferment, as did the Gila River tribes of Arizona, they could have had an alcoholic mead, but the Comanches did not know how to brew beer or ferment wines from their grapes.

Tobacco was obtained in trade with the Mexicans and not grown at all.

Honey added flavor to the Comanche diet. So highly in favor was it that one band received the name *Penatзkз* or Honey-eaters. The honey bee seems to have been abundant along the Cross Timbers of the eastern Comanchería. Honey was bagged in skin containers and could be kept indefinitely.

The original K-ration was pemmican, beloved of the Comanches and many other tribes of Indians. Wild berries, cherries, or plums, pounded well and partially dried in the sun, or walnuts, piñons, or pecans gave flavor to the dried meat, which was pounded thoroughly, softened over a fire, and then mixed with the pounded fruit or nuts. Tallow and marrow fat were added, and the mixture was stored either in parfleche bags (ɔyɔ:t), in large intestines which probably had been no more than partially cleaned, or in paunches. Before the container was firmly tied, melted tallow was sometimes poured over the whole to make it air tight. In either container, the pemmican with proper care would keep for years. It was greatly prized by the whites, particularly when sliced and dipped in honey. They called it "Indian bread," for since the Comanches had no bread, this was the nearest substitute. Children went about eating it as American children eat candy. When other foods were available, dried meat and pemmican were saved for times of food scarcity.

It was generally believed by the whites that the Comanches had no regular times for meals, that they ate at all hours of the day or night. This belief was strengthened because they prepared and set food before guests as soon as possible after their arrival, whatever the hour. Eating is a gesture of hospitality not to be postponed. "Meat is free to those who come. A man makes friends of the poor that way. They never got tired of visitors," says Slope. Nevertheless, it was customary to have a formal meal soon after arising in the morning and a much more important one in the evening. There appears to have been no regular noon meal, both children and adults helping themselves to food, if plentiful, whenever their appetites and convenience dictated. Before eating on public occasions, the chief or leader cut off a morsel and offered it to the Great Spirit by holding it first toward the sky and then burying it. Individuals did the same when eating, in lodge or elsewhere, but like our custom of offering thanks, the practice was not universal. Some interesting descriptions of Comanche meals have been left by early writers. One is that of a breakfast of the less formal type:

Outside the tent, in front of the door, two logs lay side by side. Between them the fire was kindled. A long slice of horse flesh was attached to the end of a stick some four feet in length by which the meat was held over the fire, and when barely warmed through was brought into the tent, the handle end of the stick thrust into the ground, the long slice dangling from the other end, resembling a drooping blood red flag. Kiln-dried corn was next boiled and mashed and served in a large dish made of bark. Breakfast was then ready, when, without more ado, each cut off a piece of meat, the size regulated by the appetite, and holding it between the fingers of one hand, with the fingers of the other scooped up the corn, filling the mouth alternately with flesh and vegetable.[14]

Another account is of a formal meal where visitors were present:

The company is seated, or squatted, rather, around on the matting that forms the beds at night, their feet gathered under them. Short boards or thick pieces of hide are placed before each one;

14 Lee, *op. cit.*, 132–33.

the meat is taken out of the kettle by the fingers of the woman who officiates as cook, and apportioned to each one, and placed before him; bread [this was after the government had set up a reservation and was providing some provisions] is apportioned out, and cups for the coffee furnished to each. The party is some time in partaking of the meal, which is enlivened by much conversation, amusing tales, and laughter, while the meat is torn to pieces by the teeth and fingers, sometimes with the assistance of a knife. . . . After a meal water is always offered to all who have partaken to rinse the mouth and wash the hands. After this the pipe may be in order but not necessarily. If it be introduced, the women withdraw, and some important subject discussed. The pipe is always circulated from one to another, from right toward the left.[15]

Perhaps opportunism in the life of the nomadic Comanche is best reflected in his attitude toward subsistence. Seldom were efforts put forth to make provision for the future other than preserving meat or wild fruits and nuts by drying in such quantities as could be carried when the camp moved. He ate sparingly when on a raid or a hunt. Times of hunger were frequent. He could subsist on a surprisingly small amount when game was scarce, or he could demonstrate an amazingly gluttonous appetite when food was plentiful and no danger present. Besides, the food might spoil unless quickly consumed. By practicing self-denial, he developed a quality of hardihood unequaled by other peoples who later came to his country. It was because of his surprising resourcefulness while traveling on the semiarid Staked Plains that he was able to survive where the Anglo-American invader would starve or die of thirst. And when all resources were exhausted, he could go for many hours through trying circumstances without either food or water. Indeed, his self-restraint could be quite as pronounced as his gormandizing. Clinton Smith relates that on a trip across the plains, when water was not found where expected, the most rigid discipline was enforced in the interest of the weaker members of the party. Grim warriors, with blood-shot eyes and swollen tongues, staggered on, threatening with death anyone who might attempt to

15 Battey, *op. cit.,* 322–23.

76

drink the few cupfuls of water carried in buffalo paunches to supply the children.[16]

In very early times, if we take what we know of the Shoshones as the measure, the Comanches could not have taken much interest in sartorial splendor. Even in later days their work-a-day garb was simple and crude. They hardly looked like the popular conception of the painted, beaded, and befeathered Indian. For festive occasions, however, they had their fancy dress garb, and young men, especially, liked to think of themselves as dandies. A ṭuiβItsi was much to be admired, and if asked what a ṭuiβItsi is, any Comanche will answer, "A handsome young man with shiny black hair, all dressed up on a good-looking horse." The ṭuiβItsi had his counterpart in the naiβi: a good-looking girl with long braids, painted and all dressed up in a good buckskin dress. When there were dances or when the band was moving from one camp site to another, the naiβi and ṭuiβItsi liked to parade and show off to the admiring glances of the people—and each other. Adult Comanches also liked to dress up, but they were not so self-conscious about it.

Boys, until they reached the age or eight or nine, went entirely nude unless the weather was severe. Regular attire generally consisted of breechclout, leggings, and moccasins only. The former was a broad piece of cloth or buckskin drawn up between the legs and passed under the belt both behind and before. The ends, one in front and one behind, formed loose, hanging flaps which extended almost to the knees. The length of the breechclout depended, of course, upon the size and height of the individual, but would probably average six feet for an adult male. Since blue was the favored color for formal or dress-up occasions, some early observers believed it to be the predominant color.[17]

A vestige of the breechclout is still worn by conservative Comanches in the form of a gee-string beneath their Levis. It is nothing more than a braided cord passed between the legs and wrapped about the waist. It cannot be seen, is not decorative, but is magically protective of the male's sex organs.

[16] C. and J. D. Smith, *op. cit.*, 60.

[17] Informant: Medicine Woman; also, Smithwick, *op. cit.*, 184; David G. Burnet, "The Comanches and Other Tribes of Texas and the Policy to be Pursued Respecting Them," in Schoolcraft, *op. cit.*, I, 234.

Comanche leggings were of buckskin and extended from the foot to the hip. They were close-fitting and were attached to the belt. The border of the material beyond the seam was left loose, presenting a wide margin of flapping buckskin. Those intended for dress occasions were likely to be red or blue.[18] They were distinguished among other Plains Indian leggings particularly by their long fringes. Leggings were sometimes beaded, but the ornamentation was usually attached to the fringe and might consist of bits of silver or other metal, beads, shells, elk's teeth, or anything that appealed to the wearer's fancy.

The moccasins of the Comanches had buckskin uppers with a seam down the heel, with the lower border of the upper sewed to a stiff sole of tanned buffalo hide. Like the leggings, Comanche moccasins could be distinguished by their long fringes. The fringes ran from the lace to the toe and along the seam at the heel. They were relatively short on top of the moccasin, but those on the heel were from six to eight inches in length and might number as many as fifty or more. The tail of a polecat or some other animal was occasionally used instead of the fringe of buckskin strings. In addition to the fringes, moccasins were ornamented with beads and small jinglers. Beads of various colors, including dark blue, light blue, white, and red, were strung, and the string sewed to the moccasin. Strings of beads extended along the seam at the heel and around the opening at the top of the moccasin, and from the lace almost to the tip of the toe. Small pieces of metal were often attached to the ends of the fringes.[19] Although the Abbé Emmanuel Domenech related that the Comanches extracted silver from mines near San Saba from which they manufactured ornaments for themselves and for their horses,[20] there is a lack of evidence to support his statement. Certainly most of what they used was traded from the Mexicans.

For winter foot gear the Comanches made genuine arctic boots of buffalo hide that reached to the knee. The whole boot was made with the wooly hair of the buffalo inside and with the soles folded

18 Informant: Medicine Woman; also, Burnet, "The Comanches and Other Tribes of Texas and the Policy to be Pursued Respecting Them," in Schoolcraft, *op. cit.*, I, 234; Gregg, *op. cit.*, 432.

19 Direct observation of Comanche women making moccasins by Wallace.

20 Abbé Emmanuel Domenech, *Journal d'un Missionnaire au Texas et au Mexique*, 125–26.

Drying Meat
Courtesy Oklahoma Historical Society Museum

A Comanche camp, about 1870
Courtesy Bureau of American Ethnology

A dugout in the Comanche country in 1892
Courtesy Bureau of American Ethnology

up higher at the sides than for moccasins. Unlike moccasins, they were loose fitted so that cloth could be wrapped around the feet in extreme weather. Under the boots, the buckskin leggings were always worn as well. The soles and feet of the boots were greased to waterproof them, but not the legs.[21] All in all, it must have been a good winter foot covering. Poor people, according to She Invites Her Relatives, "got pretty cold." They had no boots and had to be content with ordinary moccasins and trade cloth wrapped about their legs.

Early plainsmen claimed that they were able to identify the tribe to which a party belonged from the moccasin tracks. To some extent this was true, for the heel fringes, the nature of the soles, and the toe forms left distinguishing marks. The one-piece moccasin was typical among the Northern Plains tribes. Instead of the buckskin heel fringes, the Cheyennes, for example, used two small tails of deer skin, a buffalo tail, or a strip from the beard of the buffalo which trailed behind. The short, stubby foot of the Comanche left a track that provided an additional means of identification.

Shirts worn by the men were made from the skins of deer, antelope, or mountain sheep. They were made by sewing two pieces together in such a way that the pattern conformed to the natural contour of the skins. The ornamented shirt was more or less a ceremonial uniform of chiefs and important warriors. On the other hand, the shirt itself, stripped of its ornaments and accessories, seems to have been the precise pattern worn in daily routine in cold weather by the northern Indians. Clark Wissler believes that the shirt was not in early use among the Comanches and other southern Indians.[22] Neither Dodge, Marcy, Burnet, nor Neighbors mentions the shirt as being a part of Comanche attire, but "Dot" Babb and our informants definitely state that it was worn in cold weather prior to the reservation era.[23] The neck of the shirt was cut in a V-shape, and the shirt extended below the top of the leggings, measuring about two and one-half feet from the cut of the neck to the bottom. The garment was generally richly fringed around the collar and sleeves, the buckskin strings often extending twelve inches or more in length. It was also ornamented with beads, metal, and scalps of enemies.

[21] Informants: Holding Her Sunshade; She Invites Her Relatives.
[22] Wissler, *North American Indians of the Plains*, 47, 48.
[23] Informant: She Invites Her Relatives.

After the acquisition of bandannas, the man wore one around his neck. Instead of tying it in front, he used a button made from buffalo bone through which he pulled the ends of the handkerchief. The older men still wear bandannas in this manner.

There was a time when the art of sewing was unknown and when garments were tied together at the seams, but in modern times clothing was neatly sewed with sinew thread, which was very stout and durable. Such thread was made from the sinew lying along either side of the spine of the buffalo or deer. It was taken off in long pieces and dried, and strands of it were split off with the finger nails as needed. The strand of thread was then moistened in the mouth and rolled on the knee with the palm of the hand or between the palms, and one end of the thread pointed. With an awl a hole was made in the material, the fine point of the thread was passed through the hole, and the thread pulled through with the fingers.

Awls and needles were usually made of bone sharpened to a fine point. Steel substitutes were among the first articles traded by the whites to the Indians, but the methods of sewing remained practically unchanged so long as leather was used for clothing. Sewing implements were carried in a small case made of dressed buffalo cow or calfskin tied to the belt. Such cases usually opened at the top with a flap. The awl was also carried by the men as a part of their everyday outfit, since it was an essential tool in their work. The men carried it in a small leather pouch with a flap covering, attached to the wrist by a buckskin thong. Pouches were ornamented with variously colored beads in simple design and sometimes fringed with metal pendants.

The buffalo robe was a regular part of the wardrobe. Hides for robes were taken during the fall months of November and December. Some robes were prepared with the hair left on for use in extremely cold weather, while others were prepared with the hair removed for milder weather. Some specimens retained the holes around the edge through which pegs were driven in stretching the hide. Minor alterations in shape were made by cutting off the tail and legs and by tucking the ears through slits from the outer to the under side. The Comanche robe was usually made of two separate pieces sewed together down the center, because the buffalo was skinned by cutting down the spine. A very narrow (one-quarter to one-half inch) line of red paint down the middle concealed the stitching. Ordinarily a man's robe had no other decoration. Robes ranged in size from about twenty by thirty-six to approximately seventy-five by one hundred inches.

The robe was one of the warmest and most protective coverings that could be devised against low temperature, for the buffalo in November and December was covered with a dark, seal-brown coat of wool intermixed with hair, which on some of the bulls measured from seventeen to twenty inches in length. Plainsmen and soldiers stationed at the frontier forts claimed that one buffalo robe was warmer than four ordinary blankets. Many overcoats were manufactured by the government from buffalo robes for army men exposed to severe weather during campaigns against the Indians. Lighter robes were also made of bear skin, for which two hides were required, gray wolf, calling for four skins, and coyote, for which eight skins were needed. Rarely, even skunk fur was used. And for babies and children rabbit-skin robes were provided.[24]

There seems to have been no difference in the robes of men and women except that those worn by the wives of great warriors and chiefs were painted.

The eight Comanche robes found by J. C. Ewers in American museums in the nineteen thirties all had the so-called "hour glass" figure in the center. This figure is nothing more than a highly stylized, geometric representation of a buffalo. A geometric border runs around the outside of the field in all the women's robes. In its distribution the Comanche "hour glass" and border design is definitely Southern Plains, for it is shared for the most part only by the Wichitas, Kiowas, Apaches, and Río Grande Pueblos (presumably Taos). The feathered sun symbol, popular on robes to the north, was not used at all by the Comanches. Robes worn by the wives of noted warriors often carried markers symbolizing the coup, or war honors, of their husbands.

The preparation of a Comanche painted robe was a serious undertaking. Usually three or four women worked together under the direction of a skilled and experienced leader. Before the painting was done, they took the gelatinous scrapings from the under side of the

[24] *Ibid.*

81

hide and boiled them down in water until the concoction made a glue-like sizing. It was spread over the surface to be decorated and served as a fixer for the paint. The paints, which were mineral pigments in water, were pressed into the hide with the edge of a patella. After the design was completed, the hide was sized once again. Such robes, although they could be buried with the owner at her funeral, were usually inherited by a younger sister.[25]

Both men and women normally went bareheaded, except in bad weather when the robe was pulled up to form a kind of temporary hood, but in later years many Comanches wore fur caps made of buffalo calf or coyote skins. Warriors sometimes wore a coiffure of buffalo horns or a hood made of the scalp of the buffalo with the horns attached in proper position as a part of their ceremonial attire. For special state or ceremonial occasions, feathers were worn as plumes or woven into a hood or war bonnet. The Indians of the East wore a narrow head band into which feathers were stuck upright, but the Comanches and other Plains Indians wore a kind of cap around which the feathers were placed so as to droop and spread backward, and not infrequently the cap supported a streamer.

Clark Wissler believes the war bonnet was not regularly worn prior to the reservation period by the Plains Indians, although by 1834 feathers were worn on the head as a badge of distinguished service throughout a wide area of the Plains.[26] His conclusion regarding the use of feathers by Plains Indians in general is fairly well substantiated by evidence regarding the Comanches. Had the war bonnet been worn, some of the early visitors would certainly have noted it. It was too conspicuous to have been overlooked. David G. Burnet mentioned the buffalo-horn headdress but not the war bonnet. Several accounts relate that feathers, particularly those of the eagle, were worn in the hair by warriors. Captain R. G. Carter, who was with Colonel MacKenzie in the campaigns against the Comanches in the eighteen seventies, was one of the first to mention feathered war bonnets of the "most unique and fantastical designs" as though they were regular and proper dress on special occasions.[27] They certainly never became

25 *Ibid.*
26 Clark Wissler, *The Relations of Nature to Man in Aboriginal America*, 52–61.
27 Carter, *On the Border with MacKenzie*, 283.

nearly so important to the Comanches as they were to some tribes farther north.

The life of a Comanche warrior was rugged, but that did not keep him from spending a great deal of time at his toilet. He was especially proud of his hair, and in the village he might be seen daily combing, greasing, and braiding it. Men parted their hair from the center of the forehead back to the crown, forming a braid on each side, and made a streak of yellow, white, or red along the part. The braids were tied or wrapped with beaver fur or any other available material that appealed to the wearer's fancy. Beaver fur was worn on dress occasions. Bright-colored pieces of cloth, with red the most commonly recurring color, is used at the present time by the older men. Pieces of silver, beads, tin, glass, and single feathers were attached to the side locks as decorations. Each man also wore a scalp lock braided from the hair at the top of his head, and in it he usually wore a single yellow or black feather. Brushes, made from the tails of porcupines, were used for grooming the hair. The most common form was made by stretching the porcupine tail over a stick of wood. Hair brushes were also made by pounding out the fibres of a large yucca stalk. These fibers were gathered up and bound together with a buckskin thong and singed so as to burn off the sharp edges. The men never shaved, but carefully plucked all hair from their face and eyebrows with a pair of tweezers made of bone, leaving the whole face as smooth as a baby's cheek. A piece of door spring was used incessantly by Post Oak Jim through all the long hours of interviews in 1933. Comanche vanity went so far that narcissistic bucks begged for the hair that women cut off in mourning so that they could splice it into their braids to make them look longer. She Invites Her Relatives tells of one ɬuiβltsi who was showing off at a dance. "He threw his side lock over his shoulder—and the attached end came off. Everybody hooted with laughter; he picked it up and went home."

Paint was an indispensable article of ornamentation for both sexes. Both men and women, when circumstances permitted, painted their faces before meeting strangers and for all special occasions. The Comanches always carried paint with them. Vermilion was much sought after, but when it could not be obtained from the white trader, paint was made from clays and from weed and berry juices. Black was the war paint—the emblem of death—but red, yellow, olive green, and blue were favorite colors. There appears to have been no uniform manner of make-up. One warrior painted his face red, his eyelids white, and streaked his face with black. Another painted one side black and the other yellow down to the waist; another wore red on one side and yellow on the other, with lines of black upon his cheeks.

Tattooing was not conspicuous in the Comanche tribe, but both sexes tattooed the face and body, the chest being the most commonly used part of the torso.[28] Clinton Smith records that his chief had a black star tattooed on his chest.[29] The warriors were as proud of their battle scars as old-time German students were of their dueling wounds, and brought them out more conspicuously by tattooing around them.[30] Bears' claws, horse hair, mules' tails, beads, and other similar materials might be appended to the hair or about the body. Bands of rawhide or copper wire served to protect the wrist of the left hand from the slap of the bow string.

Another fancy of the Comanche male was to puncture his ears for rings. "A young man," says Breaks Something, "sees other men have their ears pierced. He comes home and wants to have it done too." This was in late adolescence. The young man asked one of his female relatives to pierce his ears. She took him to the lodge of a woman who had recently had a baby easily, so it would hurt less. There she heated a needle red hot (in the old days she used a cactus spine) and burned six to eight holes all along the helix of one ear. The other was punctured only three or four times. A greased straw was then run through the hole, taken out, regreased, and left in until the wound healed. The boy liked to have all the holes pierced at once, so he could wear all his earrings at once. The old-time earrings were long, thin shells obtained from the Mexicans. A few old men can still be seen who wear circles of brass or silver wire. The many shells were so heavy that the top of the ear bent over under the weight, but the discomfort was borne for the satisfaction it gave. As for the piercing service, it was done for the boy gratis.

A Comanche woman clothed herself in buckskin. The luxurious

28 Abbé Emmanuel Domenech, *Seven Years Residence in the Great Deserts of North America*, II, 281; Humfreville, *Twenty Years among Our Hostile Indians*, 184.
29 C. and J. D. Smith, *op. cit.*, 47.
30 Smithwick, *op. cit.*, 178.

fringe on sleeves and hems and colorfully beaded designs marked the dress of fashion. The dressmaker carefully worked the skins of the deer until they were soft and pliable—sometimes a muted lemon yellow and sometimes a buff color. The skirt was made in two pieces, with the legs of the deer skin making an uneven hemline reaching to the ankles. The skirt was sewed up the sides with buckskin thongs, and heavy fringe finished the hem and extended up the sides above the knees, with lighter fringe up the seams to the waist. The slightly flared skirt was broken above the knee by a narrow band of beading with long pieces of fringe at intervals below the beading. A scalloped band of narrow beading was attached just above the hem. The blouse was made poncho-style from the skin of a single animal. A slit was cut horizontally in the center, creating a high, straight neckline, which was brilliantly banded with beading extending across the shoulders to the elbow-length sleeves. Blouse and skirt were laced together at the waist with buckskin thongs, hidden beneath an ornamental skin peplum hanging in deep points to mid-thigh. Geometric medallions were beaded across the peplum in a band, and medallions of varied size and color were sewed across the front and back of the blouse. Just below these brilliant designs and continuing across the blouse were clusters of round beads, from which hung long leather and beaded thongs. A wide butterfly sleeve was formed by the loose ends of the skin. Colorful beads were scattered along the edge of the deep fringe line which finished the sleeves. Additional skin bands hung from the front and back of the sleeves, the fringed ends extending below the long, heavy fringing of the sleeves.[31]

The number-one wives of brave warriors wore an additional special decorative device, according to She Invites Her Relatives. A tongue-like appendage hung down from the neck, front and back. In the front it was fringed, while the back tongue, which was unedged, carried a painted symbol J in dark blue for each war honor of her husband.

The costume was completed by beautiful beaded moccasins. In winter highly ornamented leggings were worn to the knees, with only a knee-length buckskin dress above. In very cold weather the woman added a buffalo robe for warmth. The dress was comfortable

[31] R. I. Dodge, *The Plains of the Great West*, 342; museum specimens.

and easy to wear. Although there were variations to suit the individual taste and needs, the general pattern remained fairly uniform. A Comanche woman in motion was a graceful sight, with the gorgeous fringes swaying with every movement and the brilliant patterns of beading glittering in the sunlight or firelight.

The woman wore her hair cropped and traced the part line with vermilion, although she seldom went to the trouble of combing or otherwise caring for her hair; it just hung loose. The care that did not go into her hair was devoted to facial make-up. Her eyes were accentuated with red or yellow lines above and below the lids and sometimes crossing at the corners. Her ears were painted red inside, and both cheeks were daubed with a solid red-orange circle or triangle. She also occasionally tattooed her face and breast, and wore bracelets and necklaces. As a parallel to the strong institutional friendship between two men, two Comanche women friends might dress alike.

Little girls, unlike small boys, always wore some form of clothing. A girl wore a breechclout until near the age of puberty, when she donned the buckskin dress. She wore her hair long and in plaits.

Fine clothes were so prized for dressing up that each Comanche had a wardrobe case made of rawhide, called *nat'sak͡ʒna.* It was envelope-shaped, laced together at the edges, and had a tie-down, foldover flap. Thus it was different from the parfleche, or *ɔyɔ:t,* as the Comanche called the meat bag. In his case he kept his best suit, his leggings, moccasins, blanket, and braid wrappers. It was up to his mother to care for his wardrobe.

If he had a war bonnet or feathers, they were kept separately in a tubular bag, called *t̪unawɔs,* that could be slung from his waist as he rode his horse, so that they could be ready for instant donning in case of attack. In this bag was also carried war paint, a brush, and a mirror after mirrors became available. If the occasion arose, a Comanche wanted to look his best.

Home to the Comanche was his tipi, or conical skin dwelling. It represented a wonderful combination of utility and portability, for it could be raised or lowered within minutes. It was constructed of tanned buffalo hides sewed together and stretched, flesh side out, over a conical framework of from twelve to thirty poles. The standard number in the opinion of modern Comanches was twenty-two poles.

86

The poles were long, straight, and slender, usually of pine or cedar, peeled, seasoned, and pared down to a suitable diameter. They were sometimes pointed at the butt to prevent slipping on the ground. They varied in length from ten to twenty feet, depending on the size tipi desired. Robert G. Carter observed that hundreds of Antelope band poles were of cedar, approximately fourteen feet in length.[32]

Like the Blackfeet, Shoshones, Utes, Crows, Hidastas, Omahas, and others, the Comanches used four poles as a foundation. Many tribes, including the Cheyennes, Gros Ventres, Arapahos, Pawnees, and Kiowas, on the other hand, used a three-pole foundation. The projecting tops of the poles of a tipi erected on a three-pole foundation have a spiral appearance, while the four-pole base tends to group them on the sides. It seems evident from the fact that the Comanches used a four-pole foundation like the Shoshones, Utes, and other northern tribes, instead of the three-pole foundation of the Kiowas, Pawnees, and other southern neighbors, that they first adopted the tipi while still in their northern environment.

In erecting the tipi, the four poles were first tied together near the top and set upright. The butt ends of the poles were then pulled out and evenly spaced in a circle. Against this foundation were stacked the remaining poles, all tied together near the top with thongs of buffalo hide. They were set diagonally into the ground, as deep as two or more feet for a permanent dwelling, and three to four feet apart in a circle. Greater security was sometimes obtained by means of short stakes set at an angle across the lodge poles a few inches above the ground. A tipi thus set would withstand most of the strong winds that swept frequently across the High Plains.

The poles served as rafters. Buffalo hides, carefully fitted and firmly sewed together with sinew, were hoisted with a single pole from inside the framework. Women standing on each other's shoulders fastened the covering at the top. The covering was pinned up the front with wooden skewers the size of a lead pencil. From ten to seventeen buffalo hides were required to make a covering for the usual lodge, and rarely was a tipi larger than twenty skins, even if as many as twenty people were sheltered within. This number compares with an estimated average of fourteen and a maximum of

[32] Carter, *On the Border with MacKenzie,* 197; Lee, *op. cit.,* 128.

eighteen to twenty for the Crow tipi.[33] For the purpose of lodge-making, the hides of old buffalo cows, just shedding the winter coat in April or May, were preferred. These hides were supposed to be the easiest to tan, possibly, it is said, because the old cows were then thin in flesh and their hides thicker and hence more easily worked. The average tipi was twelve to fifteen feet in diameter across the floor. The height from the center of the floor to the peak was approximately the same as the diameter of the floor.

The tipi was tilted slightly backwards. The smoke-hole near the top, above the entrance, was made by folding the skins back or attaching flaps in such a way as to give the appearance of the lapels on a man's coat. Each flap was adjusted by means of an attached outside pole. By moving one or both of the poles, the prevailing wind could be shut out, and at most times a draft of air could be created to carry off the smoke from the fire directly beneath. Thus the smoke-hole and flaps served somewhat like a chimney.

The door, which always faced the rising sun, was simply an opening three or four feet high, covered by an extra pelt, tanned stiff. It was fastened either on the windward side or at the top, with a weight attached to the bottom. Either method provided a self-closing door.

The covering was staked down, but in warm weather it was not completely drawn to the ground, an air space of several inches being left all around. This space, together with the opening at the top, provided perfect ventilation. In cold weather the covering could be drawn completely to the ground. To keep the continual draft blowing in all around the bottom of the tent from striking those inside, a buffalo skin lining, in later times called a "dew cloth," was fastened to the lodge poles from four to six feet above the ground. The lining hung down inside the poles and was tucked under the edge of the bed. Consequently the air coming in under the outer covering was deflected upward by the lining and never struck the occupants directly. The lining also prevented rain entering the smoke-hole from falling on the bed and provided insulation against the penetrating summer heat. A very small fire was all that was necessary to provide warmth even in extremely cold weather. A narrow ditch around the outside kept the floor dry.

[33] Lowie, *The Crow Indians*, 87.

88

Compared to a good tipi, the shack of the frontiersman was a poor makeshift. The tipi shed wind and water and was warm and well ventilated. It could be set up within fifteen minutes and could be struck in less time. In hot weather the cooking was done outside. Actually, during much of the summer and autumn little shelter was really needed. In the permanent camp a brush arbor was often erected in hot weather, under which the entire family or groups of families found refuge from the summer heat. The roof was flat and made of leafy boughs supported by posts seven or eight feet high. The sides were left open to permit full benefit from the breeze. Most Comanches today, even those who have substantial houses, build brush arbors in their yards for lounging and summer sleeping. (There are no bedbugs in the arbors.) Arbors of hooped saplings reminiscent of Shoshone wickiups were also used.

Some owners painted their tipis with a number of encircling stripes and with geometric designs on both the lining and the outside cover. The average tipi, however, did not have the added touch of the artist.

The furnishing of a tipi was like all else in Comanche economic life—simple and highly adapted to mobility. Devices for comfort were a comparatively modern innovation, since it is inconceivable that in the days when the Indians were foot travelers and carried most of their possessions on their backs they would load themselves down with luxuries. In the center of the tipi a round hole was dug for the fire. It has been contended that the only difference in a Kiowa and a Comanche camp was in the fire-hole. The Comanches made their fire-hole about fifteen inches in diameter, while the Kiowas made theirs about two feet.[34]

Before the arrival of the white man, the Comanches produced fire by means of the fire drill. The method consisted of hand twirling a hard stick, held vertically in a hole in a horizontal block of softer material, until the heat ignited the Spanish-moss tinder or birds' nests packed about the hole. Fire drills were kept in cases of buffalo horn, called *na'a:*. Flint and steel for fire-making were among the first articles introduced by Mexican traders. After the introduction of gun powder, the Comanches found that a fire could be started more quick-

[34] Marcy, *Adventure on Red River*, 57.

ly and easily by placing a rag around the point of friction and sprinkling gun powder on the rag. And if rags and gun powder were plentiful, they would load an old gun and shoot it against a tree. The rags would light and could be used to start a fire. This method was especially good in wet weather.

When needed, a low fire was kept fed by wood or buffalo chips gathered by the women and children. Buffalo chips were more desirable, since they burned more slowly and the fire did not die out so readily. Their surface remained year after year, unaffected by the weather, except annually they became a little harder until at last it was almost impossible to cut them with a knife. The under side, not being exposed to the sun, retained a certain amount of moisture longer and was never quite so hard. During cold weather the same fire provided heat both for comfort and for cooking food.

The bed of the lodge owner was placed at the back of the tipi, that is, directly opposite the entrance in the place of honor. Other beds were placed on one or both sides according to need. In the permanent camp, beds were elevated above the ground from four to six inches by means of pole or rawhide slats supported by a couple of poles. Robes were spread on top to form bedding and cover. In the temporary camp the mattress was spread on the ground. Members of the family simply crawled beneath the skins needed for cover, leaving the remainder for a mattress, and, according to informants, slept with their heads to the west. Buffalo-skin partitions were frequently stretched between beds to give a degree of privacy. Pillows were made from skins of smaller animals and stuffed with grass or straw. Although such beds were soft and fairly comfortable, they were also desirable abodes for both dogs and innumerable vermin.

Mattresses served as chairs or for lounging as well as for beds. The master of the lodge always occupied the position directly facing the door. On his left was the place of honor for guests. Lodges of well-to-do persons were provided in modern times with back rests at the head and foot of the mattress.

Ample storage space was available between and underneath the beds and toward the front of the tipi. Extra food, clothing, and small articles were stored principally in parfleche bags. When many buffalo were killed, much dried meat was stored away in parfleches for use during winter and spring. Other bags contained ornaments, wooden bowls, dishes, small horn spoons, extra clothing, personal belongings, and any odds and ends. In fact, the contents of a parfleche were a perpetual surprise. It might contain anything from a tooth to a gold coin.

No tipi furnishings were complete without a supply of utensils or receptacles. They, too, were adapted to the environment and the mobile habits of the owner. No pottery was made or used, simply because it could not be conveniently handled and because more practical materials were at hand. Receptacles for carrying water during travel where water holes were far apart, as was usually the case in Comanche country, needed to be light and to pack well. The paunch of the buffalo met both requirements; therefore, before the introduction of the kettle it served well. A green paunch was hung from a limb or pole and hot stones held inside until the water boiled. Water vessels were also made from "cased" deer skins, that is, skins removed whole. The legs and necks were tied tightly with sinews. Buckets or cups could be made by tying one end of the skin of a leg and fitting a small rod around the inside of the other end. Drinking cups were made from buffalo horns and terrapin shells. A few wooden spoons and bowls were used. They were worked into shape by burning, scraping, and polishing. The Comanches, however, were little interested in this type of receptacle since it was more of a burden than an advantage in their way of life. Consequently, the workmanship was primitive. A very few crude baskets, knives of stone and bone (of metal after contact with the whites), mauls, a digging stick or two, and a few bone needles completed the tipi furnishings.

V

At Work and Play

T HE material culture of the Comanches was relatively meager, the industries few and simple. To the visitor uninitiated in ways of primitive tribal life, Comanche men might give the impression of being lazy and indolent. If meat was abundant and the men not concerned with war, raids, or ceremonies, they were likely to be found loafing in their lodges or idly working at some small task. Meanwhile their wives were occupied with domestic chores, attending to the children, and ministering to the needs of the men. Any supposition that the men were lazy, however, would be false, for in the life of the camp a division of labor between the sexes existed. If men labored less continuously than their wives, theirs were the more perilous occupations of hunting, raiding, and fighting. The wife's share in the life of the community was the care of the household; the husband was the provider. It was his duty to defend his wife and children and the tribe at large, and if the enemy were too strong to be defeated or repulsed, to hold them in check until the women and children might escape. All these activities were dangerous and hazardous. To fight at an advantage, the man must be light and active on his feet and unhampered by a load. Chiefly for this reason the men with their arms went ahead and the women followed behind, looking after the children, carrying the burdens, and attending to the animals which transported the camp equipment. Long after the need for such culture patterns ceased, it was not uncommon to see a woman walk out of a store carrying a heavy sack of flour or other supplies while the man came out unencumbered. Moreover, in the way of home industry there was indeed little for the men to do. The Comanches did not work at such specifically masculine crafts as metallurgy and wood-carving. Pottery, basketry, and weaving were unknown.

It was the woman's business to prepare the food, clothing, and shelter, and to care for the children. She made the household articles and bags, brought the wood and water, attended to packing and unpacking on moving day, and helped with making the horse equipage. She followed closely behind the hunter with pack animal and knife, skinned the animals, packed the hides to camp, and by slow, tedious processes converted them into clothing, tipi covering, bags, and other articles.

Hides were prepared differently according to whether they were to be worked into leather or made into rawhide bags. Some skins were tanned on one side only, others on both. The process was not identical for buffalo and deer skins, leather might or might not be smoked, and there were variations due to individual technique in workmanship. White influence affected the implements and technique, so that full details concerning the historic process can no longer be recovered. The essentials of tanning, however, are clear enough. To remove the hair, the skin was soaked on the hair side with a mixture of wood ashes and water, which produces lye. Lime, which was obtained from burned rock, was sometimes used in place of ashes. After the hide was sufficiently soaked, the hair side was scraped against the grain. Some women chose to shave off the hair without previously soaking the hide.

There were various kinds of scrapers. A scraper might be an oval, flat flake of flint chipped down so as to have a rather sharp and even edge all around, and it varied in size, some scrapers being large enough to use in both hands. Buffalo bones were often employed, and after the appearance of the white man, metal scrapers became common. Whether or not the hair was removed, a long and tedious process was required to tan the hide. The essential operations were the preparation of the hide, the application of the tanning mixture, and the subsequent working of the hide to make it soft and pliable.

The green hide, according to the whim of the individual worker, was thrown across a limb, laced to upright saplings (called a rack), thrown across a log flattened on top, or more often stretched upon the ground with flesh side up. If stretched upon the ground, it was made fast by means of wooden pins driven into the earth through small cuts in the edge of the hide. To get the best results in tanning, it was important that before the hide dried, it should be evenly fleshed, by which is meant freeing it of every particle of blood, fat, and flesh. This was necessary for rapid drying as well as to reduce the hide to a uniform and proper thickness.

Fleshing tools varied from a sharp flint flake or buffalo bone to an instrument similar to a drawing knife. Sometimes a wooden hoe made from the fork of a limb of a tree with the cutting part sharpened and finely serrated was employed. The most commonly used instrument was shaped somewhat like an adze. The cutting edge of this tool was bound to a handle of elk horn with strings of rawhide or sinew. It could be used with one hand. With the appearance of the white man the flint cutting edge gave way to metal blades. The rough, abrasive surface of the dried skin of buffalo tongue was preferred in some bands. As the skin clothing and the skin lodges were made by the women, the fleshing implements were very important and were handed down from one generation to another.

With the fleshing tool the worker clipped the skin, cutting off a thin shaving with each blow. The skill of this process lay in so directing and tempering the blows as to cut off the skin and yet not hack through it, and in finally obtaining a perfectly smooth inner surface of uniform thickness. Moistened wood ashes were spread on the fatty, greasy surface from time to time and left long enough for the lye to neutralize the fat. This process completed, the hide was usually left to cure and bleach in the sun for several days, although it might be saturated occasionally in water.

The next step was to make the skin soft and pliable, for if given no further treatment, it became hard and inflexible. One satisfactory method was to place it in a hole in the ground, cover it with water and then tramp it for one or two hours. Most women used a tanning mixture composed of brains, liver, grease, basswood bark, soapweed, and water. The basswood bark or soapweed root was pounded fine and thoroughly mixed with the buffalo or deer brains or liver. Grease of any available kind, except swine, might be added. The mixture was then thinned with water to the desired consistency. Brains with nothing added were used frequently. The tanning compound was applied to the hide, on both sides if the hair had been removed, and was thoroughly rubbed in with the hands or with a stone. After it had been worked into the texture, the rawhide was placed in the sun so that the heat might aid in the penetration and distribution of the mixture. The skin was then alternately stretched and rubbed with the hands, or pulled back and forth across a limb of a tree, around a sapling, through a loop of rawhide, trampled, or beaten. The friction developed considerable heat, thereby drying and softening the texture. The hide was then folded and put aside overnight. The next day it was unfolded and laid in the sun to dry. After it was dry, the process was repeated. This procedure was continued day after day until the worker deemed the skin sufficiently soft and pliable.

There was no definite time required for properly preparing a hide. The work was long and laborious, but the women were industrious and time was of little importance to them. A woman worked until she was tired, and then laid her work aside to be resumed at her convenience. The tanning might be completed in about ten days, or it might be extended over many weeks.

A worker could change a skin from its natural white to a yellowish brown on the hair side and to a light yellow or tan on the flesh side by smoking it. To do this, the skin was tied into a chimney shape around a pole or was stretched across a pole and placed over a fire pit filled with rotten wood to produce a smoldering smoke. In either arrangement the skin was placed over the fire in such a way as to prevent the escape of the smoke.[1] Tipi covers were naturally smoked by long exposure, but the women made no special effort to color them. Skins used for shirts, leggings, and moccasins were colored on both sides. According to Catlin, the smoking process kept

[1] This description of the Comanche method of tanning is compiled from the field notes of the Santa Fé Laboratory of Anthropology group and from statements by H. W. Baylor, "Recollections of the Comanche Indians," *Frontier Times*, Vol. VI (June, 1929), 373–75; E. House (ed.), *A Narrative of the Captivity of Mrs. Horn and Her Two Children with That of Mrs. Harris by the Comanche Indians*, 36; R. I. Dodge, *The Plains of the Great West*, 357; T. R. Davis, "The Buffalo Range," *Harper's Magazine*, January, 1869, 160; Carter, *On the Border with MacKenzie*, 284; Lee, *op. cit.*, 150; Smithwick, *op. cit.*, 183; Garretson, *op. cit.*, 27.

skins soft and flexible no matter how often they were exposed to moisture.

Every woman made the clothing for herself and her family, as was explained in the previous chapter. From the tanned skins the women also made various kinds of soft leather pouches, among them the long fringed ones for the men's smoking utensils. Some of these bags were decorated with beadwork after the arrival of the white traders, but informants insist that porcupine-quill embroidery was unusual among the Comanches.

Although every woman learned to make clothing and bags, it seems that there were only a relatively few who became expert at designing and cutting the cover for a tipi. A mother or wife who wanted to make a tipi gathered the poles, stripped them of their bark and pared them down to the desired size, and possibly pointed the butts. She then most likely went to an expert tipi-maker and asked for her help. She might offer her a present then, or it might be given afterwards. A day for the work was agreed upon. Other women would be invited to join the "quilting party," but the expert was in complete charge and gave the instructions. She usually did the most critical cutting and fitting. During the day the hostess provided her guests with a feast. Although the women worked together, there appears to have been no organization of tipi makers.[2]

Since the Comanches spent much of their time on horseback, horse equipage was an important item. Although both men and women worked at it, saddle-making tended to be the specialty of men who were no longer active in war. In later times, however, Mexican captives became specialists at the trade. Saddles were mostly of a modified Spanish type. They were generally made of American elm in three pieces: the bars or seat proper, the pommel, and the cantle. Each part was laboriously shaved down into the desired shape and carefully fitted. The pommel and cantle were made high with but slight pitch; the bars or seat were moderate in length so that the saddle was deep and narrow. Holes were drilled with a red hot awl, the joints daubed with glue, and then the parts were laced firmly together by means of green deer sinew. The joints were scraped and rubbed smooth, and the frame was smeared with an ochre paint. Over

2 Informants: Kills Something; She Invites Her Relatives.

96

this frame wet rawhide of deer or buffalo was stretched and sewed with green deer sinew. As the wet rawhide dried, it shrank on the frame snugly, making a tough and durable saddle. A small, soft bear skin or buffalo robe was used as a pad.[3] Women's saddles were deeper than those of the men, and the horns and cantles had longer horizontal projections decorated with fringes and brass-headed tacks and were painted red.

The stirrup was usually made of a single piece of green willow wood. On either side of the foot rest the wood was bent up and the ends brought together to form the sides and top of the stirrup. The ends were lashed in place with wet sinew, and then over this wooden frame green buffalo hide was stretched and sewed together with sinew. When riding without saddles, the Comanches sometimes used a pad, usually made of dressed buffalo hide.

Bridles or halters were made of plaited buffalo hair or strips of tanned buffalo hide. The hair bridle seems to have been the most common. No bits were used. A loop was formed just above the horse's nose, and the animal was guided by a pull on the rein or by pressure of the knees.

Pack saddles were constructed of two large, ovaloid pads made of two pieces of rawhide sewed together with a grass stuffing between them. These fitted against the two sides of the horse and were held together by two strips of wood which arched over the horse's back and also served as a base for lashing the load. The two pads came so far down and fitted so snugly against the sides of the beast of burden that no cinch was needed.

The Comanches, like most Indians, enjoyed a good smoke. Post Oak Jim thinks there was no smoking in the old days, and he is probably right. At least, a few centuries ago the Comanches had access to very little tobacco. This was changed after they had contact with Mexican traders. From them they obtained cured tobacco in large leaves, which they themselves cut into long strips and pounded to shreds and then added crushed sumac leaves. They smoked both cigarettes and pipes. Cigarettes were rolled in cottonwood leaves or leaves of catbriar or blackjack oak. Only in more recent times were cornhusks introduced.

[3] Carter, *On the Border with MacKenzie*, 277, 296.

Comanche pipes were made of bone, stone, or wood by both men and women. Many of the early pipes were straight tubes made of bone from the shank of a deer or an antelope, cut off at either end, the marrow punched out, and the mouth end pared down and smoothed. Before being used, such a pipe was commonly wrapped with the ligament from the back of a buffalo bull's neck, and this, when dried, made so complete a reinforcement of the bone that the pipe might last a long time. The straight bone pipes were easier to carry than the more bulky and elaborate stemmed pipes, and were therefore taken on expeditions. They were both long and short, and were called ɔ'mɔtɔy. Such pipes were also used by the Kiowas and Cheyennes.[4]

According to white captives, the stone pipe was most commonly used in later times. Stone pipes were made of soft stone, either white soapstone or red sandstone. Soapstone is easy to fashion, is found in various sections of the Comanche country, and answers as well as clay or meerschaum. The Comanche stone pipe bowl was made with a vertical cylinder on a flat base that projected forward and back from the bowl. This spur beyond the bowl allowed the smoker to grip the bowl without burning his hands. He had to use a two-handed grip to keep the bowl from falling off the stem, since the two parts of the pipe were not fastened together. Soapstone bowls were usually dyed red or black with a preparation concocted of poke berry and grease or walnut juice. Hard wood was sometimes substituted for stone. Pipes were often artistically engraved and designed, particularly those intended for ceremonial use.

The manufacturing of weapons and equipment for war and the hunt belonged primarily to the category of man's work. Perhaps the most important article was the bow and arrow. The Comanches made excellent bows, which they used with great skill. A good bow required a long time and much care and labor in construction. The experts were usually the old men who could no longer go to war. According to informants, they had no organization or "guild." The customary present or fee given for an ordinary wooden bow was one horse.[5]

4 Informant: Post Oak Jim; see also Grinnell, *The Cheyenne Indians,* I, 208.
5 Informant: Kills Something.

The modern bows were approximately three feet in length, most of them made of wood, although there were a few sinew-backed or compound ones made of buffalo, elk, or mountain-sheep horn. The latter were highly finished and required more time to make. They were worth from six to twenty ponies each.[6]

Not all men made bows in the same way, each workman following the method he thought best. The Comanche country stretched over a wide area, and the best bow materials found in one section might not be available in another. Methods varied with time also. Yet, in general, the process was much the same from the Pecos to the Arkansas and from the Cross Timbers to New Mexico. In making the horn or compound bow, the horns were first thrown into warm water and allowed to remain until they became flexible. They were then straightened and strips of suitable width were cut or sawed. After the strips were filed, shaved, scraped, or rubbed down until the flat sides fitted nicely, the desired length was obtained by overlapping and gluing the ends of from two to four slices. Another piece of horn was then laid on the center at the grasp, where it was glued fast. The whole was then filed or scraped down until it was well proportioned. All the joints were firmly bound with sinew to give resiliency to the bow. Several weeks were required for a skilled workman to make a good, ornamented bow of this type.

Bows were sometimes, though rarely, made of a single piece of horn. A long piece, as nearly straight as possible, was whittled, scraped, and rubbed until it was quite thin. After being made pliable by heating, greasing, and working, it was lashed to a straight stick and left until dry and straight. It was then firmly wrapped with sinew, which was secured in place with glue. Bows of buffalo ribs were sometimes made by the same process. Such bows, however, were of little practical use.

The wooden bow was the common bow of the Comanches. It was made principally from the Osage orange, or bois d'arc. Some Indian tribes called the tree "smooth bow"; the Omahas referred to it as yellowwood, but the French gave it the name *bois d'arc,* by which it is best known. It was plentiful along the Arkansas and Canadian rivers and in the eastern fringe of the Comanche country southward

[6] Garretson, *op. cit.,* 178.

into Texas. Bois d'arc is commonly recognized as one of the hardest, finest, and most durable of timbers. If it was not accessible, ash, white elm, ironwood, mulberry, or hickory were used, hickory being a highly esteemed bow wood.

When selecting bow wood, the Comanche chose a small upright sapling or a piece of timber with perfectly straight grain from a large tree. The heart of the tree was never used. The timber had to be straight and as free as possible from knots. It had to be seasoned or dried and not allowed to warp in the process. It was generally worked down to approximately the desired size while still green, since green wood worked more easily. Then followed the seasoning process, requiring weeks or months for completion. With fair use a properly made bow would last for many years, but since it might be accidentally broken at any time, timber in various stages of preparation was kept on hand. After the bow wood had seasoned, it was scraped and shaped to proper dimensions and rubbed with fat or brains to make it pliable. Then the stick was put aside, preferably in a warm place, to be worked again in a few days or weeks.[7] When worked to the proper finish, it was rubbed until it acquired a polish. Glue was spread over the bow, and fresh or wet sinew from the back of a buffalo bull or deer was applied. After the sinew had been wrapped, another coat of glue was applied and smoothed down by thorough rubbing. The bow was then laid aside until perfectly dry. In drying, the fresh sinew would shrink tightly to the wood and, with the glue, made the whole very strong and tough. A common wooden bow could be made in three days, but a week to a month was usually required to finish a fancy one.

Glue for bows and arrows was made from chippings from the rawhide of the neck of a buffalo bull, from the shavings cut from a buffalo bull hide in the process of thinning it down, or from horns and hoofs. These were boiled with water to make a strong glue. It was lobbed upon a smoothly whittled stick of mulberry or other wood and allowed to cool. The glue stick was carried in the bow case with the arrows for ready and frequent use. By softening in hot water it was ready as an instant mender for almost anything.

7 This method is still used in East Texas for making handles for hammers, axes, shovels, and the like.

Making an excellent bow string was a task for a specialist. The bow string was made of the sinew of the buffalo bull or deer, derived from the tendon which lies along either side of the spine from the shoulder blades to the hip bones. The tendon was shredded or subdivided longitudinally into fine threads of fiber. It has been estimated that each sinew had then ten times the strength of ordinary cotton thread of equal size. These sinews or threads were next soaked in glue water, and, while damp, several were twisted to form a strong, perfectly round cord of the same size and tension from end to end, and the ends knotted. Post Oak Jim said that he preferred bow strings made of horse-tail hair because "they didn't break and were not spoiled by moisture." Still, he thought bear gut was the best material of all.[8]

Arrows, next to the bow, were the most precious possessions of a Comanche. Much time was devoted to searching for arrows that had been shot. They were too hard to obtain and cost too much effort to be wasted. This was also true of points lost from the arrow shafts. Nevertheless, it is asserted on good authority that Comanches would never retrieve an arrow which had taken a human life, enemy or friend.[9] Great skill, patience, and judgment were required to make a perfect arrow. The old men who made the best arrows were highly respected for their special skill. Although there was a great difference in arrows, the proportions between the shaft, head, and feathers were quite definite. If these proportions were maintained, the arrow performed efficient and effective work in the hands of an expert bowman; otherwise, it was a failure. An arrow too light in the shaft would not fly steadily; one too heavy would not carry its force long enough. When a good, well-balanced arrow struck the mark, the feather end tilted upward. "The Cheyennes, Pawnees, and Pueblos don't know

[8] This description of bow-making is compiled from statements by informants Kills Something and Post Oak Jim; also, R. I. Dodge, *The Plains of the Great West*, 348–49; Carter, *On the Border with MacKenzie*, 295–96; Fannie M. Hughs, *Legends of Texas Rivers*, 219; Marcy, *Adventure on Red River*, 160; Anon., "Indian Bow and Arrow," *Frontier Times*, Vol. VIII (December, 1930), 141; Lehmann, *op. cit.*, 94; Gregg, *op. cit.*, 412; Wissler, *North American Indians of the Plains*, 25–27; Grinnell, *The Cheyenne Indians*, I, 174; Garretson, *op. cit.*, 178–79; Babb, *op. cit.*, 134; also, oral communication of others to Wallace.

[9] Lehmann, *op. cit.*, 46.

how to make arrows" is the opinion of Post Oak Jim. "Comanches and Wichitas make good ones."

Wood for the arrow shafts was selected and handled with the same care and patience as for the bow. Any hard, tough, straight-grained wood was used. Young shoots of the dogwood were preferred because of their straightness and freedom from knots. The second choice, but not nearly so good as dogwood, was mature ash. The young ash sapling was too pithy and soft. When neither of these was available, wild cherry, hackberry, or mulberry was used, although the hackberry required much straightening. Shafts were cut the desired length and roughly shaped, then tied in a bunch and hung near the fire place or in a dry spot to season.

When the arrow shafts had seasoned, a process which required ten days to two weeks if they were kept near a fire but much longer otherwise, they were examined by the arrow-maker for crooked places. Shafts not perfectly straight were made so. Crooked spots were greased and warmed so that the grease would penetrate readily, then quickly straightened with the hands or an implement devised for that purpose. The arrow straightener was made by drilling a hole slightly larger than that of the shaft in a buffalo bone or horn. The arrow was passed back and forth through the hole and bent until perfectly straight. Some men placed their arrows between their teeth to bend them into shape. Next, the shaft was scraped to proper size and taper, and made perfectly round. This was sometimes done by means of two grooved sandstone slabs with flat meeting faces. The arrow was placed in one groove, the other groove fitted over it. Then, holding the two stones together with one hand, the worker pulled the shaft back and forth. Most of the better arrows were grooved from the end of the feathers to the head of the arrow point. The Lipans had four straight grooves, but the Comanches usually made two straight black grooves on one side and two red spiral ones on the other. These grooves were cut with bone containing a circular hole into which extended a little projection from the margin of the hole, or with a flint with a semicircular notch and a projection. The shaft was then polished by rubbing and sometimes decorated with paintings or markings.[10]

10 This description of Comanche arrow-making is compiled from statements by

There has been much speculation about the meaning of the grooves. The most popular theory is that they permitted the blood of the victim to escape so as to weaken him. Another explanation is that the grooves symbolized lightning, which the Indians believed would make the arrows more surely fatal. It seems more probable that they were to prevent the shaft from warping.

The flight and accuracy of an arrow depended to a great extent upon the feathers. If the feathers were good and properly arranged, the arrow carried well. Those of the wild turkey seem to have been the most popular, but, when they were not obtainable, owl or buzzard feathers were used. Neither was affected by blood. Feathers of hawks and eagles were not desirable, since they were injured when wet with blood. Each arrow-maker had his own technique of winging the arrows. When the Cheyennes first began to wing their arrows, they used two feathers, but later changed to three. Some tribes used four. The Comanches used both the two- and three-feather winging technique. Some of the best-informed Comanches regard the two-feathered arrow as unsatisfactory, since it will not follow a straight line to the target. The feathers were taken from the wings, the stems split, the tip of the split stems dipped in glue, and the feathers bound in the grooves on either side of the shaft with a thread of sinew.[11]

In the distal end of the arrow shaft a notch was cut, or a cleft made, in which the arrowhead was set. Colonel Dodge believed that the Comanches placed the blade of the hunting arrow in the same plane with the notch for the string so that it would be more likely to pass between the ribs of the animal, which are up and down. For the same reason, the blade of the war arrow was at right angles to the notch, since the ribs of the human enemy were horizontal.[12] The head

informants Medicine Woman and Kills Something; also, Anon., "Indian Bow and Arrow," *loc. cit.,* 141–42; Garretson, *op. cit.,* 179; Marcy, *Adventure on Red River,* 160; R. I. Dodge, *The Plains of the Great West,* 349; Carter, *On the Border with Mac-Kenzie,* 295–96; Domenech, *Seven Years Residence in the Great Deserts of North America,* II, 270; Baylor, "Recollections of the Comanche Indians," *loc. cit.,* 374; Grinnell, *The Cheyenne Indians,* I, 178–81; Lehmann, *op. cit.,* 94.

[11] Informant: Kills Something; also, Carter, *On the Border with MacKenzie,* 295–96; Lehmann, *op. cit.,* 94; Domenech, *Seven Years Residence in the Great Deserts of North America,* II, 270; Marcy, *Adventure on Red River,* 160.

[12] R. I. Dodge, *Our Wild Indians,* 418–19.

was held in place with glue and firmly wrapped with wet sinew, which in turn was glued and rubbed to a smooth finish.

The Comanches relied almost entirely on metal for arrow points after they came in contact with the whites. Barrel hoops, bindings for boxes, even frying pans and similar pieces of metal furnished excellent material. The piece of metal was sharpened on one end and on both sides. After the point was sharpened, it was hardened by heating it in a fire and then dropping it while red hot into cold water. The Mexican traders not only supplied iron for the points but files with which to fashion and sharpen the arrowheads. Metal arrowheads became an important item of trade among most American Indian tribes.

Hundreds of thousands were manufactured yearly by eastern traders to be exchanged for furs. They were put in packages of one dozen each, cost the trader six cents a package and were the means for obtaining enormous profits. Usually one package was exchanged for a buffalo robe.[13]

There were two general types of metal arrowheads, one for game and one for war. The game point had no barb and was easily extracted, while the war point was barbed and loosely attached to the shaft. Some war points had but one barb, which, when shot into a body and the shaft pulled, caught in the flesh, and the point turned crosswise in the wound, making it impossible to extract it without tearing or cutting.

Before the acquisition of metal, arrows were made of stone, bone, or horn. Flint appears to have been the most popular, and some preferred it even after the introduction of metal. It has been claimed that wounds made by flint arrow points were more likely to be fatal than those of metal. The Comanches apparently did little grinding or polishing of flint. Indeed, the nature of much of the flint of the Comanche country rendered such treatment unnecessary. Lehmann has left an account of one method of making stone arrowheads, but whether it was Apache or Comanche is uncertain, the implication being that the method was common among both tribes.

13 Garretson, *op. cit.*, 180.

We threw a large flint stone, from two to six feet in circumference, into the fire. After the stone became very hot, small thin pieces would pop off; we selected those pieces which would require the least work to put into shape, and picked these pieces up with a stick split at the end; while these pieces were very hot, we dropped cold water on those places we wished to thin down; the cold water caused the spot touched to chip off, and in this way we made some of the keenest pointed and sharpest arrows that could be fashioned out of stone.[14]

All efforts of archaeologists to determine a Comanche-type flint arrow point have been in vain. In this connection Professor Mildred Pickle Mayhall says, "There are several mentions of distinctive points and shafts for different tribes but just what those differences were we do not exactly know. Poisoned arrows may have belonged to all the Texas tribes but there is little definite information about this save in reference to the Comanches."[15] The Comanches did poison their arrow points occasionally for use in war, by making an extract from a plant not known to our informants or by sticking them in a dead skunk.

The bow and arrow was exceptionally accurate up to fifty yards or more. The Comanche arrow shot from a good bow could wing a true flight for three hundred yards. It has been maintained on good authority that at a distance of from ten to fifteen yards, an arrow (twenty to thirty inches in length) could be driven completely through the carcass of a buffalo, providing it struck no bone, that an object the size of a doorknob could be hit by an expert marksman an average of four out of five shots, and that an expert Comanche hunter could kill twice the number of buffalo with bow and arrow as an American with a pistol.[16]

The superiority of bow and arrow over the old-type musket was recognized by the Comanches. When muskets first became known to them, they were all eager to obtain them. But when the novelty

[14] Lehmann, op. cit., 93–94.

[15] Mildred P. Mayhall, "The Indians of Texas: the Atakapa, the Karankawa, the Tonkawa" (unpublished Ph.D. dissertation, University of Texas Library), 608–609.

[16] Gregg, op. cit., 361–63, 233; Carter, On the Border with MacKenzie, 296; Marcy, Adventure on Red River, 160.

of the weapon had worn off, they realized that it was inferior to the bow and arrow both in hunting and in war. The muskets had a greater range but a much slower rate of fire, they were difficult to load on horseback, and ammunition could be obtained only infrequently. As a result the Comanches were reverting to the bow and arrow when the introduction of repeating firearms turned the tide again.[17]

A buckskin band was worn on the wrist of the left arm to protect it from the bruising twang of the bowstring. The bow and arrows were carried in a skin case by a band over the right shoulder, and in wet weather the string was kept under the armpit to keep it dry. When crossing a wide stream in flood, the Comanche shot his arrows across before swimming his horse over.

The shield, next to the bow and arrow, was the Comanche warrior's most important weapon, and it was valued above all other things. Several days were required to make a shield. There were individual differences in its structure, but the basic pattern was always the same. It was made from the shoulder hide of an old buffalo bull, since that was the toughest portion. The green hide was heated over a fire or steamed over hot water and, while still hot, was rubbed on a rough rock in order to flesh it. Scrapers were used to finish the fleshing. Heating and steaming contracted and thickened the hide, and this process was repeated as many times as necessary in order to make the hide as thick as possible. A smooth stone was then used to rub and pound the hide to efface all wrinkles and make it smooth and pliable. One or more layers of circular pieces cut from it were then stretched flesh side out over each side of a circular wooden hoop, two feet or more in diameter, and sewed together around the edge of the hoop with rawhide thongs passed through eyelets punched around the edges of the layers of hide. The space between the layers, usually about one inch thick, was packed with feathers, hair, or paper to stop the force of arrows, bullets, or blows from other weapons. Charles Goodnight relates that one shield which he captured from a Comanche warrior contained a complete history of Rome.[18] Before discover-

17 Ralph Linton, "Acculturation and Process of Culture Change," in Ralph Linton (ed.), *Acculturation in Seven American Indian Tribes*, 474.
18 J. E. Haley, "Charles Goodnight's Indian Recollections," *Plains-Panhandle Historical Review*, Vol. I (1928), 20.

106

ing that paper was used for padding inside the shields, Anglo-American pioneers were quite puzzled at the Comanche interest in books.

The surface of the shield was stretched into a convex or saucer shape with the convex surface to the outside. A convex surface would readily deflect a blow. The shield was then hung up to dry. Sometimes the shield-maker would unlace the shield and remove the wooden frame, adding, of course, additional packing. This increased the safety of the shield, since a bullet could penetrate the wooden frame more easily than the packing.

A buckskin cover was usually fitted over the flint-like shield, much as a cover is drawn over a spare automobile tire. It was drawn in on the under side by means of a buckskin thong laced through eyelet holes around the edges. Through the hide itself were bored two pairs of holes, and through each pair was passed a loop or band of rawhide or buckskin. By means of these two bands the shield was fastened to the left arm near the elbow in such a manner as not to interfere with the free use of the hand.

After the shield had thoroughly dried and cured, it was treated by setting it up as a target, and if a bullet or an arrow pierced it when fired from a distance of about fifty yards, it found a place in the debris of the camp. In times of action the Indian manipulated his arm so as to make any blow strike the shield at an angle. Very few bullets fired from old-fashioned rifles would penetrate a well-constructed shield unless the bullet struck the surface perpendicularly, a near impossibility when the shield was in the hands of one expert in the art of using it.

The Anglo-American pioneers and soldiers who knew the Comanches well relate that their shields were usually adorned with three kinds of insignia. Bear teeth worn or painted on a shield indicated that the owner was a great hunter or had the toughness of the bear; scalps attached to or painted on the shield indicated its owner to be a mighty warrior, and horse or mule tails that he was an accomplished raider. The materials were attached by means of buckskin strings to the under side of the shield. Around the rim of the outside cover feathers were attached and held in place with sinew. Comanche informants maintained that there should have been an even number, usually four but possibly six or more. The arrangement made it possible for the ruffle of feathers to be kept in constant motion when the shield was shaken, thus serving to bewilder the eye and disturb the aim of the enemy. Hair was sometimes substituted for the feather fringe. A plain cover without decoration protected feathers and paintings when the shield was not in use.[19]

Some Comanche shields were painted with simple geometric decorations. On at least one specimen which has survived the heavy lines are painted red and the narrow ones green. The great majority of shields, however, were unpainted and made without ceremony. There is not sufficient evidence either to substantiate or to disprove Professor Lowie's contention that each semi-military society had its shield which served as an insignia, symbolical of its rank and position.

Originally carried in order to ward off missiles and spear thrusts, the shield in later times rendered a protection that was not only physical but also spiritual. Indeed, according to Comanche informants, some shields possessed mystical power and were "sort of sacred." There were several ways by which a warrior might obtain such a shield. It might be a gift from an older friend or a relative, although the owner must be very careful to whom he gave his shield. Furthermore, some shields had such strong power that they could not be given away; they had to be thrown in a running stream to wash away the power. Such shields were ringed with tabus. They were rarely uncovered except in actual battle. They could never be brought within a tipi. Most of them had to be stored at least half a mile away from the camp. If this seems a foolish place to keep a shield in the event of a surprise attack, it should be realized that for a menstruating woman to come near it or for a person with greasy hands to touch it would completely destroy its power and insure the wounding of its owner. To get his shield prior to a raid, a warrior made a half-circle to the spot where it hung; he moved the shield in a circle and then returned to the camp from the opposite direction, completing a whole circle with his route.

19 This account of the construction and the utility of the shield is from statements by informants Medicine Woman and Wiley Yellowfish; also, Haley, "Charles Goodnight's Indian Recollections," *loc. cit.*, 20; Marcy, *Adventure on Red River*, 160–61; Lehmann, *op. cit.*, 25–26; Baylor, "Recollections of the Comanche Indians," *loc. cit.*, 374; Babb., *op. cit.*, 40–42; Parker, *op. cit.*, 195; Burnet, "American Aborigines, Indians of Texas," *loc. cit.*, Vol. I (June 5, 1824), 177.

The father of Rhoda Greyfoot, who was a famous medicine man, had a shield, but Rhoda never saw it. "They were very precious about them," she said.

Painted shields usually had power, and the designs symbolized that power. If a young man wanted a new shield endowed with power and was willing to encumber himself with all the burdens and limitations that power imposed, he had three choices for obtaining it. He could ask a man who had a medicine shield for a share of his power, he could go on a vision quest himself to get instructions for the design from a spirit source, or he could ask a medicine man to procure a design for him.

In the first case, the young man would visit the owner of a medicine shield and smoke with him. Not until the pipe had been smoked would he make his request, for, having smoked with him, the shield owner must grant the favor he asked. The donor gave him some power, but he still retained his own power, too. The young man then had his shield painted by the donor as an exact duplicate of his own. If, however, the young man received instructions for the design from a spirit source, he would ask a "good artist" to paint his shield according to the vision. As for the third possibility—asking a medicine man to procure a design for him—Post Oak Jim gave the following account:

« « « A boy brought his shield to a peyote meeting and asked the leader for advice. He smoked and asked assistance. He was told to leave the shield by the door at the side of the fire tender.

After the midnight water ceremony the leader took the shield, put cedar on the fire, held the shield over it, and shook it. He gave it to the boy, who was sitting on the south side. He took the shield and made a circle. The leader said he would have directions for him in the morning, and the boy thanked him. [The leader can give directions at a meeting or afterwards.]

In the morning he told the boy to bring an artist and he would dictate the design to him. "The design will be all right," he said, "so don't be afraid. If you want to know about it, go to a lonely place some night, and the shield will tell you all about it."[20] » » »

[20] Informant: Post Oak Jim.

A shield with power not only gave its owner the general protective influence due to its sacred character, but also endowed him with those qualities attributed to heavenly bodies, birds, mammals, and other living creatures from whom the design-giving vision came. It also might afford protection from the elements, for some shields were sacred to thunder and lightning.

The lance was another favorite weapon of certain Comanches. The use of the war lance has been associated with the horse, but it is evident that the tribes who came to occupy the plains in historic times were acquainted with the stone-headed lance as a hunting implement before they entered the plains. Two types of lances were used by the Comanches. One was a hooked lance, so called because the shaft was bent somewhat in the shape of the conventional shepherd's crook. The other was the ordinary lance, six to seven feet in length. It had a wooden shaft of bois d'arc armed in modern times with an iron or steel point in any shape which was convenient and easily made from the material at hand. Some lance heads were as much as thirty inches long by one inch wide, tapering to a point at the end away from the shaft. Previous to the acquisition of metal, the lance head was of chipped stone, often leaf-shaped. In either case, the head was bound to the shaft with sinew of rawhide thongs and glue in much the same way that the arrow point was bound to the shaft. The shafts of old-time spears were decorated only by a feather or a bunch of feathers attached near the butt end. Beaded shafts like the one on Quanah Parker's spear were a late fashion. Sheaths, which might or might not be decorated, were sometimes made for lances.

The battle spear was not a weapon for any ordinary man to carry. It was never hurled javelin-wise but was always thrust from under the arm. If thrust overarm, it might hit a bone and break the point or frighten the rider's horse, according to Breaks Something. Only a brave man carried a spear, because it meant hand-to-hand combat. More than this, a spear carrier could never retreat and live to face his fellow warriors. There was no alternative for him but victory or death. In Breaks Something's opinion, the war lance ranked higher as a symbol of a war chief than any headdress, and warriors who carried the spear went without a war bonnet. His own brother, after the Battle of Adobe Walls, gave up his spear, and all his family was glad.

A Comanche woman, the wife of Milky Way, in 1872
Courtesy Bureau of American Ethnology

Big Looking Glass (Pianaronit), in 1894
Courtesy Bureau of American Ethnology

"A spear is a big responsibility." A warrior returning from a successful raiding party set his lance upright before the door of his lodge with the scalps of his victims dangling from it. No one except the owner could remove the trophies.[21] As in the case of the shield, tradition records that some lances had power, and the lance carried by the leaders was a characteristic sign of office.

The Talley Sheet of Governor Anza reveals five Comanche groups, the leader of each having a lance which represented the rank of his group.[22] Robert H. Lowie asserts that the major difference in the several societies lay in the dances prior to assembling a war party and that each society had a lance and shield symbolical of a very definite position.[23] There is a possibility that straight lances may have been carried by one rank and hooked lances by another, but there seems to be no definite pattern. Both straight and hooked lances were carried with point upward.

Another weapon used by the Comanches was the war club or battle axe, called *wɜpitapu'ni*. Made of a flint stone weighing about two pounds, it was about six inches long and three inches wide on one end, tapering off to a width of from one to two inches on the other. Each end was thinned to a rough edge. The middle of the flint was grooved or thinned on either side to prevent it from slipping on the handle. The wooden handle was fourteen to sixteen inches in length and from one to one and one-half inches in diameter. One end was split, and into this incision the axe was inserted and fastened to the handle by thongs of green or wet rawhide wrapped around the flint and handle about half a dozen times. The ends of the rawhide were made fast by means of small wooden pegs passed through the rawhide and into the wooden handle. The rawhide contracted in drying and left the axe handle almost as firmly bound as a modern axe and handle. The battle axe served a number of purposes and at close range was a deadly weapon.

Despite their strenuous life, the Comanches found time for recreation and entertainment. Their diversions, like their industries, were

[21] Zoe A. Tilghman, *Quanah, The Eagle of the Comanches,* 16.
[22] Alfred B. Thomas, "An Eighteenth Century Comanche Document," *American Anthropologist,* Vol. XXXI (1929), 291–92.
[23] *Ibid.,* 293–95, quoting R. H. Lowie, "Notes on Shoshonean Ethnography," American Museum of Natural History *Anthropological Papers,* XX (1924), 283.

quite simple. Visiting, feasting, the dance, story-telling, and competitive games constituted their principal means of recreation and amusement. The Comanches were very sociable and spent much time visiting. Visiting and feasts furnished opportunity for the discussion of news and tribal welfare. The religious ceremonies were regarded by many as less an occasion for worship than an exciting and interesting social gathering.

Social gatherings in the evenings were filled with mirth, revelry, and enjoyment. Before the arrival of the white trader, the Comanches were noted for their abstinence from intoxicating drink. Most evenings were devoted to singing and storytelling, which was not only entertainment but education. By frequent repetition of stories, the tribal history, traditions, legends, and ideals were perpetuated for the young. Older people seldom grew weary of repeating the stories or of listening to them.

On other evenings young men and women gathered around a fire which had been kindled in the village, and while it reflected its dancing shadows against the yellow lodge-skins, they danced and chanted their songs to the accompaniment of the rhythmic beat of the drum. Those who did not participate in the dance sat on the ground in a circle, facing the musicians who sat in the center beating their small drums. Men and women dancers stood a short distance apart facing each other. When the music began, a man would select a dancing partner by placing his hands round her waist, while she clasped him in similar fashion. The affair lasted an hour or more. The Indian, who had been taught to dance almost from the time he had been able to lift his feet, danced with rhythm and freedom, and every movement was vivid and natural.

Competitive games continued from childhood to middle life, and when a person became too old to participate, he still enjoyed watching them.

When food was plentiful and no necessary jobs were pressing, a Comanche really liked to settle down for some good fun. Men and women alike were great sports; gambling was a passion. Their horse racing has already been described, but it was not their only athletic sport. The women liked to play double ball or shinny, a strenuous pastime, to say the least. They set up arrow-shooting contests to test speed and distance skills. With the older men they threw arrows at marks and at the wheel. The women also had a sport of their own: kick-the-ball. Younger men wrestled and in older times played at kicking each other. And adults of both sexes spent hours in games of chance. Then there were social dances of a purely recreational nature, storytelling, gossiping, and singing. A Comanche rarely had good reason to be bored, and with his usually extroverted personality his lust for life was strong.

Shinny and double ball were exclusively women's games among the Comanches. Lacrosse, definitely a man's game and important in the lives of the eastern Indians, was never taken up by the Comanche men. The two ball games played by the women were essentially similar in principle, but different in equipment required and in its use.

Ten women or girls to a side made up the usual team. The players, garbed in showy dress, were wont to gather on the ball field about mid-afternoon. If they intended to play shinny, two stakes were driven into the ground at both ends of a field a hundred or more yards long. Each player had a curved stick. The ball, made of hair-stuffed deerskin, was flattened and three or four inches in diameter. The rules of the game were essentially similar to those of our own shinny.

Double ball was a much faster variation of shinny. One stake at each end of the field formed the goal. A rawhide thong eighteen inches long was substituted for a ball. A hooked stick three feet long was used by each player to catch and throw the thong. The game started with a referee tossing the thong up between two centers as in basketball. The one who caught it had to throw it with her stick to a teammate, who ran toward her goal with it. If blocked by an opponent, she tossed it over her opponent and caught it coming down on the other side, continuing on her way, or else she passed it over to a teammate. The object was to maneuver into position so that the thong could be thrown at the stake. When it wrapped itself around the pole, a goal had been scored. This game, called *natsi'tɔ:et,* was the favorite of the Water Horse band, who were "tall, thin, and fleet of foot." When two bands gathered for games, they would bring up great bundles of goods for betting. They beat all other bands at *natsi'tɔ:et* until the others refused to play them.[24]

[24] Informant: That's It.

Shinny as a woman's game was practically universal among North American Indians, so it is hardly surprising to find it as a sport among the Comanches. Double ball was also a woman's game throughout most of the United States, except among the West Coast tribes, where it was played by men. Inasmuch as it was played by Paiutes and Shoshones in the Great Basin, the Comanches most likely enjoyed the game before their migration.

The lives and livelihood of the Comanches turned on their skill with the bow and arrow. Informal archery tournaments occurred on any festive occasion to test bow and arrow skills in several ways. One type of contest placed a premium on speed in fitting and discharging flights of arrows. The players took a certain number of arrows, which they held with their bows in the left hand. Each player in turn advanced in front of the judges and discharged his first arrow upward as high as possible. He then proceeded to discharge the others as rapidly as possible. Victory belonged to the one who succeeded in having the greatest number of arrows in the air at once.[25]

Shooting for the mark, called *wɜ'ḳɜrɜ*, was done in the manner of "bowls." Each contestant used four arrows. The first marksman sent out an arrow, near or far, as he wished. Then he and his opponent alternated in shooting their arrows. The closest to the mark arrow won the round, as in horseshoes. The loser of the round had the chance to shoot the target arrow on the next try.

Exactly the same game was played with throwing arrows specially constructed to be light and long with feathers trimmed closer than a bow arrow. This arrow game, when throwing for the mark, was known to the Comanches as *tiɾ'ɔwɔḳɔ*. Sometimes the players decided to throw for distance instead. In this case, they called the game *naɾɔ'tɔnɛ:Isɔ*, and a good throw was considered to be two hundred yards—hardly a mean distance. Players and spectators alike bet on these games.

Young men like to play the wheel game, *aɾatsi,* as a more complicated sport of arrow throwing. Among the Crows the wheels collected by Lowie were nine and one-quarter and ten inches in diameter. The Comanches called for sharper marksmanship, because their wheels, according to informants, were only four or five inches

25 Domenech, *Seven Years Residence in the Great Deserts of North America*, II, 198.

across. Otherwise, the construction of the Comanche wheel was exactly like that illustrated by Lowie.[26] It consisted of willow rim with rawhide spokes radiating from a rawhide circle, one to two inches large, in the middle. The special throwing arrow, three to five feet long, was like the Crows' in having a forked feathered butt. It differed, however, in possessing a lashed-on barb of chinaberry, a hard wood, at the point.

The wheel game called for four players, two to a side. The teams stood facing each other, five or six steps from the starter, who rolled a hoop or wheel down the line between them. The players threw their special arrows simultaneously. If an arrow hit went through the center hole, its barb made it stick and the wheel fell down. Now the side that had hit the mark had the advantage, for the other side had to throw ordinary arrows at the center hole of the fallen wheel from the spot where the successful marksman had stood. Any arrow that failed to hit the center hole was captured and kept by the other side. Any arrow that hit the center hole was recovered by the thrower. Thus the team that first put its barbed arrow in the hole while the hoop was rolling stood a chance to win up to ten arrows while not having to risk a single one of its own. Players without much skill could agree to shoot for the spaces between the spokes instead of the center hole. Spectators bet on one side or the other, and when they got excited put up their own arrows to be thrown.[27]

The old kicking game played by the boys in the legend of the split of the Comanches and Shoshones, although remembered, seems to have been dropped as a sport. The women, however, were still playing kick-the-ball in 1933. Hopping on the left foot, they keep a rag ball in the air by "dribbling" it off the ground with the instep of the right. The idea is to get as far as possible before the ball is missed and falls to the ground. One or two girls or women play on a side, and good players can carry the ball seventy-five to one hundred yards. A variation is duration kicking in place, and in this a skilled player can keep the ball in the air two or three hundred kicks.

When it was too hot for much exertion, or at night when sports were impossible, or at any time, if a person was too lazy or too old

26 Lowie, *The Crow Indians,* fig. 11, p. 102.
27 Informants: Breaks Something; Post Oak Jim.

for the more strenuous activities, there were the hand game, varieties of dice, and, in later years, card games.

One of their principal "parlor" games which was common to all the bands was known variously as "bullet," "button," and "hands." The players were divided into two parties who formed in parallel lines opposite each other or in a half-circle. A number of counters, usually sticks, were placed between the two parties and all must be gained by one side or the other before the game was won. The game was usually twenty-one points, though the players might agree upon any number. When all were ready, the players commonly sang one of the many gambling songs and several beat time, either on the ground with a stick, on a parfleche, or on small hand drums, or kept time with motions of their arms. During this performance, one player took the bullet, button, bone, or some other convenient object and, after moving his hands in time to the singing and making many gestures to confuse his opponents, thrust out his closed hands. An opposing player guessed which hand the object was in. The game could be varied by passing or pretending to pass the object from one player to another. If the guesser were successful, his party then hid the object. If during the manipulations the object were accidentally dropped, the opposing side took the object and a counter. The game was won when one side had possession of all the counters. This game could last all night or be concluded almost at once. Players bet on the outcome, sometimes staking all they possessed under the care of a neutral scorekeeper.[28] Excitement was intense as the "button" passed back and forth to the accompaniment of drumming and rhythmic hand-game songs. The winning of a game called for a special victory song.

Dice games were quite popular until replaced in recent years by card games. There were many variations. One form was played with small, square blocks of wood, each side of which was painted a different color. The bet was made on the color that would turn up when the dice were thrown.

Another form of the game, a favorite with the men, was played on the flesh side of a buffalo robe marked into sections with chalk

[28] Stewart Culin, "Games of North American Indians," B. A. E. *Twenty-fourth Annual Report*, 309; Neighbors, "The Naüni or Comanches of Texas," *loc. cit.*, 133; Bancroft, *op. cit.*, 516; Battey, *op. cit.*, 326.

lines. The dice consisted of two smooth sticks, each about four inches in length, flat on one side and curved on the other. The flat side was about an inch in width. The player held the two sticks between his thumb and forefinger and either tossed them up or dropped them on a flat stone resting in the center of the playing section. The points scored depended on the section in which the sticks fell. One tally stick for each point was taken from the pile by the winner. The player obtaining the most sticks won the game. The women usually varied the game slightly. They used twelve sticks, from six to ten inches in length. Any stick which fell and remained across another counted a point. The first player to get one hundred points won the game.

Another variation of the game, popular with the women, was played with a shallow wicker bowl or basket and six plum stones or flat pieces of bone.[29] The basket was six to eight inches in diameter, and the dice were marked in a way to make possible several combinations of colors. When several players were participating, each player bet with the opposite player. In making the throw, the basket was raised so as to toss the dice only a few inches high. Before they fell, the basket was brought sharply to the ground. Each player threw in turn. The women chatted and joked continually during the game.

The Comanches, like other Indians, had no moral inhibitions against gambling, so they went all out in their betting. After all, it was only an exchange of property between friends, and generous gift-giving was the custom anyhow. Husbands and wives were free to gamble each other's goods, and each was supposed to pay up the other's debts. Some winners, like Breaks Something, were compassionate, however. On one hunting expedition, according to Breaks Something's story, his band came upon another Comanche group and found some men gambling at dice behind a windbreak. One old man had won nearly everything and was looking for new game. Breaks Something cut in to play against him, putting up the cartridges he had brought for hunting: ten cartridges to a tally stick. He bet and won; bet and won. The old man went broke. He bet twelve hides his wife had not yet tanned. Then he bet her tipi and everything in it. Then his two horses. He lost everything he had. In desperation

[29] Culin, "Games of North American Indians," *loc. cit.*, 54–55, 159.

he offered to bet his sister. Breaks Something thought this was too much; he refused. The old man's "brother" (a classificatory cousin) broke in, "It's nothing; she's just like a dog." Whereupon Breaks Something agreed to allow twenty-five tally sticks value on the girl. He won her!

Next day Breaks Something sent his mother over to collect the goods he had won: the tipi and the girl, the horses, and everything. The women folk cried and said these were not the old man's to gamble. "I took pity on them," recalled Breaks Something. "I took pity on them and gave everything back to them except the blanket from the old man's back. So I lost my new-won wife."

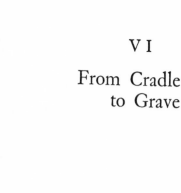

THE Comanche infant was born into a world of adults who welcomed and cherished it. It was not looked upon as a nuisance or handicap, but rather as a valuable addition to the tribe. Girls were accepted, but boys were preferred. Some families made a practice of painting a black spot on the door of the tipi if a newborn child was a boy, as a means of informing the people that the tribe had been strengthened by the addition of another "brave." Although the motherly affection that was the child's due was bestowed upon both male and female, boys received greater care than girls from their mothers and more indulgence from both parents all along the line.

There is conflicting opinion about twins. The woman who bore twin boys might be honored; other parents might regard twins as unnatural. Sometimes the parents attempted to destroy one or both of them, particularly if one or both were girls, but the more common practice was to give one away if foster parents could be found. For fear her husband might destroy both, the mother would sometimes dispose of one and not inform her husband that she had given birth to twins. In the eighteen eighties Dr. George Holley discovered and saved an infant, which was one of twins, buried in sand by its mother. There is at least one other recorded instance of such a rescue.[1]

Infanticide also seems to have been practiced in case the infant was born deformed, diseased, or a weakling. The attending women

[1] Annie M. Barnes, *Matouchon: A Story of Indian Child Life*, 11.

and the medicine woman made the decision. If it was determined that the child was unfit to live, it was left out on the plains. If the tribe was on the move, it was left near the camp site; otherwise, it was carried a distance from camp and left to die. Well-informed observers claim that they never saw an idiot or congenitally deformed Comanche in the early days.[2]

During its first days the child lay swaddled in robes in its mother's lying-in hut where it received constant attention. Soon after the mother left the hut to resume her daily round of tasks, the baby was put in its day cradle, or "papoose board," so that it could be stood out of harm's way or, if the mother was out gathering seeds or roots or on the march with the camp, it could easily be carried along on her back.

The cradle-board was either a sort of basket made of rawhide fastened to a flat, angular board or a soft buckskin sheath that laced up the front and was anchored to a back board. In cold weather the baby was wrapped in his cradle in blankets with a small opening left for breathing and for the dark, gleaming eyes. Getting babies in and out of their tight cradles to keep them dry would have been a great nuisance. The Comanches met this problem by bringing the little boy's penis out through an opening in the lashings and by providing a draining tube between the legs for a girl. Soft, dry moss was used to catch their excrement. Even so, the babies got wet and messy, but it was their lot to put up with it until they were transferred to the night cradle. Then they were washed, greased, and powdered—the powder consisting of pulverized dry rot of cottonwood. This soothing operation was done tenderfully and carefully. Bodily physical contact was thus restricted during the early months of life, and muscular activity almost wholly so. Such restriction was on a twenty-four-hour basis at first, for at night the young infant was rolled up in a stiff rawhide tube so that it could sleep on the robe between its parents without danger of being smothered if its fat mother rolled over on it. In this setting it enjoyed a snug, if not luscious, protective intimacy with both parents that was generative of strong security feelings.

Nine or ten months passed before the child was allowed out of the

[2] Marcy, *Adventure on Red River,* 167; Babb, *op. cit.,* 140, 142.

cradle for any length of time and could experience the exploratory pleasures of crawling about. From this time on, when the child was not on the board or scrambling about on the ground, it was carried on its mother's back.

A child on its mother's back seemed perfectly comfortable and at home. It ate when the mother passed food to it over her shoulder, surveyed the new, curious surroundings, or slept as its mother moved. When moving camp or when traveling, mothers carried the babies on their backs, or sometimes they hung the boards on saddles or travois poles. As a child became too large to be carried by an over-worked woman, it was generally placed on travois poles pulled by a steady old pack horse. In this manner children were usually carried until they were old enough to ride upon a pack or a horse—lashed to the saddle or held in place before the mother.

The Comanches had no surnames. At first, children were likely to be called only by pet names. Formal or real names were always bestowed, but there was no set time for doing so. Personal names were not distinctive of sex. The father might name his child, but more commonly he invited a person of distinction to do so. A child named by a medicine man or a medicine woman was supposed to have a longer and more useful life. The naming took place in a public ceremony, which was considered better performed inside a tipi. The medicine man lighted his pipe with a coal from the fire, and blowing puffs of smoke to heaven, earth, and the four directions, offered a prayer for the welfare of the child. When the prayer was finished, he lifted the child aloft to symbolize the wish that it would grow up, and addressing the parents and others present, said, "His [her] name is going to be ———." It was customary to lift the child four times, a little higher each time. The godfather was either com-pensated on the spot or told that the child would give him something later. If the child proved sickly, it would usually be given a new name, for the Comanches believed that names were closely associated with individual constitutions and that a sickly or puny child could be made strong with a strong name memorializing the great deed of a brave warrior. He Runs Directly Against The Enemy was a sickly infant who was taken to a famous warrior for a new name. It cured him, according to Greyfoot. A name commemorating a false deed was injurious to the child or its family, however. Post Oak Jim was given one of these at first.

He was taken by his mother and father to a warrior for his first name. Later he became restless and cried all night, until at last his parents took him to another brave to find out what was wrong.

« « « "That deed was false," he told them. "That fellow has no real war deeds. He can't do anything."

Then they circled his tipi and asked him for a new name for me.

"Come back in the morning," he directed them. "I cannot give it at this time of day."

In the morning my grandmother took me down before sunrise.

"Do not enter my tipi," the warrior called out. "Stay out there and look at the rising sun." He was fixing himself in his war regalia. Just as the sun arose, he came out with his spear in hand. He walked south and east of the tipi and stood facing the newly risen sun.

"You, Sun," he cried, "you cannot harm me. This thing I did was true. You, Earth, have seen me. The Big Bird [Eagle] has seen me. You cannot dispute my word. On the war path we saw the enemy on a hill. We charged and my companions outran me, for I was a poor man and my horse was slow. I was the last to come up to the battle place. My friends were doing nothing. They just sat there. I asked them what was the matter. They said the enemies on the hill were too strong for them to attack them. I went right in and charged them. I killed a man with a spear. We went home and had a Victory Dance."

He turned and came back to where my grandmother was holding me in her arms.

"His name is going to be *tɔβɔyβita*—Group of Men Standing On A Hill," he said.[3] » » »

There was a tendency for formal names to belong to a family as a sort of property. Names might be derived from some closely connected circumstance, event, or happening, trivial or otherwise; or they might reflect some experience of the godparent. The male child might be called by some term expressive of the pride or affection of

[3] Informant: Post Oak Jim.

the father. It might be named after its grandfather, uncle, or some other near relative. The person for whom the child, boy or girl, was named was expected to contribute a gift to his or her namesake. A good name was always chosen, though the child might be called by a nickname in common parlance.

Nicknames were obtained in the most haphazard way and might change at the will of associates. Greyfoot was called so because a woman got her feet covered with gray clay while crossing a creek. Even the most noted warriors were sometimes unable to control the disposition to nickname. Any unusual physical aspect or peculiar trait of character was almost certain to be seized upon. Thus Face Wrinkles Like an Old Man is an appropriate appellation for one informant. Frequently a nickname was given not because of the prospective bearer's idiosyncrasies, but after the behavior of his parental kinfolk. Such a name a boy retained until he had made a successful journey to war, a plundering expedition, or a hunt, when he received another name selected by himself or by a close friend as evidence of his newly won status as a man. Girls, however, did not regularly change their names at puberty.

Girls were unlikely to be named after the relatives of the mother, but rather after a relative of the father. Names thus remained in the family. The mother generally selected the name, which might be in commemoration of something she thought worthy. Girls, like boys, were called by nicknames. Married women did not take the names of their husbands, nor was there any equivalent of "Miss" or "Mrs." to indicate whether a woman was married or single. The name of a dead person was avoided and was not spoken in the presence of relatives for a long time, usually several years, other words conveying the same idea being substituted.

The training of children consisted almost entirely of precept, advice, and counsel. A baby soon learned that he would not have his whims gratified by crying. He was told to do, or warned to refrain from doing, certain things, not because they were right or wrong, but because they were to his advantage or disadvantage. He was taught that he would benefit by acting in a certain way. His pride and ambition were appealed to, and worthy examples among living men in the tribe were pointed out for emulation. Of abstract principles of right or wrong, as we understand them, the Comanches knew little or nothing. The approach to life was pragmatic. The child was not coaxed toward good with the hope of Heaven as a reward or frightened from evil by the fear of Hell as a punishment. Instead, he was shown by word and example that the respect and approbation of his fellow tribesmen were to be desired, and their condemnation and contempt were to be dreaded and avoided. He saw that the men who were brave and generous were applauded and respected. In Comanche society it was impossible to live a secluded life. The members were aware of the conduct of each person. Each was eager for the approval of his fellows and greedy for their praise, and public opinion promised the reward he hoped for and threatened the punishment he feared—lack of esteem among The People. This was their method of control.

The Comanches did not whip or otherwise bodily punish their children but directed them by persuasion and object lessons. However, they were, at times, frightened by threats. Breaks Something, when a small boy, annoyed his mother by whining for some mush she was making. She called in an elder classificatory sister, who simply dragged him into the tipi with a rawhide strap around his neck and threatened to hang him to the top of the tipi if he was not good. "I was really scared."

Discipline within the family usually devolved on an older sister— real or, preferably, putative—and youngsters really resented their bossiness. The Comanches knew nothing about Freud and his theory of the Oedipus complex, but they did know that parental dominance breeds resentment, and so, like most American Indians, when forceful discipline was called for, they turned the job over to a relative outside of the immediate conjugal family or to an imaginary bogeyman.

Old people covered their heads with a sheet to give a ghost scare to bad little boys and girls, and all youngsters had the fear put into them of *piamᴣmpits,* Big Cannibal Owl, the mythological creature who lived in a cave on the south side of the Wichita Mountains and ate bad children at night.

As soon as she was large enough to walk, the girl followed her mother everywhere about the camp. She imitated her in all things, playing at the tasks which her mother performed. She was given a doll, dressed usually in deer skin, which she took everywhere with her. She might be lucky enough to have a toy cradle and carry her doll on her back in the fashion of her mother. As she grew older, she learned to dress and undress her doll and to make for it the necessary articles of clothing. Little girls learned to ride almost by the time they were able to sit astride a horse and hold the reins. Although they never spent as much time as the boys in practice, they became good horsewomen, so proficient that often the white campaigner was unable in the midst of battle to distinguish men from women.

There was a very close relationship between a girl and her mother's sisters. They were not called aunt, but *pia*, "mother," and the relationship was that of a mother to her daughter. A woman called her sister's child her own and aided in its instruction. There was even less formality between a girl and her mother's sister than between the girl and her mother. It was the grandparents who spoiled the child. The maternal grandmother was the girl's favorite. She was called *kaku* and she in reciprocity called her daughter's children *kaku,* too. Their social positions were theoretically equivalent. The *kaku* was likely to be congenial and indulgent with the child, and the relationship was much more intimate than between mother and daughter.[4]

As a girl grew older, she was given small tasks. She was first required to carry water and, when still older, she began to go for wood. Parties of girls, sometimes accompanied by a few women, went out from camp to bring in the wood. They also went with the women to gather wild fruits, roots, and nuts. At about twelve years of age, the girl began to learn to cut out moccasins, to cook, to dress hides, to make and set up a tipi—all the things essential for becoming the wife of a warrior.

The passage of a girl from childhood to young womanhood was an important occasion in her life, and was hardly less so to her family and the tribe. But since there was little anxiety about becoming a woman and a girl was already well-prepared for womanhood, and since the Comanches were a work-a-day, unceremonious people, there were no puberty rites. Among well-to-do families the event was the

---

[4] For a detailed analysis of Comanche kinship relations and terminology see, Hoebel, "Comanche and Hekandika Shoshone Relationship Systems," *loc. cit.,* 440–57.

occasion for ceremonial feasting and celebration, and a daughter who was a favorite child in a well-off family might run over the prairie hanging to the tail of a fast pony so that she would be agile and active. This was the only magical activity associated with puberty. She was then ready to marry and become the mother of children and thus to contribute her part toward adding to the number and, therefore, the strength of the tribe. By the time she was sixteen the chances are her marriage had been consummated.

A boy learned to ride almost as soon as he learned to walk. From earliest babyhood he was familiar with horses and their motions, riding behind his mother, clinging to her or to the horse's mane, or strapped to her saddle. He thus gained confidence, learned balance, and, by practice, learned to ride an old gentle pack horse; by the time he was four or five years old, he was expected to be able to manage a pony of his own; and by the time he was six, he was riding young colts bareback. Sometimes while learning to ride, he was bound on the pony by a rawhide lariat while another boy held the pony by another lariat and circled the pony about until the boy literally became a part of the animal. He received the criticisms of companions, father, mother, and other relatives and onlookers. If he fell, he was laughed at by the girls and others, but he did not become angry with his critics. Soon afterwards he had to help herd the ponies. He early became expert in the use of the rope for catching horses and henceforth spent much of his outdoor time on horseback.

By the time the boy was five or six years of age, he was given a bow and some blunt arrows and taught to shoot, usually by his grandfather. This was natural enough since the father was still engaged in war and hunting, while the older man had probably passed the period of active life and thus had the leisure to make bows and arrows and to devote a good deal of his time to the education of his grandson. Consequently, there developed between the two an intimate relationship whose pattern was one of indulgence and congeniality linked with the less severe forms of authority-obedience. The grandfather taught the grandson to ride, to shoot, to make bows and arrows, and the secrets of the hunt and the trail. He told him stories of his boyhood and early manhood, instructed him in the tribal history and traditions, legends and religion, and many other things that the boy would need to know. The maternal grandparent was the boy's favorite, and each called the other *tɔk̟*.

After the grandfather, those next most likely to manifest interest in instructing the boy were his father, elder brother, and father's brothers, who were called "father," *ap'*. With the mother's brother, who was called *aɾa,* "uncle," less formal respect was customary, for the *aɾa* and the boy were on a footing of easygoing comradeship. A boy could borrow his *aɾa's* goods without asking, and he could count on his *aɾa's* aid if he got into a scrape. The uncle, also, in reciprocity, addressed his sister's son as *aɾa*. A man called a brother's child his own[5] and addressed it as "son" or "daughter."

After the boy had received his bow and had been instructed in its use, he spent much time in practice. As he improved in skill, he hunted small birds with other little fellows of his age; and as he grew older, he ranged farther and farther from camp in search of larger game. He learned that hunting was not merely for pleasure but was serious work, that his ability as a hunter might mean the difference between food, shelter, and clothing and starvation and exposure. He was encouraged to become a good hunter, and when successful, he received the coveted praise. His first great kill was celebrated as an important event in his life.

He learned to approach game with patience, caution, and quietness; learned to take advantage of vegetation, of physical features, and of the wind; learned how to make a surround—lessons which would be valuable in real hunts when he grew up. He came to understand the signs of the prairie, how to observe the habits of wild animals, to know where they might be found, and how they reacted under different conditions.

A boy was allowed much liberty, and although his parents were firm, he was seldom scolded or punished. He was not expected to perform any menial labor about the camp and was always treated with great consideration, for "he is going to be a warrior and he may die young in battle."

The Comanche boy in his daily life was learning to be self-reliant, but at the same time his play habits were fostering manly comradery. Most of the daytime hours of the pre-adolescent boys were

[5] Informant: Medicine Woman.

spent in gang play. When a new camp was set up, they set out to find a good water hole in the creek where they could play all day. Following and baiting small birds and large insects fascinated them. Hummingbirds were shot with headless arrows having a vertically split foreshaft in which to catch the birds. Boys would spend all day chasing one bird, according to Skinny and Wrinkled, in a kind of concentration that boded well for the future hunter and tracker of men and beasts. Bull bats were shot with arrows having horizontally split foreshafts. Grasshoppers were shot with hummingbird arrows, and their hind legs were eaten for lunch.

The boys had great fun by tying two grasshoppers together with a short thread and then crowding about to watch them "wrestle." They would jump and jerk each other up short. The one that first fell on its back was the loser. They liked to catch "shit rollers," tie a piece of straw to a leg, and watch them fly, running fleetly after them as they followed their courses. They would stick a small straw up the anus of a horsefly and turn the insect loose—which perhaps showed how they felt about horseflies.

Small boys, who had no real arrows, made them of reed shafts with grasshopper legs for points and a ballast daub of mud stuck two inches from the point. They killed night hawks with slings and amused themselves playing with whirrers—two strings attached to a bone and pulled taut to make a whirring noise.

Although boys were by themselves most of the time, the younger ones now and then joined the little girls to play camp. On the sand by the creek they built small windbreaks and arbors. A play group leader was made "chief," and each boy chose a wife or wives. They all swam in the creek, gathered in ponies with the girls, and rode together. Some time was spent by the boys in hunting squirrels to bring into camp for their "wives" to cook, while the girls gathered berries, edible roots, and the eggs of turkeys, ducks, quail, and prairie chickens. All this swag made for good make-believe feasts.

The more precocious dallied in sexual experimentation. "One day we played at being married. I did my best to make a baby with my wife," said Post Oak Jim.

When younger boys and girls played together (but not when they were playing camp), there were several forms of joint games.

A hilarious favorite was "grizzly bear." For this, a mound of sand, called the "sugar," was fashioned. Then one child was dragged around by his heels to smooth a circle around the "sugar." Outside the circle all the children formed a queue, holding to each others' waists and facing the mound. The leader was the "mother" protecting her young from the "grizzly," who was played by a child inside the circle. His part was to reach out of the circle and seize a child, but the mother protected the children by swinging the line back and forth. At last one child was caught and subjected to the penalty of being tickled ("eaten") by the bear in the circle. After that, players would break out of the line and try to dash in to steal some "sugar" from the grizzly's store and get out without his catching them. As each was caught, he was tickled, and the game went on until the "sugar" was all stolen or all the children were captured.

In another group game the children all sat in a row with their feet straight out in front of them. An old man had to join them in the fun. He would advance with closed eyes and feel up and down the row until he decided to choose one child. This one he picked up by the feet, head hanging down over his back, and carried him around in a circle back to the row. The other children asked the "It" many questions: "Do you have a horse, a saddle, a belt, etc?" The given answer was always "Yes." At last they rushed forward and took their playmate off the old man's back, crying that they were going to eat the old man. So they tickled the old fellow with joyous cries.

Other times they took pieces of old hide to the tops of hills. While some of the children rode on the hides, the others pulled them bouncing down with ropes. "Guess over the hill" (*nanip'ka*) was another favorite. Two older boys would organize the game. The boy who was "It" went over the hill; another stood guard at the top to make sure he did not spy while the other children hid under robes or blankets. When called by the guard, "It" came and tried to guess the names of the hiders.[6]

On rainy days all was still; the children lay quietly at home in their family tipis, for they were superstitiously afraid of thunder and lightning. Winter was the time for the telling of stories; not summer.

[6] Informant: Post Oak Jim.

As boys began to approach adolescence, there were a couple of years when they drew away from girls and ceased to play their childish games with them. They ran loose in gangs, racing, hunting, wrestling, and swimming. As their fathers stole stock, they rustled food from the camp. At night they liked to go armed with ropes and cut out riding horses from the herd to joyride on the prairie. If anyone discovered them, all they had to do was to get off and scatter. They were not encouraged by adults in these escapades; neither were they scolded. Their high spirits were tolerated, for that is as a Comanche should be, and marauding youngsters at night were a useful guard against enemy raiders.

As the boy grew into adolescence, the normal Comanche pattern demanded extreme brother-sister avoidance, even to the extent of isolating the unmarried adolescent boy in a separate tipi set up behind his parents' lodge. Here he prepared to receive power away from the contaminating grease of cooking utensils, while he was also isolated from incestuous temptation. The brother and sister could never sit close to or touch each other.[7] This social tabu was elaborated to the point where a young man might kill his sister without suffering any social disgrace or punishment if she insisted on violating it.[8]

If an older boy became unruly, disrespectful, or insolent, some of the older men made him the subject of cutting sarcasm. It usually was on such an occasion that the youth could not withdraw or save his face. This form of punishment was successful in most cases. Eventually, the youth learned to conduct himself with dignity and in accordance with the social norm set by his elders. Occasionally there was a wrangle between children, but they were allowed to fight it out to the amusement of the onlookers.

About the time a boy retired to his own tipi, he went out on his first real buffalo hunt, and should success crown his first effort, it might be an occasion for some kind of celebration. Usually a boy learned to hunt buffalo before going on the warpath. When he had shown his ability as a hunter, he was ready and eager to go on the warpath, for most boys wished to be brave and to win war honors.

[7] Informant: See How Deep the Water Is.

[8] Informant: Kills Something. Kill Something's brother-in-law shot his sister for entering his room after he had warned her not to enter.

130

But he must first make his medicine or obtain supernatural power through a vision visitation. When the moment came to fight, a boy was given every opportunity to distinguish himself. His first expedition normally occurred about the age of fifteen or sixteen. He told his father or older brother that he wanted to accompany the fighters on a raid. They were pleased, but if they thought he was not ripe and gave him a rebuff, he went sulking to his bed where he lay, head covered with his robe, refusing to eat, until his father said, "All right." His father gave him a good horse to ride only when he went into battle and another to ride while upon the trail. If he proved himself a distinguished warrior, he was likely to become a war leader, and if his success continued, he might be made a war chief by his fellow braves.

After the boy had made a success, the Give Away Dance might be held in his honor, when the father gave out presents, usually one or more horses, in honor of the occasion.[9] The dance was announced several days ahead. At the appointed time the drummers took their position facing east in the center of the circle of spectators. The honoree was certain to dance, and other young men who wished might do so. The father, mother, other relatives, or anyone else who wanted to honor the young brave pitched presents at his feet during the dance or led up horses. Blankets and horses appear to have been the most appropriate gifts. Sticks were used to represent horses. Anyone of either sex who wished could grab the gift, and it belonged to him who first snatched it. A man with power was unlikely to grab. To do so revealed to the spectators that he had lost faith in his power or had given way to greed. No man would ever desire the people to think either of him. Sometimes the host announced the name of a recipient of a gift without giving the others a chance. It was not uncommon for a family to give away until it was poverty stricken. It enhanced social prestige and indicated a belief that the giver had strong power. Consequently, he was more likely to have a stronger following on the next raiding or war party. In 1945, when the veterans returned from World War II, Comanches put on Give Away Dances for their returned heroes, just as they did of old.[10]

[9] Hoebel, *The Political Organization and Law-Ways of the Comanche Indians*, 26–28.
[10] Informant: Kills Something.

While a boy was growing up, a very close comradeship was likely to develop between him and a brother. The relationship between brothers became one of mutual helpfulness. It was based on mutual affection and interdependence in play, work, and war. There was no formality between them. An older brother gave the younger much helpful advice, and when they went on the warpath together, the older brother was likely to keep a watchful eye on a younger brother until he had become an experienced warrior. Even afterwards they remained closely associated and rendered mutual assistance. This relationship was carried to the point where they lent each other their wives; especially would an elderly married brother accommodate his younger unmarried brothers. However, he could expect reciprocity when the younger brother married. "He would never feel the same about his younger brother, if he refused to make it even."[11] This close relationship was sometimes instituted between two friends, perhaps being more common where there was no real brother. In such a case the friend took the status of a "brother" in the relationship system of his comrade's family, assuming all the privileges and restrictions which went with the new status. Then the two friends ("brothers") were likely to marry sisters and thus become brothers-in-law, or *haints,* which is the same word as "friend."

A boy's education by advice and admonition was considered to have ended with his first journey to war. He was supposed to know by this time that to gain the approbation and respect of his people he must be brave and courageous in war, wise in council, cool and fearless in the midst of danger, ardent in his friendship, charitable to the less fortunate of his community, hospitable to strangers, and enthusiastic in his patriotism and devotion to the welfare of his tribe. He was likely at that time to turn part of his attention to love and courtship and marriage. It was not uncommon for the male to marry at an early age. On the other hand, he was somewhat restrained by the desire to improve his social prestige by developing a reputation as a warrior, raider, or hunter. Also, he needed horses or other plunder to secure a wife. He might, of course, persuade his father to furnish the necessary horses, but it was far more respectable for a young man to acquire his own, so Comanche boys married at later age than girls.

11 Informant: Post Oak Jim.

In fact, girls were often married off to middle-aged men who could give a good bride-price. The average age at marriage for girls is said to have been sixteen, while for boys it was twenty-five to thirty.

Although youngsters were not subject to moral censure for sexual activity, it was not encouraged. Boys, during the period of their preadolescent gang life, ignored the girls to a great degree. At adolescence, when they got their own tipis, they became positively bashful. It was proper for girls and women to make sexual advances, but not for a well-mannered boy. "Boys seemed to stay pretty much to their tipis," said Post Oak Jim. "It was the girl's place to come to them." Bolder, unmarried older girls might crawl in a boy's tipi at night to initiate him in lovemaking. In the dark these girls commonly kept their identity anonymous, for it would not help their reputations to be known.

The Comanche pattern of social conduct, in theory, prohibited young couples from being seen together. In response to the query of what would have happened if they had been found together, informants replied, "It would have been too bad." In practice, however, they did find opportunity to be in each other's company. More romances probably began where the girls went for water and wood than any other place. When a young lover became fond of a girl, he waited near where she might pass. When she approached, he stepped toward her, watching for an encouraging sign that his attentions might be welcome. If she was not interested, the girl made the fact known through her actions, and he went away much mortified. If the girl were favorably inclined, they agreed by a sign, mutual understanding, or orally on a time and a meeting place. If no older people were near, they might spend a while together. Again, they might agree to meet after dark. Sometimes a girl allowed a boy to come to her tipi. The more bashful boys lay outside, whispering to the girls inside, but they might be bold enough to crawl under the tipi and lie with them. More often, however, the girl crawled out and went a short distance away with her suitor. Supposedly no one else knew, but informants felt that certainly the girl's mother must at times have been aware of what was taking place. Most courting was done when the girl slipped out of the tipi and met the boy at night.[12]

[12] Informants: Medicine Woman; See How Deep the Water Is. Statements by Marcy, Dodge, Parker, and others are substantially in agreement.

A youngster whose heart was too faint to approach a girl on his own account sought out an old and distantly related woman and put his plight to her. It was up to her secretly to arrange a tryst with the girl of his heart. Thomas Gladwin reports that this service was supplied by a boy's sister, but our informants specifically denied this possibility.[13] "It would make people too suspicious." Furthermore, it seems quite unlikely that a sister would be sent on a mission with sexual implications.

It was after they had got over the first pangs of adolescence that vain young men took to the *tuiβitsi* pattern of showing off. It was a show-off for the girls collectively, however, for no Comanche boy could decently reveal a public display of interest in one girl.

It was good tactics for a young man who had fallen in love with a maiden to seek the acquaintance and to cultivate the friendship of her brother, or some other near relative, or the person who controlled her marriage. If the suitor and the girl's brother were together on the warpath, the suitor might give the brother arrows or a horse and in various ways try to make things easy for him, addressing him as *n3m3aɾa,* "our children's uncle," i.e., the brother of my offspring's mother—a subtle hint of things he hoped to come.[14] This could lead the brother to speak a favorable word at home in behalf of his friend— of his bravery, his strength, his ability as a hunter or raider, and other commendable qualities. He might even extend an invitation to the friend to come to his family's lodge. The suitor was also likely to offer the girl gifts, including horses, in an effort to win her favor.

When a suitor had decided that he wanted a certain girl for a wife, he made a present to the girl's brother, her father, or her guardian. The most acceptable gift was a horse. In a few cases a boy was known to work (hunt or raid) for the family of the girl he wanted for a wife for as much as one, two, or three years.[15] In any event, sons-in-law were obligated to provide meat for their wives' parents. There was also love medicine known to certain practitioners who could be induced to charm the girl on behalf of a petitioner so that she could not resist his suit.

13 Thomas Gladwin, "Comanche Kin Behavior," *American Anthropologist,* Vol. L (1948), 73–94.
14 *Ibid.*
15 Informant: Kills Something; see also Smithwick, *op. cit.* 183.

134

Under the system of contract and sororate and levirate marriages which prevailed, a girl was often bestowed upon a man many years her senior and not of her own choosing. According to the ideal pattern she adjusted herself to the arrangement. Although it was a common belief among the older Indians that such marriages were more successful and lasting than those which were formed of romantic liaison, many young people sought love-mates of their own choosing: adultery, desertion, and wife absconding were rife and lead to a lively legal picture of strife and process.

In any case a man was not likely to press his suit unless given encouragement by the maiden or by her family. If he gave presents to her brother or father or worked for them for a time, he would eventually be asked why he had made the gifts and what he was looking for. Then he would reply that he wanted the girl for a wife. Some informants insist that when the request was made of a girl's brother in this fashion, the brother had to consent—"It was the law." He knew what the man was after and should not have taken the gifts if he did not intend to grant his request. Others say that he had to consent only in case the two were on the warpath at the time the request was made.

In most cases the suitor did not himself ask for the girl directly, but secured a mediator, in the person of an uncle, an aged relative, or a friend, to make an offer to the parents or brother as compensation for their daughter or sister. The messenger took horses or other goods to the lodge of the girl's parents. After some polite and aimless talk, he came to the point, then left forthwith, without getting an answer, so as to avoid the possible embarrassment of a refusal to his face. Sometimes the father or brother made the decision; sometimes they would call in other members of the family. The girl's wishes might or might not be respected in the matter, for she must accept the husband chosen for her. Informants maintain that a father or a brother had a legal right to kill a girl who refused to accept a husband they had selected. If the suitor was rejected, his horses were simply turned loose and driven back to his herd; if accepted, they were driven to the herd of the girl's father or brother. This was sufficient announcement of engagement.

Occasionally a boy brought the horses to the door of his prospective bride himself and waited near by without saying a thing to see if his gift were acceptable. Of course, the girl and her family knew from whom the proffered gift came even if the owner were not visible. Sometimes the girl was dressed up and brought out of the lodge right away and handed over to the suitor, who came forth to accept his prize when he saw that his gift was accepted. At other times the suitor tied his riding horse at the maiden's lodge door and waited out of her sight. If she wished to reject him, she merely turned the horse loose, but if she drove it to the herd, the act signified her willingness to accept the owner and was symbolical evidence that she was willing to take charge of his horses and other property. This simple ceremony seems to have been used frequently even after the herd had been placed in front of the girl's door.[16]

In most cases there was no further ceremony. The bridegroom took the bride to his tipi. There was no necessity for any religious ceremony, no demonstration. If circumstances permitted, there might be feasting and, occasionally, dancing. There is evidence that an occasional marriage did receive official sanction either from the chief, who had the announcement made to the camp, or from the council. The scanty evidence available does not make clear whether these were customary practices of specific bands or whether it was a matter of individual taste, as a public or private ceremony in our own society.

Another form of ceremony which has been reported is that after the horses had been delivered and accepted, the bridegroom killed one of the least valuable, removed the heart, and hung it at the door of his betrothed. After the bride roasted and divided it into equal parts, it was eaten by the couple. The heart of a buffalo or other animal could be substituted.[17]

When a girl learned that a rich suitor whom she did not care to marry was about to propose, she might elope with the man she loved. Couples occasionally eloped when the boy was poor and unable to

[16] This description of obtaining a wife is compiled from statements by informants Kills Something, See How Deep the Water Is, and Medicine Woman; also, Battey, *op. cit.*, 328; Gregg, *op. cit.*, 431–32; Daniel A. Becker, "Comanche Civilization," *Chronicles of Oklahoma*, Vol. I (1923), 250; Mooney, "Calendar History of the Kiowas," *loc. cit.*, 231–33; R. B. Marcy, *Thirty Years of Army Life on the Border*, 49; Lehmann, *op. cit.*, 177–79; Agent Charles Adams to Commissioner of Indian Affairs, September 12, 1890 (Oklahoma Historical Society Library, correspondence file K–33, p. 414).

[17] Gregg, *op. cit.*, 431–32.

furnish enough ponies or other articles of value to satisfy the parents of the girl. In such a case the relatives and friends of the boy might supply the necessary ponies to soothe the dishonor suffered by the wife's parents, or the young husband himself might later secure sufficient ponies and present them to her parents. After this he was in no danger, for when the customary gifts were sent, the marriage was made valid and the disgrace wiped out. Elopement, however, seems to have been unusual, especially in earlier times, and couples who did elope were socially ostracized to some extent.

The giving or paying of horses and other gifts for a bride was a development in the lives of the Comanches that came with prosperity. People who have goods are interested in them. The pattern was general throughout the plains in the last two centuries, and the Comanches fell in with the practice. In their earlier days of Shoshonean poverty it is unlikely that such marriage customs existed. For some Comanche boys and girls the old Shoshonean way of getting married was enough. If a couple slept together all night, they were considered married. One unscrupulous lad, known to That's It in the Water Horse band, took advantage of this fact to "frame" a girl and win her as wife.

« « « He hid his leggings under the chosen girl's bed blanket. Then he set up the frame in a gambling game. He went in and lost so that he did not have enough to pay all his losses.

He said, "Well, I have some money in my leggings," and he asked his friend to go to the girl's tipi and get them. "They are under her blanket."

His friend went over and asked the girl's father for them. He didn't know a thing about it.

So the boy went right in and pulled the leggings out from under her bed. The father then called in the girl and asked her what about it.

"I didn't know you were married," he said. She denied it, but her mother said, "Well you are old enough; you might just as well go live with your husband!" » » »

Although sleeping together was not the ideal way to get married, it was, nevertheless, idealized. Several of our Comanche friends thought such marriages were happier than the arranged ones. "In an arranged marriage the wife is likely to become angry on the least provocation and leave." Such precipitate action is explained partly by the fact that girls were given to men much older than they. "If parents give a daughter to an older man, she doesn't like it. If they do it once, nothing is said. If they do it often, people don't like it; they talk."[18]

Occasionally an up-and-coming youth who was industrious and showed promise as a warrior was sought out by a father or brother and asked to marry a girl in their family. Such a man was usually a captive; a fullblood Comanche would consider it disgraceful for him to accept advances from the girl's family. The father or brother in such a case took gifts to the prospective bridegroom. Here there was direct action—no sending of intermediaries or hiding out of sight. If the young man accepted, the girl was brought to him that night, and her parents provided most of the household necessities.

All these steps were possibilities in a first marriage. In addition, the Comanches observed several forms of affinal marriage; i.e., marriage to a relative by a previous marriage. The levirate and sororate were the strongest of these. The number of wives might run anywhere from one to six or more. It was a normal pattern for a man to take as wives the younger sister or sisters of his first wife and any women he might have captured or girls who grew up as captives in the tribe. Sororal polygyny was used by parents to induce a son-in-law to observe zealously his economic obligations to them. His reward was a second sister to wife. The contract was frequently made while the child was still quite young, even before she reached teen age. Although such a wife was treated as a child, she shared the privileges of a wife.

Polyandry as practiced by the Comanches was attenuated in form. It was a practice which might also be called "anticipatory levirate" and consisted in brothers' lending each other their wives. "One is really her husband, of course." Sexual jealousy between brothers was socially deprecated. "A man loves his brother; he knows that if his brother dies, no one can replace him; he gives him everything he can," explained That's It. "A brother therefore sends his wife over to him occasionally as a gift. She cannot go of her own free will or

18 Informant: Breaks Something.

138

meet him secretly, or her real husband will be angry." It was also expected that when a man was on the warpath, his brother could sleep with his wife. If all the brothers were out on a raid, the wives were sent to stay with their husbands' sisters. In wife-exchange the rights of the husband were fully recognized, and he was compensated for restraining his jealousy partly by social approval of his generosity, partly by his expectation of a return in kind. So strong was the idea that brothers share a wife that it logically followed that men who had sexual relations with a married woman were, in a formal sense, brothers. So it was that an outraged husband prosecuting an adulterer, demanding heavy damages, nevertheless addressed the man who had cuckolded him as "brother."

This practice indicates that brothers with their sisters formed a marriage group, which established relationships with another marriage group on the basis of inter-family exchange marriage. Although individual marriages took place between the members of the two groups (no group marriage), there was a projection of the marital rights of each member of the group to all its members of the same sex —in the present through sororal polygyny and fraternal polyandry (anticipatory levirate); in futurity through the sororate and levirate. One's father and the father's brothers were thus equated in the kinship system as *ap'*, because they were actual or potential mates to one's mother under polyandry or the levirate. One's mother and her sisters were equated as *pia*, because they were actual or potential mates to one's father as members of the same marriage group. A man called his brother's child his own (*tua*, "son," or *bɛt*, "daughter"), since they were descendants of his marriage group, but he terminologically distinguished his sisters' children, *aɾa*, because they were in another marriage group. Likewise, a woman called her sister's child "son" or "daughter" but distinguished her brother's child, *paha*. A woman who lost her husband by death was inherited by a brother of her husband. Thus brothers were potential husbands of a woman whether they ever became such in actuality. Hence, there was no separate word for brother-in-law, only *kumaxp*, "husband."

The marriage of a man to the daughter of his deceased wife's brother was not a standard Comanche practice; the custom is usually found only in societies that have patrilineal clans in which the wife's brother's daughter naturally belongs to the same clan as her father's sister. Such marriages are nothing more than the extension of the sororate to a lower generation and, like the levirate and sororate, they function to keep the bond between two families or marriage groups firm when one of the links has been snapped. In at least one Comanche instance, recounted by Slope, such a marriage was made for this explicit reason. The widowed husband was said to be a very good man, and his brother-in-law wanted to keep him in the family. As he had no other sister, he gave him his daughter instead. Previously, the widower had been his *haints* and they had joked as brothers-in-law do. Now brother-in-law had become son-in-law to his friend, and they both changed their behavior and address terms to the more circumspect relation required of son-in-law and father-in-law.

Avowedly a man could also marry his stepdaughter, but we have no examples of such marriages. So, too, he could marry his stepmother when his father died, but not his real mother. In the heinous case of attempted parricide of Old Buffalo, who had three wives, his son and grandson shot him and ran off with the two wives from whom they were not descended. They were ostracized ("people didn't like it") and had to live on the edge of the camp, but not so much for marrying the stepmothers as for their attempt on the life of their father and grandfather.[19]

Marriages between persons of any degree of recognized genetic relationship were absolutely forbidden. Most marriages took place within the band; hence, a couple lived customarily in the same group as their parents. The groom brought his wife to his private lodge, which was set near that of his parents, and there they were likely to live until a growing family made a larger dwelling necessary. Since residence in inter-band marriages was more often virilocal (residence in the locale of the husband), children usually belonged to the band of the father. When, however, a man took a first wife from another tribe, he generally went to live with her, since his own tribe held him in light esteem afterwards.

The bride's mother with other relatives and friends of the couple ordinarily helped the couple get started housekeeping. She helped make much of the furnishings and possibly a new tipi. There was no

19 Informant: She Invites Her Relatives.

140

mother-in-law tabu in Comanche society, probably because of the old Shoshonean system of pseudo cross-cousin marriages in which a boy married the step-daughter of his father's sister, thus equating mother-in-law with paternal aunt. The absence of the avoidance practice is entirely sensible, since a boy had been accustomed to treating his mother-in-law as a preferred aunt. The same relationship held for a girl and her father-in-law. The Comanches had given up the pseudo cross-cousin marriages, but the terminology and its accompanying attitudes carried on. This patterns of social conduct was quite in contrast with that of some of the other Plains tribes. Among the Cheyennes, who were neighbors of the Comanches, for example, a man never spoke to, or knowingly went near, his mother-in-law until late in life when he had presented her with a war trophy. A Comanche mother-in-law could talk or even joke with her son-in-law, although extreme familiarity was carefully avoided. The normal pattern in Comanche society was that a son-in-law should respect and help his mother-in-law. In case of an attack on the camp, a son-in-law was expected to protect his mother-in-law. In case he failed to do so, the sympathy of the group was with the abandoned mother-in-law, who could order her daughter to leave him, as in the case of the woman whose son-in-law refused to give her his horse when they were being chased by the Tonkawas. "When we get home, you don't live with my daughter any longer," was her dictum. A hunter felt obligated to share his game with his wife's parents. A father-in-law had the privilege of ordering the dissolution of a marriage when the son-in-law gave personal offense to either parent-in-law.

In polygynous families many of the secondary wives were captives whose lot in the household was that of "chore wives," helpers to the first wife. If the wives were all sisters, the oldest one usually continued as "boss," even as she had among her sisters before her marriage. This fact explains why the Comanches thought sisters made better multiple wives. There was less possibility of friction developing because a younger wife challenged the supremacy of an older one. One wife was always favored and was free to be her husband's constant companion. She was called the *paɾaiβo,* "chief" wife. The favored wife usually escaped much of the hard labor and drudgery which fell to the lot of other wives. She carried her husband's shield on the march, unless menstruating, when he carried it himself. In fact, however, plural wives tended to reduce the domestic drudgery of all through a sharing of labor.

A man with only two or three wives and not too many children kept them all in one tipi. An important man's wives ordinarily lived apart, however, each woman having her own tent for herself and her children. Among the poorer families when wives were sisters, they sometimes used only the one tipi and possibly one bed for a time, but they always constructed separate tipis as soon as possible.[20] The opening of these tents was on the main tipi which was occupied by the husband. Long buckskin strings, attached to the buffalo mattress of each woman, were laid under the fold of the tent into the tipi of the husband so that he could instantly summon any one of his wives.

Comanche women were not very prolific, and death of the mother at childbirth was not uncommon.[21] The average birth rate seems scarcely to have exceeded two children to each woman, and it was a rare case when there were more than three or four born to one woman. Births were far apart, and the newborn were usually small. Many women were barren. Contraceptives were unknown to the Comanches, but abortions were practiced by beating the belly with stones. Hard physical work and constant horseback riding also apparently induced abortions so early in pregnancy that they went unnoticed.

Giving birth to a child was ordinarily a simple affair. Cases have been reported of women on the trail dropping behind the group, giving birth to their children, and then after a few hours rejoining the group on the march.[22] Under normal conditions, however, natal preparations were made. If a woman had her own tipi, she might use it; but if it was used by other members of the family, a separate lodge was constructed. In the summer it would be of brush about eight feet in diameter and six or seven feet high. Inside the lodge the earth

20 Informant: See How Deep the Water Is.
21 R. N. Richardson, "The Culture of the Comanche Indians," Texas Archeological and Paleontological Society Bulletin, I (1929), 63.
22 Burnet, "The Comanches and Other Tribes of Texas and the Policy to Be Pursued Respecting Them," loc. cit., 234; Humfreville, Twenty Years among Our Hostile Indians, 182.

was made soft. Two pits were dug in the ground, one for the after-birth and the other for heating water and steaming. One or more stakes about four feet long were driven into the ground by the bed for the patient to grasp as an aid in delivery. A supply of sage was brought in and hot coals were prepared. A medicine woman, middle-aged or older, was in attendance. One or more additional women were likely to be on hand to give assistance. No men came near. The woman normally lay on the bed, but when the pain seemed un-bearable she walked around or squatted over the hole to grasp a stake. An attendant might try to aid nature by grasping the patient around the abdomen and exerting pressure. Hot rocks were placed against her back, and she was required to drink hot water or hot soup.

When births were prolonged and stubborn, a medicine man was called in to take over. We have accounts of the actions of two medi-cine men who were called in such cases; one had buffalo power; the other, otter. The husband of Holding Her Sunshade, when called, asked for a buffalo hide with the tail on it. He drew a white "path" down the center of it with his fingers and placed it as a door on the childbirth tipi. The mother and father also had to wear buffalo robes with tails and the hair on the outside. The doctor entered the tipi holding a buffalo tail. He waved the tail in the mother's face and then made a motion as if he were going to vomit. He was bringing up his power. Next he breathed his power into the patient's mouth and spit in the midwife's hands, had her rub them together and rub the patient's abdomen. His power was now on her and inside of her. His work was done, and he walked around the fire and out the door. "The child should be born when he puts his second foot outside the door. He was successful, and although the family was poor, they gave him their best horse."

The otter medicine man, known to Post Oak Jim, worked a little differently. He had a tabu against any other pregnant woman's being about. His method was to pull his otter skin through his teeth from left to right, after which he drew the skin down the front of the woman's body. He fanned down her whole body with an eagle feather. He then fanned her lightly above her head. A medicine song was sung, and he was ready to leave with a flying leap through the door. "When his feet hit the ground outside the tipi, the child will be born."

143

The magical associations of buffalo hides with tails is not clear, but the effect of otter medicine is obvious. Otters like to slide down slippery mud banks. With similar ease the child will slide out. A conception of the birth lodge as a symbolic womb is also there. Just as the medicine man emerges through the door (vagina), so will the child.

When the baby was born, the doleful cries and monotonous songs of the attendants immediately changed to rejoicing. After the umbilical cord had been cut, the medicine woman wrapped it and hung it in a hackberry tree when one was convenient. If it was undisturbed before it rotted, the child was supposed to have a long and fortunate life. The medicine woman carried the afterbirth and threw it in a running stream (the purifier that nullifies power). The baby was bathed and wrapped in soft rabbit skins and placed in its cradle-board. The number of days the new mother remained in bed was set by the attending midwife. In recent times, ten days is considered the customary time needed for recovery, but there are cases on record where the woman had had serious difficulty and yet was on her feet going about her way before an attendant had washed and wrapped the baby. During the entire time of confinement no man except a doctor entered her tipi. The grandfather, however, always came right away to ask the sex of the child. He stood outside the lodge, and if it was a boy, the women within would call, "ɛhaitsma" ("It's your close friend"). If a girl, they simply say, "ɜsamop'ma" ("It's a girl"). The new mother was not allowed to eat a single bite of meat; "it makes blood and would cause hemorrhage." Each day sage was burned over the coals to purify the tipi. One of the first things the woman did when she got up from her bed was to bathe in running water. A proud father usually made it a point to give away something. Normally his generosity was limited to the first person who came to see the new baby. If it was a boy and the father well-to-do, the gift would be a horse.[23]

During menstruation a woman went into confinement. If her husband had medicine (and what man did not?), she could not sleep

[23] This description of childbirth is compiled from statements by informants Medicine Woman, Kills Something, and Post Oak Jim; also, House, *op. cit.*, 59; W. T. Corlett, *The Medicine Man of the American Indians* (report of a frontier surgeon stationed at Fort Sill in 1869), 269.

in his tipi, for menstrual blood nullifies all power. If she had no tipi of her own, she moved in with her parents ("the medicine of old people was too weak to be harmed"). When an article in her tent was needed by someone, it was set or pitched out the door, and no one entered against the occupant's will. During the time, she ate no meat; it would make her sick at the stomach and cause her to flow more. She could not wash her face because that would make her get wrinkled before her time; nor could she touch or comb her hair because it would cause her to get gray young. At the end of her period she had to bathe in a running creek, no matter how cold, even if it was frozen over, before she could go back to her husband's tipi. No man could eat from the same dish or drink from the same cup as she until this had been done. An unmarried girl had to observe approximately the same restrictions. After menopause all female tabus were removed; the woman was now physiologically equal to man.

All societies recognize at least three age groupings, child, adult, and old person. The Comanches, for their part, recognized five **age groups:**

ona:—a baby
ṭuinᴣpʻ—a boy up to adolescence
ṭuiβitsi—a young, unmarried brave
ṭɛnapʻ—a grown man; also *muwɔ:* (a substitute term used by some people who had to observe the tabu on the use of the name of a dead relative when *ṭɛnapʻ* had been used as a personal name.
tsuḳupʻ—an old man; also, *naɾaβə,* a joking term of familiarity.

ona:—a baby
tuepᴣt—a girl up to adolescence
naiβi—an adolescent girl

hᴣβi—a grown woman

puʼstᴣ—an old woman

The physical difference between child and adult is easily recognizable, and the passage from childhood to maturity is marked by physiological events which make it possible to date it, exactly **for** girls and less definitely for boys. However, the physical passage from childhood to maturity does not necessarily coincide with the social transfer of the individual from one status to the other. Although the actual transition was made more quickly in Comanche society than in our own, where both men and woman remain legally children until long after they are physically mature, clear-cut lines of division between the various groupings were lacking. Age classes were lacking. In the change from boyhood to manhood, for instance, the real test was whether the boy was able to follow the strenuous life of a warrior.

The tendency for societies to emphasize the individual's first change in age status and largely ignore the change from adult to old age is due in part to the difficulty of determining the onset of old age. But in certain societies the change from the adult to the old status is made more difficult for the individual by the fact that the patterns for the new status require a different personality. This was true in Comanche society. Although society provided for old people fairly well and treated them with respect, there is abundant evidence that the transition was a difficult one for most individuals. "A brave man," said the Comanches, "dies young."

Women were able to make the change with less difficulty than men, and the line was more clearly discernible. During and before the menopause there were a number of social tabus or restrictions. They could not remain in the same room with a medicine man. Afterwards they were released from restrictions pertaining to the supernatural, and henceforth could handle sacred objects, obtain power through dreams, and practice as shamans.[24]

In the case of men, the ascribed status for old age differed radically from that for adults. The adult male was a warrior, vigorous, self-reliant, and aggressive. He took what he could get and held what he had without much regard for the abstract rights of those weaker than himself. A ready willingness to arbitrate differences or to ignore slights was a sign of weakness resulting in loss of prestige. The old man, on the other hand, was expected to be wise and gentle, willing to overlook slights, and, if need be, to endure abuse. It was his task to work for the welfare of the tribe, giving sound advice, smoothing down quarrels, and even preventing his tribe from making new

24 Informant: Medicine Woman; see also Linton, *The Study of Man*, 119.

enemies. Young men strove for war and honor; old men for peace and tranquility. Warriors did not prepare for old age, thinking it better to be killed in action than to adjust themselves to the status ascribed for old age and to eventual death on the sick bed. When waning physical powers forced them to assume a new role, many did so grudgingly, and those who were able to keep strong medicine attempted to hold the rights which belonged to the younger status. Such bad old men were a peril to young ones beginning their career, for they were jealous of them simply because they were young and strong and admired by the women. The old men could and did kill young men by malevolent magic. "It is significant that although benevolent medicine men might be of any age in Comanche folklore, malevolent ones were always old."[25]

Old men who were no longer able to go on the warpath had a special tipi, called the Smoke Lodge, wherein they gathered at the end of the day to smoke and talk. No boys or women were allowed to enter. Initiatory rites were not held for new members, and apparently no invitations were sent to prospective members. When one became old enough to be interested primarily in the past, he merely started going to the meetings. The men were free to come and go as they liked. If the camp was not permanently located, the men merely gathered at a convenient place and sat in a circle smoking and talking like a bunch of old gaffers about the cracker barrel. In permanent camps they had a lodge.

Each evening's session was opened with a ritual. The lodge possessed a large common pipe which was in the care of the leader. While the lighting of the pipe was in process, no word could be uttered. Absolute silence prevailed. The leader sat opposite the door. The firetender, a captive, sat next to the door, to the right as one entered. The leader lighted the pipe, and then offered invocation. He held the pipe up and prayed to the sun. This done, a pinch of tobacco was taken from the bowl and laid upon the ground as an offering to the Earth. If at any stage of the process the silence was broken, it was necessary to start anew. When the pipe was prepared, the firetender crossed directly to the leader and tendered a live coal. With the issuance of smoke the ceremony was done and the men could

[25] Linton, *The Study of Man*, 118–21.

lapse into conversation. The pipe was passed among them and smoked until it burned out. Then after a bit, the refilling and lighting ceremony was again solemnly performed and they were ready for another round of talk. Four times they filled and smoked the pipe out; then they dispersed for the night. The fire-tender left first; the others followed in procession, treading around the tipi to the north. But during the course of the evening a man could make nonceremonial exit from either side of the door.

The conversation dealt with matters both trivial and serious. The men exchanged ideas and related the latest camp gossip. They narrated deeds which they had performed in their younger days and stories which they had heard. They engaged in coup-counting games by forming sides and each relating a coup which he had gained. The losing side might have to furnish a feast the next day. At other times they spent the evening asking each other dishonorable and embarrassing questions. "How many times have you been divorced?" "How many times did you turn back from the warpath without meeting the enemy?" They were beyond struggling for prestige, and they made light of the prime-of-lifers to whom prestige meant so much. And although they discussed tribal matters of moment, they had no authority.

In earlier times the Old Men's Smoke Lodge was respectfully treated, but in later days they received some rough handling by practical jokers among the boys. The most common prank was to close the smoke flaps of their lodge and smoke them out. Once their old war robes with painted coup pictures were slashed by boys. Another time pranksters put excrement in the doorway and covered it with dirt, knowing that the old men always took off their moccasins to enter their sacred lodge. Yet another time, boys stood outside the door and smeared foul stuff in their hair as they came out. And once, as the old men were going through the pipe-lighting ritual and could not holler out, they backed a colt through the door and made it kick and buck. "It tore things up and the old men were awful sore. They began to talk about what they should do to the young men when they caught them, what law they should give them, but one old man spoke up.

"'Now you old fellows,' he told them, 'you were boys once.

When the sun was shining you were mighty nice. When the sun went down you were devils. Don't you remember how you were? Boys will be boys.' "[26]

They all laughed and let the matter drop. After all they were old men—peaceable, and not warriors jealous of their dignity.

Although they were a strong physical race of people, the Comanches were troubled with a number of diseases. Many of their ailments were due to their unbalanced diet, to exposure, and to the vigorous life they led. Among their more serious ailments were pneumonia, colds, rheumatism, wounds, broken bones, intestinal diseases, rattlesnake bites, smallpox, and cholera. The number with weak eyes, partially or completely blind, was appalling. Fevers often resulted from their trips to the east and south. The white intruders brought cholera, smallpox, and syphilis, which swept away many of the people. Epidemics of smallpox took heavy tolls in 1816, in 1839–40, and in the winter of 1861–62. The cholera epidemic of 1849, brought from the East by immigrants on the road to California, possibly resulted in more fatalities than the smallpox plague. In any event, whether from violence, disease, or old age, the end came inevitably to every Comanche as to every man—and the cycle was closed.

When the condition of an elderly person became hopeless, he was usually "thrown away" by all except his most faithful relatives and friends; and sometimes even they would desert him. This was not due so much to lack of affection and sympathy as from fear of the evil spirits and his ghost, which were believed to have taken possession of his body. When he felt death drawing near, he made disposition of all his property and retired to a quiet spot to die. After making medicine in preparation, an old man might take his own life, and at least one case is known where a man took the life of his wife by cutting her throat because she was hopelessly ill and lonely.

There was not a long delay between death and burial. If possible, burial took place the same day. The body was prepared with great care by anyone who would undertake the job, usually near relatives assisted by a comrade or close friend of the deceased. A woman attended to the body of a woman; a man attended to a man's. When a small child died, it was buried still lashed to its cradle-board. Before

[26] Informant: That's It.

the natural warmth had left the body of an adult, the knees were bent upon the chest, and the head bent forward to the knees. A rope was used to bind the limbs and body firmly in this flexed position. The corpse was bathed, the face overlaid with vermilion, and the eyes sealed with red clay. The corpse was dressed in the finest apparel obtainable, relatives and friends furnishing some of their own for the occasion. It was laid upon a blanket, and relatives and friends were usually permitted to take a final look at the deceased. The blanket was then folded around the body, this again tightly corded with a rope or thongs of rawhide. The body was placed in a sitting posture upon a horse. A woman riding behind, or one on either side of the horse, held the body in position until the place of burial was reached. A few near relatives and friends accompanied the body to its final resting place, wailing and weeping on the way.

The preferred burial place was a natural cave, crevice, or a deep wash among the rocks of the highest accessible peak, or in the head of a canyon, preferably to the west of the lodge of the departed. If such a place could not be found, a hole was made just large and deep enough to contain the body, or the body was set upon the ground and a pen of poles and rock erected around the grave. In either case the body was deposited in a sitting posture or on its side, facing the rising sun, and the grave was covered with rocks, sticks, and dirt, apparently with no special system or arrangement. The ideal burial place of a medicine man was high on the south side of a hill or slope— if possible, at the spot where he had received power.

During the last half of the nineteenth century the Comanches, especially those living on the Red River, away from the mountains, occasionally used scaffold or tree burial, a method commonly practiced by the Cheyennes and other Plains tribes. In such instances the body was placed in a tree and made secure by means of ropes or rawhide thongs which bound it to the branches above and below the corpse. The elevated burial was also made by binding three poles together and raising them in tripod fashion, the crossing made as high as practicable, and the body bound securely to the poles above the point of intersection. The reason for the elevated burial was to protect the corpse from wolves and other predatory animals, but it seems to have been used by the Comanches only when a satisfactory ground burial place was not readily accessible. In the elevated burial the body was extended at full length, hands to the sides, and placed on robes or blankets, which were then folded closely over it, and the bundle bound with ropes or thongs of rawhide passed many times about the whole. In a few cases war parties buried their dead comrades in a water hole. Buffalo bones or skulls, stones, or something of an identifying nature were sometimes used to mark the spot of burial.[27]

When an old person died, or one whose services were no longer useful, there was little mourning and that for only a short time. On the other hand, when a young man of established fame and prestige as a warrior and hunter was killed, the mourning was intense and prolonged. The name of the dead was not mentioned. To do so was a mark of disrespect, for it revived memories and made relatives and friends prolong their mourning. For a like reason, friends and relatives avoided passing in sight of the grave, and if the band ever came back to an old camping place where a relative had died, his kinsmen began mourning all over again, but "the second mourning was not so severe; the dead can't see them so well." Female relatives testified to their grief by wailing, moaning, and howling. They tore off or removed their customary apparel and wore rags or skin aprons only. They gashed themselves across the face, arms, legs, and breast with a knife, glass, or flint until they sometimes fainted from loss of blood, and then kept the wound raw and irritated for months. Often they cut off their hair, an ear, or a finger. The present explanations for such self-imposed torture is that the pain diverted their thoughts from their grief, but among the Shoshones and Comanches there was a time when women were killed on their husbands' graves, and self-torture may have been accepted as a satisfactory self-immolation. Black paint supplanted the customary red and yellow smeared upon their copper-colored faces.

Sometimes they built a fire and held a funeral dance by marching

---

[27] This description of Comanche burial is compiled from statements by a number of informants; also, Parker, *op. cit.,* 137; C. and J. D. Smith, *op. cit.,* 53, 132, 162, 170; H. C. Yarrow, "A Further Contribution to the Study of the Mortuary Customs of the North American Indians," B. A. E. *First Annual Report,* 99–100; Richardson, *The Comanche Barrier to South Plains Settlement,* 42; Lee, *op. cit.,* 152; Marcy, *Thirty Years of Army Life on the Border,* 56; Babb, *op. cit.,* 142, 144; Rodney Glisan, *Journal of Army Life,* 74; James Hobbs, *Wild Life in the Far West,* 33.

around it while singing a doleful song. Some would remain at the grave, mourning and refusing to eat, until relatives forceably took them away. The period of intense mourning was probably from three to fifteen days' duration. Afterwards they might continue to go out from camp at sunrise and at sunset to mourn and "feel lonely" (if in summer, until the leaves fell, or if the winter, until the leaves re-appeared). Although a year was considered to be the socially pre-scribed period of mourning for a close relative, in actual practice no set time was established. A well-to-do widow of three years who came to Marcy's camp in 1854 was still mourning her loss. It was reported that she went out every evening from camp to howl and cry and cut herself with knives. She had separated herself in a measure from the tribe and joined a group of seven other widows who were also still mourning their losses.[28]

Men sometimes cut off their hair ("they thought a lot of their hair") on one side of the head, usually the left, when a close rela-tive or friend died or was killed. Like the women, they occasionally cut their own flesh. They smoked and prayed, and for a few days offered the first morsel of food at each meal to the supernaturals for the benefit of the dead.

Ideally, the immediate family and even the brothers and sisters of the dead gave away or destroyed property, their own as well as that of the estate. Articles of intimate personal usage belonging to the deceased were buried with the corpse—ornaments, trinkets, gun, lance, bow and arrows, axe, knives, pipe and tobacco, cooking uten-sils, and tools for dressing skins. However, an object of especial value might be held out to be given to a comrade or a dear friend of the deceased with or without his request. Possessions with medicine power were either destroyed by throwing them into the river or by placing them in a tree where they would rot. Even the tipi in which the dead person—man, woman, or child (but not a baby)—lived was burned along with the less important articles. At the funeral of a prominent warrior or member of a well-to-do family, the dead person's horse was given to his best friend or it was slain near the grave. The saddle and bridle were placed in the grave with the corpse. Several horses might be killed, even an entire herd, amounting to as many as three

28 Parker, *op. cit.*, 192.

hundred or more of the deceased's best. A more economical practice, which was made to suffice in later days, was simply to shave off the manes and tails of the horses and mules which belonged to the deceased and deposit the hair at the grave. Those who did this were considered stingy, however.[29]

Outsiders who had no personal claim to a share in the estate could establish a claim by providing property of their own to be buried with the deceased.[30] Agent Neighbors observed that these helpers in grief wailed until they received sufficient gifts from the deceased's relatives to induce them to desist. "For instance," he continues, "if a man wants a favorite horse belonging to the brother of the deceased, he continues until he obtains it." Not only the deceased's estate, but the whole family property was drawn upon. If the death occurred in battle, then the demands of wailing and the value of gifts received were enlarged with the result that "from the liberality with which they dispose of their effects on all such occasions of the kind, it would induce the belief that they acquire property merely for the purpose of giving it to others."[31] For the parents, mourning continued until an enemy scalp was brought in.

When people so rendered themselves destitute, they were dependent on the tribe. They were fed and cared for until they were ready to drop their mourning. Then the men of the family went on a raid to obtain horses and start life anew. In the course of time someone was likely to provide a lodge or help make one, and the family settled back to normal life. The death of a prominent member of the band

[29] This description of Comanche mourning is compiled from statements by several informants; also Carter, *On the Border with MacKenzie*, 286; Lehmann, *op. cit.*, 152, 157; Haley, "Charles Goodnight's Indian Recollections," *loc. cit.*, 24; Yarrow, "A Further Contribution to the Study of Mortuary Customs of the North American Indians," *loc. cit.*, 99–100; Lee, *op. cit.*, 152; Marcy, *Thirty Years of Army Life on the Border*, 56; Babb, *op. cit.*, 108, 110, 136–38, 144; Wm. Bollaert, "Observations on the Indian Tribes in Texas," Ethnological Society of London *Journal*, Vol. II (1850), 271; Baylor, "Recollections of the Comanche Indians," *loc. cit.*, 374–75; Ole T. Nystel, "Three Months among the Indians," *Frontier Times*, Vol. V (October, 1927), 41; Adams to Commissioner of Indian Affairs, September 16, 1890 (Oklahoma Historical Society Library, correspondence file K–33, p. 440).

[30] Informant: Medicine Woman; also, Adams to Commissioner of Indian Affairs, September 12, 1890 (Oklahoma Historical Society Library, correspondence file K–33, p. 417); Hoebel, *The Political Organization and Law-Ways of the Comanche Indians*, 120–23.

[31] Neighbors, "The Naüni or Comanches of Texas," *loc. cit.*, 132.

generally caused the entire village to be moved. It is possible that this practice sometimes served to check the ravages of disease, but its ostensible reason was to get away from the place of death, even as the tipi was destroyed.

Death was not feared by the Comanches. It was ever present and they lived in violence and danger. But the dead caused them great anxiety. They were extravagant in the manifestation of concern. Thus, life, which was received quite casually and with mild pleasure, was closed with extreme emotional outbursts.

RELIGIOUS practice among
the Comanches consisted primarily of socially recognized
patterns for obtaining supernatural favor. There were patterns for
both individual and community ceremonials, but unlike religious
practices in our own society, group participation was extremely limited
in extent and importance. In almost every instance, it must be emphasized, the observance was a matter of individual concern. There was
no religious organization, no theocracy, no priestly class, no dogma.
Every man could be his own priest and his own prophet—the individual interpreter of the wills and ways of the spirits. A direct revelation without priestly go-between was the panacea for human ills and
aspirations, the one secure basis of earthly goods.

Every Comanche consumed with ambition set forth in quest of a
vision from which power (*puha*) was to be derived. His power, or
medicine as it is generally called, came in a mystic visitation, a dream
phenomenon or hallucinatory experience; the Comanches did not
confuse an ordinary dream with a revelation. Visions came only when
sought and under certain stringent conditions. Dreams were interesting experiences, and hardly more. Bad dreams did not portend bad
luck unless the dreamer revealed them within four days.

The vision was fundamental in the guardian spirit complex. Certainly it was to the Indian an unquestionable means of obtaining
power. Its authority was absolute. Psychic experiences were socially
recognized and regarded as the very cornerstone of cultural life. The

experience gave an individual a feeling of significance, a "thrill" of greater or less intensity. Among the tribes east of the Rockies, the emphasis was upon the vision induced by hunger, thirst, purgatives, or self-laceration; while west of the mountains a widespread attitude regarded the vision as unsought, involuntary, a thing of predisposition.[1] The Comanches recognized both forms. They retained a Shoshonean residue (the unsought dream) and had acquired the Plains method of reaching out for power. Power might come as an unsought blessing, but that was not sufficient; hence a Comanche strived for it by courting the aid of the supernaturals in the traditional way but without self-torture.

The vision was sought on continually recurring occasions: for mourning, for warpaths, for revenge, for curing disease, for success in hunting and raiding. Men who became especially noteworthy for their success in healing, procuring desired weather conditions, or ensuring a successful chase or war party, came to be singled out as medicine men, *puhaḳʌt*. The supreme test of power was whether a revelation worked. The Indian was a pragmatist. Not everyone who claimed supernatural gifts was signally successful. Either the medicine was not strong enough, or the protégé did not carry out commands accurately, or the vision-seeker had been maliciously deceived.

The selection of a man's medicine was the most important and sacred event in his life. Growing up with a firm belief in the all-sufficiency of personal visions, young men sought them without any prompting from their elders. From the stories of renowned contemporaries or mythical heroes they had learned that this was the way to make their mark. In later life there was usually some special reason, such as the desire for vengeance or worry over a sick child, that drove a man to seek supernatural aid. In any case the Comanche followed a well-established pattern.

The initial vision quest was made about the time of puberty, before the youth had gone on the warpath for the first time. The vision-seeker was usually prepared by a local medicine man for the desired experience. As a form or symbol of purification, the candidate was required to bathe, in a preliminary step to seeking relations with the supernatural.[2] It was necessary for the candidate to possess four things:

1 Ruth Benedict, *The Concept of the Guardian Spirit in North America*, 23–26.

156

a buffalo robe, a bone pipe, tobacco, and the material for producing a light. Clad only in breechclout and moccasins, he set out to find a place far enough removed that people would not disturb him, and still near enough to camp that it would not be too difficult to return when weak from hunger. He stopped four times on the way, each time smoking and praying. The spot selected was a solitary place at the top of a hill, or perhaps the site of a grave of a famous warrior or, more especially, of a medicine man who had had the kind of power the candidate desired. Medicine Bluff in the Wichita Mountains was one of the favorite locations.

The candidate preferred a position on the south slope where he could see both east and west. As darkness approached, he smoked and prayed for power, for good power, and that he might use it for good. He covered himself with the buffalo robe at night as he lay facing the east, and he had to keep his head covered the whole night through. Rising at daybreak, he faced the east to receive the benefit of the power radiating from the sun. He was required to fast during the vigil, but unlike some Plains people, inflicted no self-torture. The Comanche was confident of himself as a man: he was reverent toward the power-giving spirits, but he felt no need to debase himself before them, to lacerate and mutilate himself in sacrificial appeasement. He was quietly humble before the sources of spiritual power, but he saw no call to demean himself in lamentation and self-pity. He called not for mercy; for him there was no Siouxan self-objection as in the opening plaint of a Winnebago on the vision quest: "O, spirits, here humble in heart I stand beseeching you." For him, no Arapaho wails:

> *Father have pity on me,*
> *Father have pity on me,*
> *I am crying for thirst,*
> *I am crying for thirst,*
> *All is gone—I have nothing to eat,*
> *All is gone—I have nothing to eat.*

The Comanche on the vision quest might suffer the inner turmoil of anxiety and apprehension; yet he lay quietly waiting for

[2] Informants: Kills Something; Yellowfish; also, Ralph Linton, "The Comanche Sun Dance," *American Anthropologist*, Vol. XXXVII (1935), 424; Marcy, *Adventure on Red River*, 176.

what might come. He was not arrogant toward the helping powers—far from it—he was grateful for the help they could extend to him. He knew that he could not well do without that help, but was confident that it was forthcoming. The spirits were beneficent. They gave of their power, not in compassion but in altruism.

The regular pattern called for the candidate to remain at his solitary watch for four days and nights, but the quest might be prolonged. He remained until he received a vision, or else abandoned the quest to try again at a later time when conditions were more propitious. The vigil was completed with a vision or hallucination which made known to the candidate his personal and individual magic medium, the mysterious bond between him and that supernatural power which would henceforth act as the helping guardian of his destiny. A wind rustling through a pass or the timber, the bark of a dog, the howl of a wolf, the scream of an eagle might end the quest and send the candidate home to offer thanks to his newly found guardian spirit.

The newly acquired guardian spoke and understood the language of his ward and possessed special attributes or powers which it could transfer. On the fourth night of his search, Yellowfish heard a voice as distinctly, he vows, as if some person were standing near and speaking to him. "Tomorrow morning go take a bath in the creek below, and then go towards the east until you see a one-year-old buffalo coming across a ravine." He followed the instructions minutely and met the one-year-old buffalo crossing the ravine. Thereafter Yellowfish possessed the medicine of the one-year-old buffalo.[3]

During the revelation, the guardian spirit emphasized certain tabus and procedures which his ward must carefully follow; otherwise the medicine either would not work or would cause evil. Medicine is power, and power is not to be handled casually. Among tabus commonly noted was one in connection with medicine men's eating certain foods, or at least eating them only under certain conditions. Should anyone walk behind a medicine man while he was eating, he was certain to become ill or lose his power, unless he had "heap big medicine."[4] All medicines had to be protected from grease and the ill effects of menstruating women. Eagle medicine men could not per-

[3] Informant: Yellowfish.
[4] Informant: Medicine Woman.

mit anyone to pass behind them while they were eating because an eagle is upset by such an act. Post Oak Jim, in explaining this, said that he once had two captive eagles who took to eating back to back so as to prevent this possibility.

The newly gained power was generally referred to as "making medicine." The identification of certain powers was a life-and-death secret. Without the consent of this power, the possessor could not talk about it. The possession of power entailed serious responsibility, lest it cause harm rather than good. The owner must have faith, otherwise his power might not work. Practically every power carried with it one or more songs which the possessor had to learn and which were usually revealed during the visions. The possessor of strong medicine could, therefore, have quite a number of songs which he had to be able to sing at all times. It was not unusual in a Comanche camp to see a medicine man go out from his tipi after the evening meal, lie flat on his back, and to the music or time of a rattle sing his songs over and over again.

By association, medicines were usually similar in some respects to notable qualities possessed by the prototype of the bestowing guardian spirit. Therefore, the medicine bag which contained the material substance that served as a medium for consultation with the guardian spirit was likely to contain a great variety of objects identified with its source of the power. Among its contents might be a handful of sweet grass, certain herbs, a deer's tail, a bird's claw, small stones, the gristle of a bear snout, the dried maw of a buffalo, the skins of certain animals, particularly the buffalo, bear, or otter, plumes of certain birds, beaver oil, a smooth, round, hard ball sometimes found in the stomach of a buffalo, and so on without end. Each had a use; the sweet grass was protective; the herbs possessed healing power; the bird's claws inspired dash and courage; the stones brought health and long life since they do not wear out; the small ball from the buffalo's stomach, which this animal was believed to have swallowed, not only added great strength to its possessor but rendered him invincible in battle. These stones were reported to have been as much as three inches in diameter.[5]

[5] Battey, *op. cit.*, 332–33; Burnet, "American Aborigines, Indians of Texas," *loc. cit.*, Vol. I (May 22, 1824), 162.

Practically every Comanche in more or less varying degree possessed one or more of these amulets or charms which he carried or wore. Some were obtained from medicine men; others were discovered through visions. Men very commonly wore one or more such charms tied in the hair or about the neck. Especially did a man turn to his medicine if he had a new project of great importance in view, such as setting forth on the warpath or attempting a trading or hunting expedition into enemy territory. Charms were put on very young children by their mothers for the purpose of ensuring good health and protecting them from evil influences. Crow feathers had an especial protective power for babies; tied to the cradle-board, they kept away evil spirits. Their power was negative. In fact, we never heard of the crow's giving *puha* to a man. It was tabu to use crow feathers as flight feathers on arrows. "You absolutely cannot hit anything with such arrows," said That's It. Adding his contribution, Skinny and Wrinkled, who was interpreting, declared that he always uses the bow and arrow to hunt winter game. He is a Carlisle graduate and prone to test Comanche beliefs. "I have tried using crow-feather guides," he said. "It is no good. It does something to the shooter so he can't hit nothing."

A stuffed bat on the cradle also watched protectively over the baby. "He's little, but he's really a man."

In Comanche society practically all males and many old women came to possess medicine, but only those who possessed at least one outstanding thaumaturgic power were recognized as medicine men or women. The greater one's power, the greater the prestige he achieved. People possessing great power usually had several lesser powers as well, and they were sought after by would-be neophytes. According to Post Oak Jim, who is himself a notable medicine man, "A *puhakʌt* likes to keep his favorite medicine, which he does not use often. If a young man offers smoke and asks for medicine, he will withhold his favorite and give him another."

This asking for medicine was an interesting aspect of Comanche practice and attitudes. From the Comanche point of view a good citizen should help his fellow tribesmen. Medicine was primarily to bring success in war and the hunt, activities in which the triumphs of each redounded to the benefit of all. Medicine, like a helping hand, should be offered to a comrade. Good health was the other great boon sustained by power. Curing and health-giving medicines should also be shared. To the Comanche this meant not only that a medicine man ought to use his power to protect, cure, and serve his fellows, but that he should also teach them how to use it themselves, if they so desired. Thus it was that a medicine man who was asked for power could not very well refuse. If he smoked the pipe that was brought to him, he was contractually bound to deliver some of his medicine.

A famous old Comanche medicine-man warrior was Bear Claws Marks on His Shield (*masitɔtɔp*). From Post Oak Jim we have a detailed and formalized account of a transfer of his power.

« « « The mother of a boy may arrange for the boy's first medicine. A boy's mother went to the wife of Bear Claws to ask for the power. This woman told her what her husband would want—the sort of horse, blankets, bridle, her husband would prefer.

No matter what it was going to cost, they were going to have that medicine.

The mother then told the boy's father what was needed. The father loaded a horse with the proper gifts and tied the horse a short distance to the east of Bear Claws' lodge. He walked around the tipi from east to south to west to north in the usual ritual pattern and then entered the door. There he offered his pipe to the medicine man and spoke of his desire.

Bear Claws prepared to perform the ceremony. He had his wife raise a new tipi on the south side of the camp. He enlisted a young brave with good arrows and another with a good spear. They stood with Bear Claws at the rear of the tipi.

The boy was standing outside the door. He circled about the tipi around the south to the north, and passing through the door, he did the same thing inside. Dressed only in his breechclout, he assumed a stooping posture, facing northward, from his position just south of the door. Bear Claws sang a bear medicine song. Then he blew across the room four times. Now he was ready to tell his arrow assistant to make his shot. He had worked up his power and sent it over to the neophyte. Using his knee to bend the bow, the archer took three practice pulls; on the fourth he let the arrow fly at the medicine seeker. The steel pointed arrow struck the boy. The point was bent, and the arrow flew up toward the top of the tipi.

The spear man's turn was next. He ran up to the neophyte, took three practice jabs, and thrust with all his force on the fourth. The spear point was bent, but the candidate was not fazed.

During all this action, the boy was grunting like a bear. It was proven that the power of this medicine was very strong.

Next the boy gave his new shield to Bear Claws, who painted it like his own with bear claw marks—stripes of blue paint applied with fingers of the hand and running vertically. Bear Claws gave the boy his instructions: "When you are using this medicine, ride a horse with yellow skin and a black mane; look up to the clouds; you will see that when the rain falls, it does not hurt the body; bullets will be like that to you; in battle, ride across the firing line four times from left to right." » » »

Post Oak Jim did not acknowledge that he was the boy who received the power; however, we suspect he was on two counts: first, he had intimate knowledge of the reputed details of the event; and, second, he claimed invulnerability to bullets. Once in a saloon shooting, according to his story, he was hit in the mouth. The bullet knocked out a couple of teeth. "I just spit the lead out. Like that. It didn't really hurt me."

In this account no mention is made of a general principle laid down by a number of informants and substantiated by several other cases of power transfer. The medicine man did not give the power itself. He merely prepared and instructed the candidate so as to make him ready for the power. The neophyte, after instruction, had to go out in the regular way to get a vision bestowal of the actual power from the guardian spirit who controlled it.

A medicine man not infrequently preferred to share his power with a close friend or relative—brother or wife—without his seeking or wanting it. He could even be importunate about it. Breaks Something had such an experience with his own elder brother.

« « « He wanted me to have his medicine. Twice I refused

him, because I didn't want the tabus. He could not eat beef heart or leg muscle.

When I was a young man, still living with my mother and two sisters, my brother and his wife lived in another tipi. Early one morning my brother's wife called to me from outside my lodge. She said my brother wanted me in his tipi—for me to bathe in the creek and come over.

I heard my brother singing in his tipi. I bathed and went in. There I found him sitting at the west side of the lodge; he told me to sit on the north. He was painting his face. Then he started to paint my face in the same way according to the dream he had had in the night. I did not want his medicine, so I did not go through with it.

When I got married, I had a daughter. Then my brother forced his medicine on me. "You need it especially, now," he said. "If anyone gets sick in your family, you won't have to hire another medicine man. It will save you goods and trouble."

So my brother called me in again. He took a stick and bent it in a circle, making a little medicine wheel about this big [two inches]. He strung white beads and covered the wood of the wheel with them. Then he fastened two strings of beads across the middle, like spokes, with one string lying down at the bottom. He fastened this to my side medicine lock. He also gave me an eagle feather to wear.

My brother said the medicine would come to me in a vision. I would learn how to use it there. When I felt my power, I could swallow that ring.

I knew this medicine would be bad for me; it was borne out later.

When I was coming home from the hospital at Anadarko after I had cut my leg while cutting timber on Washita Creek, a Kiowa invited me in to eat. I was very weak. Another Kiowa was with me. That first Kiowa's wife got the meal while we rested.

When we sat down to eat, we had beef heart. I could not eat it. It was the same with my friend. Our host tried to call our attention away, so we would eat the meat. He joked with us.

I had a piece of bread, and I stuck it in the meat gravy twice. Right away I noticed it. Cold chills ran up and down my back. The woman came to take away the dishes; she said, "These men aren't hungry. They would not eat." The Kiowa ate no meat or gravy whatever.

When I got home, I felt all right for three nights. On the fourth night I got a pain in my stomach. A knot formed there, so I decided to go see my brother from whom I had received that medicine.

It was about sundown when I got there. I told him I was sick. His wife removed all dishes and cooking things.[6] Then he told me to sit at the west side of his tipi. We smoked. He got up and stood at the foot of his bed where I lay. He held eagle feathers over me and prayed; he was finding out what was wrong. When he was through, he sat down and told me I should not eat beef heart.

I said, "I haven't eaten any."

He knew better, and said the beef heart had formed a knot in there. He would cure it early the next morning. We went to sleep.

When I came out the next morning, I found they had a sweat lodge already built and a fire burning outside. We went in. My brother told me to squat on the west side, but I could not bend over; I could only lie down, facing the fire, with my head toward the sun.

Four times his wife brought in hot rocks over which he dropped water while singing. I nearly smothered in the steam. I wished I were somewhere else. My sister-in-law opened the door to let in a little air for a minute. Then three more times she brought in rocks on which my brother poured water. He sang. Finally, picking up the last red hot rock in his hand, he rubbed the knot in my stomach with it. That rock felt like ice to me.

"This rock has power," my brother said. "It will melt the knot and pain away."

When I staggered out of the sweat lodge, I could not see at first, but after I rode to the creek and lay in the water to cool, I found the knot was gone and I had no more pain.   »   »   »

This situation reveals a nice example of psychosomatic compliance with the dictates of a dogma: violation of a medicine tabu causes illness or death. Breaks Something got ill on the magic fourth day. His cure combined thermotherapy—a sound technique for muscular-vascular relaxation—plus partial removal of the guilt through the therapeutic services of the power giver. The cure was not permanently effective, however, for the stomach pains, beginning with a numbness

[6] This was a precaution against tabued contamination by grease or greasy things.

in the legs, came back a month later and have recurred at intervals ever since. Breaks Something now relieves himself by lying on his stomach over a grass hummock. He thinks he will never get over the effects of eating the beef-heart gravy. It would seem to be apparent that from his not wanting the power and his conviction that it would be bad for him, he saw to it that he suffered the ill effects he predicted for himself and masochistically "revenged" himself on his brother, who forced the power on him.

Such reluctance to assume power, or particular powers, was common among the Comanches. Powers were always accompanied by tabus; tabus were onerous restrictions on the freedom of action that the Comanche male cherished. The result was an ambivalent attitude toward the possession of medicine. Because of the onerous nature of the tabus, a man who had power could, if he wanted to be rid of it, go back to the place where he had his vision; there he thanked the guardian spirit for his blessing, saying that he no longer wished to use the medicine. Having thus returned the power to its source, he took his amulets and paraphernalia to a stream of running water for disposal. He was then free of the power and its tabus.

The sharing of power between medicine men led to the spontaneous formation of simple medicine societies of no more than twelve persons. Division of a power among a greater number so weakened its strength that it was believed to be useless. All the members of a medicine group possessed similar amulets and painted their shields alike. They made medicine in the same manner and observed the same tabus. Of course, this practice applied only to the medicine they shared in common. Individual members could also have their individual medicines.

The original procurer of the power was the society leader. Of course, he was a great medicine man. On his death, the surviving members chose a successor from among their members.

It was always proper to approach a practitioner through an intermediary when seeking a cure or a share of his power. For example, Bear Claws' wife was used. Wives were preferred for this role by many Comanche medicine men for the simple reason that their wives served in the manner of medical technicians and office assistants. (Note the role of Breaks Something's sister-in-law.) These women knew the "way" of the medicine. Other medicine men preferred to be approached through a particular friend, who was usually the formal friendship partner. This overcame the handicaps connected with a wife, who in her menstrual period was barred from associating with the medicine. Some busy medicine men, like Breaks Something, preferred also to set up a medicine tipi separate from the living quarters. Like the adolescent tipi of the boy, it was always free from greasy and menstrual contamination. "My office," Breaks Something, not without a touch of humor, likes to refer to his old medicine tipi.

The acquisition of medicine power by a Comanche woman was always through the indulgence and aid of her husband, although no Comanche woman could make medicine on her own until after menopause. "It is impossible for a single woman to get power," according to the observation of She Invites Her Relatives. Even a married woman who had her husband's power could use it only after his death. "A brave warrior, if sensible," she proclaimed, "will show his wife how to use his medicine, so that when he dies, she can use it in his place and keep his clientele." As an afterthought she added, "He will do this only if kind and sensible." Then, after his death, the wife could go to his grave to receive his power. His guardian spirit might come and give it to her. Extremely solicitous medicine men sometimes instructed their wives and took them out to the lonely place where their power had been received. The wife could then get the power directly from the source.

She Invites Her Relatives was instructed in the medicine of her husband, but she refused to seek the sanctioning vision. "My husband wanted me to have it, but I did not want it. It had too many tabus. It might have killed me."

The procuring of the services of a medicine man has something of the nature of a contract in it. It was expected that the doctor would receive four articles in return for his efforts. He, on his part, was expected to make a gift of a part of his receipts to the intermediary through whom he was approached. And because he was an important man on whom the obligations of generosity bore heavily, other people could "horn in" on the gifts he received. "They might even ask him for his gifts before he went to make the cure. It depended upon how much nerve they had. He could not refuse them."

166

Sometimes, if no cure was effected, the family of the patient withheld the promised gifts, but "an honorable medicine man would forget it." A mean medicine man could retaliate with sorcery, but in the opinion of Post Oak Jim this was quite unusual. It was felt by the Comanches that if a doctor tried his best and failed, it was still the honorable thing to give him his fee. In the case in which Been to See His Son (*patuawu'nikwai*) received a fine horse for doctoring a sick man, the patient subsequently died. Been to See His Son was riding this horse in a race one day when a disgruntled relative of the deceased patient demanded the return of the animal. Upon being refused, he pulled out a pistol and shot the horse dead. Been to See His Son did nothing.[7]

The cures effected by the Comanches included the use of pharmaceuticals, mechanical manipulation, thermotherapy, and psychosomatic therapy. Various medicine men used one or another or all of these techniques in accordance with the nature of the illness and the dictates of their guardian spirits.

The crude psychosomatic effect of tabu violation in the case of Breaks Something has already been described along with its cure by means of heat therapy and suggestive ritual. Two brief case histories of simple hysteria also illustrate the process.

« « « Wolf medicine makes a person invulnerable to bullets. You can't kill a wolf with a gun; only with a bow and arrow.

The father of a girl named She Blushes (*ɛkarɔ'ro*) was killed in battle. She went out alone to mourn by a tree. A wolf came along and attacked her. She tried to escape up the tree, but the wolf got her and pulled her down. She cried for help, and the wolf ran away, but not before it had bitten her.

The wolf bite made her insane. When people touched her, she howled like a wolf. They sent for Not Enough to Eat (*kewɜ'tsəmi*). He had wolf medicine.

He told some men to track down the wolf and bring it in to remove the medicine. They went out with guns and shot at it. Yet they could not kill it until one warrior shot it with an arrow. When they skinned the wolf, they found powder marks on the skin from

[7] Informant: Post Oak Jim.

167

the bullets that had hit but not hurt it. After they skinned it, they painted its nose red as directed by the medicine man. Then he told them to hang the skin in the tipi doorway with the head hanging toward the inside.

Right away the girl quieted down from howling. Not Enough to Eat then doctored her. She came to and asked for a drink.

He asked for a gray horse, a saddle, a blanket, and a bridle in pay. He also got the wolf skin, which his wife tanned for him. He painted the picture of a wolf on it and used it as a shield cover.[8] » » »

In yet another situation a woman showed hysterical symptoms for which the cause was unknown, according to *Kɔwino*.

« « « They took her to a peyote meeting to try to cure her. She ate peyote. During the night she was delirious—out of her head—so they went for another doctor. He wasn't able to help her, and she said she was not going to live until morning.

They sent me to get *Pihune*. When I got to his tipi, I found he was not at home. I went looking, and I found him with some other men, gambling. I told him my mission.

"Oh, must we hurry?" he asked.

"Yes," I told him. "Right away." So we rode back together at a lope. *Pihune* called for me to stop.

After a while, when he caught up to me, he said, "This thing is not really serious. That woman is not really sick. I knew you were coming for me. I know from a dream I had what is going on, and I knew the route we would have to take to get there. Now when we get there and that woman is talking out of her head, you tell her that I am no real medicine man. Tell her that I have no power. Tell her that she really isn't sick at all and that I am just a fake who is pretending to cure her."

When we arrived in the tipi where the woman lay, I gave *Pihune* a smoke. Then he asked for a drink of water before he started to doctor her. She watched him closely while he worked. She called him an untruthful man—no doctor.

"Yes, you are right," he confessed. "I have no power at all. How-

8 Informant: She Invites Her Relatives.

168

ever, you take a drink now, and you will come out of your delirium."

However, she refused the drink and started to fight him, so that I had to hold her back. She called him a liar again. He just told her to drink and she would get better. He was finally able to give her two drinks. Right away she began to quiet down.

When she was calm, he laughed at her, chuckling, "Now I have cheated you, and you have come to. I do have power."

She got well. There was nothing more to do, so that night *Pihune* left.[9]))))))

The tables could also be turned on a medicine man who carried his "monkeyshines" too far, however. Breaks Something told of a medicine man who, whenever he had the notion that someone was working against his medicine, would climb up the poles inside his wife's tipi and growl like a bear. It was his bear power protesting. This was all very well, except for one thing. He was so heavy that he broke several poles. These "fits" of his began to come so often that his wife ran out of poles. At last, she had to trade a good horse to an Arapaho or Cheyenne for some more poles.

He had a close friend who, when he heard about it, asked the wife of the medicine man what could be done to break these "climbing spells." She confided that her husband had told her to have someone shoot him when he was in a spell. So the friend went home to get a gun. He loaded it and put a spear in it (bear medicine gives immunity to bullets). He came in the tipi and asked the wife if she was sure that she was right. Yes, she was sure. "Go ahead and shoot," she replied. Just then the husband stopped his growling and called down from the top of the tipi that she was wrong. He promptly climbed down—and, says Breaks Something, "He had no such spells after that."

For simple ailments some medicine men used direct, practical techniques. As a preventative of croup, children were given necklaces to wear made of beads strung alternately with bisected segments of the ring cartilages from the windpipe of a turkey. When they were choking with actual croup, because an adult's finger is not long enough to reach down the throat to open the obstructive passage, a thong

9 Informant: Kowino.

wrapped with sinew and softened in water was pushed down the throat to clear it.[10]

Although buffalo medicine was worked to cure bloody wounds, especially gunshot wounds, mechanical tourniquets were used when necessary. Surgery was also relied upon. Slope tells of a battle casualty whose intestines protruded from a belly wound. A medicine man stopped the bleeding by putting his buffalo tail in his mouth and blowing on the wound. He then pressed the intestines back into place, and after burning the spines off a prickly pear cactus, split it. The open surfaces of the cactus were pressed against the flesh on both sides of the wound to compress it. It was then bound up and left to heal.

For patients with rheumatism or headaches some doctors dug a trench and heated it with a fire until the ground cracked. Raking out the fire, they laid a bed of sage, poured cold water on to steam it, and felt to see that it was not too hot. The patient lay down in the trench and was covered by a buffalo robe or blanket for a good baking.

For toothache they heated tree fungus and held it to the aching jaw. Cavities were treated by stuffing a dried mushroom of a certain variety in the hole. A laxative was made by boiling the cambium layer of the willow tree. Healing by means of herbs was practiced by men and women alike, whether professional doctors or not, just as was the case with whites in pioneer America. Almost every man and old woman had a bundle of medicines peculiarly his own, the secrets of which were known only to the owner. One such remedy used by a doctor was about as follows. With the liquid obtained from boiling certain herbs, he bathed the patient. With a paste derived from the liquid he also painted dog tracks on the patient and on a large dog.[11]

Some of the owners of medicines were supposed to have learned of the various medicinal plants by means of dreams or through some mythical hero who went out on the prairie with the individual and pointed out various plants for use in treating diseases. Fasting was a common treatment for most ailments. The Comanches are credited with "being expert in curing gun-shot wounds, and in the treatment

10 Informant: She Invites Her Relatives.
11 Informant: Medicine Woman.

170

of fractured limbs, which they bandage with neatness and good effect," but they did not attempt amputation. If blood flowed too freely, it was checked by packing the wound with grass. Likewise, it is claimed that they had one or more good remedies for rattlesnake bites. Several formulae were concocted from roots and herbs, but possibly the most effective treatment was to cut out the injured part and then suck the wound to draw out the poison. A poultice made of prickly pear leaves was applied to check inflammation and was a common remedy applied to wounds, as in the abdomen case just cited.[12] The prickly pear poultice is still a home remedy in our own society.

Petroleum was also considered to be an excellent healing salve. A Comanche chief once took Thomas C. Battey to a place on Medicine Creek, Oklahoma, where there was a "heap of medicine—good, black medicine." It was oil on top of water.[13] Near by, on top of Adams Hill, they found a heavy exudation of petroleum which they used as a salve on the sore backs of their horses.[14]

The "madstone" or medicine bone was used for wounds, infections, boils, and pains. It was a small piece of the leg bone of the giant prehistoric mammoth, believed by the Comanches to be bones of *piamꝫmpits*—the cannibal owl. Placed over the affected spot, it was supposed to draw out the poison.[15] In case of internal pain, some doctors treated by cutting the patient where the pain seemed to be and then attempting to suck out the pain or evil spirit. The sucking was done through a small horn prepared for the purpose, which was placed over the incision. The doctor would spit out whatever he sucked from the wound. The clever medicine man might show the patient some small stones, which he had placed in his mouth, and pretend that he had sucked them from the wound with the aid of his spiritual power, claiming that the stones had been the cause of the pain.

[12] Burnet, "The Comanches and Other Tribes of Texas and the Policy to Be Pursued Respecting Them," *loc. cit.*, 233; Neighbors, "The Naüni or Comanches of Texas," *loc. cit.*, 129; C. and J. D. Smith, *op. cit.*, 56; J. Lee Humfreville, *Twenty Years among Our Savage Indians*, 242.

[13] Battey, *op. cit.*, 189.

[14] Nye, *Carbine and Lance*, 99.

[15] Informants: Medicine Woman; Yellowfish. Medicine stones are still in use among the Comanches.

The vapor bath or sweat lodge was used extensively in medical treatment as in the cure of Breaks Something.

Beyond curing and lending their protective power to others, the Comanche medicine men served to make rain and as seers. The rain-making medicine of Big Bear called for the use of an outside tail feather of a black eagle. With his power it was necessary only to dip the feather into water and sprinkle towards the sun four times. "A cloud will soon appear and shortly it will rain." Big Bear overdid it once when living in a tipi northeast of Cache, Oklahoma. He made medicine for a rain with some wind in it. Came a cloud. It grew bigger. Then came rain and a big wind that blew his tipi down. "His wife got after him for not asking for a nice, soft rain."[16]

A seer might be called upon to learn the fate of overdue war parties. In one simple method the medicine man "dreamed" on it and gave the answer in the morning. The other method was a regular séance. Post Oak Jim's account of such a séance is as follows.

《 《 《 A war party was gone for a long time; they wanted to find out about it.

The medicine man had them clean up a nice place on the ground for a special tipi west of the camp. He selected about seven special men to go in with him. The camp was ordered to remain quiet. He had a fire built, and they went in just before midnight. They smoked and told the medicine man what they wanted to know.

He told them to put out the fire and close the smoke vent from outside.

Then he put on his blanket and went out into the night. He made a call. From way off an answer came back. He called again; the answering call was closer. He called a third time; it was closer yet. On his fourth call the answer was near by.

Then he re-entered the tipi and sat down.

"Everyone remain quiet," he told them. "The ghost is coming. That was his call."

The ghost, in the form of a bird, lit on top of the tipi. They could hear it was heavy.

From inside the tipi, the medicine man talked to it. "What we

16 Informant: Slope.

want to know is what has become of these people on the war party. You are wonderful. You know everything.

The answer came in a clear voice—

"They are all killed."

A sickly man with them asked if he would get well.

"You will die in the fall," came the answer.

Then they asked the bird who he was. It was the spirit of an evil medicine man who had died of tuberculosis.

After a while one of them went out to open the flaps of the tipi.

He came back in to light the fire.

They could hear the ghost calling as he went. That was all.))))))

This is the Algonquian spirit séance without the shaking of the tent at the visitation of the spirit. Inasmuch as the northern Shoshones did not have this rite, it is probable that it was borrowed from the neighboring Cheyennes.[17]

Ghosts did not generally bother the Comanches, but the Comanches definitely were uneasy about them. The tabu on the use of the names of dead people has already been mentioned several times. Hunters, raiders, and campers often saw and heard groups of people who were there one moment and gone the next. They were ghosts who haunted battlefields or scenes of annihilation.

Ghosts gave great power to the men who could stand up to them. Such ghosts appeared either as bare-bone skeletons or as bloody, scalped spectres waving long knives. Several stories are told of men who were chased all the way home from their vision vigils right into their own tipis by terrifying ghosts, who came with the rising moon.

Not all ran away, however. Slope knew one who got ghost power.

((((((A bunch of Comanches camped near a haunted spot. They asked a young man to go down to the spring for water. He just stalled around.

"Are you afraid?" They asked him.

He said he wasn't, so he took up a cow paunch and started for the water, thinking about ghosts. He heard something behind him; then he felt arms about his neck; he could see only bones—no flesh on

<hr>

[17] Cf. K. N. Llewellyn and E. A. Hoebel, *The Cheyenne Way: Conflict and Case Law in Primitive Jurisprudence*, 91.

them. He dropped the paunch and seized the arms fast, so he could carry the ghost on his back.

The people heard him coming. They heard the squeaking of the bones.

"Coward, what are you doing out there?" they called. "Bring us that water."

He just threw the skeleton in at them. They all fled and fell in a heap. The ghost disappeared.

That night it came back to the young man. It gave him medicine. "You will be hard to hit," it told him. "Bullets will never kill you. Keep a ball of white clay with you. When there is going to be a fight, paint yourself white all over."

"Never go into the battle first. Wait until your friends retreat. Then go right in."

The next day the party went on. They made a good raid on a herd of Mexican horses, but the Mexican pursuit caught up with them. The battle started. He went off to one side to prepare himself. Another young man came up to ask for the protection of his medicine. He gave him some and told him how to wait.

At the right time, they charged, and they turned the tide by killing several Mexicans. After that he became a famous warrior. » » »

Sorcery with ghost medicine is supposed to cause paralysis. In a case of epilepsy, recounted by Breaks Something, a medicine man with power over ghosts was called in. He looked at the patient and said, "This disease has nothing to do with ghosts; it is not in my line; must be something else." He could not help this sickness; it seemed to be something inside of the sick man.

Another source of great power for the Comanches, and Shoshones, too, lay in the "little men"—the *nɜnəpi*. They were believed to be no more than a foot high. They were armed with little shields, bows, and arrows, which killed every time they shot. They also threw little spears with points made of alligator spines. The Comanches say that the *nɜnəpi* made all the little stone arrowheads that they found all around. A few daring medicine men sought power from the little men, but most people did not want to possess it, for it was too dangerous: a man might kill someone when he did not want to kill.

Buffalo Hump
Courtesy National Archives

Horse Back (Kiyou)
Bureau of American Ethnology Photograph
Courtesy Denver Art Museum

The Shoshone notion that *nɜnɘpi* power gives Herculean strength (a little man can pack a deer on his back) seems to have been dropped by the Comanches. At least, it was not mentioned.

Comanche religious beliefs and practices, although they were socialized, remained almost wholly individualistic. Group rituals were few and far between until the introduction of the peyote cult.

Of group rituals practiced in the mid-nineteenth century by the Comanches, we know of only two—the Beaver Ceremony and the Eagle Dance. The Sun Dance was not tried until 1874, and that, apparently, no more than once.

The Beaver Ceremony is known as *pianahuwait*, "Big Doctoring." It was performed under the direction of a powerful beaver medicine man assisted by others with beaver power. Other people joined in the ceremony to share in its general effects of well-being, although the cure was held only at the request of a family who had a member suffering from tuberculosis or sorcery.

An extra-large tipi was raised and carefully prepared inside. Placed erect in the very center of the lodge was the trunk of a cottonwood tree, which reached to the top of the tipi. Slightly to the east of the pole, toward the door, was the fireplace. North and south of this were dug two elongated ponds, filled with water and edged with willows. They were beaver ponds. On the outside of each pond a little effigy mound of earth was made in the form of the beaver facing westward.

Just outside the tipi, to the south of the entrance, was dug a pit two feet deep by six or seven feet long, with the long axis running north and south. At the edge of the northwest corner of the pit (the corner nearest the door of the medicine lodge) was set a vertical pole, ten feet high, from which an eagle feather was hung.

When the ceremony began, the patient was laid at the extreme western edge of the tipi, with two women assistants to the doctor taking their places to the north of him. The doctor worked from the south side of the patient. A group of song leaders filed in to their places at the south side, and a band of drummers sat along the edge of the tipi in the southeast quadrant. Spectator participants filled all the remaining space to the east and north.

In the cure, the fire was lighted after the patient was brought in.

The medicine man, dressed according to the dictates of his medicine, approached the tipi from the east, swinging a bull roarer (*yuanɛ:*[18]) as he came and calling to the people, inviting them into the lodge.

After circling the tipi in the clockwise direction, he leaped into the pit from the east; on climbing out on the west side, he was ready to enter the lodge.

All persons who wished to be spectators (everybody was welcome —sickly or puny ones were most likely to participate) gathered around. They first had to remove all metal objects from their persons; then they circled the lodge and jumped in and out of the pit as the medicine leader had done. After entering the lodge, anyone going to sit on the north side had to circle the fire clockwise to get there.

Now the ceremony began. The medicine man ordered the music to start. The drummers gave four beats, finishing with a yell. The song leaders followed with four special beaver medicine songs, after which the medicine man dismissed the singers, who moved over among the drummers.

The time had arrived for the invocation of the pipe. The assistants (the women who had summoned the medicine man) filled the pipe. They lighted it with an ember offered from the fire by a spectator. Each took a puff before handing the pipe to the medicine man. He drew four puffs of smoke and prayed according to the dictates of his medicine. The pipe was now returned to the women, who cleaned it and laid it on the ground before them.

The medicine man next took up his feathers. First they were dipped in the north beaver pond; next in the south. Circling as always in the clockwise direction, he returned to the patient, whom he fanned with the dripping feathers. The two assistants once more filled and lighted the pipe, smoked it, and passed it to the medicine man. He smoked as before. When he had done, he again passed it back to the assistants for cleaning.

Now standing at the feet of the patient, the doctor worked over him with herbs. When he had finished this process, he flung off his buffalo robe and shinnied up the cottonwood tree to stick his head

18 *Yuane* means "warm wind," the soft whirring noise of the bull roarer. It consists of a flat cedar board "in the shape of a beaver tail" swung above the head by means of a thong attached to a handle. In battle it was whirled, or else carried close to the shield, for power to stop bullets.

176

out the top of the tipi (Does his spirit rest up there as in the séance?). Descending the pole, he ran around the fire and stepped into the bed of coals from the east, fluttering his arms as a burrowing owl flutters its wings. This spectacular feat completed, he stepped back out of the fire to the east, and walking to the south to complete the circle, he resumed his place at the west edge of the lodge.

His next step was to circle around to the south pond and take some bark from the willows. This he chewed like a beaver. He exhaled upward, blowing out perfume of the beaver.

The first night's curing was over. The medicine man ordered the drummers and singers to start the closing song—a song in which everybody joined. At its end, the fire was extinguished, and everybody milled about in the tipi for a while. On leaving, each participant jumped into the ditch and climbed out on the east side of it. The service was over at midnight.

Early the next morning, the medicine man was out announcing when the next session would begin. The same procedure was repeated, except that it ended at noon. That night it was all done over again, and again the next morning. The whole ceremony lasted two nights and two days, ending at noon of the third day.

Before the people left the tipi on the third day, they sang the closing song four times. Meanwhile, the tipi stakes were loosened, so that at the close of the last song, while still singing, they could lift up the tipi cover and run out in all directions.

Thus was the most powerful of all the curing ceremonies of the Comanches consummated. It must have been an impressive rite, and one which stood out in the stark simplicity of Comanche ritualism. Ralph Linton suggests that the Beaver Ceremony may have been derived from Pawnee sources. He also calls attention to its Earth contacts (the entering into the pit) as an implication of a use of Earth medicine as well as of beaver.[19] We would add that the inclusion of the burrowing owl reinforces the weight of this suggestion.

Two versions of the Beaver Cure were given: one by Post Oak Jim, a member of the Those Who Move Often band, and one by Kɔwino, a Yɛp Eater. Kɔwino's version described a much more at-

---

[19] Ralph Linton, "The Comanche," in A. Kardiner (ed.), *Psychological Frontiers of Society*, 67.

tenuated ritual than that of Post Oak Jim's, which has been presented here. *Kɔwino* said that he described the ceremony as it was performed in later years. That's It, a Water Horse, had heard about the Beaver Ceremony, but had never seen it because it was not performed in his band.

Of the dances used by the Comanches in search of power, the Eagle Dance was outstanding. It was sponsored by a prominent member of the band, usually the father or uncle of a youth turning warrior. The sponsor sought out a medicine man with strong eagle or war power and offered a smoke. If the medicine man accepted, he assumed complete charge of the ceremony. The decision was for him a serious one. If he accepted, his own power would be diminished somewhat, since it would be spread among the dancers. On the other hand a refusal might be interpreted as lack of confidence in his own power, as fear to risk spreading it out. In such a case, the medicine man would suffer loss of prestige among his own people. Furthermore, there was the factor of remuneration. Relatives and friends of participants contributed gifts. The medicine leader could keep what he preferred for himself, leaving the remainder for the dancers.

After the medicine man accepted the request, he announced the time and place of the ceremony. He and the dancers arose before daylight, went to the creek, bathed, stripped to the breechclout, put on war paint, let their hair down and put eagle feathers in it, and rubbed themselves with sage. After that they sat in a semicircle, with the opening toward the east, and smoked ceremoniously.

When the smoking was over, the leader arose and, followed closely by the dancers, sneaked silently to a near-by camp to "capture" a girl. Spectators remained some distance apart. In the old days the girl had to be a captive. The girl's family made a pretense of defending their camp against the attacking party, but the "victorious raiders" carried the "captured" girl to their own camp where preparations had been made for the remainder of the ceremony.

A tipi or brush lodge was used. The medicine leader provided two, four, or six drummers and singers to help—never an odd number. They sat close together facing the east. The girl sat beside the leader. The dancers first assumed a position directly in front, facing east, but when the music began, they formed a circle around the musicians.

Each dancer carried in his right hand a rattle, decorated with feathers, paint, and beads; and in his left hand he carried a wand or fan prepared from the wing feathers of an eagle. The dancers were young eagles attempting to leave their nest and parental care in order to soar away, masters of the sky. The dancers did not sing, but attempted from time to time to imitate the cry of the young eagle. When a dancer lagged or wearied, the leader either blew his eagle-bone whistle as a warning for him to speed up or reinvigorated him with new power by waving the eagle fan above him. When the music ceased, the dancers dropped on their knees and sat back against their legs to rest, but the moment the music resumed they sprang to their feet and began dancing again.

Between dances a warrior would rush into the circle and recite an outstanding coup or deed which he had performed. At the close of his recital a deafening applause of yells, drum beats, gourd rattles, and the stamping of feet went up. These speeches were like pep talks to encourage the young dancers to acts of bravery. During the dance, the warriors of the girl's people rushed up and made a sham attempt to recapture her. In actual practice they rushed in and recited some coups of their own. These recitals had to be true, because the power of eagle medicine was so strong that misfortune would befall any who on this solemn occasion falsified the facts. Spectators looked on in reverential silence.

About mid-morning, the mother of one of the dancers brought water for the participants and set it down near the circle. The leader drank and then offered the water to the dancers, each drinking in turn and passing it to the one on his left. After the "failure" of the girl's relatives to recapture her, they brought in presents, which they deposited before her in the circle. Relatives and friends of the dancers might also provide some of the gifts.

The medicine man retained a portion of the presents and gave the others to the dancers. One informant had received a horse when he danced. Not infrequently a dancer went through the ceremony without gaining power. "There had to be something inside stretching and pleading, reaching and grasping for power, if it were to be obtained."

The dance ended shortly before midday. No ceremonial departure is remembered, but the feather wands and rattles used by the dancers were given to the girl, and then the dancers rushed to the creek to bathe. They dived into the water upstream four times. They then dressed in their best attire and returned to camp to partake of a feast prepared by the women.[20]

The Medicine Dance reported by J. Lee Humfreville was probably a slight variation of the Eagle Dance. Unfortunately Humfreville gave few details, but in those there are only two significant points of difference: the ceremony he witnessed began in the afternoon and ended late in the night, and the dancers carried their medicine bags during the ceremony.[21]

All attempts to piece together a definite picture of the Buffalo Hunting Dance have been almost futile thus far. One informant was of the opinion that it was the most important communal ceremony. Others were aware of its existence, but remembered none of its ritual or symbolism. Apparently it varied much in form and detail from tribe to tribe. It was rarely held, and only when the camp was in desperate need of buffalo for food or other necessities. It was a band or village affair, under the supervision of a shaman who possessed buffalo medicine. The dance was a prayer to the guardian spirit to direct the buffalo in plentiful numbers to their hunting grounds. Furthermore, the participants danced for power to be successful in the chase. Those going on the hunt could participate. Usually the dance was held in the main camp on the evening before the departure of the hunting party, but if buffalo were scarce, the hunting party sometimes danced after leaving camp. The dancers wore masks made of the whole skin of the buffalo head with the horns left attached.

Smoking was also associated with power, as has already been demonstrated in the accounts of curing; it was therefore a sacred and ceremonious act. It is true that the Comanches smoked for pleasure, but never casually; and when smoking ceremoniously, it was an oath, a signature to an agreement, a pledge on the part of the smoker, or a prayer for power. In smoking for pleasure, they customarily used

20 Informant: Yellowfish. Yellowfish danced the Eagle Dance when he was a young man. On another occasion the ceremony was observed by the Reverend John Melville while visiting the Comanche chief, Talaquitnamse, in the Wichita Mountains. Melville's unsatisfactory account of the ceremony is related in Barnes, *op. cit.*, 55–57.

21 Humfreville, *Twenty Years among Our Savage Indians*, 438.

cigarettes, which were rolled in various materials. One of the favorites is the soft, inner leaves of the corn shuck or the leaves of the blackjack oak. They rarely smoked cigars, and according to most accounts, tobacco chewing was not adopted until reservation days. Although smoking was done in various ways, ceremonial smoking was customarily done with pipes. There were common pipes for general use, council pipes for state occasions, a specially dedicated peace pipe, a special pipe used by the old men in the Smoke Lodge, and a most sacred medicine pipe for solemn religious ritual. Etiquette forbade the use of special pipes for any purpose other than that for which they were intended. To touch the consecrated medicine pipe to profane lips would have amounted to sacrilege so profound as to bring on a general catastrophe. However, in the absence of a special pipe, another was substituted, or cigarettes might serve the purpose. Each ceremony required its own special ritual in handling the pipe.

When a group engaged in ceremonial smoking, they ordinarily seated themselves in a circle or a semicircle. The opening was toward the east. If within a lodge, they sat around it in a semicircle facing the door, which was usually on the east. On most occasions, the women withdrew when the pipe was introduced. The fire tender, when present, sat just to the right as one entered the opening of the circle or door. Opposite the opening was the medicine man or leader of the ceremony. When the time for offering the invocation to the supernatural powers arrived, the leader ordered the fire built up. He then filled the pipe. The next step was the invocation. Holding the pipe with stem pointed to the sky, he made offering to the sky, then to the ground, then to the four points of the compass in order. This done, a pinch of tobacco was taken from the bowl and laid upon or buried in the ground as an offering to Mother Earth. Then the pipe was lighted, and the leader blew the first puff of smoke toward the sky, then to Mother Earth, to the four directions, and afterwards to his guardian spirit or whatever supernatural power he desired to propitiate. While the lighting of the pipe was in process, there was a tabu on spoken words. Absolute silence prevailed. If at any stage of the ceremony the silence was broken, it was necessary to dump all the tobacco from the pipe on the ground and begin anew. On some occasions the silence prevailed until the pipe had completed the round;

on others, the smoker addressed one or more of the supernatural spirits in prayer; and at other times it appears that with the issuance of smoke the ceremony was finished and the group could enter into conversation. The smoker sought power: power to heal, to triumph over enemies, to become a better hunter, to gain more horses, or to live a long and useful life.

When the leader had completed his invocation, he passed the pipe to the person on his left, who repeated the same smoking ritual, and then on to the next until everyone had smoked. When the man sitting next to the door had smoked, he could not pass the pipe across the doorway; it must be handed back entirely around the circle (no one smoking) to the man on the opposite side of the door. The pipe was handled only according to prescribed ritual.

To refuse to smoke under certain situations was disrespectful and might be regarded as an insult or an offense. Likewise, it was disrespectful for an unqualified man to smoke ceremoniously. In some cases, no one might leave or enter the lodge during the smoking ceremony. No one was permitted to stand up or walk about the lodge. Sometimes smokers anointed themselves with the smoke. Medicine men anointed patients with it by passing their hands through sacred smoke and then rubbing the patient. It was strong medicine. The smokers gave special attention to pipe ashes, which were usually deposited according to prescribed ritual.[22]

The Sun Dance, which loomed so large in the lives of the tribes of longer standing in the plains, was not an established part of Comanche socio-religious activities. When it was introduced in the eighteen seventies, it was seized upon as a mechanism of Messianic revivalism—a story that will be presented in a later chapter. The peyote cult was also worked up in later days as an integrative device to replace the collapsing system of native supernaturalism. And that, too, will be treated later on, as a part of the problem of readjustment to new conditions imposed by the white conquest.

The Green Corn Dance was a late cultural innovation borrowed from the Caddos and Wichitas. It was a thanksgiving ceremonial for

[22] This account of the smoking ritual is compiled from statements by informants Medicine Woman and Kills Something; also, Neighbors, "The Naüni or Comanches of Texas," *loc. cit.*, 126–27; Battey, *op. cit.*, 323–24; Parker, *op. cit.*, 59; C. and J. D. Smith, *op. cit.*, 108; Lee, *op. cit.*, 146; Smithwick, *op. cit.*, 180.

first foods. All informants hasten to emphasize that it is not an original Comanche rite and that it has seldom been used by them. According to observers, the Comanches did not follow the customary procedure and ritual of their neighbors, but adapted the ceremony to their own fancy and practical situation. The ceremony was sponsored by the village headman, who secured the services of a prominent medicine man for the occasion. Instructions were issued, and at the appointed time all the people of the camp gathered at the accustomed meeting place. During the afternoon, the medicine man mixed his herbs and roots and boiled them until he had a thick broth. When the mixture was ready, he scattered his coals and addressed the people who had seated themselves around him in the customary fashion—the principal men immediately around him, the young warriors just back of them, and the women and children on the outside of the circle. He told them of the benevolence of the Great Spirit who had given them food in season and exhorted his listeners to be thankful for it.

After he had finished speaking, the people joined hands in two circles, one inside the other, and danced and sang to the accompaniment of drum and rattle. After about thirty minutes the headman had them line up and file past the medicine man, who gave each in turn a spoonful of his medicine. Stubborn children were compelled to swallow by holding their chins up until the medicine went down. The medicine was a strong purgative used for cleansing the system before eating the first green corn of the season.

That night or the next evening a number of fires were kindled near the circle, and the women roasted a quantity of green corn, which they piled on buffalo hides. After the roasting was finished, all the people sang and danced. When the dancers wearied, they sat in a circle, and the medicine man again addressed them. At the close of the address, he stood over the piles of corn and with his hands and eyes lifted toward the sky prayed for the Great Spirit to continue to give his people strong power. The people then ate the corn and returned to their lodges.[23]

So it was that the Comanches sought and manipulated power. If religion is the complex of man's interrelations with the supernatural

[23] Lee, *op. cit.*, 155–57; Barnes, *op. cit.*, 66–68, gives a disappointing account of a ceremony witnessed by the Reverend John Melville.

powers in which man believes, the direct, personal search for power and the control of power is the essence of Comanche religion. What of his conception of the universe? Did he believe only in spirits? Had he no conception of higher deities? In a vague and poorly defined way, Yes. This concept we shall attempt to formulate in the next chapter.

VIII

Cosmogony
and Folk Beliefs

NO subject is more difficult to
treat than one which deals
with the beliefs of a people
concerning abstract matters. It is not easy to learn from intimate
associates their inmost religious ideas; it is obviously much more
difficult to determine the beliefs of an alien race speaking an unfamiliar tongue and having a wholly different inheritance, training,
and point of view.

The Comanches have often been designated as the skeptics or un-
believers of the plains. This conclusion has been based largely upon
the fact that they had comparatively few well-established visible and
externalized customs of religious meaning such as were found among
other Plains Indians. Since their religion was largely individualistic,
there was, as there is among our own people, great diversity of faith
and feeling. They had no dogma and no professional priestly class
to formulate a systematic religion.

It was not in the nature of the Comanche to be introspective. Nor
was it in his nature reflectively to state his motives or ways of acting
in formulae. The Comanche was oriented to see things as isolated
episodes, not as a patterned unfolding of a great scheme.

We have already seen that the Comanche took the spirit beings
with whom he had formal contact pretty much for granted. He
hardly bothered at all to concern himself with the nature of the universe beyond them. It is to be expected, consequently, that the vague

185

and scanty information that is available will reveal divergent and conflicting opinions concerning the supernatural.

Comanche religion was exceedingly simple, highly vital, and based on no more than casual attempts to explain satisfactorily the mysterious operations of nature by which he was confronted every day.

After burial, according to the somewhat fanciful account of an adopted Comanche, the spirit of the departed warrior mounted the spirit of his slain pony, his ghostly quiver of bow and arrows at his back, the spectre of his lance in his hand, the shadow of his shield on his arm—to gallop skyward, followed by his phantom herd loaded with ghostly possessions heaped by his relatives and friends in and about his grave. Straight into the sun and the pastures of the Happy Hunting Ground he sped, there to remain an extended time. But eventually, after an excursion in celestial pastures, the spirit of the departed must be reborn of the Earth Mother and return to keep up the population and power of the tribe.[1]

There is no doubt that the Comanches had an unwavering faith in a future existence. As to the nature of their after world, their accounts are fairly uniform. Their after world was generally conceded to be beyond the sun where it sets in the west. It was modeled after the imperfect reality of their everyday existence with all the disagreeable features absent, for all things there were perfect. It was a "valley ten thousand fold longer and wider" than their own valley (this specific reference was probably to the Arkansas), covered with groves, streams, and meadows. There was no rain or wind; the climate was always mild and the water cool. There the great chiefs of all the Comanches held their assemblies, and they and all the warriors were young. They followed the chase, but the war whoop never penetrated those sacred realms. There was no darkness there, for the Great Spirit was everywhere. In this heavenly valley there would always be plenty without the necessity of expending much energy or effort to obtain it. The "shade" of the Comanche could there experience to the fullest measure all the pleasures the material body had experienced or hoped for while on earth. There were buffalo, deer, elk, and antelope in abundance; pounded corn was forever at hand; and horses were fleeter than the wind. Beautiful birds warbled

[1] Hobbs, *op. cit.*, 33–34.

from the treetops for his entertainment. And to add further to a condition conducive to a supremely happy after life, there was no suffering or sorrow there.

The Comanches knew that all this was so from what they thought was genuine observation. Death and resurrection were not uncommon. The mothers of Post Oak Jim and Slope both died, visited the land of the dead, and returned to life, because it was not yet their time to depart.

((((((My mother died from a fever. An iron grey horse was waiting for her. She got on and rode away.

After awhile, she came upon a travois trail. Many Indians had passed that way. The horse noticed something by the smell and trotted off down the trail neighing.

She came to the top of a high hill. There she looked to the west; the sun was low. Below her she saw a big camp in a grove of tall cottonwoods by a clear creek. The land looked so beautiful. Lots of Indians rode around on horseback. There were women playing old-time games [shinny].

Two men on horseback left the group and began to race toward her. As they approached, she heard them whooping and guns shooting. As they came, she was thirsty and got down to drink from a near-by spring. Scooping up the water, she splashed some on her face. It felt cool.

Then she came to. Her husband was blowing on her face, making a medicine. They gave her water and food; she felt better, got well, and lived a long time.))))))

That was Post Oak Jim's story. Slope's story, told quite independently, reveals the same simple belief. This was the experience of his grandmother, *Ya:ai,* who finally died in 1890, after a long life.

((((((When my grandmother was young, she got very sick. A medicine man worked on her, but he could accomplish nothing. Her time had come. So she died. People began mourning. They buried her possessions.

She started walking toward the other world. At last she came towards a creek bordered with tall cottonwood trees in which was a big camp. Just before she got to the camp, she looked ahead and saw a large herd of horses. As she came closer to the horses, she saw a man approaching her on horseback. As he came nearer, she saw he was a relative long since dead.

Then she noticed a certain grey horse which had died and which had belonged to her family. The relative roped it for her and told her to mount and hurry to get on, as they had to get along.

She tried to mount the horse, but it balked. The man kept urging her to hurry, but the horse kept balking and balking. She couldn't get there.

Finally, she came to while still trying to get on the horse.

She opened her eyes. She saw people weeping for her. She told them she had come back. She was alive again. She lived a long life after that. » » »

Although Comanche ideas were fairly harmonious concerning the nature of the after world, there was some uncertainty about who might be eligible to enjoy its pleasures. Some early observers thought the Comanches had no idea of accountability; that they believed they would all go to Heaven (except in special cases, as when one happened to be so unfortunate as to lose his scalp after death). Such was the concept generally held by their neighbors on the plains. Among the Cheyennes the "Brave and cowardly, good and bad alike go there. All who have died are equal. After death there is neither reward for virtue nor punishment for sin."[2] On the other hand, nineteenth-century observers flatly reported that the Comanches did believe in future rewards and punishments.[3]

The Comanche's religion taught him that it was his duty to be courageous, to be brave in battle and faithful to his comrades in arms, to be generous to his friends, and to walk upright among his tribesmen. For that he would reap the reward of existence after death. The warrior who died in the fray and the woman who died in childbirth

2 Grinnell, The Cheyenne Indians, II, 91.

3 Interesting comments on Comanche religion are found in these volumes: Marcy, Thirty Years of Army Life on the Border, 57; Carter, On the Border with MacKenzie, 258, 260; Battey, op. cit., 331; Lee, op. cit., 153; Bollaert, "Observations on the Indian Tribes in Texas," loc. cit., 267; Rister, Border Captives, 26; Glisan, op. cit., 74; Burnet, "American Aborigines, Indians of Texas," loc. cit., Vol. I (May 15, 1824), 154; R. I. Dodge, Our Wild Indians, 102–103, 178, 180–81.

were expected to receive special consideration on arriving in the eternal home beyond the sun. Mortal wounds or mortal illness vanished at death, leaving the victim free of their effects in the after world. But the spirit of the bad, the lazy, the coward, or the thief would be driven before the Great Spirit into a region that was barren, cold, and desolate, with rugged and sterile mountains infested with noxious animals and insects. There game was scarce, meager, and unsavory, and the soul had to wander through thorns and among rocks, thirsty, hungry, and in pain.

Our own Comanche informants revealed no such notions at all. Nor do the Shoshones have any such conception of post-mortem immanent justice. We suspect these assertions should be taken with a grain of salt, if not rejected.

Believed limitations of immortality included loss of scalp, strangulation, death in the dark, and mutilation. If the scalp were taken after death, the Comanches looked on life as annihilated. A scalp removed before death, whether by accident or design, affected immortality not in the least. To preserve the scalp on the head of a dead comrade was of more consequence than the preservation of one's own life; while by the same token, scalping a foe was of much greater merit than simply sending his spirit out of this world into the next, whence it would eventually return to plague the Comanches anew. "Dot" Babb says the Comanches did not scalp a Negro since they believed he had no soul, but they might kill him to prevent his killing Comanches. But the dance leader's scepter, given to Ralph Linton in 1933, had several scalp symbols on it—tokens of scalps taken by its original owner—and a couple of them (colored differently) were pointed out to represent Negro scalps.

Fear of strangulation arose from the belief that life (spirit or "soul thing") issued from the mouth at the moment of death. Thus if death occurred through choking, the passageway was closed and the spirit, unable to free itself, remained in the mortal body and was forever imprisoned in the ground at burial. Next to fear of strangulation came the fear of death in the dark, for the spirit that left the body in the dark might be unable to find its way to the after world and thus wander forever in darkness. Although the majority believed that mortal wounds or mortal illness vanished at death, there were some who believed that such indignities as the body suffered after death, other than the removal of the scalp, permanently affected the spirit or shade. Thus, if the feet were cut from the body after death, the unhappy spirit was forced to dispense with them henceforth.

The Comanche who failed to approach the camp of the after world well mounted might also be refused admission into those celestial pastures. A current legendary story taught the importance of providing the deceased with a good mount. Once an old Comanche died who had no relatives or worldly goods. The villagers, concluding that almost any old nag would serve to transport him to the next world, killed at his grave an old, ill-conditioned, lop-eared horse. A few weeks after the burial of this friendless one, he returned, weary and hungry, riding the same old worn-out horse. He first appeared at a neighboring camp of Wichitas, where he was well known, and asked for something to eat; but his sunken eyes and his strange appearance frightened all who saw him, and they fled from his presence. Finally, one bolder than the rest placed a piece of meat at the end of a lodge pole and extended it to him. Shortly afterwards, he appeared at his own camp, creating even more dismay than in the Wichita village, so that the entire camp moved to Rush Creek, not far distant from the present site of Fort Sill, Oklahoma.

Some of the Comanches, however, were bold enough to question the unwelcome, ghostly visitor about his reappearance among the inhabitants of the earth. When he had come to the "gates of paradise," he told them, the people would on no account permit him to enter upon such an ill-conditioned beast as he rode, and thus in sadness he had returned to haunt the homes of the greedy, stingy people who had not properly provided for him. Since then, no Comanche has been allowed to set out for the after world without a steed which would do honor to the rider and his friends.[4]

The nature of the cosmos was only vaguely conceived, and contemporary Comanches have no notions what the people thought about it in the old days, if they had any thoughts at all. The Comanches, so far as we can tell, had no star lore, and only the sun, moon, and earth were looked upon as semi-deities.

4 Yarrow, "A Further Contribution to the Study of Mortuary Customs of the North American Indians," *loc. cit.*, 100.

Nineteenth-century observers of the Comanches (Dodge, Neighbors, Babb, Burnett, and others) attributed a strong belief in a Supreme Deity to the Comanches, whom they generally addressed as the Great Spirit, but at times as "Our Sure Enough Father."[5] The Great Spirit was a vague, omniscient, all-powerful being, who was credited with creating and governing the earth, sun, moon, and stars. He was the chief god, the creator, the first of all addressed in prayer, and to him the first smoke was offered. The person who prayed looked upward and perhaps held his hands toward the sky. While some maintained that the Comanches believed that the Great Spirit dispensed good and evil, life and death, at his will, others insisted that they believed also in an Evil Spirit who was the antithesis of the Great Spirit. The supposition was that there was eternal conflict between the Great Spirit leading the forces of good and the Evil Spirit controlling the forces of evil. It was argued that the unhappy thought of a father who, though all powerful, permitted ills and sorrows to afflict his children, was forever irreconcilable with Indian philosophy. So strongly did the Comanches feel about the subject of the bad god, says Colonel Dodge, that it was practically tabu as a subject of conversation—a reticence shared by other Plains Indians, but which gave rise to the supposition that the Comanches did not believe in the negative element. The Evil Spirit was not equally powerful with the Great Spirit, however, for he shared with the Great Spirit in control of the earth only. Believing as he did in the immortality of the soul, the Comanche could not conceive of god rivalry in a perfect world. Hence for those who adhered to the philosophy of a dual power, much of the individual outward religious forms revolved around invoking the aid of the Great Spirit and appeasing the wrath and enmity of the Evil Spirit.

Through the medium of a host of inferior evil spirits, the Evil Spirit, it was claimed, brought about every mortification or disaster—droughts, disease, hunger, distress, and discomfort—and was the author of unhappiness, sorrow, and defeat. He made such animals as the panther and venomous serpents, reptiles, and insects for the injury of man.

Although there may be some question as to the source of all the

[5] Babb, *op. cit.,* 44.

bad and evil visited upon man, there was none as to the source of all that was good and beneficial in life. Through the medium of a host of inferior spirits, the Great Spirit brought about all that was good or beneficial to the Comanches, such as health, peace, plenty, and happiness. He aided a worthy warrior in all his undertakings, delivered his enemies into his hands, protected him from danger, privation, and pain, and provided all good and pleasurable things. All good and useful animals were made by him for their use. All their success in hunting was the result of his benevolence. They thought that if they lied to the Great Spirit, or displeased him, he would withdraw his guardianship, allowing them to die or suffer other punishment.

The origin of the Comanches was credited to the Great Spirit, according to the early reporters. In one version, another race inhabited the country before them, but a great flood of waters covered the whole earth, and the inhabitants, whom they supposed were white, saved themselves from being destroyed by turning into white birds and flying away. After this the Great Spirit sent down to earth a secondary spirit to create the Comanches. When first made, the Comanches were imperfect. The spirit returned to the Supreme Being and told what he had done. Thereupon, the Great Spirit directed him to return to the earth and complete his work by giving intelligence to the beings he had created and to instruct them how to live. The secondary spirit carried out the instructions. He taught the Comanches how to make the stone arrow points and knives of stone and bone for cutting. He taught them how to put the arrow points on shafts, showed them how to make a bow, and how to use the arrows for shooting. He told them that the buffalo, deer, and the elk—all the animals that are on the earth—were for their use. He taught them to make fire by rubbing two sticks or by knocking together two hard stones until the fire started.[6]

Another account of the creation of the Comanches as told by a long-time adopted Comanche warrior, although differing somewhat in details, likewise credits the work to the Great Spirit. According to this story, the Great Spirit collected the dust from the four corners of the earth to make man, so that when man died the earth would not refuse him a burying place by saying, "Thou hast not been taken from me, hence I cannot receive you in my bosom." When the Great

Spirit created man, the earth shook and trembled and said unto the Great Spirit, "How can I feed the vast multitudes of man that will issue from the first created?" And the Great Spirit replied, "We will divide the maintenance of man; you will feed man during the daytime with all that you produce, while when the night will come, I will send my sleep upon man, and he will rest, and he will be fed by me with the peace of slumber, and he will awake refreshed in the morning."

The Great Spirit took eight parts to form man: the body from the earth, the bones from the stones, the blood from the dew, the eyes from the depth of the clear water, the beauty from his own image, the light of the eyes from the sun, the thoughts from the waterfalls, the breath from the wind, and the strength from the storms. The first man was of such gigantic size that his head reached the skies and his eyes looked from one end of the earth to the other, but menial labor and unwholesome food diminished his size and made him vulnerable.

After the Great Spirit had created man, he ordered all of the inhabitants of the spirit world to go and prostrate themselves before man as recognition that man was the greatest of the Great Spirit's creations. All obeyed the command except one, who as a result of his failure to do so was cast out from the spirit world and made to roam around on earth. To seek revenge, this demon took refuge in the tooth of the serpent, the fang of the spider, the legs of the centipede, and in other poisonous animals, insects, and reptiles to torment and harm man on earth at every opportunity.[7]

Inasmuch as the Shoshones and other tribes of the Great Basin had some conception of an otiose Supreme Being, who in the minds of some was equated with Wolf, the big brother of Coyote, it is not unreasonable to accept the basic validity of these early nineteenth-century descriptions of Comanche beliefs in a Great Spirit. Wolf was wholly beneficent; his acts of original creation made all things perfect and good. Coyote, the mischievous Til Eulenspiegel of Shoshonean folklore, was the spoiler of all things, however. His was the role

[6] Neighbors, "The Naüni or Comanches of Texas," *loc. cit.,* 127.

[7] Narrated by Herman Lehmann, Comanche captive, who became a respected warrior and member of the tribe. Jonathan H. Jones, *A Condensed History of the Apache and Comanche Indian Tribes,* 199–200.

of the transformer who undid the good works of his big brother. He brought hardship, travail, and effort into the lives of men. He represented the force of Evil as we conceive it—and yet the Shoshones in no way thought of him in his relationship to Wolf as a conflict of good and evil. Coyote was not bad; he was no more than wantonly mischievous.

When we consider the writings of the early whites among the Comanches on the Great Spirit and the Evil One, we are plagued by serious doubts. We cannot but feel that they, who lived in a time of great religious conviction in this land, projected something of their own ideas of what the Comanches ought to have believed into their descriptive accounts.

At any rate, the old Comanches living in 1933 who served as informants for the Santa Fé Laboratory group revealed only the slightest vestiges of such ideas. The Great Spirit was only occasionally mentioned by them; none showed any concern with the problem of evil. Coyote, in the folk tales recounted by these later-day Comanches, had moved almost entirely from the realm of myth and legend to assume a position of no more than a power-giving animal—except that the old Shoshonean tabu against killing coyotes retained a good deal of its force. The transformer tales, except for the Comanche story of the release of the buffalo, were lost, one and all. What remained of the old Coyote folk tale and myth cycle was only that part which told of Coyote as a harmless bungler and trickster. And the hero in all these tales, as told by Slope, Post Oak Jim, and That's It, was no longer Coyote but Fox, Coon, and Bob Cat. As for the Creation, the typical attitude was expressed by Post Oak Jim: "We never gave much consideration to Creation. We just knew we were here. Our thoughts were mostly directed toward understanding the spirits."

The Comanches were not quite certain of the relationship existing between the Great Spirit and the Sun. Sometimes the two were closely associated, while at other times a distinction was made between them. Robert S. Neighbors makes a clear distinction, saying that they offered the first puff of smoke to the Supreme Being, the second to the Sun, the third to the Earth, and so on to the lesser objects of

[8] Neighbors, "The Naüni or Comanches of Texas," *loc. cit.*, 127.
[9] Bollaert, "Observations on the Indian Tribes in Texas," *loc. cit.*, 268.

veneration in whatever order they might choose.[8] Bollaert states that the Great Spirit was supposed to live in the Sun,[9] but other accounts have it that he lived beyond the Sun. Some Comanches explained that he was so far distant in the sky that they could not hear him speak, and that when they wished to communicate with him, they were obliged to do it through the medium of the Sun, which was nearer and which they could see and converse with. Josiah Gregg thought that the Sun was their principal deity. His conclusion was based partly upon the fact that the Comanches, when preparing for a campaign, ceremoniously placed their arms in the early morning on the east side of their lodges that they "may receive the blessing of the fountain of light at his first appearance."[10]

Apparently the Sun represented the visible medium through which the Great Spirit revealed himself. No doubt the Comanches found it extremely difficult to separate the two, and in their worship of the Sun were paying humble reverence to the Great Spirit at the same time. Their veneration of the Sun cannot be doubted. To this fact practically all those who have commented on Comanche religion have left testimony. It was certainly the most dominant single feature of Comanche belief. The Sun was worshiped as the primary cause of all living things. Contrary to Agent Neighbors' statement, most informants insist that the first puff of smoke was blown toward the Sun. "Smoking to the powers, he first addressed the Sun . . . ," explained That's It, in describing the conditional curse. His religion taught him that the Sun was his father, and he addressed it as such in prayer. "He went above them to the Sun. 'Father,' he swore, 'early in the spring let the first lightning and thunder take my life if this thing be true!' The brothers sat back. They were satisfied. 'If you say such a thing, we can't dispute you.'"[11]

The conditional curse appears to be typical of the reverential attitude toward the Sun; it is called *taβeβekʌt,* "sun-killing." E. Adamson Hoebel has recorded several similar cases where the defendant appealed to the Sun, who knew all and could pass and execute judgment.

The Sun, however, was not the only body worshiped. Next after

[10] Gregg, *op. cit.,* 438.

[11] Hoebel, *The Political Organization and Law-Ways of the Comanche Indians,* 89–90; Smithwick, *op. cit.,* 180.

the Sun, the Earth was named in prayer. It was worshiped as "Mother" because it was the receptacle and producer of all that sustains life. The Earth was the mother not only of men, but of animals. The mother is the natural protector of the young. The buffalo, by loosening the earth with his horns and pawing or rubbing the loose earth upon his body, and the Comanche, by praying to it and covering himself with paint taken from it, each calls the attention of his mother to her child. It has been said that some Indians would not kill a person while he was digging in the earth—while he was making his medicine, for it might be too strong; but he would distract the attention of his intended victim; then when he looked up, they were on equal terms.

Mother Earth was implored to make everything grow which they ate, that they might live; to make the water flow, that they might drink; to keep the ground firm, that they might walk upon it; to make certain herbs and plants grow, that they might be able to heal the sick; and to cause the grass to grow on which the animals fed. The Great Spirit put the Earth here and put them upon it. Without the Earth nothing could live; there could be no animals or plants. Such reverence for the earth was not unique with the Comanches, but was common among the Indians of the plains. The Earth was addressed in prayer after the Sun and, like the Sun, was regarded as having power to look down on earthlings and pass and execute judgment.

Smoking to the power, he first addressed the Sun saying, "You, Father, know the truth of the matter. As you look down on them don't let them live till fall." Then to the earth he said, "You, Mother Earth, as you know what is true, don't let them live a happy life on you." Whereupon he gave his pipe to his wife that she might make her self-curse.

She swore to the powers, "Sun, if you don't believe me, then let me perish. Mother Earth, if you don't believe me, let it be true that I won't live right upon you! Whatever he says, let it be true."[12]

Needless to say, not all those who invoked the judgment of the

[12] Hoebel, *The Political Organization and Law-Ways of the Comanche Indians,* 100.

powers had great faith in the fulfillment of their prayers. In this particular case the woman later admitted that she did not believe in the power of the Sun and had lied. Yet, the many cases remembered by the people where divine judgment had been implored and executed upon the guilty party is evidence that the philosophy was strongly implanted in Comanche society.

The Moon also had the quality of a deity. "She is the Mother—as is the Earth." She was particularly the guardian of the raid. A group of Comanche marauders bent on stealing horses laid a rope on the ground and sat within it. They made smoke to the Moon, praying, "Mother, if it be your will, let this rope take many horses."[13]

Although Sun and Earth and Moon were active in the affairs of men, they were akin to deities and as such were above individualized pity. They gave no personal power and did not come forth as guardian spirits. They were tribal deities who loomed pre-eminent in an individual's consciousness, except when ousted from that position by a special spirit to which a Comanche looked for protection and guidance. Comparison of the latter in strength with the Sun and Earth did not spontaneously arise. It became significant only when and if there was a clash of interest; and then the assurance with which a Comanche relied on his individual patron against the rest of the universe was amazing. Yet there is little suggestion that the visitants were sent by higher authority. They conferred bounties in their own right. The supernaturals might come to loggerheads on behalf of their mortal protégés, or again they might co-operate to aid a favorite. Nothing prevented a man from gaining power from several supernaturals. All were living spirits who spoke the language of man and who possessed the power to assume various forms. The transformation from one being into another could be instantaneous, and the reverse process could occur as suddenly. The guardian spirit was most likely to confer on its ward a blessing or power corresponding to its own natural gifts.

The spirits dwelled in springs, in rivers, on the prairies, in the hills, or in high bluffs. Any phenomenal object of nature was likely to be the residing place of a spirit.

A place was told of, far to the north, where there were always

13 Informant: Post Oak Jim.

clouds which the sunlight never penetrated. This was the home of a powerful spirit that brought the winter. He came in a cloud, forcing the Sun back, and as he approached, he spread the cold over the country. Then in the spring the Sun grew higher and higher and told the spirit of the cold to move back, for he must heat the earth and make the grass and all other things so that the Comanches could prosper.

The thunder often appeared as a great bird, somewhat like an eagle, but much larger. The Thunderbird made the thunder and lightning and storm and rain. It was dark blue, or showing the color of cut lead like a thundercloud, with red zigzag markings extending from its heart to the tail and wing tips. It went south at the approach of winter and returned from the warm country with the Sun, bringing the heat and the rain. In its talons the bird carried arrows with which to strike its enemies; therefore, the Indians believed that the eagle on our coins is a Thunderbird. Its shadow was the thunder cloud; it produced lightning by rapidly opening and closing its flashing eyes; thunder was the sound made by the flapping of its enormous wings; and the downpour which followed was from the lake carried on its back.

The Thunderbird supposedly had its dwelling on some high mountain or rocky elevation difficult of access. It discharged arrows, but they could not be seen even when they killed people or animals. Although the Thunderbird myth was common to most Plains Indians, the Comanches have given it variation. They had evidence other than thunder and rain of the existence of the great bird. They told of a spot on the upper Red River where the grass remained permanently burned off over a space having the shape of a huge bird with outspread wings. They claimed that the Thunderbird once alighted there. A hunter shot and wounded a large bird which fell to the ground, but because of its large size, he was afraid to go close enough to kill it. He returned to camp for help. When his party approached the ravine where the bird had fallen, they heard thunder and were blinded by terrific flashes of lightning coming from the ravine. While attempting to approach nearer, one of the hunters was struck dead by a flash. Realizing that their victim was the Thunderbird, the rest became frightened and fled back to camp.[14]

The Comanches had great fear of thunder and lightning. It gave them no power and was dangerous in a way that the Sun, Earth, and Moon were not. It was malicious and wantonly prone to tease mankind. "In a thunderstorm you have to remain quiet; you must not say anything to thunder and lightning, as it has no pity."

They were afraid, but they were Comanches and they did not like to be pushed around. So every now and then one of them got defiant.

« « « I was out riding once when a rainstorm came up. I got off my horse and got down among some weeds and put my head down. The thunder was making noise all around. Finally I decided it was making fun of me—lightning and thunder likes to make fun of someone—so I got on my horse and made a war whoop in defiance. Then I ran away. The lightning struck right near me. I got away, but thunder and lightning has no pity. » » »

This was Post Oak Jim's personal experience. He reverted to the same theme later on. His lesson impressed him greatly, but it was reinforced by what happened to one of his friends.

« « « Thunder and lightning has no pity for them who talk back. We were out in a bunch branding. When we were eating our breakfast, a thunder shower came up. A tough guy, who was with us, went out and shot at the lightning with his gun to show that he was not afraid. The lightning struck and killed him. » » »

A belief of more recent days is not to look in a mirror when it thunders. The lightning may look in, too, and strike you.

Like most prairie tribes, the Comanches greatly revered the buffalo. It has been reported that the dry buffalo head was their idol. Before the entrance of a sweat-lodge there was likely to be a buffalo skull. Out on the prairie might be seen the skulls of buffalo turned so as to face the main camp, the idea being that the guardian spirit would direct the herd to move in the direction the skulls were facing.

[14] Mooney, "The Ghost Dance Religion and the Sioux Outbreak of 1890," *loc. cit.*, 968-69.

Sometimes when they were ceremoniously smoking, after puffs had been blown to the Great Spirit, Sun, and Earth, a puff was blown to a near-by buffalo skull with a prayer that it provide the people with meat to eat and skins for their lodges and clothing. At times they prayed to the buffalo in general to range where hunting would be good.

Sometimes buffalo talked to a person. Although in Cheyenne mythology it was only the buffalo male that talked, in Comanche mythology it could be either male or female, old or young. A buffalo might turn into a human being and through its supernatural power reveal the location of the herd to the people or otherwise perform good deeds. A Comanche story which has survived not only is interesting but explains how the guardian spirits functioned through the medium of the buffalo.

« « « Once when a party of Comanches went on a buffalo hunt, they were accompanied by a young boy. He was a handsome child, and his family, who were well-to-do, dressed him in the finest regalia and provided him with the best of equipment and a swift horse. When the hunters charged and scattered the herd, the boy selected and followed a small group which contained a beautiful young calf. The boy selected this buffalo for his kill. His first arrow hit beneath the lowest rib. He shot again, and again his arrow found its mark, but the buffalo did not fall. The boy decided to retrieve his arrows, but the buffalo ran into a stream and stopped in the middle of it. The boy would not go into the water because he did not wish to spoil his fine clothes, so he abandoned the chase.

Ordinarily a buffalo shot as this one had been would die, but through its supernatural power the young buffalo maintained life, as it had fallen in love with the boy. It rejoined the herd and in time gave birth to a calf. The boy by means of the two arrows was father of the calf. The other members of the herd would not play or associate with the calf. The calf noticed that the other calves stood around their mothers and fathers, and he wondered about his father. When he asked his mother about his father, she explained to him that his father was "one of those who eats us, and it was I who desired that he be your father." The calf then insisted on seeing him, even after his mother warned that they would be killed should they upon the long journey meet scouts from his father's people. They traveled by night, and after many days came in sight of the village. The mother told the calf to do as she did. She rolled herself about on the ground, and there stood a woman dressed in a buffalo-robe with peg holes or eyelets about the edges. The calf rolled on the ground and became a handsome boy, wrapped in a beautiful yellow calf robe. Then the woman told the boy to go forward to the center of the village; there he would find his father and his relatives in his tent. The boy found everything just as his mother had said, and told his father his story. His father remembered the incident, and asked for the boy's mother. They went for her, and the father said that both were to live in his house. The woman returned the two arrows to the father and cautioned him not to drink from any stream except as she directed.

The people in the village were starving. As soon as the buffalo woman learned of this, she took a piece of dry meat and fat and gave it to the man. Although the portion was small, he satisfied his appetite without consuming it all, and passed the remainder to another. When they had all eaten their fill, a portion of the dry meat still remained. When the father again spoke to the buffalo woman about the plight of the tribe, she directed every family to pack a parfleche as if it were full of dry meat. When morning came the parfleches were full of dry meat. After they had again eaten, she directed them to break camp and follow her. She led them to a herd of buffalo, and they made a rich killing. They were aware that the strange woman was the cause of their success; also they noticed that neither she nor the calf boy ever ate.

Some time had passed, and the Comanches were prosperous. One day the father of the buffalo calf, while traveling across the prairies, became very thirsty. He remembered the warning given him by the woman, but thought he would merely wet his mouth. As he did so, there occurred a great confusion in the camp, and the people saw the woman and the boy, who had been instantly transformed into a buffalo cow and calf, fleeing from the camp. The father was very sad, for the woman had made him very prosperous through her supernatural power. Likewise, the people were sad, for they had learned to love the buffalo woman and the calf-boy."[15]   ))   ))   ))

The coyote was regarded by the Comanches as a brother, who often warned those who possessed power to speak and understand its language, of impending trouble. "Coyote medicine was for knowing things ahead or in the future."

When Skinny and Wrinkled was staying with an old man north of Medicine Park, Oklahoma, the old fellow asked him one night, "Well, have you heard from our friend yet?" Skinny and Wrinkled had heard nothing. The old man admonished him, "Well, you better listen hard now. I believe he is coming around pretty soon."

Not long after, they were talking one night when the dogs began to bark. The old man told Skinny and Wrinkled to shut them up. "I believe there's our friend."

Sure enough, there was a coyote howling.

"I could not interpret what he was saying, but the old man could."

"You better start saving up your bread," was his version of the message. "He says there is going to be a hard winter this year. We aren't going to have much to eat."

That is the way it was, according to Skinny and Wrinkled. The winter before, the Comanches had more flour than they knew what to do with. That winter there were hardly enough rations to give them what was due them.

The coyote also predicted good fortune. One night a coyote howled, and at breakfast the mother of Skinny and Wrinkled said it was telling the tribe that they were all going to get a lot of money soon. Her husband, who was quite a skeptic, laughed and said, "How do you know?"

She insisted, however, and warned, "You wait and see. If the old man talks again before the week is out, it sure is coming true."

On Friday they heard him again. The very next day there were checks for $180 each at the agency for every member of the tribe.[16]

If, when the Indians were on a journey, a coyote jumped up before them, looked at them, and barked or howled, they would likely change their course and travel no farther in that direction that day. A friendly spirit in the form of a wolf was warning them of danger,

[15] Gene Weltfish, "The Man Who Married a Buffalo Wife, A Comanche Story," *Caddoan Texts* (*Publications* of the American Ethnological Society, XVII), 218–23.

[16] Informant: Yellowfish.

and they must heed the warning. The enemy was generally found just where the coyote told them.

Eagles possessed power in matters concerning war. Because of this power their feathers were attached to shields, worn tied in the hair, and during the later period they were placed on the war bonnet. Owing to the protective power of the bird, those wearing the feathers believed that they would not be hit by either bullets or arrows.[17] When eagle feathers were attached to the shield, it could not be pierced by either bullets or arrows. The Comanches secured a part of their feathers by taking young eagles from their nests and keeping them in captivity. (Young eagles were easily kept by tethering them by the legs to a pin driven in the ground.) After the eagles had reached full size, they pulled out the tail feathers. War whistles were made from wing bones of eagles.

The deer had much power which might be used for good or evil. It had the power to cause or cure disease. It could say to its favorite: "Of all things on this earth that step on the ground, there is nothing that beats me in running. By that save yourself in time of trouble." At times it was a helper in love affairs. Possibly because the elk had great vitality and was hard to kill, it was credited with having great strength which could be transmitted to those whose guardian spirit it happened to be. The bear possessed power to cure wounds. The skunk possessed great power. Doctors used its hide to hold their medicine. Men tied its tail to their horses' tails in war. For a member of a war party to kill and skin a skunk while on the way to attack was likely to nullify some of the most powerful war medicine.[18] The roadrunner had the power to reinvigorate and give speed, since it was a speedy bird. The owl was unpopular, for it brought bad news, but the Comanches never shrank nearly so much with fear and horror at the sound of its hoot as did the Kiowas. The wolf gave power to walk barefoot on the cold snow. Medicine men who had this power painted the flesh between their toes red like that of the wolf. And if a person would howl like a wolf before eating red haws, there was no danger of foundering on them.

In like manner, in an ever lessening degree, practically all animals

[17] *Ibid.*

[18] This was the reason attributed by the leader for the failure at Adobe Walls.

and insects were attributed certain powers by someone. One of the very few animals known to the Comanches which never gave supernatural power was the horse. Although of extreme economic value, horses had no place in the ceremonial life of the tribe; nor did they ever appear in visions or significant dreams except as incidental details. This was also true of the dog. It would seem that the dog and horse, as everyday parts of the Comanche household, were too profane to be thought of as power givers. Man had control of them. Givers of power had to be outside his realm of dominance.

Just as animals, birds, and insects might be guardian spirits, so was any unusual phenomenon of nature likely to be the abiding place of a spirit. Some of these places, because of the extraordinary power of the spirit abiding within, became rather famous among the Comanches. One such place is Medicine Mounds.

Medicine Mounds are a line of rounded hills in Hardeman County, Texas, between the Pease and the Red rivers. They are rather conspicuous, the cones rising about 350 feet above the surrounding plain. Flanking them to the west is a gully-washed scar of an ancient buffalo trail. On the top of the highest of the four mounds is a flat cap rock, a protector against erosion. It was believed by the Comanches to be the dwelling place of a powerful and benevolent spirit.·

A Comanche medicine man first discovered its great power when once his band came to hunt in the vicinity of the mounds. He had a young and beautiful daughter who was ill of fever and was growing weaker day by day. Her father had sucked worms and evil spirits out of many a brave and many a squaw, had chanted away the pains of many a girl, and had smoked the weakness from many a boy, but he could not cure his own daughter. He had rattled his gourd all night long while he prayed and chanted. From his medicine bundle he had prepared cures, while the moon was dark and while it was full. He had mixed and tried his formulae in every way he knew. He had consulted other medicine men. But all without results. One morning he came out of his tipi and in despair was gazing silently into the distance when suddenly his eyes came to rest on the rock-capped peak of the highest mound. Here was a powerful spirit that could help him, he thought. So without touching water or food, he went apart to pray and fast until the spirit should send him a revelation. At length it came. He was instructed to take his medicines to the high rock and there mix them so that the power of the good spirit should enter into them. He prepared the medicine as directed by the vision, gave it to his daughter, and then again went out and prayed to the mound spirit—prayed with the patience of those who live under the sun, and watch shadows, and note day by day the greening and the browning of the grass. At length he heard the voice of his daughter. He bounded into the tipi. Her eye was bright, her color almost healthy. She had slept deeply, she said. From that hour she mended steadily and soon was able to return to her work.

Thereafter this medicine man made regular visits to the mound, made offerings to the mound spirit, and performed his cures through its aid. The fame of the mound spirit spread. Other medicine men came. From the gypsum waters of a spring at the base of the mounds, the ailing Comanches came to drink. The spirit came to be a protector for the Comanche bands. Here it could view the country for miles around, and from this lofty point directed arrows of hunters to the vitals of buffalo and deflected those of enemies shot at his wards, the Comanches. And today the name of the four extraordinary hills lined against the ancient buffalo trail that runs down to Pease River remains as a testimonial of the associations they had for the native people who lived by and vanished with the buffalo—Medicine Mounds.[19]

Medicine Bluff is another place commemorated in name and held in great reverence by the Comanches as being the abode of a powerful, benevolent spirit. It is located in Comanchería at the confluence of Cache and Medicine Bluff creeks. The two creeks empty into Red River and are overlooked by a precipitous bluff—Medicine Bluff. It is a mile in length, forming a perfect crescent, rising at once from the bed of Medicine Bluff creek, which flows at the base of the perpendicular scarp, to the height of 310 feet. The surface of the face of the bluff is perfectly regular and smooth. Moss covers the sides with a garb of pale green. The greater portion of the face is perfectly bare, though at some places a few stunted cedars have found lodgment in the crevices. From the rear the bluff presents three knolls, the center one being the highest. Mount Scott, about eight miles dis-

[19] J. Frank Dobie, "Stories in Texas Place Names," *Straight Texas*, 32–34.

tant, stands forth with its pyramidal outline like a sentinel guarding the eastern gate of the Wichita Mountains.

There, from the bluff, according to a Comanche legend recounted by Thomas Battey, a powerful spirit looked over and cared for his people, saw that game was abundant and that his children were prosperous and happy. Comanche medicine men erected a cairn about six feet in height upon the summit of the principal knoll. Here the sick repaired or were brought by their relatives or friends, and here they were left to its invisible and subtle power. Especially those who were past the cure of the medicine men were deposited on the altar and left to be disposed of by the spirit. If the sick had not offended the supernatural powers, they were suddenly healed and returned to their kindred. Sometimes they were transported bodily to the after world. But if they were notoriously bad, they were allowed to die, and the ravens descended from the air, and the wolf came up from the valley and devoured the body, and the bones were gathered up by the Evil Spirit and deposited in the land of terrors.[20] At times the vicinity of the bluff became suddenly lighted up as by a great fire. The dews of night, the rain, and the wind circled about the spot of the altar at the very summit, but none of these agencies of nature trespassed, and the patient was thus left sheltered better than in his own tipi.

To the spirit was attributed the power of resurrection. Once an old warrior, who had long lived among the women of the village, having ceased to hunt or go on the warpath and having been turned out to wait his time to join his fathers, had struggled to the top of the bluff to die and be borne away to the after world. Each night after his departure, when darkness covered the face of nature, the awe-stricken people of the village below observed a great blaze, as if a fire had been built to alarm them. On the morning after the third night, a young man equipped as a warrior was seen descending the bluff, along the trail to the village. He approached the chief's lodge and sat by the fire. The warriors gathered around, but no one recognized him and so remained silent, waiting for him to speak. Lighting his pipe, decorated with beads and feathers of strange birds, the stranger, after all had made the ceremonial smoke, began his story.

When he had reached the top of the hill, he could see the village

20 We read this to be un-Comanche-like embroidery supplied by Battey.

206

and hear the laughter of children, the mourning of his kindred, and the barking of the dogs. He could see the buffalo and deer in the distance, and the young warriors in all their pride and strength. Then he asked himself, "Why do I live any longer? My fires have gone out. I must follow my fathers. The world is beautiful to the young, but to the old it has no pleasures. Far away to the setting suns are the hunting grounds of my people. I will go there." After these words, he had mustered all he could of his failing strength and leaped into the air from the giddy height before him. He knew no more of the woes of life. He was caught up in midair and transported into a smiling country where there was no rain and no wind, where the great chiefs of all the Comanches were assembled. They were all young and chased the buffalo and feasted. There was no darkness. The Great Spirit was everywhere and everybody was happy.

The story captivated the minds and imagination of the listeners, and the strange young warrior became at once an oracle and a big medicine man in the tribe. His counsel was all-powerful, and his abilities to cure were considered infallible. Reverence for the bluff was enhanced; and in the years that followed no Comanche would ascend to the summit of the hill except for a most sacred purpose. When white soldiers fired shots at the cliff to hear the echoes, the Comanche guide, Blue Leggings, was horror stricken, and he refused to scale the peak with the soldiers, saying, "Me no sick!"[21]

At times a young man, eager to take the warpath for the first time, ascended to the sacred spot in quest of his vision. Having provided himself with a shield, in accordance with ceremonial instructions the youth proceeded to the highest point of the bluff, remaining for three successive days. A part of the ceremony included presenting the face of the shield to the rising sun each morning, as if warding off an arrow or a spear. The sacred surroundings of the place and the Sun, the emblem of the Great Spirit, casting its rays upon the shield were supposed to endow it with supernatural protective powers.

On principle no Comanche worshiped the entire animal life or physical phenomena of his country. But accounts of recent and legendary visions prove that no wild species or type can be ruled out as a possible source of power. The world view precluded nothing from

[21] Nye, *Carbine and Lance*, 98.

the range of the mystically potent, but the individual consciousness ascribed power to a relatively narrow selections of beings, their identity being determined by chance experience.

To discuss Comanche religion in terms of a definite pantheon would therefore be preposterous. Comanche "gods" were not clear-cut beings with sharply defined cosmic or social functions. Divine power was not concentrated in a few major personalities, but diffused over the universe and likely to crop up in unexpected places. A Comanche did not first envisage a god and then worship him; he started with the thrill, with the sense of a supernatural agency, and objectified his emotional stirrings. There were, nevertheless, certain supernaturals that appeared rather frequently both in ritual and in visionary experiences, notably the eagle, the bear, and the buffalo.

Religion and ethics were largely divorced. The really vital social canons had no supernatural sanctions. When a vision-seeker called upon the supernaturals to favor him, he hardly ever stressed his moral worth, but his desire for aid. What he pleaded for was not moral elevation, but some material benefit; and it was compassion that animated his patron in granting it. Often, to be sure, the visitant laid down rules of conduct, but they had no bearing on social considerations. Good intentions were no safeguard against the consequences of transgression. A man who unwittingly broke rules imposed upon him had to bear the brunt of the catastrophe, for ignorance of the "law" was no safeguard against punishment.

IX
Government and Law

I N a society as simple and as homogeneous as was that of the Comanches there is little need for the development of governmental institutions. Add to this the extreme individualism of the Comanches, and a situation exists in which neither social needs nor ideology work to stimulate the development of government. Consequently, Comanche government was at a minimum, legal precepts were rudimentary, and the enforcement of the simple substantive law remained the responsibility of individuals rather than of officials.

Just as the Comanche made no attempt to organize a philosophy of religion or to systematize a conception of man's place in nature, so he made no attempt to generalize or formalize the rules underlying his legal system or the constitutional structure of his state. For instance, when That's It was asked about the Comanche peace chiefs, he said, "I hardly know how to tell about them. They never had much to do except to hold the band together."

To the Comanche, law was not an expression of social policy, but rather a series of individual responses to threatening situations. Descriptively we can note the Comanche point of view. Analytically we are not content to stop at this level. The Comanches had more law than they themselves recognized.

Ralph Linton has expressed that thought in these words: "Different cultures show a tremendous amount of difference in the degree to which their patterns are consciously formalized. My experience with Polynesians and Comanches illustrates this: Polynesians can give you practically an Emily Post statement of what proper behavior should be on all occasions, whereas Comanches, when asked how they do anything, immediately answer, 'Well, that depends.' They genuinely think of behavior as a range of unlimited, individual, freedom of choice, although when you take a series of examples of behavior, as Hoebel did, you actually find quite a high degree of uniformity. But you have to check Comanche behavior to arrive at this."[1]

In other words, to learn about Comanche law, it is necessary not to talk about "law" when doing field work with the Comanches, but rather, through utilization of the case-law method of legal recording and analysis, to accumulate a sizeable body of case histories of dispute situations from which the regularity of legal patterns can be abstracted.[2]

Before presenting the facts of their law, it is necessary to describe the nature of the Comanche state.

The basic principle of Comanche political organization was the constitutional separation of civil and military leadership. For a warlike people this separation was quite remarkable, although, of course, it was a general North American Indian practice for which the Comanches cannot be singled out for credit.

The peace chief was known as *pařia:βo* and each family encampment had its *pařia:βo*, whom we shall call either "peace chief" or "headman." There was reluctance on the part of the Comanches to accord him formal recognition, but genuine recognition of his powers was reflected in the attention given to his advice and in the general subordination to his influence. It was one of these family headmen who was elevated to the position of head peace chief of the band; the remainder of the chiefs functioned as an advisory council for the band as a whole and at the same time maintained their positions as family headmen to their own group of followers. The chief, or headman, was chairman, so to speak, of the group. He was *primus inter pares*.

There is no explicit way of saying how a man became a civil

1 Ralph Linton in S. S. Sargent and M. W. Smith (eds.) *Culture and Personality,* 123.
2 Cf. Hoebel, *The Political Organization and Law-Ways of the Comanche Indians,* 181.

chief. When asked, "How did you *select* your peace chiefs?" That's It, misunderstanding the phrasing of the question, answered with a touch of annoyance, "We did not *elect* them. We were not like you white people, who have to have an election every four years to see who is going to be your leader. A peace chief just got that way." His idea was echoed quite independently by Kills Something, who said, "No one made him such; he just got that way."

A peace chief rose to his position of leadership by combining generosity, kindness, evenness of temper, wisdom in council, and knowledge of his territory with good sense and the ability to speak persuasively on matters at issue. The man whose advice was most consistently followed was a peace chief for his group. He emerged gradually as a leader, and when his ability to influence his group was surpassed by that of another man, he ceased to be its *paɾia:βo*. Another had taken his place. The position was not competitively sought, at least not openly, for aggressive behavior was not part of the pattern of action of the man who was acceptable to the people as a peace chief. He epitomized the ideal of order and tranquility, not strife.

Josiah Gregg observed a tendency for sons of chiefs to acquire the position with more than average frequency, but explained that it was not due to any established rule of hereditary succession or legal pattern, but rather that it resulted from the fact that sons of chiefs, by virtue of the training and example set by their fathers and the expectancy of high standards within their families, attained the qualities of the chieftain. Competition was open, and the office was granted on performance solely.[3] Our own data confirm Gregg's penetrating perception. Here we see the roots of the hereditary principle as it can arise in any society. We would add that not only are the sons of chiefs more apt to act in the chiefly pattern, but the chief is merged to some extent in his family, and people get used to looking to that family for leadership. The son, who is identified with the father, tends to become the focus of leadership expectancies.

The authority of a peace chief, as has already been indicated, lasted only so long as he was able to maintain it. His position was more nominal than positive, more advisory than compulsive. The man made the office and not the office the man; he perforce relied

[3] Gregg, *op. cit.*, 343.

more upon personal influence than upon delegated authority. In addition to the qualities of kindness, generosity, and wisdom in tribal affairs, physical fitness, a record for dash and daring, valor, and firmness, whether in camp or in battle, were also desirable characteristics of such leaders, but were not absolutely prerequisite to the attainment of office.

While it was not necessary for a man to have a war record to become a peace chief, it was not uncommon in later years for a war leader to achieve that rank. Certainly one who had attained leadership by personal bravery and exhibitions of courage and skill, either in the chase or on the field of battle, had added prestige. The peace chief was usually a man whose raiding days were over, although he might occasionally take to the warpath, designating someone to act in the capacity of civil chief during his absence.

When a man emerged as a civil chief, he had become a kind of revered patriarch. To all the band he was "father." The People were his "children." Although he wisely refrained at times from intervening in disputes, there were times when his judicious words brought satisfaction to both parties. Judge he was not, but mediator he seems to have been at times. It was in situations where the problem was a question of what ought to be done that the civil chief was important. That his advice was followed means no more than that his ideas appeared to be right and proper. He spoke the custom. Under no circumstances did a civil chief have the power to order an adjustment to be made. He had no power over the life of any member of the tribe. His influence was limited to internal and civil matters only. No peace chief had authority to prevent by force a war party from taking the trail. His only really definite power was that of deciding the time and place of camp moving.[4] The chief who proved tactless, cowardly, or inefficient would soon be supplanted; but the readjustment would take place gradually and by common consent rather than by formal procedure. Should the chief disgrace himself by an act of cowardice or maladministration, the band might quickly depose him and elevate another.

An important peace chief had his personal herald or camp crier, who served as the chief's mouthpiece in announcing the daily news

4 Informants: Kills Something; That's It.

and comments of the chief. Each chief kept a staff of young men to serve him as aides and counselors. These young men protected their chief at all hazards; they risked their lives to rescue his body from the enemy, for it was a great honor to be chosen as a bodyguard to a civil chief. It was customary in the larger camps to send two of these young men out each day to circle the countryside looking for signs of enemies in the vicinity.

There is some difference of opinion as to the relative power of civil and war chiefs. The bulk of the evidence indicates that the head civil chief was superior to the war chief in theory, but that if the civil chief was aged and decrepit and the war chief vigorous and popular, the authority of the civil chief would be more theoretical than real.

Important policies were determined in council. In theory, at least, the council was supreme, but its decisions were often indefinite. Generally the majority made little effort to impose its will on the minority, for, as in most Indian tribes, it was thought that agreement should be unanimous. The council was composed of all the old men of the tribe who had shown exceptional ability as warriors, leaders, or guides. As in the selection of chiefs, there was no formal procedure for admission; one "just got that way" because of his achievements. During the later period the authority of the counselors might be indicated by the "sun-rayed" buffalo robe dropping regally from the shoulders, even on a hot day, and by the feather war bonnet with its plumed train worn at times by members whose military achievements entitled them to wear it.

Within the council, experience and rank were usually given preference. The talking was done principally by the older men—those with the greatest experience. After the elders had stated their views, middle-aged men expressed theirs, and even younger men might speak a few words. Boys were generally allowed to attend the meetings, but only as respectful listeners. For them to intrude opinions in weighty matters was to invite scorn and ridicule; consequently, they maintained silence. They learned by watchful listening. If either the young men or the boys were called upon to speak, they did so with moderation and with a feeling of pride that they should be so honored. They wished to prove themselves first by action, then by speech. In this school of training, qualities of restraint, dignity, and reserve were generated which enabled them to become respected counselors in later years. Women sometimes attended the meetings and on rare occasions were permitted to speak,[5] but these appear to be exceptions to the normal pattern. The final decision was made by the recognized members in good standing, generally by acclamation.

Any principal chief had a right to call a council meeting of his own band. A joint council of two or more groups could be convened, provided the separate chiefs of each band concerned called a meeting. There was no regular tribal council or head tribal chief, and it is doubtful that all the bands were ever brought together in a single assembly. The first assembly of chiefs representing all the bands that was convened, in the belief of Echo of the Wolf's Howl, was at the time of the proposal of the Medicine Lodge Treaty in 1867.

Usually the subject of the council meeting was known in advance and had to some extent been privately discussed. The members were informed of the meeting by the official crier or messenger, who also had the duty of filling the official council pipe. The entire meeting was conducted with strict formality and with a degree of courtesy that could hardly be exceeded. When all the members had assembled, a few minutes of silence ensued, during which time the council pipe was passed from one to another around the circle of counselors as an invocation to the Deity to preside. When this part of the ceremony was completed, one of the older men arose and introduced the subject at issue. His remarks were followed by a brief silence for consideration before a second speaker began. Each counselor spoke or politely declined as his turn came. Questions were considered carefully and deliberately, especially if important, and frequently considerable time elapsed before a decision was rendered. During the meeting, members might consult each other as well as address the group as a whole. Sometimes there were vast differences of opinion among the men, yet each was heard gravely and respectfully; and no matter how earnest the debate might become, no man ever interrupted the speaker, nor did anything like wrangling occur.[6] The Comanches had no

[5] Rister, *Border Captives*, 28–29.

[6] Linton, *The Study of Man*, 235; Neighbors, "The Naüni or Comanches of Texas," *loc. cit.*, 130.

214

Roberts' Rules of Order, but their procedure was on a very high level of parliamentary decorum.

Such a council was held in 1843 to decide the fate of the ambassadors sent by President Sam Houston of the Republic of Texas to invite the Comanches to discuss a treaty. Each speaker, as his turn came, delivered a vociferous oration, but was never interrupted. When all who were entitled to speak had finished, the head chief, whose turn it was, remained silent, and no one moved or spoke from noon until four o'clock. Either the chief was pondering the weighty matter or seeking by his silence to impress upon his audience the importance of the decision before the body. When he spoke, he gained such support that when the vote was taken the ambassadors were spared.[7]

The council considered such matters as moving the camp, undertaking a tribal war, making peace, seeking an alliance with other tribes for the purpose of proceeding to war against a common enemy, the selection of the time and place of the summer hunt, community religious services, the disposition of spoils belonging to the band (but not of spoils acquired by a raiding party), the allocation of supplies to widows and the needy, and the regulation of trade with outsiders.

When any important decision had been reached, it was announced by the camp crier, who, mounting his horse, heralded the news as he rode through the village. If by any chance the decision was not in accord with public feeling, the action was likely to be modified. In practice, however, this seldom happened, for public sentiment had been well ascertained before the council met. The older men were always slow to take any radical action.

Decisions of councils generally were regarded by the warriors as sacrosanct. Punishment for violating these decisions was certainly neither common nor necessary. The warriors obeyed more from fear of arousing the anger of their chiefs and the displeasure of the supernatural powers than because of any respect for authority in the abstract. The nomadic character of the Comanches, however, made it impossible for the chiefs to keep in touch with their warriors at all times, and when a warrior committed an offense, his punishment, so far as the chief and council were concerned, usually went no further

[7] M. M. Kenney, "Tribal Society among Texas Indians," *The Quarterly* of the Texas Historical Association, Vol. I (1897), 31.

than rebuke and admonition. The people in general, however, showed great respect and obedience to their chiefs and headmen.

While warfare was still going on, the exactions of the chiefs, headmen, and counselors who stood at the top of the scale of society were kept in check by fear of reprisals should some man of lower rank later rise to supremacy. Thus the warriors prevented the tipping of the scales toward undue governmental authority. The end of warfare froze the social system, depriving able young men of all chance of social advancement, since this primary means of achieving status was blocked. As a result, the old men became arrogant in a way that they dared not in earlier times.[8]

War chiefs were men who had war records and who had won leadership by personal bravery and exhibitions of courage and skill. Each band seemed to have recognized one individual as the leading war chief. Apparently his elevation to the position was given official recognition by the council of elders. Yet, again, in this matter the council apparently followed public opinion, which in this case would be the wishes of the warriors. The war chief was apt to be a younger man than the civil chief and in times of war might possibly overshadow the leading civil chief.

In the event of the death or decline and withdrawal of a war chief, the warriors in council selected one of their number and installed him as their leader. The discussion and the expressions of opinion usually showed clearly who was the most popular man for the place. There appears to have been no formal balloting; the discussion continued until sentiment had crystalized around one man. In addition to the number-one war chief, each band had a number of war leaders of lesser rank.

The prosecution of warfare was very much a matter of individual discretion. Any Comanche was theoretically eligible to lead a war party, and there was no power to restrain him. A warrior who wished to organize a war party made known his intention. If his military reputation had been established in combat, if his "medicine" was powerful, and if he was known to be liberal in the division of the spoils, he seldom had difficulty in securing a large following. Continued successes would lead to his elevation to the chieftainship.

[8] Ralph Linton, "The Distinctive Aspects of Acculturation," *loc. cit.*, 506.

216

A heroic and possibly legendary story of the making of a war chief in the Water Horse band, full of the flavor of the Comanches, was told by That's It. It reveals his influence and reflects Comanche marital and legal attitudes.

《 《 《 There were two young brothers about sixteen and twenty-five years old. Neither was a medicine man.

In the old days lots of trouble began over women. The oldest brother was out wandering about the camp one day when he met a young woman coming down a cow trail. She proposed to him that they go on the warpath. They had seen each other at the dances; she wanted him and had plotted the meeting.

"I am a young man," he rebuffed her. "I take orders only from my people. You are beautiful and married. If we do this thing, there will be trouble."

Later she accosted him in the same spot.

"For a young man, you're an awful coward," was her taunt.

This made him kind of sore. He answered her, "Well—you come at sundown with your stuff. I shall be here with two horses."

Her husband was in the habit of having some old men in for a smoke in the evening. He told her to clean up the tipi. When the old men were all there, he told her to bring the fire stick and then to lie down and listen.

While she was lying there, the sister of her lover came over with a rare blanket, which she slipped to her under the edge of the tipi.

After a while she told her own sister she was going out to get some air. Putting the blanket over her head, she walked right by the men smoking outside.

One of them remarked, "My, there goes a boy with a beautiful blanket."

She met her lover at the rendezvous and they made their get-away.

In the morning her husband missed her. He went up to the boy's tipi and asked his father where the lad was. He got the answer that they did not know; he had not been in all night.

"Well," said this man, "he has run off with my wife." The father told him he was sorry, and the husband went away.

Later on, when nothing was seen of the couple, the husband came back again.

217

"What is it you want," he was asked.

"I want *nanɛwɔkə* (damages)," he declared.

The father agreed to this, telling him that he could have his pick of all their herd. The younger brother gave his assent, too, saying, "That is all right, if only you leave my favorite."

The husband laughed, "That's just the very horse I want."

"Well, in that case, it's just as good as yours. But I won't give it up until my brother comes back."

His mother pleaded the same thing, so finally the husband agreed to let the whole matter of the settlement rest until the elder brother returned.

Before long a war party was being organized.

The youngest brother wanted to go to war. He was a strong young man. It was time, he thought, to show his worth to the people.

He went to his father, telling him of the feeling he had, saying that he wanted to go with the fighters on the raid. His father was glad that his son had such thoughts. "It is good," he said. "And furthermore, my son, I will give you a powerful pony with which to meet our enemies. You shall have a good mule to ride upon the trail, for you must respect your pony. He must be ridden only in battle. Ride upon the mule and lead the pony by its halter until the proper time. When you get to the territory of our enemies it will be time. Leave your mule and get on that pony. Ride him hard like you were meeting the enemy. Do this a short way and stop. Rest! Charge again. Rest once more. Do this four times, my son. Do this, and you will have a pony which will never tire. It will be a famous war pony among the people."

When the boy did these things the people wondered, but it was as his father had told him.

A couple of nights later they set up a camp, and the leader put a scout upon the hill to look for enemies. When he got there, he saw two tipis on the other side. He turned back and came zigzagging down the hill. When the war party saw him making the signal, the fighters ran for their horses, grabbing their spears and stringing their bows. The scout came in to report to the chief. He had seen two men returning to the tipis; it seemed as though they had seen him as he turned to leave the hilltop.

218

The mounted warriors were off in a pell-mell rush about the hill. They came out there in the open. Yes! There they went. Three families of the enemy were scudding away in flight—like rabbits. The women were in front. The three men were riding behind them to cover their flight. Down on them the Comanches rode. One of the enemies had a fast horse. He circled back and forth trying to keep off the Comanches. Around he came. The boy on his war pony drove at him, his spear in hand. The enemy fell from his horse dead. The other two jumped from their horses; they began shooting with guns. The young Comanche turned his pony on them; in an instant he speared them both. It was over like that. He turned then and looked about. There were the dead enemies. Way back, the Comanches were coming strung out in a line. The fast ones were ahead, but his pony had left them far behind. The first man up hit all the victims and cried, "*ahɛ!*" The others came and took the scalps.

It had been a successful raid, so they all turned back to the main camp. When they got there, the people held a Scalp Dance. On the next morning some fine young maidens dressed up like warriors. They went over to the young brave's tipi before he was awake. They did the Shakedown Dance there and sang the songs. The boy's father came out. He knew what they were there for. He was proud of his son, so he gave these girls what they wanted. He gave them two horses.

The next time the boy went with a war party he was its leader. They were going west. When they got to the enemy territory, he got on his pony and worked it as he had before. After a while they came face to face with a party of Utes out looking for trouble, as they were. There was pause while the two lines stood facing each other.

Then the boy rode out alone, circling before the waiting Utes. The Ute chief came out and chased him back.

"Now," said the youth to one of his followers, "you do as I have just done." Then he waited. When the Ute chief came chasing that Comanche, the young leader dashed down on him and killed him with his spear. That was his strategy. With a yell, he rode straight into the rest of the Utes. He killed two more of them—like lightning. When his fighters saw his brave example, they followed him in. The Utes broke and fled. It was too much for them. Our people chased them a long way. Lots of them were killed, but the rest got away. After a while, when the Comanches got tired, they turned back. They scalped the dead bodies of the enemy and took what they wanted besides.

The people were pleased when they got back to the camp with their great deeds. They had a big Victory Dance, celebrating almost until morning. The young girls came again to give a Shakedown Dance; the boy's father gave them three horses.

Later on the warriors gave a Horse Dance. It was a sign they were going on a raid. The boy was with them. This time they had a battle with the Osages. The enemy had three chiefs to lead them; they were out in front, so the young boy charged, killing them all. A regular dog fight followed. But the Osages were without their chiefs, so they could not last very long. When it was over the Comanches cut off the roaches of the Osages for scalps.

The people gave dances just as before. This time the boy's father gave away four horses. Three years had passed. The boy was now a young man of great renown. He was a mighty fighter, a killer of chiefs.

The wearers of the war bonnets held a meeting about him. They talked about the famous things he had done. It was decided the young man should be raised to the status of war chief.

They got ready and set up a buffalo-hide tipi painted over with white clay. The people knew they were going to make a war chief of the young man. He was only nineteen years old, but he was very brave.

They laid buffalo robes and blankets on the smooth floor for the warriors to sit upon; all was ready.

The wearers of war bonnets were first to enter. The bravest went in first; the others followed after. They turned to the left as they passed through the entrance, walking all the way about the tipi until the first one came to the place at the right side of the door. They came in until they lined the edge of the floor. The leader sat at the west side. Then they waited for the young man.

When his turn came he went through the door of the tipi and walked to the left until he came to a vacant space at the side of the leader. The leader got up to address the warriors. He repeated everything the brave had done, closing his speech with these words,

"This young man has done enough brave deeds. He is honorable and brave. He shall be one of us. He is as brave as any of us and we make him one of us. What is more, I honor him ahead of myself. Hereafter, he is chief in my stead."

Turning to the young man, he took in his hands a fine war bonnet with two rows of feathers as a special honor. Putting the bonnet on the boy's head, he said to him, "This is nothing but a bunch of feathers given by your friends."

The boy was now a war chief. Because the leader had made him chief in his stead, the young warrior walked right to the place to the north of the door and took his seat. The newest member usually had to sit at the end of the line to the south of the door, but he was the greatest fighter they had ever had.

Then it was over. The young war leader rolled up his blanket and walked out; the others followed him.

Ten years later (he was then twenty-nine), he led another big raid—this time to the Mexican border. They attacked a small camp beside an elbow-shaped hill. What they did not notice was that there was another camp—a big one—around the crook of the elbow. They met a lot more resistance than they expected. The Comanches were driven off, their leader surrounded and forced into a draw. He fought fiercely and killed a good many of the enemy until they went away and left him. He was himself shot in the legs.

After he had recovered his strength, he followed slowly after his companions. He traveled eleven days, but could not find them. The eleventh day, he put in at a creek at sunset. He climbed a hill to look about. On the other side he saw some horses and located the smoke from a fire. Leaving his horse behind, he stole up on the lone lodge— a brush hut. He listened and heard a man speaking to a woman. Their talk was Comanche!

He took off his weapons and walked up to them. The man greeted him. He invited him in; he fixed him up with new clothes and gave him a blanket to sit on. This man was an old man; he was living out all alone with his family. He was glad to have some one to talk to him. Supper was served up right away. When it was finished he said, "Now we'll tell stories."

The chief remarked that his host had been telling his wife that he was going to shoot a hawk to get some feathers for their boy. "Well, I have some feathers over there in my bundle. Go get him some."

The man was pleased with this offer, and he told his wife to get some of them. When she opened the visitor's bag, he was surprised at all the war materials in it; he saw he had a war chief with him. He wanted to know who he was, so he asked his guest for the name of his father.

"Well, my father is nobody," was the reply he received. "But I got these feathers"—and then he told of all his war deeds that his feathers represented. He also told how his brother ran away.

Then this lonely man knew that here was his own brother. They were happy to be together again.

The older brother asked what had been done about the *nanɛwɔkə* for the wife he had. He learned that it had never been settled because he had never come back to the band. Now was the time to go back.

Together with his younger brother, the chief, he started back to look for their people. His wife and children were with them.

When, at last, they approached the camp, they were met by a look-out. He told them to wait where they were while he rode into the camp to warn their parents. The chief had been given up for dead; his family was in mourning for him. His mother fainted when she heard the good news, but she recovered and washed the caked blood from her gashes. She dusted herself all over with red powder. She was overjoyed.

Then the two brothers came in; after thirteen years the family was reunited. The old man, the father, traded four horses for two large tipis—he got them from a Kiowa who was present. These were the new homes for his sons.

They were waiting for the old man, whose wife the elder brother had stolen, to come up and collect that *nanɛwɔkə*. They wondered why he did not come.

The younger brother, the great chief, told his older brother he would have to give his wife back. "If you can't get another wife, I shall take care of your children myself."

Their mother talked to the older brother.

"Your brother is a big war chief now," she admonished him. "What he says must go."

222

So they sent down for the old man to come up. He did not want to go, but one of his wives urged him into it—he now had four wives.

The young chief dictated the whole thing. When the old man came into the tipi he told him to sit between his brother and his wife. The old man hesitated. He was afraid.

"It is all right," he was assured by the elder brother.

When he was seated, he hugged the children and was very pleased.

"We are going to give you back your wife," the chief told him, "Tomorrow when you come back, we shall have a feast here. Bring one of your wives. Then when we have eaten, you can take this woman and her children to your lodges."

The old man and the woman were not as one once again until they were on their horses and ready to go the next day.

Thereafter the old man told the two brothers to pitch their tipis back of his. "We are brothers now. My wives are yours any time you want. Just for the asking." » » »

On the raid or warpath the leader of a war party was in supreme control of all the activities of his followers as long as they remained in his party. With so loose and voluntary a collection of personnel, disobedience might be expected, but a warrior seldom refused to obey his leader. It was said that a brave leader never asked of his men what he himself would not readily do. Each knew this. Each knew, too, that disobedience might bring disaster to the party. The leader did not use force or punishment. If a man did not trust the ability and wisdom of the war leader, either he did not join or he separated himself from the party. A warrior followed only the leader in whom he had confidence; when he lost confidence, he withdrew from that leader's sphere. This, be it noted, was also the procedure when a man and his friends did not like the way in which things were being run in the band in times of peace.

The powers of the war chief included determining the objectives of the raid, designating the scouts, deciding upon the camping places and periods of rest, appointing the cook and water carriers, formulating the general tactics of attack, ordering the expedition to turn back, making a truce with the enemy, and dividing the booty.[9]

[9] Informant: Yellowfish; see also Hoebel, *The Political Organization and Law-Ways of the Comanche Indians*, 25.

The warriors of most of the Plains tribes were organized into a series of fighting societies or military fraternities. These organizations were secondarily arms of the tribal government or, at least, they functioned as strong pressure groups.[10] The Comanches, however, in keeping with their lack of internal segmentation, possessed only the slightest trace of military fraternities. Informants explained that their societies were something like a combination of our present-day army regiment and lodge organization. Their dearth of historical data and the paucity of material, combined with the lack of information on the part of contemporary Comanches, indicates that the associations were not a developed and integrated part of Comanche culture. There is no evidence that they played an important role in social control and government.

Such formal government as existed was limited to the activities of the peace chiefs and war leaders, who acted separately or through the medium of the band councils. The Comanches, like almost all of the tribes east of the Rockies, militarists though they were, wanted no military *junta*. They knew the value and need for constitutional separation of civil and military power. From their point of view, that government was best which governed least.

The law system of the Comanche tribe was primitive but dynamic —and exciting. It lacked the maturity and balance of the Cheyenne way. It was crude and lacking in juridical subtlety, but it was fluid, inventive, and colored with its own ideals of justice.

Comanche law-ways functioned without benefit of courts. As might well be expected, in view of the ambiguity of powers of the political chieftains, there were no public officials endowed with law-speaking or law-enforcing authority. Comanche law was neither legislated nor judge-made. It was hammered out on the hard anvil of individual cases by claimant and defendant pressing the issues in terms of Comanche notions of individual rights and tribal standards of right conduct.

It was almost exclusively a system of private law—a law in which the responsibility for instituting legal actions rested with the aggrieved party—a law in which the aggrieved and his personal supporters had

10 J. H. Provinse, "The Underlying Sanctions of Plains Indian Society," in F. Eggan (ed.)., *Social Organization of North American Tribes*, 341–449.

to push the process to its conclusion, or nothing would be done at all to provide relief or redress.

Nevertheless, a system of law it was. It was absolutely sure that certain forms of wrongs would be prosecuted. There were proper procedural patterns to be followed in the prosecution of a case. There were quite specifically understood sanctions to be applied to the different categories of offenses. And if the defendant was adamant beyond the point of reasonableness, he was, after due process, subject to a violent attack upon his person.

The essence of law, whatever specific forms it may take from one social system to another, comprises regularity, force, and official authority. Comanche law-ways had all those essential attributes.

"Dot" Babb's statement that on the whole there was little infringement on the rights of others among the Comanches, that they did not fight, quarrel, and commit murder as did the white man,[11] is contrary to the facts as we know them. The Comanches were most litigious, not, it is true, from any love of going to law for the savor of it, but because they were extreme individualists given to crowding each other in the unceasing struggle to outrank each other in personal prestige. A man could climb the social ladder by piling up a war record at the expense of enemies, and this was the legitimate way. But he could also reach toward his goal by aggressively challenging the status of a rival through stealing his wife, or seducing her, or taking his horse. This was the illegitimate way. It was illegal, but it was also customary enough. Forty-five cases of old-time legal actions arising from adultery and wife stealing alone were recorded from Comanche informants by one of the authors in his study of Comanche law-ways. Of these, twenty-two were wife-absconding cases and twenty-three were cases of simple adultery.

If the Comanches were lawless, it was not through an absence of law, but rather because of a reckless tendency to break the law in the face of certain and severe penalties. Seven of the forty-five erring wives paid the death penalty: four for running off with another man, three for committing adultery. Of the remaining twenty adulteresses, five were mutilated by their husbands: four had the tips of their noses cut off and one had the soles of her feet slashed so that she could not

[11] Babb, *op. cit.*, 102–104.

walk. A cut nose was a social disgrace which was extremely difficult to live down. However, since these public marks had a tendency to decrease the value of a woman should the husband transfer her to another man, erring wives were not always disfigured. Nevertheless, Colonel Dodge reported seeing one Comanche woman with four separate gashes in her nasal organ,[12] while Kills Something claims to have known a woman with five. These were all legal penalties which it was the privilege-right of the husband to impose.

As for the offending male correspondent, in every case save four, he had, in conformity to law and custom, to pay damages to the husband. Comanche law required the aggrieved husband to prosecute. Public opinion forced him to, for if he held back, he would stand as a lily-livered coward before all The People. No man risked that. Thus, although the aggrieved husband was in fact prosecuting a wrong against himself, he was also put in a position of maintaining the public standards, whether he wanted to or not. He was in a sense a public prosecutor as well as the protector of his own private interests.

The payment of damages loomed so large in the interests of the Comanches that they coined a word for it—*nanɛwɔkə*. Such settlements were ideologically in sets of four different kinds of articles: horses, guns, blankets, and clothing. More often than not, they were paid only in horses, numbering from one to ten. Almost inevitably the demands of the husband, if he was a warrior of any consequence, included the favorite horse of the defendant as essential to his satisfaction. His personal prestige had been hurt by the affront, and it was his intent to re-establish it by forcing the aggressor into the humility of giving up that which was most dear to him. It was more than a "money" equivalent that was sought, for it was all part of a prestige battle.

In initiating the procedure, since there were no courts or assizes to be waited upon, action could be instituted at any time. The case was carried to the offender wherever he could be found. The aggrieved could prosecute by accosting the defendant himself, stating the offense and the amount of damages necessary to satisfy him; he might send a third party to prosecute for him; or he might send or accompany a group who stated the charges and then negotiated.

12 R. I. Dodge, *The Plains of the Great West*, 304.

Prosecution procedure was by bargaining. The defendant was seldom confronted with witnesses. The aggrieved had to ascertain the guilty party before he took steps against the defendant. In wife-absconding the presence of the woman with the absconder was sufficient evidence. In case of adultery, evidence came from witnesses or by confession of the wife. When the evidence was obtained and the guilty party had been revealed, the defendant could then be confronted. The bargaining normally began with the guilt accepted by both sides. When the defendant denied guilt, the legal prosecution of the case was ended unless proof of guilt was at hand. The aggrieved might take extralegal steps by committing some act of violence, but that would likely lead to retaliation.

It was possible, if the absconder was afraid of the erring woman's husband, for him to place himself under the protection of an outstandingly brave warrior. This made his chances in the bargaining much better. As another possibility, the aggrieved was allowed the privilege of obtaining the aid of friends. A show of force on the side of the plaintiff was a strong factor in checking illegal action. Such an institutionalized procedure made possible a sort of justice by assuring that the guilty and the wronged parties were placed on a bargaining level.

Cases were opened with formal politeness·and smooth words. The defendant was told the charges and what must be given in damages to satisfy the plaintiff. Ordinarily the negotiation took place outside the door of the defendant's tipi, since the defendant was usually aware of the nature of his visitor's business and did not invite him inside. The damages rendered were those which the defendant agreed to give and which the aggrieved agreed to accept. There was no judge to set the amount, nor was there any rigid customary code regulating the amount of damages in accordance with the degree of wrong, except as it placed a ceiling of ten horses on any settlement. Only by agreement could the case be settled. Naturally, if the defendant were a brave warrior and the plaintiff a timid soul, the compensation would be low. If the aggrieved were a brave warrior, the defendant might acquiesce to the first demands. Damages were also concluded in accordance with the wealth of the offender; the prosecutor "stuck" the defender for the most he believed he could squeeze out of him.

Although it was unusual to resort to fighting and killing over the loss of a woman, society theoretically recognized the right of the offended male to take the life of the offender if he refused to make settlement after guilt was established.

Should the accused deny his guilt, either party might appeal to the supernatural powers as a way out. When accused by an irate husband, one informant denied that he "had broken the law." His accuser proposed that they make smoke and call on the Sun. The informant smoked and then addressed the Sun: "Sun, if what I say is not true, strike me dead. If I am not guilty, strike my accuser dead." When he heard these words, the accuser withdrew his charges and thereby ended the whole affair.[13]

It was, as we have already noted, incumbent upon the husband to seek damages. If he demanded damages and received a satisfactory settlement, his claim upon his wife could be released, thus making legal a divorce and consequently freeing her to change her marital status. In case of divorce or separation, the children legally remained with their father. In many cases the husband took the wife back.

A woman who remarried after the death of her husband without first getting a verbal, but formal, quit-claim from her husband's youngest brother was technically guilty of desertion; her new husband was subject to *nanεwɔkə* demands, and·he had to pay up.

Breaks Something was the unwitting victim of such an action, as his own account shows.

《 《 《 Mexican was a friend of Touched with a Closed Fist. They called each other brother. When Touched with a Closed Fist died a long time ago, Mexican went to claim the widow for his wife. That was Woman. Woman didn't want to live with him, so she came to me.

We were living down at Red Store when one day two men came to see me. They were Mangy Coat and Atsaci. We talked, and then they said they had come to get damages for Woman. I was surprised. I asked them which one of them had a claim on her.

They answered, "We have come to you from Mexican. He was the brother of Touched with a Closed Fist and this woman is his wife."

13 Informant: Kills Something.

I called her and asked her if she were married to another man.

"No," she said. She denied having anything to do with him or wanting to have anything to do with him.

I was satisfied. Then I turned to those two men and asked what Mexican wanted in claim.

They answered that he wanted a certain horse I had got from a dead friend, another horse, a saddle, and a Winchester.

I told them that I would not part with that first horse. It was dear to me. I told them I would give them another just as good.

Atsaci answered, "We want that horse or none."

I tried three times to get them to agree on another horse, but they refused. Finally, I told them, "All right, if you take that horse, you get nothing but that horse. It is enough." I had something else to say, too, and I told Atsaci I wanted to tell him something after we finished.

"What?" he said.

I told him not to forget that he was married to two of my "daughters" (they were daughters of my brother). In these words I spoke to him. "If I accept these terms, and you insist on that horse, you can have it. But if you do, you will lose your two wives. I will take back my daughters from you. You are my son-in-law and yet you are not caring what you say; you are trying to get the horse I love."

Then Mangy Coat broke in right away. He said that Atsaci wasn't thinking about what he was saying. He said they would agree to take another horse.

That was what I wanted. Atsaci was silent. He was ashamed. He was really older than I was and he had forgotten about being my son-in-law in that way. Then I asked him what he had to say to the agreement.

He mumbled, "Well, it's up to Mangy Coat. He is older than I am. It's up to him to have the say." Well, I told them I was willing to do the right thing, so I gave them a gray mare, a bay horse, a good saddle and a gun. Later on that gray horse got to be a very good racer and won lots of money.[14]))))))

The role of intermediaries in damage-seeking actions is the most

[14] Hoebel, *The Political Organization and Law-Ways of the Comanche Indians,* 56–57.

229

interesting theoretical aspect of Comanche law. A really strong man pressed his own cause. Yet in the nature of the Comanche scheme of things, the wife-stealer or adulterer was frequently a man of more aggressive courage than the husband he victimized. Men who had brothers to rally to their side could muster their aid as a matter of course. For some men of weak families this was not always possible, however, although if they failed to collect even token damages, neither they nor the tribe would consider them worthy of being Comanches. It was socially required that they act, yet by themselves they could not do so. In the crude legal genius of the Comanches this was recognized as an impossible demand upon some men; hence they devised a way out that could be used without disgrace. Any man of faint heart could call upon a great warrior to act as his surrogate, his champion at law. His response was assured; no warrior of reputation would have it imputed that he was afraid of any other man. He stood ready to pit his prestige against the aggressor on behalf of any weaker plaintiff. He received no fee or compensation in kind for risking his life in intervention. The *nanɛwɔk*ə that he wrested from the defendant went to the plaintiff. The reward of the champion was the praise of the people and added luster to his name.

The case of Red Crooked Nose (ɛ*kamuɾawa*), as given by She Invites Her Relatives, reveals the champion in action; it also displays the suicidal *beau geste* of the Comanche who died honorably against the enemy, so to recover in perpetuity the prestige he had lost when outfaced within the tribe. He also set a check against unreasonable overpenalizing of future defenders. Comanche law was law with limits, as is any good law system.

《 《 《 The wife of Red Crooked Nose absconded with a young, good-looking warrior. In the raiding party were four other men and another woman. For two years the pair remained away, and no one in the main camp knew where they were living. But one day some hunters found their camp and reported it to Red Crooked Nose. He was determined to get his wife back, but he had few war deeds to his credit. So he asked a brave, well-known warrior to go with him. The warrior consented to go.

When they reached the absconder's camp, the woman saw them

coming and ran to her young husband, saying that she wanted to stay with him. But when the young man saw Red Crooked Nose's champion he said, "Against such a man I have no chance to keep you."

So they met outside the tipi. Red Crooked Nose picked up a quiver of arrows belonging to the young man, but his wife told him, "Put them down. You can't do any better with them than their owner can."

Food was offered the newcomers, and they stated their mission. They said that they would accept no damages in place of the woman, that Red Crooked Nose needed her to care for their young child. So the young man ordered her horse brought, upon which was a good saddle, a silver-braided bridle, and good blankets. He told the woman to dress up. He told her, "Take everything nice that belongs to you. This old man can't get things like these for you."

She gathered all her belongings, including fifteen horses. She was ready to start back with them, but she cried pitifully to have to leave her young lover. After they started, she lagged behind sullenly.

They had gone. The young absconder broke camp. He mounted and rode on past them. As his horses ran by, Red Crooked Nose killed one of them and called upon his party to take the meat he had shot for them. Then the owner of the dead horse scorned him, "My feelings aren't hurt. I can get plenty of horses—like the grass, so many!" and he rode on.

He knew that Red Crooked Nose would not have dared to kill his horse without the warrior as protector.

While stopping one night, they heard that enemies were coming. The women were sent on. The men prepared for war. Before the battle started, the young man donned his best war paraphernalia. With his feathers flying, he rode past the camp of Red Crooked Nose. He fought conspicuously and was killed.

The champion saw him go down.

He called to Red Crooked Nose, saying, "It was we who caused him to be killed. I know you are a coward, but you have to go and walk in front of the enemy to protect us while I carry off his body."

Thus they took the young man off the field and put his body on a horse. When the woman saw his body brought back, she tore her dress apart, slashed her body all over with her knife, and cut her hair off short. She embraced his body and wanted to throw her jewelry away in mourning. But the people pulled her away, telling her to keep it in remembrance of him.

Red Crooked Nose and his champion rode up and mourned him. Then he was wrapped in blankets and buried. The camp broke up and continued on its way.[15] » » »

In a few rare instances an inversion of the institution of the champion was employed, as in the case of the husband who was so afraid of the warrior who stole his wife that he sent an *old woman* to try to get his wife back for him. The absconder said he was going to keep the woman, but he sent back a horse loaded with goods in her place.[16]

Whether by force or by insinuating himself upon the grace of the great aggressor, Comanche law and custom guaranteed compensation to a husband, if not necessarily the return of his wife.

For murder, however, there was no adjudication or compromise. Indeed, the murder of a fellow tribesman was most unusual, but it sometimes happened. In such an event, the *lex taliones* was invoked; the punishment of the murderer was primarily the concern of the murdered man's relatives. The case was not closed until the kin of the dead man had taken the life of the murderer. But the privilege of a revenge killing might not be recognized by the kin of the murderer. Kinsmen could legally strike back.

However, kin organization was weak; the principle of kinship liability was not sufficiently pronounced to result in feud. There was no ruthless taking of life of whoever happened to be related to the murderer. The kin feeling was strong enough, however, to induce the kin of the murderer to protect him for some time. As long as vigilance was maintained, an attempt on the life of the murderer was unlikely, for legal right usually gave way to determined resistance. In actuality it was extremely unlikely that a murder resulted in a deadly clash between groups of kin. Tribal consciousness checked a possible internecine war. But note that the responsibility for obtaining justice rested with the relatives and friends of the dead. This is the first principle of collective liability.

15 *Ibid.*, 62–63.
16 *Ibid.*, 53.

A group might intervene to stop a fight, yet it had no legal authority to do so. The offended party, if disposed to compromise, had the privilege of accepting a commutation and releasing the murderer, according to David G. Burnet's observation in 1824.[17] This was seldom the case, however, and by mid-century, if our informants are correct, it was out of the question. Comanche law was hardening through the decades in this one respect. The murderer might flee the camp to another band and thereby escape vengeance for an indefinite period, if he was lucky. Whether or not any kind of settlement was reached, the man who had done the killing was usually more or less ostracized by his fellows. It made no difference how prominent the man might have been or how good his family, should he shed the blood of a fellow tribesman, a stigma was cast over his family and his relatives shared in the disgrace. The matter was not only talked about, but might even blight the lives of his children after his death.

Those who committed murder were often men of great bravery whose success in war and whose standing in the tribe had made them somewhat arrogant and impatient of those who did not do as they demanded. Other men committed murder in revenge.

In Comanche law the killing of a murderer by the kinsmen of the victim was a privileged act. *It did not lead to feud.* A killing called for a counter-killing. And there it stopped. The society at large and the kin of the murderer also recognized and granted the privilege-right of the execution of the murderer by the hand of his victim's brothers. This made it a truly legal sanction. No single case contravening this norm in action is remembered by any Comanche informant. The Comanches in this remarkable (in the light of the usual feudal tendencies of primitives) self-imposed restraint raised this aspect of their law to a higher than ordinary level for people of their general cultural attainments.

Favorite horses were so endowed with personality that killing a man's favorite horse was akin to killing his brother. The owner might, and sometimes did, kill the horse-slayer in return.[18]

A wrong committed by one member of a kin group against an-

[17] Burnet, "American Aborigines, Indians of Texas," *loc. cit.*, Vol. I (May 15, 1824), 154.

[18] Cf. Hoebel, *The Political Organization and Law-Ways of the Comanche Indians,* 68–72.

other individual within the same group was not punishable in the same way as a wrong done by an out-grouper. Public opinion might be strongly antagonistic to the wrongdoer, but the settlement of even murder was not considered a matter for "legal" interference by society. Therefore, murder was essentially a wrong and only vaguely a crime. The family group or kin could punish a member of their own group. There does not appear to have been any definite custom. What happened inside the kin group was the business of nobody outside the group; and inside the group, the way of handling a situation depended largely on personality and temperament.

One variation of the in-group character of in-group action was the privilege-right of the husband to kill his wife. For this, retaliation appears to have been abnormal. The legal position of woman was largely that of chattel, and upon marriage she passed from the original family to the husband. That the kinship group showed no inclination to retaliate when a husband killed his wife—their genetic relative— can mean nothing else than a true relinquishment of the kinship bond upon marriage in favor of a supreme marital bond. The kin of the erring wife might plead with the husband or offer him gifts to prevent the killing, but there was nothing to compel him to accept them and forego meting out punishment. Furthermore, society recognized the right of a brother to kill his sister who, disregarding the recognized social pattern of brother-sister avoidance, came into his presence in violation of his wishes. The brother-in-law of Kills Something shot his sister for such an offense.[19] Apparently, in such a case the killer suffered no social disgrace.

The privilege-right of a husband to kill his wife was paralleled by his privilege to handle her most cruelly in an attempt to force her to name a suspected lover. He could take her out to a lonely spot and choke her until she informed. Or he might prefer to hold her prone over a fire, slowly lowering her closer and closer to the flames, until she in anguish confessed and named her lover. There was no device in Comanche law by which a husband with a grievance could seek an impartial judgment on the alleged male miscreant in the case. Guilt had to be certain before the legal suit could begin. When there was doubt as to the facts, the hapless women were the goats.

[19] Informant: Kills Something.

Men also killed their wives at times when they suffered chronic ailments and medicine cures had failed. A case is reported of a chief who cut the throat of his wife, who had been ill for a long time, to avoid the inconvenience of caring for her. After making "medicine of preparation" to fit her for a happy reception in the land of spirits, he took her life, though mourning her untimely death. Such deeds were rare, however.

In spite of the legal right of a husband to kill his wife, a man who killed his wives too recklessly was considered "mean" by the people. Yet, if he were insensitive to such disapproval, and particularly if he were brave enough to maintain his status through coups, there was little to stop him, except that new wives became more difficult to get. On the other hand, attempts of wives on the lives of husbands were rare indeed.

Of acts taking on a criminal tinge there was only one category—excessive sorcery. Among other Plains tribes violation of the communal buffalo-hunt rules, i.e., going out to hunt alone or beating the signal for the mass charge, was one of the most severe public offenses. The military society police in charge of the hunts were wont to handle any such miscreant roughly. But the Comanches were the great exception.

Ralph Linton has suggested that a superabundance of bison on the Southern Plains made formal police sanctions functionally unnecessary for the Comanches; however, the historical evidence cited earlier indicates that food was not always easy to come by. However this may be, it is quite evident that the Comanches felt no need to make a crime of violation of the rules of the communal hunt. Furthermore, unlike the other Plains tribes, who felt the need and also had an admirably suited mechanism at hand for fulfillment of the need, the Comanches with their Shoshonean background possessed no military societies. They let the matter ride.

Sorcery that got out of hand was another matter. The Comanches were only slightly plagued by witchcraft. As Ruth Benedict once observed, "Sorcery is a fear-projection, and the Comanches were not ridden by fear."[20] Ralph Linton has emphatically reiterated that only old men, who could no longer compete on a warrior basis, turned to

[20] In conversation with Hoebel.

black magic as a means of defending their positions when their physical prowess had failed.[21] Ideally, a Comanche male who had passed beyond fighting age should have emulated the peace chief in behavior. Most men relaxed and did so. A few whose egos were too strong did not; from medicine men they transformed themselves into evil medicine men.

It was not necessary that they learn any new formulae of black magic to achieve their evil purposes. All they had to do was to direct their once-good powers to antisocial ends. Instead of healing the sick, they used their powers against victims of their jealous spleen to bring them sickness and death.

"The life of a young man was very dangerous," said Breaks Something in discussing sorcery. "If he hung around the wives of a medicine man, he would be jealous and paralyze the young man's legs."

"My grandfather had four wives, but none of them ever ran away or got into trouble," observed Rhoda Greyfoot in a reflective mood. "He was a great medicine man, and other men were too much afraid of him to bother his wives."

In the youth of Herman Greyfoot, his band harbored a "crazy young man, who was harmless, just wandering about on foot; he never rode a horse." He lost his mind "because he paid too much attention to the wife of a medicine man, who witched him."

As the young warriors expressed their rivalry in coup-counting, older medicine men expressed theirs in occasional formal medicine jousts. There is extant among the Comanches a legendary account of one such "battle of sorcerers."

《 《 《 Arapaho and Cheyenne medicine men used to use their power in an evil way. Once, when the Comanches and Cheyennes were camped together, the Cheyennes pointed out a medicine man who was using his power to cause deaths.

A Comanche medicine man heard about this, and he decided to go and see the Cheyenne. He got on his war horse, which he rode without a bridle, and rode over to the camp of the Cheyenne medicine man.

The Cheyenne came out and greeted him; he asked him what

21 Linton, "The Comanche," *loc. cit.,* 67.

236

he wanted. The Comanche answered that he wanted to smoke. So the Cheyenne invited him into the tipi and sat down on the north side after putting the Comanche on the south, next to the sun.

Then the Cheyenne got his long pipe. He filled it with tobacco, and lit it with a coal from the fire burning in the center of his lodge.

"How should I pass this pipe to you?" he asked his visitor.

"Oh, any way is all right," the Comanche answered, as he took it with both his hands. He smoked, inhaling four times. On the fourth draw the Cheyenne poison went right into him. He could feel it.

He blew in the pipe before handing it back to his Cheyenne host. Then he rubbed his own belly, and blew a yellowhammer feather out of his mouth and into his hand.

"What does this mean?" he asked the Cheyenne. "I found this in the stem of your pipe."

"Huh, I don't know anything about that," was the answer that came back. "You may do anything you want with it."

Now it was the Cheyenne's turn to smoke. He drew three puffs. On the fourth puff he felt a pain in his side. He wiggled and blew. Out of his mouth and into his hand came an eagle feather.

"What do you mean by this?" he demanded of his guest.

"Why, I don't know anything about that," came the innocent answer from the Comanche. "That must be your feather; it's your pipe."

"Well, here, I give this feather to you." The Comanche's turn to smoke came again. He smoked three times. On the fourth smoke he felt a pain, and he blew out a black bug.

"What is this?"

"Why, I don't know," his host answered. "It must be yours."

"No, its not mine. It must be yours; this pipe belongs to you."

Now the Cheyenne smoked again. On the fourth puff he blew out a tarantula.

"What is this?" he asked in wonder. "It must belong to you."

"Oh, no, that bug isn't mine. That is your pipe you are smoking. That bug must belong to you."

Then the Comanche took his fourth turn with the pipe. He smoked three times. On the fourth puff he felt a terrible pain, and he blew out a cockleburr. The Cheyenne said he did not know a thing about it.

The Comanche medicine man handed the pipe back to him for his fourth turn. This time, on his fourth puff, a barrel cactus lodged in the throat of the evil Cheyenne medicine man. It lodged there. He blew and blew, but he could not get it out.

"Well, this has been a nice day," said the Comanche. Then he mounted his horse and went home.

When he was back at his lodge, he heard cries arising from the Cheyenne camp. The medicine man had died; he had found a medicine man with better power than he had; he had died of the cactus in his throat.

The next day the Cheyennes brought the Comanche medicine man a horse loaded with presents. They were thankful to him for killing their bad medicine man.[22]   »   »   »

As a note of caution the reader is reminded that this is a Comanche and not a Cheyenne story. As such it projects Comanche attitudes upon the Cheyennes. The Cheyennes knew sorcery, but it was an exceedingly minor factor in their lives—more so than in the case of the Comanches. The Cheyennes had smoking tournaments, but only for coup-counting bouts. Cheyenne old men inverted the warrior ideal of their youths to try to outdo each other in burlesquing war honors by boasting of "dishonorable" deeds. But they did not engage in sorcerers' rivalry.

The Cheyenne old men could laugh serenely at themselves, because their place in life was secure. The Comanches, who never achieved lasting security of personal prestige, could not stomach self-ridicule. They turned the coup bout into the sorcerers' duel for old men.

Most Comanche sorcery was, of course, not done in open contest. A sorcerer simply willed an illness upon a victim with his power, or he shot in a feather or other thing secretly. His victim could be an object of sexual jealousy or merely a rival medicine man toward whom he bore a grudge. Or it could be a woman who had at one time rejected him. A sorcerer might also use his power to kill a man in order to get his wife.[23] In a few cases the sorcerer had nothing against his victim of which he was consciously aware. It was simply that his

[22] Informant: Breaks Something.
[23] Informant: Kills Something.

238

Quanah Parker and one of his wives, in 1892
Courtesy Bureau of American Ethnology

Quanah Parker's children, in 1892
Courtesy Bureau of American Ethnology

power had shown him a victim in a dream, and it was believed, if this occurred, that the sorcerer had to kill the person or his power would kill him instead.

The sorcerer would be revealed in the diagnosis of a medicine man when he was called in to cure. "When a feather is shot into a person, a medicine man can see just like reading a newspaper who put it there." When the sorcerer was announced, it was usual for the brothers of the sick person to pay him a visit in order to ask him to remove the power. In most of the specific cases of which we have accounts, the sorcerer denied his guilt. Then his petitioners either went away and engaged their own medicine man to counteract the witchcraft or they threatened bodily injury to the sorcerer. If their curing doctor was strong enough and was willing to go on with the case, he turned the power back, and the sorcerer died of his own malefactions.

The sorcerer who maintained his innocence, when threatened with force, in each recorded case immediately forestalled further legal steps by throwing the whole affair over to supernatural judgment. He swore his innocence with a conditional curse. If he was guilty he was killed by powers of the Sun and the Earth. If he survived, his innocence was accepted as proved.

The sin for which he died was perjury before the supernatural powers. The penalty was not imposed by man, but by the "gods." Isolated instances were not, therefore, legal offenses.

Excessive and repeated sorcery was another matter. It built up a condition of social anxiety that led to a fairly dispassionate and quite deliberate execution of the sorcerer by general consent. In two instances, sorcerers were lured into ambush on the pretext of engaging them to make cures. In one of these cases the sorcerer was assassinated by two delegates chosen by the people. In the other, he was shot just as he left the tipi.

In a third case, the members of the Those Who Move Often band were afraid to assault a dangerous sorcerer, so they contrived a successful ruse to cause him to break his tabus. Thus they destroyed him.[24]

Many forms of social conduct which are considered abnormal in

[24] Hoebel, *The Political Organization and Law-Ways of the Comanche Indians,* Case 23, 89–90.

239

our own society were not considered criminal by the Comanches. Their attitudes toward illegitimacy, which seems to have been rare, show no vindictiveness, although the feeling prevailed that every child should have a recognized father.

Premarital sex relations were common, but in case a child was born as a result, the father usually married the mother. The father could claim the child at any time.

Incest, which consisted of sexual relations between two persons within three degrees of relationship, was tabu, but there was no legal control. The few men who were known to have committed incest were called *pɔsa,* "crazy." Beyond this, there was only informal ostracism—and more sneering references. Thus, when Pointing to the Rising Sun married his sister's beautiful daughter, Wide Feet, his own sister refused to address him as *monapə,* "son-in-law," which would have been the respectful and proper thing to do, had it been a proper marriage. The People did not let it pass, however; they made it a point always to refer to him, her elder brother, as her son-in-law.

The Comanches actually had strong feelings against incest— brother-sister avoidance was enjoined on this basis—but they felt no need to impose strong sanctions against it. Most men were too concerned with the maintenance of their personal prestige to mar it with such an act. And perhaps more important is the fact that Comanche supernaturals were in no sense projected images of a rewarding and punishing father. Incest was not a sin against the gods any more than it was a crime. There was no need to punish the offender in order to protect the community from supernatural wrath. The act remained an offense against good taste, nothing more.

Rape, except upon captives, occurred infrequently and was not part of the general pattern. Sleep-crawling by either boy or girl was legitimate if the recipient did not object to quiet night visits. But before the advent of the white race's demoralizing influence, Comanche women rated high in chastity.

Theft was so unusual that no provision was made for it in the legal scheme. Consequently, it must fall into the vague class of unapproved, abnormal acts which were outside the scope of the law. Generosity was so highly valued that he who had need of something had only to indicate his desire, and he would receive it as a gift.

Among settled peoples with fixed property and diversified economics, the institution of land tenure, the disposition and inheritance of property, the treatment of chattels, and the obligations of contract form the most important aspects of civil law. Yet among the Comanches these had almost no significance. The Comanches had no concept of land value. As herding hunters, land was a matter of unconcern for them, being held neither individually, jointly, nor communally. One may speak of their country as being merely communally occupied. There are no records of any disputes between the bands over hunting grounds. The external boundaries of the Comanchería were not firmly fixed, but vaguely felt. Allies and friends were welcome to hunt and visit, but other outsiders entered on peril of their lives.

Wealth for the Comanches centered largely in horses, as has already been shown; horses were individually owned by both men and women. They were acceptable as a medium of exchange and could be used as payment of obligations in damage suits. Women, too, might be listed in the category of chattel property—first of father and brother and later of husband. Dogs must also be included under the heading of private property. They abounded, but after the acquisition of the horse had little economic value or importance save as camp scavengers and sentries. The idea of liability for the acts of animals did not exist. There was no recompense for a dog bite; nor could damages be collected for injuries received from a kicking horse.

The Comanches owned a number of captives who were chattel property until adopted as brothers by their owners if they were boys or married by their captors if they were girls. There were a few personal slaves held by blood covenant by individual warriors. They were generally captives, Mexicans forming the bulk of the number. A blood ceremony, according to Josiah Gregg, was performed with blood taken from a vein on the back of the captive's hand or arm. The ceremony was repeated whenever ownership of the slave changed. The slave had the right of life, food, and protection, since no one dared molest the property of another, and the owner could sell or transfer him at any time to whomever he chose.[25] There are indications that the Comanches captured and sold slaves merely as articles

25 Gregg, *op. cit.,* 434.

of trade, and poverty-stricken Shoshones often sold their children to their more prosperous Comanche cognates.

Some captives became naturalized, free members of the tribe, even respected warriors. The changed status was recognized by a solemn ceremony only after the Comanches felt they ran no risk by such a step. According to the customary procedure, the pipe was passed around the council circle. After smoking, all stood up, each placing his right hand over the heart, then raising it toward the sun, repeating the process while marching around the circle. Then the captive was led before the chief to take the oath, wherein he promised faithfully to perform all the duties of a Comanche warrior, to help provide for, protect, and obey the chief in all things in both peace and war. The person taking the oath was then given a Comanche name and was required to select a family and be adopted by a brother.

Objects of material culture were personally owned, but the test of ownership was not production so much as use. Clothing was made, for example, by the women, but was owned by the person who wore it. The medicine formula was privately owned, but could be transferred. War honors were a sort of property which might on occasion be transferred, but rather as a mark of esteem and not for economic consideration. Objects jointly used, like the tipi, were usually considered to be the property of the husband.

At the time the Comanches were confined upon the reservation, their practices in regard to inheritance were in a chaotic condition. Apparently the whole problem of inheritance was so new to their culture that no established norms had evolved. The Plateau tribes from whom the Comanches had separated themselves when they entered the plains were accustomed to destroy all a man's property at his death. This included clothing, weapons, saddles, tools, war paraphernalia, and horses customarily ridden by the deceased, and in ancient times even the wife. In the early days, the Comanches also sometimes killed the favorite wives of a deceased warrior. Articles of intimate personal use were buried with the corpse; other less important articles were burned. This destruction entailed few hardships and no serious economic loss, since the property was limited to clothing and a few weapons and utensils. When the Comanches acquired horses, inheritance became a serious problem. To slaughter the entire herd at the death of the owner was prejudicial to tribal interest, for, since the animals were freely lent, several people might be dependent upon one man's herd for their mounts, and they would be seriously handicapped in hunting and in war if the animals were killed. Also, in case of food shortage, horses were food. By 1870 it had become customary to kill only the deceased's favorite mount and to distribute the remainder of his horses among the surviving relatives and friends. No absolute rule governing this distribution had been developed, with the result that there was often hard feeling among the heirs. The culture apparently was moving toward a settlement of the problem through bequests and recognition that certain relatives and close friends had the right to take their choice of the property, but the lines were not yet clear.[26]

Although there seems to have been no absolute consistency in rules of disposal, property appears to have passed to the widow, upon whom the obligation to share with others was imposed. She could not retain all the property herself. The first outside claim could be that of the deceased's best friend. He was entitled to the favorite horse, if it was not slaughtered at the grave. During the later period, a man often expressed the desire that his horse be given to a specified friend rather than slaughtered. Surplus horses went to the wife, father, mother, brothers, and other relatives according to the degree of relationship. Outsiders who had no personal claim to share in the estate could establish an obligatory claim either by providing property of their own to be buried with the person or by being helpers in mourning who "wailed a dead person until they received sufficient gifts from the man's relatives to stop."[27] If death occurred in battle, the amount of wailing and the value of goods demanded in payment might be increased.

Contract occurs when a party assumes a definite and limited obligation by virtue of agreement. The contractural arrangement is ended when the obligation has been fulfilled. Included among Comanche contractural agreements were the transfer of medicine powers, curing, the obligation to lead a revenge war party, occult prophecy, sorcery for hire, and hiring a specialist to help in the making of material objects such as arrows, saddles, and tipis. In the making of most con-

[26] Linton, *The Study of Man*, 297.
[27] Neighbors, "The Naüni or Comanches of Texas," *loc. cit.*, 133–34.

tracts there were certain solemn steps customarily followed. The most common method of sealing the contract was by offering smoke. If the second party took the smoke, it was an acceptance and the deal was closed. The failure of one of the parties to meet the terms of the contract terminated the contractural obligations of the other. In cases where such a procedure worked an injustice on one of the parties, the legal procedure followed the same general pattern as in other cases of disputes—if the aggrieved party felt inclined to act. He was, however, under no social pressure to proceed, as was the man who had suffered impingement on his rights as a husband. The contract situation rarely involved prestige rivalry and did not contain the spark plug that ignited legal action as in the highly charged adultery and wife-absconding situations.

Warfare

THE motives which led the Comanches to go to war were plunder, love of fighting, a desire for glory as a means of achieving personal status, eagerness for revenge, and a determination to take and afterwards to hold free from all trespassers, both white and red men, the hunting grounds of the South Plains. Their bravery and their desire to win prestige for themselves inspired them to take many risks. Prior to the introduction of the horse, Plains warfare was sporadic and not bloody; but the introduction of the horse furnished all the Plains tribes a new and strong motive for war, for by war men might acquire something of great value and they now had the mobility with which to strike at each other. Concomitantly with the horse came another new factor: the pressure of the whites on the eastern frontier, setting in motion a chain reaction of tribal displacements that caused group after group to fight for a place under the western sun. War became the pattern of life; the military cult became the ideal of the aspiring young man. The old peace chief ideal still survived, but it was destined to be overshadowed by the ideal personality type of warrior.

War honors provided the basis of the whole system of rank and social status in Comanche society. Consequently, the life of the male came to be centered around warfare and raiding. The men were all warriors. War was regarded as the noblest of pursuits, one which every man should follow; and from earliest youth boys were taught to excel in it. They were taught that success in war brought in its train the respect and admiration of the men, women, and children of the tribe, and that the most worthy virtue for a man was bravery. They were taught that death in battle, aside from being glorious, protected one from all the miseries which threatened later life and were inevitable to old age.

The Comanches, in conformity with the general Plains pattern, adhered to institutionalized procedure in giving social recognition of war honors: the practice of counting coup. The coup was an individual exploit, made in any contact with the enemy, after it had been socially and publicly recognized as worthy of distinction. In some respects it was a rough equivalent of an official citation after a modern engagement. It required more bravery to hit an adversary with a spear or a war club than to pierce him at a distance with an arrow or a bullet. Since the quality most highly esteemed was courage, striking an enemy thus gave ground for an honored coup, while long-distance killing did not necessarily do so. To scalp an enemy was not especially creditable, for anyone could scalp a dead man; hence scalping was only of secondary importance. But if the scalping were done under danger, it was considered worthy. How much of the scalp a Comanche took depended upon circumstances. He preferred to take the whole scalp, but if he were pressed for time or the situation were very dangerous, he seized only what he could get. The scalp was a trophy, proof of success to be used in the Victory Dance, and it was also desirable as a decorative fringe for shirts, shields, and tomahawks.

The bravest act that could be performed was to count coup on a live enemy. When hunting, if a dangerous animal was killed or wounded, boys and young men might race to see who could be the first to touch it, just as women sometimes raced to see who could be the first to touch the first fallen animal in a buffalo hunt. The stealing of tethered horses from within a hostile camp ranked as a very high honor, but it was not so valued as striking a fallen enemy who lay near his own lines or as drawing blood from an enemy in hand-to-hand combat. In addition to the standardized honors, any audacious deed performed against the enemy could be claimed as a coup by the Comanches.

Contemporary Comanches tell a tall tale of two warriors who

246

went on a coup-seeking expedition to see which was the better man. They traveled until they came to a Ute camp.

"Tonight I'll go in to see what I can do," said one.

After dark, he drew his blanket over his head and sauntered into the Ute encampment. From within one of the lodges he heard the songs of a hand game in progress. Protected by his disguise, he walked right through the door to join the spectators. Nobody paid any attention to him. Casually and slowly moving about, he touched one after another of all the Utes in the lodge. When he had touched them all, he strolled out and rejoined his friend.

"He had counted coup on twenty enemies at one time. It was a great deed," said Post Oak Jim.

His friend was put to a real challenge. They traveled on, it is said, until late the next day they came to a lone ranch homestead.

"Tonight I'll go in to see what I can do," said the second Comanche. When the lights were out in the cabin, he crept forward. He entered the little house and found the rancher and his wife sleeping together in their bed. With all the stealth he would have used in untethering a picketed horse before the lodge of an enemy chief, he lifted the sleeping woman from the side of her unsuspecting husband. Without wakening her, he brought her to the side of his friend. Together they took her back to the main camp. The People said this was the greatest coup of all. No Comanche had ever done anything like that before!

It sometimes happened that a man, if he had been ill for long without hope of recovery or if some misfortune of such significance that he no longer wished to live had befallen him, determined to give his life by some daring act of bravery against the enemy. This was suicide, but a socially recognized way of ending one's life in a most honorable manner. He went out in one grand coup.

A daring exploit was not of itself in the strictest sense a coup. Rather it was the raw material for one. If unrecognized, the deed remained only a matter of individual memory, for only recognition in due "legal" form turned the deed into a coup. It often happened that an exploit claimed by an individual was unwitnessed, not believed, or claimed by one or more other warriors. The man who believed he had a right to claim a coup made a strong fight for recog-

247

nition of his deed. Other than securing witnesses or presenting circumstantial evidence in support of his claim, he might take a formal oath that what he claimed was true. It is evident that in the confusion of battle a man might believe himself entitled to honors claimed by others. At the first opportunity after the fight, the chief called the warriors together, preferably before they arrived at the main camp.[1] But the procedure varied from band to band and according to circumstances. One account has the leading warriors seat themselves in a semicircle. Near the opening of the circle was placed a buffalo hide. Some of the Indians danced to the beat of drums. A warrior rode into the circle, stopped suddenly, and plunged his spear in the buffalo hide. Music and dancing stopped, and the warrior under oath narrated in detail the circumstances connected with the deed which he claimed as a coup. When he had finished, he dismounted and joined his comrades in the semicircle, and the dancing and drumming were renewed. Then a second warrior was called upon. The same procedure was continued until each claimant for honors had told his story. Those seated in the semicircle either publicly recognized the deed as a coup or rejected the claim.

A scout who was out alone sometimes ran unexpectedly into an enemy, perhaps killing or counting coup on one. In such a situation there was no one to witness his deed; it was necessary for him to attest its truth. If he was a member of the Water Horse band, he did so by taking the buffalo-chip oath. On returning to the band, he signaled that he had important news. Before entering the camp, he waited for all the warriors to assemble. They all lined up in a row behind three or four buffalo chips, which were stacked on end, tipi wise. When they were ready, the scout rode in and speared a chip for each man he had killed or struck. With each blow he cried, *"A:he!"* If he had counted no coup, he merely walked around the pile and then scattered it as a sign that the news he was bringing was true. The false asseveration of a coup brought bad luck and death.

The Comanches recognized two coups struck on the same victim by different persons. Subsequent coups received no credit. The Cheyennes counted coup on an enemy three times, while the Arapahos touched four times. In battle, members of one tribe counted coup

[1] Informant: Yellowfish.

248

without reference to what had been done by those of another allied tribe in the same fight. Recognition of plural coups on the same victim was, of course, an efficient way of providing enough coups to meet the cultural demands of the society. It is worth noting that the warlike Comanches engaged sufficient enemies to make unnecessary as great an inflation of the currency of war prestige as that of their neighboring tribes, but in later days they devised a method to spread their coups around. The first man to touch a fallen enemy with his weapon or hand uttered the cry, *"A:he"* ("I claim it"), thus receiving credit equal to or greater than that which accrued to the man who had done the actual killing. If a bow or a gun had been used to bring down the enemy, the second coup-counter received greater honor for his deed than did the slayer himself.[2]

Opinions are somewhat at variance as to why the Plains Indians counted coup. Robert Lowie emphasizes the play aspect of this phase of warfare. From one angle, he says, Plains Indian warfare "loomed as an exciting pastime played according to established rules, the danger lending zest to the game. The primary goal was to score, only the loss of kindred prompting reprisals on a major scale. Whenever men fight for glory, practical ends become secondary."[3] George Bird Grinnell sees in it a cultural survival of the old feeling that prevailed before the Indians had missiles, when they were obliged to fight hand-to-hand with sticks, clubs, and stones. Under such conditions only those who actually came to grips with the enemy could inflict injury and gain glory. "After arrows came into use," he continues, "it may still have been thought a braver and finer thing to meet the enemy hand-to-hand than to kill him with an arrow at a distance."[4] The game aspect and the survival elements are both a part of the complex, but more important is the functional adjustment of an institution to a social end. The deeds honored are in good part the kind of deeds that toughen a warrior to stand when he is needed, and the numberless opportunities afforded for coup-counters to boast of their exploits were strong ego builders and the sort of social device that could not but encourage men to fight and fight recklessly.

[2] Hoebel, *The Political Organization and Law-Ways of the Comanche Indians,* 22.
[3] R. H. Lowie, *An Introduction to Cultural Anthropology,* 222.
[4] Grinnell, *The Cheyenne Indians,* II, 36.

A coup was regarded as a type of incorporeal property, which could be transferred by the owner to a comrade in public ceremony. The practice may have emerged only since the advent of the reservation, when the restrictions upon fighting imposed by the whites made the coup a commodity of scarcity, so that the ingenious Comanches devised the transfer technique. It was done in public in order that the recipient's right to the honor would be witnessed and duly recognized. It was considered best if the giver of the honors announced a dance, inviting all members of the band to be present. After the dance had continued for a time, the host, walking to the center of the ring, called a halt. There, in the presence of all the people, he narrated the details of a coup, swearing to the powers that the deed was his, and concluded by saying, "I now give this to my brother, ———." The man named then stood and claimed the deed, with the following words, "I now take this deed. Sun, Father, Moon above, and Earth, Mother, witness that it is mine." The drum was struck a resounding blow. If those present gave their assent, the transfer of the coup was complete. The coup was bestowed only upon brave men; it could be neither sold nor inherited.[5]

The prosecution of warfare was a matter of individual discretion. Any Comanche was theoretically eligible to lead a war or raiding party, for there was no legal authority to restrain him. Although a vision was not deemed necessary as a sanction for starting a war party, it was in many cases the effective stimulus. Should a man inexperienced in warfare and without an established reputation attempt to organize and lead a party, he would be unlikely to secure a following. A young warrior was usually content to serve under others until he had gained experience. He must know when and how to attack and how to retreat without loss of men when the fighting went against him. On the other hand, a man whose qualities of bravery and leadership had been demonstrated in combat seldom found any difficulty in mustering a following when he announced his intention to go on the warpath. Nobody would risk leading a party without power. He may have received it through a vision or a dream. When a man declared that he knew how, he certainly felt that he did, else he would be afraid to say so. It was for each individual to determine for himself whether his own and the leader's power was working for success.

Ordinarily, a man contemplating leading out a war or raiding party made medicine to determine when and where the raid should take place. Then he called his friends and some older men into his lodge to discuss the matter. After they had eaten, a pipe was filled and the host made known his plans. Those who did not care to join the enterprise let the pipe pass without smoking.

If the leader had received sufficient encouragement from his guardian spirit and his comrades, he put on his war paint and all his war paraphernalia. During the afternoon he began to drum and to sing war songs in his tipi. Some of the men going with him were already prepared, and it was only necessary for them to go over and join the leader in the drumming and singing. About sundown the party mounted their horses and paraded through the village to enlist other volunteers. The parade signified that the party was leaving that night. The warriors paraded the village four times in single file, singing war songs. There were as many parades as there were leaders planning to take out a party. Men who had performed the honorable act of carrying a dismounted or wounded comrade out of battle danger rode double. This was a method of giving public recognition for meritorious service. No onlooker could forget this ever present obligation or the public recognition to a man who had fulfilled it.

When the party was a popular one, men, women, and children turned out to join in the singing and to encourage the warriors. Young maidens sometimes serenaded the lodges of popular warriors whom they wanted to join the party, chanting the victories of ancestors and the valor of contemporaries and imploring or goading them to join.

Both maidens and old women who promoted a successful raiding party expected a horse or other plunder for their efforts. During the period of preparation, shields belonging to volunteers hung by day on racks before the warrior's doorway to absorb the all-powerful medicine of the sun. Each rack was either a lance or a tripod of three lances.[6]

The night before departure, the War Dance was held. If the leader was going forth to avenge the death of a friend, it was also

[5] Informant: That's It.

[6] Informants: Yellowfish, See How Deep the Water Is, Kills Something, and Face Wrinkling Like Getting Old; see also Gregg, *op. cit.*, 436; Babb, *op. cit.*, 107–108; Hoebel, *The Political Organization and Law-Ways of the Comanche Indians*, 24; Burnet, "American Aborigines, Indians of Texas," *loc. cit.*, I (June 5, 1824), 177.

called a Vengeance Dance. The dance did not begin until dark, and it ended in time for the party to take its departure before day, although the Comanches did not rely on dancing to arouse the war spirit of the group as much as some of the other Plains Indians. The tendency of the Comanches to make a decision quickly and to leave the same night as the dance were additional factors tending to eliminate unnecessary details. As darkness settled over the village, the people gathered around a fire, leaving an opening in the circle toward the proposed objective of the party. The volunteers were attired in all their war dress and paint. Only braves leaving on the raid could dance, but each was aided by a woman partner. A dancer might carry a rattle, but it was not essential. The warriors danced when they felt the urge, unless ordered to dance by a whip wielder. Sometimes there was little actual dancing. The spectators formed a circle outside the dancers, and joined in the singing.

The War Dance in some respects compares to the modern college pep rally preceding a football game. Some songs were merely musical and without words. The songs with words were known by most people. Popular love songs, of which there were many, were sung. It is very difficult to render the songs into English without sacrificing the rhythm, but a sample verse of a popular song goes as follows:

> *Going away tonight;*
> *Be gone a long time.*
> *While I'm gone,*
> *I'll be thinking of you.*[7]

The dance would be interrupted at intervals by an old warrior, who approached the drummer and announced that he wanted to tell a story while the dancers rested. Having received recognition, he would recite the details of a coup which he had gained and take an oath that what he told was true. "Sun, Father, you saw me do it. Earth, Mother, you saw me do it. Do not permit me to live until another season, if I speak falsely." When the speaker finished, he was given an enthusiastic ovation: a mingling of war whoops, drum beating, gourd rattling, stamping of feet, and clapping of hands. Be-

[7] Informant: See How Deep the Water Is.

fore the noise subsided, the drummers would strike up the next war song and the dancing would be resumed, shortly to be interrupted again. Dancing warriors might occasionally interrupt the dance to narrate exploits of their own. Finally, the leader spoke of the necessity of the war party and its aim, and ended by appealing to his followers to display their accustomed courage while on the raid, that their people might be proud of them and not consider them cowards.

Shortly afterwards, the leader silently and without ceremony left the dance. The dance continued for a time, but occasionally a warrior and a maiden quietly slipped away into the dark for a few minutes together before parting, for the Comanches enjoined no continence, although they must not be seen leaving together. There might be several parties going out under as many leaders. In such a case, instead of having so many War Dances going at once, each party might end its dance in a short time and make way for another leader and his party. The leader had previously designated a rendezvous outside the village, and after the dance, the warriors returned to their lodges to get their horses and equipment; then silently they stole off to the gathering place. The raid was under way.

Under no circumstances could the War Dance or departure occur in daytime. That was bad medicine. On one occasion a group of warriors held their dance and left during the day. Not a single member of the party returned. The case was never forgotten nor repeated.[8]

Each man who gathered at the rendezvous had provided himself with arms, lasso, food, clothing, a robe if the weather was disagreeable, and horses. The food consisted of dried meat, in sheets or pounded fine, and mesquite meal. Both were very strengthening, packed well, and were convenient to carry. This food was taken only as emergency rations, for they were expected to subsist on the flesh of animals killed along the route.

When the raiders planned a quick thrust at the enemy and a hurried get-away, they left their women, children, and lodges at the main camp and traveled as unencumbered as possible. The leader and men with sacred shields might each take along a woman to help with their equipment, but they seldom exercised the privilege. It was not uncommon, however, for some women to accompany them for the

[8] Informant: Yellowfish.

fun of a little fighting; they could snipe with bows and arrows from the fringe of the fray, although Rhoda Greyfoot says they never went on the "hardest" raids. For a married woman to join up with some man who was going on the warpath was, as has already been shown, the commonest manner of absconding.

When the entire band intended a series of onslaughts upon a distant enemy (three to four hundred miles from headquarters was a commonplace distance for a raid), they not infrequently took women along. The women carried small lodges and a few supplies to set up a temporary camp, the preferred location being one which provided a convenient place from which to strike at the enemy and was at the same time far enough removed to be safe from pursuit. Although the Apaches took their best medicine men along and the Kiowas included in the party a buffalo doctor who had power to heal wounds and an owl doctor with power to tell what was going to happen, the Comanches encouraged their medicine men with the greatest healing power to remain in camp and care for the wounded as they were brought in.[9]

A war party carefully studied and mapped any unfamiliar country that it expected to traverse. All those needing information about the route and the terrain were assembled and instructed by the well-informed elders. After they were seated in a circle, a map was plotted on the ground showing rivers, hills, valleys, water holes, and any other identifying or unusual features. Then a line was drawn to represent the route planned for the first day. From a bundle of sticks, marked consecutively beginning with "one," a stick with a single notch was stuck at the point where the party was to camp at the end of the first day's journey. When the novices had committed this much to memory, the second day's journey was illustrated in the same manner. Instruction continued in similar fashion until it was felt that each man could follow the route satisfactorily. Thus a group could usually traverse without difficulty a region entirely new to members of the party. It is reported that one such instructed party, none of whom were over nineteen and none of whom had ever been in Mexico, were able to travel from their main camp on Brady's creek, Texas, and raid as far as the city of Monterrey without mishap and

9 Lehman, op. cit., 38, 148; Alice Marriott, The Ten Grandmothers, 35.

with no other guidance than the instructions furnished before starting out.[10]

The leader of an organized war party was absolute dictator of all the activities of his followers as long as they remained with the party. The legal governmental powers of the leader have been considered elsewhere, but for the sake of clarity some repetition here is essential. The men obeyed their leader implicitly and willingly. Each knew that a brave leader never asked of his men what he himself would not readily do. Each knew, too, that to disobey might bring disaster on the party. If, on the other hand, disaffection did set in, the disgruntled warrior and those who sided with him merely withdrew to go their own way.

It was the duty of the leader to determine the objective of the raid, to plan the routes, to determine the camping places and the periods of rest, to designate the scouts, to appoint the cook and water carrier, to plan the general strategy of the attack, to divide the booty, and to order a retreat or make a truce with the enemy.

One or two scouts were kept from a one-half to a day's march ahead. A war party rarely traveled at night by choice, and the men rode without much talking, steady and quiet, all intent on where they were going. About midday they stopped to rest and water the horses. At night they camped, preferably in a grove near fresh water. If they were in enemy territory and a hill was available, the war party circled gradually up and around the hill until it reached a camping spot halfway up the hill on the side opposite the direction from which it had approached. The leader sent two sentries to the top of the hill, and the rest of the party slept soundly through the night. An enemy following their trail was exposed on the side of the hill under the view of the sentries in plenty of time to warn the sleeping encampment.

The leader carried a sacred pipe. When the evening meal was over, the pipe was formally filled, lighted and, after the usual offerings to the spiritual powers, passed to each warrior in turn. Then the leader talked to his men, telling them of the country, the best routes, and the safest places of retreat, giving them advice and telling them how

[10] R. I. Dodge, *The Plains of the Great West*, 414, from an account by Pedro Espinosa, a Mexican-Comanche warrior.

they should act. Sometimes they sang. Perhaps before going to sleep the leader sang a spiritual song—a prayer to the guardian spirits for help and wisdom. Occasionally the leader might carry the pipe and have the men dance at night along the route. Ishatai carried the pipe around and had each society dance every night while on the way to Adobe Walls in 1874.[11]

War parties are difficult to distinguish from raiding parties, for the Comanches conducted both in much the same manner. The distinction rested for the most part in the stated objective of the undertaking, although a raiding party, if confronted with enemies, would fight; and a war party was not likely to pass by a chance to make off with horses or booty.

Only the vengeance party moved with a singleness of purpose. The Comanche parent who had lost a son to the enemy "never rested in his mind until he had an enemy scalp to make things even." If he was still of a fighting age, he could seek a scalp or organize his own vengeance raid. But if this was beyond his abilities or if the aggrieved person was a widow who had lost a son or a husband, he or she would take a pipe to a war leader and offer smoke. If he accepted, the war leader bound himself to organize a vengeance expedition. He had a camp crier announce the project to all the camp. "The young people don't care if they get killed on this raid," he cried for all to hear. "They want revenge."

With the taking of a single scalp, the revenge raid accomplished its mission and was inevitably turned back by its leader, even if bigger prospects were near at hand. One scalp was all that was necessary for the Scalp Dance, and this was what they were after.

In their most destructive raids, the Comanche war party proceeded to some convenient point within striking distance of the settlements to be raided and established a temporary camp in which they left most of their supplies, horses, guards, and women. The leader sent out scouts to gather information. If their report was favorable, he informed the warriors of the plan of attack. The party often broke into a number of small bands, and the destructive work was begun. The preferred time was the period following the full of the moon. They

11 Informant: Yellowfish. Yellowfish's father went to Adobe Walls with Ishatai, and afterwards told him the details of the raid many times.

256

never by choice made an offensive attack in the dark; they never raided when the moon was a crescent with the horns pointing upward, for the moon was then "full and running over" and there was the likelihood of rain, after which their trails could be easily traced on the moist earth.[12] They struck swiftly on moonlight nights or surprised undefended, isolated settlers by day when circumstances were favorable, killing or capturing their victims and driving their stolen animals back to their rendezvous, where they were attended until such time as they could return to the main camp. When approaching the camp or settlement, the warriors separated and entered it by pairs or small groups. If an enemy dog barked, the raiders tossed it a piece of meat to quiet it. The older, experienced men cut loose the more valuable horses and led them out, while the younger men gathered up the loose animals. At times it was understood that the horses taken by each man were to be his own; at other times, they were common property to be divided by the leader of the expedition. By means of signals, the raiders kept in touch with one another and would reunite when they had completed their foray or when considerations of safety demanded.

Frequently, of course, the Comanches engaged an enemy prepared to offer resistance. One simple strategy was to send forward a small party on swift horses to lead the enemy into an ambuscade. Sometimes this plan was successful, but often those hidden in ambush were unable to restrain their eagerness and rushed out too soon, causing the stratagem to fail. Although the leader planned the attack, when the battle began each man was free to fight according to the dictates of his own medicine and his personal inclinations.

As a rule the Comanches relied upon surprise, upon the effect of a sudden and furious dash, accompanied by an unearthly, blood-curdling war whoop. They avoided a pitched battle when they were matched by an equal or greater number. They preferred to surprise a much smaller party. If the enemy was not surprised or put to flight at once but stood his ground, the wedge-shaped mass of Comanches quickly assumed battle formation. The wedge turned into the shape of a huge ring or wheel without hub or spokes, whose rim consisted

[12] Julia Estill, "Indian Pictographs near Lange's Mill, Gillespie County, Texas," Texas Folklore Society *Publications*, IV, 105.

of one or more distinct lines of warriors. This ring, winding around and around with machinelike regularity and precision approached nearer and nearer the enemy with each revolution. As a warrior approached the point on the circle nearest the enemy, he dropped into the loop around his horse's neck on the side opposite his target and discharged his arrows from beneath the neck of his horse while traveling at full speed. If his horse was shot down, he generally hit the ground on his feet, and holding his shield in front of him for protection, he shot from beneath it. Such strategy not only provided a difficult target for the enemy, but it gave the Comanches opportunity to reload while riding the circle safely out of danger of enemy fire.

One purpose of the Indian was to draw the fire of the enemy prematurely, and then to charge him while he was reloading. In this type of attack the bow proved not inferior to the musket. For a time the Comanches were eager to get muskets, but their inferiority for this mode of warfare was soon recognized. Muskets had greater range, but a much slower rate of fire, were difficult to load on horseback, and required ammunition which could not always be obtained.[13] Not until the whites adopted the use of the revolver were they able to cope successfully with this type of Indian strategy.

The Comanches never received a charge and rarely met one. If charged, the line immediately in front of the charge broke and melted away, reforming on either flank of the enemy to continue the attack or break again when charged. In one battle with a superior force of Utes the Comanches let the Utes chase them fifty or sixty miles, engaging and disengaging themselves while they traded ground for freedom of action. Occasionally a young warrior, anxious to display his bravery and gain prestige, might leave the line and dash dangerously close to the enemy. The attack might continue until the ponies gave out or the enemy fire became too hot, when they withdrew to attempt another surprise.

Naturally, when the attack occurred on rough terrain or where there was timber, brush, rocks, or holes, the strategy had to be altered. A common procedure in such a position was to leave part of the horses at a safe distance and then approach the enemy with two riders to a horse. While circling the crucial spot, the extra warriors slipped

13 Linton, "Acculturation and Process of Culture Change," *loc. cit.,* 474.

off the horses, if possible unnoticed by the enemy, whose attention was distracted at the time. While the riders continued to draw the attention of the enemy, the dismounted warriors slipped silently to a position from which they could strike a mortal blow.[14] Another plan of strategy was to take up a position in a creek valley where there was a thicket of bushes and stunted trees and where the low, steep banks of a meandering stream afforded a measure of protection. In such a place their concealment was so complete that it would have been difficult to believe any Indians were there had it not been for the twang of a bowstring or the swish of an arrow. In such a position they were known to have fought without giving or asking quarter until there was not one left to bend a bow.

When a comrade was killed or wounded, the Comanches endeavored to retrieve his body or carry him to safety if he were still living. Two Indians riding abreast, one on each side of the prostrate warrior, would reach down and take hold of the warrior as they passed, either dragging him to safety or swinging him up beside one of them. If he could not be removed by mounted comrades, he was sometimes lassoed and dragged to a spot where he could be recovered.

To the white man the Comanche appeared to be a cruel, savage warrior. But in all fairness it must be remembered that he knew nothing of the white man's code of war and his so-called humanity. He could not take many prisoners for the simple reason that he had no prison to hold them and perhaps no food to sustain them. He killed the men, took the women when he could, and adopted into the tribe children who were too young to run away. His courage was superb. Since he gave no quarter, he asked none in return. Sometimes, when the fight became desperate, a warrior dismounted and took off his moccasins in token of his resolve never to retreat.[15] Even when surrounded, with no hope of escape, he always refused to surrender and fought as long as any strength remained in his body.

Although it was not their custom to torture unfortunate enemies, at times when the Comanches became unusually angered, they resorted to extreme forms of barbarism in seeking revenge. For the most part, the treatment an individual captive received depended on

[14] R. I. Dodge, *The Plains of the Great West*, 380, 381.
[15] Informant: Face Wrinkling Like Getting Old.

the personal character of his captor. Slope knew of a man who regularly castrated his boy captives, crucified one prisoner, and killed a Navaho because the victim was diseased. Adopted captives who became warriors are reputed by the Comanches to have been more cruel than the Comanches themselves. The father-in-law of Breaks Something was adopted, and it is said that he more than once threw captured babies into the air to catch them on his spear. Rhoda Greyfoot's father, the feared medicine man, turned loose the first Mexican boy he took to tend his horses, "because it was too much trouble teaching him the language." Thereafter he let his captives go or gave them away. On one occasion, when a war party of Comanches surprised a small group of Tonkawas roasting a Comanche warrior preparatory to a ceremonial meal, they scalped the Tonkawas, amputated their arms and legs, cut out their tongues, and threw the mangled bodies of both living and dead upon the campfire, piled more wood on the fire, and while the victims moaned for mercy as the grease and blood ran from their cracking bodies, they danced around the fire.[16]

Although most accounts of the Comanches are filled with stories of the atrocities they committed, these wandering nomads of the plains often revealed kinder aspects of behavior. They had great admiration for any white who exhibited bravery in combat with them and always spoke with great praise of such men afterwards. Those captives whom they admired and who accepted their way of life were treated usually with great consideration and received a liberal share of anything their captors might possess.

In 1933 there lived with her seventy-five-year-old daughter, not far from Indiahoma, Oklahoma, a remarkable old woman of ninety years. She was Carrying Her Sunshade. She was a Comanche captive who had been taken from her home in old Mexico in the eighteen fifties, when she was a little girl of six or seven. The rest of her long life had been lived as a Comanche, and at fifteen she had borne her first child, the daughter who seventy-five years later was still living a hale and hearty existence with her mother. A fragment of the old woman's autobiography as taken by the Hoebels offers a first-hand account of personal experience of a Comanche captive.

16 Lehmann, *op. cit.*, 156.

« « « My former home was near the highest mountain in Mexico. I do not remember my parents' names or who they were.

The Comanches were raiding our country from the top of that mountain. They had already taken some of my friends when they came down to the school one day. They rode around the school on horses and threw firebrands into it. As the children ran out, they snatched them up and carried them off. The teacher they killed. It was the custom of the Indians to cache their stuff up on that mountain when on a raid; also to leave their captives up there when out gathering more.

I was captured in the summer by a war leader, *Tɔyɔp,* who was himself a captive—it's funny they had no pity on their own people. I was sitting in my grandmother's arms on a log outside our house. An Indian came and pushed our fence down. He rode up, grabbed me from my grandmother's arms and put me behind him on his horse. I was the only one in my family who was captured, for my parents were gone that day.

When it was nearly night, we joined up with some Indians. They came on a boy sheepherder, whom they killed, and they ate his lunch. Then they rode on toward the high mountain. It was a four-day trip, and when they ran out of food, they killed a horse. When we finally got there, it was raining hard, and I went to bed soaked. As soon as we had entered the camp, other Indians had run up and snatched off my earrings and clothes for souvenirs. Other little captive girls told me not to be afraid. "They won't really hurt you," they said.

The next morning the sound of a wagon moving at the foot of the mountain was heard. Four men were sent down to see about it. Then we heard shots. After a while the scouts came back, bringing some food and Mexican blankets. I knew from this that they had killed some more Mexicans.

It was a big camp there on the mountain, and we stayed there quite some time while the Comanches made some more raids about the country. They didn't seem to be the least bit afraid. We captive girls had to eat by ourselves so we would not disturb the men's medicine.

On the last raid, all the Comanches went, including the women. They left all us captive children in charge of one man, himself a captive. He cooked a whole horse for us, and we ate as much as we could.

When the raiding party returned with more horses, they all got ready to go back north. It was probably in September.

Each family camp left when it got ready, driving off its own bunch of horses. *Tɔyɔp,* my captor, had about thirty people in his camp. He was not satisfied with his horses; he wished to capture more; so his bunch stayed behind. Everybody had gone, but a man named *Wahaɔmɔ* came back to get something. As he rode by me, *Tɔyɔp* said to him, "We are going on another raid. This girl is in the way, so we are going to kill her."

Wahaɔmɔ felt sorry for me. He thought of his own children; his wife was dead. So he picked me up and put me on his mule. He gave *Tɔyɔp* a few arrows, and *Tɔyɔp* gave him three blankets, plus one for me to ride on.

On the route we passed a girl lying in the road about to die; she had been raped. Later we passed a boy captive—dead.

Wahaɔmɔ told me no harm would come to me. "When you grow up, you'll be my wife," he said. His wife was dead and his niece was running his camp for him. He told his niece to be good to me (sometimes the women were very mean to captives); he told her to look after me so no men would harm me.

One night when we were camping and my captor was out looking after his horses, a young brave came along and pulled me out there against my will. He lay down and exposed himself, and I saw he had a diseased scrotum. I didn't do anything. I just stood around.

Then my captor saw me and ran to me. He scolded that fellow and took me back to camp. After that he always took me along when he went places. I was tied on a horse, and he led me with him.

We were still traveling when we came to a camp of Kiowas. *Wahaɔmɔ* sent his niece and me to get some food; we were pretty short of it. He dressed me in a blanket and painted my face. We looked for the largest lodge and went there.

"Are you a warrior's wife?" they asked.

"No," I told them, "I'm only a captive."

Those Kiowas loaded us up with dried meat. They also told us there was a large Comanche camp not far away. When we got there, we found the fires still smoking at the old camp place, but they were gone.

All the next day we followed their trail until we came upon them at dusk. It was the main Comanche camp that my captor had been seeking; his wife's parents were there. I noticed that their hair, and that of his sister, was already long. He must have been gone on this raid for several years.

He led me into their tipi—all fixed up with blankets—and he bade me sit down at the west side (my regular place was next to the door). The women of the family struck me with whips, as was the custom on the arrival of a new captive in camp.

My job was to care for his children. The little crippled one I had to carry on my back; the other one I led about. Wherever they went to play, I had to go with them.

Wahaɔmɔ slept regularly with his former wife's younger sister, *Puki.*

That winter a party left on a hunting trip to get some more meat. In their absence we had trouble keeping the horses. A big snow storm came up and completely buried some horses. In the main camp we were short of wood and food. The captive boys had to dig paths in the snow and dig for frozen horses for us to eat. They fed the living horses cottonwood shoots; the bark is good food, but it was frozen and cut the horses' mouths. After the horses had eaten the bark, the captive boys brought in the twigs for fuel.

The hunting party was out for nearly a month on account of the storm. They lost many horses, and they nearly starved to death. Still, they brought back a little meat. The people out on the party invented snowshoes made of woven sinews. One man on snowshoes shot an animal with an arrow, and when he ran up to it, he slid right past it. Others borrowed his snowshoes, because they didn't have enough sinew to make shoes for all the hunters.

That was a hard winter.

Wahaɔmɔ taught me to hunt during the next spring. He had not yet married me. He was just kind to me. His wife would take a stick out of the fire and poke it at me out of jealousy to scare me and make me cry, but her step-children would help me against her.

By the fall of the second year I knew the language and was familiar with the customs.))))))

Captive white children were generally initiated into the tribe by a series of terrifying experiences in which the Indians tried their courage by brutal treatment and threats of destruction. They would sometimes be tied to a stake while their captors, with slashes and menacing gestures, punctuated by hideous yells, threatened to cut them to pieces, shoot them, or even burn them at the stake. Some of these unfortunate children never lived to recount their experiences. If the victim survived the initiation to the satisfaction of his captors, he became a slave and was compelled to do menial tasks, like Carrying Her Sunshade. If he proved his mettle according to Comanche standards, better days awaited him. He would likely be adopted as a member of a chief's or warrior's family. Later he was permitted to take part in raids and battles. If he proved a brave fighter, he might become an honored and respected warrior and rise to any position open to a natural-born Comanche. The captives, mostly Mexicans, who did not become warriors tended the horse herds and practiced such specialized industries as gun repairing and saddle-making. The captive woman who made a dutiful and faithful wife and the captive man who had won war honors were sometimes publicly honored.[17] Ordinarily the Comanches refused to surrender a captive without the payment of a reward. Some of the more responsible chiefs tried to stop the taking of white women and children as captives, and some went so far as to buy captives from other Comanches and liberate them. Some of the most hardened warriors are known to have wept because a captive of whom they had become fond returned to his own people.

All the accounts agree that a Comanche felt obligated to lodge, entertain, protect, and feed, even to his last morsel, any person, regardless of nationality, even though it might be his bitterest enemy, who happened to ask for lodging.

When a Comanche raiding or war party found itself hard pressed by an enemy force too large to resist, or if it feared pursuit, it divided and subdivided its forces until each fleeing warrior left a separate trace and pursuers found it impossible to follow the trail. Scattered Comanches were adept in communicating with one another through means of signals. After a night raid when the warriors knew them-

17 Linton, "The Comanche Sun Dance," *loc. cit.*, 421; Burnet, "American Aborigines, Indians of Texas," *loc. cit.*, Vol. I (May 22, 1824), 163.

selves to be in close proximity, they communicated by imitating an owl or a coyote. Writing of one occasion when the members of a party had become separated during a night raid on the settlements, one of the raiders said, "When all was quiet we hooted like an owl for our missing companion; when he failed to answer, we knew he was dead."[18] They would build fires and surround them with blankets, forcing columns of smoke to ascend as signals. Different numbers of columns had various meanings. Mounds of stones were arranged to indicate routes followed and the time of the moon when they were arranged. When buffalo bones were available, they were certain to be used to convey messages to comrades. Herman Lehmann has left an interesting paragraph on signaling.

> We found buffalo bones and on them pictures representing a fight with the white people. On some bones properly arranged were the pictures of seven men pierced with arrows, also a wagon burning up; the bones pointed upward. Twelve bones peculiarly arranged represented twelve days journey. We traveled twelve days and saw smokes a long way apart in a row pointing westward which indicated that the Rangers had made it too hot for them and they had gone on west.[19]

The scattered warriors would seek some point where the chances were good that their trail would be discovered. Providing themselves with a thin piece of birch bark, which can be folded without breaking, they placed upon it the information which they wished their comrades to have, then striking a hatchet deep into the trunk of a tree and withdrawing it, they placed the bark in the incision, the outer part pointing in the direction they had taken.

After an expedition the Comanches normally had plenty of mounts, and they kept going night and day at a high rate of speed until they believed themselves out of danger of pursuers. On one occasion they kept going so long that one captive "began to think they had quit eating."[20] During a fast retreat, old, slow, and weak

18 C. and J. D. Smith, *op. cit.,* 64.
19 Lehmann, *op. cit.,* 119.
20 C. and J. D. Smith, *op. cit.,* 35.

horses that fell behind were abandoned. No time was lost hunting for food. If necessary, old horses were killed and consumed. Captives who retarded the speed of the retreat might be abandoned or killed. To avoid surprise, they stopped to rest for only an hour or two and then moved on again, making three or four such stops within a day. To discourage pursuit, they would take a route on which they knew there was no water. When they became very thirsty, they killed horses and drank the blood. The meager supply of water carried in buffalo paunches was rationed, well guarded, and conserved for the children and women when they were along, or for wounded warriors. Clinton Smith declares that on one occasion the warriors did without water until their throats became too swollen for them to swallow readily.[21]

After an engagement or a stealthy garnering of horses, the leader and war-bonnet wearers covered the escape with rear-guard actions. The leader designated two men to remain on fast horses some distance behind, yet close enough to signal, in order to watch the back trail. They sometimes set fire to the grass to blot out their trail against both men and dogs, or they emptied pouches of skunk musk on the trail to prevent dogs from following in pursuit. After the advent of the white trader, the rear-guard scouts carried field glasses.[22]

When raiders had put two or three days of safety between themselves and possible pursuers, they halted. They needed rest and the wounded required attention. In most cases there were spoils to be divided, and the division was made as soon as convenient. The leader's eyes had been open to industry, willingness, and bravery. He noted or was soon told of the actions of his followers while in battle. Unless previously agreed otherwise, to the man who had excelled he allowed first choice of the horses to be divided. Each member of the party chose in turn according to his services as determined by the chief, the cook usually having high priority. The leader took his pick of what remained. The succession of choices was repeated in the same order as before. A reputation for fairness in dividing the spoils enhanced the prestige of a war leader and gained him followers. Liberality was

21 *Ibid.,* 60.
22 Informant: Yellowfish; see also Hoebel, *The Political Organization and Law-Ways of the Comanche Indians,* 25; C. and J. D. Smith, *op. cit.,* 34, 39, 40.
23 Linton, *The Study of Man,* 142–43.

one of the surest forms of insurance against ill fortune, for where one had given he could legitimately expect a return.

In theory the leader could retain as much of the loot for himself as he wished.[23] Actually, leaders rarely kept more than a small share for themselves and often gave all the loot to their followers. Success in war, with its attendant spoils, was believed to be due to the leader's medicine, that is, his supernatural powers. Such power came and went capriciously, and its presence was revealed to a man by a subjective reaction which he could immediately recognize. If the leader kept the bulk of the spoils, that act was tantamount to a confession that he felt his power was waning. He was keeping what he could, because he knew that he might not be able to get more. The selfish leader was likely to lose prestige and have difficulty in recruiting his next war party. If he gave freely, it showed that he knew his medicine was strong. It is said that Quanah Parker, the last great Comanche chief, was not always liberal toward his followers; he frequently made favorites of his relatives and took the best horses for himself. Some of the warriors refused to go on raids with him for this reason.[24] If a man on a raid was killed before the spoils were divided, his heirs were not included in the division, but if he had personally taken any horses singlehanded, they were supposed to be turned over to his family.

About the time of the Civil War, when the cattlemen were pushing westward beyond the line of settlements across Texas into the Comanche country, Texas cattle became an important article of plunder. Stolen cattle were exchanged for goods with the *Comancheros,* or traders from New Mexico. Cattle constituted a commodity easily procured and transported, and they could be obtained in almost unlimited numbers. The Comanches felt that if only the raiders could succeed in driving off enough of the intruders' cattle, it would discourage further encroachment into their country. There were regular meeting places where traders with their cart-loads of commodities met the Comanches to trade for horses and cattle. So abundant was the trade that it was reported in 1867 that the territory of New Mexico was "filled with Texas cattle."[25] In exhange for these cattle the Co-

[24] Informants: Post Oak Jim; Whitewolf.

[25] A. B. Norton (superintendent Indian Affairs, New Mexico) to Commissioner of Indian Affairs, August 24, 1867, Commissioner of Indian Affairs, *Annual Report,* 1867, 194–95.

manches received ammunition, knives, calico, coffee, arrow points, tobacco, whiskey, and gewgaws. An idea of the enormous extent of this trade may be gained from the fact that in 1867 Charles Goodnight found six hundred head of his cattle, which had been stolen sometime before from his range near old Fort Belknap, on Gallinas Creek in New Mexico. He was firmly convinced that at least three hundred thousand head of Texas cattle had been stolen and sold or traded to New Mexicans during the Civil War. A later and more conservative estimate by another Texas ranchman set the loss for the two decades preceding 1873 at one hundred thousand head.[26] Most of these cattle were driven to New Mexcio by the Comanches and their Kiowa allies. The most active band of Comanches engaged in plundering cattle was the Antelope of the *Llano Estacado.*

If a returning war or raiding party had been unsuccessful, it was customary to bury those who died on the road. They laid the deceased in a crevice or shallow grave and piled rocks over it to prevent the corpse's being disturbed by predatory animals. The warriors separated upon approaching the main camp and, with their faces painted black and the tails of their horses shaved, dropped into it one by one quietly and without fanfare. If several warriors had been lost, the entire camp broke forth in a pandemonium of wailing; recent captives were in danger of being abused, tortured, or slain; violence and frenzy reigned supreme. The female relatives of slain Indians were expected to evidence their grief by shrill lamentations and self-torture, continuing the demonstrations for weeks, months, and even years. They cut their legs and arms and cut off finger tips and hair, painted their faces black, and piled ashes on their heads. Usually they tore down the tipis of the dead warriors and destroyed or gave away their property. "A war leader will always comfort the survivors of a casualty on his party," said Post Oak Jim, "and will sometimes give them a horse or other gift."

A successful returning party timed its arrival so as to enter the village during the morning hours; they halted on an elevation a short distance from the village and sent a messenger ahead to inform the

26 J. E. Haley, *The XIT Ranch of Texas,* 26; C. C. Rister, *The Southwestern Frontier,* 82, n.73.

people. It was usually one of the youngest members of the party who carried the good news.

While waiting for the people in camp to make ready for the occasion, the victorious warriors put on their war paint and war dress. The horses were rubbed with grass so as to look their best. The death of a warrior after he had counted coup did not prevent the celebration, for it was considered an honor for a person to count coup first and afterwards be killed in the same fight. His relatives joined in the dance. When the people learned that the party had returned, they were greatly excited and expressed their exultation with shouts and yells. All was joy in the village. The women sang songs of victory as they went forth to greet the returning heroes. An elderly, respected woman, carrying a long lance or a slender scalp pole, might lead the parade to meet the warriors, and the victorious warriors might honor her by fastening their scalps to her lance or pole. On other occasions the leader of the party was allowed the honor of being scalp bearer. At other times, it would be the member of the party who had most distinguished himself on the raid. But more often, each warrior was permitted the honor of flourishing his own scalp pole. The scalps were tied to the point end of the lance, and the latter was held with scalps up as they rode into camp. In the absence of a lance, a tomahawk would serve. He who had achieved the greatest success in the raid was entitled to tie the scalp lock on which he had taken first coup to the lower lip of his horse. This signified disdain for the enemy.

The scalp when taken might be small, only a little larger than a silver dollar, but like any piece of fresh skin it stretched greatly. Many Comanches preferred, however, to take the whole skin of the head. The preparation of the scalp took place as soon after it was taken as convenient, the same day if possible. Preparation was a ceremonial procedure, and young warriors who had never before scalped an enemy were taught to prepare the scalp under supervision. Smoke was made and a prayer offered to the spiritual powers before the work on the scalp itself was begun. The flesh was shaved from the skin. A willow twig was secured and bent into a hoop, somewhat larger than the scalp, and the ends were lashed together with a sinew. The margin of the cleaned scalp was then sewed to the hoop, the sinew threads being pulled taut in order to stretch the scalp. The proper procedure in sewing was from east to south, to west, to north, to east, or in the same direction in which a Comanche entered a tipi. The hair was oiled and combed, and the scalp-loop attached to a slender pole. The other end of the pole was stuck in the ground and the scalp was allowed to dry. Lances, tomahawks, and shields were sometimes used instead of poles.

With the scalp poles high, so all could see, the warriors led the parade into the village. The leader and any other person receiving special recognition led the way. Behind them were those who had shown the greatest courage, counted coups, or performed creditable acts. The remaining warriors came next. On both sides and in the rear were the relatives, friends, and other villagers, who had come forth shouting, yelling, and dancing. They sang songs in which they mentioned the names of their favorite heroes. On entering the village, the warriors turned off as they came to their own lodges, turned their horses and weapons over to a wife, mother, or sister, and went inside to rest and prepare for the big Victory Dance.

When there were scalps it was a Scalp Dance; if only plunder and captives had been taken, it was a Victory Dance. There was little difference except for the presence of the scalps. The dance was likely to continue all night, and when the victory had been a brilliant one, dancing and feasting were apt to be kept up for several days.

These dances varied from band to band, and even within the same village, but certain characteristics were evident in all. The dance took place in the center of the village in the evening following the return of the successful war party. The villagers put up a large pole in the center of the dance circle. The scalps were attached to the pole. Wood was gathered and stacked in a conical pile with dry grass beneath, so it could be easily fired. The fire was lighted after dark when the singers and drummers, old or middle-aged, had arrived and seated themselves near the scalp pole. Both men and women painted and dressed for the occasion. Black was the predominating color for women; red for men. Men entitled to wear war bonnets donned them. The men and women dancers at times formed in lines facing each other, each line dancing forward and backward; a moment later they formed a circle, dancing around the scalp pole and the musicians. At intervals the spectators joined in the singing.

Ten Bears, in 1872
Courtesy Bureau of American Ethnology

Mumshukawa
Bureau of American Ethnology photograph
Courtesy Denver Art Museum

Captives were bound and placed in the center of the circle, possibly tied to the scalp pole. Frequently one of the dancers left his position and in pantomime killed and scalped the captive. Sometimes captives were tortured by the dancers, even to death. When the dance began, the singing was low and the dancers moved in a slow to moderate pace, but as it continued, the pace was accelerated and the singing grew louder. The dance continued from two hours to two or more days, but normally terminated before the light of day.[27]

The contemporary Comanche Brush Dance still retains some of the features of the old Scalp Dance.

In 1933, at a Brush Dance put on by Mʌmsɜkə, the men and women danced back and forth in the old way before a tall pole on which Old Glory flew.

"That used to be a pole for scalps. At sunset we will bring down the flag," they said. "The man who brings down the flag has to be a good warrior. He has to tell about a coup first."

In each Comanche band there was a dance whip-holder. His whip was a wood blade with a serrated edge, and upon it were carved scalp symbols for the owner's victims. At the end of the whip were two short otter-skin lashes. In the old days there were one or two of these, owned by the bravest men in the band.

At any dance, the owner of the whip, which is called *pianɜ'ɜpai'i* (big whip), may stop the dance and recite a coup, ending his recital with a sun curse upon himself in testimony of its truth. He is a kind of master of ceremonies at the dance. He can dance up to any lounging spectator and point his whip. That person has to jump right in and dance—or be whipped.

Sometimes a warrior who could not dance for certain reasons wished to be excused; nevertheless, when the whip was pointed, he had to get up and dance. Then he could recite his strongest deed. The whip wielder next countered with his. If his deed was as good as the warrior's, the brave had to dance the rest of the time; if not,

[27] This account of the return of a successful party is compiled from statements by informants Yellowfish, Face Wrinkling Like Getting Old, and See How Deep the Water Is; also, Nystel, "Three Months among the Indians," *loc. cit.,* 38; Gregg, *op. cit.,* 436; Lee, *op. cit.,* 150; R. I. Dodge, *Our Wild Indians,* 359–60; Möllhausen, *op. cit.,* I, 184; Hoebel, *The Political Organization and Law-Ways of the Comanche Indians,* 27–28.

then the brave was excused, and the whip owner had to dance himself.

On the fourth day of *Mʌmsɜkə's* Brush Dance in 1933 Ralph Linton was adopted into the tribe. In a simple ceremony his war record (World War I) was praised and he was named *Ekakuɾa,* Red Buffalo, the buffalo who had so much power that he had thrown the Comanche "witch" up to the moon with a toss of his horns. She can be seen there yet. And then in a touching tribute and climax *Pinedapoi,* the Whip Owner, stepped forward and, placing his whip in the hands of Ralph Linton, announced that he was relinquishing it to a younger and greater warrior.

In pre-reservation days successful raiders who reached the village with many horses sometimes gave a part or all of them away. A young man who was courting a girl might drive all his horses to her father's lodge and leave them there. A young warrior who had gained high distinction while on the warpath was likely to be serenaded upon his return. On the morning after the Scalp or Victory Dance, young maidens of the camp dressed like warriors. They congregated before the young man's tipi to do the Shakedown Dance and sing the songs. The boy and his father knew why they were there. They were paying honor to the young warrior, and it was customary to present gifts to the serenaders in return. The boy's father, proud of his son's exploits, came out and gave horses to the girls. Later, when the boy had accumulated a supply of horses, he made the gifts himself.

Military fraternities did not become a developed and integrated part of Comanche culture to the extent that they did among other tribes of the plains. Most of the Comanche warrior groups appear to have been informal organizations compounded of mutual friendship and interests, and they were not continuous or permanent. Although not formally organized into an association, the wearers of full-feathered war bonnets formed a special class, called war leaders, similar to top-ranking military men in our own society in wartime.

The buffalo-scalp-bonnet wearers were of a lower order. The buffalo-scalp hat was decorated with a row of eagle feathers. The breast feathers were tied about the bottom of the quill and reached down to the waist of the wearer. At the top of the buffalo scalp was a bunch of magpie feathers set back on the center of the head. The bonnet was assumed and worn by any brave, not necessarily a chief, who felt worthy and desired to accept the responsibility it imposed upon the wearer. There was definitely no ceremonial bestowal. Usually the bonnet was made by friends of the warrior and presented to him as a token of esteem. The acceptance of a buffalo-scalp bonnet was a serious matter, for the people afterwards expected him to prove himself really worthy of their confidence. Failure meant ridicule and disgrace. After the surrender of the Comanches at Fort Sill, Gets to Be a Middle-aged Man hung his buffalo-scalp bonnet in a tree, never to wear it again. "A man who is beaten has no right to wear such a thing," he said.

Women sometimes made a war bonnet in secret to bestow upon a braggart whose words spoke louder than his deeds, and the presentation was made in public at an opportune moment. The recipient of such a war bonnet had to live up to the obligations of that war bonnet or else lose it and become an object of ridicule and scorn.

The Comanche war leader was under obligation never to retreat except under certain conditions which were well understood, and then only when the other warriors were safe first. He protected the rear as they retreated. The war bonnet was a symbol of tribal integrity and honor to the Comanches to be protected at all costs, "just like the flag." The mere fact that he assumed such responsibility made the war leader a rallying point for all other fighters. The war-bonnet wearer could be rescued with honor by a fellow warrior who dared to dash in and carry him from the field. It was also the duty of a war leader to help a dismounted comrade. Should he fail to do so, any other war chief who observed his disloyalty could publicly upbraid him with the act and thereby cause him to lose his status and right to wear the war bonnet if judged guilty. If a war-bonnet wearer cast off his bonnet and fled, he lost his right to wear it, and all other men would address him as *paβi*, "elder sister." An aspirant brave who wished to obtain the status of war leader might immediately do so by dashing in and recovering the bonnet. He hung it on a bush and protected it all day in the face of the enemy. At sundown, if he charged the enemy four times, the bonnet and all its honors and obligations were his. The lower-rank bonnet could be picked up by any one who saw it and was willing to assume the obligations adhering thereto.

Young warriors who had not attained the rank of war-bonnet

wearers sometimes seem to have banded together into semi-military fraternities or dance groups. Among those noted in more or less descending popularity, according to informants, were the Crow, Shield, Big Pony (Big Horse), Little Horse (Little Pony), Fox, Buffalo, Gourd, and Drum. These groups seem, however, to have been limited to the northern bands. A youth was likely to join the group of his brother or father, but there was no obligation to do so. He made known his choice, and if the group was willing to accept him, he was admitted. There was keen rivalry among the dancers to secure members who gave evidence of becoming brave warriors. Sometimes the pipe was forced into their mouth. Members were somewhat like brothers. They went on the warpath together and helped bury and mourn a dead fellow member. They had their own distinguishing insignia, songs, and dances, which could not be used by anyone else. When a group sponsored a dance, none but members could attend, except by invitation. They had social get-togethers and held dances in the day or evening, but more frequently in the evening. Dances occurred more often immediately preceding the departure or following the return of a war party or at the time of the communal hunt. Both men and women took part in their social dances. The warrior groups also competed in athletic events, sports, and military exercises. When a member determined to lead a revenge or raiding party, he could usually rely on the support of his own group, but other warriors were welcome to join a party. And when a leader had the support of the majority of the members of his dance group, the War Dance was referred to by the name of his society.

There were minor differences in the purposes and interests of the several organizations, but in general they were much the same. All the members of the Shield group carried identical shields which had been inspired by a vision. The shields were sacred, and among the many requirements for handling them was the one that they could not be permitted to touch the ground. The sacred-shield bearer often found it essential to have a wife accompany him on the warpath to care for his shield.

The Crow Tassel Wearers wore a special type of war bonnet made of fine feathers clipped short except for one large one which was trimmed to scalloped edges. The wearers prepared their own emblem under the tutelage of a man who possessed one, as in the case of the Shield group. They placed a tassel on their left shoulder and one in the hair, taking the Crow Tassel pledge to dedicate themselves to unceasing war. A man who had no surviving family or a man who had a family tradition with a fighting reputation to uphold might become a member. The members dedicated their lives to war. War was their business. They recognized no family ties of restraint. Loyalty to one another was a superior obligation. They fought and raided together as a unit. They pursued the war goal with such singleness of mind and purpose that they were apart from the larger society. Yet they were free to dissolve the band when they so desired. If they had been successful, when they dissolved the band, they became leading men in the community by virtue of their prestige.[28]

Among many of the Plains tribes there were "crazy" warriors who did everything backwards. The Cheyennes called them Contrary Ones; the Crow Indians, Crazy Dogs Wishing to Die. The Comanches, too, had a few of these men, called *pukutsi*.

Any man brave enough and desiring to do so could become a *pukutsi* on making up his mind, according to Frank Moeta. He carried a buffalo-scrotum rattle in his hand and would go about the camp singing, no matter what else might be going on. Everything he did was in inversion, but no one ever molested a *pukutsi,* because he was so recklessly brave.

He wore a long sash over his shoulder and rolled up under his arm. In battle, he rolled out his sash, stuck the free end into the ground with an arrow, and there took his stand. With bow in one hand and rattle in the other, he stood singing, tethered by his sash. He neither fought nor charged, but sang his songs until victory was won or death took him. Only a friend could come and free him. Should he give way in battle or release himself after the fight was done, the other warriors would taunt him in an attempt to egg him into an overt act against them so they could kill him.

There were not many of these men among the Comanches. Carrying Her Sunshade in all her long life knew only one. Of him she had the following story.

[28] Informant: Kills Something.

《 《 《 This *pukutsi* was going through the camp, singing as usual.

An old woman stopped him and said, *"Pukutsi,* I want you to kill me a buffalo. I need the hide to use for my saddle; I have no boys to get one for me."

He went and was gone from the camp for a long time. Finally he came back at night with the whole skin of a Pawnee, even with hands and feet still on it, and he hung it up like a man standing there against her arbor.

Some man saw it there and called in to her in her lodge, "That *pukutsi* is back. Your hide is out here on the arbor."

Early in the morning she got up and went out to get it. That human skin frightened her. Then that man came by and told her she should not have asked a *pukutsi* to do such a job. "He is afraid of nothing."

"Well, I didn't ask him to bring me an enemy," she complained. But that's the way it is with *pukutsi.* You ask them to do one thing and they do just the opposite.

When she got over her first scare, the old woman jumped up and down and sang. She had an enemy scalp, which she kept. 》 》 》

The waging of war was a matter of individual initiative, but the making of peace was a matter for the chiefs. A war leader on a raid could make peace in behalf of his own party on his own authority, but such a peace was not binding upon other members of the band or upon the tribe. Band peace was made only upon consent of the war leaders, the council of elders, and the head chief. Tribal peace could be attained only when agreed upon and recognized by all the bands.

For all their devotion to war, the Comanches accepted the fact that a people cannot fight everybody on all fronts at once. The home base had to afford some measure of security for hunting and everyday living. Thus the Comanches worked out a sort of national policy of defensive alliances with their more powerful neighbors to their north, keeping their southern, western, and eastern frontiers open for far-ranging aggressive action.

Peace with the Kiowas was cemented in 1790 through the good offices of a mutual Spanish friend.[29] No details of this step are known, but it established a co-operative alliance that grew into the firmest of intertribal friendships, unbroken to this very day.

The Kiowas and Comanches together achieved peace with the Cheyennes in 1840. The details of the steps leading up to this agreement have, from the Cheyenne side of the picture, been recorded by Grinnell[30] and analyzed by Llewellyn and Hoebel.[31] Earlier in this book we described the gift exchanges that signalized the binding of the peace. From 1840 on, there were no disturbances between the Comanches and Cheyennes, although between these tribes there never developed the close symbiotic relations that characterized the Comanche-Kiowa ties.

Back to back, territorially speaking, the Southern Cheyenne, Kiowa, and Comanche combine formed a hard, solid core of security from which each tribe could push its warlike activities against outsiders.

There do not seem to be any accounts or memories of how the Comanches established peaceful relations with their eastern neighbors, the Wichitas. Perhaps they never regarded these people as objects of aggression.

Sporadic and limited peace gestures were made toward the Utes and Apaches in later years. They were never the consequence of a national policy but rather of individual motivations, as the following accounts indicate.

《 　《 　《 　Once there were a bunch of Comanches out looking for trouble. They came upon a bunch of Utes and started a fight.

There was a captive Ute woman with the Comanches whose son was a Comanche warrior. Because she got scared for her son's safety, she rode out between the fighters, holding up her hands and calling for them to stop.

"I am on both sides," she cried. "I am a Ute. My son is a Comanche. I don't want my kinspeople to be killing each other."

One of the Ute chiefs rode up to her. The woman held out her hand, but the Ute chief would not accept it.

[29] Mooney, "Calendar History of the Kiowa," loc. cit., 162–65.
[30] Grinnell, The Fighting Cheyennes, 60–66.
[31] Llewellyn and Hoebel, op. cit., 91–94.

He said, "No, not until I know if your chiefs have sent you."

Then her son, who was a war chief, rode up. He was willing that they should stop fighting. And so a truce was made.

The two bands went into camp, the Utes on one side of a hill, the Comanches on the other.

Some Comanche hunters returning to their camp did not know about the truce. They came upon a Ute, whom they killed and scalped. Then they went right on into the Ute camp by mistake, singing the Victory Song and carrying his scalp.

The chief of the Utes calmed his people. "This is a mistake," he told them. "It is all right. We are at peace. We shall not get mad about this thing."

So the Comanche hunters went back and found their own camp.

When he heard the news, a Comanche chief went over to see the Utes. "This was a mistake," he told them. "However, it is not necessary to do anything about it. One of our men was killed in that battle we were having. Things are now even."

The Utes agreed.

The next day a council of ten Ute chiefs came to the Comanche camp to visit the Ute woman, and they found that she was a sister to one of them. They took her and her family back to the Ute camp to visit her parents, who were still living. There they gave her a special tipi with an antelope skin tied to a pole as a special sign.

At the end of four days, the Utes said, "Four days are now up. Now we shall separate."

The Utes wanted the Ute woman's son to stay with them. At first he refused, staying alone when the camps moved, to decide what to do. Finally, he took the Ute trail.

He came to the Ute camp and asked for their chief. The chief invited him to dismount, and told his wife to serve him a supper. The Comanche captive, his mother, was sent for to interpret. He told the chief of his desire to become a Ute.

This chief replied, "All right, you can be my son. But these Utes are bad. They might kill you sometime."

The Ute chief made him his son, and he named him *Wasape Sɜmanɛtɛ*. After a while the chief gave him a pack horse and sent him back to the Comanches.

278

Our people renamed him *Paɾuwa Sᴣmɛno,* Ten Bears.[32]))))))

Greyfoot added a poignant scrap of detail as an epilogue to this account. The son of the Ute chief was dying of an incurable illness. He was not old enough to go to war, but his father wanted him to die the glorious death of a warrior. He did not want to see him waste away to nothing.

Acceding to the chieftain's wish, Ten Bears and a friend dressed in their war regalia, ready to meet the enemy. The sickly boy was dressed for war. In a pantomime of battle Ten Bears and his friend killed him. The Ute chief, in thanks for honoring his son, gave the boy's horse and clothing to them. That was when Ten Bears returned to the Comanches.

Except for the Kiowa and Cheyenne relations, Comanche peace pacts were touch and go. The temporary Ute peace could have been destroyed in the making by the Comanche hunters' killing the Ute had not the Ute chief been a man of power and forbearance. The delicate nature of such negotiations and the low level of mutual trust is revealed in Slope's account of a Tonkawa peace overture.

((((((A Comanche girl had died. Her mother wanted to leave the tribe so that she would see no more Comanche girls. There were only seven left in the family.

They were camping all by themselves when they were attacked by the Tonkawas, those man-eaters. Four of them were killed, and the mother and two of her children were captured.

After a year had passed, the Tonkawas decided they wanted peace with the Comanches, so they sent thirty warriors to escort the woman back to the tribe.

When they came to Comanche territory, they made a camp, and a Tonkawa chief and one warrior set out with the woman to look for the Comanches.

A Comanche war party, including some Kiowas, met them on a hill top. The Tonkawa signaled for friendship, so the Comanche leader came right up and shook hands before anything was said. The woman was glad. "This is what the Tonkawas want," she said.

[32] Informant: That's It.

While they were talking, some of the Comanche and Kiowa warriors drifted on and found the Tonkawa camp. The group on the hill heard a shot fired.

"Well, it's too late," said the Tonkawa chief, and he whirled his horse and rode off. The Comanche woman, who had become his wife, took a spear and scattered the Comanches. Thus the Tonkawa chief got away.

They started a general fight right then, the Tonkawas beat up that Comanche-Kiowa war party that day. They chased the Comanches a long way.

One Tonkawa was outstanding. The brother of Eagle Tail Feather shot his horse, but he was not hurt. » » »

The Comanches seldom took the initiative at treaty-making with the whites; rather, it was the whites. In later days the preliminary procedure in getting the Comanches to make a treaty was about as follows: An agent acting under orders from Washington decided that a treaty was desirable. He then went into the Comanche country to visit with as many of the bands as he could locate. He told them that the "Big Chief" wanted to make peace and be friendly with them; that he hoped to see them at a certain time and place, probably in the vicinity of a trading house. He made a number of promises, gave a few presents, and got some Indian messengers to carry the news to other bands and tribes. If the chiefs promised to come in, and some nearly always would agree, preparations were made on a grand scale for the assembly.

Quantities of beads, hatchets, mirrors, fine combs, matches, cloth, and other articles which the Indians desired or needed were provided. A company of soldiers was sent along (in Texas, Texas Rangers, if available), commissioners to make the treaty, and the agents. By the date set, the council ground was alive with activity, but most of the time the only Indians present were those who hoped by their early arrival to secure more than their share of the spoils. A Comanche seldom kept an appointment on time; to do so sacrificed a measure of his independence. Some of the Comanche bands would not appear at all, because they had no confidence in the white man's treaties or in their own ability to achieve a diplomatic victory over them in council. An agent might work for months to bring the Indians into council and have all his efforts thwarted by a wild rumor set afloat by some unscrupulous trader. The Indians who did come were fully armed and dressed in all their war paraphernalia and paint. Both the white and the red men tried to make as formidable an appearance as possible to impress the other. The Comanches usually maneuvered in such a way as to make a test of the good faith of the white man. Some Comanches failed to show up for fear of the intentions of the whites. *Huwia,* who was a medicine man, was instructed to go to Fort Sill to attend a council to be held with an army officer. He was afraid to go, because he feared a trap, and *Tsi:vas* went in his stead. The People then elevated *Tsi:vas* to the chieftainship for which *Huwia* had been in line.

Dealing with the whites on other than a war footing taxed all the abilities of the Comanches. Bull Elk (*paᶜuwa ḳum*), who was the top war chief of the Antelope band, turned his chieftainship over to Wild Horse and Black Mustache when the Comanches were placed on the reservation. He said he did not know how to deal with the white man.[33]

Finally, when all was ready, the council convened for business. Matters were conducted with much gravity, on the part of the white men in order to impress the Indians, and on the part of the Indians because gravity in council was in keeping with their nature. The chiefs, commissioners, and other officials seated themselves in a circle. Behind stood the respective warriors of each group, fully armed. The peace pipe was ceremoniously lighted and passed around the circle from lip to lip in silence. After it had made the round, the commissioner or agent made a talk in which he stated the purpose of the council, reminded the Indian that he had been making depredations upon the white people, expressed his love for the red man, and made known the overwhelming power of the Great Father. Then the Indians were urged to state their side of the case and to tell the whole truth. If they had been wronged by the white man, the commissioners wished to know it, and if they themselves had committed acts of hostility, they were to confess.

Then the Indians spoke, always with simplicity and often with

[33] Informant: Eagle Tail Feather.

impressive eloquence and beauty. (Knowing that they would likely have to speak in public council at some time, the Comanches had trained themselves to speak well. Before delivering a speech, if there were opportunity, the speaker spent much time in preparation and rehearsal.) He represented himself as a man of peace, but he made it understood that he wanted no encroachment of either red men or white men upon the vast expanse of territory south of the Arkansas River which he considered his own. He did not want it disfigured by soldiers' camps and "medicine homes." His country was small enough already. There was time enough to consider reservations and the building of homes when the buffalo were gone, and there were plenty of buffalo if only enough to supply the Indians' needs were killed. As to trusting to the agents for food, he had no confidence in that. He called attention to the "white" Indians, those who had come in contact with the whites and had made treaties in accord with white man's wishes. Formerly they had been powerful, but now they were weak and poor. He had little respect for them, for "They are an old dirty, inefficient-looking set, hardly capable of managing their own affairs," who had degenerated to the point where the Comanches had no desire to associate with them. The speech of Ten Bears, of the Ute peace episode, who spoke for the Comanches at the Council of Medicine Lodge Creek in 1867, may well be given in full, not only because it presented the case of the Comanche well and forcibly, but also because it is a masterpiece of oratory that would be a credit to one trained in the classroom.

My heart is filled with joy when I see you here, as the brooks fill with water when the snows melt in the spring; and I feel glad as the ponies do when the fresh grass starts in the beginning of the year. I heard of your coming when I was many sleeps away, and I made but few camps before I met you. I knew that you had come to do good to me and to my people. I looked for benefits which would last forever, and so my face shines with joy as I look upon you. My people have never first drawn a bow or fired a gun against the whites. There has been trouble on the line between us, and my young men have danced the war dance. But it was not begun by us. It was you who sent out the first soldier and we who sent out the second. Two years ago, I came upon this road, following the buffalo, that my wives and children might have their cheeks plump and their bodies warm. But the soldiers fired on us, and since that time there has been a noise like that of a thunderstorm, and we have not known which way to go. So it was upon the Canadian. Nor have we been made to cry once alone. The blue-dressed soldiers and the Utes came from out of the night when it was dark and still, and for camp-fires they lit our lodges. Instead of hunting game they killed my braves, and the warriors of the tribe cut short their hair for the dead.

So it was in Texas. They made sorrow come in our camps, and we went out like the buffalo bulls when the cows are attacked. When we found them we killed them, and their scalps hang in our lodges. The Comanches are not weak and blind, like the pups of a dog when seven sleeps old. They are strong and far-sighted, like grown horses. We took their road and we went on it. The white women cried and our women laughed.

But there are things which you have said to me which I do not like. They were not sweet like sugar, but bitter like gourds. You said that you wanted to put us upon a reservation, to build us houses and make us medicine lodges. I do not want them. I was born upon the prairie, where the wind blew free and there was nothing to break the light of the sun. I was born where there were no enclosures and everything drew a free breath. I want to die there and not within walls. I know every stream and every wood between the Río Grande and the Arkansas. I have hunted and lived over that country. I live like my fathers before me and like them I lived happily.

When I was at Washington the Great Father told me that all the Comanche land was ours, and that no one should hinder us in living upon it. So, why do you ask us to leave the rivers, and the sun, and the wind, and live in houses? Do not ask us to give up the buffalo for the sheep. The young men have heard talk of this, and it has made them sad and angry. Do not speak of it more. I love to carry out the talk I get from the Great Father. When I get goods and presents, I and my people feel glad, since it shows that he holds us in his eye.

If the Texans had kept out of my country, there might have been peace. But that which you now say we must live in, is too small. The Texans have taken away the places where the grass grew the thickest and the timber was the best. Had we kept that, we might have done the things you ask. But it is too late. The whites have the country which we loved, and we only wish to wander on the prairie until we die. Any good thing you say to me shall not be forgotten. I shall carry it as near to my heart as my children, and it shall be as often on my tongue as the name of the Great Spirit. I want no blood upon my land to stain the grass. I want it all clear and pure, and I wish it so that all who go through among my people may find peace when they come in and leave it when they go out.[34]

After both the Indians and the whites had talked too much and told a good many lies along with a great deal of truth, the treaty would be drawn and signed by the white men. The Indians made a mark opposite their names, which were phonetically written, after a fashion, by the white men. Yet there is no evidence to indicate that the Comanches were ever convinced that it was best for them to sign. Presents were distributed and the council ended. The Comanches returned to their buffalo tipis and the whites to their cabin homes, but neither had any confidence that the other would do what had been promised.

[34] Ten Bears, Comanche chief, "Speech," October 20, 1867, "Record Copy of the Proceedings of the Indian Peace Commission Appointed under the Act of Congress Approved July 20, 1867" (MS, National Archives, Office of Indian Affairs, Washington), I, 104.

The Lords of
the South Plains

WHATEVER may have been their disposition in earlier times, the Comanches were constantly in conflict with certain of their neighbors on the Great Plains. When they lived in the forks of the Dismal River and in Nebraska, they engaged in incessant warfare with the Pawnees, their neighbors on the east. The Cheyennes, Arapahos, and Dakotas were pressing against Comanche territory from the east and north.

The Kiowas and Kiowa-Apaches were migrating southward at the time. These people are known to have lived at one time as far north as the Yellowstone country, from which they may have been driven by the Cheyennes and the Dakotas. At any rate, they drifted southward, clashed with the Comanches, and for many years there was war between the two tribes.

There is a Kiowa tradition explaining their southward migration. The Kiowas lived where it was very cold most of the year—far beyond the country of the Crows and Sioux. They knew nothing of ponies, but used dogs to carry their burdens. In time one of their men went far to the southward where he was taken prisoner by a band of Comanches. The latter took council to put him to death, but one of the headmen prevailed upon the others to spare him, for if they treated him well, he might later befriend some Comanche who might fall in with his tribe. It was then decided to send the Kiowa home with honor. He was given a pony, saddle, and bridle, which became objects of general admiration and envy among his own tribesmen. The returned traveler gave his tribesmen a glowing description of the country he had visited. It was a land where the summer lasted nearly all the year and was stocked not only with large game but also with large herds of ponies. So intrigued were the Kiowas with the report that their council unanimously decided to follow the old man to the country he had seen. Accordingly, upon the opening of the following spring, most of the Kiowas commenced their migration to the southward until they encountered a party of Comanches, who made war upon them.[1]

During the course of the ensuing Comanche-Kiowa conflict, the Comanches gradually drifted south of the Arkansas River. In the manner described in the previous chapter peace was achieved in 1790. The Kiowas and Kiowa-Apaches thus became the friendly northern neighbors of the Comanches. Other frontier relations of the Comanches have already been indicated, but it is pertinent to restate them here in more detail.

On the extreme northwest were their kinsmen, the Utes. Throughout the years from 1749 to 1786, the Utes and Comanches fought constantly, except for sporadic and localized truces. The Jicarilla moved westward at this time and no longer formed a barrier between these hostile tribes. The Utes formed an alliance with the Spaniards, and the two co-operated in attacks against the Comanches. When, in 1786, the Spaniards succeeded in making peace with the Comanches, the Utes persuaded the Jicarillas to join with them in a defensive and offensive alliance against the Comanches and Kiowas.[2]

The Cheyennes and Arapahos appeared in great numbers along the upper Arkansas River about 1820. War broke out immediately thereafter between them and the Comanches. The failure of the Comanches at the decisive battle of Wolf Creek in 1838 left the intruders firmly entrenched beyond the northern border of Comanchería.

To the east and northeast of the Comanche country were the Osages, a tribe of the Sioux family. A band of these Indians drifted as far south as the Arkansas River about 1802. They were less numerous than the Pawnees, but more formidable because their associ-

[1] Battey, op. cit., 104–105.
[2] M. K. Opler, "The Southern Ute of Colorado," in Ralph Linton (ed.), *Acculturation in Seven American Indian Tribes*, 162–63; A. B. Thomas, *Forgotten Frontiers*, 68–77.

286

ation with the whites and immigrant civilized tribes enabled them to possess firearms. However, the Osages had already begun the process of ceding their territory to the United States. In 1808 they had transferred a portion of their lands comprising a large part of what is now the state of Missouri and the northern section of Arkansas, and in a few years the Cherokees from east of the Mississippi settled in part of that territory. By 1825 other concessions had reduced the Osages to a small area along the Neosho River, and the area east of the Comanches came to be occupied largely by more advanced Indians from the east. Wars interspersed with periods of peace occurred between the Comanches and the Osages until the groups were brought under government control.

From the Washita and Red River valleys southward almost to the location of Austin, occupying a strip of territory about two hundred miles wide, were the Wichitas or Pawnee Picts, the Wacos, and a few Tawakonies and Kichaies. Estimates made in 1824 gave this whole group a population of 2,600. They were Caddoan stock, but were generally friends and allies of the Comanches, and their attitude toward the white people was governed largely by their powerful friends from the plains. In fact, by 1840, the Comanches occupied this country jointly with these weaker tribes. There grew up a considerable trade between them, the Wichita village on the Red River becoming the trading center.[3] The Comanches exchanged Apache slaves and horses and mules for French weapons and Wichita agricultural products. To the east of the Wichitas were remnants of other tribes belonging to the Caddo family. From time to time, these bands, pressed upon by white settlers, drifted over to the middle Brazos region; and Caddos, Anadarkos, and Ionies (Hainaies) were living along the border of the Comanche country after the eighteen thirties.

The Tonkawas, who formed a separate linguistic family, lived in central Texas. The coming of the Anglo-American settlers drove them westward and northward, and they were forced to occupy the country along the Llano and San Saba whenever they were not suffered by the colonists to reside closer in. By the time of the Republic of Texas, they numbered but a few hundred. Their later enmity with the Comanches was proverbial.[4]

[3] H. E. Bolton, *Athanase de Mézières and the Louisiana-Texas Frontier*, I, 47.
[4] J. T. DeShields, *Border Wars of Texas*, 275.

The tribe which suffered most at the hands of the Comanches was the Apache. The Apaches, like the Comanches, were composed of a number of bands, ranging along the whole southern and western border of the Comanche country. The most important were the Mescalero and the Faraon, along the lower and middle Río Grande, and the Jicarilla on the upper Río Grande and in the mountains to the east. The Lipan band occupied the country along the San Saba, Llano, upper Guadalupe, and Nueces rivers, and occasionally it retreated into New Mexico or across the Río Grande into the northern Mexican states. The enmity between the Apaches and the Comanches had its beginning with the southern migration of the Comanches. The two became implacable foes, and warfare prevailed between the two tribes most of the time to 1875. On the plains the Comanches were victorious, but in the hills and mountains the Apaches were able to resist successfully.

As early as 1706 the Spaniards in New Mexico reported the collapse of Apache power northeast of the province, and thirteen years later they stated that the Jicarilla were in full retreat before the Comanches. By 1748 the sweep was complete, for the Jicarilla had been driven from their ancient lands.

Coincident with the attacks upon New Mexico, the Comanches hammered the Apaches southward in Texas. To mark the beginning of the southern advance, they defeated the Lipans in the early eighteenth century in a nine-day battle on the Río del Fierro, a stream which seems to have been the Wichita River.[5] As a result of this and other victories, the Comanches came to occupy their southern range. Other Apache relations can best be discussed in connection with relations with the whites.

The Comanche migration southward no doubt checked the French expansion to the southwest as well as the Spanish advance to the northeast. French goods had begun to reach the settlements in northeastern New Mexico as early as 1706. By 1718–19, La Harpe, Du Tisne, and other traders were edging westward along the Red River, while Bourgemond in 1721–23 lived among the Missouri tribes and schemed to open up trade with New Mexico. However, the Comanches blocked French attempts to reach New Mexico, because they

5 Bolton, *Anthanase de Mézières and the Louisiana-Texas Frontier*, I. 25.

288

were loath to see them arming their Apache enemies. They waged war against the Jumanos, allies of the French, far to their east and pushed them back. By 1746 the Comanches had defeated the Apaches of northeastern New Mexico, and there was no longer any reason to fear the expansion of French trade. In fact they would benefit most from it. Consequently, they made peace with the Jumano and allowed the French to open the Arkansas River route to New Mexico.

Toward the Spaniards in New Mexico the Comanches adopted a policy of war or peace according to whether plunder or trade appeared to offer the greater remuneration. The Spaniards aided the Jicarilla against the Comanches on the ground that the Jicarilla were Christians. From time to time the Spaniards made punitive expeditions against the Comanches, but the "Nomads of the Plains" always returned to attack and plunder the settlements. Don Juan de Padellao attempted to crush the Comanches in 1717. With a powerful force disguised as Indians, he surprised and killed many and took several hundred prisoners, some of whom were taken to Spain. They were later returned to Cuba, but were unable to survive the hot, damp climate. In 1748 and 1749 the Comanches were admitted to the fair at Taos, but even the reciprocal need of trade did not prevent hostilities. Within three years the government was fighting them again. The Spaniards were aware of the advantage of the Comanche barrier against French-English intrusion, and it was for this reason that they followed a relatively lenient policy.

After the transfer of Louisiana to Spain in 1762, however, the Spaniards set out to reorganize the defenses of their northern frontier. The Marquis de Rubi, who inspected the northern frontier for this purpose, recommended that peace be established with the Comanches in order that they might be turned against the Apaches. This policy was executed in New Mexico by Governor Don Juan Bautista de Anza in 1786. Since there was no longer any French trade, the Comanches desired to trade with the New Mexico settlements and to receive Spanish aid against the Apaches. In accordance with the treaty of 1786, the Spaniards set out to erect the village of San Carlos de los Jupes on the Arkansas River for a group of Comanches. They spent nearly seven hundred pesos on the project. Artisans built houses, and farmers were sent to teach the Indians to farm, but the Comanches abandoned San Carlos almost before it was completed. The Spaniards could not make pueblo Indians of the Comanches, but from that time until they were compelled to give up their nomadic existence and come into the reservation, the Comanches were comparatively friendly with New Mexico. Their wrath was vented upon the Spaniards, Mexicans, and Texans to the south.

Before the Spaniards had reversed their frontier policy, the Apaches in Texas, hemmed in between Spaniards and Comanches, turned to the former for an alliance against their more fearful enemy, the Comanches. The Spaniards, wanting to expand their frontier and carry the gospel to the Apaches and not realizing the tremendous strength of the Comanches, established a mission and a small presidio about one hundred miles from their outlying post, San Antonio, on the San Saba River near present Menard. The Apaches never could find time to attend the mission and be converted, but they were glad to have the Spaniards bolster them in their losing struggle with the Comanches.

The Comanches did not long delay paying the newcomers a visit. In March, 1758, they attacked the mission and killed several persons. In an attempt to avenge the insult, the Spaniards were disastrously defeated the following year on the Red River near the present town of Ringgold, Texas. As a result of the defeat, Spanish extension into Comanchería ended. Throughout the rest of the century Comanche attacks on the Spanish settlements became almost a matter of regular routine, and their operations were extended south of the Río Grande.[6] They overawed the feeble garrison and village of the Spaniards at San Antonio, often thronging the streets and squares with insolent bravado and defiance or raiding and plundering, as fancy dictated.

As in New Mexico, the report of the Marquis de Rubi was followed by an attempt to make peace with the Comanches in Texas. Rubi recommended that the Spanish settlements on the East Texas frontier be abandoned, that strong garrisons be maintained at San Antonio and at La Bahía, and that the San Saba mission be abandoned. The recommendations were carried out for the most part, and in 1785 the Spaniards succeeded in drawing the Meat-eater and Wasp

6 Wm. E. Dunn, "The Apache Mission on the San Saba River, Its Founding and Its Failure," *The Southwestern Historical Quarterly*, Vol. XVII (1914), 379–414.

bands into a formal treaty of peace in return for a huge quantity of presents. The Spaniards, however, were loath to furnish them with guns and ammunition which they desired, and as a result, the Comanches continued to steal Spanish horses and to trade them to the New Mexico settlements or to other tribes of the North for the articles they wanted. The treaty furnished the Spaniards some relief, but it was not until the close of the century that the declining power of Spain, in a final effort to hold dominion over Texas, succeeded in overawing the Comanches for even a brief time. With the appearance of the Anglo-American traders in the early nineteenth century, the Comanche-Spanish relations became more openly hostile.

But neither were the Anglo-Americans able to keep peace with the Comanches, for they were bold, aggressive, and intolerant, and they had little understanding of the Indian or sympathy for him. Until about 1820 there was little contact between the Comanches and the Anglo-Americans, but about that time traders began to push west and settlers moved into the Spanish province of Texas. In 1825 a trading expedition of Americans visited and traded with the Comanches on the Clear Fork of the Brazos.[7]

When the eastern Indians were removed to Indian Territory, the Comanches objected to encroachment upon their hunting grounds and threatened a war of extermination. The United States government on its part decided to attempt a policy of peace. In 1832 a large number of Comanches met Sam Houston, an agent of the United States, to discuss the possibility of peace. As a result of this apparently good beginning in council at San Antonio, the United States in June, 1834, sent an expedition from Fort Gibson to invite the chiefs to the fort for a general council. A Comanche village was found about ten miles north of present Fort Sill, but the chiefs insisted on holding the council in their own country and refused to return with the expedition. Finally, a group of Comanches and Wichitas were persuaded to attend a council at Camp Holmes on the Canadian. A group of their headmen met the United States commissioners on August 24, 1835, and concluded a treaty whereby the Indians agreed to share their hunting grounds with the eastern tribes, citizens of the United States

[7] M. M. Kenney, "The History of the Indian Tribes of Texas," in Dudley G. Wooten (ed.), *A Comprehensive History of Texas, 1685–1897*, I, 763.

were permitted to pass and repass through their country without molestation, and restitution was to be made by either party of property stolen from the other.[8] Although both parties remained friendly for a time, the treaty proved of little value, for they soon forgot it.

Meanwhile, it was the Anglo-Americans in Texas whom the Comanches had come to regard as their real enemy. The first Anglo-Americans in Texas were not seriously troubled because they settled largely outside the Comanche land range, and the Comanches preferred to direct their raids against the Mexican settlements. They continued to take horses from the Mexican settlements and to sell them to Anglo-American traders, and the advantage of these transactions tended to keep them friendly toward the white man.[9]

But gradually the Anglo-American settlers in Texas scattered fearlessly over the face of the country; each one built his cabin and plowed his field wherever his fancy dictated, without much regard to means of defense beyond his individual arms and without apparent desire for near neighbors. They brought with them a superior breed of horses, much larger, stronger, and more enduring than the neglected breed which had grown from Spanish stock. Such a situation made it easy, attractive, and relatively safe for the Indians to take horses and scalps for trophies. It invited raids.

The year 1835 marks the beginning of the hostile raids against the Anglo-American settlements in Texas. During the Texas Revolution most of the Southern bands remained relatively quiet, but a group of Northern Comanches and their Kiowa allies made a destructive raid on the Texas frontier in May, 1836.[10] In the spring of 1837 the Cherokee chief, Bowl, was commissioned to visit the Comanches. He found those near the settlements friendly, but those along the upper Brazos, Wichita, and Red rivers apparently hostile. Texas President David G. Burnet, who had lived with the Comanches and understood something of their loose tribal organization, appointed Major A. Le Grand to visit the Northern bands and negotiate a treaty with

8 M. Stokes and M. Arbuckle to Secretary of War, September 15, 1835 (National Archives, Office of Indian Affairs, Western Superintendency file, Washington); Charles J. Kappler, *Indian Affairs, Laws and Treaties*, 57 Cong., 1 sess., *Sen. Doc. 452*, II, 435–39.

9 Mary Austin Holley, *Texas*, 155–58.

10 This was the attack on Parker's Fort in which Cynthia Ann Parker was captured.

them. Major Le Grand made contact with the Indians, but they refused to enter into a treaty agreement.[11]

President Sam Houston of the Texas Republic then urged a system of regulated trade as the best means of bringing about better relations with the Comanches, but Congress ignored the President and proceeded to enact laws for the protection of the frontier.[12] Although no open war occurred for a time, there were a few irregular conflicts. In 1838 the Wasp band asked for a treaty of peace, but insisted on a definite boundary between themselves and the Texans which would give them undisputed possession of the country north of the Guadalupe Mountains. The Texas commissioners refused to discuss the boundary question, but it was agreed that a general council should be held at San Antonio. At that meeting the Comanches again insisted on recognition of their right to certain lands and, further, on a ban against trading posts in their country, but again the Texas government's refusal to concede that right prevented any formal peace agreement.

While the negotiations around San Antonio were going on, Noah Smithwick accepted the invitation of a band living on the Colorado River, near the present site of Austin, to come to their village to talk peace. He spent some time at their village and persuaded them to visit President Houston. The result was the treaty of May 29, 1838, but it contained no provisions of consequence other than a promise that an agent would be appointed to protect the Indians and supervise the trade among them. The treaty was never ratified by the Senate.[13] The failure of the agent to maintain contact with the Indians, plus the failure to establish the trading house, made it appear to the Comanches that the Texas government was not keeping faith with them.

President Mirabeau B. Lamar, who succeeded Sam Houston in 1838, favored an aggressive war of extermination against the Indians. In fact, war already existed. The continued westward expansion of the whites had angered the Comanches more than ever and had left the white settlements less protected. The Texas Congress promptly

[11] H. Yoakum, *History of Texas*, II, 228 ff.

[12] H. P. N. Gammel (compiler), *Laws of Texas*, I, 1480.

[13] Anna Muckleroy, "The Indian Policy of the Republic of Texas," *The Southwestern Historical Quarterly*, Vol. XXVI (1923), 23.

provided for a system of frontier forts, authorized the placing of over a thousand men in the field, and appropriated one million dollars to be used in the defense of the country.[14] There were some raids and counterattacks during 1838, but the following year was generally quiet.

Early in 1840, three Comanches appeared in San Antonio with a request for peace. As a result, twelve Comanche chiefs met with Texas commissioners on March 19, 1840, at Bexar, where General Hugh D. McLeod was in command. In the course of the proceedings, the Texans demanded that the Comanches give up their white prisoners. This they refused to do. A body of troops was then brought into the council room to intimidate the Indians. In the fight which followed the twelve chiefs were killed. The struggle was shortly transferred to the grounds surrounding the council house, and there twenty followers of the chiefs were slain. The Council House tragedy provoked severe retaliatory raids by the Indians and destroyed whatever confidence the Comanches had in the integrity of the Texas government. The success of the Texas militia at Plum Creek in August and Colonel John H. Moore's surprise attack on a Comanche village, probably as far in the interior as Colorado, Texas, where the Comanches felt secure, were decisive in discouraging the Comanches. During the remainder of Lamar's administration the Texas settlements were comparatively free from Comanche raids.

In his message to Congress in December, 1841, President Houston indicated that his administration would return to the pacific policy of his first term. He recommended that trading posts be established along the frontier, that traders be allowed to traffic with the Indians at these posts, and that a force of some twenty-five men be stationed at each. He further recommended the making of treaties with the Indian tribes, declaring that when the latter found that the Texas government was disposed to treat them kindly, confidence would be restored and the interest of trade would keep them quiet. He firmly believed that with less than one-fourth of former appropriations he could procure and maintain peace with all the tribes on the Texas borders by this method.

Messengers were sent out early in the following year to inform the Indians of the change in policy, but the Comanches were dis-

14 Gammel, *op. cit.*, II, 15–20, 29, 30, 78, 84–85.

trustful and remained away from the councils. Finally, Houston sent a commission composed of J. C. Eldredge, Hamilton Bee, and Thomas Torrey to find the Comanches and bring them into council. The Indian guides believed that the Wasp band chief, known as Paha-yuca, was camped on the headwaters of the Brazos, but he was found in August, 1843, on the upper Canadian River. The commissioners did not receive a very friendly reception. This was the occasion mentioned in Chapter IX when the Comanches debated all day in council the fate of the peace messengers. At one time the voice of everyone in the council except that of the principal chief favored putting the envoys to death. Paha-yuca, after detaining the council for many hours, brought over a bare majority to respect the flag of truce. The messengers were dismissed with a negative answer, but Paha-yuca expressed a desire for peace and promised to attend a peace council at a later date.[15] However, Paha-yuca controlled only a small part of the Comanche bands, and it was too late in the year for the commissioners to make contact with the other bands.

After more unsuccessful efforts, the general council finally convened at Tehuacana Creek in October, 1844. After some delay the Comanches arrived. President Houston attended and conducted the proceedings. A mutual pledge of friendship was made and the Texans agreed to establish official trading houses and to appoint Indian agents. The Comanches were to cease plundering, and certain provisions pertaining to warfare were agreed upon in case war should again develop. The Comanches also agreed to attend a council once each year. In return, the Texas government promised the Indians presents from time to time. But the main question, that of a satisfactory boundary, could not be settled. The Comanches refused to accept President Houston's proposal, and he in turn refused to accept their demands. Trading houses were established by Houston at Bird's Fort (near Fort Worth), at Comanche Peak west of the Brazos in Hood County, and at old Fort San Saba. The Comanches and other tribes came regularly to trade their peltries for such goods as they fancied, but peace was not maintained for any considerable time. The Texas government was not strong enough to prevent expansion; the Comanches would not have been satisfied with anything less than a

[15] Kenney, "The History of the Indian Tribes of Texas," *loc. cit.,* 769.

complete cessation of frontier extension. Moreover, the treaty bound only a part of the Wasps and none of the other Comanche bands.

President Houston's hope of peace was not realized, for the Comanches came in only when it suited them. His pacific policy achieved some worthwhile results, but it did not solve the Comanche problem for even the time being. The Indians continued to fight the Mexicans, and in passing to and from Mexico they came in contact with the Texas settlements and committed a number of depredations along the trail. Reports of peace with the Texans, together with a scarcity of buffalo on the northern range and a plentiful supply near the Texas settlements, caused many of the Northern Comanches to drift south near the settlements. By 1845 relations were again strained. The outbreak of hostilities began when a group of renegade Delaware Indians, whom the Comanches regarded as allies of the whites, murdered some Comanches. Depredations on the settlements followed. As a result, most of the chiefs remained away from the next annual council, but the Wasps soon afterwards came in and agreed to keep the peace.

After annexation to the Union, the people of Texas believed that once the protecting arm of the United States had been extended to their frontiers, their Indian problems would soon be ended. On the contrary, however, troubles with the Indians continued for another thirty years. The federal government set out at once to establish a uniform and consistent policy toward the aborigines. Through its agents and soldiers it sought to control the Indians, protect the frontier, and avoid clashes; but there were too many factors beyond its control. It could forbid the Indians' entering the settlements, but it could not prevent the whites' going into Indian country whenever they desired. Also, the ineffective tactics of the army on the frontier caused both Indian and settlers to be impressed more with the weakness of the government than with its strength. In some instances costly forts were built where temporary camps would have sufficed; frequently the posts were manned by infantrymen who were helpless in a contest with mounted Indians. Many officers and troops were strangely ignorant of the rudiments of warfare as carried on by Indians of the plains.

To achieve its purpose of establishing peace, the federal government in January, 1846, sent commissioners to meet the Indians. So few Comanches appeared for the first council meeting that another was set for the following April. Although late in arriving, the Indians gathered in large numbers in April at Tehuacana Creek. It was the most representative council of the Wasps that had yet assembled, but they were the only division of the tribe represented. A treaty was signed whereby the Wasp band agreed to accept the jurisdiction of the United States, to trade with licensed traders only, to surrender culprits on demand, to restore all horses that might be stolen in the future, to co-operate in the suppression of the liquor traffic, and to give up all captives. The government of the United States on its part agreed to permit no whites to go among the Indians except with a pass from the President, to establish trading houses near them, to furnish blacksmiths to repair their arms and utensils, and to present to the Texas Indians signing the treaty presents to the value of ten thousand dollars.[16]

The Comanches were not entirely pleased with the treaty. They wanted to have a boundary established between them and the whites. That was no simple matter, however, for by the terms of annexation, Texas retained ownership of its public lands and the United States could not guarantee the Indians permanent rights to any part of it. Failure to make such a guarantee appeared to the Comanches as merely one more example of broken faith. Whites continued to enter the Indian territory in violation of the treaty, yet the Texans were unwilling to allow the Comanches to pass through their settlements on the way to attack the Mexicans. Because of the outbreak of war with Mexico, the government of the United States hesitated to place soldiers of its regular army on the frontier, but when it appeared that Indian trouble was imminent, it authorized the government of Texas to raise companies for frontier defense. Before the end of Governor J. P. Henderson's term in December, 1847, nine such companies were in the federal service along the frontier.[17] No doubt they were a strong persuasive force upon the Indians to keep the peace.

However, to Robert S. Neighbors, who became special agent for

[16] *United States Statutes at Large*, IX, 844–48; Kappler, *op. cit.*, 554, 557.

[17] R. N. Richardson, *Texas: The Lone Star State*, 202; see also Clarksville, Texas, *Northern Standard*, January 22, 1848.

the Indians of Texas in the early part of 1847, belongs much of the credit for the period of comparative peace along the Texas frontier. The tireless efforts of this patient and tactful agent gained the friendship of some of the great old Comanche chiefs, who seriously endeavored to preserve the treaty. They restrained their warriors from acts of hostility, and at times when it appeared that they would be unable to prevent the outbreak of disturbances, they removed with their followers far away from the white settlements. The friendliness of these groups tended to restrain the Northern bands.

Agent Neighbors continued in the Indian service under the federal government, until his death in 1859, except for the period from 1849 to 1853.

About the time Neighbors left the Wasps in 1849, the Southern Comanches suffered from a siege of smallpox and cholera which carried away a large number, including their head chief. From that time on, the Wasps had no common leader. Congress had not appropriated funds for presents, and the Wasps intensified their raiding both in Texas and in Mexico. The Comanches maintained that they had not ended their war against the Mexicans, regardless of which side of the Río Grande they lived on. The chiefs also insisted that the depredations against the Texans were carried out by irresponsible young men who could not be restrained, so matters drifted from bad to worse, and by 1851 war appeared imminent. Agent John H. Rollins decided that a new treaty might help the situation. He signed a proposed treaty on December 10, 1850, practically a duplicate of the old one. One new concession made by the Comanches was that they would not go south of the Llano River without the approval of an army officer.[18] Although the Senate failed to ratify it, some of the Northern Comanches were angry at the Wasps for making the treaty, and they began to make depredations on them. They also turned up for the few presents that were distributed and were dissatisfied that they did not receive more. The tension was lessened somewhat in 1851 when Congress made annuities available for the Texas Indians.

Confusion was also increased by the great amount of trespassing

18 J. H. Rollins, special agent for Texas, to Commissioner of Indian Affairs, December 22, 1850 (National Archives, Office of Indian Affairs, Treaties, Talks, and Councils file, Washington).

across Comanche territory in the years following the discovery of gold in California. Some three thousand persons crossed by way of the Canadian River route, making a trail through the heart of the Comanchería.[19] A road from San Antonio or Austin to Fredericksburg, thence north to the head of the main Concho, westward to the Pecos, and from there to El Paso cut across the southern Comanche range.[20] Many emigrants, rather than follow the regular routes, cut overland wherever it seemed most convenient. The movement of so many whites across their country increased the distrust of the Comanches, and they grew more and more hostile.

At the same time, white settlement continued to encroach upon the Comanche hunting grounds. The pressure of the settlers forced the more eastern Indians like the Wichitas, Wacos, Tawakonies, Tonkawas, and Lipan Apaches west into the Comanche range. A more serious problem still was the coming of the partly civilized Indians—Delawares, Shawnees, Seminoles, Cherokees, and Kickapoos—which the United States moved from their homes east of the Mississippi to new lands along the eastern border of the Great Plains. Groups of these Indians became wanderers and hunters. Sometimes the Plains Indians united against the eastern intruders. On one particular occasion in the spring of 1853, a great party estimated at 1,500 warriors, composed of Comanches, Osages, Apaches, Kiowas, Arapahos, and Cheyennes, undertook to wipe out all frontier Indians found on the plains. The Great Plains force met about one hundred Sauk and Fox Indians near the Kansas River and received a humiliating defeat, for the Sauk and Fox were armed with rifles while the Plains Indians had very few firearms and most of those inferior in quality.[21]

Comanche hostility to the encroachments was intensified because the buffalo were becoming more and more difficult to find and kill. There was not enough game for the border Indians, white hunters, and Plains tribes combined. When the supply failed, the white men

[19] R. P. Bieber, "The Southwestern Trails to California," *Mississippi Valley Historical Review*, Vol. XII (1925), 360.

[20] Clarksville, Texas, *Northern Standard*, February 16, 1850.

[21] Whitfield to Commissioner of Indian Affairs, September 27, 1854, 33 Cong., 2 sess., *Sen Exec. Doc. 1*, Part 1, No. 29, 298. A Cheyenne version of this fight is given in Grinnell, *The Fighting Cheyennes*, 80–92.

and the border tribes had other means of subsistence, but the warriors of the plains had nothing left.

The United States government was not willing to resort to open warfare on the northern frontier without first attempting to restore amicable relations by negotiation. For this purpose Thomas Fitzpatrick was sent to the frontier. Fitzpatrick, as sole commissioner for the United States, on July 27, 1853, signed a treaty with the Comanches and their Kiowa and Kiowa-Apache allies. The United States reserved the right to build roads, to establish depots and posts, and to protect emigrants passing through the Comanche country. As compensation for these concessions, the federal government was to distribute among the Indians merchandise, provisions, agricultural implements, and other goods to the amount of $18,000 annually for a period of five years, or as long as the President deemed necessary and proper. On their part, the Indians pledged themselves to cease their attacks on the emigrants and frontier settlements, to restore all captives they held, and to refrain from any further raids into Mexico.[22]

This treaty did not solve the problem any more than the others. Like the previous ones, it was not kept by either of the two contracting parties. The Indians captured and killed citizens of the United States and continued their raids into Mexico. They did allow the construction of the military posts, if they were strongly protected during construction. On the other hand, the government made no effort to build roads in the territory or to protect the Indians, but it did send supplies, most of which were of little use to them.

Meanwhile, the United States government already had begun to assume the responsibility of a forceable keeping of the peace on the frontier. When it withdrew its forces from Mexico in 1848, dragoons took the place of state troops on the frontier. In 1849 the army began to put into effect a permanent plan of defense. Eight outposts were established from Fort Worth, at the site of the modern city of that name, to Fort Duncan, at Eagle Pass on the Río Grande. The posts were to serve in controlling the Indians and preventing them from harassing the settlements.

22 "Treaty between the United States and the Comanche, Kiowa, and Apache Indians in 1853" (original draft dated November 19, 1853, and treaty as ratified by the Senate, National Archives, Office of Indian Affairs, Washington).

So rapid was the advance of settlement, however, that within less than two years the line of frontiersmen's cabins had passed beyond this cordon, and a new series of forts was established about one hundred miles west. Beginning with Fort Clark near the Río Grande, posts were erected at strategic points in or near the Comanche range to the northward. These included Fort Chadburne, Fort Phantom Hill, Fort Belknap in present Young County, Fort Arbuckle in the valley of the Canadian, Fort Mann, and, later, Fort Atkinson far out on the Arkansas River. The garrisons, it is true, were small, but the fact that there were always some troops present caused the Indians much annoyance. By 1855 the frontier line of settlements ran roughly through the Texas counties of Grayson, Denton, Parker, Palo Pinto, Eastland, Brown, Lampasas, Burnet, Gillespie, Kendall, Bexar, and thence southeast to San Patricio.

A close correlation existed between the number of troops stationed on the frontier and the extent of marauding operations by the Indians. During 1853, for instance, there were 3,265 soldiers in Texas, the greatest number at any time before the Civil War, and the frontier was comparatively tranquil. During the following year, after many troops had been withdrawn and the country between the Colorado and Red rivers was left defended by only four small companies of infantry and two of dragoons, conditions became so bad that a call was made for state troops.

In an effort better to provide for the Indians and to co-operate with the federal government in restraining them, two reservations were established in Texas in 1855. The act of establishment authorized the general government to survey and set up reservations out of twelve leagues of land, to be selected from any vacant lands within the state. The amount was pitifully small, but the state insisted that caring for the red man was a federal problem and thought the grant to be quite generous. Surviving members of the Caddo, Anadarko, Ioni, Waco, Tonkawa, and Tawakoni tribes, totaling about one thousand, were located on an eight-league reservation at the junction of the Brazos and Clear Fork rivers near Fort Belknap. The second reserve was located on the Clear Fork, in what is now Throckmorton County, where Camp Cooper was later established. There were collected here by 1857 about 430 Comanches of the Wasp band, or not much more than half of that band. The remainder stayed at large, and some united with the Northern bands and became even more troublesome.[23]

Conditions near the Indian country improved greatly in 1856. The change may have been due in part to the reservations, but more likely it could be traced to the presence of the great number of competent military men stationed on the frontier, plus the fact that since game was becoming scarcer, the Comanches broke up into small thieving and marauding bands. More than ever, small squads of irresponsible warriors carried on their operations without restraint. But, most significant of all, retreat into the heart of the plains country no longer offered security. Heretofore white men had considered this northern and western region impenetrable, and in its semiarid fastness the Comanches had felt secure. But during 1858 both the Texas and the federal forces penetrated to the Comanches' farthest retreat with sufficient strength to destroy the Indians wherever they set their lodges. Three times during 1858 the Comanches were defeated north of Red River. Thus it seemed to the Comanches that on every front they were met by aggressive foes; the hand of every white man was against them. In despair they huddled their families together near the agency on the Arkansas, while they sent their young warriors in small parties to harass the settlements from Red River to Corpus Christi. A German settlement twenty-five miles from Fredericksburg was completely broken up, and the citizens of Kerrville had to organize a company of rangers on their own initiative.

In spite of the loyal aid given by the reservation Indians, the whites of the frontier charged that the reservation Indians were taking part in the raids, and they demanded that they be removed from Texas. The evidence available does not sustain the charges of the white settlers, but bloody conflicts had provoked in them a hatred for the red man that made them blind to reason. Angry settlers threatened the lives of reservation people, and only the presence of federal troops prevented a massacre. To avoid catastrophe, the federal government in July, 1859, at a council held at Fort Arbuckle, granted the friendly

23 Commissioner of Indian Affairs, *Annual Report,* 1854, 158–66; R. N. Richardson and C. C. Rister, *The Greater Southwest,* 283.

Indians a tract of land near Anadarko in the Leased District.[24] In the late summer of 1859, the Indians of both reservations were removed to their new home. However, since reservation Indians had not been engaged in the raids, relocation of the reservation did nothing to solve the Indian problem.

Dissatisfaction with conditions on the frontier led to the defeat of Hardin R. Runnels and the election of Sam Houston as governor of Texas in 1859. Houston had made a campaign promise to quiet the Indians, and he proceeded with an ambitious program for defense. By a series of orders he authorized the raising of ranger companies, until by the end of March, 1860, more than five hundred men were in active service. He also authorized the chief justice of each frontier county to raise a company of not more than twenty-five minute men, and for a time in 1860 twenty-three such companies were available for service. In addition to the state forces there were 2,651 federal troops in Texas in 1860 and others were on their way.[25] With such forces available, the state of affairs which had existed along the frontier could not long have continued but for the outbreak of the Civil War and the consequent slackening of the merciless pursuit of the red men by the whites. With the outbreak of civil war the frontier was temporarily forgotten and the center of diplomacy shifted north of Red River, although the people of Texas continued to pay in blood and plunder.

The Comanches were not a factor of great importance during the war as far as either the government of the North or South was concerned. They forced both the Federal and the Confederate governments to maintain military forces to watch them, but neither government cared to spare the men and money necessary to fight Indian wars. In order to avert such a conflict, both North and South made overtures to the Indians. The Comanches, on finding themselves sought after by both governments, accepted peace with one or the other, as it suited their convenience. Neither side tried to use them against the other, but each attempted instead to hold them as passive allies so as to prevent their joining the foe.

[24] The Leased District was land leased from the Choctaws and Chickasaws. It was bounded on the east by the ninety-eighth meridian, on the west by the one-hundredth meridian, on the south by the Red River, and on the north by the Washita River.

[25] Richardson, *Texas*, 205.

The Confederate government was the more successful in diplomatic dealings with the Comanches during the first few months of the war. In May, 1861, Albert Pike was appointed by President Jefferson Davis as special commissioner to treat with the Indians west of the Mississippi. His task was made easier, since the United States government had been virtually at war with the Kiowas for two years and their annuity goods had not been delivered to them.

Pike was acquainted with the Comanches and was well aware that peace with them would mean that troops could be withdrawn from the Texas frontier to be used in the East. So, with the aid of the Creeks, who were friends of the Comanches, he induced the latter to meet him at the Wichita agency on August 12 and 13, 1861. He there negotiated two treaties, one with the Indians of that reservation and the other with the "Comanches of the Prairies and Staked Plains." The treaty with the Indians of the agency included, among others, the Wasp Comanches; and the treaty with the prairie Comanches included four bands, the Those Who Move Often, Yep-eaters, Meat-eaters, and a remnant of the Liver-eaters (*Tanima*). More than a dozen chiefs signed the treaty on behalf of these wild bands. Every important band except the Antelope had a part in these treaties, and it was probably the most representative gathering of Comanches ever assembled up to that time.

The treaties, however, did not differ widely from those the United States had made with them in former years. Each side was to give up the prisoners then held, and the Comanches were to be paid for theirs. The Confederate government was to maintain at least one agency in the Leased District. The whites promised to furnish the Comanches with supplies until they should become self-sustaining, as well as with cattle to enable them to start herds. "The Confederate states ask nothing of the bands of the Nerm [Comanches] except that they prepare to support themselves, and live in peace and quietness."[26] In short, nothing was asked of the Comanches except that they should no longer be Comanches. This was too much to expect of the restive Lords of the South Plains. As long as there were buffalo to chase and unprotected ranches to despoil, it would take more than

---

[26] Commissioner of Indian Affairs, *Annual Report*, 1861, 634; *War of the Rebellion, Official Records*, Series IV, I, 542–54.

their crude marks on a piece of paper to hold them to such an agreement.

The agent was instructed to do everything possible to make the reserve inviting to the Indians, and in the autumn of 1861 the Confederate Congress voted $64,862 for the Comanches in order that the government might comply with its treaty obligation. But the prairie Comanches never came to the agency except occasionally to ask for presents. Agent Mathew Leeper provided well for the agency Wasps, but the Comanches off the reservation did not envy their reservation brethren; nor was Leeper able to keep all the Wasps on the reservation. The relations between the Confederate government and the Comanche bands practically collapsed with the destruction of the Wichita Agency in October, 1862, by a band of Delawares and Shawnees in sympathy with the Union government. The Wasps then took up their abode in the Wichita Mountains.[27]

The treaty, coupled with an effective frontier defense, resulted in a marked decline in raids along the Texas border. But with the collapse of Comanche-Confederate relations in the latter part of 1862 and a simultaneous decline in the efficiency of frontier defense because of reduction of personnel and the lack of good horses, conditions became much worse than before the war. Cooke, Clay, Jack, Palo Pinto, Denton, Montague, Wise, and Parker counties suffered most heavily from attacks. The Indians drove off more than ten thousand head of cattle, which they sold to Yankees, doubtless contractors for the armies. By 1864 the attacks were fewer but heavier.[28]

The federal agent had withdrawn from the Comanche country at the outbreak of the war, but in August he returned and made an armistice pending the negotiation of a permanent treaty. The Comanches saw no reason why they could not be friendly with both governments, one along the Arkansas and one in Texas. Two Comanches, one Apache, and four Kiowa chiefs were consequently taken to Washington, where they signed a treaty on April 6, 1863, agreeing to make perpetual the agreement signed at Fort Atkinson on July 27, 1853. The Washington treaty defined more clearly to the Indians

[27] *War of Rebellion, Official Records,* Series IV, II, 335.

[28] Cf. W. C. Holden, "Frontier Defense in Texas during the Civil War," *West Texas Historical Association Year Book* (1928), V, 16–31.

the matter of staying away from the Santa Fé road, and in return the United States was to furnish the associate tribes $25,000 in annuity goods. The treaty, however, was never ratified.[29] The failure of Congress to ratify this treaty may have been largely responsible for the outbreaks that followed the generally peaceful years of 1862 and 1863. Comanches had drifted in from the south to receive a share of the anticipated presents and annuity goods, and although most of the chiefs said they intended to adhere to the treaty of Washington, it is believed that there was formed in the autumn of 1863 an alliance of the Comanches, Kiowas, and Kiowa-Apaches of the South with the Cheyennes, Arapahos, and Sioux of the North. Widespread disturbances occurred in 1864. Numerous attacks were made along the route to Denver. Emigration was stopped and much of the country was depopulated.

These attacks were largely the work of the Cheyennes and their allies, but the Comanches and the Kiowas were active along the Arkansas and to the south of it, particularly along the Santa Fé Trail. Finally, a punitive expedition under Christopher (Kit) Carson was sent against the Comanches. The Indians, principally Kiowas and a small number of Comanches, Kiowa-Apaches, and Arapahos, gathered at Adobe Walls on the Canadian River to resist him. Since they greatly outnumbered the whites, but for two howitzers, Carson's force might have been overwhelmed.[30]

While the army was planning further campaigns against the Southern Indians, the Comanche and Kiowa agent, Colonel J. H. Leavenworth, persuaded authorities in Washington that more could be accomplished by following a policy of kindness and peace than by war. Leavenworth was able to get Comanche and Kiowa chiefs to a council in August, 1865, at the mouth of the Little Arkansas.[31] There the Indians agreed to cease all acts of violence or injury to the frontier settlements and to travelers on the Santa Fé road, or other lanes of travel, and to remain at peace. They further agreed to meet in council

29 "Treaty with the Kiowa and Comanche April 6, 1863," and "Resolution of Senate" relating to the treaty (MSS, National Archives, Office of Indian Affairs, Treaties, Talks and Councils file, Washington).

30 *War of the Rebellion, Official Records,* Series I, XLI, Part 1, 939.

31 J. H. Leavenworth to General John B. Sanborn, August 4 and 10, 1865, *ibid.,* XLVIII, Part 2, 1164, 1176.

with commissioners of the United States in October. Accordingly, on October 18, 1865, a treaty between the Comanches, Kiowas, and Apaches on the one hand and the United States on the other was signed at the mouth of the Little Arkansas, at approximately the present location of Wichita, Kansas.

Like all preceding treaties with the Comanches, the agreement was defective because some of the bands were not represented. The Meat-eaters band did not sign except by proxy, and the Antelopes were not represented at all. The great chiefs of the Yɛp-eaters, Those Who Move Often, Liver-eaters, and Wasps were there. The commissioners reported that "six of the nine bands which compose the Comanche tribe" were present. By the terms of the treaty, the Kiowas and Comanches who signed agreed to remove within a territory whose boundary, beginning with the northeast corner of New Mexico, was to run southward along the eastern boundary of the state to its southeast corner, thence northeastward to a point on Red River opposite the mouth of the North Fork, thence down the Red River to the ninety-eighth meridian, thence due north to the Cimarron River, thence up the Cimarron to the southern boundary of Kansas, and thence westward along this line to the place of beginning.[32]

The purpose of the United States in making the treaty was to secure peace with the Indians, to stop their attacks on the overland wagon trains and on the frontier settlements, to secure the release of prisoners held by the Indians, and to confine them to a narrower range. The government succeeded for a time, but, as usual, neither the government nor the Indians kept the agreement. The Indians determined to keep the Texans from encroaching further upon their domain; the Texans disputed the Indians' claim to any portion of the territory within their state.

By slowing up emigration into and across their territory, the Civil War gave the Indians a breathing spell, and if they were not more numerous, they were more insolent and desperate at its close than at its beginning. For a few months after the breakup of the Southern armies, state troops managed to afford some protection, but the federal government refused to allow the Texas government to protect

[32] Kappler, *op. cit.,* II, 891–93. The commissioners could not legally award any area within Texas.

the state frontier, nor would it do so for a time. The Comanches and their allies were not slow to learn of the unprotected condition of the frontier, and raids became so destructive and frequent that in some places the line of settlement was driven back a hundred miles. The country west of a line drawn from Gainesville to Fredericksburg was abandoned, except by a hardy few who moved into stockades. Although Sheridan refused to allow Governor Throckmorton to raise the thousand rangers authorized by the legislature, the Governor's persistent efforts to have the federal government place a part of its troops on the Texas frontier did meet with a measure of success. Before the end of the year, two regiments of cavalry were covering the line from the Red River to Fort Clark on the Río Grande. During the next two years the army established, with some modifications, the old cordon of posts it had maintained before the war, but the soldiers were inexperienced and ineffective and the policy was defensive rather than offensive.

Meanwhile, the federal government had turned to treaty-making again. Although officials at Washington did not realize the extent of the depredations, they were aware that affairs in the Indian country, north of Texas as well as in Texas, were not satisfactory. Accordingly, in the autumn of 1866, agents were sent to investigate. They reported that a large part of both the Comanche and the Kiowa tribes were flagrantly violating the treaty of the Little Arkansas; and that they did not even come in to receive their annuity goods, goods which were of inferior quality, the blankets being "hardly fit for saddle blankets." The majority of the army officers were charged with "utter ignorance of the Indian character and of the proper method of dealing with Indians." The report recommended the establishment of permanent agency headquarters with adequate buildings for residences, officers, and storehouses, and the prompt delivery of annuity goods that would be useful to the Indians. It was believed that there would be an outbreak of hostilities in the following spring unless precautions were taken.[33]

As a result of the investigation, in June, 1867, Congress authorized

[33] Charles Bogy and W. R. Irwin, special agents, to Commissioner of Indian Affairs, December 8, 1866 (National Archives, Office of Indian Affairs, Treaties, Talks, and Councils file, Washington).

a peace commission to correct the causes of Indian complaint by securing a lasting peace. This necessarily meant the segregation of the Indians at points remote from the settlements and lanes of travel.

The commissioners met the Indians somewhere near the present site of Medicine Lodge, Barber County, Kansas, and on October 21, 1867, signed a treaty. The treaty was proclaimed August 25, 1868. It was the last ever made with the Comanches, Cheyennes, Arapahos, Kiowas, and Kiowa-Apaches, and was the occasion of one of the last old-fashioned Indian gatherings. Both whites and Indians made great display. The commissioners distributed many gifts; food and coffee were free and plentiful so that no time might be wasted by the Indians in preparing food. When the council opened, the Indians were told that they had been violating the treaties and were urged to state their side of the case. Satanta of the Kiowas was the first to speak. Warlike and arrogant, he scorned the suggestion of houses or schools or labor. Ten Bears of the Yɛp-eaters spoke for the Comanches. His presentation of the Comanche point of view, a fragment of which we have already quoted, is a masterpiece of logic and oratory. He had seen the numbers and wealth and power of the white man on his visit to Washington two years before. He believed in the friendship and good intentions of the government, and to some extent he understood that it was unable to stop the westward drive of its people. He knew that the proposals represented an alternative between refuge on the white man's terms or utter destruction. But he pleaded that the United States leave the Comanches unmolested.[34]

The treaty provided that the Comanches and their Kiowa allies should refrain from further attacks on the whites, permit the construction of railroads and other roads, as well as military posts, in their country; and that they should accept an agency, schools, farms, a physician, and a carpenter—none of which they wanted. They were to be furnished implements, seed, and instruction in farming—over which they were not enthusiastic. The government agreed to provide annuity goods as may "seem proper to the condition and necessities of the Indians" for a period of thirty years. The Comanches, Kiowas,

[34] "Record Copy of the Proceedings of the Indian Peace Commission Appointed under the Act of Congress Approved July 20, 1867" (MS, National Archives, Office of Indian Affairs, Washington), I, 109, 104–106.

and Kiowa-Apaches were restricted to an area bounded on the east by the ninety-eighth meridian, on the north by the Washita River westward to a point thirty miles above Fort Cobb, and thence by a line due west to the North Fork of the Red River, and on the south and west by Red River and its North Fork.[35] It included the present counties of Comanche, Cotton, Kiowa, and Tillman, and parts of Grady, Stephens, and Jefferson. This area of only 5,546 square miles was small indeed compared to the vast Comanchería of old. The Lords of the South Plains were about to become the wards of the federal government.

[35] Kappler, *op. cit.*, II, 977 ff.

XII

On the Reservation

THE reservation assigned to the Comanches and their allies by the treaty of Medicine Lodge in 1867 was a beautiful country of 2,968,893 acres carved from lands ceded by the Chickasaws and Choctaws in 1866. Although the greater portion of the old reservation is wide, rolling plains, the topography ranges from level valleys to mountainous terrain. Slightly toward the northwest the granite masses of the Wichita Mountains lift abruptly, wrapped always in purple haze. Beautiful streams carry away the water drained from their heights, and in the grassy flats deer and buffalo once abounded. Small blackjack trees cover the hills in the northern part of the reservation, while cottonwood and elm, with sparsely scattered oaks and pecans, are found along all the streams and in low spots where water collects. There is a wide variation of soils—mainly flood plain, second bottom, colluvial, high terrace, and residual. The highest point is Mount Scott in the Wichita Mountains, which has an elevation of 2,400 feet, while along the Red River valley the elevation is about half as much. The average elevation is 1,262 feet above sea level. The average precipitation for a thirty-five year period ending in 1937 was thirty-one inches. The average date for the first killing frost is October 30 and the last in the spring falls on April 3, thus providing an ample growing season.

There is no evidence that the Indians were ever convinced that it was best for them to deed away the greater portion of their lands, but the treaty signers probably realized that if they refused they would receive no annuity goods and would have to fight soldiers besides. Even so, only ten Comanche chiefs representing the Yɛp-eaters, Those Who Move Often, and Wasps signed the treaty. The powerful Meat-eaters and Antelopes did not sign. Probably a third of the Comanches were not represented at all, but in the end they had to accept the inevitable. They all became reservation Indians.

The conduct of the United States Indian Service and the military forces after the treaty was signed was such as to puzzle the Indian's mind. The treaty was ratified in Washington in 1868, but the government was slow in meeting its obligations. It failed to send troops to protect the agency and maintain order among the Indians who gathered near by. As a consequence, neither life nor property was safe in that vicinity. Nonresident Comanches gathered near the agency, demanded food and presents, and plundered the reservation Indians. The agent, because of either fear or disgust, deserted his post. Those Comanches who in times past had frequented the region of the Arkansas Valley left for their old haunts, while other bands took to the *Llano Estacado* where they had been wont to roam in earlier times.

The first annuity day finally arrived on December 30, 1868, and great numbers of Comanches came in to Fort Cobb on the northern edge of the reservation for the occasion. But by that time the Cheyenne war had broken out along the Arkansas and to the north of that stream, and the military authorities feared that the Comanches and their allies might join the Cheyennes. To prevent such a possibility, they escorted those who had gathered on the northern edge of the reservation southward to the vicinity of Medicine Bluff. There they established Fort Sill near by on Cache Creek for the purpose of holding the Comanches and their cohorts in check. The first stake of the new post was set on January 8, 1869, and shortly afterwards Colonel W. B. Hazen located the agency site three miles from the post. One small adobe building had been provided for the agency plant when Agent Lawrie Tatum arrived on July 1. This became the headquarters for the Comanches, Kiowas, and Kiowa-Apaches.[1]

While waiting for the new agent to arrive to replace the deserter,

1 Supt. W. B. McCown, *Annual Report: Narrative Section,* 1935, 4 (Kiowa-Comanche Agency, Anadarko). The Wichita and Affiliated Bands were also there, but they soon became so annoyed by the thievery and wildness of the prairie Indians that they moved north of the Washita. They were granted a separate agency in 1872.

Colonel Hazen started to train the Comanches as farmers. But most of the money given him by the army had to be used for food. He had intended to use it for fencing, plowing, buying fruit trees, and constructing houses and schools. He hired a white man to plow up a tract of land near the agency and plant corn, melons, beans, and squashes as a starter, but the Comanches and Kiowas were not interested, except to plunder the fields. After eating the green watermelons and getting the "Devil inside my belly," they were even less desirous of agricultural pursuits, for they thought farming bad medicine.[2] The more independent Comanches, approximately 1,500 of an estimated population of 2,416, remained off the reservation, but some of them were willing to come in whenever goods and presents arrived. Even while they were waiting for a distribution, troops from New Mexico struck them in the very heart of their range in the dead of winter at a time when the majority were trying to obey the instructions of their white guardians.[3]

Because of its failure to deal satisfactorily with the Indian problem and because of fraud, the Indian Office brought upon itself so much criticism that, in 1869, Congress, in an effort to correct some of the abuses charged against the Indian administration, authorized the President to organize a board of Indian commissioners, who were to exercise joint control over appropriations with the Secretary of the Interior. This new body became at once a dominant force in determining the Indian policy of the government. Simultaneously, President U. S. Grant made another important change in Indian administration by appointing Quakers as Indian agents and employees. Other denominations were, however, allowed to participate in the Indian work, and most agents, teachers, and employees at the Indian agencies came to be nominees of some church or religious society. This was the era of the Peace Policy.

On July 1, 1869, Lawrie Tatum, an unimaginative but courageous and sensible Quaker, took up his duties at Fort Sill as the agent of the Comanches, Kiowas, and Kiowa-Apaches. Tatum felt that God

[2] Agent Lawrie Tatum, *Annual Report*, August 12, 1870, 41 Cong., 3 sess., *House Exec. Doc. 1*, Part 4, No. 94, 725.

[3] Agent W. B. Hazen, *Report*, 1869, Commissioner of Indian Affairs, *Annual Report*, 1869, 338–96; Agent J. H. Leavenworth to Commissioner of Indian Affairs, May 21, 1868, 41 Cong., 2 sess., *House Misc. Doc. 139*, III, 5–7.

had called him to this new work, about which he knew nothing, and declared that the necessary information would come to him as needed! The Friends believed that kindness and honesty would solve the Indian problem, but not all the white elements in the picture were Friends. The Friends proposed to make the Indians secure in their legal rights, to locate them on the reservation, and to assist them in agriculture and the arts of civilized life.[4] They strongly opposed the use of military forces against the red men and forbade the troops to attack them on the reservation. They were, on the other hand, allowed no control over the Indians who failed to come on the reservation.

Tatum began his work with the firm conviction that such a policy would succeed, but he soon came to the conclusion that force was the only kind of treatment that some Indians understood and respected. From the very beginning, he found that soldiers were necessary to control the Indians on issue day and that nothing short of armed force would command respect. Without the presence of the army, the reservation became a sanctuary for marauders, and raids into Kansas and Texas continued. Farming operations did not turn out well, nor could the majority of the Indians be induced to come on the reservation.

Mow-way (Shaking Hand), a Meat-eater chief, whose natural inclination was friendliness, expressed the view of many of the prairie Comanches when he said, "When the Indians in here [the reservation] are better treated than we are outside, it will be time enough to come in." Chief *TaβenanIka* (Voice of the Sunrise) told Special Commissioner Henry Alvord in 1872 that he would rather stay out on the prairie and eat dung than come in and be penned up in a reservation. W. S. Nye says that because he proclaimed his sentiments in a stentorian voice, the Commissioner and everyone else in a radius of a quarter of a mile knew that he meant what he said. And this was the man who died of a heart attack while running to catch a train at Anadarko, Oklahoma, years later.[5] In 1869 the government sent less annuity goods, much of the annuity money being withheld to pay for depredations, and the Indians concluded that it was more

[4] Tatum, *Annual Report*, August 12, 1869, Commissioner of Indian Affairs, *Annual Report*, 1869, 385–86.

[5] Nye, *Carbine and Lance*, 205.

profitable to raid and to obtain a new treaty, for treaty meetings always meant presents and a liberal supply of goods.[6]

Hence it came about that during 1870 the Indians were especially insolent and defiant. Colonel B. H. Grierson was busy building Fort Sill early in the year and paid little attention to the Indians. When some prairie bands moved near the farms on Cache Creek, he thought they desired to begin farming, that they realized that the buffalo were disappearing. But he was wrong. They had no idea that the buffalo would not be sufficient; all they intended was to plunder the reservation.

In June the Comanches sat in council with the Kiowas during their annual Sun Dance and the question of peace or war was discussed at length. Prevailing sentiment was for peace, but some of the chiefs were determined to have war. After the council, a number of bands stayed out and organized raiding parties which went to harass the Texas frontier until checked by cold weather. Voice of the Sunrise insolently sent Agent Tatum word that he wished the soldiers from Fort Sill would come out and give him a fight. But it was the Kiowas rather than the Comanches who molested Fort Sill during the summer, stealing horses and mules, shooting cattle, and plundering fields. They took seventy-three mules from the corral at Fort Sill, and Colonel Grierson was unable either to catch the culprits or to ascertain who they were. Late in the summer, the Indians told Grierson and Tatum that they would not disturb Fort Sill any more that season. "The white people need not sit trembling in their tents, peeping out to see if our warriors are coming. You can now send your horses out to graze, and your men out to chop wood." These were the favors granted to the fort where five hundred men were under arms.[7]

When the Indians began killing the agency commissary beeves, Agent Tatum put soldiers on guard, but some visiting Quakers, horrified at seeing soldiers at the agency, forced him to remove them to the fort. Tatum then attempted to restrain the Indians by withholding half the rations as punishment. But at the very same time, the policy of giving one hundred dollars' reward for the return of each white captive only encouraged the Indians to raid for more victims.

[6] Tatum, *Annual Report*, August 12, 1870, *loc. cit.*, 725–28.
[7] Nye, *Carbine and Lance*, 150.

The experience of 1870 proved beyond doubt that as long as game was plentiful and the Indians could secure arms and ammunition from the traders, they could not possibly be kept on the reservation without the use of force. This was borne out by the number of audacious raids which occurred in 1871. Best known is the Salt Creek "massacre" of May, 1871, when a band of Kiowas attacked a wagon train between Jacksboro and Fort Griffin, killing seven teamsters. For the Indians the time of the attack proved unfortunate. William Tecumseh Sherman, commander of the Army of the United States, and R. B. Marcy were at Jacksboro on a tour of inspection to see for themselves whether conditions were as bad as reported. The Indians were followed to the reservation and the raiding chiefs arrested, tried, convicted of murder, and sentenced to be hanged; but Governor E. J. Davis of Texas commuted the sentence to life imprisonment.

The incident was instrumental in causing the government to abandon its peace policy. In fact, Tatum himself requested that the Meat-eaters and Antelopes be forcibly brought to the reservation. Colonel R. S. MacKenzie, who was in Texas and unhampered by the Quaker peace policy, led an expedition from old Camp Cooper northwest up Blanco Canyon against the Comanches under Quanah Parker. MacKenzie, however, was unsuccessful, for the Comanches, after holding the troops at bay, moved out upon the *Llano Estacado,* and cold weather prevented the soldiers from following them. The prairie Comanches had not even been punished.

During the winter months of 1871–72 the Comanches remained quiet. All except the Antelopes came in for rations. But when the grass became green and the ponies fat in the spring of 1872, the young warriors of the wild bands could not be restrained from their perennial raids. The principal reasons for this year's outbreak were the urge for personal glorification and prestige, the desire to obtain revenge for relatives killed by whites, the slaughter of the buffalo by the whites, and their determination not to live on the reservation. On a June night a young warrior of the Meat-eater band, named *Teneβ3ka* (Gets to Be a Middle-aged Man), and four other warriors under cover of a thunderstorm raided the government corral at Fort Sill and got away with all fifty-four horses and mules that were inside.

None of the group were ever apprehended, and when Gets to Be a Middle-aged Man was visited by Ralph Linton, E. A. Hoebel, and G. G. Carlson of the Santa Fé Laboratory of Anthropology party in 1933, he was most suspicious of them. He thought they were government spies sent to get evidence against him. In all the intervening years he had given Fort Sill a wide berth. But when Professor Linton arranged a peace gesture with the commandant of the fort, the old Comanche accepted the invitation to be the honored guest at a dinner and receive his "pardon."

In the eighteen seventies the Quakers resorted to their peace policy again. Two councils were held in an effort to persuade the wild bands to make peace and come on the reservation, but the Indians either did not show up or were defiant. Representatives of the Five Civilized Tribes joined the whites in a council at Fort Cobb in July in an effort to persuade the wild bands that the buffalo would soon be gone and that they must take up the white man's ways lest they starve. But the Comanches refused to believe that such a calamity was imminent; if such a danger was impending, they would abstain from killing the buffalo for a year or two. Meanwhile they could manage to subsist on cattle stolen from Texas.

When the peace efforts of the summer failed and raiding continued, the military campaigns were renewed, this time with much greater success. In September, Colonel MacKenzie set out from near Fort Griffin. On September 29 he surprised and destroyed a camp on McClellan Creek near the mouth of Blanco Canyon, taking a large number of prisoners and three thousand horses and mules. The Indians stampeded and recaptured their animals the following night, but the spirit of the band was broken. Although they refused to go to the agency at once, they assumed an attitude of humility and gave assurances of friendship. Shortly afterwards they sent representatives to offer to exchange captives for the return of their own people. During the winter of 1872–73 the wild Antelope band camped near the agency at the present site of Lawton, while the other Comanches were north of the post on Chandler Creek, and the amount of raiding was negligible.

The use of the military against the Indians aroused Quaker sentiment against Tatum, and the days of his service were numbered. Although Tatum insisted that the Indians had made progress towards passivity as a result of the punitive measures against them, his co-religionists did not share his views. On April 1, 1873, he was succeeded by J. M. Haworth, a thoroughgoing Quaker and a firm believer in the Peace Policy. Haworth's first act in accordance with his convictions was to remove the military guard which Tatum had kept at the agency. In its place he tried using an old Indian to perform police duty on issue day, but in May he found it necessary to ask for a night guard.[8]

In the spring of 1873 when the government was surveying the reservation lands, some of the Indians feared that the land was about to be divided for settlement. This led Comanches to join the Kiowas in their annual Sun Dance on Sweetwater Creek. The Kiowas were considering going to war if the chiefs Satanta and Big Tree were not released. In June, Haworth released the prisoners taken by Mac-Kenzie in 1872, hoping that it would keep the Indians quiet; but no sooner had the prisoners been released than the Comanches renewed their destructive raids into Texas and Mexico. However, some of the chiefs attempted to keep their renegade warriors in hand and brought in to the agents the stolen horses. Despite this action the raids into Texas continued during the winter of 1873–74.

Heavy rains interfered with freight service at the agency in the spring of 1874, and at a critical time the agent was forced to issue half-rations. The rations were so meager that the Indians on the reservation had to kill their horses and mules for food. The Indians at the agency became unruly and joined with the outside bands to hold a tribal medicine dance. This was a new thing and portended evil.

The backs of the Comanches and their neighbors, the Kiowas and Cheyennes, had not yet been broken, but they were deeply disturbed and desperation was settling in their hearts. The old way was not yet gone, but it was slipping rapidly away from them. They were ripe for a movement of nativistic revivalism.

On the West Coast, among the Indians of California and Oregon, similar conditions prevailed. During the long period of Spanish occupancy the Indians of California had not found their way of life too seriously disturbed. But 1849 had come and two decades of American

[8] Agent J. M. Haworth to Lt. Col. J. W. Davidson, May 9, 1873, "Kiowa Military Relations" (Oklahoma Historical Society Library, correspondence files).

influx. The Oregon Trail had been opened, and in the seventies the Prophet Dance, a cult of revival of old ways, was sweeping the Northwest.

The Comanches had no contact with this remote phenomenon, but their crisis was similar. Through all their time they had felt no need for tribal integration, but now it was stand together or go under.

As so often happens in the history of oppressed peoples, a messiah came forth in answer to the need. This was none other than a young and as yet untried warrior—medicine man, *Ishatai,* Coyote Droppings. Coyote Droppings gave evidence of strong powers. He was immune to bullets—not in itself an outstanding trait, for many great warriors had over the years been possessed of such medicine. More significant was his claim to have "ascended above the clouds, where he had communed with the Great Spirit."[9] This was unusual. Also, he had, as had other medicine men before him, brought back the dead from the After World. He had power all right. But what really gave him prestige was his successful prediction that a comet which was attracting much attention early in 1873 would disappear in five days and would be followed by a summer-long drought. These things are reputed to have occurred in accordance with his prophecy.

In their despair the Comanches were willing to turn to him for the kind of leadership their established chiefs could not give. When he belched forth a "wagonload" of cartridges and swallowed them again in the presence of several Comanches, they believed that they had really seen this thing. Word spread that Coyote Droppings had such powers as no other Comanche had ever before possessed.[10]

In the hard spring of 1874 the Prophet felt that the time had come for the great endeavor. He announced that the Comanches should gather for a tribal Sun Dance. They should make a great medicine and save themselves. The call, according to R. N. Richardson, "was widely heralded, and when the tribesmen assembled in May at a point on Red River near the agency boundary, every band was represented, several of them by almost one hundred per cent of their people. . . . The great chiefs of the past had never been able to bring the scattered

9 Richardson, *The Comanche Barrier to South Plains Settlement,* 373.
10 Battey, *op. cit.,* 302–303.

threads of the people together, but now a youthful warrior was about to accomplish that."[11]

The Sun Dance, as it was worked out for the occasion by the Comanches, was a much simplified version of the elaborate complex that existed among the Cheyennes, Arapahos, and Kiowas. The Comanches had been interested spectators of Kiowa Sun Dances for some seventy-five years, and they had from time to time watched the Cheyenne spectacle in the years following the making of the peace in 1840. They were familiar enough with the external forms of the dance.

Certain features of the social structure that supported the Cheyenne and Kiowa dances were lacking in the cultural equipment of the Comanches, but this did not bother them. They were always a highly adaptable people and not in the least form-bound. If they had no military societies to police the camp and the dance, as did their neighbors, that was quite all right with them. They did not use police on the buffalo hunt—and they could do without them here. The fact that a little fetish doll was essential to the Kiowas in their form of the dance did not worry the Comanches, who had no such doll. They made no effort to procure a Sun Dance doll; they simply did without one. That the Cheyennes possessed trained Sun Dance priests, each of whom owned an inherited Sun Dance Medicine Bundle, without which no man could direct a Sun Dance, was of no moment. A respected shaman could direct the ceremony.

What was wanted was the Sun Dance—an invocation of the Great Power. The will and the general form of the dance would achieve the goal. Comanche thinking was running in the Comanche way.

The Comanche Sun Dance lodge had the traditional forked center pole surrounded by a circular wall of twelve upright posts, from each of which a streamer ran to the crotch of the center pole. The wall, with an opening between the two easternmost poles, was filled in with brush. Four ceremonial days were used to gather the materials and prepare the lodge.

The common Plains Indian practice of treating the tree that was to yield the center pole as though it were an enemy—i.e., "scouting" for it and counting coup upon it—was not done by the Comanches. They did, however, choose an honored, virtuous woman to do the

11 Richardson, *The Comanche Barrier to South Plains Settlement,* 374.

cutting, as did the other tribes. The Comanches followed the Kiowa practice of delegating the honor to a captive woman who had been faithful to her captor husband. This was but one of the ways of integrating the alien members into the tribal whole.

The ritual of raising the center pole with three false starts before hoisting it into place was done in the common Plains manner. A freshly killed and stuffed buffalo was mounted on the center pole. It is significant that in the crisis of the disappearing herds the Comanches in formulating their Sun Dance placed more than usual emphasis upon the bison.

On the last day of preparation, a scout was sent out to locate a "herd," and on the evening of the fourth day it was announced that it had been located. The Sun Dance proper began with an impounding of the buffalo. Four brave warriors went out some distance from the camp disguised as buffalo. One of them wore the robe of a mangy old bull. An especially outstanding warrior, carrying a bow and a torch, set forth to find them. In time, he found the herd and drove it back to the camp and into the dance lodge, just as used to be done with the old-time corral. Then the dancing could begin.

There were two other bits of dramatic by-play that took place on the fourth day of preparation and thus preceded the hunt. One of them provided comic relief, and the other provided an important bit of symbolism, as did the buffalo hunt. The first of these was the invasion of the clowns, or Mud Men (*sɛkwitsit puhitsit*). Here was something the Comanches had almost certainly picked up in their visits to the Pueblos, possibly at Taos where they were not infrequently peaceful visitors. This they grafted on to their version of the Sun Dance. The Comanche clowns were "masked" dancers akin to the *koshare* of the Eastern Pueblos. They prepared themselves by the creek, smearing their hair, faces, and bodies with mud. On their heads they wore willow-leaf "helmets" that hung down to their shoulders like semi-masks. About their bodies they wore leaves. On their visages they built up large noses of mud, and each carried a club of willow withes and a wicker shield made of the same material.

Mounting their mud-bedaubed ponies, they charged into the camp, swatting people with their "clubs," chasing dogs about, and generally acting funny. People who were whipped could not remonstrate; they could only escape by dodging into the lodges where the mounted Mud Men could not follow them.

The clowns performed no police functions at the dance, as do the Pueblo *koshare*,[12] for the Comanches had no use for tribal police. Neither were they an intrinsic part of the dance itself, as are the *koshare*. They provided a simple comic relief in the serious activities of the Sun Dance preparations; they were a light-hearted gesture in an act of desperation—the inauguration of the Sun Dance for the earthly salvation of the Comanche way of life. As soon as they were done with their clowning, they returned to the creek to cleanse themselves so that they could be back in time for a more serious drama—the sham battle.

While the dance lodge was being finished, a group of warriors went down to the creek to build a symbolic fortified enemy encampment of a circular rail fence. When all the work on the dance lodge was finished, a scout who had served as a real scout went out to find them. He rode back to the main camp signaling the discovery of enemies. All the warriors in the main camp prepared as if for battle, and together they sallied forth to the attack, women and children following to see the show. In the assault on the enemy camp each man attempted to re-enact his own great war deeds before the eyes of the woman and children, who, according to Post Oak Jim, "got scared by the real way they seemed to fight." When the enemy was destroyed, the whole tribe marched back to the camp singing the Victory Song.

It is most probable that the rail-enclosed mock enemy camp was not intended to represent an Indian encampment. Plains Indian villages were not stockaded. Could this have been the white settlement at Adobe Walls, Texas, with its surrounding adobe enclosure, that the Comanches were going to annihilate as soon as the Sun Dance was over? If so, this dramatic by-play was a projective wish-fulfillment of their plan to destroy the whites who were destroying them, just as the symbolic buffalo hunt was a wishful recapture of the herds that were no more.

The integrating nature of the Sun Dance for the Comanches is

---

12 E. C. Parsons and R. L. Beals, "The Sacred Clowns of the Pueblo and Maya-Yaqui Indians," *American Anthropologist*, Vol. XXXVI (1934), 491–514.

in part revealed by the closing act of the four-day period of preparation. After the victory rejoicing following the sham battle was over and just as twilight was drawing in, a crier rode through the great encampment, telling the people to get ready. Each band assembled before its lodges. Then, all starting together, each doing its favorite dance and singing as it came, all the bands of the whole Comanche nation (save the Wasps, who had gone back to their homes in Texas) moved in unison toward the dance lodge in the center of the great camp circle. When finally they reached the lodge, they clustered in one great mass before its eastern entrance. In a solid body they danced with a slow stomping step. The People for the first and last time in all their history were together as one.

After the buffalo hunt on the morning of the fifth day, the Sun Dancers prepared themselves. The crier called for them to bathe, and for anyone who was going to go into the lodge to watch or drum or sing to do likewise. While the dancers were preparing themselves, their wives, mothers, or aunts made beds of sage along the wall on the western half of the lodge. These beds were on the floor of the little compartments formed by a screen of cedar or cottonwood set out about four feet from the wall of the lodge. Here the dancers could stand or lie down to rest when not dancing.

After the sun had reached its noon position, the dancers, drummers, and chorus filed into the lodge. A huge round drum, upon which a half-dozen older men could thump in unison, was placed just south of the entrance. Each drummer had his stick—and some drummers had rattles.

The dancers retired behind the screen and painted themselves, and when all was ready, the drummers began their first song. The dancers stepped forth, and with gaze fixed on the center pole, they made little jumping movements in time to the beat; with each jump emitting a short blast on the eagle-bone whistle held between their teeth. It was just like any other Plains Indian Sun Dance. So it went until late at night and through the following three days.

Men with power performed miracles, and people came forward to hang gifts on the center pole. Boys who were learning to be warriors tied their little gifts to arrows which they shot up into the pole.[13]

13 See also Linton, "The Comanche Sun Dance," *loc. cit.,* 420–28.

In keeping with the lack of masochism in their approach to the supernatural, the Comanche Sun Dancers made no effort to torture themselves by hanging from the center pole with rawhide thongs through their breasts, as did the tribes to the north. Nor was there any dragging of buffalo skulls around the lodge by means of thongs passed through the back muscles. The only self-denial was of water and food for the duration of the dance, and even this was mitigated by chewing the bark of the slippery elm and a bath in the creek each night.

Visions came to some individuals who fainted in the course of the dancing—an important feature of the Sun Dance for most Plains tribes. In their dances the Comanches did not bother to make vision-seeking a primary interest, however. It was not the reason for which they were dancing. They were dancing to revive the power of the tribe, to weld themselves into one cohesive unit that would launch forth on the great military venture that would sweep the whites from all their land. That was what Coyote Droppings had brought them together for. That was why they were dancing.

There had been much strong talk by Coyote Droppings before he had got the Sun Dance under way—inflammatory talk. Coyote Droppings preached that the Caddos, Wichitas, and other tribes who had accepted reservation life were "going down hill fast" in numbers and well-being. Was this what the Comanches wanted? It would be their fate, he warned them, if they gave in to the lures of the government to get them on the reservation. But he knew, he exhorted his tribesmen, from his visits to the Great Spirit, that if they would all turn to the warpath and annihilate the whites in one fell swoop, the buffalo would come back in numbers. The People would flourish and once again they could live the old life—powerful and prosperous as they had been of yore. These things they could do, he assured them, because he in his great power would share his immunity to bullets with them all. Over them he would shed his protective mantle. They could not fail. They would have the Sun Dance and then go to war. That is why they danced, all except the Wasps, who went back home to Texas when they heard this strong talk in which they had no faith and which they felt boded no good. A few other small groups also pulled out before the dance, being either too prudent or too skeptical to follow the path of the fiery prophet.

Although a few of the Comanches refused to accept the Prophet, a host of Kiowas, Arapahos, and Cheyennes fell under his spell. They were ready for the great "putsch."

On the day after the Sun Dance was finished, a large party of Comanche and Kiowa warriors "charged" the great Cheyenne camp which stood near by at the head of the Washita River. They were led by Coyote Droppings and four war chiefs. When their charge was done, the Cheyennes charged in turn, and that evening all the warrior societies of the several tribes danced. "There was much excitement," notes George Bird Grinnell.[14]

The next day they took off for Adobe Walls, nearby an old trading post built by William Bent's men in the eighteen forties on the South Fork of the Canadian in Hutchinson County, Texas, a center of operations for the encroaching buffalo hunters. It was to be the starting point of the war of extermination. At daybreak on the morning of June 27, the attack was made by a long line of Indians in such numbers that "the noise of the horses' hoofs was like thunder."

Twenty-six white men stood inside the houses. Two were sleeping in a covered wagon outside the walls. With the men in the post was one white woman. It so happened that most of the men had been working all night on the repair of a roof beam, and so they were still up and around when the Indians charged. It also happened that they were armed with new large-bore, long-range buffalo rifles. They were resolute and stout-hearted. In the first charge they killed two Cheyennes and a Comanche. One Cheyenne charged within the walls and was killed. The others turned back and milled around. They charged again and again throughout the morning, and although there were more than enough warriors to overwhelm the little party in the adobe houses, it was not the Plains Indian way to take a bastion by storm.

Coyote Droppings, his naked body painted yellow, sat throughout it all upon his white horse on a distant hill. A Cheyenne father who had lost his son in the fighting taunted him with a dare to go down and bring out his son's body, if he really had immunity to bullets. He refused to move. As though to mock him further, a long-range shot from one of those deadly rifles knocked a member of his party from his horse as he sat with the Prophet watching the fiasco.

[14] Grinnell, *The Fighting Cheyennes*, 312.

Early in the afternoon the discouraged Indians gave up. They had killed three white men—they who with the Prophet's protection were going to scour them from the earth. Nine of their own number had been killed and a number wounded. Not a very sanguine battle as battles go in the histories of nations, but it was a crushing spiritual defeat for the Comanches and their friends whose hopes had been so falsely raised. Coyote Droppings had no real power.

But the fighting on the Southern Plains was not yet over. The defeat at Adobe Walls did not check the war spirit, for the Indians plundered and raided for a time over a wide area—Kansas, Colorado, New Mexico, and Texas. In order to distinguish between friendly and hostile Indians, army officials issued an order for all friendly Indians to place their camps on the east side of Cache Creek. Many Kiowas and a large majority of the Comanches failed to obey, and the military regarded them henceforth as "hostiles." One group of the Those Who Move Often band, not wishing to surrender or to remain out on the prairie where they would be attacked, went to the Wichita agency to seek protection. Hearing of their presence there, the army officers went to demand their surrender as prisoners of war. An incident during the parley led to a fight and was the opening signal for new campaigns. Other Indians now joined the renegade bands, and probably one-half of the Comanche, Kiowa, and Cheyenne tribes were openly hostile during the early autumn of 1874.

Meanwhile, in July the government in Washington had given its consent for the army to attack the Indians in their own territory and to subdue them wherever they offered resistance to constituted authority. The outbreak of 1874 had put an end to the Peace Policy. From all sides, troops poured into the Comanche and Kiowa range. Colonel Nelson A. Miles moved south from Camp Supply. Major William Price moved east from Fort Union in northern New Mexico. Lieutenant Colonel J. W. Davidson operated to the west from Fort Sill. Colonel MacKenzie operated north from Fort Concho, Texas, to his old Supply Camp on the Fresh Water Fork of the Brazos. Colonel G. P. Buell pushed up Red River in the region between Davidson and MacKenzie. Their concerted purpose was to drive all the Indians on the reservation.

Davidson marched north of the Wichita Mountains and headed for the North Fork of the Red River; he skirted the edge of the Staked Plains south to Red River, and returned to Fort Sill on October 16. Most of the Indians fled from him into the rough area along the headstreams of Red River. MacKenzie operated along the eastern edge of the High Plains as far as the head of the Palo Duro Canyon. At the junction of the Palo Duro and Blanca Cita canyons, on September 28, he looked down upon hundreds of tipis stretched for miles along the bottom of the canyon. The Indians were in a perfect trap, if resolutely attacked. In the battle that followed he captured 1,424 of the Indians' mounts, and, having learned by sad experience that it was almost impossible to prevent their recapture by the Indians, he brought them to his camp on Tule Canyon, where on the next day he had 1,048 killed. The Indians were hobbled without horses. Nearby, on October 9, Buell defeated another group, and four days later Price, another group in Hemphill County, Texas. On October 21, Davidson took the field again to receive the surrender of the Indians near the agency, while Miles drove the hostiles from their old haunts north and east of Palo Duro.

Very few Indians were killed in these engagements, and virtually none of the braves were captured. However, their mounts and supplies were so depleted that they could not continue their existence on the plains, and as cold weather approached, the bands straggled in one by one to surrender unconditionally. This time there were to be no peace councils, no presents. The Comanches were licked. They were in no position to ask for terms. They were placed in a concentration camp on Cache Creek east of the post; some of the warriors were locked in an unfinished icehouse, and once a day a wagon pulled up by the walls and hunks of raw meat were pitched over the fence, "like we were lions," said one of them. Horses, mules, and weapons were taken away from them. Some animals were shot, some given to the whites and Indian scouts, and about 5,500 were sold at an average of four dollars a head. The Indians lost more than 7,500 head of horses and mules as a result of the campaigns that fall.

A few hostiles remained out during the winter. In February, 1875, about 250 came in. In April, approximately 175 additional ones surrendered. Quanah Parker at the head of a large band of Antelopes arrived at Fort Sill on June 2. There remained only a few Comanches still at large, and occasionally others stole away from the reservation to stay out a short time. But the damage done by these small groups was negligible. An enrollment made at the agency on August 5 showed that 1,076 Kiowas, 763 of whom were classed as "loyal," and 1,597 Comanches, 938 of whom had recently been hostile, were on hand. About 50 Comanches were still at large at the time of the enrollment.

The Comanches never again participated in an outbreak, nor was there ever again an organized effort to defy the authority of the government. For several years, many Comanches were frequently off the reservation. It was some time before they ceased entirely their depredations in Texas, for they raided and pretended to the agent that they had merely been hunting. In June, 1879, however, they made their last raid. A group went to the Staked Plains on a buffalo hunt, and, while out, raided a ranch south of Big Spring.

They could no longer stay out in large parties without risking a renewal of the wretched wars. Other influences more powerful than armies were also at work. The buffalo hunters were making the plains dangerous for them, and hunting out there was becoming more and more fruitless because of the increasing intensity of the buffalo slaughter. And when that slaughter, which ceased so suddenly as to astonish the nation, was completed, the very basis of Comanche tribal life had disappeared. If the braves followed their old trails to Texas, the Rangers were certain to pounce upon them. Great herds of cattle driven by armed cowboys were seeking new ranges. Barbed wire fences were being stretched for hundreds of miles. Immigrants in long lines of covered wagons, like vast marching armies, were steadily penetrating the Indians' hunting grounds, filling the West with a sturdy and capable population. The white settlements in Texas advanced more in the decade from 1874 to 1884 than in the fifty years preceding. Yet with bow and spear and shield and horse the Comanches had held their own. Not until they were surrounded and outnumbered a thousand to one, when the iron horse sped across their hunting grounds with a speed and endurance which set at naught the Indian pony, did they at last succumb to civilization and to fate.

The cultural change demanded of the Comanches was too rapid

and too great for simple adjustment. They were called upon to pass within the span of a single life from the Stone Age to that of steam. Men trained for war and raiding and communal hunts found themselves idle, faced with the problem of adopting the white man's way of life. For some of them there was no problem. They simply refused to consider a change.

The reservation was not a liberal grant and was entirely too small for the Indians to live as they formerly had. Of this the government had been well aware when the treaty was made and the reservation established. Consequently, a provision to furnish the Indians a limited amount of necessities had been included in the treaty. Seeds and agricultural implements were to be supplied each Indian during the first three years of his farming efforts. Congress was to appropriate $25,000 each year for a period of thirty years "to be used . . . in the purchase of such articles . . . as from time to time the condition and necessities of the Indians may indicate to be proper." Certain enumerated articles of clothing were to be provided. Each man and boy over fourteen years of age was to be given a suit of clothing, consisting of shirt, pants, coat, hat, and a pair of socks. For each woman and girl over twelve years of age, the government allowed one woolen skirt, twelve yards of calico, twelve yards of domestic, and one pair of woolen hose. Material was to be distributed for making children's clothes.[15]

Only a person with a distorted sense of humor could have regarded the selection of articles issued as less than tragic. The black, shoddy suits given out to the men were practically worthless, but some government contractor had been enriched. The trousers were all the same size, made to fit a man of two hundred or more pounds. The shirts were red flannel, and the hats were of a high, puritanical pattern. The Comanches, unaccustomed to the white man's clothes, quickly discarded the hats, although today hardly one can be seen without a hat. The coats were converted into vests by cutting off the sleeves, which the children wore for leggings. The seat was cut from the trousers and the feet from hose to convert both into leggings. Some wore the hose without shoes, and women wrapped the cloth around them-

[15] Kappler, *op. cit.*, II, 978–80.

selves without the trouble of subjecting it to either scissors or needle and thread.[16]

According to the treaty, the government was to begin by allowing for each one hundred rations 150 pounds of beef, 70 pounds of corn meal, 4 pounds of sugar, 1 pound of salt, 2 pounds of coffee, and 1 pound of soap. The sugar and coffee were the only items of the rations that the Comanches really desired. Having lived by the hunt, they subsisted mainly on meat. Yet they would eat the salt pork which was given out at times only if they had no other meat. For several years they were able to secure a limited supply of meat by hunting. They had to learn gradually the uses of grain, vegetables, and bread. Corn meal they detested at first, frequently feeding it to their horses.

The amount of rations issued was presumably according to need. It was intended that rations would be only supplementary to farm products and food obtained on the hunt. Bacon, beans, flour, salt, rice, and hominy were sometimes added to the list or substituted for other articles. The quantity of rations was accordingly adjusted upward or downward from time to time. The winter of 1876–77 was extremely cold and the stock poor, so the agent increased the amount of beef to four pounds a week. During the early reservation period, the agent attempted to curtail raiding by withholding rations, but it was not entirely effective, for while the buffalo lasted, the raiders obtained more and better meat off the reservation than was issued to them on the reservation. When withholding failed to restrain the Indians, Agent Haworth held a roll call every three days, the men by name and the women and children by count. If any Comanches left the reservation for over three days, they had to have a military escort or a pass from the agent.[17]

The government allowed the Comanches and their allies the privilege of augmenting their government provisions by continuing to hunt off the reservation, but when some of the Indians abused this privilege by pretending to be hunting when actually they were raiding, the military authorities, in 1878, proposed to stop the Indians from leaving the reservation even to hunt. The Indians, however, depended upon the

16 Nye, *Carbine and Lance,* 107–108; Tatum, *Annual Report,* 1869, *op. cit.,* 386.

17 R. S. MacKenzie, to Haworth, May 5, 1875, "Kiowa Military Relations" (Oklahoma Historical Society Library, correspondence files).

hunt to obtain a portion of their winter supply of meat, and the sale of buffalo robes was the source of a large part of their income. They preferred their own clothing obtained by means of the hunt to that provided by the government. The agent defended their cause, and the final decision was that they might continue to hunt off the reservation, but must be accompanied by a military escort when they did so.[18]

The regulation was tardy, for the day of the old-time summer communal hunt was past. Nevertheless, the whole tribe set out eagerly for their old hunting grounds. But there were no buffalo. Only white bones gleaming ghostlike in the sun, victims of the white hunters' long-range rifles, remained as a reminder of the vast herds that once covered the plains. And even the bones were not to lie undisturbed for long; they were to be ground up for fertilizer. From creek to creek the Comanches journeyed. Their scouts ranged far and wide seeking the herds. The few antelope they met hardly provided them with daily food. Still there were no buffalo, no feasts of marrow bones and tidbits, no racks of meat drying for their winter needs, no buffalo robes to turn the cold north wind.

"They will come when the leaves fall," the Indians said. But the frosts came and the weather grew colder, and still the plains were empty. The time allowed by the agent for the hunt expired. Some gave up hope and returned to the reservation, glad to get their rations of flour, sugar, rice, and beeves. The agent sent an emissary with food to bring the others back to the reservation. The aid came in good time, for they were starving. They had killed some of their ponies and were suffering in the season's early snowstorm. They accepted the inevitable and returned sadly with the emissary to the agency. Sullenness and despair fell upon them. The buffalo had failed, and they now began to realize for certain that their old way of life had ended. Several war chiefs abdicated, and there followed a noticeable trend away from communal life toward family life.

Now the Comanches began to turn in all seriousness to a source of religious solace that could not and has not failed them. The Sun Dance had failed them and they felt that their power-giving spirits

18 Agent P. B. Hunt, *Annual Report,* 1878, in Commissioner of Indian Affairs, *Annual Report,* 1878, 60; Hunt to Commissioner of Indian Affairs, May 11, 1878, and reply, October 14, 1878.

had all but forsaken them. Their accustomed guardian spirits, and even the Sun, lacked sufficient power to turn back the whites and to preserve their old tribal way of life; they needed and sought new power. The answer was peyote.

It was strong power, and it could always be invoked. Visions could always be had through peyote; it was reassuring to The People.

Peyote worship developed as essentially a group experience. It always has been, and still is. The old camp life was broken up. The Comanches were having to learn to live on isolated farmsteads. They yearned for the companionship of each other. In the peyote meetings they were brought together in the warm intimacy of the sacred tipi. They sat shoulder to shoulder in common experience. There they knew that they were not alone, and they could feel that all was not lost.

R. N. Richardson records the general belief that peyote was first used by the Comanches near Fort Sill, about 1875, shortly after they had been confined on the reservation.[19] D. P. McAllester, in his excellent study of Comanche peyote music, also sets the eighteen seventies as the period in which the Comanches first took up peyote.[20] This, it is true, is the time when the use of peyote in the form of a religious cult really took hold among the Comanches. Until their collapse and the failure of their venture with Coyote Droppings there was no functional reason for them to rely on a drug as the means to supernatural power, although they had access to it and, indeed, had used it in a limited way for some time.

There is ample evidence in the data given by Post Oak Jim, Breaks Something, White Wolf, Kɔwino, and Frank Moeda to make it quite certain that the Comanches "knew" peyote before the middle of the nineteenth century. In those days it was used exclusively as a war medicine—especially as an aid in seer-seeing to determine what dangers to expect or where to find horses or enemies.

Peyote, a small, gray-green, spineless, napiform cactus, is botanically known as *Lophophora williamsii*. It contains pharmacologically a complex number of alkaloids capable of producing a variety of physiological effects, including visual and auditory hallucinations, as well

19 Richardson, *The Comanche Barrier to South Plains Settlement*, 34, n.55.
20 D. P. McAllester, *Peyote Music*, 13.

as a number of medicinal specifics for an as yet undetermined series of illnesses and pathological states. It is not, so far as has been determined, a habit-forming drug of the sort that requires continuing and increasing doses in order to meet a physiological craving. Unlike alcohol it does not cause a loss of muscular control or co-ordination, although it does produce a slowing down of reaction time accompanied by a sensation of euphoric relaxation and a feeling of absolute social harmony toward everyone present in the peyote session. Among the American Indians, at least, the effect is sedative and it has not the least tendency to rouse its partakers to violent behavior. It banishes fatigue and produces no "hangover" effects.

The ritual use of peyote goes far back into old Mexico. The *conquistadores* found it in religious contexts in Central Mexico, and it flourishes among the Cora-Huichol and, to a lesser extent, among the Tarahumara. The word "peyote" is corrupted Nahuatl (Aztecan) for the word for caterpillar, "peyotl," so called because the fuzzy white tufts on the rounded top of the plant look like the fuzzy back of a caterpillar.

By 1716, according to a note of Velasco, the Indians of South Texas were using "pellote." The Carrizo Apaches are believed to be the group through whom it was transmitted to other Apaches; and the Comanches believe that they first got it from either the Carrizo or White Mountain Apaches.

McAllester presents a full and detailed Comanche version of the acquisition of peyote from the Carrizo Apache. According to this account, a young Comanche war leader lost all his followers in a fight with the Carrizos. He himself was scalped, stripped, and left for dead. The Apaches were holding a peyote meeting sometime later when the scalped Comanche entered their lodge. He told them that in four days seven Comanches would arrive among them. "When those seven arrive you are to have a peyote meeting. When you have the meeting I command you to give them my bow and this peyote. They shall take these things from you with them." This the Carrizos agreed to do; and thus it came to pass that the Comanches learned about peyote.[21]

As McAllester points out, his version, which was recorded in

21 *Ibid.*, 14–17.

1940, is "more of an historical account than a myth," for it lacks the usual diagnostic characteristics of Plains Indian mythology. But when set against a hitherto unpublished and more pristine account, given to the Laboratory of Anthropology researchers by White Wolf in 1933, it may be seen to what degree the myth-making tendency has built up the story in the McAllester version.

« « « A war party of Comanches was returning from a raid in the country far to the west. When they were camped in the country of the White Mountain Apaches, they heard a drumming different from any kind they knew. Their leader said, "I shall go to see what kind of a thing this is. If I do not return, you will know that I am dead."

An Apache had had a dream that an enemy Comanche was to appear, so they were not surprised when this war chief showed up. Their leader had said they should bring him right in when he appeared.

When he came into their meeting, the Apache leader asked him why he was there.

"I wanted to follow up the drum," was his reply.

They were holding a peyote meeting, and the peyote leader told him to observe closely all that happened. In this way he learned the ritual. When the meeting was over, they gave him the drum and the Father Peyote. They told him where to find more peyote for the use of the Comanches. This is how we learned about this herb.

I was told this when I was a small boy by an old man who had been told it by an old man. » » »

White Wolf, at the time of the telling of this simple account was himself eighty ears of age.

Greyfoot observed that although the Comanches first got peyote from the Apaches "a long time ago," they dropped it "because some medicine men began using it in an evil way."

In the eighteen sixties it was coming into limited use again as war medicine, as indicated in the following account given by Breaks Something, who had been told it by *Mʌmsɜka*.

334

Gets to Be a Middle-aged Man (Tenewerka), in 1933,
one of the Comanches who stole the horses from the stone corral
at Fort Sill in 1878

Photograph by E. A. Hoebel

Voice of the Sunrise (Tabananika), chief of the Yamparika
Courtesy Bureau of American Ethnology

《　《　《　Charcoal led us on a trip to find where the peyote plants grew. The Apaches knew where it was, and they gave the directions to Charcoal.

On the road Charcoal finally recognized the place which the Apaches had described to him. All the Comanches spread out to search for the plant. They had never seen it growing before, but *Mʌmsɜka* recognized some. He called the others to come look.

They all gathered around the patch and arranged themselves in the peyote-meeting formation. Charcoal was the leader. He made smoke to the peyote. He addressed it, saying, "We are going to take you for protection against the enemies."

Then he cut off the head of a big peyote plant just below the ground. He cleaned the dirt off of it, wrapped it in a clean cloth and put it in his pocket over his heart. Now he told the others to cut all the peyote they needed. He said they would have a meeting that evening.

For their peyote lodge they cut brush which they formed in the shape of a tipi and covered with robes. Charcoal formed the earth crescent and fireplace in the center. All prepared for the meeting; they bathed and returned to the camp to get painted up. Then they entered the tipi in the ceremonial fashion. *Mʌmsɜka* was the fire tender. Charcoal placed the first button he had cut on the crescent for the road medicine, Father Peyote. He lit a cigarette with a coal, and then he spoke to the peyote. He told it he heard it had power; he was going into enemy territory; and he told it he was going to carry it for protection. He put his cigarette down and chewed some wild sage which he rubbed over his body as a purifier. The other men did the same.

Now a bag of peyote buttons was brought in. Charcoal took four. Each of the other men was also given four.

Then each man chewed a piece of peyote into a pulp. He spewed it out into his hand, made four circular motions toward the fire, and swallowed it. Then he spit in his hands and rubbed them over his head, arms, and ears to take away aches and pains, and to hear better.

Charcoal used his bow for the singer's staff. A rattle and drum had been brought along for the occasion. Each man sang four songs as they passed the staff and the rattle and drum around the circle.

Then they passed out more peyote.

Finally, Charcoal spoke up: "*MΛmsɜka,* stir the fire. I have learned that tomorrow we shall all be killed."

He smoked again and spoke to the peyote, telling it that he did not expect anything bad like this from it. Now he was in a very dangerous place, he said.

Next he talked to his followers.

"Tomorrow we go over a certain hill. I have seen that there will be two companies of soldiers there. We might as well die now. Let this peyote kill us right here! Eat a lot of it."

With tears in his eyes, he ate more and more.

At midnight the water was brought in, and they all smoked. Charcoal again upbraided the peyote for treating him thus, and he ate more and more peyote.

After a while Charcoal spoke again.

"I have learned more," he said. "Tomorrow we shall meet some enemies, but no harm will come to us. We shall go on and capture some horses and get home safely. There will be a gray one for me."

The next morning they ate breakfast and prepared to leave. They traveled a bit and went up a hill. On an opposite hill, across a creek they saw two companies of soldiers. After a drill, the soldiers left. Our people went down the hill and traveled southwest all day long. At night they came upon an enemy camp where there were many horses, among them a gray one. Cried Charcoal, "That's *my* horse."

They gathered up the horses and made for home, Charcoal riding the gray.

This shows the wonderful power of peyote. It all came true. » » »

Charcoal's first peyote button was preserved by him until his death, when he gave it to a friend, who in time gave it to *MΛmsɜka,* who still preserved and cherished this famous button in 1933.

With such powers, peyote took firm hold of the Comanches as soon as they settled down on the reservation. Its worship flourished, until in the early part of the present century it suffered from opposition emanating from missionaries and government officers.

The old leaders were waging a losing fight to retain their religious practices through the peyote sacrament until James Mooney, a representative of the Smithsonian Institution, became interested in its continuance as an aid to the psychological integration of the Indians. Renewed interest and agitation resulted in a charter, granted by the state of Oklahoma on October 10, 1918, which placed the peyote ceremony on a basis of legal equality with other religions by providing constitutional protection through the establishment of a Native American Church charged with the responsibility "to establish a self-respecting and brotherly union among the men of the native race of Indians and to foster and promote their belief in Christian religion with the practice of peyote sacrament as commonly understood among the Indians."

From the Comanches the worship of peyote spread to the Kiowas, Wichitas, Pawnees, and Shawnees before the turn of the century, and between 1900 and 1907 to the Poncas, Kickapoos, and Kansas. This was perhaps the most important cultural contribution of the Comanches to the lives of other American Indians; for from these tribes, who received the cult directly from the Comanches, the peyote complex has spread throughout the plains and, in recent years, into the Great Basin and the deserts of the Southwest, where the Navahos are now beginning to adopt the faith.

The peyote ritual as practiced by the Comanches today differs only in minor details from the early session presided over by Charcoal.

Thus in time of their travail the Comanches found a new faith to help them through their great emotional and spiritual crisis. It did not solve their problems of adjustment to confinement on a reservation, but it helped to ameliorate their suffering and to prevent total disintegration.

As life on the reservation settled down, the Comanches were not always satisfied with the way the government fulfilled its obligation to supply rations and annual provisions. Contractors were slow in getting supplies to the point of delivery, and the freighters were slower still. The goods were often misdelivered and had to be reshipped. It was difficult for freighters to cross the swollen streams. Sometimes delivery was months behind, causing tremendous suffering on the part of the Indians.[22] When they did arrive at the reservation,

[22] Hunt, *Annual Report*, 1885, in Commissioner of Indian Affairs, *Annual Report*, 1885, 7.

the goods were often of a most inferior quality and could not be used. Many agents and contractors connived at rewarding themselves from government contracts at the expense of the Indians. When Agent Hugh Brown, who assumed his duties in June, 1893, attempted to force the contractors to deliver in full according to the terms of their contracts, he was removed before the year was out.

At first the policy was to issue the rations to the chiefs, who in turn distributed them among the people of their respective bands. This policy did not always assure a fair distribution. Agent Tatum in 1871 made a count and found 4,444 actual eligible residents as compared to a count of 8,746 claimed by the Indians as being entitled to rations. To remedy this situation, the Commissioner of Indian Affairs ordered a change in the distribution system so that each family would receive its own rations directly. Each family was given a card with the family name at the top and the number of persons in the family. The card was punched when rations were issued. A military officer was also required to be present when rations were given out.[23]

Issue day, once a week at times and once every two weeks at others, was a gala occasion. The women with their ration cards filed by various clerks who served them much as in a modern cafeteria. The beef was issued sometimes on the hoof, and here the men came in for participation. The animals were penned in a great corral near the agency, from which they were turned loose one at a time. The waiting men and youths pursued them, making a pretense of their old buffalo hunt. Firing at the fleeing animals from the backs of running ponies, they presently brought them down. They seemingly were not as effective with pistols as their fathers and grandfathers had been with bow and arrow and lance. Waiting women and children hastened to skin and cut up the animals as soon as they were killed. Considerable trouble often arose over the issue of beef, since obviously each family could not have the choice parts.

Issue days were times of feasting, gambling, and entertainment. The trend developed rapidly during the administration of Captain J. Lee Hall, who became agent in 1885. Captain Hall was generous,

23 Hayworth, *Annual Report,* September 20, 1876, in Commissioner of Indian Affairs, *Annual Report,* 1876, 52.

hospitable, and a heavy drinker who allowed the agency to go on sprees. One principal amusement when not eating or gambling was horse racing, as it had been of old. The long, straight road between the agency buildings was the favorite track. But this was the only street of the village. Freight wagons rumbled along it, children played in the middle of the road, and the women crossed back and forth. Fearing someone might be injured, the agent ordered the Indians to hold their races in a near-by pasture. On a level place they laid out two straight tracks side by side, about ten yards apart and one-half mile long. Only two horses raced at a time. When one race was over and the bets paid, another would follow as long as there were any one who would race. Not infrequently a loser left without money, blanket, or food.

Sometimes the entire week's supply of rations was gone before a family left the station, and it was not unusual for them to beg for more. In 1892, the agent estimated that the Indians were 50 per cent self-supporting, with government rations making up the other 50 per cent of their subsistence.

Those families who lived some distance from the agency spent most of their time going to and from the agency for the purpose of drawing their rations. To avoid this situation, Agent P. B. Hunt issued rations for more than one week to those who were farming and found it a handicap to come to the agency so frequently. In 1886, a ration station was opened at Fort Sill as a means of helping solve this problem. As the Indians became adjusted to the white man's mode of living, only one member of a family went to the station for rations. Before the close of the ration period several families or a community might send in only one or two persons to obtain their supplies.

The thirty years set by the Treaty of Medicine Lodge for issuing rations and supplies ended in 1897. By this time the Indians were becoming established with farms and cattle, supplemented by income from grass leases and from wages received from hauling and for other odd jobs. The end of rationing was delayed, however, until the opening of the reservation to settlement in 1901, when it was rapidly discontinued. Afterwards only those Indians unable to work were given rations. During the fiscal year 1909–10 only eighty-seven, all of whom were unable to work, received rations, to the amount of $4,335.90.[24]

The breakdown of established norms of behavior and the change to new patterns of conduct resulted in many social conflicts and disturbances. The whites were not sufficiently well acquainted with the Indians always to apprehend the guilty parties and mete out justice as well as some of the Indians. Horse thieves preyed on the Indians' herds. It was easy to round up a bunch of ponies in the isolated portions of the Comanche lands and run them off into the Chickasaw country or into Texas, where they had a ready sale.

To assist the agents in maintaining order on the reservation, Congress in May, 1878, provided for a system of Indian police. They were to be provided with badges, uniforms, and guns, and each officer was to receive eight dollars and each private five dollars a month in addition to full rations.[25] Their business was to ride over the country and keep watch for thieves and trespassers, to report any troubles that might arise among the Indians of the reservation, and to keep watch over the Indians' cattle and horses. They would work under the agent's orders.

Agent P. B. Hunt, whose task it was to organize the first police force, found it difficult to secure men willing to serve. He wanted young men, but the compensation was too small to induce men to volunteer for the service. Furthermore, the chiefs declared that it was not right for younger men to arrest the older members of the tribe. The agent reminded the leaders that the police were to work for all their people, to guard their livestock, to carry information to the agent and from him to their people; they would do work similar to the Cheyenne Dog Soldiers. In order to win the support of those objecting to the police, the headmen were commissioned to arrest anyone committing a crime on the reservation, thus satisfying them with a semblance of their old authority.[26] To complete the police rolls, Hunt found it necessary to refuse the Comanches the permit for their annual

24 Supt. Kiowa-Comanche Reservation, *Annual Report,* 1910 (Oklahoma Historical Society Library, correspondence files).

25 Commissioner of Indian Affairs, *Annual Report,* 1878, p. xlii; Commissioner of Indian Affairs to Hunt, September 28, 1878.

26 Agent J. Lee Hall to Commissioner of Indian Affairs, June 19, 1886 (Oklahoma Historical Society Library, correspondence files).

buffalo hunt until the required number of men had agreed to serve. The necessity and eagerness of the Indians to continue their annual hunts compelled them to fulfill the agent's demand.[27]

When the force was organized on October 1, 1878, it consisted of one captain, two lieutenants, four sergeants, and twenty-two privates. Their authority was seriously limited, and they were not adequately equipped for effective service. Yet, they consistently rendered commendable service and managed to settle without trouble many cases which might have led to serious consequences had a white peace officer attempted to make the arrests.

Matters of justice and punishment were partially entrusted to the Indians also. Much of the agent's time was consumed in hearings and adjustments of smaller troubles, while serious cases made necessary a journey to the federal court at Wichita Falls. The Indians refused to use voluntarily the available courts in Texas. Both Agent Hunt and Agent Hall recommended the establishment of an Indian court in which matters pertaining to the reservation could be handled. Both relied upon the aid of tribal headmen like Quanah Parker to help with difficult cases.

Situations that were new to the Comanches were handled by the Indian officers on the lines of old Comanche principles. As an example, we have a case remembered by Eagle Tail Feather.

« « « One Comanche beat another to a claim for a half-section of land. This one who lost out was making a big complaint about it, and the man who had received the land said that if he lost the land because of this fellow's objection, he would kill him.

Quanah Parker decided the case on old lines.

He called in two well-known warriors to decide on the war records of the two men. One of these warriors was late in coming in, so he sent me out in his place to get the record of the man who felt he was being beat out of his claim. I was chief of the Indian Police. The man who had the claim asked if he could go along too.

When we found the warrior, this man who had the land said, "Who is the better man, I or this other fellow?" He thought the warrior would give him the credit.

[27] Hunt, *Annual Report,* 1879, in Commissioner of Indian Affairs, *Annual Report,* 1879, 64, 68.

341

"All right," the warrior answered him, "you asked me. I'll speak right out. This other fellow is the better man. I was in a battle where I saw him get off his horse and help a dismounted comrade out of the midst of the enemy. He is a brave man and did a great deed. You had better look out or he will whip you or kill you!"

I took this report back to Quanah. It was then up to this fellow to come out with a true account of a braver deed or else give up the land and abide by the decision.

He could not do this, so Quanah and the two warriors decided for the complainer. That man had to give up the land and keep quiet.))))))

This is hardly the way a white court would have decided the validity of a land claim in dispute. And we have strong doubts as to its being the way that it would have been settled by Comanche peace chiefs, if they had been called upon to adjudicate by the Anglo-Americans. But it was sound Comanche reasoning from a war leader's point of view, and in terms of the Comanches' premises it was just.

In 1886, provision was made for the establishment of the Court of Indian Offenses with power to try minor cases. The court as constituted that year was composed of three judges who were selected by the Indians with the assistance and approval of the agent. The presiding judge was paid thirty dollars a month; the other two, twenty-five dollars each. The agent certified Quanah Parker of the Comanches as presiding judge, Lone Wolf of the Kiowas and Jim Tehuacana of the Wichitas as the first members of the newly created court. The court was to have jurisdiction over both the Kiowa-Comanche-Apache and the Wichita-Caddo reservations. It was to meet twice a month.

The plan worked well. The judges fully appreciated the dignity of their positions, and the Indians were more willing to submit difficulties or complaints to their own court presided over by their own chiefs. The presence of two of the three judges from other tribes was intended to assure impartial hearings and sentences. The court assessed fines or jail sentences which sometimes were more severe than the white man's law assigned for like offenses, and a few times

342

the agent asked the court to reduce the sentence. Cases of murder were subject to trial in the federal courts in Texas under the Act of 1887. Offenses handled by the court included the holding of Sun Dances, Scalp Dances, polygamy, medicine making, timber selling, disturbances, fighting, stealing, and selling girls. The constitutional jurisdiction of the court in the first four of these "offenses" is highly doubtful, but nobody bothered to challenge the issue in those days. The dance penalty was loss of rations for ten days for the first offense, and fifteen to thirty days for the second. The court functioned until the opening of the reservation to settlement, when it was officially abolished on July 1, 1901.[28]

After the Comanches and their Kiowa allies had been subdued and placed on the reservation, the buffalo disappeared so rapidly that the Indians could not comprehend what had happened. Without them there was no hope for their old way of life. With longing, many told themselves that the buffalo had gone into hiding and could be brought back by proper power. In 1881, a Kiowa medicine man claimed to have gained the power to make the buffalo return, but his medicine failed him.[29]

While still hoping for a miracle before the inroads of white civilization should sweep the last vestiges of the old way of life from them, there came in 1890 whispers—good tidings from the north. It was the promise of the Ghost Dance prophet. The Comanches first heard the story from the Cheyennes. High Wolf, a chief of the Sioux, and Sitting Bull of the Arapahos came to teach the new message to the Kiowas and the Comanches. These people were told by the visiting teachers that the Great Spirit had taken pity on his children. Wovoka of the Paiutes, alias Jack Wilson, had had a vision. When the sun was darkened in the daytime, his spirit went away from his body, ascended to Heaven, and learned the word of the Great Spirit. It returned with a message to Wovoka. Jesus had once come to the white people and they had killed him. He was now coming to the Indians on top of a new earth which would cover the old earth. He

---

[28] Supt. J. A. Buntin, *Annual Report: Narrative Section,* 1930, I, 4 (MS collection, Kiowa-Comanche Agency, Anadarko, Oklahoma); Agent G. D. Day, *Annual Report,* 1893 (Oklahoma Historical Society Library, correspondence files).

[29] A truly beautiful narrative of this event may be found in Marriott, *op. cit.,* 142–54.

would bring back the spirits of the dead Indians, the buffalo, wild horses, and all the other animals which had formerly been on the plains. Indians and whites would live together in brotherly forbearance. But the Sioux, as they took up the Paiute-Christian pacifism of the Prophet, transformed it into a doctrine of aggressive retribution. All peoples except the Indians were to be pushed off the earth into the seas whence they came, and be drowned. All that the Great Spirit required of the Indians was to have faith in the teaching and to dance strange new dances. It would not be necessary to go to war. The dance prepared the people for the Messiah and would bring forth the new earth.

Far out on Elk Creek, away from the agency, a camp was set up for the Ghost Dance. The ceremony was strange and solemn. The dancers, both men and women, sang a plaintive and pathetic song, representing their struggles and hardships. It was a ceremony of despair. Some dancers wore white clothes so that the ghosts of the departed would not be afraid to come back and live with their people. With hands clasped, the dancers moved around a center pole to the cadence of a chant, while the medicine man in the center strove to induce a hypnotic trance in each of the dancers. As the dance progressed, the dancers succumbed, falling on the ground in a stupor and remaining there for as long as an hour. During the trance they saw visions of the antelope and bison in numbers, and the dear, departed dead.

Sitting Bull was sincere, although he was also getting wealthy from the fees he charged. Many Indians were deeply affected and followed him around trying to touch the hem of his garments or grasp his hand and pray, frequently with tears rolling down their cheeks.

Most of the Comanche leaders, including Chief Quanah Parker, had no faith in the new prophecy. They recalled another day in 1874 when a young medicine man claimed great power and had made promises to save his people from destruction if they would only follow him. They had made medicine and followed him to Adobe Walls, where their faith and dreams were shattered and they learned to their sorrow that their leader had no more power than themselves. It had been a bitter and unforgettable disappointment.

344

Almost the only Comanches to become converts to the new Ghost Dance religion were the Wasps and a few on the northern edge of the reservation who were influenced by their northern neighbors. The rest remained indifferent. James Mooney attributes the refusal of the Comanches to accept the Ghost Dance religion to their "general skeptical temperament," to their "tribal pride against borrowing from others," to their carelessness in regard to ceremonial forms, and to their faith in their own mescal (peyote) rites.

That the Comanches were not inherently skeptical is shown by their earlier gullible acceptance of Coyote Droppings' pretensions. To say they had a tribal pride against borrowing from others is manifestly absurd. Although they never abandoned some of their Shoshonean orientations, most of that which typified their culture as Plains was borrowed, and Ralph Linton feels that of all the peoples he knows, the Comanches were one of the most adaptable.[30] The evidence set forth in this book certainly sustains his judgment. It is true that the Comanches were originally unceremonial; they cared no more for ritual form than they did for philosophical or political formality. But they were not averse to incorporating the ritualistic Beaver Ceremony into their culture, and at the end they were grasping for ritual to solidify the quicksands that were engulfing them. They had tried the Sun Dance, and by 1890 they were deeply committed to the Peyote cult—a highly ceremonial form of religion. It could not have been the ceremonial features of the Ghost Dance that repelled them. The fact is that they had been "immunized" to messiahs and salvation by miracle through their experience of 1874. That this is so, is indicated in the fact that the only group of Comanches who embraced the Ghost Dance as a unit were the Wasps, the one band that had gone home in 1874, refusing to participate in Coyote Droppings' Sun Dance. On one point Mooney was right. Peyote was meeting the Comanches' need with sufficient effectiveness to reinforce their immunization against the last, wild desperate appeal to a new messiah.

For many of the Comanches there would still be Christianity, and although the first missionary efforts among them had been begun by the Episcopalian J. B. Wicks in June, 1881, Christianity in 1890 was not a present hope for them.

[30] Personal communication from Linton to Hoebel, September 26, 1950.

The old way of life was nearer an end than they feared. The whites were rapidly pushing in. When the Indians and the buffalo had been removed from the plains of Texas, the cattlemen quickly covered the area with vast herds. Many thousand head of cattle were driven northward to market. By 1877 the Comanches were troubled with trespassing cattle, and the agent was instructed to have these cattle removed. A penalty of one dollar a head was to be collected from the owner of such cattle when the animals were driven on the reservation to graze, but nothing was to be collected for what the cattle ate while being driven through the reservation, since "this is incidental."[31]

Some of the cattlemen took advantage of this decision by driving their herds across the reservation where the best grass was to be found, and although the herds might not be turned loose to graze, they traveled at a much slower rate across the reservation than was customary for herds on the north-bound trail. To remedy this situation, the Commissioner of Indian Affairs in 1881 established a definite trail across the reservation leading toward Fort Dodge. It crossed the reservation for a distance of about twenty miles, northwest through Greer County. The Abilene Trail followed the east line of the reservation. The Commissioner opposed the opening of a trail in 1883 from Doane's store north by way of Fort Sill on the ground that the cattlemen would start their cattle in the spring and fatten them on the grass of the reservation, which would interfere with efforts to build up the herds of the Indians.[32] Cattle were to move along the trails at the rate of not less than ten miles a day. It was the duty of the soldiers and police to see that the herds were kept on the trail and that they traveled at the required rate of speed.

There was a drought in 1881, and about the same time the government reduced the ration of beef to the Indians. Agent Hunt offered to allow the cattlemen to graze their herds on the reservation during the winter and spring in return for a specified amount of beef for the Indians. They paid willingly, for they received more in return than the value of the animals donated. They were certain that the

31 Commissioner of Indian Affairs to Haworth, March 30 and April 16, 1877 (Oklahoma Historical Society Library, correspondence files).

32 Hunt to Commissioner of Indian Affairs, December 31, 1883, P. B. Hunt, "Copy of Record of Commissioner's Copy Press Book of Kioway Agency, 1882–1884" (MS, Oklahoma Historical Society Library, correspondence files).

Indians would take what they needed anyway. The agreement was unofficial, but to the cattlemen it gave an aspect of legality to their enterprise, and as such it constituted the first paid grazing leases contracted for the reservation. The cattle of the ranchers who paid were allowed to cross the river to the reservation unmolested, but those of the others were driven off. This plan was followed for several years, the twenty or more cattlemen with whom the agreement was made each taking a portion of the range.

Once the cattle had been placed on the reservation, the owners were slow to remove them at the designated time or to continue to pay for their right to pasturage. There was, after all, much unused grass on the reservation, and to Texas cattlemen the use of the grass was very important. They could see no reason why it should go unused. Consequently, they drove their cattle to the border of the reservation, and allowed them—possibly with some urging and guidance—to wander or stray on to the reservation. The Indian police attempted to guard the border, but the line was long. Each week the chief of police was instructed to remove the cattle illegally grazing the reservation; the government employees tried and failed to keep the cattle off; the troops tried and failed. Agent Hunt said that it would have required an army to keep them off.[33]

Cattlemen resorted to other schemes to get their cattle on the reservation. Emmit Cox, a white, came to the tribe and married the daughter of Quanah Parker and secured his bride's right to graze. In 1881, Cox had a large herd of steers, which he claimed as his own, near Lawton, but it was rumored that they belonged to a Texas cattleman who paid Cox $1.50 a head annually to get them on Comanche land.[34] When the cattlemen failed to obey the orders, Hunt gave them a thirty-day notice and then proceeded to levy fines on violators. But the fines were so small, and it was so difficult to prove that the owners purposely drove the cattle on to the reservation, that most cattlemen disregarded the orders and paid the fine, if they were found guilty. Since Hunt was unable to keep the cattle off, he called upon outside assistance. One of his last official acts before leaving the agency was to post notices in the post offices and stores along the

[33] Hunt, *Annual Report*, 1885, *loc. cit.*, 89.
[34] Claude Southward, *Nocona's Nest*, 30.

Texas border that no cattle were to be driven on to the reservation and to call upon the Texas sheriffs to assist in enforcing the order. Agent J. Lee Hall reported that during his first summer of tenure the Indian police removed from the reservation ten thousand head of trespassing cattle.[35]

It was only a short step from paying for grass with beeves to contracting a lease for grazing, but even so there were difficulties involved. By 1885, both the agent and a number of the Indians realized that they could not prevent trespassing and that it would be better to lease grazing privileges than to try to enforce the ban on grazing. In February, 1885, a delegation of Indians were told that they might make their own arrangements with cattlemen, but that the government would not handle the business for them. An arrangement was made with several large cattle firms, and the first money payments to the Comanches were made under this agreement in the summer of 1885. The Kiowas and Kiowa-Apaches for a time refused to accept money for fear that a scheme to deprive them of their lands was involved. In February, 1892, the Indians in council appointed a delegation to go to Washington to discuss grass leasing. As a result, the agent was granted authority to submit one-year contracts for approval. Six leases, aggregating 250,580 acres, were approved for the year beginning September 1, 1892.[36]

Agent W. D. Myers took a census of the Indians for the purpose of paying the lease money due them. To complete the census required several months, for definite and permanent names had to be decided upon and enrolled as such. Very often confusion arose over the spelling of a name; the Indian might use one name among his Indian friends and still another on the ration rolls. Births and deaths were not always reported. The Indians' share of the "grass" money was paid twice each year. The Commissioner of Indian Affairs directed that all heads of families were to give receipts for their own shares, shares of their wives and of their minor children. In the absence of the husband, a wife might sign for him. In case of minor orphans, guardians were designated by the tribal headman.

[35] Hall, *Annual Report*, 1886, in Commissioner of Indian Affairs, *Annual Report*, 1886, 131.

[36] Commissioner of Indian Affairs, *Annual Report*, 1893, 29.

All leases presumably were to be made through the Anadarko office and referred to the Commissioner of Indian Affairs at Washington for approval. However, some cattlemen used their political influence to secure leases in Washington without the knowledge of the agent. Fear of increasing encroachment of the land-hungry "boomers" made the cattlemen eager to lease large tracts at the government price of six cents an acre, with the result that the Indians of the Kiowa-Comanche reservation in 1893 leased 1,304,958 acres.[37] Most of the requests were for grazing cattle, but sheep and hog owners also asked for permits, although no permits were allowed for hogs.

In 1894, the crops were poor but the grass was excellent, and the agent persuaded the Indians in council to agree to use the semiannual payment of about $50,000 for purchasing fine young cattle. However, the project met with such a storm of protest from the traders to whom the Indians were indebted that it was set aside. The agent then devoted much effort to encouraging the Indians to be thrifty and buy their own individual cattle from their savings.

Meanwhile, the "boomers" made stronger and stronger demands for opening the Kiowa-Comanche reservation. Their principal argument was that the lands were not being used. The cattlemen joined the Indians in opposing the opening of the reservation, since they desired to continue leasing the grass for pasture. They employed an attorney in Washington and brought pressure upon congressmen to prevent it, but with little success, for on October 6, 1892, the Jerome Agreement was made at Fort Sill between the Comanche, Kiowa, and Apache tribes and the United States. According to the agreement, each Indian man, woman, and child was to secure 160 acres of land by allotment. Church, agency, school, military, or other public land could not be claimed by an individual. Sections thirty-six and sixteen of each township were to be held for school purposes, and sections thirteen and thirty-three for public institutions and welfare. The allotments were to be held in trust for twenty-five years, after which they were to be conveyed in fee simple to the holder. The period of trust could be extended if the government of the United States deemed it necessary for the best interests of the Indian.[38] During the trust

[37] *Ibid.*

[38] The Agency records show that twenty-eight were given fee patent (complete

period the allotments were to be free from taxation and could not become subject to any indebtedness. In addition, four tracts were reserved to the Indians collectively: the "Big Pasture" lying along Red River, an area adjacent to the Wichita-Caddo reservation, an area east of the Big Pasture and adjoining the Chickasaw country, and a small area near Fort Sill for a wood reserve. The four tracts amounted to 551,680 acres; the Big Pasture with 414,720 acres was by far the largest.

For the surrender of their rights to all other lands of the reservation, the government agreed to pay the Indians two million dollars in installments of $500,000 each at such times as the "Secretary of Interior shall deem the best for the said Indians." The money was to draw 5 per cent interest while in the United States Treasury, the interest to be paid annually. The agreement was to become effective when approved by Congress.

Many leading Indians protested that the agreement was secured unfairly. They accused the interpreter, Joshua Givens, son of Satank, of falsely translating their statements. It is reported that the Indians were so infuriated with Joshua that they made medicine to cause his death as well as the commissioners'. They made an image of Joshua and threw mud at it. The fatal ailment would occur where the mud hit. The mud struck his chest. On the way home from the council, Joshua had a hemorrhage of the lungs. Shortly afterwards he died, and the commissioners did not long survive him.[39]

Since only a part of the Indians had been present at the signing of the agreement, opponents argued that it was illegal. The opposition party was supported by the cattlemen, and they did not concede without a fight. They sent a delegation headed by General Hugh L. Scott and Lone Wolf to Washington. The delegation obtained a hearing with President Grover Cleveland, who is said to have listened to their case and exclaimed, "I will not permit it. I will see justice done

ownership) in 1926, and possibly a half-dozen since then. The trust period has been extended from time to time by executive order. The latest order extends it for twenty-five years from August, 1946. Personal communication from Supt. W. B. McCown to Wallace, June 12, 1945, and Executive Order 9659, Federal Register, November 24, 1945.

39 J. J. Methvin, missionary teacher who went to the reservation in 1887, to Lillian Cassaway, June 22, 1937, Indian-Pioneer Papers (MS collection, Oklahoma University Library), Vol. XLII, pp. 415–16.

Albert Atocknie (Lone Tipi), in 1924
Courtesy Bureau of American Ethnology

Hair Hanging Down, in 1930
Courtesy Bureau of American Ethnology

these Indians as long as I am in power."[40] They hired an attorney in Washington and left him in charge of their fight to block ratification of the agreement.

They were fighting a losing battle. One by one the various chiefs were won over by the "boomers." They saw the futility of protesting longer, for nothing could hold back the mass of land-hungry whites clamoring for admittance. At most they merely delayed the opening, for on June 6, 1900, an act of Congress made the Jerome Agreement the law of the land, and on July 4, 1901, a Presidential proclamation ordered the execution of the agreement. According to the agreement, allotments were to be made as soon as possible. The Secretary of the Interior, acting within his rights, had delayed the execution of the agreement while awaiting the decision of Congress. The agent was not ordered to have the lands surveyed until 1895. But as soon as Congress acted, the work was rushed. Each Indian was allowed to select his or her own 160-acre allotment. Tracts for minors were selected by the parents or by the agent. As soon as a choice was made and the authorities informed, it was recorded and the Indian's title evidenced by the issuance of a trust patent.[41] By the next year the allotments had been completed. The Indian court was abolished on July 1, 1901, by the Commissioner of Indian Affairs in anticipation of the new status.

The lands not allotted to the Indians were surveyed into homesteads of 160 acres each and thrown open to the public. This opening was more orderly than preceding ones in that it was by lottery rather than by a run. Everyone who wished to get a claim was required to register between July 10 and 26. Prior to the registration, cattlemen were required to remove their herds and pasture fences from the reservation. Two registration booths, one at El Reno and another near Fort Sill, were set up. At El Reno 11,556 registered. The drawing of names from two large iron boxes was held at El Reno on July 29, 1901, before a crowd of 30,000. In a few weeks the country was full of whites who were plowing fields and building homes. Three townsites were laid out—Lawton, Hobart, and Anadarko, the last at the

[40] H. L. Scott, *Some Memoirs of a Soldier*, 201.

[41] Agent J. F. Randlett, *Annual Report*, 1901, in Commissioner of Indian Affairs, *Annual Report*, 1901, 255.

site of the Kiowa-Comanche agency. The auction of town lots occurred on August 6.

The change took place so rapidly that a corn field was converted overnight into the town of Anadarko. Other towns sprang up almost as rapidly. Lawton, the largest of the new towns, was for months a wild frontier place, with open saloons, gambling, and frequent fights. Roads leading through the reservation were filled with homeseekers and traders in covered wagons, on horseback, and on foot. The Indians were forced to change their way of living overnight, also.

But the "boomers" were not satisfied with a partial opening of the reservation. They continued to use the same argument—that the Indians were not using the lands. The demand could not long be delayed. Congress on June 5, 1906, provided for the opening of the remainder of the reserve lands of the reservation, the last big opening in Oklahoma. The law specified that these lands were to be sold under sealed bids to be opened by the Secretary of Interior. Before the sale could take place, the 517 Indian children of the reservation born after June 5, 1901, when allotments were completed, had to be given their 160 acres each. The men to whom the pastures were leased were allowed time to remove their cattle. Surveys divided the lands to be sold into 2,531 tracts. The sealed bids were to be placed in the Lawton land office between December 3 and 8, 1906, later extended until December 15.[42] Thus were the Comanches finally stripped of the last of their once vast tribal holdings.

The Geronimo band of Apaches, after having been held captives in Florida and Alabama, were removed to the Fort Sill military reservation in 1894, where they were held as prisoners until 1913. They were then permitted to decide whether they preferred to go to the Mescalero Reservation in New Mexico or remain in Oklahoma. The majority returned to New Mexico, but eighty-five chose to remain. Those who remained received allotments of land and cattle and were joined in 1913 to the Comanche-Kiowa agency. They are located largely in the vicinity of the town of Apache, north of Fort Sill.

Simultaneously with the opening of the last of the reservation, a

42 Agent J. P. Blackmon, *Annual Report,* 1906, in Commissioner of Indian Affairs, *Annual Report,* 1906, 309; Blackmon to Commissioner of Indian Affairs, September 20, 1906; Commissioner of Indian Affairs *Annual Report,* 1906, 159.

movement was on foot for bringing statehood to Oklahoma and Indian Territory. On November 4, 1906, an election was held throughout the two territories for delegates to a constitutional convention. On November 20 that body met and began its work, and on November 16, 1907, Oklahoma was formally proclaimed a state of the Union. Verily, the phase of reservation life had passed, a short interlude of forty years. The Comanches had entered the White Man's Road. They were Lords of the Southern Plains no longer.

Bibliography

ORAL AND UNPUBLISHED MATERIALS

Anthropology Museum, University of Texas, Austin. Comanche specimens.

Apauty, Adeline (Comanche), Lawton, Oklahoma, to Ophelia D. Vestal, November 16, 1937, Indian-Pioneer Papers *(q.v.)*, I. University of Oklahoma Library, Norman.

Banks, Dick, to Bessie L. Thomas, March 29, 1938, Indian-Pioneer Papers *(q.v.)*, V.

Buntin, Martha Leota. "History of the Kiowa, Comanche, and Wichita Indian Agency." MS in the University of Oklahoma Library, Norman. 1931.

Comanche-Kiowa Agency Records. Agency Headquarters, Anadarko, Oklahoma. The agency records constitute the most important source for recent years. They contain data on tribal customs, geography, land titles, leases, crops, labor, schools, churches, and health. The "Narrative Section" of the 1930 *Report* of Superintendent J. A. Buntin and the "Narrative Section" of the 1935 *Report* of Superintendent W. B. McCown were very valuable.

Gilcrease, Thomas, Foundation Museum. Comanche specimens. Tulsa.

Hoebel, E. Adamson. Cheyenne Field Notes. Unpublished.

Indian-Pioneer Papers. 116 vols., MS collection, University of Oklahoma Library, Norman. 1937.

Informants (Comanche). Those used in 1933 by the Santa Fé Laboratory group were Breaks Something, Eagle Tail Feather, Gets to Be a Middle-Aged Man, Holding Her Sunshade, George Kewino, Post Oak Jim, She Invites Her Relatives, Slope, That's It, and Howard White Wolf. Those used in 1945 by Ernest Wallace were Josephine Comah, Face Wrinkling Like Getting Old, Kills Something, Medicine Woman, See How Deep the Water Is, and Wiley Yellowfish.

Linton, Ralph. Communication to E. A. Hoebel, September 26, 1951.

355

McCown, W. B. (superintendent of Kiowa-Comanche Agency). Communication, oral and written, to Ernest Wallace, 1945, 1948.

———. Program. Kiowa Reservation. MS. Anadarko, Oklahoma, 1945.

Mayhall, Mildred Pickle. "The Indians of Texas: The Atakapa, the Karankawa, the Tonkawa." Unpublished Ph.D. dissertation, University of Texas, Austin. 1939.

Methvin, J. J. (missionary teacher on the Comanche Reservation). Communication to Lillian Cassaway, June 22, 1937. Indian-Pioneer Papers *(q.v.)*, XLII.

Moore, Scott B. (in charge of Kiowa-Comanche farm loans). Communication to Ernest Wallace, 1945.

Oklahoma Historical Society Library, Oklahoma City. Kiowa-Comanche Records. The correspondence files contain a considerable amount of original or copies of correspondence and reports of agents, superintendents, military officials, and others pertaining to the reservation and agency periods.

Penrod, Max (principal of Riverside Indian School, Anadarko, Oklahoma). Communication to Ernest Wallace, 1945.

"Record Copy of the Proceedings of the Indian Peace Commission Appointed under the Acts of Congress Approved July 20, 1867." MS. National Archives, Office of Indian Affairs, Washington.

Riverside Indian School, Anadarko, Oklahoma. Records. 1945.

Taylor, Martin (supervisor of education for the Comanche-Kiowa Agency). Communication to Ernest Wallace, 1945.

Ten Bears (Comanche chief). "Speech at Medicine Lodge Peace Council, October 20, 1867," in "Record Copy of the Proceedings of the Indian Peace Commission Appointed under the Act of Congress Approved July 20, 1867" *(q.v.)*, Vol. I.

Texas Technological College Museum, Lubbock. Comanche specimens.

Thomas, R. B. "Kiowa-Comanche Experiences," Indian-Pioneer Papers *(q.v.)*, CX.

Underhill, Ruth (Office of Indian Affairs). Communication to Max Penrod (principal of Riverside Indian School), Anadarko, Oklahoma, October 2, 1943.

United States Commissioner of Indian Affairs. See entry under Published Materials.

United States National Museum, Smithsonian Institution, Washington. Comanche specimens.

United States Office of Indian Affairs. Records. National Archives Building, Washington. Many papers are originals; others are copies. The files drawn from most extensively are labeled: Treaties, Talks, and Councils (special file); Western Superintendency; Indian Territory Miscellaneous; Upper Arkansas Agency; Central Superintendency; New Mexico Superintendency; Wichita Agency.

Abel, Annie Heloise. *The American Indian as Slaveholder and Secessionist*. Cleveland, 1915.

—— (ed.). *The Official Correspondence of James S. Calhoun while Indian Agent at Santa Fé and Superintendent of Indian Affairs in New Mexico*. Washington, 1915.

Allen, J. A. "History of the American Bison," United States Geological and Geographical Survey of the Territories, *Annual Report*, IX. Washington, 1875.

Anon. "Indian Bow and Arrow," *Frontier Times*, Vol. VIII (1930).

Anon. "Reminiscences of Service among the Comanches," *Frank Leslie's Popular Monthly*, June, 1882.

Atkinson, Mary Jourdan. *The Texas Indians*. San Antonio, 1935.

Babb, T. A. ("Dot"). *In the Bosom of the Comanches*. Dallas, 1912.

Bancroft, H. H. *The Native Races*. 5 vols. San Francisco, 1886.

Barnes, Annie Marie. *Matouchon: A Story of Indian Child Life*. Philadelphia, 1895.

Battey, Thomas C. *The Life and Adventures of a Quaker among the Indians*. Boston, 1875.

Baylor, H. W. "Recollections of the Comanche Indians," *Frontier Times*, Vol. VI (1929).

Becker, Daniel A. "Comanche Civilization with History of Quanah Parker," *Chronicles of Oklahoma*, Vol. I (1923).

Benedict, Ruth. *The Concept of the Guardian Spirit in North America*. American Anthropological Association *Memoir 29*. Menasha, Wisconsin, 1924.

Bieber, Ralph P. "The Southwestern Trails to California," *Mississippi Valley Historical Review*, Vol. XII (1925).

Bollaert, William. "Observations on the Indian Tribes in Texas," London Ethnological Society *Journal*, Vol. II (1850).

Bolton, Herbert E. *Athanase de Mézières and the Louisiana-Texas Frontier*. 2 vols. Cleveland, 1914.

——. "Tonkawa," in Frederick W. Hodge (ed.), *Handbook of American Indians North of Mexico (q.v.)*, II.

Burnet, David G. "American Aborigines, Indians of Texas," *The Cincinnati Literary Gazette*. 2 vols. 1824–25.

——. "The Comanches and Other Tribes of Texas and the Policy to Be Pursued Respecting Them," in Henry R. Schoolcraft, *Historical and Statistical Information Respecting the History and Prospects of the Indian Tribes of the United States (q.v.)*.

Buttree, Julia M. *The Rhythm of the Red Man*. New York, 1930.

Carlson, Gustav G., and Volney H. Jones. "Some Notes on Uses of Plants by the Comanche Indians," *Papers* of the Michigan Academy of Science, Arts, and Letters, Vol. XXV (1940).

Carter, Robert G. *On the Border with MacKenzie.* Washington, 1935.
———. *The Old Sergeant's Story.* New York, 1926.
Catlin, George. *North American Indians.* 2 vols. Edinburgh, 1926.
Clark, W. P. *The Indian Sign Language.* Philadelphia, 1885.
Cook, John R. *The Border and the Buffalo.* Topeka, 1907.
Corlett, William T. *The Medicine Man of the American Indians.* (Report of a frontier surgeon stationed at Fort Sill in 1869.) Springfield and Baltimore, 1935.
Culin, Stewart. "Games of the North American Indians," Bureau of American Ethnology *Twenty-fourth Annual Report* (1902–1903). Washington, 1907.
Davis, Theodore R. "The Buffalo Range," *Harper's Magazine,* January, 1869.
DeShields, J. T. *Border Wars of Texas.* Tioga, Texas, 1912.
Dobie, J. Frank. "Stories in Texas Place Names," in J. Frank Dobie and Mody C. Boatright (eds.), *Straight Texas.* Austin, 1937.
Dodge, Richard I. *The Plains of the Great West.* New York, 1877.
———. *Our Wild Indians.* Hartford, 1882.
Dodge, T. A. "Some American Riders," *Harper's New Monthly Magazine,* May, 1891.
Domenech, Abbé Emmanuel. *Journal d'un Missionaire au Texas et au Méxique.* Paris, 1872.
———. *Seven Years Residence in the Great Deserts of North America.* 2 vols. London, 1860.
Dunn, William E. "The Apache Mission on the San Saba River, Its Founding and Its Failure," *The Southwestern Historical Quarterly,* Vol. XVII (1914).
Estill, Julia. "Indian Pictographs near Lange's Mill, Gillespie County, Texas," Texas Folk-Lore Society *Publication,* No. IV. Austin, 1925.
Ewers, John Canfield. *Plains Indian Painting.* Stanford University, 1939.
Farnham, Thomas J. *Travels in the Great Western Prairies.* 2 vols. Vols. XXVIII and XXIX of R. G. Thwaites (ed.), *Early Western Travels (q.v.).*
Fletcher, Alice C., and Francis La Flesche. "The Omaha Tribe," Bureau of American Ethnology *Bulletin No. 27* (1905–1906). Washington, 1911.
Folmer, Henri. "Etienne Veniard De Bourgmond in the Missouri Country," *Missouri Historical Review,* Vol. XXXVI (April, 1942).
Foreman, Grant. "Red River and the Spanish Boundary in the United States Supreme Court," *Chronicles of Oklahoma,* Vol. II (1924).
Gammell, H. P. N. (compiler). *Laws of Texas, 1822–1897.* 10 vols. Austin, 1898.
Garretson, Martin S. *The American Bison.* New York, 1938.
Gladwin, Thomas. "Comanche Kin Behavior," *American Anthropologist,* Vol. L (1948).

358

Glisan, Rodney. *Journal of Army Life*. San Francisco, 1874.

Goldstein, Marcus S. "Anthropometry of the Comanches," *American Journal of Physical Anthropology*, Vol. XIX (1934–35).

Gregg, Josiah. *Commerce of the Prairies*. (Reprint.) Dallas, 1933.

Grinnell, George Bird. *The Cheyenne Indians*. 2 vols. New Haven, 1923.

———. *The Fighting Cheyennes*. New York, 1915.

———. "Who Were the Padoucas?" *American Anthropologist*, Vol. XXII (1920).

Haines, Francis. "The Northward Spread of Horses among the Plains Indians," *American Anthropologist*, Vol. XL (1938).

———. "Where Did the Plains Indians Get Their Horses," *American Anthropologist*, Vol. XL (1938).

Haley, J. Evetts. "Charles Goodnight's Indian Recollections," *The Panhandle-Plains Historical Review*, Vol. I (1928).

———. *The XIT Ranch of Texas*. Chicago, 1929.

Harrington, John Peabody. "The Ethnogeography of the Tewa Indians," Bureau of American Ethnology *Twenty-ninth Annual Report* (1907–1908). Washington, 1916.

Hasson, Alex B. "Post Surgeon at Fort Phantom Hill Report for 1852," West Texas Historical Association *Year Book*, I. Abilene, Texas, 1924.

Hobbs, James. *Wild Life in the Far West*. Hartford, 1872.

Hodge, Frederick W. (ed.). *Handbook of American Indians North of Mexico*. Bureau of American Ethnology *Bulletin No. 30*. 2 vols. Washington, 1907, 1912.

Hoebel, E. Adamson. "Comanche and Hekandika Shoshone Relationship Systems," *American Anthropologist*, Vol. XLI (1939).

———. "The Comanche Sun Dance and Messianic Outbreak of 1873," *American Anthropologist*, Vol. XLIII (1941).

———. *The Political Organization and Law-Ways of the Comanche Indians*. Memoir No. 54 of the American Anthropological Association. Menasha, Wisconsin, 1940.

Holden, W. C. *Alkali Trails*. Dallas, 1930.

———. "Frontier Defense in Texas during the Civil War," West Texas Historical Association *Year Book*, V. Abilene, Texas, 1928.

Holley, Mary Austin. *Texas*. Lexington, 1836.

House, E. (ed.). *A Narrative of the Captivity of Mrs. Horn and Her Two Children with That of Mrs. Harris by the Comanche Indians*. St. Louis, 1839.

Hughs, Fannie May. *Legends of Texas Rivers*. Dallas, 1937.

Humfreville, J. Lee. *Twenty Years among Our Hostile Indians*. New York, 1903.

———. *Twenty Years among Our Savage Indians*. Hartford, 1897.

Inman, Henry. *The Old Santa Fé Trail*. Topeka, 1899

Jefferson, Thomas. *Message from the President of the United States Com-*

municating Discoveries Made in Exploring the Missouri, Red River, and Washita by Captains Lewis and Clark, Doctor Sibley, and Mr. Dunbar. Washington, 1806.

Jennings, Jessie D. *Plainsmen of the Past: A Review of the Prehistory of the Plains.* National Park Service, Region Two, 1945.

Jones, Jonathan H. *A Condensed History of the Apache and Comanche Indian Tribes.* San Antonio, 1899.

Kappler, Charles J. (ed.). *Indian Affairs, Laws and Treaties,* 57 Cong. 1 sess., *Senate Document 452.* 3 vols. Washington, 1903.

Kardiner, Abram (ed.). *The Psychological Frontiers of Society.* New York, 1949.

Kenney, M. M. "The History of the Indian Tribes of Texas," in vol. I of Dudley G. Wooton, *A Comprehensive History of Texas, 1685–1897.* 2 vols. Dallas, 1898.

———. "Tribal Society among Texas Indians," *The Quarterly* of the Texas State Historical Association, Vol. I (1897).

LaBarre, W. "Potato Taxonomy of the Aymara Indians of Bolivia," *Acta Americana,* Vol. V (1947).

Lee, Nelson. *Three Years among the Camanches.* Albany, 1859.

Lehmann, Herman. *Nine Years among the Indians* (1870–79). Austin, 1927.

Lewis, Meriwether, and William Clark. *History of the Expedition of Captains Lewis and Clark, 1804-5-6.* Hosmer edition, 2 vols. Chicago, 1902.

Linton, Ralph. "Acculturation and Process of Culture Change," in Ralph Linton (ed.), *Acculturation in Seven American Indian Tribes.* New York, 1940.

———. "The Comanche," in A. Kardiner, *The Psychological Frontiers of Society (q.v.).*

———. "The Comanche Sun Dance," *American Anthropologist,* Vol. XXXVII (1935).

———. "The Distinctive Aspects of Acculturation," in Ralph Linton (ed.), *Acculturation in Seven American Indian Tribes (q.v.).*

———. *The Study of Man.* New York, 1936.

Llewellyn, K. N., and E. A. Hoebel. *The Cheyenne Way: Conflict and Case Law in Primitive Jurisprudence.* Norman, 1941.

Lowie, Robert H. *The Crow Indians.* New York, 1925.

———. "Dances and Societies of the Plains Shoshone," American Museum of Natural History *Anthropological Papers,* XI. New York, 1916.

———. *An Introduction to Cultural Anthropology.* New York, 1940.

———. "The Northern Shoshone," American Museum of Natural History *Anthropological Papers,* II. New York, 1909.

———. *Primitive Society.* New York, 1920.

————. "Property Rights and the Coercive Powers of Plains Indian Military Societies," *Journal of Legal and Political Sociology,* Vol. I (1943).

McAllester, D. P. *Peyote Music.* Viking Fund *Publications in Anthropology No. 13.* New York, 1949.

MacLeod, William Christie. "The Distribution and Process of Suttee in North America," *American Anthropologist,* Vol. XXXIII (1931).

Marcy, Randolph B. *Adventure on Red River.* Ed. by Grant Foreman. Norman, 1937.

————. *Exploration of the Red River of Louisiana in the Year 1852,* 32 Cong., 2 sess., *Senate Executive Document 54.* Washington, 1854.

————. *Thirty Years of Army Life on the Border.* New York, 1866.

Marriott, Alice. *The Ten Grandmothers.* Norman, 1945.

Maximilian, Prince of Wied. *Travels in the Interior of America.* Vol. I of R. G. Thwaites (ed.), *Early Western Travels (q.v.).*

Methvin, John Jasper. *In the Limelight; or, History of Anadarko (Caddo County) and Vicinity from the Earliest Days.* N.p. (Anadarko, Oklahoma?), n.d. (Copy in the Oklahoma Collection, University of Oklahoma Library, Norman.)

Möllhausen, Baldwin. *Diary of a Journey from the Mississippi to the Coast of the Pacific with a United States Government Expedition.* 2 vols. London, 1858.

Mooney, James. "The Aboriginal Population of America North of Mexico," *Smithsonian Miscellaneous Collections,* Vol. LXXX, No. 7. Washington, 1928.

————. "Calendar History of the Kiowa," Bureau of American Ethnology *Seventeenth Annual Report,* Part I. Washington, 1898.

————. "The Ghost Dance Religion and the Sioux Outbreak of 1890," Bureau of American Ethnology *Fourteenth Annual Report* (1892–93), Part II. Washington, 1896.

Muckleroy, Anna. "The Indian Policy of the Republic of Texas," *The Southwestern Historical Quarterly,* Vol. XXVI (1923).

Neighbors, Robert S. "The Naüni or Comanches of Texas," in Henry R. Schoolcraft, *Information Respecting the History, Condition, and Prospects of the Indian Tribes of the United States (q.v.)*

Northern Standard (newspaper), Clarksville, Texas. 1848, 1850, 1853.

Nye, Wilbur S. "The Annual Sun Dance of the Kiowa Indians" (as related by George Hunt, a Kiowa), *Chronicles of Oklahoma,* Vol. XII (1934).

————. *Carbine and Lance: The Story of Old Fort Sill.* Norman, 1937.

Nystel, Ole T. "Three Months among the Indians," *Frontier Times,* Vol. V (1927).

Opler, Marvin K. "The Origins of Comanche and Ute," *American Anthropologist,* Vol. XLV (1943).

————. "The Southern Ute of Colorado," in Ralph Linton (ed.), *Acculturation in Seven American Indian Tribes (q.v.).*

Parker, W. B. *Notes Taken during the Expedition Commanded by Captain R. B. Marcy through Unexplored Texas, in the Summer and Fall of 1854.* Philadelphia, 1856.

Parsons, E. C., and R. L. Beals. "The Sacred Clowns of the Pueblo and Maya-Yaqui Indians," *American Anthropologist,* Vol. XXXVI (1934).

Powell, J. W. "Indian Linguistic Families of America North of Mexico," Bureau of American Ethnology *Seventh Annual Report* (1885–86). Washington, 1891.

Provinse, J. H. "The Underlying Sanctions of Plains Indian Society," in F. Eggan (ed.), *Social Anthropology of North American Tribes.* Chicago, 1937.

Richardson, Rupert N. *The Comanche Barrier to South Plains Settlement.* Glendale, 1933.

————. "The Culture of the Comanche Indians," Texas Archeological and Paleontological Society *Bulletin,* Vol. I (1929).

————. Texas: *The Lone Star State.* New York, 1943.

————, and C. C. Rister. *The Greater Southwest.* Glendale, 1934.

Rister, Carl C. *Border Captives.* Norman, 1940.

————. "Indians as Buffalo Hunters," *Frontier Times,* Vol. V (1928). Republished from *The Cattleman* (Fort Worth).

————. "The Significance of the Destruction of the Buffalo in the Southwest," *The Southwestern Historical Quarterly,* Vol. XXXIII (1929).

————. *The Southwestern Frontier.* Cleveland, 1928.

Ruxton, George F. *Adventures in Mexico and the Rocky Mountains.* New York, 1848.

St. Clair, H. H. "Shoshone and Comanche Tales," *Journal of American Folk-Lore,* Vol. LXXXV (July–September, 1909).

Sanchez, José María. "A Trip to Texas in 1828" (trans. by C. E. Castañeda), *The Southwestern Historical Quarterly,* Vol. XIX (1926).

Sapir, Edward. "Southern Paiute, A Shoshonean Language," American Academy of Arts and Sciences *Proceedings,* LXV. Boston, 1930.

Sargent, S. S., and M. W. Smith (eds.). *Culture and Personality.* New York, 1949.

Schmeckebier, L. F. *The Office of Indian Affairs, Its History, Activities, and Organization.* Baltimore, 1927.

Schoolcraft, Henry R. (ed.). *Information Respecting the History, Conditions, and Prospects of the Indian Tribes of the United States.* (Collected and prepared under the direction of the Bureau of Indian Affairs in 4 parts.) Philadelphia, 1853.

Schultes, Richard E. "The Appeal of Peyote (*Lophophora williamsii*) as a Medicine," *American Anthropologist,* Vol. XL (1938).

Scott, Hugh L. *Some Memoirs of a Soldier*. New York, 1928.

Smith, Clinton and Jeff D. *The Boy Captives*. As told to J. Marvin Hunter. Bandera, Texas, 1927.

Smithwick, Noah. *The Evolution of a State*. Facsimile reproduction of the original. Austin, 1935.

Southward, Claude. *Nocona's Nest*. N.p., n.d.

Spier, Leslie. "The Sun Dance of the Plains Indians," American Museum of Natural History *Anthropological Papers, XVI*. New York, 1921.

Steward, Julian H. "Basin-Plateau Aboriginal Socio-political Groups," Bureau of American Ethnology *Bulletin No. 120*. Washington, 1938.

Tatum, Lawrie. *Our Red Brothers*. Philadelphia, 1899.

Teit, James A. "The Salishan Tribes of the Western Plateaus: The Flathead Group," Bureau of American Ethnology *Forty-fourth Annual Report* (1928). Washington, 1930.

Thomas, Alfred B. "An Eighteenth Century Comanche Document," *American Anthropologist*, Vol. XXXI (1929).

———. *Forgotten Frontiers: A Study of the Spanish Indian Policy of Don Juan Bautista de Anza, 1777–1778*. Norman, 1932.

Thrall, Homer S. *A Pictorial History of Texas*. St. Louis, 1879.

Thwaites, Reuben Gold (ed.). *Early Western Travels, 1784–1897*. 32 vols. Cleveland, 1906.

Tilghmann, Zoe A. *Quanah, the Eagle of the Comanches*. Oklahoma City, 1938.

Twitchell, Ralph E. *Spanish Archives of New Mexico*. 2 vols. Cedar Rapids, 1914.

United States Commissioner of Indian Affairs. *Annual Reports* for 1841, 1854, 1855, 1857, 1858, 1861, 1867, 1868, 1869, 1870, 1871, 1875, 1876, 1877, 1878, 1879, 1881, 1883, 1884, 1885, 1886, 1890, 1892, 1893, 1900, 1901, 1906, 1910, 1930, 1935, 1945. Reports of agents, superintendents, special agents, and commissioners, as well as the general report and recommendations of the Commissioner of Indian Affairs are included. Each available report was examined, but those here listed were especially valuable.

United States Congress. *House Documents:* 27 Cong., 2 sess., *Exec. Doc. 2;* 41 Cong., 2 sess., *Misc. Doc. 139*, Vol. III; 41 Cong., 3 sess., *Exec. Doc. 1*.

———. Senate Documents: 32 Cong., 2 sess., *Exec. Doc. 54;* 33 Cong., 2 sess., *Exec. Doc. 1*, Part 1, Vol. I; 34 Cong., 1 sess., *Exec. Doc. 1;* 35 Cong., 1 sess., *Exec. Doc. 11;* 35 Cong., 2 sess., *Exec. Doc. 1*, Vol. I; 57 Cong., 1 sess., *Doc. 452*, Vols. I, II.

United States Federal Register. Executive Order 9659, November 24, 1945.

United States Statutes at Large. 47 vols. Washington, 1845–1933.

Vestal, Stanley. *Short Grass Country*. New York, 1941.

Voegelin, C. F. and E. W. "Map of North American Indian Languages," *American Ethnological Society Publication No. 20*. New York, 1944.

War of the Rebellion: Official Records of the Union and Confederate Armies, Series I, Vols. XLI, XLIII, XLVIII, LI: Series IV, Vols. I, II. Washington, 1881–1901.

Webb, Walter Prescott. *The Texas Rangers: A Conflict of Civilizations.* New York, 1935.

Wedel, Waldo R. "An Introduction to Pawnee Archeology," *Bureau of American Ethnology Bulletin No. 112*. Washington, 1936.

Weltfish, Gene. "The Man Who Married a Buffalo Wife, A Comanche Story," *Caddoan Texts (Publications* of the American Ethnological Society, XVII). New York, 1937.

Winship, George Parker. "The Coronado Expedition," *Bureau of American Ethnology Fourteenth Annual Report* (1892–93), Part I. Washington, 1896.

Wissler, Clark. *North American Indians of the Plains.* New York, 1927.
———. *The Relation of Nature to Man in Aboriginal America.* New York, 1926.

Wooten, Dudley G. (ed.). *A Comprehensive History of Texas, 1685–1897.* 2 vols. Dallas, 1898.

Yarrow, H. C. "A Further Contribution to the Study of Mortuary Customs of the North American Indians," *Bureau of American Ethnology First Annual Report* (1879–80). Washington, 1881.

Yoakum, H. *History of Texas.* 2 vols. Facsimile reproduction of the original. Austin, 1935.

Zingg, Robert M. *A Reconstruction of Uto-Aztekan History.* University of Denver, *Contribution to Ethnography,* II. New York, 1939.

Index

Bandelier, Adolf: 9

Banks, Dick: 5, 355

Bands, Comanche: 22; Antelope, 24, 28, 39, 87, 268, 304, 316f., 327; Burnt Meat, 26; Down Stream, 29; Hill Wearing Away, 30; Liver-eaters, 26, 29, 304; Meat-eaters, 26, 304, 307, 316; Those Who Move Often, 26, 304, 326; Wasp, 24–27, 30, 74, 293, 296ff., 301f., 304f., 323, 345; Water Horse, 30, 113, 137, 248; Wormy, 30; Yap-eaters, 26f., 304

Bannock Indians: 6, 21

Barber County, Kansas: 309

Barnes, Annie Marie: 119, 180, 357

Barton, Mrs. Ernesteen: *xi*

Basketry, absence of in Comanche culture: 93

Battey, Thomas C.: 68, 71, 76, 116, 136, 159, 171, 182f., 188, 206, 286, 319, 357

Battles: Wolf Creek, 286; Río del Fierro, 288; of Plum Creek, 294; with Sauk and Fox (1853), 299; with U. S. Army, 302; Kit Carson at Adobe Walls, 306; Adobe Walls, 325ff.; Palo Duro Canyon, 327

Baylor, H. W.: 95, 103, 108, 153, 357

Beals, R. L.: 322, 362

Bear Claws Marks on His Shield (personal name): 161f.

Becker, Daniel A.: 136

Bee, Hamilton: 295

Been to See His Son: 167

Benedict, Ruth: 156, 235, 357

Bent, Charles: 32

Bexar County, Texas: 301

Bieber, Ralph P.: 299, 357

Big Bear: 172

Big Cannibal Owl: 124, 171

Bird's Fort: 295

Birth practices: 142ff.

Blackfeet Indians: 10, 38

Blackmon, Agent J. P.: 352

Black Mustache: 281

Blanco Canyon, Texas: 316

Blue Leggins: 207

Boas, Franz: 45

Bogy, Charles: 32, 308

Bollaert, William: 153, 188, 194, 357

Bolton, H. E.: 70, 287f., 357

"Boomers": 349, 351f.

Bonville, Capt. B. L. E.: 31

Bosque, Fernando del: 37

Bourgemond, Étienne Veniard de: 6, 288

Brazos River: 12, 26, 291, 301
Breaks Something (personal name): *xi,* 36, 84, 110, 115, 118, 138, 162 ff.,
    169, 174, 228, 236, 238, 260, 334
Brown, Agent Hugh: 338
Buell, Col. G. P.: 326 f.
Buffalo: 54 ff., 199 f.; Comanche use of, 50; extinction of, 63 ff., 298, 327, 342
Bull Elk (personal name): 281
Bull-roarer: 175
Buntin, Supt. J. A.: 343, 355
Buntin, Martha Leota: 355
Bureau of American Ethnology: *xi*
Burial, Comanche: 149 ff., 190 f., 268
Burnet, David G.: 23, 77, 78, 82, 108, 142, 159, 171, 188, 191, 233, 253,
    264, 292, 357
Burnet County, Texas: 301

Cabeza de Vaca, Álvar Núñez: 54
Caddo Indians: 25, 38, 182, 301
Cameahwait: 11
Camp Cooper: 301, 316
Camp Supply: 326
Canadian River: 9, 12, 27, 99
Camps: 14
Cannibalism: 70, 260
Captives, among Comanches: 241 f., 259, 261 ff., 271, 321
Carlson, Gustav G.: *xi,* 73, 316, 357
Carrying Her Sunshade: *xi,* 260, 275
Carson, Kit, at Adobe Walls, Texas: 306
Carter, Robert G.: 71, 72, 82, 87, 95, 97, 101, 103, 105, 153, 188, 358
Casa Grande, Joseph: *xi*
Cassaway, Lillian: 350
Castañeda, Pedro de: 54
Catlin, George: 15, 17, 358
Cattlemen, on Comanche reservation: 346
Ceded lands: 350
Ceremony, beaver: 175 ff., 345
Chaat, Robert: *xi*
Charcoal (personal name): 334 ff.
Cherokee Indians: 287, 299
Cheyenne Indians: 4, 14, 63, 98, 103, 141, 188, 238, 249, 285, 299, 306,
    325; Comanche peace with, 277; Sun Dance, 320
Chiefs, Comanche: 24; hunt, 57, 61; band, 183; peace, 209 ff., 276 f.; war,
    213, 216 ff., 220 f., 223, 250 ff., 255, 267, 273 f., 281
Childbirth: 278 ff.

Child training: 48, 119 ff.
Chouteau, Agent P. L.: 9, 12, 31
Christianity: 345
Cimarron River: 12
Civil War: 64, 303, 307 f.
Clark, Agent E. L.: 26, 29
Clark, W. P.: 28, 358
Clark, Gen. William: 4, 11
Clay County, Texas: 305
Clear Fork River: 301
Cleveland, President Grover: 350
Clothing: 77 ff.; women's, 85 f.
Clowns, in Comanche Sun Dance: 321
Colorado: 8; Indian depredations in, 326
Colorado River: 12, 38
Comanche: meaning of, 4; origin of, 5, 8, 9 f.; physical appearance, 17 ff.; tribal organizations, 22; *see also subject headings for other items of Comanche culture and history*
Comanche County, Oklahoma: 310
Comanchero: *see* trade, Mexican
Confederate States Indian policy: 303 ff.
Contract, in Comanche culture: 135, 160 ff., 166
Contrary Ones: 275 ff.
Cook, John R.: 66, 358
Cooke County, Texas: 305
Cora-Huichol Indians: 323
Corlett, William T.: 144, 358
Coronado: 6, 37
Corpus Christi, Texas: 302
Cortez, Hernando: 54
Cosmogony, Comanche: 190 ff.
Cotton County, Oklahoma: 310
Council: Comanche, 213 ff., 215, 242; with United States representatives, 291, 297, (1859) 302 f., (1865) 307; with Republic of Texas representatives, 293 ff.
Coup: 179, 219, 246 ff., 269
Court of Indian Offenses, on Comanche reservation: 342, 351
Courtship: 132 ff.
Coyote, mythological character: 69, 193, 202
Coyote Droppings (personal name): 256, 319 ff., 324 ff., 345
Cradle board: 120
Creek Indians: 304
Crier, camp: 211, 215
Cross Timbers: 12, 14, 25

368

French, trade relations with Comanches: 8, 288
Friendship, formal, in Comanche culture: 132

Gainesville, Texas: 308
Gambling: 49, 112f., 117
Games: 112ff.
Gammel, H. P. N.: 293f., 358
Garretson, Martin S.: 55, 67, 95, 99, 101, 104, 358
Garth, T. E.: 89
Geronimo, Oklahoma: 30
Gets to Be a Middle-aged Man (personal name): *xi*, 273, 316f.
Ghosts: 173
Gift-giving: 59, 108, 109, 134, 136ff., 152, 179, 220, 240, 243, 250, 268, 272
Gilcrease, Thomas, Foundation Museum: 355
Givens, Joshua: 350
Gladwin, Thomas: 134, 358
Gold rush, effect on Comanches: 300
Goldstein, Marcus S.: 18, 29, 359
Goodnight, Charles: 106, 268
Grady County, Oklahoma: 310
Grant, President U. S.: 313
Grayson County, Texas: 301
Gregg, Josiah: 47, 59, 78, 101, 105, 136, 195, 211, 241, 251, 271, 359
Greyfoot, Herman: *xi*, 121, 123, 236, 279, 334
Greyfoot, Rhoda: 108, 236, 253, 260
Grierson, Col. B. H.: 315
Grinnell, George Bird: 9, 41, 98, 101, 103, 188, 250, 277, 299, 325, 359
Group of Men Standing on a Hill (personal name): 122
Guadaloupe River: 288
Guardian spirit: 158, 181, 197; *see also* vision quest

Hadley, J. Nixon: *xi*
Haines, Francis, 37f., 359
Haley, J. Evetts: 106, 108, 153, 268, 359
Hall, Capt. J. Lee: 338, 348
Harrington, John Peabody: 6, 359
Hasson, Alex B.: 64, 359
Hayworth, Agent J. M.: 318, 330, 338
Hazen, Gen. W. B.: 312ff.
He Runs Directly Against the Enemy (personal name): 121
Henderson, Gov. J. P.: 297
Hertzog, George: *ix*
Hides, preparation of: 93
High Wolf (personal name): 343

371

Llano River: 287f., 298
Llewellyn, K. N.: 173, 277, 360
Lockett, Claiborne: *xi*
Loup River: 6
Lowie, R. H.: 21, 24f., 62, 88, 108, 111, 114, 115, 224, 250, 360f.

McAllester, D. P.: 332ff., 361
McAllister, J. G.: *xi*
McClellan, Capt. George B.: 73
McCown, Supt. W. B.: 312, 349f., 355, 356
MacKenzie, Col. R. S.: 28, 40, 316f., 330
McLeod, Gen. Hugh D.: 294, 359
MacLeod, William Christie: 361
Magic: 77
Maps, made by Comanches: 254
Marcy, Capt. Randolph B.: 17, 25, 26, 39, 44, 47f., 73, 79, 89, 101, 103, 105, 108, 120, 134, 136, 151, 153, 157, 188, 316, 361
Marriage: 132ff.; affinal, 138ff.; to wife's brother's daughter, 139f.; to step-daughter, 140; residence in, 140; cross-cousin, 141
Marriott, Alice: 254, 343, 361
Massacre, Salt Creek: 316
Maximilian, Prince of Wied: 39, 361
Mayhall, Mildred Pickle: 105, 356
Medicine (supernatural power): 61, 152, 155ff., 183, 203f.; shield, 108; love, 134; medicine bag, 159; societies, 165f.; stones, 171; Earth, 177; coyote, 202; *see also* ceremony, curing, medicine man, peyote, religion, sorcery, spirits, Sun Dance
Medicine Bluff, Oklahoma: 15, 157, 205
Medicine man: 121, 143, 155ff., 175ff., 182, 183, 203ff., 236f., 254
Medicine Mounds, Texas: 204
Medicine Woman (personal name): *xi,* 69, 70, 77, 78, 103, 108, 127, 133, 136, 144, 147, 153, 158, 170f., 182
Melville, Rev. John: 180, 182
Menard, Texas: 290
Mendoza-López Expedition: 38
Messianism: 33, 319ff., 343f.
Menstruation: 144f.
Methvin, J. J.: 350, 356
Mexico: Comanche raids in, 45, 261ff., 296ff., 318; peyote in, 333
Miles, Col. Nelson A.: 326
Miller, Robert: 64
Mirsky, Jeanette: *ix*
Missouri River: 6
Moccasins: 78

Möllhausen, Baldwin: 43, 47, 271, 361
Moeta, Frank: 275
Montague County, Texas: 305
Monterrey, Mexico: 254
Mooney, James: 5, 8, 25, 27, 29 ff., 136, 199, 277, 336, 345, 361
Moore, Col. John H.: 294
Moore, Scott B.: 356
Mount Scott: 311
Mountain (personal name): 40
Mourning, Comanche: 151 f., 222, 231 f., 242 f., 268
Muckleroy, Anna: 293, 361
Mud Men (Comanche clowns): 321
Mumshukawa (personal name): 271, 334 ff.
Mun, Joseph de: 9
Music: 178 f.
Meyers, Agent W. D.: 348
Mythology: 51 ff., 69, 124, 129, 192 ff., 198, 200 f., 206 f., 236 ff.; origin of peyote, 333 ff.

Naming: 121 f.
Native American Church (Peyote cult): 337
Navaho Indians: 3
Neighbors, Agent Robert S.: 5, 25, 30, 79, 116, 153, 171, 182, 191, 193 f., 214, 297 f., 361
Neosho River: 287
New Mexico: 8, 39, 288 ff.; Indian depredations in, 326
Norton, A. B.: 267
Not Enough to Eat (personal name): 167
Nueces River: 288
Nye, Col. W. S.: 15, 40, 171, 314 f., 330, 361
Nystel, Ole T.: 153, 271, 361

Oath: 242, 248
Oklahoma: 9; admission to statehood, 353
Oklahoma Historical Society Library: 356
Omaha Indians: 14, 40
Opler, Marvin K.: 4, 286, 361
Ortiz, Francisco Xavier: 27, 31
Osage Indians: 3, 14, 40, 220, 286 f., 299

Padello, Juan de: 289
Padouca Indians: 4
Paha-yuca (personal name): 295
Palo Duro Canyon: 40, 65; Battle of, 327

Palo Pinto County, Texas: 301, 305
Paiute Indians: 20
Parfleche: 74
Parker, Cynthia Ann: 292
Parker, Quanah: 5, 110, 267, 316, 327, 341 ff., 344
Parker, W. B.: 24, 32, 47, 71, 108, 134, 151, 152, 182, 362
Parker County, Texas: 301, 305
Parker's Fort: 292
Parsons, E. C.: 322, 361
Pawnee Indians: 3, 38, 40, 177, 285
Peace-making: 40
Pease River: 12, 26
Pecos River: 12, 25, 27, 31
Penrod, Max: *xi,* 356
Personality, ideal: 146 f.
Peyote cult: 109, 168, 332 ff., 345
Pike, Albert: 304
Pike, Zebulon: 9
Pipes: 98, 214; use of, 176, 255; peace, 281
Plains Indians: cultural characteristics, 33; prehistory of, 34
Platte River: 4, 8
Pointing to the Rising Sun (personal name): 240
Political organization, of Comanches: 210 ff.
Police: military fraternities as, 56 f.; Indian police on reservation, 340 ff.
Polyandry: 138, 223
Polygyny: 138, 141
Ponca Indians, tradition of contact with Comanches: 39
Population, of Comanches: 31 ff.
Post Oak Jim: *xi,* 9, 36, 42, 47, 60, 62, 69, 83, 97, 98, 101 ff., 109, 115, 122 f.
    128 f., 132 f., 143, 144, 159 f., 167, 172 f., 177, 187, 194, 197, 199, 247,
    267 f., 322
Pottery, absence of in Comanche culture: 91
Powder River: 64
Powell, J. W.: 6, 8, 362
Prayer: 181, 195 f., 214
Property: 247; horses as, 47; disposal of, 152; incorporeal, 250 f.
Provinse, J. H.: 224, 362
Puberty: 125 f., 129 f., 145 f.
Pueblo, Colorado: 9
Pueblos: 321; Pecos, 3, 31; Taos, 9, 81

Quaker Peace Policy: 313 ff., 317, 326

Raiding: 45 f.; *see also* warfare

376

Randlett, Agent J. F.: 351
Rape: 240
Red Crooked Nose (personal name): 230
Red River: 12, 27, 287, 302, 310, 319
Religion: 155 ff., 186 ff.; *see also* cosmogony, medicine, medicine man, mythology, prayer, spirits, vision quest
Reservations, Indian: 310 ff., 329; in Texas, 301; life on, 337 ff.; Wichita-Caddo, 350; opening of Comanche, 351 ff.
Residence, Comanche practices: 140
Resurrection, Comanche belief in: 186 ff., 206, 319 f.
Richardson, Rupert N.: *ix, xi*, 11, 24, 29, 142, 151, 297, 302 f., 319 f., 332, 362
Ringgold, Texas: 290
Río Grande: 8, 13, 288, 290
Rister, Carl Coke: 15, 58, 60, 63, 71, 188, 214, 268, 302, 362
Riverside Indian School: 355
Robes: 80 f.
Rollins, J. H.: 298
Rubi, Marquis de: 289 f.
Runnels, Hardin R.: 303
Ruxton, George Frederick: 45, 362

Saddles: 96 f.
Sadelmeyer, Jacob: 45
St. Clair, H. H.: 51, 362
San Antonio, Texas: 12, 290; council at, 291, 293
San Carlos de los Jupes, village of: 289
Sanctions: in child training, 124, 130, 215, 273; death, 232 f.
San Patricio County, Texas: 301
San Saba Mission: 290
San Saba River: 287 f.
Sanchez, José María: 362
Santa Fé Laboratory of Anthropology: *ix* ff., 9, 25, 30, 73, 95, 317
Santa Fé, New Mexico: 3, 12, 31
Santa Fé Trail: 6, 306
Sapir, Edward: 20, 362
Sargent, S. S.: 362
Satanta: 309
Sauk Indians: 299
Scalping: 111, 189, 219 f., 246, 269 f.
Schmeckebier, L. F.: 362
Schoolcraft, Henry R.: 362
Schultes, Richard E.: 362
Scott, Hugh L.: 350, 363

377

Scout, Comanche: 218, 255 f.
Séance: 172 ff.
See How Deep the Water Is (personal name): *xi,* 130, 133, 136, 142,
    251, 271
Seminole Indians: 300
Sewing: 80
Sex relations: 128, 133 f., 240; contraceptives, absence of, 142
Shaking Hand (personal name): 314
Shawnee Indians: 14, 299, 305
She Blushes (personal name): 167
She Invites Her Relatives (personal name): *xi,* 79, 83, 85, 96, 140, 166, 168,
    170, 230
Sheridan, Gen. Philip H.: 55, 66, 308
Sherman, Gen. W. T.: 316
Shoshone Indians: 5, 10 f., 38 f., 70, 141, 193, 242; physical characteristics,
    18; territory of, 20; Wind River, 30
Signals: 265
Sioux Indians: 14, 344
Sitting Bull: 343 f.
Skinny and Wrinkled (personal name): *xi,* 128, 160, 202
Slavery: 287; *see also* captives
Slope (personal name): *xi,* 47, 60, 67, 140, 173, 187, 194, 260, 279
Smith, Clinton and J. D.: 39, 43, 71, 76, 83, 84, 151, 182, 265, 266, 363
Smith, M. W.: 362
Smithsonian Institution: 337
Smithwick, Noah: 43, 71, 72, 77, 83, 95, 134, 182, 195, 293, 363
Smoke lodge: 147 f.
Smoke River: 6
Sorcery: 147 f., 167, 174, 235 ff.
Sororate: 135
South Platte River: 64
Southward, Claude: 347, 363
Spaniards, relations with Indians: 3, 8, 11, 27, 286 ff.
Spier, Leslie: 63, 363
Spirit: Supreme, 183, 191 ff.; Sun, 195; Earth, 196; Thunderbird, 198;
    see also guardian spirit
Staked Plains: 12 f., 28, 312, 316
Status, age: 145, 213 f.
Stephens County, Oklahoma: 310
Steward, Julian H.: 363
Stokes, Gov. Montfort: 12, 292
Suicide: 231, 247
Supernaturalism: 155 ff., 203 ff., 323 f.; *see also* ceremony, conditional curse,

divination, medicine, medicine man, mythology, oath, peyote cult, religion, spirits, tabu, vision quest
Surgery: 170
Sweat lodge: 172

iards (1786), 289, (1785) 290; with United States, 291f., 297, (1853) 300, (1863) 305f., (1868) 309; with Republic of Texas (1838), 293; with Confederate States, 304
Twitchell, Ralph E.: 8, 363

Underhill, Ruth: 356
United States: Commissioner of Indian Affairs, 64, 302, 304, 313, 338, 346, 348, 351, 362; relations with Comanches, 291ff., 303ff.; Army, 296, in Texas (1853), 301f., (1860) 303, (1865) 308f., 312; Indian Service, 312f., 356; Secretary of the Interior, 313, 350, 351f.
United States National Museum: *xi,* 356
University of Texas, Anthropological Museum: *xi,* 254
Ute Indians: 3, 5, 20, 219, 286; peace with, 277f.

Vernon, Ida: *xi*
Vestal, Ophelia: 355
Vestal, Stanley: 363
Villasur Expedition: 8
Vision quest: 109, 130f., 155ff., 207f., 324
Voegelin, C. F. and E. W.: 21, 364
Voice of the Sunrise (personal name): 314

Waco Indians: 287, 299, 300
Wallace, Ernest: *x,* 18, 78, 101, 350, 355
War bonnet: 82, 86, 220f., 272f.
Warfare: 48, 130, 216, 218f., 245ff.; organization of war parties, 250ff., 335ff.
Washita River: 12
Wealth, Comanche: 36
Weapons: bow and arrow, 98ff., 114; poisoned, 105; guns, 105f.; shield, 106f., 203; lance, 110; war club, 111
Weaving, absence of in Comanche culture: 93
Webb, Walter Prescott: *xi,* 35, 364
Wedel, Waldo: *xi,* 6, 364
Weltfish, Gene: 202, 364
White Wolf, Howard: *xi,* 61, 69, 267, 334
Whitfield, Agent J. W.: 64, 299
Wichita Agency: 304f., 326
Wichita Indians: 25, 81, 182, 277, 287, 299
Wichita Falls, Texas: 341
Wichita, Kansas: 307
Wichita Mountains: 12, 15, 124, 157, 311
Wicks, J. B.: 345
Wide Feet (personal name): 240

Wife-lending: 132, 138
Wife-stealing: 216f.
Wild Horse (personal name): 281
Winnebago Indians: 157
Winship, George Parker: 6, 364
Wise County, Texas: 305
Wissler, Clark: 19, 32f., 79, 82, 101, 364
Woman (personal name): 228
Women: work of, 60, 80, 92ff., 96, 166; position of 147, 234, 241; role of, 214, 252f.
Wovoka (Jack Wilson): 343
Wooten, Dudley G.: 364
Wright, Robert M.: 55

Yarrow, H. C.: 151, 153, 190, 364
Yellowfish, Wiley: 108, 157f., 171, 180, 202, 223, 248, 251, 253, 257, 266, 271
Yoakum, H.: 293, 364

Zingg, Robert M.: 19, 364

UNIVERSITY OF OKLAHOMA PRESS

NORMAN AND LONDON

PRENTICE-HALL
HISTORY OF MUSIC SERIES
H. WILEY HITCHCOCK, editor

MUSIC IN THE MEDIEVAL WORLD, *Albert Seay*
BAROQUE MUSIC, *Claude V. Palisca*
MUSIC IN THE CLASSIC PERIOD, *Reinhard G. Pauly*
NINETEENTH-CENTURY ROMANTICISM IN MUSIC, *Rey M. Longyear*
TWENTIETH-CENTURY MUSIC: AN INTRODUCTION, *Eric Salzman*
FOLK AND TRADITIONAL MUSIC OF THE WESTERN CONTINENTS, *Bruno Nettl*
MUSIC CULTURES OF THE PACIFIC, THE NEAR EAST, AND ASIA, *William P. Malm*
MUSIC IN THE UNITED STATES: A HISTORICAL INTRODUCTION, *H. Wiley Hitchcock*

FOLK AND TRADITIONAL
MUSIC OF THE
WESTERN CONTINENTS

second edition

FOLK AND TRADITIONAL MUSIC OF THE WESTERN CONTINENTS

BRUNO NETTL

University of Illinois

with chapters on Latin America by
Gérard Béhague (University of Illinois)

PRENTICE-HALL, INC., ENGLEWOOD CLIFFS, NEW JERSEY

Library of Congress Cataloging in Publication Data

NETTL, BRUNO
    Folk and traditional music of the western continents.

    (Prentice-Hall history of music series)
    Includes bibliographies and discographies.
    1. Folk music—History and criticism.   2. Music,
Primitive.   I. Behague, Gerard.   II. Title.
ML3545.N285 1973   781.7'09182'1   72-10010
ISBN   0-13-322941-6
ISBN   0-13-322933-5 (pbk)

FOR GRACE

Printed in the United States of America

10   9   8   7   6   5   4   3   2   1

© 1973, 1965 by Prentice-Hall, Inc.
Englewood Cliffs, New Jersey

PRENTICE-HALL INTERNATIONAL, INC., *London*
PRENTICE-HALL OF AUSTRALIA, PTY. LTD., *Sydney*
PRENTICE-HALL OF CANADA, LTD., *Toronto*
PRENTICE-HALL OF INDIA PRIVATE LIMITED, *New Delhi*
PRENTICE-HALL OF JAPAN, INC., *Tokyo*

FOREWORD

Students and informed amateurs of the history of music have long needed a series of books that are comprehensive, authoritative, and engagingly written. They have needed books written by specialists—but specialists interested in communicating vividly. The Prentice-Hall History of Music Series aims at filling these needs.

Six books in the series present a panoramic view of the history of Western music, divided among the major historical periods—Medieval, Renaissance, Baroque, Classic, Romantic, and Contemporary. The musical cultures of the United States, Latin America, and Russia, viewed historically as independent developments within the larger western tradition, are discussed in three other books. In yet another pair, the rich yet neglected folk and traditional music of both hemispheres is treated. Taken together, the eleven volumes of the series are a distinctive and, we hope, distinguished contribution to the history of the music of the world's peoples. Each volume, moreover, may be read singly as a substantial account of the music of its period or area.

The authors of the series are scholars of national and international repute—musicologists, critics, and teachers of acknowledged stature in their respective fields of specialization. In their contributions to the Prentice-Hall History of Music Series their goal has been to present works of solid scholarship that are eminently readable, with significant insights into music as a part of the general intellectual and cultural life of man.

H. WILEY HITCHCOCK, *Editor*

PREFACE

Dividing the world into two halves for the purpose of investigating and discussing its traditional and folk or its so-called ethnic music is perhaps a dangerous proposition. But if such a division must be made, it seems logical to group together Europe, sub-Saharan Africa, and the Americas. During the last several centuries, these areas have come greatly under the influence of Western civilization and its music—and they have influenced Western high culture also—while the rest of the world appears to have been more under the aegis of the oriental high cultures. Moreover, in an American publication it seems appropriate to treat together those areas of the world which, broadly speaking, are responsible for the musical culture of the Americas today: Europe, Negro Africa, and aboriginal America. Finally, the areas covered here can be thought to have produced about half of the world's music and musical styles, if such concepts can be quantified at all. On the other hand, there is not much unity but there is a tremendous variety of musical styles, values, functions, and instruments in the part of the world that is the subject of this volume.

Our approach is essentially geographic. After two chapters dealing with the general characteristics of traditional music and its cultural context, and with some of the methods used to study folk music, we devote four chapters to Europe, one to sub-Saharan Africa, and three to the Americas. It has been impossible, of course, to survey comprehensively the music of each area, nation, and tribe, and we must content ourselves with examples of the kinds of musical styles that are found, and with sampling the types of songs that are sung, the various uses to which music is put, and the plethora of instruments past and present. The musical examples are intended to illustrate points made in the text rather than to serve as a representative anthology of musical forms; but most of the things discussed are musically illustrated, and a few of the most important and unusual instruments are depicted.

This revised edition differs from the original in a number of respects. Wherever possible, errors have been corrected. Several chapters have been substantially expanded, largely in the direction of providing more discussion of the role of music in culture and of recent developments in the traditional musics as they continue their existence in modern urban culture. Most important is the inclusion of an entirely new chapter on folk music in Latin America by my colleague, Dr. Gérard Béhague, who has also revised and added to the section of music of Afro-American peoples in South America and the Caribbean, in Chapter 10.

I should like to express my thanks to the various publishers, collectors, and authors who have given permission to quote musical and textual material; individual credit is given with each quotation. I am indebted to William P. Malm for advice and criticism and for arranging to have the exquisite line drawings of instruments by the prominent Japanese artist Masakazu Kuwata. I am also grateful to H. Wiley Hitchcock for advice and guidance and to my wife for technical assistance.

B.N.

CONTENTS

ONE

FOLK AND TRIBAL MUSICS
IN THEIR CULTURAL SETTING

INTRODUCTION

We are concerned here with a body of music called ethnic, folk, or traditional, as it is found in Europe, most of Africa, and the Americas. This music consists essentially of two groups of styles and repertories: (1) folk music, which is found in those cultures and areas in which there is also a longtime development of urban, professional, cultivated musical tradition, something that is often called "art" or "classical" music, and (2) tribal music, the music of nonliterate cultures, i.e., those without a tradition of literate, sophisticated musical culture living alongside the musical folk culture. The latter kind of music is frequently called "primitive," but the term is to be used with caution. The world's tribal musical cultures are not in essence different from the cultivated ones, except that they have less in the way of music theory and of professionalization of

1

musicians; and they have no musical notation. Quantitatively, their musics are simpler than the art musics of the world. (But even this statement is only generally true; for example, the rhythmic structures of African music are often much more complex than those of nineteenth century European classical music.) Nevertheless, the musical creations of tribal cultures are genuine works of art; they can be analyzed, judged, and appreciated in much the same terms as can the great masterpieces and all other compositions of Western music, if one views them in the context of their own cultural background.

Although we really have no way of telling just what happened in the musical history of all the world's cultures, we may perhaps assume that an earlier stage of the musical development of all cultures, including the modern ones, was something like the musical culture of contemporary tribal and folk societies, in the sense that it involved mainly people who were not professional musicians, and that it consisted of music that all of the people could understand and in which many or most could participate. Then, among some peoples, there must have taken place the development of a separate musical life for an educationally sophisticated and economically or politically powerful segment of the population, while the rest of the people held on to the older musical tradition. In Western civilization, we tend to be dominated by this more sophisticated musical culture, which includes our concert music and also the vast body of popular music. We are much less aware of the folk traditions that, before the invention of recording and radio, were dominant, especially in the rural parts of Europe and the Americas, and that still live in relatively isolated pockets of society. But we are beginning to realize the great influence that folk music has had on urban musical culture, and we are also beginning to understand the ways in which the musical folk culture has changed under the influence of the urban mass media, but still remains somewhat intact.

We are concerned, then, with two kinds of music, the folk and the so-called primitive, which really—when they are first heard by the novice—have very little in common. European and American folk music is, after all, part of our own cultural tradition as members of Western culture. The traditional music of the American Indians and Africans is generally quite outside our experience. Moreover, each nation, each tribe, has its own music, and one kind of folk music may sound quite unlike another; Indian and African music are quite dissimilar, indeed, as different as two kinds of music can be. Our only justification for including such a large group of music in a single volume is the fact that in each culture in the Western half of the world this is the music that is used by a large number of people.

Contemporary academic musicians tend to concentrate on the

degree to which a piece of music is unique and on the complexity of its structure and texture; and they may not care particularly whether it is understood by many listeners, by a few professionals, or even by the composer himself. In tribal and folk musics, the values are usually turned around. Uniqueness may not be important, and the innovator may be discriminated against; but a new song must be acceptable to others in order to live. This distinction is important, even if the case for it has sometimes been overstated.

Early students of folk music believed that in a tribal or folk community all individuals knew all of the songs in the repertory and could perform them more or less equally well. It is true that in order for a song or other music to be viable in such a culture, it must be understood and accepted by a large segment of the population. But we know that in African societies there have for a long time been musicians recognized as such; we know that American Indian shamans or medicine men knew more songs than other members of their tribes; and we are aware that in European folk cultures individuals who knew many songs and could sing well were singled out for recognition. Moreover, in all of these cultures, there was a tendency for certain songs or pieces to be reserved for specific groups, such as men, women, children, members of religious cults, political subdivisions, etc. Thus it is impossible to conclude that there is a difference *in essence* between the musical cultures of primitive tribes and those of the modern Western city. The simplest tribal group and the most advanced group of avant-garde musicians (which throughout the world has perhaps only a few thousand adherents) are at different ends of one continuum, and most of the world's musics fall at various points between them. And a great deal of the world's music is at borderlines between such conventional categories as tribal, primitive, folk, popular, and classical.

If there are specific features common to all of the musics discussed in this volume, they are (1) ready acceptability to large segments of the society in which they exist, and (2) the fact that they live in and are preserved by oral tradition.

ORAL TRADITION

To say that a culture has oral tradition means simply that its music (like its stories, proverbs, riddles, methods of arts and crafts, and, indeed, all its folklore) is passed on by word of mouth. Songs are learned by hearing; instrument making and playing are learned by watching. In a literate musical culture, music is usually written down, and a piece conceived by a composer need never be performed at all during his lifetime; it can be discovered centuries later by a scholar and resurrected. But in a folk or a nonliterate culture, or even in a sophisticated culture without musical notation, a song must be sung, remembered, and taught by one generation to the next. If this does not happen, it dies and is lost forever. Surely, then, a piece of folk music must in some way be representative of the musical taste and the aesthetic judgment of all those who know it and use it, rather than being simply the product of an individual, perhaps isolated, creator.

As we have just indicated, a folk song must be accepted or it will be forgotten and die. There is another alternative: if it is not accepted by its audience, it may be changed to fit the needs and desires of the people who perform and hear it. And since there is not, in the case of most folk or tribal music, a written standard version which people can consult, changes made over the years tend to become integral to the song.

Of course this kind of change occurs for several reasons and at various levels. Imagine, for instance, that a Kentucky or an Alpine mountaineer makes up a folk song—both melody and words. He may compose the melody by putting together snatches of other songs he knows, or simply by humming aimlessly until he hits upon something that strikes his fancy, or by systematically changing a melody he already knows. (We know very little about the way in which composing is done in folk and nonliterate cultures, just as we really know next to nothing about the mental processes involved in composing sophisticated music.) This man then teaches his song to his three sons. Son number one is a musical fellow who has a television set and occasionally goes to the city (where he hears more complicated music) and over the years, he whittles away at the song, changing notes here and there, adding ornaments, and evening out the meter, until he has made very substantial changes, which he no doubt considers improvements. Son number two likes to sing, but has a poor musical memory. He forgets how the song begins but remembers the second half of the tune. In his rendition, the song, which originally had, say, four different musical phrases (ABCD), consists only of a repetition of the last two and now has the form CDCD. (This is what evidently happened in the case of an old English and American song, "The Pretty Mohea," which is often sung to a tune with the form AABA. The last two lines, repeated, seem to have become the tune of a popular hillbilly song, "On Top of Old Smoky.") Son number three moves to Mexico, and while he likes to sing his father's song, he becomes so saturated with Mexican popular and folk music that his version of the song begins to sound like a Mexican folk song with the kind of rhythmic and ornamental structure characteristic of that country's tradition. You can imagine what might happen at a family reunion: the three sons sing their three versions, and while a person who knew the old man and his song the way it was first sung would surely realize that the sons have sung three versions of the same song, a newcomer to the group might hardly guess that the sons' songs actually were descendants of the same original. Add a few generations, and one song has become a large number of variants. The original form is forgotten and can no longer be reconstructed from the later versions.

HOW DOES TRADITIONAL MUSIC ORIGINATE?

We have looked at the way in which folk music comes to us. Most of it is quite old, but it has changed. To be sure, new songs are made up in most cultures at all times. In some cultures, many new songs are composed every year or every generation; in others, only a few new ones may appear in a century. But a great deal of the material, in all cases, is old, and thus we frequently hear about the great antiquity of folk and primitive music. But we must keep in mind the fact that this music, no matter how far back its roots, has probably undergone a great deal of change—because people wanted to improve it, because they forgot parts of it, or perhaps because they felt it necessary to make it sound like other music that they were hearing. Folk and primitive music, then, have for us the fascinating quality of being both old and contemporary, of being representative of a people's ancient traditions as well as an indicator of current tastes. And they are simultaneously the product of individual composers and of the creativity of masses of people. This historical development—far more than the artistic merit of the individual composition, which may be considerable in the opinion of some, but which may also seem insignificant in comparison to Bach fugues and Brahms symphonies—is the main justification for a detailed consideration of traditional music on the part of modern urban students and musicians.

We have implied that folk music is composed by individuals, but that subsequent to the original act of composition, many persons may make changes, thus in effect re-creating a song. This process, called "communal re-creation," is one of the things that distinguish folk music from other kinds. But the way in which folk music is created has not always been recognized. Among the earlier definitions of folk music, that which stresses the anonymity of the creator is one of the most persistent. According to this definition, a song whose composer is unknown is a folk song. Of course there is a fallacy here; should our ignorance of the identity of a composer make such a difference in our classification of musics? Still, there is some truth in this view, for the composers in European folk music and in most nonliterate cultures are indeed not known to scholars. Moreover, they are not usually known to the members of their own culture; in most of the cultures with which we are concerned here it makes little difference just who makes up a song. There are exceptions, of course; in some Plains Indian tribes people remember very specifically who "made" a particular song, or who "dreamed" it (some tribes believe that songs come to people in dreams).

It was believed by some nineteenth-century scholars that folk songs were made up by people improvising in groups. Actually this is rare, if indeed it occurs at all. Controlled improvisation under the leadership of a music master does seem to occur here and there—in the gamelan orchestras of Java and Bali, for instance, and among the Chopi of Southeast Africa. We have reports of American black slaves in the nineteenth century making up songs by calling to each other and gradually arriving at a song-like formula. But this kind of "communal creation" is rare. Nevertheless, those who formulated the theory that folk songs are the product of the communal mind were not unwise, for they must have realized the importance of the contributions of generations of singers, players, and listeners in determining the final form of the song (but is it ever really final?). Of course, folk songs are normally composed by individuals, and in the case of Western European folk music these may be professional composers, popular song writers, churchmen, and sometimes even the great masters of music. There are many instances of tunes from the classics—Schubert's "Linden Tree" and Papageno's aria from Mozart's *Magic Flute* come to mind—which have been taken over by the folk tradition.

When speaking of the importance of change, in folk and tribal music, that is due to communal re-creation, let us not fail to realize that the amount of change that a song undergoes is also determined by the culture's view of change. Some of the world's cultures regard change as a positive value—the modern United States is certainly a good example—while others regard an adherence to tradition as immensely important; the culture of India is one of many possible examples. On the whole, folk and tribal cultures have tended to avoid rapid change, at least until confronted with modern technology. But there is variation even within a group of related and similarly complex societies. For example, the Pueblo Indians of the southwestern United States resisted change much more than did the Indians of the North American Plains, and this difference in attitude affected many aspects of their history, including the recent history of their music. Thus, while we must assume that we never find complete stability and that some change always results from oral tradition and communal re-creation, rapid and dramatic change occurs in some cultures, while slow and often barely perceptible change occurs in others.

FOLK MUSIC AS NATIONAL EXPRESSION

The idea that folk music is closely associated with a people, a nation, or a culture has long been widely accepted. In some languages, the words for "folk music" and "national music" are the same. This popular notion is quite opposed to that which deems music a "universal language." Neither is really correct or objective. Of course, it is possible to identify music as music, whether it is in a style known to us or not. Music is a universal phenomenon, but each culture has its own, and learning to understand another culture's music is in many ways like learning a foreign language. No culture can claim a body of music as its own without admitting that it shares many characteristics and probably many compositions with other neighboring cultures. But we must also assume that some of the essential and distinctive qualities of a culture somehow find their way into its music. Balancing the idea of traditional music as a national or regional phenomenon against the concept of folk music as a supranational kind of music is one of the fascinations of this field.

At the root of the concept of uniting nation and musical style is the idea that a nation's folk music must somehow reflect the inner characteristics of that nation's culture, the essential aspects of its emotional life—its very self. This feeling has at times given rise, among the general population as well as among folk song scholars, to a politically nationalistic view of folk music. Unfortunately, folk music has at times been made the tool of aggressive and racist policies. This was to an extent the case in Nazi Germany, where the high quality of German music was extolled and the "poorer stuff" of Slavic folk song was denigrated, and in the Soviet Union during the 1950s, when traditional folk tunes of all peoples, including the non-Slavic minorities in Soviet Asia, were fitted with words praising Lenin and Stalin, collective farms, and the dictatorship of the proletariat. Although we may question the authenticity of music treated or arranged in this way, and while we may wonder whether it is really representative of or accepted by a nation's culture, it behooves us to study this use of folk music in order to understand its importance in the political and cultural processes.

There is some validity to the notion that the folk music of a nation or a tribe has a special relationship to its culture. We have spoken of the need for general acceptance of a song if it is to be remembered. There

are other points. For example, it seems likely that the general characteristics of a language—its stress patterns, its patterns of intonation, and of
course the structure of its poetry—are reflected in the music of its people.
Moreover, if we plotted the characteristics of the folk music of each
people—the characteristics of its scales, its melodic movement, its rhythm,
and so on—and if we fed this information, nation by nation, into a com-
puter and examined the results statistically, we would probably find that
no two peoples have identical styles of music. And while various musical
characteristics may be present in the music of many peoples, each people
has its own particular proportion and combination of musical traits, and
these interact in a unique way.

Studies of this sort have actually been carried out by a group of
scholars headed by Alan Lomax.[1] Using many characteristics of music,
they plotted the typical stylistic "profile" of many musical cultures, finding correlations between certain kinds of music and certain culture types,
but also finding each unique. According to Lomax, the favorite song
style of a culture reflects its style of social relationships. Thus he believes that the difference between Middle Eastern music (which is prevailingly soloistic and has long, drawn-out, ornamented melodies) and
African music (which is frequently performed by ensembles or choruses,
requires close cooperation by the musicians, and contains a lot of polyphony) is due to differences between these cultures in their attitudes towards
cooperation, sex, and the stratification of social classes. Whether this
theory will in the end prove correct is not yet known, but it does make
us aware of the fact that each culture has its distinctive music, and that
this distinctiveness is probably in some way related to the basic values
and attitudes of the culture.

Despite the distinctiveness of each people's music, the musical
relationships between neighboring peoples may be very close. It has
been shown many times that melodies and songs travel from people to
people. A tune may appear as a ballad in Germany and (in slightly different form) as a Christmas carol in Poland, as a dance song in Slovakia, and
so on. It is possible, of course, that the same tune was made up separately
in each of these countries, but this is not likely. The more complex an
idea or a cultural artifact is, the smaller the possibility that it was invented more than once by different people. And a song, even a very
simple one, is, after all, a complicated creation. Very likely a melody
found in several countries was simply taught by people on one side of
the border to friends on the other side, or taught in many communities
by a wandering minstrel. The tune could be easily learned, but the words
were strange, could not be readily translated, thus were replaced by a

[1] Alan Lomax et al., *Folksong Style and Culture* (Washington: American
Association for the Advancement of Science, 1968).

poem in the language of the second country. But since the tune did not fit perfectly into the repertory of the second country, since it did not have the characteristics of that country's preferred musical style, it was gradually changed to make it conform. If the styles of the two countries involved were very different, the song would probably not take root at all in the second country but would be dropped. It so happens that the various folk music styles of Europe are rather similar, and probably for this reason there are many tunes that have spread from people to people until they covered the entire continent, In contrast, when Spaniards and Englishmen settled North America, they did not absorb into their repertories many, or perhaps any, tunes of the American Indians, probably because, among other reasons, they were too strange for absorption into their style.

We see that songs can be passed from culture to culture. The same is true, to an extent, of musical characteristics or, as we frequently call them, stylistic traits. A type of scale, a kind of rhythm, a way of singing can be passed from one people to another without a simultaneous passing of songs. If one country has a particular kind of technique—for example, antiphony, the alternation between two groups, each singing a phrase at a time—that technique can be taken up by the people in a second country, who may then impose it on their own songs. There is some evidence that this actually happened in North America. Antiphonal technique is highly developed in some African cultures, and when Africans came to America as slaves, some began living with certain Southeastern Indians, both as slaves and as refugees from slavery. The Indians, who already practiced some singing in which a leader and a chorus alternated, seem to have started using the specifically African variant of this technique in their own songs. It is obvious that in spite of the national or tribal identity of a folk music style, there is much sharing of songs and of ways of performing music among the peoples of the world.

Discussion of the uniqueness of each people's musical style brings us to a consideration of authenticity. This concept is rooted in the idea that each culture has a primordial musical style of its own, and that songs and traits learned at a later date in its history are not properly part of its music. An authentic song is thought to be one truly belonging to the people who sing it, one that really reflects their spirit and personality. To be sure, each culture has its unique musical style, but within this there may be subsumed a number of varieties, some of them resulting from the introduction of new techniques of composition and of new inventions, such as instruments, or from contacts with other cultures. All of the kinds of music that reside within a culture are worthy of study and are important for an understanding of that culture. We are entitled and, indeed, obligated to find out and interpret the differences in age among certain songs, the difference in complexity among various strata of the repertory of a culture, and the attitudes that members of a culture take towards various kinds of music that they perform. But that is quite different from deciding that a particular kind of music is the "authentic" music of that culture, and that other kinds of music, particularly those that have come about under the pressure of outside influences, are somehow inferior, debased, or contaminated, and not worthy of attention. We may even be justified in saying that the majority of the musics in use in the world today are in some way hybridized, as a result of contact among widely divergent cultures. Surely this is true of most of the "popular" musics in use; Western popular music has elements of African musical styles, Middle Eastern popular music is a mixture of traditional and Western. The same is true of older and less modernized tribal or folk musics. A too narrow identification of one kind of music with each culture or nation is, in the long run, related to the gross and widespread misconception that simple cultures, folk and tribal, are capable of learning only one kind of music. The facts seem to provide another picture: the culture type, economic development, and range of long-term outside influences of a people help to determine the limits of its musical development and its favorite style, but within these limits there is ample room for variety and change.

HISTORICAL PERSPECTIVE

A characteristic of folk and tribal music that is frequently stressed is its great age, although often it is not certain whether the age of individual songs or of musical styles is meant. But to assume that each people is, for all time, tied to one kind of music is to assume that no change has ever occurred in its tradition. This view we cannot accept, for we can observe change in the world's folk music traditions going on constantly. And while change may have been accelerated in recent times by the rapid Westernization of many non-Western cultures and by the growth of mass media, we must assume that change also occurred in the more distant past. After all, migrations of peoples have always taken place, cultural diffusion and acculturation have occurred at all times, and there is no reason to believe that peoples who have learned from each other to use the wheel, to construct instruments, and to smelt iron should have refrained from exchanging songs.

It is rarely possible to reconstruct the music history of a culture with oral tradition alone, but we can find out something about the growth, change, and geographic movements of musical styles, instruments, and even specific songs from their geographic distribution throughout the world, from archeological investigation of instruments, and from observation of the types of change that have occurred recently. But the fact that a culture has, today, a limited repertory does not mean that it may not, in prehistoric times, have possessed musical styles that were later forgotten or that merged with new materials learned from outside influences.

About the history of folk and tribal musics, then, we can make only the most general sorts of statement. We must assume that there has been a history, that change, rapid or slow, took place. In general, but probably not always, simple musical styles were followed by more complex ones. Several kinds of change were involved: changes in the repertory, brought about by the introduction of new compositions; changes in the uses of music and of attitudes towards music; and changes in individual compositions, e.g., the addition of new musical phrases, or of ornamentation, or of harmony to an extant song, or perhaps the changing of a song from one mode to another, as from major to minor. And finally, we must assume that in general (but certainly with exceptions), those cultures which are exposed most to outside influences also had a more rapidly changing music history than do the more isolated ones, and that societies whose culture changes rapidly also exhibit more rapid musical change than do those with greater cultural stability.

MUSIC IN CULTURE

The foregoing paragraphs may give the impression that we reject the concept of authenticity outright. To be sure, there seems to be little to justify some of its implications. We are approaching the study of folk music with the assumption that we are studying the musical expression of many people. And we cannot neglect any aspect of this expression simply because it is not ancient, or because it was brought from the outside, or because it does not seem to reflect the personality of the culture. On the other hand, we are not concerned here with music that is disseminated primarily by the mass media of radio, television, and records, although this music today has an enormous role in the world, and although some of it is closely related in style to the orally transmitted musics that are our subject. Similarly, we shall not deal with arrangements of folk songs as performed by professional urban musicians, nor shall we deal with rock, jazz, and country and Western music, except to mention their ultimate derivation, in part, from folk styles. This exclusion may seem arbitrary, since there is an unbroken historical line connecting rural folk music and urban popular music, but the entire field of world music is historically interrelated and arbitrary lines must be drawn for practical reasons. Thus the concept of authenticity has its practical uses: we are discussing, in this volume, that part of the music of the world's Western continents which was and is entirely or largely maintained in oral tradition.

But we are also interested in the music of particular groups of people. Those classified as nonliterate or tribal cultures can be defined with no great difficulty. Until recent times, for instance, there was no doubt that all American Indians were in this category. In the nineteenth century, there were individual Indians who learned to read, and some became learned; later, some became anthropologists who studied their own cultures. But the Indian languages were not written down except under the stimulus of white missionary scholars, and in each Indian tribe, more or less all the people shared one kind of music.

In the folk cultures of Europe and America it is more difficult to separate the folk music from the sophisticated, cultivated, or fine art of music, or from popular music. The distinction is gradual and unclear. The musical life of cities and courts, directed by trained professional musicians with the use of written music, is certainly different from that of the villages in which music is passed on by oral tradition and in which most of the people participate actively without much specialization. But some folk music also exists in the cities, and some influence from the cities has always trickled down to the villages and at times inundated them. Everyone has a bit of folk heritage; on the other hand, the folk songs of most areas in Europe and America have for centuries undergone some influence from the sophisticated music of the cities. The popular music of the cities seems to occupy a sort of middle ground. We can draw no sharp line.

Much has been said about the differences between folk and art music as far as their use or functions in the culture are concerned. We frequently hear the statement that folk and primitive music are "functional," while art music is not, or less so. This would imply that folk and primitive music always accompany other activities in life, and that art music is always "art for art's sake." There is some truth in this distinction, but the overall picture is a very complex one.

If we scrutinize the role of music in Western civilization, we find that music is not at all solely a giver of pleasure and a device for aesthetic edification. On the contrary, it is frequently designed to accompany activities of all sorts. We need to mention only church music, dance music, marching music, and the background music of drama, film, and television. On the other hand, the ideal kind of music, the music generally considered as best and greatest by those most concerned with music, is the music designed primarily for hearing in recital or concert. Thus we would be right in stressing the role of music in Western civilization as being one not involving other activities, but only because this is the idealized role of music, not because most music necessarily conforms to this image. And, to be sure, we generally respond by describing music as beautiful rather than judging its suitability for its particular function.

The converse picture is, on the whole, found in folk and tribal cultures. We are frequently told that all folk music accompanies other activities, that it never fills a role of entertainment, that it does not provide simple enjoyment. Of course this is not the case; there are many examples, in European folklore and in African and American Indian cultures, of music's being used as entertainment. Individual singers may entertain groups or themselves with music. In some African cultures, music is performed by professional or semi-professional musicians to entertain. But generally speaking—and here there are great differences among the world's cultures—the traditional music is focused towards functionality. Songs are typically referred to as "good" or "powerful," indicating that it is not the aesthetic quality of the song but the manner in which it fulfills its task (persuading the spirits, accompanying a dance, or giving an account of history) that is essential. Is it possible to indicate for any culture the main function of its music? No doubt, in any culture, music has many uses. But seen in the overall perspective of a culture, and compared to other activities, music may in each society have one special role. In some tribal cultures, music has essentially an enculturative function, that is, it serves to introduce members of the tribe to various aspects of their own culture. Elsewhere, its main function may be specifically religious in the strict sense, that is, it may be used as a language in which the supernatural or divine is addressed. Elsewhere again, music is the tribal "stamp of approval" for an activity; the activity must be accompanied by the appropriate music in order for it to be carried out correctly. Or music may be an important force for tribal unity and cohesion. In modern Western culture, all of these functions are present, but the fact that our most valued musical creations are intended for concerts and for entertainment (in the broad sense of that word) indicates that in our lives music has a different role from that which it has in most tribal and folk societies.

THE GENESIS OF FOLK MUSIC

The way in which Western folk music (or, for that matter, the folk music of Asian civilizations) came about is a fascinating one. The question whether "the folk creates" or whether it only utilizes material created by a higher social stratum has frequently been asked. We have already stated that all music is composed by individuals. The old belief that folk music rises, like a mist, from the collective consciousness of the village or band is hardly worth an argument. But the source of the materials used in folk music is still a bone of contention. Tribal cultures, of course, must have acquired their songs and the musical components of these songs from their own creativity or possibly from occasional outside contacts, although it is sometimes argued that even the remote primitives have had contact with the high cultures of the world, and that they have derived their musical accomplishments by absorbing the music of the high culture, diluted though it may be by passing through tribes and nations. Thus it may be argued that the Indians of South America, some of whose music is exceedingly simple, must in primordial times have derived their style from that of China; and there are remote similarities to substantiate this theory. This, however, is quite different from the everyday contact that has existed between folk and art music in some European countries. In Europe, it is sometimes thought, both the songs and the style of music in each nation are derived from the same nation's art music. This idea, based on a theory known by the German term *gesunkenes Kulturgut* (debased culture), assumes that the folk communities are inherently incapable of creating music or literature or art, and that instead they assimilate what trickles down to them from the sophisticated society of the cities. A time lag is assumed as well, so that the kind of style found in German art music in one century, for instance, is likely to turn up in its folk music centuries later. No doubt there has been a great deal of influence bearing from the cities on the folk culture. We know of folk songs that had their origin in the city, and we know of sophisticated dances that decades later became folk dances. But we cannot accept the notion that all folk music is simply debased city culture. The evidence of folk song influencing the sophisticated composer—from Schubert and Liszt to Bartók and Enesco—is too great. Rather, let us accept a theory of mutual give-and-take to describe the relationship between folk and art music.

Let us now summarize, on the basis of the considerations given in this chapter, the criteria we shall use for determining the materials to be discussed in the rest of this volume. Defining tribal music is not too difficult, but defining folk music is not an easy task. Several criteria can be used, but each, applied alone, is unsatisfactory. The main one is the transmission by oral tradition. Folk music, in its native setting, is not written down. As a result its compositions develop variants, and the original form of a folk song is rarely known. Folk music may originate anywhere, but it is most frequently created by untrained, nonprofessional musicians, and performed by singers and players with little or no theoretical background. Folk song is frequently old, and the style of folk music may be archaic. But folk and nonliterate cultures do have a music history; they allow their music to change, their compositions to be altered, and their repertory to be turned over. Folk music is frequently associated with other activities in life, but it also serves as entertainment. And most important, since folk music is the musical expression of a whole people or tribe, or a significant portion of a culture, it must be performed and accepted in order to remain alive.

BIBLIOGRAPHY AND DISCOGRAPHY

Introductions to the general nature of traditional music and its functions in society and as an aspect of human behavior are not numerous. Among the best are some of the articles in Funk and Wagnalls' *Standard Dictionary of Folklore, Mythology and Legend,* edited by Maria Leach (New York, 1949–50): "Song" (by George Herzog), "Dance" (by Gertrude P. Kurath), and "Oral Tradition" (by Charles Seeger). An overview of traditional musics, nation by nation, appears in *Grove's Dictionary of Music and Musicians,* 5th ed. (New York: St. Martin's Press, 1954), under the heading "Folk Music." A survey of non-Western music, especially in its historical perspective, appears in the first volume of *The New Oxford History of Music* (London: Oxford University Press, 1957). Alan P. Merrian, *The Anthropology of Music* (Evanston: Northwestern University Press, 1964), provides much material on the role of music in various nonliterate cultures.

Several scholarly periodicals specialize in non-Western and folk music; among them, we should note *Ethnomusicology* (Journal of the Society for Ethnomusicology); *Journal and Yearbook of the International Folk Music Council; Asian Music; Jahrbuch für musikalische Volksund Völkerkunde; Selected Reports* of the UCLA Institute of Ethnomusicology; and *African Music.* Bruno Nettl, *Reference Materials in Ethnomusicology* (Detroit: Information Service, 1961) is a bibliographical guide to the whole field.

Some articles of interest that explore specific aspects of traditional music everywhere and that are relevant to points made in this chapter are Alan Lomax, "Folk Song Style," *American Anthropologist,* LXI (1959), 927–954; Maud Karpeles, "Some Reflections on Authenticity in Folk Music," *Journal of the International Folk Music Council,* III (1951), 10–16; and K. P. Wachsmann, "The Transplantation of Folk Music from one Social Environment to Another," *J-IFMC,* VI (1954), 41–45.

A number of records and record sets give examples of the music of many of the world's cultures. These are listed here, although they could also have been listed following Chapter 2 and in some cases later chapters: *Music of the World's Peoples,* ed. Henry Cowell (4 albums), Folkways

FE 4504–4507; *Primitive Music of the World,* ed. Henry Cowell, Folkways FE 4581 (a smaller selection overlapping with the former); *Columbia World Library of Folk and Primitive Music,* compiled by Alan Lomax (over 20 records, partly reissues of older recordings, partly new material collected by Lomax and others); *The Demonstration Collection of E. M. von Hornbostel and the Berlin Phonogrammarchiv,* Folkways FE 4175 (reissue of an early collection that attempted to show the great variety of the world's musical styles); *Man's Early Musical Instruments,* Folkways P 525; *An Anthology of the World's Music,* Anthology records; and the UNESCO Collection, comprising sets of African and Asian music.

TWO

STUDYING THE STYLE
OF FOLK MUSIC

Music of any sort, but folk and tribal music especially, should be examined in two ways: (1) for itself, that is, its style and structure, and (2) in its cultural context, its function, and its relationship to other aspects of life. Eventually, of course, a blending of the two approaches should be achieved. The second has been briefly covered in Chapter One. We have tried to show how folk music and the music of nonliterate cultures, despite their diversity, differ as a group from other kinds of music in their origin, transmission, and cultural role. We should now like to devote a few pages to the question of musical style. In order to talk about music we need to develop a vocabulary, and talking about or describing folk music and the music of non-Western cultures requires special adaptations of the technical vocabulary normally used for describing the music of Western civilization. Also, in order to distinguish the various styles of folk music throughout the world from each other, we should have some idea of what is common to all or most of them. Here, then, we wish to talk about the music itself, not about the use that is made of it, nor about the words of the song, nor about the instrument used to play it.

We are interested in finding out how a piece of music is put together, what makes it tick. We also want to know what aspects of music characterize a repertory of a community or a country or a tribe, and we want to know what it is that distinguishes the musical sound of one culture from that of another. Answering these questions, i.e., describing musical styles, is something that ultimately requires great sophistication. Some published descriptions of music seem to defy understanding even by trained musicians. On the other hand, a layman with no background at all can, by listening and repeated listening, learn a great deal about how a piece of music is put together. In the case of folk and tribal music, which tends to be quantitatively simpler than the sophisticated music of the trained composer, analysis by listening rather than by examining a score is normally not too difficult. The reader of these pages is advised to listen to records of folk music as much as possible.

It is important to realize that a music is something like a language. It must be understood to be appreciated. The listener must know that certain kinds of sounds are signals, for example, of points of tension, of relaxation, of beginnings or endings of musical thoughts. A music, or perhaps we may say a musical repertory, is a system with an internal logic, structure, and typical modes of expression. And this is true whether the music is written by professional trained composers, as in Western classical music; whether it is composed by sophisticated professionals who do not use musical notations, such as the composers of Indian classical music; whether it is by the formally untrained composer of folk and tribal cultures who may not be able to explain what he is doing; whether it is an improvisor of Middle Eastern music who, as it were, composes on the spur of the moment; etc. In no music is material made up simply at random. The absence of an articulated music theory does not imply the absence of rules which a composer must follow; on the contrary, the composer in a folk or tribal culture is likely to be surrounded with musical limitations, to which he feels it necessary to adhere. (This is partially related to the need of having one's compositions accepted by performer and listener in order for the music to remain alive.)

Since in folk and tribal cultures "rules" of composition are not stated by music theorists and composers, we must derive them from the music itself, and the statements in the following chapters regarding the characteristics of various musics may be regarded as partial or introductory statements of the rules and logic of their musical systems. These brief statements are of necessity superficial, for if we delve with sufficient depth into any musical repertory, we discover that it is a system of communication with a complicated "grammar," "syntax," and "vocabulary" of musical materials and devices.

SOUND AND SINGING STYLE

The first thing that strikes a listener when he hears an unfamiliar musical style is the overall sound, which has many components but among whose chief traits are tone color and texture. Musical cultures differ in their sound ideals. The way in which the human voice is used, particularly, is characteristic of a culture and tends to be maintained throughout the variety of forms, scales, rhythmic patterns, and genres in its repertory. The way in which American Indians sing is quite different from that of Africans; Spanish folk singers sound different from English ones. One needs to hear only two seconds of Arabic singing to identify it as Middle Eastern. The characteristics of singing in a culture may reflect characteristics of speech and language, but there are sufficient exceptions to make us suspicious of any simple explanation that automatically relates these two methods of communicating.

Describing the characteristics of a singing style in words is difficult. We speak of such things as degrees of vocal tension, use of vibrato or tremolo, presence or absence of sharp accentuation of tones, loudness, ornamentation such as trills and grace notes, nasality, and so on. It is interesting to find that in many cultures, the sounds of instruments have characteristics similar to those of the singing style. Thus the violin playing of India sounds very much like Indian singing, and very different indeed from European violin playing.

The overall sound of music characterizes a musical culture in other ways as well. Sub-Saharan Africa, for example, may be characterized by a multiplicity of simultaneous sounds, and we find polyphony, that is, part-singing or ensemble music. But in addition we also find attempts by single musicians to produce several simultaneous sounds even when the means to do so are limited, and we find that there are always attempts to make these simultaneous sounds contrast with each other, as in the use of unrelated instruments in an ensemble or in the simultaneous use of widely divergent rhythms. In contrast, the music of South and West Asia is usually soloistic, and when several instruments play together, they tend to approximate each other in their tone colors.

It is important to realize that while the musical style of a culture may change rapidly, its singing style and overall sound patterns change very slowly; thus this is one of the traits of music that is most characteristic of a culture and that is closely tied to the value structure of other aspects of life.

Realizing the relative stability of singing style and sound ideals in a culture, we may be tempted to tie them to heredity and race. We may assume that the way in which the voice is used by Indians or Africans is related to the peculiarities of their race, their appearance, the color of their skin. But there is no evidence to support this view. Africans and Indians can learn to sing in the styles of other cultures, and indeed, Europeans and Americans, with sufficient effort, can learn to sing in Indian, African, and Chinese styles. The integrity of national or tribal singing styles has other roots. Every people has musical traits which are of great importance for maintaining its cultural identity, whether the musicians are able to verbalize about this or not; and singing styles and sound ideals in music are evidently among these traits. On the other hand, all aspects of music are definitely parts of culture, and the cultural and racial boundaries of the world do not coincide precisely, if at all.

FORM

Having noted the general character of the sound of a music, perhaps the best way to begin analyzing it, whether one hears it or sees it written out, is to find the large subdivisions and the broad tendencies of formal design. Is it made up of several large sections which contrast markedly? Are the sections of equal length? Does the tempo change considerably or suddenly in the course of the piece? Are any of the sections repeated? Is the whole piece repeated several times? If so, are the repetitions more or less exact, or are they variations of the first rendition? Do the sections correspond to sections or lines of the same length in the verbal text? These are the kinds of questions an intelligent listener must ask.

Simultaneously, we should watch for the arrangement of the performance, and this is especially important in studying music from a recording. We want to know whether the piece is performed by a single performer or a group, and whether there is alternation. Do several performers sing or play in unison, or does each have his own part?

Having identified the several sections of a piece, we must try to establish the relationships among them. One way to do this is to give each of them a letter, and to repeat the letter when the section is repeated. When one section is a variation of a previous one, we give it a superscript number: thus A^1 is a variation of A. When a section is new but seems somewhat reminiscent of a previous one, we can indicate this by a super-script letter so that B^a is a section reminiscent of A. For example, the song in Example 2-1 could be analyzed with the following letters: AA^1BA^1.

EXAMPLE 2-1. German folk song, "O du lieber Augustin," learned by the author from oral tradition.

Sometimes the interrelationship is more complex, as in Example 2-2, where a section reappears at different pitch levels. It could be described by letters $AA^1{}_5A^2{}_5A$, A_5 being a transposition, a perfect fifth higher, of A.

Forms such as AABB, ABBA, and ABCA appear frequently in European folk music. All these forms have in common the use of four musical lines, perhaps of equal length. But the internal differences are significant. Example 2-1 presents a theme, then a contrasting line, and returns to the theme. Example 2-2 is based on a single theme which, perhaps for the purpose of providing variety, is presented at different pitch levels. But they both share a quality of being rounded off, which most typically forms the basis of strophic songs, in which a melody is repeated several times with different words.

EXAMPLE 2-2. Hungarian folk song, from Zoltán Kodály, *Folk Music of Hungary* (London: Barrie and Rockliff, 1960), pp. 61–62.

Tempo giusto

In the music of some non-Western cultures, songs don't have clearly marked endings or forms that are precisely predetermined. The following Navaho song (Example 2-3) is made up of an occasionally regular, but sometimes irregular, alternation of three sections (marked A, B, and C in the transcription). The sequence of the sections is AABBCBAB-BCBAABABBCB, etc.

EXAMPLE 2-3. Navaho Indian song, from Bruno Nettl, *North American Indian Musical Styles* (Philadelphia: Memoir 45 of the American Folklore Society, 1954), p. 47.

In the discussion of musical styles of tribal and folk cultures, we must keep in mind the limitations that are imposed by the lack of a musical technology (i.e., notation and music theory) and the absence of intensive training of the musician by professionals. These limitations amount to relatively simple forms as well as the use of strong unifying factors which act as mnemonic devices. A drone (as in the lowest pipe of the bagpipes), the use of the same musical material in each voice of a part-song, the reappearance of a musical motif at different pitch levels throughout a song, a repeated rhythmic pattern, a simple tonal structure with clearly marked tonic and reciting tones—all of these are devices that are arrived at unconsciously but are eagerly accepted by the folk community because they help the folk singer and his audience to organize the musical material in their minds and clarify its structure, thus making oral tradition a more feasible process.

POLYPHONY

Most of the music we deal with in this volume is monophonic, which means that only a single tone is heard at a time, and there is no accompaniment except that of drums, rattles, or other percussive sound. But there is a good deal of European, American, and Latin American folk music, and a great deal of African music, that has more than one tone sounding at a time or more than one melody at a time or has perhaps accompaniment with chords. Several terms have been used to describe such music; perhaps the most satisfactory one is "polyphony," which we will use here to include all music that is not monophonic, whether it consists of a singer's own simple accompaniment with his guitar or of a chorus or of a group of different instruments playing a complex interrelationship as in chamber music.

In a style of polyphonic music that is strange to one's ears, it may be difficult to describe just what is going on. There is not much point, when describing folk music from Russia or from South Africa, in trying to apply labels used for Western art music, such as "organum," "fugue," "conductus," and the like, to music that developed quite outside Western European musical culture.

A better way to begin describing a polyphonic piece is to decide whether the various parts being sung or played at the same time are of equal importance, or whether one stands out as the leading or solo part. Then one can try to describe the melodic relationship among the parts. For example, do they use material based on the same tune or theme, or do they use more or less independent tunes? If the latter is the case, one should decide whether the relationship among the different voices or instruments produces imitation or canon, the most common manifestation of which is the round (the same tune performed at different time intervals); or parallelism (the same tune performed at the same time at different pitch levels); or heterophony (something like variations of the same tune played or sung simultaneously). At this point, also, one would like to know how much of the music is composed, and what aspects of it, if any, are improvised. It would also be important to know which aspects of the music had to be performed the way they are, and in which the performer had a choice and the right to make changes on the spur of the moment.

A further point to be considered is the way in which the musicians and listeners in another culture perceive polyphony. Do they concentrate on the effects of the simultaneities, such as chords, and on their progression, or do they listen to the progression of the individual melodies as they proceed side by side? We can hardly make judgments about this on the basis of simple listening, and extensive field research is necessary in order for us to be sure of our ground. But we must at least be aware of the fact that different cultures may perceive the same music differently, and that our own perception may or may not be relevant.

RHYTHM AND TEMPO

We can learn a good deal about the rhythmic character of a culture's music, or of a single piece of its music, also simply by listening. We want to know, for example, whether the music is organized in measures that recur more or less regularly throughout, and where exceptions occur. If we can perceive a repeated unit of beats and accents, we may conclude that the music is "metric." We can check this by tapping our foot regularly and seeing whether the tapping fits the music. We also want to know whether a drum or rattle accompaniment, if any, coincides with the rhythmic units of the melody. Then, quite aside from the meter, we may also describe rhythm in terms of the lengths of the notes found in a piece. This is something that cannot be found out quite so easily by listening, but can be described with the use of written notation.

We want to know, for example, whether most of the notes are of one length, whether two note-lengths predominate (as, for instance, quarters and eighths, in Example 2-4), or whether perhaps there are notes of all sorts of lengths, from half notes to sixty-fourths.

The tempo of a piece is also important here. We want to know whether it is fast or slow. Here our intuitive judgment cannot always be trusted. A piece that a Western listener considers fast (perhaps because of the speed of the drum accompaniment) may be considered slow by a person from the culture that produced it. One way to find an objective measure of tempo is to divide the number of notes in a melody by the number of minutes the piece takes; this would express the tempo in terms of average number of notes per minute. Another way is to ascertain the speed of the "pulse" or "beat," if there is one; it may be the most frequently used note-length in the melody, or the length of stroke of the percussion accompaniment.

There are many other factors that make up the rhythmic character of music. The degree of accentuation of stressed notes, already mentioned above as an aspect of singing style, is a characteristic feature of rhythmic style. The very presence or absence of meter, the degree to which performers deviate from it, the use of different meters simultaneously, the amount of contrast between the longest and shortest notes, and typical rhythmic motifs, such as dotted rhythms (♩. ♪ ♩. ♪) or more complex patterns that recur, are examples of things to look and listen for.

EXAMPLE 2-4. Shoshone Indiane Peyote song, from David P. McAllester, *Peyote Music* (New York: Viking Fund Publications in *Anthropology*, no. 13, 1949), song no. 73. Reprinted by permission of David P. McAllester and Wenner-Genn Foundation for Anthropological Research.

MELODY AND SCALE

We come now to the aspect of music that has been of greatest interest to students of folk and nonliterate cultures—melody. This aspect is probably the most difficult to study or describe. A simple approach to an understanding of melody involves consideration of the melodic contour. We wish to know whether the melody of a piece generally rises, falls, remains at the same level, proceeds in a curve, or moves in large leaps, and so on. Listening to the overall movement of the tune is thus important. We are also interested in the ambit, or range, of a tune—that is, the distance, in pitch, between the highest and lowest tones. This can be found with little difficulty by listening. Then we come to consideration of the scale.

The uninitiated listener to non-Western music, and to the folk music of Eastern Europe and even perhaps some Western European folk music, is often struck by the curious, possibly unpleasant sound of it. It may sound out of tune to him, and he will have trouble reproducing the tones and intervals if he tries to sing it. Also, he will be unable to reproduce the tones correctly on a piano. The reason for this is that the tone systems and scales of much non-Western music do not conform to these scales used in the music of Western civilization. Under no circumstances should this statement be taken to imply that the Western system of music is somehow a world standard, that it is more natural or more rational than other systems. While certain musical systems may appear to correspond more closely to natural laws (e.g., acoustical, biological, or psychological), we must assume that all musics are man-made to an equal extent, and that all of them are in some way based on the rules of nature. In this respect, all of them are equally worthy of independent study, and the fact that some diverge from the average more than others is not to be the basis of value judgments. Thus the "peculiarity" of certain scales or tone systems to our ears is due to the "particularity" of the tone system with which we have grown up.

A scale may be defined as the pitches used in any particular piece of music such as song. A tone system, on the other hand, is all the pitches used in a whole body of songs or pieces in the same style. One way to describe a scale is to count the number of different pitches or tones that appear in it. From this kind of description are derived such terms as "pentatonic," which denotes a scale consisting of five tones; "tetratonic," a scale of four notes; "tritonic" (three tones); "hexatonic" (six); and "heptatonic" (seven). The mere number of tones, however, doesn't really determine the character of a scale to any great extent; the reason for the curious sound of some non-Western music is not to be sought in the number of tones used.

The distance in pitch between the tones is probably a more important indicator of tonal character than their number. Thus we may find one pentatonic song that uses the scale, A-B-D-E-G and another one that uses the tones, A-B♭-B-C-D. Each uses five tones, but one uses large intervals, the other very small ones. The number of interval arrangements that can be found in folk music is almost infinite, but the listener should decide whether the intervals he hears are, on the whole, large, small, or medium, and get an idea of the character of the scale that he is hearing.

In some cultures there are intervals smaller than the half tone, that is, smaller than anything that can be produced on the piano. More commonly we find intervals intermediate in size between those used in the Western tempered system. Thus the "neutral third," an interval found in various cultures, is halfway between a major and a minor third. Of course, in Western civilization we use several different pitch standards. The intervals on the piano are somewhat different from those produced on the violin. But we have a range within which an interval is considered "in tune." Although "A" is normally supposed to be 440 vibrations per second, a pitch of 435 or 445 would still, by most persons, be considered "A." Presumably a similar range of acceptability exists in the musical system—expressed, or unconsciously taken for granted—of each culture. And probably one may deviate from pitch more in some musical styles than in others and still operate within the acceptable norm.

Another important feature of musical scales is the hierarchy in importance and function of the individual tones. Most frequently there is one tone which is the basis of the scale; it is apt to appear at the end of a piece and is called the tonic. Another tone, perhaps higher and used with great frequency, may be called "dominant." Other tones may appear with average frequency, and still others may be rare. Individual tones may also have particular functions, such as appearing typically just before or after certain other tones, thus providing the listener with signals indicating points of the musical structure.

In short, the scale of a composition can and should be a capsule diagram of its melodic materials and rules.

In many ways, the music of non-Western and some folk cultures sounds strange, confusing, and downright unacceptable to the uninitiated listener. There is a tendency in earlier musical writings, and in present-day remarks of the uninformed, to assume that such music has no structure and no laws, that it is chaotically improvised. The frequent tendency to label it "chant" indicates an assumption that the music is simply a vehicle for ceremonial words, and that it has little interest of its own. Nothing could be farther from the truth. The intricacy of much of this music—its consistent and logical structure—makes much of it a marvel of artistry. Its simplicity is dictated by the fact that it must be memorized, and by the lack of notation available to the composer. Careful listening can, however, clear up much of the apparent confusion. Intervals that sound out of tune will not, once they are heard recurrently in several songs of one tribe, sound so harsh. Of course, all non-Western and folk music is not alike, so that learning one musical language, such as that of the Plains Indians, does not by any means assure knowledge of another, such as West African. But as in learning languages, so in learning musical styles, each succeeding "foreign" style is easier to assimilate than the previous one.

DESCRIPTION OF A CULTURE'S MUSIC

The sections just completed—dealing with sound, form, polyphony, rhythm, and melody—have concentrated on understanding the musical style of an individual piece of music. We find it perhaps even more necessary to describe the style of a whole body of music—all Sun Dance songs of one Plains Indian tribe, or all music of the Basongye tribe, or even the whole body of music in the Plains, or of one European folk culture such as the Rumanian. Of course, we cannot assume that all music in a culture will sound like the one example included on a single record, or even that all songs of a given tribe exhibit the same characteristics. Nevertheless, we frequently hear statements such as "the Ibo have this kind of music" or "Spanish folk music sounds like that." Fortunately for the serious scholar in our field, there is a good deal of stylistic unity in the folk music of each culture. Such unity is probably greatest in the world's simplest cultures and gives way to increasing diversity as the cultures get more complex.

The description of the musical style of a whole culture is bound to be essentially a statistical statement. There are few traits of music that don't occur at least to a small degree in many cultures, but the extent to which they occur varies and is important. When we say, for example, that most of the scales of the Arapaho Indians are tetratonic, that is, they have four tones, we must add that there are also many songs with five or six tones, some with three, and a few with seven. When we say that English folk songs are essentially modal, which implies seven tones to the scale, we must realize that all sorts of other scales also appear. We also face a problem in distinguishing among several kinds of a culture's music: the oldest and perhaps most authentic music, the recent imports and the results of outside influences, and the atypical creations which don't really belong. (Or can we make this distinction?)

In the other chapters of this survey, we will be describing musical styles along with their cultural background. We must admit at the outset that we don't really know enough about the folk music of Europe, Africa, and the Americas to give a reliable or definite description. Many songs have been collected, many recordings are available; but the job of analyzing the songs and of describing the styles in scholarly terms has actually just begun. The statements that will be made in this volume will sometimes have to be impressionistic, based on knowledge of only a small segment of a people's music. We can only indicate examples of the kinds of things that occur. We cannot give a complete picture, but we hope that the partial picture presented will stimulate the reader to strike out on his own in order to learn more.

RESEARCH IN TRADITIONAL MUSIC: ETHNOMUSICOLOGY

Perhaps a few words about the way in which research in folk and non-Western music is done will help the reader to understand some of the procedures and statements in the following chapters. The field that provides research in this area is now known as ethnomusicology. Before about 1950 it was commonly called comparative musicology, and it is a sort of borderline area between musicology (the study of all aspects of music in a scholarly fashion) and anthropology (the study of man, his culture, and especially the cultures outside the investigator's own background). Research in ethnomusicology consists essentially of two activities, field work and desk or laboratory work. In past decades it was customary to keep these activities quite distinct. Those who went into the "field"—to villages, reservations, or colonies, to make recordings—were not necessarily trained in the techniques of analysis and description that form the main part of the "desk work." Conversely, the armchair ethnomusicologists rarely went into the "field." In recent times it has been assumed that the best work would result if the same person did both the field research and the later analytical work. It is now taken for granted that almost every ethnomusicologist is, at various times, both a field and a "desk" worker.

The distinction between the field worker who is interested only in recording music and the one who is interested in music as a factor of culture and as a form of behavior is also disappearing. It is true that these two different approaches to ethnomusicology are and continue to be recognized, but recently ethnomusicologists have come to realize that one cannot record and study the music of any people effectively without understanding the cultural context in which the music lives. At the same time, they realize that discussing the uses that a culture makes of music, its attitudes towards music, and the way in which music reflects the values of the society is likely to be meaningless without an understanding of the music itself. Thus it is true that ethnomusicology has two sides, or two approaches, the musicological and the anthropological, but they are both essential, at least to some degree, for each individual scholar and student; they are complementary.

There are many different types of field projects that an ethnomusicologist may undertake. He may go to study the music of an entire people, such as the Yoruba of Nigeria or the people of Afghanistan, but aside from providing an introductory survey, such a project would be useless in the context of the amount of knowledge available today because it would be superficial. More fruitful is the study of a particular type of music or the musical culture of an individual community, of a particular group (such as a minority) in a community, or even of an individual musician. The approach of the field worker varies with the project and the emphasis. He may simply record music and take down, from the statements of his informants, the necessary information on its cultural background. Or he may observe musical events as they occur. He may learn aspects of the musical system by learning how to perform the music himself; this can be done particularly effectively in those cultures which have established formal musical training. He may devise techniques, such as musical aptitude tests based on the people's own music, questionnaires or various approaches involving statistics. In general, we may divide field research into several categories: (1) eliciting material (music and information about it) from informants in special recording or interviewing sessions; (2) observing culture as it operates, from the field worker's view as an outsider; (3) participating in the culture as a student and performer; and (4) gaining insights from special tests which oblige the informants to think about their culture in ways to which they are not accustomed.

Obviously, the complexity and difficulties of ethnomusicological field work are considerable and not to be underestimated by the novice who tries his hand at it. The person who goes off to record the music of an African tribe or a Balkan village must know, in advance, a good deal about the culture of the people he will visit. Once there, he must use certain techniques to be sure that he gains access to the individuals who know songs, and that he makes representative samplings of the music. He should not, for example, try to record only one kind of song. Thus a collector of folk songs in the Virginia mountains should not try to record only old English ballads. If he does so, not only will he miss much other valuable material, but he may also alienate the singers, since they will probably consider other songs equally valuable, and he may not even succeed in hearing as many old English ballads as he would if he had taken a more broad-minded approach. He must get to know people in the community very well. A three-day field trip is usually not very successful; ideal field work requires months and years of stay, with follow-up visits to see how songs and also how attitudes toward music have changed.

Whatever the field worker's specific approach, he should take a broad view of his task. Turning on the tape recorder or learning how to play an instrument is only a small part of his job. He should find out what his informants think about the songs they sing; what they consider a good song or a bad one, and why; how they learn songs; how they compose; who the good musicians are and what makes them good musicians; what kinds of songs the culture has (according to the tribe's own classification; what kinds of terms they use, if any, to talk about music; what kinds of music outside their own they have had contact with; what activities each song is designed to accompany, if any; what the status of the musician in the society is; and so on. The field worker may have to use special eliciting techniques. David McAllester, for example, widely known for his collecting of Navaho music, says that he persuades the Indians to sing for him by singing folk songs or even Indian songs to them.[1] It may be useful to find an informant who will assume the role of teacher to the field worker. It is necessary to record the same song as it is sung by different people in a community, or by the same person at different times, in order to find out what aspects of a song remain stable and which ones are subject to change by improvisation; also how much a song changes in a given period of time. But no matter how much an ethnomusicologist prepares himself before a field trip and how much he learns from books and records, the first week in the field will convince him that somehow everything is different from his expectations, and that there is no substitute for seeing the situation at first hand.

TRANSCRIPTION AND ANALYSIS

Arriving back at his office with a collection, the ethnomusicologist must set about analyzing and describing the music. He may do this simply by listening with techniques something like those described in the first pages of this chapter. More likely he will want to set at least some of the music down on paper in notation. This process is called transcription.

Since our ordinary system of notation was devised essentially for the music of Western civilization, and since its purpose is to help a performer carry out the composer's intentions rather than to describe the musical actions of the performer, it is not surprising that the system is rather imperfect for the descriptive use to which it must be put in ethnomusicological transcription. The fact that the rhythms and scales of non-Western and folk music do not always fit into the Western system makes it all the more difficult to reproduce such music in conventional notation. Yet, although various special systems have been devised, most scholars have returned to the conventional one despite its shortcomings.

[1] David P. McAllester, *Enemy Way Music* (Cambridge, Mass.: Peabody Museum of American Archaeology and Ethnology, Harvard University, 1954).

It is one, after all, that can be easily mastered and that is already understood by individuals who are acquainted with music. It can be used in folk song collections that serve the double purpose of being scholarly descriptions of music and providing music to be performed. Some transcribers have added special symbols where the, conventional system of notation is wanting. For example, intervals smaller than half-steps are frequently indicated by placing a "plus" (higher) or a "minus" (lower) above a note.

Careful listening to even a simple folk tune indicates that a considerable number of musical events take place in every second of singing. The question is whether we should try to capture each of these or whether we should restrict our notation to the main lines. The ethnomusicologist, careful and thorough, would like to capture all. If he has a talented ear and enormous patience, he will come up with a very intricate notation. This procedure was followed by Béla Bartók, not only a great composer but also one of the most important scholars of folk music, who collected vast numbers of Hungarian, Slovak, Yugoslav, and Rumanian folk songs. Example 2-5 shows one of his transcriptions of Yugoslav folk music. Below the melody in all its detail is a less complicated version of the song that gives only the main notes.

EXAMPLE 2-5. Serbo-Croatian folk song, with complex and simplified transcriptions by Béla Bartók and Albert B. Lord, *Serbo-Croatian Folk Songs* (New York: Columbia University Press, 1951), p. 154.

Of course, the important thing in transcribing is to be objective, to write down what actually occurs and not what the transcriber, with his ear used to a particular musical idiom (usually the Western one), may think he hears. And make no mistake about this: what one hears is conditioned not only by what sound is actually produced, but also by what sound one's ear is attuned to and expects. Consequently, transcribing is a process that requires hearing and rehearing a piece; a minute of music may take two hours to transcribe.

In order to save time and increase accuracy and objectivity, several attempts have been made to devise machinery that would measure pitch and transcribe music. These range from a monochord—simply one stretched string with a graduated table to show vibration rates—invented by Jaap Kunst, to elaborate electronic devices based on the oscilloscope and on computers. The most recent devices are usually called melographs. There are three important forms, one invented by Charles Seeger and used at the University of California at Los Angeles, another developed in Israel, and a third invented by a group of Norwegian scholars headed by Olav Gurvin.[2] These machines produce detailed graphs, as shown in Example 2-6 (in which the top section indicates amplitude or rhythm, which is derived from volume; the series of dots in the middle indicates the time, the space between two dots equalling one second; and the bottom section indicates pitch movement or melody). Such graphs must be retranslated into a more musically meaningful form—like conventional notation with all its deficiencies. Even so electronic transcription holds great promise for future research in music that lives in oral tradition.

2 Charles Seeger, "Prescriptive and Descriptive Music Writing," *Musical Quarterly,* LXIV (1958), 184–95; Karl Dahlback, *New Methods in Vocal Folk Music Research* (Oslo: Oslo University Press, 1958).

EXAMPLE 2-6. Graph of an automatic transcription of part of a Norwegian folk song; from Karl Dahlback, *New Methods in Vocal Folk Music Research* (Oslo: Oslo University Press, 1958), p. 127.

Transcription of the musical sound into some kind of notation system is only one of the techniques used by ethnomusicologists to prepare their material for analytic conclusions. Processing musical data with computers, counting various kinds of intervals and note values, tracing the development of a musical motif from the beginning to the end of a performance, comparing various versions of one song, classifying a repertory in groupings that are internally related, comparing the structure of a melody with that of its accompanying verbal text—all of these are examples of the kinds of things that are frequently done together with, or in some cases, instead of, transcription.

All of these techniques are, however, only stepping stones for the ethnomusicologist to get at the central questions of his field: What is the nature of music throughout the world? What does music accomplish in culture generally? Why do different cultures produce different musics? And in each individual culture? What are the conditions under which music changes? By what processes does it change?

BIBLIOGRAPHY

Methods of analysis and approaches to describing musical styles in their various phases are set forth in Curt Sachs, *The Wellsprings of Music* (The Hague: M. Nijhoff, 1962); Alan Lomax, *Folk Song Style and Culture* (Washington: AAAS, 1971); several articles by Mieczyslaw Kolinski, especially his "Classification of Tonal Structures," *Studies in Ethnomusicology* I (1961), 38–76, and B. Nettl, *Theory and Method in Ethnomusicology* (New York: Free Press, 1964). Many publications deal with methods of analyzing individual aspects of music. Among them are Sirvart Poladian, "Melody Contour in Traditional Music," *J-IFMC*, III (1951), 30–35; Mieczyslaw Kolinski, "Consonance and Dissonance," *Ethnomusicology*, VI (1962), 66–74; Kolinski, "Determinants of Tonal Construction in Tribal Music," *Musical Quarterly*, XLIII (1957), 50–56; and Curt Sachs, *Rhythm and Tempo* (New York: Norton, 1953), chapters 1 and 2.

General works about the field of ethnomusicology, its history and theories, are Jaap Kunst, *Ethnomusicology*, 3rd ed. (The Hague: M. Nijhoff, 1959) and Bruno Nettl, *Theory and Method in Ethnomusicology*, Mantle Hood, "Music, the Unknown" in *Musicology* (Englewood Cliffs, N.J.: Prentice-Hall, 1963), and Hood, *The Ethnomusicologist* (New York: McGraw-Hill, 1971). Other discussions of research methods appear in Alan P. Merriam, "Ethnomusicology, Discussion and Définition of the Field," *Ethnomusicology* IV (1960), 107–14; and his "Ethnomusicology Revisited," *Ethnomusicology* XIII (1969), 213–29. A special issue of *Ethnomusicology* (vol.

VII, no. 3, Sept. 1963) is devoted to questions of identification and methodology of the field.

A directory of ethnomusicological archives in the United States and many other nations is currently being published by the Society for Ethnomusicology. For an earlier view of such archives, see George Herzog, *Research in Primitive and Folk Music in the United States, A Survey* (Washington: ACLS, 1936). The standard work on musical instruments is Curt Sachs, *The History of Musical Instruments* (New York: Norton, 1940); important dictionaries of musical instruments are Curt Sachs, *Real-Lexicon der Musikinstrumente* (New York: Dover, 1964) and Sibyl Marcuse, *Musical Instruments: a Comprehensive Dictionary* (Garden City: Doubleday, 1964). The basic book on dance, despite its considerable age, is Curt Sachs, *A World History of the Dance* (New York: Norton, 1937). An excellent survey of recent research in non-Western dance is Gertrude P. Kurath, "Panorama of Dance Ethnology," *Current Anthropology*, I (1960), 233–54. *Ethnomusicology* VII (1964), 223–77, contains a detailed symposium on transcription and analysis on the basis of a single Bushman song.

THREE

THE GENERAL CHARACTER
OF EUROPEAN FOLK MUSIC

"What is Europe? Is it an aggregate of separate cultures or an integral unit? And what is European folk song? A single body of music or simply a group of separate styles as large in number as the continent's nations and languages?" These questions are asked by Walter Wiora,[1] a leading authority on folk music, and they are good questions with which to begin a discussion of European folk music. Of course, a qualified "yes" can be said to each of these questions. In some ways, European folk music is indeed a single corpus of musical style. The various European folk musics have much in common, but each country—in some cases each region, each district, and each community—has its own music and its own style. In this chapter we would like to devote ourselves to exploring the unity of European folk music. In Chapters Four, Five, and

---

[1] Walter Wiora, *Europäischer Volksgesang* (Cologne: Arno Volk Verlag, 1950), p. 5.

Six we will try to discuss the special characteristics of regions and countries.

We have pointed out that it is very hard to state concretely just how much difference there is between one kind or style of music and another. One way of telling that a musical style is similar to another one, the second of which you already recognize, is that the first of the styles also appeals to you. If this is true, and a person who is acquainted with British folk music finds Russian folk song more appealing than the music of Polynesia, then Russian and English folk song are indeed more similar to each other than are the English and the Polynesian. This has to do, of course, with the fact that folk music styles, like languages, exhibit greater or lesser degrees of relationship. Just as it is usually easier to learn a language that is closely related in structure and vocabulary to one's own, it is easier to understand and appreciate a folk music style similar to one that is already familiar. (This hypothesis does not, however, explain the fascination that an utterly strange music may immediately hold for a previously unexposed listener; but obviously there are many things that determine what kind of music will speak to an individual. Familiarity, however, is one of the strongest criteria.)

If we use this only very moderately reliable measuring device, we must admit that most of the European styles are rather similar to each other. And, on the whole, those that are geographically close to each other are also the most closely related in terms of musical style. There are a number of characteristics which we find to be present throughout Europe—with the usual pockets of exception, of course—and throughout that part of the world inhabited by descendants of Europeans.

We really know very little about the history of European folk song. We have little evidence as to the age of individual songs, although some idea can be gained from the notations of folk songs made by composers ever since the Renaissance. But in such cases we don't know whether a song was really part of the folk tradition, or whether it was an art or popular song that later moved into the realm of folklore. We also know little about the age of the various styles of folk music in Europe. Still, we are sure that for centuries there has been a close relationship between the art music of the continent and its folk music. How could it be otherwise? Villages and cities could not live without some mutual contact. In the early Middle Ages, wandering minstrels carried their tunes from court to village and from country to country. The villagers of the Middle Ages attended church and heard Gregorian chant. The composer at the court of a minor duke in seventeenth-century Germany drew his performers from the village musicians living on his lord's estate. We have ample evidence for assuming a constant relationship between the folk musician and his sophisticated counterpart.

All of this contact was accelerated by the invention and rapid dissemination of printing after the fifteenth century, especially in Western Europe. We tend to think of the folk and the art music traditions as living essentially separate lives, but this is surely erroneous not only in a consideration of European culture but also in the case of those Asian civilizations that have similar stratification. The folk musics of China, India, the Islamic world, and elsewhere all bear important similarities to the art musics of their countries. And in Europe, where printing provided a particularly good and rapid method of dissemination, especially of the words but to an important extent also the music of song, the relationship has been especially close.

Of course the effect of art music on folk music is dependent on the existence of a well-developed fine-art tradition in music. Such a tradition evidently did not exist to a large degree before the Middle Ages, and it did not come to Eastern Europe until even later. There are those who believe that the styles of European folk music evolved to a state similar to their present one before the time (perhaps a thousand years ago) when sophisticated composers first began to influence folklore; that the folk styles are an invaluable remnant of precultivated times, even of prehistoric eras. This belief can be neither substantiated nor negated. But we are probably safer in believing that the styles of European folk music developed sometime in the Middle Ages, and that this happened to some extent under the influence of the art music that was also developing at the time. This, after all, might account for the rather considerable degree of homogeneity in European folk music.

THE STROPHIC FORM

The most characteristic trait of European folk songs is their "strophic" structure. We tend to accept such a structure in which a tune with several lines is repeated several times, each time with different words, as normal. But this kind of arrangement is not so common elsewhere in the world, and it ties the European nations together as a musical unit. The length of a song with stanzas (called strophic song in technical terminology) can vary greatly, from a short bit such as that in Example 3-1 to a relatively elaborate piece such as that in Example 3-2.

It is important to realize, however, that strophic songs are found also in other parts of the world. They appear in some North American Indian cultures, in the Middle East, in Asia and Africa. Their basic principle is that a tune, or a portion of a tune, can be sung more than once, with different words; and this principle is accepted at various

EXAMPLE 3-1. Slovak folk song with short stanza, learned by the author from oral tradition.

EXAMPLE 3-2. Irish folk song, "Patty McGinty's Goat," collected in Newfoundland by MacEdward Leach, transcribed by Bruno Nettl.

levels in a multitude of musical styles. Indeed, in some of the world's simplest styles, the repetition of a single musical motif, with slightly or completely different words, is common. But the more or less exact repetition of a fairly detailed musical organism with several different sets of words as the basic and by far predominant type of organization is unique to Europe; and, interestingly, it is important in all types of European music—folk, art, and popular music; East and West, North and South.

The special character of the strophic song is derived from a peculiar trait of European poetry—folk poetry as well as that of the sophisticated poets. This is the tendency to arrange poems into units of two, three, four, five, six, or more lines. Such units, called stanzas or strophes, have a form that is repeated; the interrelationship of the lines is repeated, but the words—or at least most of them—are not. The lines may be interrelated by the number of syllables or of poetic feet per line, or, more commonly, by a rime scheme. But in any event, some sort of structure is given to the stanza quite aside from the meaning of the words. The words themselves, of course, progress through the poem, telling a story or expressing the poet's feelings about practically any subject. But the structure of the stanza is repeated. We don't know, of course, whether such a strophic structure in the poetry came first, or whether it was invented to fit the music of a song; this may be a case of the "chicken-and-egg" dilemma. But logically, it is a simple transition from a repeated poetic structure to a repeated melody, with the words and their content changing from stanza to stanza.

For example, the following stanza of the famous English ballad, "Barbara Allen," shows us some of the traits of the poetic unit typical in European folklore:

> *Oh yes I'm sick, I'm very sick*
> *And death is in me dwelling;*
> *No better, no better I ever shall be*
> *If I can't have Barb'ry Allen.*

Even if we saw the complete poem without music and without the printer's divisions into stanzas, we could easily figure out that it is arranged into stanzas, because: (1) lines 2 and 4 rime (also lines 6 and 8, lines 10 and 12, etc.), and (2) every fourth line ends with the words "Barb'ry Allen." In other songs and in other languages, there are different characteristics of the stanza, different ways of identifying the stanza as a unit. But the same kind of musical structure, strophic, with its repetition of a few musical lines, is found throughout Europe (if not in all songs) and is simply an accompaniment to and analogue of the poetic structure.

The close relationship between the words and music of a song is carried even further in European folk song. The lines of music and text usually coincide, and the points at which the music comes to a temporary rest are also those at which a sentence, phrase, or thought in the words is completed. There is, moreover, a close relationship between the smaller segments of musical and linguistic structure, for example, between stress and accent, and between the length of tone and of syllable, although the nature of this relationship varies from nation to nation because of the differences in structure among the various languages. In art song, this relationship has often been refined, and the rough edges resulting from oral tradition are smoothed out.

CHARACTERISTICS OF EUROPEAN SCALES

We have mentioned its basic strophic structures as a reason for our belief that European folk music is essentially a stylistic unit. Let us also briefly discuss the unity of the continent with regard to individual elements of music—scales, meter, intervals, and manner of singing.

The scales of European folk song exhibit great variety. Most typically, there are songs with only two or three different tones (these are most frequently children's ditties or game songs), there are songs with five tones (pentatonic scales), and others with six or seven tones. But the kinds of intervals, the distances in pitch, among the tones are not quite so diverse. The tendency is for European folk songs to use intervals that fit into the diatonic system, a system of tones that we can hear by playing the white keys of the piano. The diatonic system consists of major and minor seconds and of intervals produced by adding seconds. Throughout Europe, it seems that the most common intervals in folk music are the major seconds and the minor thirds. Unfortunately, we do not yet have statistics to prove this definitively, but a thorough inspection of a few representative song collections would be convincing. Other intervals are also found, of course, and occasionally there are intervals that do not fit into the diatonic system and which could not even be reproduced approximately on the piano. Also, in folk singing the intervals are not sung with the degree of precision found on the piano, and deviation from a standard norm seems to be somewhat greater in folk than in concert music. Nevertheless, adherence to the diatonic intervals seems to be one of the great general characteristics of European folk music.

Of course, other cultures also use scales which fit into the diatonic system. In some Asian civilizations, music theory that is almost parallel to that of Europe (so far as the arrangement of pitches in a scale is concerned) has been developed, and intervals approximately the size of major seconds are probably found in the vast majority of world musics. Nevertheless, the almost perfect adherence of European folk song to this diatonic system is one of the chief characteristics of the continent.

Going into a bit more detail, we find that a great many of the songs that use seven tones can be explained, as far as their tonal material is concerned, in terms of the modes (Dorian, Phrygian, Lydian, Aeolian, Mixolydian, Locrian, and Ionian) that are used to classify Gregorian chant (in slightly different form) as well as other medieval and Renaissance music. This fact has led some scholars to believe that the styles of European folk music actually originated in the chants of the church. While we must concede the possibility of a great deal of influence of church music on folk song, it seems useful to consider these modes as only a system for classifying the latter. As such, it can be used to classify only those songs which actually have seven tones. For instance, Example 3-3 could be considered a Mixolydian tune transposed up a fourth.

EXAMPLE 3-3. Russian folk song in the Mixolydian mode, from Elsa Mahler, *Altrussische Volkslieder aus dem Pečoryland* (Basel: Bärenreiter-Verlag, 1951), p. 43.

We might be tempted to classify tunes that have only five tones according to the same system of modes, pretending that two tones of the mode are simply absent. The trouble is that we could not prove which tones are lacking. A song with the scale A-C-D-E-G that ends on A could be considered either Aeolian or minor, if the tones that are lacking were B and F. But if they were B-flat and F the tune would have to be called Phrygian. And if the missing tones were B-flat and F-sharp the scale would not fit any of the above-mentioned modes at all. (See Example 3-4 for the various modes that can be fashioned out of a nucleus of five tones in the diatonic system.) Thus we can hardly accept the blanket statement, made so frequently, that folk music is "modal" in the sense of the Gregorian modes. But a great many European folk songs do fit into the modal system.

EXAMPLE 3-4. Diatonic modes based on a single group of five tones.

Anhemitonic Pentatonic

Aeolian   Phrygian   Dorian

Not in the traditional diatonic mode system

Pentatonic songs make up a large proportion of the European body of folk song; their scales are usually composed of major seconds and minor thirds, as in Example 3-5.

Pentatonic songs cannot, however—even with the special kind of pentatonic scale illustrated here—be considered as primarily a European phenomenon. This type of scale is one that Europe shares with a large part of the world, particularly with Northern Asia, with the American Indians, and with Negro Africa.

The same is true of the songs with two or three tones, illustrated in Example 3-6.

This very limited kind of scale is found in repertories throughout the world. There are some tribal cultures, particularly in the Americas and in Northern Asia, whose music hardly goes beyond it. This is true, for example, in the music of the Vedda of Ceylon (a people whose traditional music is now extinct, but whose songs were recorded, in rather small number, around 1900), and the songs of the last member of the Yahi

EXAMPLE 3-5. English folk song with a pentatonic scale, from Jan P. Schin-han, ed., *The Music of the Ballads* (Durham, N.C.: Duke University Press, 1957. *The Frank C. Brown Collection of North Carolina Folklore*, vol. 4), p. 184.

Scale:

EXAMPLE 3-6. Tritonic children's ditty, found in various nations with different sets of words.

Indians, the famous Ishi. In these cultures, however, an occasional fourth or fifth tone appears as well. We may feel that these cultures did not have the intellect to invent more complex scales, or to comprehend them when they heard them from other tribes. But this judgment is almost certainly false. In each culture, certain limitations are placed on musical development, and in these, the limitations were placed on the number of tones in the scale. The songs of Ishi exhibit considerable sophistication in other respects.

Cultures with more complex scale systems nevertheless tend to have some songs with only two or three tones, and this is also true of European folk cultures. In most cases (in Europe and elsewhere) these are children's songs, game songs, lullabies, and old ritual melodies. The melodies of epic poetry also frequently have few tones. The widespread geographic distribution of these scales, coupled with the simplicity of the songs which they usually accompany, has led some folklorists to believe that in Europe they constitute a remnant of an ancient musical culture. These scholars believe that all music must at one time have been as simple as this, and that such songs were driven into a corner of the repertory, just as those cultures which use only such songs were driven into the geographical corners of the world as newer, more complex music was invented. But this is only one of several possible explanations. The simple children's ditties of Europe may have nothing to do with the limited scales of the Yahi Indians, whose history may have included, in earlier times, more complex scales which gradually become more and more restricted in order to make possible the greater development of other aspects. It would be a mistake to take for granted the assumption that music everywhere moves consistently from simple to more complex forms. Thus the simplest songs of Europe may be the most archaic, but they are probably not representative of a stage in world music in which all music was based on two-tone and three-tone scales. If ever there was such a stage, it must have occurred many millenia ago, for we know that human culture, in many varieties, has been present in sophisticated forms for that long.

In summary, then, the seven-tone scales, with their modal arrangements, are a hallmark of European folk music, but they are not really limited to Western culture. The pentatonic scales are important in most if not all European traditions, but they are equally important in a large variety of non-Western cultures, in some of which they constitute the dominant scale type. The restricted two- and three-tone scales are found throughout the world, but except in a few isolated cultures, they constitute a small minority of the repertory.

METER AND SINGING STYLE

Most European folk music adheres to the concept of meter. This means that there is some regularity of recurrence in the accent pattern of the music, though such regularity does not by any means imply the predominance of common or triple meters without deviation. A good deal of European folk music can indeed be classed as isometric; that is, a single metric pattern, such as 4/4, 3/4, 6/8 (or even 5/8, 7/8, etc.), dominates the song. When several meters are used, these tend to appear in recurring sequences; thus a song, particularly one in Eastern Europe, may have a meter consisting of the regular alternation of 3/8, 4/8, and 5/8 measures (see Example 5-3). Music in which no metric pattern can be detected is not common in European folklore. Deviations from a metric pattern—for example, the elongation of tones at points of rest, near the endings of lines or of phrases—are common, as for instance that in

Example 3-7; but these deviations tend to reinforce the metric character of the music rather than to negate it. Thus another trait, found also, to be sure, elsewhere in the world, ties European folk music into a homogeneous unit.

EXAMPLE 3-7. English folk song, "Lady Isabel and the Elf Knight," from Cecil Sharp, *English Folk Songs from the Southern Appalachians* (London, New York: Oxford University Press, 1952), vol. 1, p. 7.

The metric character of European folk music is closely related to the metric organization of much of the poetry. Those peoples in which metric poetry is well developed are also those whose music most typically adheres to a simple meter. Those peoples in Europe (and they are mainly in Eastern Europe) whose poetry is organized in terms of syllable count rather than metric-foot count are also those which have a certain amount of nonmetric music, and which have more complex and more varying metric patterns in their folk music.

The manner of singing—use of the voice, movements and facial expressions, types of tone color—is another important feature. We have few guidelines according to which we can describe this phenomenon. Alan Lomax[2] is one of the few scholars who have paid attention to this important aspect of music. Lomax believes that it is possible to divide the world into relatively few areas each of which has a particular manner of singing that exists independent of the geographic distribution of other aspects of musical style such as melody, rhythm, and form. Europe, he finds, is rather complicated, for it possesses a number of singing styles that do not have contiguous distribution.

What we are interested in assessing, in a discussion of singing style, are those things that go into the singing of almost every tone, the things that make the sound of a singer and of his entire culture distinc-

---

[2] Alan Lomax, "Folk Song Style," *American Anthropologist*, LXI (1959), 927–54. See also his *Folk Song Style and Culture* (Washington: American Association for the Advancement of Science, 1968).

tive and recognizable immediately. Among the parameters of singing style already mentioned in Chapter Two are these: (1) degree of tension, or its opposite, called by Lomax "vocal width"; (2) amount of ornamentation; (3) raspiness; (4) accentuation, that is, degree to which individual tones are attacked with strength, and degree to which stressed tones are distinguished in loudness and sharpness from the unstressed ones; (5) nasality; (6) pitch level, i.e., the level of singing within the singer's natural vocal range; (7) vocal blend, i.e., the degree to which singers in a group blend their voices; (8) ornamentation; and others. Before Lomax, the Hungarian composer and folk song scholar Béla Bartók divided Hungarian and other European folk singing into two basic singing styles, "parlando-rubato" and "tempo giusto." The first of these is a singing style in which emphasis is on the words, there is not much strict adherence to tempo and meter, and there is a substantial amount of ornamentation. "Tempo giusto" implies greater stress on musical meter and tempo, and less on the words. Bartók found that both of these singing styles were found in Hungarian folk music, and both appear to be present in many European countries, although their definition must generally be adjusted somewhat differently for each culture. According to Lomax, however, there is in each culture one dominant singing style, and it can be identified rather easily in any small sampling of singing. His view is that the main singing style of each culture is determined by the character of that culture, and in particular by the types of relationships among people that are typical of that culture.

The three singing styles that Lomax assigns to European folk music are termed by him "Old European," "Modern European," and "Eurasian." The "Eurasian" style, which is found primarily throughout most of the high cultures of Asia, is represented in Europe in parts of the British Isles and France, in South Italy, and in the Mohammedan parts of the Balkans. The singing is high-pitched, strident, and harsh, and the singers' facial expressions are rigidly controlled or sad. The style lends itself well to long, ornamented tones and passages, and the character of the music is sweetly sad and melancholy. Lomax equates singing styles with certain types of social structure and, according to him, the Eurasian area is one in which the position of women is below that of men; they may be put on a pedestal, but they do not have equality.

The "Old European" style, according to Lomax, is found in the Hebrides, Northern England, Scandinavia, the Pyrenees, Czechoslovakia, Western Yugoslavia, Northern Italy, Germany, parts of the Balkans, the Ukraine, and the Caucasus. Here the singing is done with the throat relaxed, and the facial expressions of the singers are lively and animated. The tunes are simple and unornamented, and group singing is common. Cooperation among the singers in a chorus seems to have allowed polyphony to develop, and, says Lomax, possibly some of the polyphonic types of folk music antedated the development of polyphony in European cultivated music. In these areas, in any event, harmony was easily accepted. The idea of cooperation in music seems to have something to do with social cooperation, for the position of women in the "Old European" areas, according to Lomax, has been one of equality with men.

The "Modern European" style is, according to Lomax, a later layer which seems to have been superimposed on some of the other styles, perhaps because of the influence of the cities. It is found in most of England and France, in Hungary, Central Italy, and colonial America. This is the area of ballads and lyrical love songs. Singing, in contrast to the Old European style, is normally done by soloists or in unblended unison. The vocal quality is harsh and strained. Interest is more in the words than in the music.

Lomax's observations are certainly stimulating. He believes that the way in which people sing is more likely to remain constant than is the musical content of their songs. And he believes that a small sample of singing from a particular area or country will indicate the total singing style of that area. He seems to feel, accordingly, that each culture can sing in only one way (which is a theory that has been proved incorrect in various cultures, as for instance among the North American Indians). Lomax's observations lead us to conclude that Europe is not a unit as far as singing style is concerned, but that two or three styles of singing and voice production are found, and that each of these is supranational in character and cuts across the boundaries of politics, culture, and language. Also he shows that the two main European singing styles are not found to a great extent on other continents (except among descendants of Europeans).

WANDERING MELODIES

Quite aside from the characteristics of the elements of music, the content of the tunes found in Europe indicates that Europe is a historical unit. In the nineteenth century, some scholars began to be intrigued by what they came to call "wandering melodies," that is, by tunes whose variants were found in the folk traditions of widely separated countries. The existence of these melodies, or melody types, is also proof of the close relationship of art, church, and folk music. Melody types found in European folk music are also frequently found in hymns and art songs, particularly of the periods before 1700. They are probably not simply quotations of folk songs, in the sense of "quoting" something strange or exotic, as in nineteenth- and twentieth-century art music, but part and parcel of the basic material of art music.

Example 3-8 illustrates the phenomenon of "wandering melodies," or of widely distributed melody types. More extensive examples of related tunes found in larger numbers of countries, and including art

EXAMPLE 3-8. Tunes from Spain, Rumania, and England similar in structure and possibly genetically related, from Walter Wiora, *Europäischer Volksgesang* (Köln: Arno Volk Verlag, ca. 1950), pp. 50–51.

music, can be found in various publications, particularly in Walter Wiora's *Europäischer Volksgesang*.[3] In a good many cases, it is quite likely that the similar tunes found in several nations are indeed wandering melodies or, rather, variants of a single wandering melody. Whether or not the three tunes in Example 3-8 are genetically related we cannot say. Curiously, the variants of a tune found in separated countries are usually accompanied by widely varying verbal texts. An English ballad tune that has related forms in other countries will hardly be found outside England with a translation of the same ballad story. This very fact may lead us to suspect that the existence of similar tunes in different countries is not always, and perhaps not even frequently, simply the result of a tune's migration. In any event, we cannot *prove* in most cases that the tune has actually migrated. It is likely that traveling singers of the early Middle Ages (their existence is documented) taught to the peoples of many lands the original forms of many songs which developed into groups of melodies related in the manner of Example 3-8.

Another way of explaining the phenomenon of "wandering melodies" is that the musical characteristics of European folk song have been so homogeneous and have developed so much in the same direction throughout the continent that similar tunes were composed independently in several countries. Given a certain restricted set of musical characteristics—for the sake of argument, let's assume melodies composed of five tones with seconds and thirds predominating, regular metric structure, the tendency for the final sections of songs and of phrases to be lower in pitch and more drawn-out rhythmically than the rest, and a range of about an octave—it might be possible and even necessary for similar tunes to spring up independently in several places at various times. Thus the fact that there are some obvious similarities among the tunes in the foregoing examples does not prove that all of them are descended, through the use of communal re-creation, from a single parent

---

[3] Wiora, *Europäischer Volksgesang*, p. 5f.

tune. Whichever explanation is the correct one (and we may never know in many specific cases), the existence of similar tunes throughout the continent again shows us that Europe is an entity as far as its folk music is concerned.

SOME SONG TYPES FOUND IN EUROPE

Europe is a unit not only in the purely musical aspects of folk song. The cultural background and context as well as the words of the songs also indicate the essential integrity of the continent. There are certain types of songs that are found throughout Europe, though they are not present everywhere in the same proportion of quantity and importance.

One important song type is narrative song. Two main styles of songs that tell a story have been developed in Europe: epics and ballads. Narrative songs, particularly epics (distinguished from ballads by their length and heroic quality), are found outside Europe, in areas as divergent as the Great Basin of North American Indian culture, Persia, Borneo, and Japan; but only in Europe do they constitute one of the most important, indeed, perhaps, the preeminent, folk song type.

The ballad was developed in Europe in the Middle Ages—first, presumably, by song composers of city and court—and evidently passed into oral tradition and the repertories of folk cultures thereafter. The musical characteristics of the ballad are not different from those of most other kinds of folk song. Usually there are three to six musical lines and a number of stanzas. As far as the words are concerned, the ballad tells a story involving one main event. In contrast to the ballads, the epic songs are long, complex, and involve several events tied together by a common theme. Typically, the epic, as exemplified perhaps by the heroic songs of the Southern Slavs, does not have a strophic arrangement but tends rather to use a line which, with variations, is repeated many times. But there are sub-types of these genres and it is at times difficult to distinguish between them. (See Chapter Four for more detail about ballads, Chapter Six for epics.)

Love songs are important in many European countries (they are relatively rare in the folklore of other continents). They are more common in Western Europe than in the East, and characteristically they express love for another person in a melancholy or tragic setting. The music of love songs does not, on the whole, differ in style from that of other folk songs.

A number of ceremonial song types are common throughout Europe. Of course, the use of folk songs in an ecclesiastical setting is found. There are areas in which genuine folk hymns are sung; in Germany, a body of spiritual folk song became a partial basis of the Lutheran hymn, and the singing of "Kyrieleis" (a corruption of "Kyrie Eleison") in the rural communities was reported in medieval sources. But more typical are songs involving ceremonies that may have been practiced long before the advent of Christianity in Europe. Thus there are songs which revolve around important events or turning points in a person's life: puberty, birth, marriage, and death. In some countries these proliferated, as in France, where special songs for various events in a child's life (first words, first walking, etc.) were developed. The French have songs to urge a child to eat, to teach him to count, and so on. These are songs accompanying the so-called rites of passage which are important in practically every culture.

Also, there are songs involving the turning points in the year, such as the advent of spring, the summer and winter solstices, and the equinox. These have frequently been associated also with agriculture, and some have been attached, since the introduction of Christianity, to Christian festivals. Thus some pre-Christian winter solstice songs have become Christmas songs, as may have been the case of the popular German "O Tannenbaum." Pagan spring songs have sometimes become Easter or Whitsuntide songs. Again, these calendric song types are common in several nations of Europe.

Songs involving agriculture are also common, more so in Eastern than in Western Europe. Perhaps these songs should be generally regarded as work songs, since some of them actually aid in the rhythm of work, while others, such as the short tunes used by the Lapps to call reindeer, are functional in labor but not in a rhythmic sense. Another type of agricultural song, simply describing the work, is not sung during work but perhaps at social gatherings in the evening. Again, work songs are found also on other continents, but they are more common in Europe than in most other areas. As before, we cannot say that their style differs appreciably from the styles of European folk songs at large, although a few types of work songs do have special musical styles. Thus the Tribbiera of Corsica (Example 3-9), a type of work song sung while driving oxen around a small enclosure in which threshing is done, always has a form consisting of two sections with words, followed by a long, melismatic call.

Another characteristic type in European folk music is the humorous song. Musically this type does not differ especially from other songs, and of course humorous words can be associated with all sorts of song functions—ballads, work songs, children's songs, and so forth. One special type of humorous song found in many countries is the cumulative song.

EXAMPLE 3-9. Corsican "Tribbiera," from Wolfgang Laade, "The Corsican Tribbiera, a kind of work song," *Ethnomusicology* 6 (1962), 185.

It is not always uproariously funny or even mildly amusing, although some elements of humor are usually found and perhaps even the process of cumulation can be considered as having a humorous effect. A cumulative song is one in which each stanza, while presenting something new, also incorporates elements from the previous stanzas. Among the best known of these songs are "The Twelve Days of Christmas" and, of course, "Alouette."

Dance music is of course one of the main types of folk and ethnic music throughout the world. In Europe it is one of the important genres, and accompanies two main types of dance. According to Herzog,[4] the older dances are involved with rituals and ceremonies (round dances are especially characteristic here); these tend to be accompanied by relatively simple music. Dances that came into the European folk repertory at later times—and this includes most of those danced by couples, and many of the other kinds of social dances—have more complex music which shows, as does the dance itself, the influence of sophisticated musical cultures. However, while we can in good conscience make such broad generalizations about folk dance and dance music, we must also stress the tremendous variety of dances which exists in Europe. The dance seems to be one area of culture in which European trends are similar or closely related to those in other continents. Possibly this means that the older layers of European culture, those which antedate the introduction of Christianity and stem from a time when the European folk cultures would have been classed as primitive or nonliterate, have remained present in the dance more than in some other aspects of culture.

At any rate, mimetic dances (those which choreographically repre-

---

[4] George Herzog, "Song," Funk and Wagnalls' *Standard Dictionary of Folklore, Mythology, and Legend* (New York: 1949–50), II, 1035.

sent actions, events, feelings, persons, or animals) are found throughout European folk culture and in other continents as well. The same is true of dances with weapons (sword dances, for instance, performed in Scotland, Central Europe, and India), dances having sexual symbolism, and acrobatic dances, to name just a few. Gertrude Kurath[5] has made a survey of European folk dances and has managed to divide the vast array into several types, according to the form and style of dancing. For example, she distinguishes among circle, longway (line), and quadrille (square) dances, according to the formation used by the dancers. The point is, again, that each of these forms is found all over Europe, and that similar dances are performed in areas and countries with sharply contrasting cultures. Thus, Kurath cites the Maypole as used in dances of Spain, England, Germany, and Hungary; the "Hey," a technique in which two lines of dancers wind in and out of a circle, is found in England, Germany, Czechoslovakia, and Spain. Thus, in spite of national and regional peculiarities, we see again the basic unity of European folklore.

INSTRUMENTS AND INSTRUMENTAL MUSIC

Although singing accounts for a preponderance of music making, formal and informal, in the European folk music tradition, musical instruments are important, and instrumental music is of very great interest. While we can state with confidence that the participation of the population in singing is quite general, that is, most people in a folk culture can sing some songs and recognize many more, instruments are to a much larger extent the property of specialists. As we have pointed out, truly professional musicians, who have theoretical training and who make their living entirely through music, are not common in folk cultures. When they are found, they are usually instrumentalists. Instruments are typically played by only a small number of persons in a folk community, and these are usually professionals at least in the sense that they are recognized for their skill and called upon to perform on special occasions.

According to Curt Sachs[6] and others, the primitive instrumental styles of the world did not come about through simple imitation, on instruments, of vocal melodies. To be sure, vocal music must have come into existence before instrumental. But instrumental music presumably

---

[5] Gertrude P. Kurath, "Dance," Funk and Wagnalls' *Standard Dictionary of Folklore, Mythology, and Legend* (New York: 1949–50), I, 276–96.
[6] Curt Sachs, *The Wellsprings of Music* (The Hague: Martinus Nijhoff, 1962), p. 110f.

came about through the elevation of noise-making gadgets to really musical artifacts, through the coincidences of acoustic phenomena accidentally discovered, and through visual criteria used by craftsmen. For example, the maker of a flute may, in positioning the finger holes, be guided by the visual effect of the design more than by the pitches and intervals which a particular arrangement of these holes will produce. If this assumption is correct, it should not be surprising that the instrumental music of European folk cultures often seems quite unrelated to the songs found in the same area and sung by the same people. Also, there seems to be more stylistic variety in the instrumental music of Europe than in its vocal music, perhaps because of the limitations of human voice and ear as compared with the relative freedom allowed the instrumentalist, who needs to know only the right motions to make, but not necessarily how the music will sound before he plays it. Random improvisation and toying with an instrument may have a considerable effect on developing the styles of instrumental folk music.

Regarding the instruments themselves, we can make very few generalizations. They vary enormously in type, design, and origin, to say nothing of the musical materials which they produce. In so far as their origin is concerned, we can divide them roughly into four classes. (1) Among the simplest instruments are those which European folk cultures share with many of the simplest tribal cultures throughout the world, including rattles, flutes (with and without finger holes) usually made of wood, the bullroarer, leaf, grass and bone whistles, and long wooden trumpets such as the Swiss *Alphorn*. These (like the songs with the most restricted scales) tend to be associated with children's games, signalling practices, and remnants of pre-Christian ritual. Many of them actually function as toys, much as do their counterparts in simpler cultures. They are evidently archaic and became distributed throughout the world many centuries ago, but the fact that they are used as toys and for pre-Christian ritual does not necessarily mean that these rituals were, in earlier times, accompanied only by the simplest of musics. (2) A second group consists of instruments that were brought to Europe from non-European cultures in more recent times. They are much more complex, and evidently many of them were changed substantially after they were brought to Europe. Among them are bagpipes, simple fiddles such as the Yugoslav one-stringed gusle, the folk oboes and double-oboes of the Balkans, the banjo, and the xylophone. In general, the sources of these instruments were the Middle East and Africa. (3) Another group consists of instruments developed in the European folk cultures themselves, usually made from simple materials. A characteristic example is the Dolle, a type of fiddle used in Northwestern Germany, made from a wooden shoe. A more sophisticated one is the bowed lyre (sometimes also called the bowed harp), once widespread in Northern Europe and the British Isles, but now mainly confined to Finland. (4) A final, and perhaps the most important, group includes the instruments that were taken from urban musical culture and from the traditions of classical and popular music, introduced into folk cultures, then sometimes changed substantially. Prominent among these are the violin, bass viol, clarinet, and guitar. Some instruments used in art music during the Middle Ages and other early periods of European music history continued to be used in folk music into the twentieth century. Examples are the violins with sympathetic strings, related to the viola d'amore and still used in Scandinavia, and the hurdy-gurdy, related to the medieval organistrum and still played in France.

In Chapters Four through Six we shall explore European folk music in somewhat more detail. Unfortunately, even if comprehensive information were available we could not give the whole story on these pages. We cannot even give samples of the music of each nation. All we can do is to give some examples of what is typical, what is common, and what is particularly noteworthy, and then hope that the reader will continue delving into the specialized literature and, above all, proceed with listening in order to broaden his understanding of this fascinating area of European culture.

BIBLIOGRAPHY

The only general and comprehensive book on European folk music is in German, and it approaches its field from a very special viewpoint, attempting to show various historical layers evident in present-day traditions. Nevertheless, it is worth reading: Werner Danckert, *Das europäische Volkslied* (Bonn: Bouvier, 1970). Several collections of folk music in Europe that make it possible to compare the various styles are Leonhard Deutsch, *A Treasury of the World's Finest Folk Song* (New York: Howell, Siskin, 1942); Maud Karpeles, *Folk Song of Europe* (London: Novello, 1956); *Europäische Lieder in den Ursprachen* (Berlin: Merseburger, 1956), a collection published under the auspices of UNESCO; and Walter Wiora, *European Folk Song; Common Forms in Characteristic Modification* (Cologne: Arno Volk, 1966), a collection that illustrates the unity of European folk song by presenting variants of the same tunes or tune types from many countries.

Important general bibliographies of European folk music are Karel Vetterl, *A Select Bibliography of European Folk Music* (Prague: Czechoslovak Academy of Sciences, 1966) and *Annual Bibliography of European Ethnomusicology* (Bratislava: Slovak National Museum, 1966–). Ruth

Tooze, *Literature and Music as Resources for Social Studies* (Englewood Cliffs, N.J.: Prentice-Hall, 1955) provides material for the public school teacher. Walter Wiora, *Europäischer Volksgesang und abendländische Tonkunst* (Kassel: Hinnenthal, 1957) surveys the role of folk music in the history of European art music. *Handbuch der europäischen Volksmusikinstrumente*, a multi-volume encyclopedia of European folk instruments, is in preparation.

Introductions to the field of European balladry are Gordon H. Gerould, *The Ballad of Tradition* (Oxford: Clarendon Press, 1932) and William J. Entwistle, *European Balladry* (Oxford: Clarendon Press, 1939). The many variants of a single ballad text in several European nations are studied in Iivar Kemppinen, *The Ballad of Lady Isabel and the False Knight* (Helsinki: Published by the author, 1954). A short discussion of European epics is Felix Hoerburger's "Correspondence Between Eastern and Western Folk Epics," *J-IFMC*, IV (1952), 23–26. The entire epic tradition is discussed, but with emphasis on the Yugoslav forms, in Albert B. Lord, *The Singer of Tales* (Cambridge: Harvard University Press, 1960). Finally, a classic on folk song as a living artifact is Phillips Barry, "The Transmission of Folk Song," *Journal of American Folklore*, XXVII (1914), 67–76.

FOUR

THE GERMANIC PEOPLES

The Germanic peoples—that is, those peoples which speak Germanic languages—can be divided into three groups on the basis of their folklore: (1) the English, including Scotland and Ireland; (2) the Scandinavians; and (3) the Dutch and the German-speaking peoples of Germany, Austria, most of Switzerland, and other areas in Eastern Europe. Although these three groups of peoples speak related languages, their cultures cannot be considered particularly similar, and this is also true of the styles of their folk music. Of course, the folk music of the Germanic peoples is known in different phases and varying degrees. For the English-speaking peoples there exists a vast body of ballads, collected in America as well as in England; and the study of ballad variants, their interrelationship, structure, and origin, has been carried further for English material than elsewhere. Of German folklore we know best the songs that have come into the repertory rather recently. Swedish folk music happens to have available a large collection of fiddle tunes, because some Swedish collectors have concentrated on this aspect of music. Also, the Germanic peoples have been strongly influenced by their neighbors. For example, English folk song shows considerable relationship to that of the Low Countries and France, while German folk music is at times similar to that of its neighbors to the east, Czechoslovakia, Poland, and Hungary; Austrian folk songs have some common features with those of Italy. Thus, while we are treating the Germanic peoples as a unit in this chapter, it should not be assumed that their folk music is necessarily a stylistic unit. We should avoid the corresponding conclusion that the style of Germanic musics goes back to the time when all Germanic peoples were one and spoke one tongue, and the equally erroneous assumption that the Germanic-speaking peoples possess a psychic unity. The heritage of Germanic languages goes back much further than the style of present-day folk music, and whatever similarities are found are due almost certainly to cultural contact in recent times, that is, from the early Middle Ages on.

THE ENGLISH CHILD BALLADS

The most characteristic type of British folk song is the ballad, and the most famous ballads are the Child ballads. These have nothing to do with children but rather bear the name of Francis James Child (1825–96), who organized, published, and classified those ballads which he assumed were of popular (that is, rural and truly anonymous) origin. He avoided, in his classification, those ballads in the folk tradition which could be traced to the cities or to professional song writers, and those which he thought did not have high literary quality. It turns out, however, that many of the Child's ballads can now be traced; still, as a whole, these ballads are, textually and to an extent musically, a stylistic unit which contrasts with other bodies of English-language song. Because the different variants of each ballad do not bear identical titles or first lines, Child gave each ballad (or group of variants) a number, and for this reason the most famous ballads are known by their "Child numbers."

The stories of some of the most famous ballads are widely known to students of literature. Child 10, "The Two Sisters," deals with jealousy between two girls over a lover; the man chooses the younger sister, who is thereupon drowned by the older one, who in turn is punished for her crime. In an epilogue, various parts of a musical instrument are made from the younger sister's body. "Lord Randall" (Child 12) is perhaps the best known of the Child ballads and tells in a dramatic retrospective dialogue the story of a young man who is poisoned by his lady-friend.

This type of dialogue is also used in "Edward" (Child 13), in which a young man confesses that he killed his brother and that he will now leave his family. "The Maid Freed from the Gallows" (Child 95) finds that no one in her family is willing to rescue her from punishment by paying her fine, until her lover arrives.

Love ballads, especially tragic ones, are important among the Child ballads. "Mary Hamilton" (Child 173) is an historically founded story of a lady-in-waiting at the English court who is condemned to death because she becomes pregnant by the king. "Little Musgrave" or "Little Mathy Grove" (Child 81) is seduced by a noble lady; they are discovered by the husband, who kills Musgrave in a duel. In "The Gypsy Laddie" (Child 200) a noble lady runs off with a gypsy, and when her husband finds her, she tells him that she prefers to stay in poverty with the gypsy band. Some of the ballads have very simple stories. This is true of "Barbara Allen" (Child 84) in which a girl who has spurned her lover has second thoughts when she hears that he is sick with love, but arrives too late to save him from death. The eternal triangle is exemplified in Child 73, "Lord Thomas and Fair Elinor," in which a man jilts his fiancee to marry another; the unhappy girl comes to the wedding, kills her rival, and is in turn killed by her former lover, who ends the story by committing suicide. "Lord Lovel" (Child 75) is one of a number of ballads in which separated lovers are reunited in a meeting resulting from an outrageous coincidence.

Ballads of the sea are common. They can be exemplified by Child 286, "The Golden Vanity," in which a cabin boy is promised the hand of the captain's daughter if he will swim to and sink an enemy ship; but when his mission is accomplished, the captain leaves him to drown in the sea. "Lord Bateman" (Child 53) is imprisoned by the Turks but aided in his escape by a Turkish lady, whom he promises to marry; seven years later, she seeks him out just as he is about to marry another, and he finally keeps his word. In the "House Carpenter" (Child 243) we see remnants of the supernatural elements which once were common in ballad texts. A married lady is persuaded to run off with a former lover who, it turns out, has become a demon and destroys his ship and her when he finds that she wants to return to her husband and child. Remnants of medieval superstitions are also found, for example, in Child 155, "Sir Hugh," in which a young boy happens into the garden of a Jewish family and is sacrificed by the Jew's daughter in a satanic ritual. Humorous ballads are also known, as for example Child 277, "The Wife Wrapped in Wether's Skin," in which a man, afraid to beat his aristocratic wife, wraps her in a sheepskin, which he is able to whip. "Our Goodman" (Child 274) comes home drunk and finds his wife in bed with another man, but she insists that the evidence—the man's horse, hat, and head—are ordinary things he should expect to find in the house, such as a cow, a chamber-pot, and a cabbage.

A few of the ballads, as they are found in tradition today, consist only of a vestige of the original story, or of a set of formulas which accompanied the story. Child 2, "The Elfin Knight," is a dialogue between two lovers who ask each other to prove their love by committing extraordinary feats, as making a Cambric shirt without any needle or needlework. Religious stories are also found. The best known is the "Cherry Tree Carol," an apocryphal story in which the unborn baby Jesus commands a cherry tree to bow down and to give cherries to his mother, after which he announces his birth and identity from the womb.

There are about three hundred Child ballads, but for only about two hundred has any music been collected; for the rest, only words survive. The famous ballads we have enumerated share some characteristics, and they are representative of the whole Child group (with the exception of a number dealing with Robin Hood), although most of the ones mentioned here are tragic, while the majority of the whole group of Child ballads actually do not have unhappy endings. The stories of these ballads are easily available in most of the large array of folk song collections made in the United States, and in Child's own collection, which dates from the late nineteenth century.[1] The stories usually revolve around one incident, names of places and characters change from variant to variant, and setting and background are only briefly stated. The narrator does not take an active part in the story but tells it dispassionately. There is some dialogue, and there is also a tendency for whole verses to be virtually repeated, as in the following excerpt from Child 200:[2]

(He says):   *Take off, take off those milk-white gloves,*
               Those shoes of Spanish leather,
               And hand you down your lily-white hand,
               We'll bid farewell together.

(Narrator says): *Oh she took off those milk-white gloves,*
               Those shoes of Spanish leather,
               And she handed him down her lily-white hand,
               They bade farewell forever.

Other characteristics of ballads are also found in this example. We see the use of conceits, that is, of descriptive phrases which appear re-

[1] Francis James Child, *The English and Scottish Popular Ballads*, 5 vols. (Boston and New York: Houghton Mifflin Company, 1882–98); reprinted, New York: Folklore Associates, 1956.

[2] Cecil J. Sharp, *English Folk Songs from the Southern Appalachians* (London: Oxford University Press, 1952), I, 235.

peatedly as if they were formulae. Thus hands are often described as "lilly-white" (as are gloves), horses are "milk-white," and so on. Many ballads have refrains, the origins of which are sometimes obscure. Flowers, plants, and spices are sometimes mentioned, as in Child 1,[3] which has been made famous in another variant, by the popular singers, Simon and Garfunkel.

> (*Verse*) *Go tell her to make me a cambric shirt*
> (*Refrain*) *Setherwood, sage, rosemary and thyme,*
> (*Verse*) *Without any needle or needle's work,*
>   *And then she'll be a true lover of mine.*

Refrains, incidentally, are a feature of song shared by all regions of Europe. Some refrains mention dancing or movements that can be interpreted as parts of a dance. Here is an excerpt from "The Two Sisters" (Child 10):[4]

>   *There lived an old lord in the North countree*
> (*Refrain*) *Bow down, bow down.*
>   *There lived an old lord in the north countree*
> (*Refrain*) *Very true to you. . . .*

"Bow down" is thought to be derived from dancing. The reason for mentioning this is a theory that the ballad, narrative though it is, began as a dance song type. The name may, of course, be derived from the Latin *ballare* (to dance), and there is some evidence that ballads were once used as dance songs in medieval Scandinavia. On the Faeroe Islands, between Scotland and Norway, this tradition is still in existence, and lively group dances using the "Faeroe step" (two steps left, one right) may be performed while the dancers sing Norwegian ballads. We know of no ballad dancing in the English-speaking world, but this practice may once have existed there as well.

A look at the collections of Child or of some of the more recent great American collectors makes it obvious that the differences among variants of one ballad can be very great. Take Child 12, the popular "Lord Randall." Randall's name appears in all sorts of variant forms, Randall, Rendal, Lorendo, Durango, William, Tyranty, Nelson, Elson, King Henry, Willie Doo, etc. The person who poisons him may be his sweetheart, his grandmother, or his stepmother. It has even been estab-

[3] Sharp, *English Folk Songs*, I, 1.
[4] Sharp, *English Folk Songs*, I, 27.

lished that the children's song, "Oh where have you been, Billy boy, Billy boy?" which ends, "She's a young thing and cannot leave her mother" was derived from one version of the more dramatic "Lord Randall." Thus it would seem that formulae are very stable elements, while the details of a story are more subject to change. The lengths of the variants also differ greatly. A story told in one ballad with the use of fourteen stanzas may, in another version, be summarized in four, through elision, omission of events, and omission of stanzas giving background information.

Similar variety is found in the tunes. Bertrand H. Bronson[5] has assembled all of the tunes used for the Child ballads, and he finds that for each ballad story there seem to be two or three basic tune types to which all of the variants must be sung. For example, most of the tunes of "The Golden Vanity" (Child 286) are related to one of the two in Examples 4-1 and 4-2.

EXAMPLE 4-1. English folk song, "The Sweet Trinity," from Jan P. Schinhan, ed., *The Music of the Ballads* (Durham, N.C.: Duke University Press, 1957. *The Frank C. Brown Collection of North Carolina Folklore*, vol. 4), p. 120.

There was a lit-tle ship in the North A-me-ri-kee, It went by the name of the Gol-den Wil-low Tree, As she sailed on the low-land lone-some low As she sailed on the low-land sea.

While ballad stories evidently moved from nation to nation in the Middle Ages, the tunes did not accompany them. For example, there is the ballad of "Lady Isabel and the Elf-Knight" (Child 4), in which a knight courts a lady but really intends to kill and rob her; when she discovers his false intentions, she foils him and causes him to drown. This ballad is known throughout Europe except for the Balkan area, but its tunes are largely national in provenience, and the tunes used with the English versions are evidently not related to those used in Dutch, Scandinavian, German, or other versions. On the other hand, variants of a tune used for one ballad in the English repertory may be found in other English ballads or songs.

---

[5] Bertrand Harris Bronson, *The Traditional Tunes of the Child Ballads* (Princeton, N.J.: Princeton University Press, 1958–   ).

EXAMPLE 4-2. English folk song, "The Little Cabin Boy," from Phillips Barry, Fannie H. Eckstrom, and Mary W. Smyth, *British Ballads from Maine* (New Haven, Conn.: Yale University Press, 1929), p. xxxiii.

BROADSIDE BALLADS

Besides the Child ballads, for which no written original can usually be found, the English-language repertory possesses other types, particularly a group of later origin, the broadside ballads. This type, so named because it appeared printed on large sheets of paper called broadsides, became popular throughout Western Europe. Written frequently by professional song writers, the broadside ballads tend to deal with historical events more than do the popular ballads, and they contrast with the Child ballads also in their concern for detail, in their more complex plots, and in the involvement of the narrator, who frequently appends a moral. The words are often shamelessly sentimental and usually do not have the literary value of the older ballads. But the broadside ballads (which were still being written in the twentieth century) functioned somewhat as newspapers in areas in which illiteracy was common. All of them did not, of course, pass into oral tradition, but a good many did and have thus become true folk songs. Some of our best-known songs originated as English broadside ballads: "The Foggy Dew," made popular by Carl Sandburg, "Brennan on the Moor," "Devilish Mary," and "Sam Hall." Some of the broadsides are even derived from the Child ballads. Thus a broadside ballad called "The Turkish Lady" is obviously just a variant of "Lord Bateman" (Child 53), in which a Turkish lady saves an English prisoner in her father's jail and marries him. The tunes of the broadside ballads are of diverse origin. Many of the printed broadsides did not include music but simply named the tune of this or that popular song, folk song, or hymn. Finally, the practice of printing broadside ballads and their dissemination into folk tradition is found not only in Britain but also in most European countries and, of course, in America.

THE STYLE OF ENGLISH FOLK MUSIC

As we have pointed out, the music of the English ballads does not differ greatly from that of English folk song in general; thus the discussion of ballad tunes below can be said to apply to English folk song at large. Many of the older tunes have, as one characteristic, a melodic contour which forms, roughly, an arc, starting low, rising in the second phrase, remaining on the higher level of tessitura in the third phrase, and moving down to the level of the first in the fourth phrase. Four phrases or lines are common, but five (usually through repetition of the fourth), six, and eight are also found, as well as two and three. Three examples of English folk song follow (Examples 4-3, 4-4, and 4-5); they may be considered representative of the whole style to an extent, but certain song types, such as dance songs, game ditties, children's songs, and humorous songs, are not represented. Example 4-3 is a Scots version of Child 76, as sung by Ewan MacColl, the well-known folk singer. Example 4-4 is a variant of the same song collected in Southern Indiana. It is essentially the same melody, but is sung in quite a different manner. Example 4-5 is the tune of a broadside ballad, "Girls of Newfoundland," of Irish origin, collected in Labrador. Perhaps we should point out here that much more British folk music has been collected in North America than in Britain, and that, for material collected in England itself, published collections with reliable transcriptions are difficult to come by. Thus we must rely to some extent on American versions for a picture of British folk music.

EXAMPLE 4-3. English folk song, "Lord Gregory." Reprinted from *The Traditional Tunes of the Child Ballads,* vol. 2, by Bertrand Harris Bronson by permission of Princeton University Press, Copyright 1962.

EXAMPLE 4-4. English folk song, "The Lass of Loch Royal," from Bruno Nettl, "The Musical Style of English Ballads Collected in Indiana," *Acta Musicologica* 27 (1955), 83.

She wet her cheeks___ with fallen___ tears And then she kissed__ my hand, Said, Willie dear, re - mem - ber me When you're in___ some dis -tant land.

Examples 4-3 and 4-4 use the so-called "ballad meter," that is, iambic lines alternating in four and three-foot lengths (- / - / - / - / ; - / - / - / ;) and so forth). This is common, though by no means universal, in British folk song and tends, in music, to be translated into one of three types of rhythm: (music notation) or (music notation) (with several variants, such as (music notation) and (music notation) or (music notation)). Example 4-3 uses the first of these, and Example 4-4 a variant of the second. There is, however, a tendency in those songs that are sung in the parlando-rubato singing style to include elongation and shortening of measures, and even a systematically heterometric structure. Thus, in Example 4-4, the measures have, respectively 3, 5, 5, 7, 5, 7, 6, 6, and 5 eighth-note equivalents.

Songs whose words are not cast in ballad meter nevertheless tend to use the same rhythmic types, with minor adjustments, in their tunes. Thus, Example 4-5 has a structure rather similar to that of Example 4-3, but the text has eight lines instead of four. This type of stanza is most frequently set to variants of the first or second rhythmic types given above, and is more common in the broadsides than in the Child ballads, and particularly widespread in the English-language ballads sung by the Irish.

British folk song is frequently said to be modal, but the great majority of the songs fall into the major or Ionian mode. (Our three examples are all major.) There are also many songs in the Mixolydian (major with lowered seventh) mode, in Dorian (minor with raised sixth),

EXAMPLE 4-5. English folk song, "Girls of Newfoundland," collected in Newfoundland by MacEdward Leach, transcribed by Bruno Nettl.

There's a girl in Saint John ci - ty I'm go - ing__ now__ to

see No__ fel low in the__ reg' - ment do

know her, on - ly__ me She__ cried so when I left__ her I

thought she'd break her__ heart But__ if we__ e - ver

meet a - gain we ne - ver__ more__ shall part.

and in Aeolian (natural minor). The other modes are not common. Some modulation may occur (though this is often hard to identify because the music is monophonic) as in Example 4-3, in which the first two phrases seem to have G for a tonic, but the last one D.

Much has also been said of the pentatonic nature of English folk song. A rather large minority of the songs are pentatonic, while the majority (again, except for the old layer of children's and related songs) seems to be heptatonic or hexatonic. It is sometimes revealing to examine the functions of the various tones in a scale, however, for often it will be evident that the most important and most common tones are indeed five in number, while the other two are subsidiary or used only in ornaments. Also, the scale structure of the individual phrases or lines may be pentatonic. For instance, in Example 4-3, the first half of the song uses a common kind of pentatonic scale—D, F-sharp, G, A, B; the other tones, E and C-sharp, are brought in only later. Similarly, in Example 4-4 important tones are B, C (tonic), E, F, and G. Example 4-6, a version of Child 53, uses six tones, but one of them, F, appears only in ornaments. This song also is a good example of the kind of pentatonism found in English folk music.

The emphasis on pentatonic structure does not seem to be an ingredient of the newer layer of British song. The tunes that were introduced into the folk culture more recently, perhaps since the advent of music printing and the broadside ballad in the sixteenth century, are both more varied in style and more closely related to popular and art music. This is to be expected, of course, with regard to the broadsides, since their writers frequently set them to tunes of any sort that were widely current. Thus the later tunes are more frequently in major or harmonic minor, rarely pentatonic, and they do not deviate, as does Example 4-4, from a standard and consistent metric structure.

EXAMPLE 4-6. English folk song, "Lord Bateman," from Bruno Nettl, "The Musical Style of English Ballads Collected in Indiana," *Acta Musicologica* 27 (1955), 83.

The_____ turks they had but one lone daugh-ter And she was of some high de-gree, She stole the keys of her fa-ther's dwell-ing And vowed young Ba-ker_____ she'd set free.

As we noted above (p. 48), Béla Bartók divided Hungarian folk singing into two types, which he called "parlando-rubato" and "tempo giusto."[6] The distinction between these two ways of singing does not always emerge from printed music, since it involves the singer's interpretation of rhythm and tempo. And although the distinction was derived for use in describing Hungarian folk music, it applies also to singing in other countries, especially those of Northern and Eastern Europe. Example 4-3 is a sample of tempo-giusto singing, while Example 4-4, a variant of the same song, exemplifies the parlando-rubato. In Hungarian folk music, parlando-rubato is used mainly for ballads and tempo-giusto for dance songs, but both styles are found in British ballad singing.

At this point we must mention also the Celtic-speaking inhabitants of the British Isles, particularly the Irish and the Welsh, peoples whose musical culture has played so important a part in their history that the Irish national emblem is the harp. Irish folk song today is almost entirely in the English language, and, indeed, the songs of Irish origin have contributed greatly to the English-language heritage of the United States,

[6] Béla Bartók, *Hungarian Folk Music* (London: Oxford University Press, 1931).

Canada, and Australia. On the whole, their musical style does not differ greatly from that of the English folk tunes of eighteenth- and nineteenth-century origin. Yet, certain minor traits characterize the singing of these ethnic groups. For example, Irish singers will take a conventional major ending (e.g.,) and change it to end on a repetition of the tonic ( ).

The Welsh have developed—partly through their folk heritage and partly because of the influence of hymn-singing—a tradition of choral singing of folk songs; this is done largely in the style of nineteenth-century hymns, with conventional chord progressions and triadic harmony. They also preserved, into the nineteenth century, an instrument that evidently was widespread in medieval art music, the *cruth* or *crowd*, a lyre with six strings—four over the fingerboard, two as drones—which was usually bowed. It evidently accompanied the songs of the bards, whose importance among the Welsh and Irish was very great. A similar instrument, the *tallharpa*, was used in Finland and Estonia, and today, Finland is the only country in which bowed lyres are still widely used.

SOME NETHERLANDISH FOLK DANCES

Of course, the ballads are not the only kinds of folk songs in the British Isles; we have chosen them as one representative group. The same sort of thing is true of the Dutch and Flemish folk dances, which are briefly discussed here because we have space to discuss only one of the categories of Dutch music, and because we must pay some attention to the dance music of the Germanic-speaking nations, despite the importance of ballads and lyrical songs.

Evidently folk dancing has indeed been a prominent activity in the Low Countries for centuries. An edict of Charlemagne outlawed dancing in churches and ceremonies, indicating the popularity of such activities. The practice of religious dance, including dances on the occasion of death, particularly by young girls, is attested by various documents from history, and appears to have remained in the folk tradition until relatively recent times. The religious dances are almost always round dances.

In other ways, also, Dutch folk music seems to have had a close relationship to the practices of Christian worship. There are many religious folk songs and carols of various kinds (Christmas and Easter), and the style of a great deal of Dutch folk music reminds us of the styles of Christian monophonic hymns and Lutheran chorales. To a considerable degree this is true of German folk music, as well, for in many instances it also adheres to the style of the hymn, with its typical lines consisting mainly of quarter notes except for the final long tone.

Many European folk dances have their origin in pre-Christian ritual dancing. An example from Holland is the "Seven Saults" dance, described by Kunst,[7] and known also in other parts of Western Europe. It was evidently once a sacrificial dance, but after the introduction of Christianity it was danced at harvest festivals, fairs, and wedding parties. These functions are, of course, residual of pre-Christian ceremonies involving the life cycle or changes in the year's cycle. Kunst reports seeing the "Seven Saults" still performed in the twentieth century on the Dutch island of Terschelling. The dance involves seven motions of a mildly acrobatic nature: stamping with each foot, touching the ground with each knee, then with each elbow, and finally with the nose. It was evidently performed—as are many European folk dances—with the accompaniment of group singing, such as that found in Example 4-7.

EXAMPLE 4-7. Dutch folk dance tune, from Jaap Kunst, "On Dutch Folk Dances and Dance Tunes" in *Studies in Ethnomusicology*, ed. M. Kolinski (New York: Oak Publications, 1961), vol. 1, 32.

The tune in Example 4-7 shows us some of the traits common in Western European folk dance music. Of course, since the music is used for dancing, and since it is sung by a group, it could not easily partake of the parlando-rubato singing style with its distortion of tempo and emphasis on words. It tends to be rigid in this aspect of music, to have simple

[7] Jaap Kunst, "On Dutch Folk Dances and Dance Tunes," *Studies in Ethnomusicology*, I (1961), 35.

rhythms consisting largely of two- or three-note values (as in this case, quarter, eighth, and sixteenth notes). The tune is in major, with an implication of harmony in the Western tradition, based on tonic, subdominant, dominant, and dominant seventh chords. Note also the repetitive refrain, whose words count off the "seven saults."

Holland, being near the center of the Germanic-speaking area, exhibits musical relationships to England, Germany, and Scandinavia. In both dance and dance music, some similarities between Dutch and Scandinavian folk music are striking. Variants of the same tunes and dance movements are found in both areas, as well as in Scotland, which was at one time under strong Danish and Norse influence.

SAMPLES OF SCANDINAVIAN
INSTRUMENTAL FOLK MUSIC

The folk music of Scandinavia is of great interest because in some ways it seems to exhibit very ancient traits, and yet in other ways it has been very much under the influence of the cultivated tradition of the cities. An example of ancient practice frequently cited is the use of parallel fifths in Iceland, which has evidently preserved some traits of medieval Norwegian culture. For a long time there raged an argument, mentioned in Chapter Three, about the origin of Icelandic "organum," whether it represents a case of medieval church music practice which trickled down to the folk tradition or whether it is an example of ancient and generally forgotten folk practice which in the Middle Ages was taken up by the Western church. Similar historical arguments have been going on for decades about the relationship of other folk polyphony— that of Russia, the Ukraine, Yugoslavia, the Caucasus, the mountains of Italy—to that of medieval art music. The arguments have brought no conclusions, and today the interest in primacy has dwindled, especially as various kinds of polyphony have been discovered in many European folk traditions, but we may still marvel at what must surely be a musical tradition of great age. Aside from simple parallel fifths, Icelandic music seems to have used other forms similar to the earliest polyphony in Western church music, such as the so-called free and melismatic types of organum.

There is no doubt that many of the folk dances of Europe were originally dances of medieval and later towns and courts. This is true of the square dances, which grew out of quadrilles; of the polka, a more stately dance; and of the waltz, which originated in part in the slower and more dignified minuet. Frequently, of course, a dance almost completely changed character when it moved from court to countryside or vice-versa. Thus the sarabande, one of the slowest and most stately dances of seventeenth-century Western Europe, is thought to have been derived from a quick and violent Spanish folk dance which, in turn, had been brought from the Spanish-American colonies in the sixteenth century. More rarely, the music accompanying folk dances can also be traced to earlier forms of art music. In such cases we have musical instances of *gesunkenes Kulturgut*. Examples can be found in Sweden, where one of the important folk dances is the "polska," which is a form of the polonaise. Anyone familiar with Chopin's polonaises or with those of late Baroque composers such as G. Ph. Telemann or J. S. Bach will recognize the characteristic rhythm in Example 4-8, which is played by violins. Aside from rhythm, moreover, the melodic configurations are also definitely in a style reminiscent of baroque and pre-Classical music: note the arpeggios and the triad-like figures in the second section, reminiscent of the Alberti bass. The form, in which each phrase is repeated with first and second endings, is common in Western European instrumental music and similar also to the earliest known examples of medieval instrumental music, the *estampie* or *stantipes*. (Only the melodic line—not the accompaniment—is given in Example 4-8.)

EXAMPLE 4-8. Swedish "Polska" playel by two violins; melody only, transcribed by Bruno Nettl from recording issued by Sveriges Radio (Radio Sweden), RAEP 8. Collected in Halsingsland.

Tunes of various sorts, frequently more ornamented, are played in other Scandinavian countries on folk instruments such as the Norwegian "Harding fiddle." Typical of the multifarious forms of folk instruments in Europe, this is a violin with four or five sympathetic strings under the fingerboard (which are not played but are caused to vibrate by the vibrations of other strings activated by the bow). The four main strings are tuned in various ways, for example 𝄞, 𝄞, or 𝄞.

Another instrument prominent in Scandinavia is the dulcimer, which in Sweden is known as the *Hummel* and exists in a great many forms. Unlike the dulcimer of the Southern United States, it is used more as a solo instrument than as an accompaniment to singing. It produces melodies with drone accompaniments, or tunes in parallel thirds. The dulcimer, basically, is a string instrument that lies flat on a table and is plucked or struck; it has anywhere from three to over a dozen strings, and usually one or more of them are fretted. The shape varies from that of an oblong violin to rectangular and irregularly triangular. Sometimes it is bowed as well as plucked. It seems likely that the American dulcimer was brought from Scandinavia or Northern Germany, though similar instruments do, of course, exist elsewhere in Europe, particularly in Hungary, whose Csimbalom (derived from the Persian *santour*) is something of a national instrument.

Throughout Europe, folk music enthusiasts are deploring the gradual disappearance of folk singing and the knowledge of folk music on the part of the rural population. Attempts to reintroduce folk music through schools and festivals have been only moderately successful. Nevertheless, there still seem to be many people who know and can sing folk songs from their family or village traditions. Denmark seems to be such a place, for we have available in a case study, made over a period of time by the Danish musicologist Nils Schiørring,[8] all of the songs known by one woman, Selma Nielsen. Mrs. Nielsen produced some 150 songs from memory, including material of every diverse origin—ballads from the Middle Ages, sea shanties, soldiers' songs, humorous ditties. It is possible to see throughout her repertory the close relationship between the development of folk and art music, for we find modal materials, jaunty songs in major and somewhat in the style of the lighter art songs of the pre-Classical period, and sentimental tunes obviously from nineteenth-century popular music. Scandinavia offers good illustrations of the interdependence of folk and art music in Europe.

[8] Nils Schiørring, *Selma Nielsens Viser* (Copenhagen: Munksgaard, 1956).

Swedish dulcimer.

GERMAN FOLK SONG

Nowhere, however, is the interrelationship between art and folk music stronger than in the German-speaking nations. The influence of the sophisticated musician on his rural counterpart has sometimes been so great there that the old practices of the German countryside seem to have disappeared and can be traced only through old documents or through the music of Germans whose ancestors emigrated from their homeland centuries ago. This is analogous, of course, to the study of British folk music through American folk song. The types of German folk song are similar, so far as text and function are concerned, to the English—medieval ballads, work songs, sailors' shanties, dances, year- and life-cycle songs, and so forth. In Germany proper, the vocal music seems to have developed much more strongly than the instrumental. But in Switzerland and Austria, instruments as well as special forms of singing have flourished. In the period since World War II, the emigrants from German-speaking communities in Hungary, the Balkans, and parts of Russia who returned to West Germany after centuries of isolation have produced singing informants with a knowledge of many older songs thought to have disappeared from the tradition.

The influence of the church on German folk song is of early medieval origin. Many of the German ballads with medieval themes have words of partly or entirely religious character. There are folkloric descendants of mystery plays in the modern moralities and in children's religious pageants. Much of the music fits in with the system of church modes as well as with the rhythmic structure of the early Lutheran hymns. The singing style is more frequently tempo-giusto than it is in the oldest British ballads.

German ballad texts remind us of the British ones, but the proportion of ballads with religious background is larger than in the English repertory. A greater dimension of tragedy seems to be present as well. Indeed, the historical and cultural differences between Germany and England can very well be illustrated by the differences in their ballad texts, although many of the story types used in these texts are identical in the two countries. For example, a German version of Child 95, "The Maid Freed from the Gallows," tells the story of a merchant who gambles away his son's life in a game of cards. The boy's sister is told by the judge that she can redeem him by running naked around the gallows square nine times, and she does this to save her brother. The dramatic impact of this detailed account is quite different from the formulaic recitation of the dialogue between the maid and her relatives in the English version, in which the listener never finds out how the maid came to be condemned in the first place, and in which ordinary payment of a fine, rather than humiliation of the sister, is the conclusion. German ballads contain more rape and seduction, more violence on the part of authorities than the English ones, and, generally, reflect the stormier and less isolated history of their country.

If the music of some of the old German ballads has medieval roots, the majority of extant German folk songs seem to stem from a later period, from the time—beginning in the seventeenth century—when the German countryside was dotted with minor courts, many of which had a sophisticated musical life, with court composers, orchestras, and opera. In this way even the smallest hamlets and the most remote farms began to have contact with art music, and the result seems to have been the assimilation of elements of the art styles into folklore. The folk music from that period, typically, is in major mode and has melodies making liberal use of triads with implied harmony. Tempi and meters are even and constant, and the singing style is definitely tempo-giusto. There is also a later layer of song, that of the German broadside ballads, mainly from the nineteenth century. Here the style is that of nineteenth-century popular music, with some chromaticism, modulation, instrumental accompaniment, and what we today feel is a sentimental quality.

A children's song still widely used is shown in Example 4-9. It is sung in autumn by children while walking in pairs or small groups, carrying lanterns. The structure, which consists essentially of one line

EXAMPLE 4-9. German children's song, "Laterne, Laterne," from pamphlet accompanying the recording, *Deutsche Volkslieder, eine Dokumentation des Deutschen Musikrates,* ed. Deutsches Volksliedarchiv, Freiburg (Wolfenbüttel: Moseler Verlag, 1961), p. 19.

repeated with variations, is typical of children's songs throughout Europe and may, historically, represent an archaic layer of style that preceded the various national folk styles, which are evidently mainly of medieval origin. Especially typical is the scale, which is tetratonic, but which emphasizes the tones, E, G, and A. The added C may be interpreted as a result of the importance of the triad in German folk song style.

In contrast to England and Scandinavia, polyphonic singing is common in Germany, Austria, and Switzerland. Canons are, to be sure, found throughout Europe, but a form of polyphony characteristic of Germany is parallelism, particularly parallel thirds. Whether this came about through the influence of art music or whether it originated as a folk practice cannot be said. Most likely it was once exclusively a folk practice that was reinforced by similar forms in art music. Much of the part-singing (which is concentrated in Southern Germany and the Alpine region) is definitely in the category of chordal harmony. This is surely the case in Example 4-10, a woodcutters' song from Bavaria. But at one point it leaves the widely accepted art music tradition: line 4 has several parallel fifths, which are performed consistently stanza after stanza. This song also, of course, indicates the importance, in German folk song, of triads in both harmony and melody.

EXAMPLE 4-10. German woodsmen's song, from pamphlet accompanying the recording, *Deutsche Volkslieder, eine Dokumentation des Deutschen Musikrates,* ed. Deutsches Volksliedarchiv, Freiburg (Wolfenbüttel: Moseler Verlag, 1961), p. 11.

M.M. ♩ = 132

Im Fruah jahr, wann der Schne e weggeht, gehn Holz-knecht mir an Wald; An Ko - bi, der aus Rin - d'n ist, da bleibn ma jung und alt. Mir hak - ka Baam die gros - cht'n her, fur so an Holz - knecht ist's an Ehr, wann er im Schlag is nit da letzt, und ar - bet frisch und gsetzt.

Ho la - ro, ho la ro, rü - di - rü ru dl ja,   rü - di - rü - ru - dl ja, ru - di - ru ru dl - ja,   rü !

rü - di - rüru - dl - ja

GERMAN FOLK MUSIC IN THE ALPS
AND EASTERN EUROPE

The Alpine region of South Germany, Austria, and Switzerland has developed a regional body of folklore and folk music, including certain unique practices, which contrast with those of Germany proper. It is sometimes thought that the extreme isolation of the mountain dwellers as well as their exceptional physical environment are responsible for this regional peculiarity, and some scholars have tried to draw parallels between Alpine folklore and that of other mountain regions in the belief that geography plays an important role in determining the nature of a people's traditions. Two characteristic aspects of the Alpine musical heritage are the *alphorn* and yodeling.

The *alphorn* is a Swiss instrument, a wooden trumpet from four to twelve feet long, used to call cattle and to signal across valleys; it is played also at sunset rites. Similar instruments are found in other countries, including Estonia, Poland, and Rumania. Its repertory is mostly short calls, but there are also a few traditional tunes. Since its sound can be heard for miles, especially with the help of echoes, its presence in the Alps can be explained, at least partly, by the geographic environment. The fact that the player uses the higher partials has caused its music to make use of a peculiar scale—C-D-E-F sharp-G (transposed, of course, to various pitches when the instrument varies in size)—which has also been used as the basis of some Swiss folk songs.

Yodeling, the rapid alternation between chest and head voice while singing meaningless syllables, is also a practice due partly to the possibility of communicating over long distance from one mountainside to another. While we do find the use of falsetto in various continents, true yodeling is rare outside the Alpine region. Yodeling usually appears in the refrains of songs, although there are also some songs which consist entirely of yodeling. There is in the Alps also some polyphonic yodeling with parallel thirds or triads, for polyphonic singing of the type described for Germany is particularly strong in the Alps. The practice of yodeling has led to the emergence of a class of semiprofessional musicians in the Alpine region, for certain individuals achieve fame as yodelers and give paid performances.

Brief mention of European Jewish folk music is perhaps suitable here. The Yiddish folksongs are related to German folklore, for Yiddish is essentially a German dialect of the late Middle Ages that has been penetrated by words borrowed from Hebrew, Polish, Russian, and other languages. During the late Middle Ages, the Jews were driven out of Germany and sought refuge in Eastern Europe, keeping their special brand of German folk culture. Thus the songs of the Yiddish-speaking Jews have retained some of the German medieval character. But to a greater degree their songs partake of the styles of the nations to which they moved—Russia, Poland, Rumania, and elsewhere. And there are also traces of Hebrew liturgical music in their folk songs. Thus the styles of Yiddish folk song have great variety, and the whole corpus of Yiddish folk music is not a homogeneous one. A similar development, incidentally, occurred among the Sephardic Jews who, during the Middle Ages, lived in Spain but were driven out in 1492 and carried with them a Spanish-derived language, Ladino, and songs partially Spanish in style. (For a discussion of Israeli folk music, see William P. Malm's book in this series, *Music Cultures of the Pacific, the Near East, and Asia*.)

There are—or there were, before World War II—many enclaves of German population in various parts of Eastern Europe (Russia, Hungary, Yugoslavia, Rumania), in South America (particularly Brazil and Argentina), and in the United States and Canada. These consist largely of descendants of individuals who left Germany in quest of religious freedom between the sixteenth and the nineteenth centuries. Their folk music has occasionally been collected. As we might expect, it has sometimes been influenced by their new surroundings; German-Americans have, for instance, incorporated English tunes into their repertory. But, more important, these groups tended to keep intact some of the styles and many of the songs that were evidently once current in Germany proper, but that have disappeared in the original center of their distribution.

There is much variety in the music of the Germanic-speaking peoples of Europe, but their styles stand together when compared to those of the Slavic and Finno-Ugric speaking peoples of Eastern Europe, or to those of Italy, France, and the Iberian peninsula. No doubt peoples who speak related languages very frequently share other aspects of culture such as music, but it is not always so. And while we can perhaps speak of a Germanic style of folk music, we must also be aware of the interchange of materials and styles between these and neighboring peoples—the impact of German and Austrian music in Czechoslovakia and Poland, the similarity between Dutch and Belgian songs and styles, the impact of Italy on Austria, and the relationship between Scandinavian and Russian music.

BIBLIOGRAPHY AND DISCOGRAPHY

Cecil J. Sharp is the author of a number of fundamental works on British folk music. One of the important ones is *English Folk Song, Some Conclusions*, 3rd ed. (London: Methuen, 1954). A readable survey of the British ballad is Evelyn Wells, *The Ballad Tree* (New York: Ronald Press, 1950), and a very useful introduction to both texts and tunes is a book by Roger D. Abrahams and George Foss, *Anglo-American Folksong Style* (Englewood Cliffs, N.J.: Prentice-Hall, 1968). The most comprehensive collection of British ballad tunes, because it reprints the tunes in many other important collections, is Bertrand H. Bronson, *The Traditional Tunes of the Child Ballads* (Princeton, N. J.: Princeton University Press, 1958–1970). Bronson's article, "About the Commonest British Ballads" *J-IFMC*, IX (1957), 22–27, is important reading. Donal J. O'Sullivan, *Songs of the Irish* (New York: Crown Publishers, 1960), is a standard collection. A number of Bronson's important studies are reprinted in his *The Ballad as Song* (Berkeley: University of California Press, 1969).

A short survey, with examples, of Dutch folk music is Jaap Kunst, "On Dutch Folk Dances and Dance Tunes," *Studies in Ethnomusicology*, I (1961), 29–37. For Norwegian folk music, a monumental set of volumes covering the entire repertory is being published under Olav Gurvin, *Norwegian Folk Music* (Oslo: Oslo University Press, 1958–   ).

An interesting collection of Danish folk music collected from one informant is Nils Schiørring, *Selma Nielsens Viser* (Copenhagen: Munksgaard, 1956). Many collections of German folk music are available. A classic is Ludwig Erk and Franz Magnus Boehme, *Deutscher Liederhort* (Leipzig, 1893–1894, reprinted by Olms, Hildesheim, 1962). A more recent publication, still incomplete but with comprehensive notes, is *Deutsche Volkslieder mit ihren Melodien*, edited by John Meier and others (Freiburg: Deutsches Volksliedarchiv, 1935–). Many publications by German scholars on German folk song are worth reading; those by Walter Wiora and Erich Stockmann are particularly to be noted. In the field of musical instruments, Stig Walin, *Die schwedische Hummel* (Stockholm: Nordiska Museet, 1952) is an excellent, profusely illustrated study of the Swedish dulcimer.

The number of records of British folk song, both field collections and artistic interpretations, is enormous. To be mentioned especially is a set of Child ballads produced by British traditional singers, A. L. Lloyd and

Ewan MacColl, for class and other educational use: *English and Scottish Popular Ballads,* Washington Records 715–723. Also worth hearing are *Sussex Folk Songs and Ballads,* edited by Kenneth Goldstein, Folkways FG 3515; *Songs and Pipes of the Hebrides,* Folkways P 430; *The Art of the Bagpipe* (with elaborate annotations), Folk-Lyric Records FL 112; and, as a selection of Gaelic songs, *Songs of Aran,* Folkways P 1002. Child ballads as sung by American informants are available on many recordings published by the Library of Congress. See particularly *Child Ballads Traditional in the U. S.* (AAFS 57–58).

Songs and Dances of Holland, Folkways 3576, and *Songs and Dances of Norway,* Folkways FE 4008, are both educational and entertaining selections. For German folk song, a set produced by the famous Freiburg archive is to be recommended: *Deutsche Volkslieder,* Deutsche Grammophongesellschaft 004–157 to 004–160 (2 disks), with a pamphlet giving texts, notes and complete transcriptions.

It must be noted, however, that most recordings of the European music discussed here are not field recordings sung by rural singers, but by professional folk singers; the tunes are thus authentic, but the singing style is frequently not.

FIVE

EASTERN EUROPE

If the area east of Italy, Germany, and Scandinavia has any internal unity in its folk music style, this must be due to the fact that on the whole this area has been much less under the influence of art music than has the western half of Europe. Peoples as diverse as the Greeks, the Russians, and the Finns can hardly be expected to have one style of folk music. For many centuries, parts of Eastern Europe have repeatedly been conquered and re-conquered from several peoples from the outside —Mongols, Turks, Romans, Germans. Its culture has many roots, among them Hellenistic, Islamic, Oriental, and North Asian. It is inhabited by peoples speaking languages of several distinct families and groups: Slavic, the largest group; Finno-Ugric (Finnish, Hungarian, Estonian, and several minority languages in Russia); Turkic (the Turks, the Chuvash of the Russian interior, etc.); Romance (Rumanian); Albanian; and Caucasian. Musical influences have come from sources as diverse as the chants of the Byzantine Church, the pentatonic tunes of Mongolia, and the complex rhythms of the Arabic and Hindu spheres. And certainly there are important links between Eastern and Western Europe, tunes found in both areas, identical uses and functions of music in the culture.

In view of this great diversity, this chapter makes no attempt to discuss these individual nations one by one. Some, indeed, are entirely omitted. Instead, we discuss certain techniques of composition and certain types of song which are found in several of the cultures. But let us bear in mind that each of the Eastern European countries, from gigantic Russia to tiny Albania, has a rich folk music heritage; each has enough songs to fill a multi-volume anthology and a musical culture of sufficient wealth to keep scholars busy for several lifetimes. It is also important to bear in mind the fact that while there is a common flavor to East European folk music, there is probably more variety of practices and styles in each of its nations than there is in the typical Western European country.

MELODIC SEQUENCE:
HUNGARIANS, CZECHS, CHEREMIS

East European scholars have studied intensively their native musical traditions, and nowhere has this been more true than in Hungary. For decades in the nineteenth century it was thought that the folk music of Hungary was the music of the gypsies who supplied ethnic entertainment in the cities, but in the twentieth century the great wealth of true Hungarian peasant music (which has little in common with the gypsy tunes) was discovered, largely by Béla Bartók and Zoltán Kodály. Since the Hungarians are linguistically related to the Finns, it was thought that the styles of these two peoples would have something in common. This turned out to be only partially the case, but other Finno-Ugric speaking peoples living for centuries in isolation from the Hungarians, inside Russia, do have music somewhat similar to that of Hungary. The most important of these groups is the Cheremis, who live in a semi-autonomous republic of the Soviet Union some five hundred miles east of Moscow.

These peoples have something in common that is also found far to the east, among the Mongolians, and even to some extent further on, in American Indian music; and this strengthens our belief that the essential features of the oldest Hungarian folk music are very old, and that they were brought by the Finno-Ugric tribes when they moved westward in the early Middle Ages. The most striking of these features is the practice of transposing a bit of melody, once or even several times, to create the essence of a song. Many Hungarian songs have the form $A^1A^2A^1$(a fifth lower)A^2(a fifth lower), for example. Transposition is usually up or down a fifth, perhaps because this interval is an important one in the series of overtones, or perhaps because this practice may have originated long ago, in the Far East, where fifths are also significant, or for any of several other possible reasons. In Hungarian folk music, and even more in that of the Cheremis, pentatonic scales composed of major seconds and minor thirds predominate. Such scales have sometimes been called "gapped scales" on the assumption that they are simply diatonic scales in which gaps have been made. Of course such a label is not really justified, for there is nothing any more "natural" about a scale made up of seconds (of two sizes) than there is about one made up of seconds and thirds, or, for that matter, one made up of quarter tones or augmented fourths. To demonstrate the integrity of the kind of pentatonic scale we have mentioned, let us examine a Cheremis song that makes use of the principle of transposition, (Example 5-1).

EXAMPLE 5-1. Cheremis song, from Bruno Nettl, *Cheremis Musical Styles* (Bloomington: Indiana University Press, 1960), p. 37.

The song consists of three lines, the last two of which are identical. The first consists of two halves, the second of which is derived from the first (and is therefore designated as B_a). The first half of the second line is a downward transposition of the first half of the first line, by a fifth (and is therefore designated as A_5). But there are further ramifications of this notion of transposition, as the analysis in the next paragraph indicates.

First we assign to each of the notes in the scale a number: beginning with the lowest tone, B–1, C sharp–2, E–3, F sharp–4, G sharp–5, B–6, C sharp–7, E–8. Then we compare the section labeled A with that labeled A^5. Obviously their melodic contours are similar, but at some of the points at which A has a minor third, A^5 has a major second, and A^5 begins a minor sixth below A but ends on a perfect fifth below A. Now, if we translate the tones into the numbers we have assigned, and compare musical lines A and A⁵, we have the following sequences:

Line A⁵   5 5 4 5 4 3 2 3 3 2 3 2 1
Line A   8 8 7 8 7 6 5 6 6 5 6 5 4.

The relationship between the number sequences is constant because the principle involved in this transposition is not a constant relationship of the frequencies (which would occur if the method of transposition were an exact one), but that of tonal transposition. Presumably the scale used in this song existed, in an unconscious sense, in the mind of the composer when he was making up the song, and when he began transposing he did so within the framework of the scale, which is made up of both thirds and seconds.

To some degree, the use of transposition as a structuring device is found in a great many cultures throughout the world, and certainly everywhere in Europe. It takes on special significance in parts of Eastern Europe because of its greater frequency there. The practice of transposing as an integral part of the composition process seems to have radiated from Hungary to its neighbor countries. The Slovaks and, to a small extent, the Czechs make use of it also. The Slovaks transpose sections largely in the manner of the Hungarians (up or down a fifth), the Czechs more frequently up or down a third or second. Perhaps the difference between the Czech and Hungarian practice is due to the greater frequency of diatonic, especially major, scales among the Czechs. Or the influence of neighbor nations may be at work, for the Czechs have lived in an area surrounded by Germans and they participated, more than their neighbors to the east, in the development of art music. Thus their songs sound more like Western cultivated music, and they have variants of many tunes found also in Germany. Example 5-2 is a Czech song using transposition.

EXAMPLE 5-2. Czech folk song, "Vrt sa devca," learned by the author from oral tradition.

WORDS, MUSIC, AND RHYTHM:
THE BALKANS AND CZECHOSLOVAKIA

It is natural to look to the characteristics of a language to explain the characteristics of the songs sung by its speakers. Indeed, the structure of folk songs is frequently determined by the form of their texts, and the rhythmic, even the melodic, quality of a musical repertory may be substantially influenced by the stress, length, and the patterns of the words to which it is sung. Of course we could not claim that the rhythmic structure of a folk music style automatically comes from the language, and we could easily find examples in which the rhythm of folk songs contravenes that of their language. However, there is no doubt that the nature of a language has much to do with shaping the style of the folk songs for which it is used.

It is interesting, in this light, to compare the rhythmic structure of Czech and German folk songs. That of the Czech songs frequently is more accented, while the German flows more smoothly. The German songs more frequently have an anacrusis—a pickup or up-beat, as it is popularly called—while the Czech ones rarely do. These distinctions may come from one of the major phonological differences between the two languages. Czech speakers tend to accent their stressed syllables heavily, and the Czech language automatically places an accent on the first syllable of each word. Also, Czech has no articles such as "a" or "the" that would be unstressed. As a result, Czech utterances begin with accents, and so do Czech songs and instrumental folk compositions. German, with its accents coming on any syllable, and with its unstressed articles preceding nouns, has given rise to a musical structure in which an unstressed beat in the music often precedes the first measure.

The rhythm of Czech and Slovak songs is relatively simple, with the meter typically an isometric duple or triple. Hungarian folk songs are frequently in similarly simple meter, but there are also many Hungarian songs with irregular metric patterns, and some that move steadily in 5/4 or 7/4 meter. One of the common features of Hungarian rhythm is the use of dotted figures— ♩. ♪ or, even more typically, ♪♩. —with heavy stress on the first note. Perhaps, again, the rhythmic structure of the language is evident here, for in Hungarian, as in Czech, there are no articles, and the first syllable is automatically accented. Also common in Hungarian and some other Eastern European folk styles is the use of isorhythmic structure. This means that a rhythmic pattern is repeated for each line. The meters may vary and the measures may have irregular numbers of beats, but the sequence of note values remains the same from line to line in this type of song. The following rhythmic patterns appear in some of the Hungarian as well as the Rumanian folk songs with isorhythmic structure:

① ♫♫♩♩ ② ♩♩ ♩♩♩

③ ♩♩♩♩♩♩ ④ ♩♩♩♩♩♩♩♩♩ |

The reason for the frequency of this kind of structure in some Eastern European styles may lie, again, in the structure of the poetry. In Western Europe, it is the number of metric feet (iambic, trochaic, dactylic, anapestic) which are constant. Each foot corresponds to one or to a half measure of music. The actual number of syllables per line may vary, since a line consisting of iambic feet may suddenly be broken by a foot of anapest:

"*Thĕre wás ă yoúth aňd ă jól-lў youth*" ("aňd ă jól-" is the anapest foot).

But in most Eastern European styles of poetry it is not the number of accented syllables that is constant, but the number of syllables in toto. Thus an isorhythmic arrangement, even if each phrase has several measures of different lengths, is better for accommodating the kind of line sequence that makes up the poetry.

On the whole, the Balkan countries have in common an unusual degree of rhythmic complexity. It appears in three forms: (1) freely declaimed melodies, which can only with difficulty be classified as to meter, and which are performed with extremes of the parlando-rubato technique; (2) tunes with few different note values, but with frequently changing meter; and (3) tunes with a single dominant meter which, however, is based on the prime number of beats—5, 7, 11, 13, and so on. The first type is well exemplified in the Yugoslav epic, which is discussed further on in this chapter. The second and third types are especially common in the Rumanian and Bulgarian traditions, so much so that songs in 11/8 or 7/8 have been called tunes "in Bulgarian rhythm" among Balkan folk song scholars. Example 5-3 gives some of the rhythms found in these songs.

Example 5-4 is a Rumanian Christmas carol with the meter of 10/16 kept consistently throughout the song. Actually it might be possible to divide the song into measures of different lengths, but in spite of the rather complicated relationship between such note values as eighths and dotted eighths, or sixteenths and dotted sixteenths, there is a steady rhythmic pulse which is followed throughout: ♪ ♪. ♪. ♪ . The curious

EXAMPLE 5-3. Examples of metric patterns found in Bulgarian folk songs.

EXAMPLE 5-4. Rumanian Christmas Carol, from Béla Bartók, *Die Melodien der rumanischen Colinde* (Wien: Universal Edition, 1935), p. 68. Reprinted by permission of Boosey and Hawkes, Inc., New York, and Universal Edition, Ltd., London. Copyright 1918 by Universal Edition, Renewed 1945. Copyright and renewal assigned to Boosey and Hawkes, Inc., for U.S.A.

thing is that the pulse is not regular. It alternates between eighths and dotted eighths. Perhaps this is the key to the rhythmic complexity of some Balkan songs as, for instance, the one given in Example 5-4. There is a meter—10/16 in this case—but the denominator of the fraction does not indicate the length of the beat, as it would in most Western European music, because the length of the beat varies, depending on its position in the measure.

It would seem almost that ♪♪. ♪. ♪ is another version of ♪♪♪♪ and that ♪.♪.♫ is simply an elongation of a simpler figure, ♫♫ . We should point out, incidentally, that there is a vast body of Christmas carols in the Rumanian folk repertory. Bartók collected several hundred tunes, and they seem to be particularly archaic, being short, with forms that do not correspond to the simple line organization of Western European, Czech, or Hungarian songs and are irregular not only in the structure of the measures but also in the number of measures and phrases per song.

One might expect the dances of the Balkan countries to be based on simple metric schemes; after all, people have two legs and two arms, to which movement in duple meter lends itself; no one has seven feet. Nevertheless, among the five most important folk dances of the Bulgarians, only one is in duple meter. The Bulgarians have (1) the *Pravo Horo,* a simple round dance, in 2/4 meter; (2) the *Paiduška,* in quintuple meter, with two beats— ♩ ♩. ; (3) the *Povărnato Horo,* a back-and-forth round dance, in 9/16, with four beats— ♪ ♪ ♪♪. ; (4) *Račenica,* danced by couples in 7/8 meter, with three beats— ♩ ♩ ♩. ; and (5) *Eleno mome* ("My Helen"), a more recent introduction, also in 7/8, with four beats— ♩ ♩ ♪♩. The metric structure of these dances, once established, is quite consistent.

The tunes with frequently changing meter are illustrated by Example 5-5, a simple Rumanian Christmas carol with the range of a sixth, with alternation of 3/8, 4/8, and 5/8. The simple yet irregular rhythmic structure of many Balkan songs is illustrated by the fact that the rhythm of the first three measures reappears in the last three. The transcription by Béla Bartók gives the way in which the first stanza was sung, and

EXAMPLE 5-5. From Béla Bartók, *Die Melodien der rumänischen Colinde* (Wien: Universal Edition, 1935). Printed by permission of the copyright owner, Dr. Benjamin Suchoff, Successor-Trustee, The Estate of Béla Bartók.

then, by means of numbered references, indicates the ways in which subsequent stanzas differ from the first. There are seven stanzas, and the variants are given in the order in which they appear.

We are not able, in this short book, to discuss the words of folk songs to any significant extent, especially as far as their content is concerned. In general, however, it must be pointed out that there are broad but recognizable differences between Eastern and Western European folk song texts. Thus, for example, the widespread importance of the ballad in Western Europe, particularly in the Germanic-speaking countries, is balanced by the greater importance in Eastern Europe of lyrical songs, particularly of songs involving activities of and feelings about tilling of the land. Both types of songs are found throughout Europe, but it is in Eastern Europe that songs truly reflective of a peasant economy are found in large number. Possibly this reflects the earlier and greater urbanization of the Western part of the continent. As samples of Eastern European lyrical songs, we present here a few Czech folk song texts, in English translation,[1] from the many that deal with agricultural life and are among the most popular. They are usually not real work songs, but lyrical poems sung after work.

> *Around Trebon, around Trebon*
> *Horses are grazing on the lord's field.*
> *Give the horses, I'm telling you,*
> *Give the horses oats.*
> *When they have had their fill*
> *They will carry me home.*

Often the songs concern love among young peasants. For example:

> *Come, young man, to our house in the morning.*
> *You shall see what I do.*
> *I get up in the morning, I water the cows,*
> *And I drive the sheep to pasture.*

The fruits of agriculture may be used as special symbols in the text:

> *Under the oak, behind the oak*
> *She had one or two*
> *Red apples; she gave one to me.*
> *She did not want to give me both,*
> *She began to make excuses,*
> *That she hasn't, that she won't give, that there are too few.*

---

[1] Czech folk song texts quoted from Bruno Nettl and Ivo Moravcik, "Czech and Slovak Folk Songs Collected in Detroit," *Midwest Folklore*, V (1955), 40–48.

Many of the Czech lyrical songs deal with or mention music, such as this—

> *In the master's meadow I found a ducat.*
> *Who will change it for me? My sweetheart is not at home.*
> *If she won't change it I'll give it to the cimbal (dulcimer) player.*
> *The music will play until dawn.*

FORM IN BALKAN FOLK SONGS

The forms of Balkan songs exhibit similarities to, but sometimes also considerable differences from, those of Western Europe. In the latter area, we are overwhelmed by a large number of four-line stanzas, in which there is either progressive development (ABCD, each line a new melody with no repetition) or some recurrence of the first line. As we have seen, AABA is very common in German folk music, in British broadside ballads, and in modern popular and popular-derived songs. ABBA is common also in the older British ballads, especially in relationship to the curved melodic contour. The reverting forms—AABA and ABBA—are common also in the western part of Eastern Europe, in Czech, Polish, and Hungarian song. AABA especially is found in Czech and Polish music, perhaps because of strong German influence. ABBA is found in Hungarian and other Finno-Ugric groups, but more common is a variant of this form, A A(5) A(5) A, indicating transposition of the first section up or down a fifth for the second and third sections. The use of three sections, such as ABA, with the middle section longer or shorter, and sometimes at a tempo different from the first, is sometimes found in the Balkans and sometimes among the Czechs. (Example 5-5 has a shorter middle section, for instance.) Songs with two, five, and six or more lines are found throughout the Balkans and in the Baltic area. Often these can be subdivided into asymmetrical units (like the measures in Bulgarian rhythm). Simple general principles may govern the development of greatly varied groups of forms. Many Rumanian Christmas songs can be divided into two parts, the first longer than the second, with both having common material. The second part is often a condensation of the first (e.g., ABC-AC; A^1A^2B-A^1B).

An area of the world as rich in both folk tunes and folk song scholars as the Balkans was perhaps bound to produce pioneer work in the classification of musical forms. Bartók devised a system which he used for his collections of Hungarian, Slovak, Rumanian, and Serbo-Croatian songs. In his Slovak collection, the songs are first divided according to the number of melodic lines (normally two, three, or four) without counting repetitions of material. Thus a tune with the form ABBA has two different melodic lines, but the form ABCD has four. Each class is then subdivided according to the position of the final tones of the lines in their relationship to the last tone of the song. For example, a song in which all lines end on the same pitch is in one class; one in which the sequence of final tones of lines is GAAG would be in another; and so on. Beyond this, each of the categories is then divided according to rhythm—dotted rhythms are separated from even rhythms. Finally, each of these groups is subdivided according to the number of syllables per line, distinguishing the songs that have the same number of syllables in each line from those in which the number varies from line to line. Bartók's scheme of classifying melodies differs greatly from that used by most students of British folk song, such as Cecil Sharp, who classified tunes according to mode. The reason for this difference is probably related to the fact that there is in the British (and other Western European) styles less formal variety than there is in East European folk music, for the former, being based on poetry with metric feet, relies on more or less constant meter and length of line.

Folk song scholars in Eastern and Central Europe, particularly in Hungary and Czechoslovakia, have followed Bartók's lead and continue to work with great energy to find more adequate methods of classifying folk tunes, now frequently using computers to process the vast amounts of data at their disposal as a result of the wealth of collected tune material. The purposes of classification are (1) to make it possible to find tunes by the musical characteristics; (2) to show that tunes are related genetically, that is, that they are members of one tune family; and (3) to provide a basis for broad analytical and descriptive surveys of the style of a folk music repertory. The folk music scholars who are most involved in questions of classification have made great strides, but their methods still do not easily and automatically provide solutions for these problems.

EPIC SONG:
YUGOSLAVIA, FINLAND, RUSSIA

Traditions of epic poetry are important in a number of European folk cultures, but especially in those of Eastern Europe. An epic is a narrative poem, distinctly longer than the ballad, usually sung, with a main character who is usually a national hero, and who has many adventures in war and love. Its basic unit of organization is usually the individual line of poetry rather than a stanza consisting of several lines. In the Middle Ages the epic was fairly widespread in Western Europe; the French "chansons de geste" and such famous works as the "Song of

Roland" are examples. In Western Europe, the epic tradition was evidently one in which folk and sophisticated traditions shared and mixed, for it was presumably carried by professional minstrels who at least occasionally used written texts. In Eastern Europe the epic tradition is today much more alive and much more closely associated with the genuine folk culture. We find epic material in the Slavic world, and also in Albania and Finland, where the main body of folk epics, the *Kalevala*, consists of songs dealing with the Finnish mythical culture hero, Väinemöinen. The *Kalevala* is structured in couplets, and the songs were performed by pairs of bards who would alternate, which is probably responsible for the peculiarly repetitive form of the text, as shown in this excerpt:[2]

> *O thou wisest Väinemöinen,*
> *O thou oldest of magicians,*
> *Speak thy words of magic backwards,*
> *And reverse thy songs of magic.*
> *Loose me from this place of terror*
> *And release me from my torment.*

Of course the reader will recognize the style as that also used in Longfellow's "Song of Hiawatha." The influence of the *Kalevala* on nineteenth-century poets was certainly considerable. The Finnish bards sang to the accompaniment of the *kantele*, a psaltery with 20 to 30 strings.

The Russian tradition of epic poetry is, typically, unaccompanied. The Russian poems are called *byliny;* they are slow-moving, unrimed, and performed in a rhythmically free style. Their stories—in contrast to the mythical past of the Finnish *Kalevala* cycle—deal with historical or semihistorical events of eleventh-century Russia and of the wars against the Tartars which took place for the next two hundred years. Of course there are literary motifs that are found in many nations: for instance, the poor and neglected prince who becomes a hero, found in all European folklore but perhaps without historical foundation. The practice of singing *byliny* seems to have reached a peak of artistic perfection in the seventeenth century, when like the epic tradition of Western Europe in the Middle Ages it was penetrated by professional minstrels. The Ukrainian version of the epic is a body of songs called *Dumy*, dealing largely with the struggles of the Ukrainians against the Tartars and Poles in the late Middle Ages.

One of the most interesting folk song types of the Greeks is the "Klephtic song." The Klephts (meaning bandits in Turkish) were the men who fought against the Turks from the fifteenth to the nineteenth centur-

---

[2] From the book *Kalevala: or, The Land of Heroes*. Trans. from the Finnish by W. F. Kirby. Everyman's Library Edition. Published by E. P. Dutton & Co., Inc. Used by permission of E. P. Dutton & Co., Inc., and J. M. Dent & Sons Ltd.

ies for Greek independence. Klephtic songs deal with these fighters, who have become folk heroes, in a way somewhat similar to that of the Yugoslav epics. The songs are performed in a rubato manner, with much ornamentation and complex metric arrangements. They do have a strophic structure, but the melodic and poetic forms do not coincide; in fact, the musical line ordinarily covers one and a half textual lines. Thus, in a sense the modern Greeks share in the epic traditions of Eastern Europe.

The most accessible body of epic singing today, however, is that of the Yugoslavs (mainly the Serbs, but also the Croatians and Montenegrans whose style is also found in Bulgaria and Albania). Their songs deal mainly with the struggles against the Turks from the thirteenth to the seventeenth centuries. Some of the epics are told from the Christian point of view, others from the Muslim. The songs deal mainly with the rulers and the leaders in war. That the tradition is still alive is attested to by the mention of modern appliances such as the telephone, and by the existence of an epic about the shooting of Archduke Ferdinand at Sarajevo at the beginning of World War I. That it is also ancient is proved by the songs' musical structure. There have been attempts to link the Yugoslav tradition to that of the Greek Homeric epics, and certainly we can learn a great deal about the possible genesis of the *Iliad* and *Odyssey* and about the way in which these great epics must have been performed from the structure and cultural context of the Yugoslav epics.

The Yugoslav epics take from less than one to perhaps ten hours to perform; they are performed by semiprofessional minstrels in cafes, and they are sung only by men. They are accompanied on the *gusle* (which the singer himself plays), a simple fiddle with one string made of a strand of horsehair, a belly of stretched skin, and a crude bow. The *gusle* usually plays a more ornamented version of the singer's melody, or it performs a drone and plays ornaments between the singer's lines.

It would be surprising if songs of such length were sung exactly the same way by any two singers, or even twice alike by the same one. To a considerable extent they are improvised, re-created each time. Thus the process of creation and performance are to a degree united.

There are points where adherence to a norm is required, of course; a particular epic has certain themes, certain motifs, and certain formulas —similar to the "conceits" of the British ballads—which recur. In the structure, one of the typical arrangements is the ten-syllable line, which remains constant throughout the hours required to complete the poem. Just how a singer who is partly improvising can consistently and undeviatingly produce lines of exactly ten syllables is one of the mysteries of this ancient tradition. We know that he must learn to sing in accordance with certain patterns, mastering first the stories and the formulas, then singing single episodes, and only later being permitted to sing full-blown songs. Even more exacting than the overall structure is the requirement of a "word boundary" after the fourth syllable in some of the Yugoslav styles; that is, the fourth syllable always ends a word, and no word occupies both fourth and fifth syllables. Here is a sample of this kind of poetry:[3]

> *Beg sad priđe|đamu đo penđera,*
> *Pa dofati|knjige i hartije,*
> *Kaljem drvo|što se knjiga gradi,*
> *A mastila|što se knjiga piše,*
> *Pa načinje|knjigu šarovitu,*
> *Sprema knjigu|ljićkom Mustajbegu.*

(*Translation*): *Now the bey went to the window*
And he took letter paper,
A quill with which letters are made,
And ink with which letters are written,
And he prepared a well-writ letter;
He directed the letter to Mustajbey of the Lika.

Example 5-6 gives a short sample of the music, showing its very ornamental style of singing and playing, and its use of some small intervals. The scale could not be notated without the use of additional marks; arrows indicate slight (quarter-tone) raising or lowering. The notes played by the *gusle* include, consistently, a tone between C-flat and C, and one between G and G-sharp. Several possible reasons for this use of microtones have been advanced: the influence of Turkish and Arabic music; the ancient Greek tradition, with its enharmonic genus; and the use of the *gusle*, which, when fingered by the human hand in natural position of tension, produces such intervals.

The rhythm of Yugoslav epics is also worthy of discussion. If the many vocal ornaments were disregarded, we would find two main types of line:

♩ ♩ ♩ ♩ | ♩ ♩ ♩ ♩ | ♩ ♩ 𝄾 | and ♩ ♩ | ♩ ♩ ♩ | ♩ ♩ ♩ | ♩ ♩ 𝄾 | .

But near the beginning of a song or an episode (usually preceded by introductions played on the *gusle*) the rhythm varies more, the first note of each line is elongated, and the singing has an even more dramatic character than it does in the remainder of the song.

Finally, we should point out that regional and individual styles of

[3] Albert B. Lord, *The Singer of Tales* (Cambridge, Mass.: Harvard University Press, 1960), p. 84.

EXAMPLE 5-6. Sample of Yugoslav epic song (transcribed by Béla Bartók), from Milman Parry and Albert B. Lord, *Serbo Croatian Heroic Songs,* vol. 1 (Cambridge, Mass.: Harvard University Press, 1954), p. 440.

Šè - nluk ći - nî   jod Zä - da - ra   ba - ne,

I,   u - fä - ti - jo   slú - gu Ra - do -   jï - cu,

Ej,   Ra - do - jï - cu   tür-skú pri - dvö -   ri - cu,   (17) Ej,

singing are very highly developed in Yugoslav epic poetry. Two singers will sing the same song with many points of difference. Albert Lord narrates an incident of great interest which affords unusual insight into the relationship of tradition and individual creativity:

> When [the epic collector and scholar Milman] Parry was working with the most talented Yugoslav singer in our experience, Avdo Mededović in Bijelo Polje, he tried the following experiment. Avdo had been singing and dictating for weeks; he had shown his worth and was aware that we valued him highly. Another singer came to us, Mumin Vlahovljak from Plevlje. He seemed to be a good singer and he had in his repertory a song that Parry discovered was not known to Avdo; Avdo said he had never heard it before. Without telling Avdo that he would be asked to sing the song himself when Mumin had finished it, Parry set Mumin to singing, but he made sure that Avdo was in the room and listening. When the song came to an end, Avdo was asked his opinion of it and whether he could now sing it himself. He replied that it was a good song and that

Mumin had sung it well, but that he thought he might sing it better. The song was a long one of several thousand lines. Avdo began and as he sang, the song lengthened, the ornamentation and richness accumulated, and the human touches of character, touches that distinguished Avdo from other singers, imparted a depth of feeling that had been missing in Mumin's version.[4]

SCALES AND INTERVALS:
BULGARIA, GREECE, POLAND

If we measured the intonation of genuine folk singers anywhere we would probably find that their intervals do not coincide as well with those in Western music theory as our notations indicate. Especially in Eastern Europe, and perhaps more in the Balkans than elsewhere, would we find intervals smaller than the minor second, thirds which are neither major nor minor, and the like. The Balkans have for centuries been under the cultural influence—now strong, now weaker—of the Near East, where small intervals are common. But they have also conformed to a degree with the diatonic system found in Western folk and art music, and with the widespread pentatonic modes which use minor thirds and major seconds and can be derived from the circle of fifths. Thus we find a great deal of variety in the melodic material used in Balkan folk music.

The use of small intervals—some microtones, but more frequently minor seconds—is an important feature of some Balkan styles outside the epic tradition. The importance of ornamentation seems to have contributed to this predilection, for vocal ornaments as well as instrumental ones seem especially made for the use of small intervals. Thus a Macedonian song uses a scale with the tones E-flat, D, C, B, and A-sharp. The fact that the ranges of Balkan songs are, typically, small may also be a contributing factor. According to Kremenliev,[5] Bulgarian songs rarely exceed an octave in range, and a great many of them are within the compass of a fifth. Occasionally one even finds two-tone melodies with only a minor second between the tones. Ornaments in Bulgarian folk song are improvised; they vary from stanza to stanza and, in any single song, from singer to singer. Their purpose may be that of pleasing the audience through vocal virtuosity, of calling attention to the song or to particular words (this is evidently the purpose of melismatic passages preceding a

[4] Lord, *The Singer of Tales*, p. 78.
[5] Boris Kremenliev, *Bulgarian-Macedonian Folk Music* (Berkeley and Los Angeles: University of California Press, 1952), p. 78.

song, a practice common also in the Yugoslav epics), or of imitating instrumental passages.

Greek folk music, like that of some other Balkan countries, seems to be a combination of archaic and more recent melodies and contains a great diversity of styles. It is possible to find traces of the ancient Greek modes, and many Greek songs fit perfectly into the system of the diatonic modes. Many other songs, however, are more chromatic. Perhaps the combination of these two concepts—diatonic modes with small, chromatic steps—is responsible for the existence of heptatonic scales that have four minor seconds, such as the so-called Gypsy scale: C-D-E flat-F sharp-G-A flat-B. In most ways, however, Greek folk music seems to show the influences of centuries of Turkish and Muslim occupation. What remains of the ancient Greek traits seems best preserved in Asia Minor and the islands of the Aegean.

Polish folk music is quite different from that of the Balkans and is quite distinctive, but in some ways it is close to that of Russia, while in others it is obviously related to the music of Western neighbors, the Czechs and the Germans. It is also similar to the folk song style of two Slavic-speaking peoples, the Wends and the Jorbs, who lived in Eastern Germany, first as a numerous group and, by the nineteenth century, as a small minority, eventually becoming completely absorbed by the Germans. The folk songs of these peoples were collected in the middle of the nineteenth century; they form something of a link between the German and Polish styles.

The oldest layer of Polish songs is pentatonic, but the majority make use of seven-tone scales, which can be classed as church modes. Those modes similar to the modern minor mode, with lowered sixth and seventh or lowered third, are the most common; that is true also of Russian folk music. But both Poland and Russia also have many songs in major. In contrast to Russia, Poland has little polyphonic folk music and what part-singing there is seems to be of recent origin and emphasizes parallel thirds. The range of the songs is relatively small. A peculiarity of the singing style—typical perhaps of many and varied peculiarities of singing through Europe that never seem to appear in the printed collections of folk songs—is the practice of holding the final note of a song for several seconds, or of trailing off with a downward glissando.

MUSICAL INSTRUMENTS

Perhaps the most characteristic feature of East European folk music is its wealth of instruments and instrumental music. There are far too many instrument types to enumerate or describe, so again we must be content with a sampling. Instruments may serve as clues to the musical past of a nation or region. For example, the association between ancient Greek and modern Near Eastern and Slavic cultures is evident in their use of similar instruments. The ancient Greek *aulos* was a reed instrument with two tubes; similar instruments are today found among the Persians, Arabs, Turks, and Southern Slavs, and in India and Central Asia. In Yugoslavia, an instrument of this type is the *dvojnice* which is, in effect, a double recorder or plugged flute. The right-hand tube has, typically, four or five finger holes and is used for playing simple, embellished melodies; the left-hand side has three or four holes and is normally used to play an accompanying drone. Sometimes the two pipes are played in unison.

The Czechs, Slovaks, and Hungarians all have a large number of instruments. One of the most widely used is the bagpipe, which (perhaps to the surprise of some) is by no means limited to the British Isles; on the contrary, it is found throughout Europe and parts of Asia, and evidently it was brought to Scotland from the East. The kinds of bagpipes found in various countries differ, of course, from the very simple kinds found among the semiliterate tribes in Russia (such as the Cheremis) to the beautifully fashioned and sonorous instruments with three and four pipes found in Western Europe. In Scottish and Irish piping, the tunes are most frequently unrelated to the vocal music, and complex compositional forms, such as *Pibroch*—a kind of theme with variations—make up the repertory. In Eastern Europe, however, much of the bagpipe music consists of the same tunes as are used in vocal music, and some Hungarian folk songs, for instance, appear—with richer ornamentation—in the bagpipe repertory.

In Czechoslovakia and Hungary we also find many instruments related to those of other areas; for example, the Hungarian Csimbalom, a large, hammered ducimer; many kinds of flutes; the ordinary violin, especially prominent in Bohemia; and the accordion.

Folk music instruments seem to be especially numerous in Poland. Many forms of several basic types—flutes, fiddles, bagpipes—exist, each with regional variants. For example, among the stringed instruments, there is a one-stringed *diable skrzypce* (devil's fiddle); a musical bow with three strings; several types of *gensle* (fiddles in various shapes with four and five strings, some held on the knee, some under the chin); the *suka,* with four strings tuned in fifths; the *mazanka,* a small fiddle with three strings tuned in fifths; and the *maryna,* a very large fiddle, also with three strings tuned in fifths, a form of the medieval Western European *tromba marina.*

Yugoslav double recorder.

Cheremis bagpipe.

Perhaps because of the proliferation of instruments, Polish folk music is dominated by instrumental tunes, most of it used, of course, for dancing. There is an immense number of dance types, each with regional provenience. Some of these have been taken over into art music by composers such as Chopin—the polonaise, the mazurka, the polka, the krakowiak. Typically, the Polish dances are quick, and the majority use triple meter.

While many Eastern European peoples have instruments that are derived from art music, or closely related to it, one finds pockets in which the instruments closely resemble some of those in the world's simpler cultures. This is the case among the Cheremis of Eastern European Russia, where we find long, wooden trumpets without finger holes, simple bagpipes and flutes, horns made of bark, a one-string fiddle, a simple drum, and whistles made of fired clay.

POLYPHONY:
THE SLAVIC COUNTRIES AND THE CAUCASUS

Polyphony is one type of music that characterizes all of Eastern Europe. It seems to exist everywhere except among the Finno-Ugric and Turkic peoples; its development has been greatest in Russia and the Caucasus. The existence among the Georgians of polyphonic songs similar to the *organa* of medieval Europe has long tantalized the historian of Western art music, who can hardly assume that the Caucasus could have had an influence on Western European practices and who finds the East too remote to have received stimuli of such a specific nature from the medieval West, but who also believes that the two forms are too similar to have been invented independently twice. This is one of the riddles of historical ethnomusicology that may never be solved. The existence of organum-like folk music in Iceland and of other polyphonic types in Spain, Italy, and elsewhere (sporadically) indicates a possible solution: that polyphonic singing was once widespread in folk practice but receded to the marginal areas of Europe. Example 5-7 is a song of the Gurians, a tribe in the Caucasus, in three voices. The solo phrase at the beginning is typical also of Russian and Ukrainian polyphony. The first part of the song makes liberal, though not consistent, use of parallel triads. The second part also uses the principle of the drone, above which parallel thirds appear.

The role of Eastern (Orthodox) Church music in the development of this kind of polyphony may have been considerable. Polyphony was

EXAMPLE 5-7. Gurian polyphonic folk song, from Robert Lach, *Gesänge russischer Kriegsgesangener* Band 3, 1. Abt. (Wien: Wiener Akademie der Wissenschaften, 55. Mitteilung der Phonogrammarchivs Kommission, 1928), p. 108.

officially adopted by the Eastern Church in the seventeenth century, and its style was strongly influenced by Western European polyphony, with its absence of parallel fifths or triads. Russian folk polyphony must have felt the impact of this polyphonic singing in the churches, for while there are occasional parallel fifths and fourths, the tendency is to have four voices which sing harmony largely in the Western tradition. In Russia and the Ukraine, the practice of polyphonic singing is extremely important. Singing is typically a group activity, except in the case of narrative poetry, and even in the 1950s we hear of young people in Russian cities walking in groups and singing informally. The polyphonic songs are traditional, but some improvisation in the lower parts seems to be acceptable. In the

Russian songs, the upper voice is definitely the melody; but in the Ukrainian ones, the two or three voices seem to be roughly equal in importance. Parenthetically, we should point out the rather unusual developments in Russian folk music since World War I. The Soviet government has attempted to preserve the folk heritage not only of the Russians but also of some of the many minority populations in the Soviet Union, at the same time making their songs servants of the communist ideology. The result is a large body of folk song in the traditional musical styles—although the traits of Russian songs per se have to an extent penetrated the domain of some of the minority groups—with words of recent origin, often mentioning the leaders of the Soviet Union and the communist ideology.

The Cossacks of the Don River basin (who have produced the famous professional Don Cossack choruses) have developed the art of polyphonic singing to especially great heights; evidently even the epic *byliny* were sometimes sung by them in chorus. Another area of Russia in which polyphony flourishes is the North, especially the area around the monastery of Pečory. The Ukrainians also have a polyphonic style of great interest; Example 5-8 is typical of those Ukrainian songs which make use of parallel fifths. The polyphony of the Eastern Slavs, while

EXAMPLE 5-8. Ukrainian polyphonic song from Poltava, collected by Ossyp and Roman Rosdolsky, transcribed by Bruno Nettl.

essentially relying on parallel movement, does not follow this principle throughout. There is occasional oblique and contrary motion, use of the drone and even of imitation. Nor does the interval between the voices remain constant in one song. Example 5-8 contains parallel thirds as well as parallel fifths, with an occasional fourth and seventh. The beginning by a soloist is typical, and the choral parts may be doubled at the octave when both men and women sing. Tonality, in the case of the parallel fifths, may be difficult to identify, for each voice retains its own distinct tonality in order to preserve strict parallelism. But a common closing formula that establishes the final tonality proceeds from a third or triad built on the second degree of the scale to an octave on the tonic.

As we move westward, polyphony decreases in prominence, and the vertical intervals become smaller. Poles, Czechs, and Slovaks use parallel thirds (and occasionally sixths), perhaps under the influence of the Alpine style with its emphasis on triadic harmony and melody. In the Balkans we also find vertical seconds and, occasionally, parallel seconds.

In Yugoslavia, there are also various types of polyphony, the most distinctive emphasizing major and minor seconds not only as passing intervals but as the main supports of polyphonic structure. For example, there are vertical and even parallel seconds in the type of singing called "Ojkanie," whose melodies are sometimes similar to the melodic lines of the epics. The members of the Balkan folk cultures evidently do not consider the parallel seconds complex or difficult to perform, for in Bulgaria even children's songs may contain them.

Although polyphony is not common in the Baltic area, it does occur in some interesting forms also using vertical seconds. Example 5-9 is a Lithuanian round, sung by three groups, in which only two tones are sung simultaneously. The reason is that one of the three groups is always resting. Thus, the tune, consisting of phrases A and B and the rest, X, has the following form when sung as a round:

Voice 1	A B X A B X
Voice 2	A B X A B
Voice 3	A B X A.

Our examples have shown that Eastern Europe possesses one of the richest traditions of folk music. Variety and regional diversity are tremendous, but if we had to divide the area into geographic subdivisions with some stylistic homogeneity, it would have to be into four groups: (1) the Western Slavs—Czechs, Slovaks, Poles—who tend to show Western European characteristics and the influences of Western art music; (2) the Russians, Ukrainians, and Caucasians, whose main characteristic is highly developed polyphony; (3) the Balkan peoples, with music of small intervals and a strong influence of the Near East; and (4) the Hungarians and other Finno-Ugric peoples who, in spite of their isolation from each other, have retained some elements of their common heritage, such as the prominence of the pentatonic scale without half tones and the practice of transposing phrases as an essential part of song structure.

EXAMPLE 5-9. Lithuanian round in three parts, from pamphlet accompanying the recording *Lithuanian Folk Song in the United States* (New York: Folkways Records P 1009), pp. 4–5.

BIBLIOGRAPHY AND DISCOGRAPHY

The folk music of some of the Western nations in Eastern Europe is a field that was thoroughly studied by Béla Bartók and Zoltán Kodály, and their publications are to be recommended, among them the following. Bartók's *Slovenske ľudovne piesne* (Bratislava: Slovakian Academy of Sciences, 1959–) is a monumental collection of Slovak folk song which also shows Bartók's method of classifying the songs. Zoltán Kodály, *Folk Music of Hungary* (London: Barrie and Rockliff, 1960) is an important discussion. Bartók's *Melodien der rumänischen Colinde* (Vienna: Universal Edition, 1935) includes the melodies of hundreds of Rumanian Christmas carols.

Among the many good readings on Yugoslav folk music, we suggest Bartók and Albert B. Lord, *Serbo-Croatian Folk Songs* (New York: Columbia University Press, 1951); Albert B. Lord, "Yugoslav Epic Folk Poetry," *J-IFMC*, III (1951), 57–61 and *The Singer of Tales* (New York: Athenaeum, 1965); and George Herzog, "The Music of Yugoslav Heroic Epic Folk Poetry," *J-IFMC*, III (1951), 62–64. Two important discussions of Greek folk music are Solon Michaelides, *The Neohellenic Folk-Music* (Limassol, Cyprus: Nicosia, 1948) and Rodney Gallop, "Folksongs of Modern Greece," *Musical Quarterly*, XXI (1935), 89–98. A detailed discussion of one Balkan style is Boris Kremenliev, *Bulgarian-Macedonian Folk Music* (Berkeley: University of California Press, 1952). *Treasured Polish Songs with English Translations*, published by Polanie Club, selected by Josepha K. Contoski (Minneapolis: Polanie, 1953), is a collection for practical use, as is Rose Rubin and Michael Stillman, *A Russian Song Book* (New York: Random House, 1962). Polyphonic Russian songs are collected in A. Listopadov, *Pesni Donskikh Kazakov* (Moscow: Musgys, 1949–). Aspects of Caucasian folk music are discussed in Victor Belaiev, "Folk Music of Georgia," *Musical Quarterly*, XIX (1933), 417–33. The music of one special ethnic group in the USSR is presented in Bruno Nettl, *Cheremis Musical Styles* (Bloomington: Indiana University Press, 1960).

The following records give samplings of Eastern European folk music: *Czech, Slovak and Moravian Folk Songs*, Monitor MF 389; *Czech Songs and Dances*, Apon 2473; *Folk Music of Hungary*, collected under the auspices of Béla Bartók, Folkways P 1000; *Folk Music of Yugoslavia*, Folkways 4434; *Folk Music of Rumania*, collected by Béla Bartók, Folkways 419; *Folk Dances of Greece*, Folkways FE 4467; *Folk Music of Greece*, Folkways FE 4454; *Polish Folk Songs and Dances*, Folkways FP 848; and *Russian Folk Songs*, Vanguard VRS 9023, a recording performed by professional interpreters.

SIX

FRANCE, ITALY,
AND THE IBERIAN PENINSULA

The area comprising France, Italy, Spain, and Portugal is distinguished by its particularly long and close association with art music. This is especially true of France and Italy, the nations which, since the Middle Ages, have perhaps more consistently than any others had a tradition of urban civilization, of learned courts and monasteries, and of the trappings of art music such as notation and written theory. It has often been thought that these countries, as a result, now have little folk music except for a residue of earlier art music which has somehow trickled down to the rural communities. Indeed, certain song and dance types now part of folklore turn out to have originated in the art music tradition of the Middle Ages; for that matter, this art music tradition (for example, that of the Troubadours and Trouvères) certainly had more in common with folk traditions than did later art music traditions in Europe, such as the symphony orchestras of the nineteenth century and their music. Some of the forms of contemporary folk music, such as that of the French *branle* in Example 6-1, are pointedly similar to forms found in medieval instrumental music—in this case the *stantipes*, which also consists of a series of repeated musical lines with first and second endings. Whether this form originated in folk or art music, it is obviously an example of the close relationship between the two traditions. But recently, folklorists have also uncovered enclaves in which folk music seems to have developed with much less influence from the cities, and styles which appear to have grown with an amazing degree of independence.

FRENCH FOLK MUSIC AND ITS TIES
TO ART MUSIC OF THE PAST

In France, the main areas preserving old traditions are in the South, near the Pyrenees, and Brittany—relatively isolated regions, as one might expect. On the whole, the French folk songs have the same kinds of functions and uses as those in England, Germany, and the Low Countries. Ballads are not quite so numerous, nor are songs involving religion, while lyrical love songs, humorous songs, and dance music are among the most prominent types.

A large number of dances—whether they were used in the peasant culture, in the towns, or at the courts we don't always know—are described in Thoinot Arbeau's *Orchésographie* (1589); and a number of these dances are still alive in folklore today. Notable among them is the above-mentioned *branle,* performed either as a round dance or by two lines of dancers facing each other, in moderately quick duple meter.

Example 6-1 is a *branle* performed on a hurdy-gurdy. The tune exhibits some interesting characteristics. It is in straight duple meter. (Most French folk music is in duple or triple meter, with little evidence of the parlando-rubato style in either instrumental or vocal music.) The tune is heptatonic and, if it made use of the note A, could be considered as alternating between the major and Lydian modes. It contains a tritonic tetrachord (e.g., C-D-E-F♯), which is also common in several styles of instrumental folk music, particularly in the Alps, and which composers of art music have sometimes consciously introduced to impart a folk flavor.

The form of this piece is related not only to Western European medieval forms, but also to instrumental folk music forms found throughout Europe, even as far away as the Cheremis in interior Russia.

EXAMPLE 6-1. Excerpt from "Branle carré," French instrumental piece, played on the hurdy-gurdy. Transcribed by the author from the recording, *Folk Music of France*, edited by Paul Arma, with introduction and notes on the recordings by Paul Arma (New York: Ethnic Folkways Library P 414, 1951), Side A, Band 1.

The hurdy-gurdy performing Example 6-1 is not to be confused with the barrel organ also known by that name, for it is a stringed instrument. It has a number of strings, all but one of which are used only as drones. Instead of fingering the instrument, the player uses a kind of keyboard with mechanical stops which shorten the melody string. And instead of a bow, a rosined wheel is cranked; this touches all of the strings and automatically produces a melody with drone accompaniment. The unbroken character of the music gives it a bagpipe-like effect. The hurdy-gurdy is known in France as the *vielle,* but this should not be confused with the simple medieval fiddle also known by that name. Indeed, known by a Latin name, *organistrum,* the hurdy-gurdy was important in the Middle Ages, and was evidently used (probably in a somewhat larger form, played by two men) in churches. It was evidently once much more widespread in Europe, and variants of it appear in corners of the continent as, for example, in Sweden, whose *Nyckelharpa* is almost identical with the French hurdy-gurdy except that it is played with a bow instead of a wheel.

The importance of melodies accompanied by drones is remarkable in European folk music, perhaps sufficiently so to make this one of the special characteristics of Europe. However, the drone is of great importance in Middle and Near Eastern music as well. A number of other-

French hurdy-gurdy (eighteenth century).

wise unrelated instruments seem fashioned especially for use as drones. Besides the hurdy-gurdy there is, of course, the bagpipe (which, known as *cornemuse,* is common in France and has evidently been popular there for centuries, as is attested to by the many pieces entitled "Musette" in seventeenth- and eighteenth-century art music). The double flutes or clarinets of the Balkans, such as the Yugoslav *dvojnice,* use one pipe for melody, the other for drone. The dulcimer is frequently used in similar fashion. But even in the music of instruments that because of their structure are not especially suited to drones, the drone principle is often present. Thus Anglo-American fiddle players and the performers on the Norwegian Hardanger fiddle often strike open strings in addition to the melody tones, producing a kind of interrupted drone effect. And the chordal accompaniment on instruments such as the banjo and the guitar frequently revolves around a single chord, which gives an effect related to the drone.

In spite of regional diversity and even though archaic styles of French music exist in isolated pockets, the predominant style of French folk music shows the powerful impact that art music through the centuries must have had. The typical tunes are isometric, they have major or (much less commonly) melodic minor tonality, they are monophonic or accompanied by chord or drones, and they move briskly in strophic forms. Singing is with relaxed voice and with little ornamentation. The fact that some of the French forms can be related, whether through the etymology of their names or through their structure, to some of the genres of music (such as the dances) of the Renaissance and Middle Ages should prove to us the close contact that exists between art and folk music. In the last three or four centuries, this relationship can also be shown in the diffusion of the quadrille and its relative, the square dance. This type of dance evidently originated in France some time before the eighteenth century and was a sort of transition between round and couple dances. It became a dance popular in the cities and at the courts, had a period of being stately and dignified, and then was again accelerated. In the nineteenth century it gradually declined as a dance of city folk but found its way again into rural folk culture, eventually becoming the typical folk dance of the English-speaking world. Similarly, remnants of medieval forms of troubadour song seem to have found their way into contemporary folk culture. Thus Carlos Vega[1] believes that he has found variants of medieval troubadour melodies from Provence in Argentine folk tradition.

---

[1] Carlos Vega, in a paper read at the First Inter-American Conference on Musicology, Washington, D.C., May, 1963.

ITALIAN FOLK MUSIC—
THE ANCIENT AND THE MODERN

For several decades in the twentieth century it was widely believed that Italy had no folk music, that the country had been in the grip
of musical sophisticates for so long that no folk heritage with its characteristic traits—oral tradition, communal re-creation, and the like—still
remained. In the 1950s, however, through the collecting efforts of several
scholars including Diego Carpitella and Alan Lomax, a great treasure of
folksongs quite different from art music and exhibiting great variety of
style and forms was uncovered. Carpitella[2] believes that a rather sharp
division exists between an ancient style, which is found largely in
lullabies, work songs, and funeral laments, and a modern style, found
largely in lyrical songs. The ancient style is characterized by the church
modes and, occasionally, by scales with five and fewer tones. The later
style (which evidently really did come about through the growth of art
music) is characterized by the use of major and of harmonic and melodic
minor scales, as well as by the use of harmonic accompaniment and of
melodies constructed on a latent harmonic background. The ancient style
is found mainly in those regions of Italy which have remained relatively
undeveloped and unmodernized, and which, even after 1950, had a
noticeably lower standard of living than did the rest of the nation; these
regions are the mountains of South and Central Italy, and the islands of
Sicily and Sardinia.

     Among the most interesting finds of the recent upsurge in ethno-
musicological research in Italy is a rich tradition of polyphony. Among
the simpler instances is Example 6-2, a kind of duet recitative. A beginning by a soloist who is joined by a second voice is typical of this
style, though not found in this example (see Example 5-8 for a Ukranian
example of this feature which is found in many European countries and
in Africa). In Example 6-2, the movement is largely in parallel thirds,
which is a feature also common in Italian popular and light classical
music. Of special interest is the divergence of the two voices from
unison to fifth in the second half of the first line, the parallel fifths in the
middle, and the ending on a unison: these are reminiscent of medieval
organum.

     A characteristic of some of the more complex Italian polyphony is
the alternation of melodic movement among the voices. While one voice

[2] Diego Carpitella, "Folk Music: Italy," Grove's Dictionary of Music and
Musicians, 5th ed. (New York: St. Martin's Press, 1960), X, 137.

EXAMPLE 6-2. Italian polyphonic folk song, from Alberto Favara, *Corpus di Musiche Siciliane* (Palermo: Accademia de Scienze, Lettere e Arti, 1957), vol. 1, 225.

Mas - sa - ru Ma - ri - a - nu, mi vog - ghiu spi - a - ghè,

Se suo ch'a vi 'na fig - ghia, se'a vu - li— ma - ri - è.

sings a bit of melody, the other one is sustained; in the next phrase, the previously sustained voice becomes the carrier of the melody, and so on in alternation. The use of different kinds of rhythmic structure in each voice is also typical; one voice may carry the main tune, another may sing sustained notes supplying harmony, while a third may sing a rapid rhythmic figure with meaningless syllables on one tone perhaps imitating a drumbeat. Polyphonic singing is found in various kinds of Italian song—shepherds' songs, songs of dock workers and sailors. Some of the polyphony makes use of instruments as well as of voices; in such cases the singers are often accompanied by instruments that can produce a drone, bagpipes, a small organ, or the *launeddas*, which is discussed below.

The influence of cultures outside Italy on Italian polyphony may explain some of the regional differences. The north of Italy, which is dominated by the more modern style of folk song and by singing in parallel thirds and sixths, has had close contact with the Alpine musical cultures with their love of triadic structures. The South has had less contact with Europe and has preserved older forms. Influences from Africa and the Near East can perhaps also be felt in the South. According to Carpitella,[3] a type of song sung in the tunny-fishery areas near North Africa is characterized by the kind of call-and-response patterns common also in Black African music and found sometimes in North Africa as well. If he is correct in his belief that this song type actually came from Africa, he has come upon an interesting early example of the kind of influence on Western music that African music has come to exercise so strongly in the last two centuries, for it is precisely this call-and-response pattern which has been one of the cornerstones of the various Afro-American styles in folk and popular music.

The instruments most evident in Italian folk music are those which

[3] Carpitella, "Folk Music: Italy," p. 140.

have been taken over from the cultivated tradition: violin, guitar, mandolin, clarinet, accordion. But there are also much older instruments, some of which seem to have remained relatively unchanged since classical times, in the more isolated parts of the nation: various percussion instruments (clappers, rattles), conch trumpets, the Jew's harp, panpipes, simple bagpipes with up to three drone pipes, recorder-like plugged flutes, reed pipes, and ocarinas made of fired clay. One of the most intriguing, found mainly in Sardinia, is the *launeddas*, which consists of three reed pipes. The longest and shortest of these are fastened together and held in the left hand (these are called *tumbu* and *mancosedda*, respectively); the middle-sized one, *mancosa*, is held in the right hand. The *launeddas* is used for polyphonic music of the drone type, similar to that played on the Yugoslav *dvojnice*. One of the problems faced by the player is the need to keep blowing without pausing for breath; it is solved by a technique of blowing air out of the mouth while inhaling with the nose, called "circular breathing," also found in distant parts of the world such as Australia, whose aboriginal *didjeridu* players use the same technique. A boy learning to play the *launeddas* learns circular breathing, as have Mediterranean musicians since Egyptian antiquity, by blowing through a straw into a pail of water. The teacher can see whether the pupil is succeeding by observing the bubbles in the water.

The close relationship between Italian folk and art music during the past few centuries is also illustrated by the sources of the words of some of the songs. In Central Italy, a type of song (or perhaps a sequence of songs) known as *maggio* is sung during May. Its words are frequently taken from the works of famous poets, Ariosto, Tasso, Dante, even Classical poets such as Virgil and Ovid. Its structure is evidently related to some of the earliest manifestations of opera around 1600. The form of the *maggio* consists of a choral or instrumental introduction, recitatives, and instrumental or choral interludes which recur, functioning rather like refrains or *ritornellos* (instrumental refrain-like pieces in early opera). In thematic content the various parts of a *maggio* are not necessarily related; the recitative may be in the modal style of ancient Italian folk music, the choral section may have some features found in the part-songs of Renaissance Italian art music, and the instrumental sections may be popular dances such as polkas or tarantellas.

THE BASQUES—EUROPE'S OLDEST FOLK CULTURE?

Legend has it that the Basques are the oldest people in Europe, but they seem to have retained little of their ancient heritage of folklore.

On the contrary, they seem to have partaken of the traditions of Northern Spain and Southwestern France, and their culture is a repository of archaic forms of that region, both French and Spanish. For example, young Basque men have a custom, also found in other parts of Europe, of going from house to house on the last Saturday of January, wishing the inhabitants good health and a good life, and singing songs to them. Elsewhere, this may be done before Christmas and even at Easter, and the singers may be young boys and girls. Another custom shared by the Basques with some other areas of Europe is the singing of "rough music" around the house of people who have engaged in some presumably immoral act.[4] An adulterous couple, an old man who marries a young girl, or a wife who beats her husband may be visited by a group who use pots, pans, cowbells as rhythmic accompaniment to improvised, insulting songs. In Germany and other countries, similar "music" is performed on a wedding night or on the night before a wedding.

We know very little about the ways in which European folk songs were composed. This applies to words as well as music, although we realize that some of the material is composed by sophisticated song writers and then passed into oral tradition. Among the Basques, improvisation is particularly important; it is even thought that most of the Basque folk songs originated on the spur of the moment. Evidently the Basque language (which is said to be so difficult that not even the devil can learn it) lends itself easily to improvisatory riming. Many improvised poems of the Basques have a humorous or satirical character and deal with recent events of village interest, politics, and the church. Many are anticlerical in sentiment. Evidently the improvised text was sung to a traditional tune, and most Basque men participated in the practice of improvising words. A few of them gained preeminence, and some of their songs still carry their names after years and decades. This is one of the few examples in a folk culture of a composer's being recognized and associated with works years after he composed them. The most famous Basque improviser, or *kolaris*, was known as Etchahoun and was born in the valley of Soule in 1786.

Like a large proportion of the Spanish and French songs, Basque songs are frequently in 6/8 meter and make use of the church modes; the latter is true of the ballad in Example 6-3, which is Dorian. More complex meters, such as 5/8, are also common, as are songs without ascertainable metric structure. The most famous illustration of quintuple meter in Basque folk music is the *zortziko*, a type of melody used mainly for dance tunes. The forms of Basque songs consist of from four to six

[4] Rodney Gallop, "Basque Songs from Soule," *Musical Quarterly* XXII (1936), 461.

EXAMPLE 6-3. French singing game, "Yan petit," from Violet Alford, "Dance and Song in Two Pyrenean Valleys," *Musical Quarterly* XVII (1931), 253.

phrases, interrelated in various ways. Lullabies frequently consist of varied repetitions of a single musical line (A¹ A² A³ . . .), while love songs and dance songs have forms such as ABCC, ABCB, AABCD, AABB, and AABCDC.

Instrumental folk music among the Basques features a three-holed flute (*chirula*) and the *ttun-ttun*, an instrument with six strings, similar to the dulcimer but held in the arm. The same player uses both instruments, accompanying the tunes of the *chirula* with a drone on the *ttun-ttun*. Instrumental music is used in dances and for "mascaradas," processions accompanied by dances performed at carnival time. This custom is one found throughout Europe, but it is preserved in very elaborate form in the Basque country. Ceremonial dances are performed by certain stock characters—the hobby horse, which is surely a remnant of the tournaments of the Middle Ages, the fool, the sweeper, and the lord and the lady. Similar practices are found among the Negroes of Uruguay, where the *candombe*, interestingly enough, features a broommaker analogous to our "sweeper" (see Chapter Nine). There is a sword dance which, like those of France, Spain, and England, was probably originally a representation of the century-long struggle between Christians and Moors. There is also an acrobatic dance in which dancers leap and turn in complicated steps around and over a tumbler of wine without upsetting it. Basque instrumental music is similar in style to the songs, but the song tunes themselves do not normally seem to be used by the instrumentalists.

The Basques have also retained a form of the medieval mystery play, called *Pastorales*. These folk plays make use of interpolated songs which appear at particularly important points in the plot. The themes of the *Pastorales* are biblical or legendary and frequently hark back to the battles of Christians against Moors in the Iberian peninsula. No matter what the plot, the characters are divided into Moors or Turks dressed in red costumes, and Christians, in blue. The battles for national or cultural survival in Spain and France have evidently had just as great an impact on the development of folklore as have the struggles against the Turks in Yugoslavia, with its epic tradition, or as did the fights between Christian and Tartar in Russia.

SPAIN AND PORTUGAL—
A REGION OF GREAT DIVERSITY

There is great variety in the folk music of the Hispanic peninsula. Particularly, there is a great difference between the North, which is closely related to France and Italy, and the South, which bears much resemblance to North Africa and the Middle East, and, thus, also to the Balkan peninsula (due to the importance of Arabic influences on Spanish culture throughout the Middle Ages and to a smaller degree ever since). Beyond this major difference, each area has its own folk music repertory and styles. Nevertheless, there is also considerable unity: few listeners would fail, after some experience, to recognize a Spanish folk melody. Of course, the many kinds of folk songs have also spread to Latin America, where together with Afro-American and, to a smaller degree, American Indian elements, they form the basis of a huge wealth of folklore.

It is difficult to identify and separate those traits which make Spanish or Portuguese folk music sound Hispanic. Triple meter abounds: slow triple meter, usually noted as 3/4, and quicker, compound meters such as 6/8 and 9/8 are very common. But songs in duple meter are also found, as are some in quintuple. There is also a great deal of recitative-like singing, without metric structure, and with considerable ornamentation, similar to types of song found in the Eastern Mediterranean. Scales tend to be diatonic and the tonality major, natural minor, or characterized by the

use of augmented and minor seconds, thus:
Intervals are small, and large leaps are rare, as with the anhemitonic
pentatonic scales so common in England and Eastern Europe. The forms
of the songs are often strophic, like those of Italy and France but in
many cases somewhat less regular as far as the relative length of the
lines is concerned. But other kinds of formal organization, less tight and
less standardized, are also found. There is a good deal of polyphonic
singing, mainly in parallel thirds or sixths or with the accompaniment of
a drone.

The influence of Arabic music on Spanish folk song seems to have
been considerable, which is not surprising when we remember the
long period of Arab rule over the peninsula (ninth through fifteenth
centuries). Specific tunes from the Arabic tradition do not seem to have
remained in any large numbers, however. The scales with augmented
seconds may have been introduced by the Arabs, or they may have developed as a result of Arabic influence, since such intervals are a typical
feature of much Arabic music. The great amount of ornamentation found
in some of the melodies that have no metric structure may also ultimately
be of Near Eastern origin, for singing of a related sort is found in some
Arabic music of today. Example 6-4 is such a melody from Santander.

Perhaps a more important feature common to both Spanish and
Arabic music is the manner of singing, which is rather tense, nasal,
and harsh-sounding. Again, similarities to the Balkan styles of singing
may be noted. Ornaments of a modest sort are found in many songs; the
mordent and the turn are particularly common. The tempo of Spanish
songs may be rapid, vigorous, and downright driving, or, on the other
hand, slow and stately.

Among the many kinds of song in Spain and Portugal we should
mention the *copla,* which is a short, lyrical type, usually with only one
stanza. Ballads are also found in Spain; they deal, frequently, with the
heroism of medieval warriors such as Charlemagne and El Cid, and
their content has more in common with the epics of Eastern Europe than
with the old tragic ballads of Britain, impersonal as the latter usually are.
The arrangement of a group of ballads around a hero is rather like the
clustering of epic tales around a leader such as the Serbian Kraljevic
Marko (Prince Marko), and it has something in common with the cycle
of Robin Hood ballads, which were once sung throughout Great Britain.
Some of the themes of Spanish balladry are of wide provenience, however; the same stories have been found, on occasion, in French and
Scandinavian songs.

When one thinks of Spanish folk music one perhaps thinks
automatically of dancing, and, of course, there are many Spanish folk

EXAMPLE 6-4. Spanish folk song, from Kurt Schindler, *Folk Music and Poetry of Spain and Portugal* (New York: Hispanic Institute in the United States, 1941), song no. 530.

dance types: the *jota,* the *gitana,* the *seguidillas,* the *bolero,* the *fandango,* the *murciana,* and others too numerous to mention. Each district has its own version of the dance types of national provenience. The *jota,* a combination of song and dance, is one of the most interesting. In rapid triple meter, it is danced by a couple—originally it was probably a dance of courtship—whose complicated footwork and tricky castanet rhythms are especially fascinating.

The *flamenco* tradition of Andalusia in Southern Spain is perhaps the most widely known aspect of Spanish folk music. It is not typically Spanish, for it is particularly the music of the Spanish gypsies, although it probably did not originate with them but was simply taken over by them. The gypsies, who inhabit many countries of Southern and Eastern Europe, have a tradition of entertaining and, evidently, a talent for emphasizing and exaggerating the most characteristic elements of the folk music in each country in which they live (in addition to continuing their native tradition). Thus, for example, the Russian gypsies have developed a style out of the Russian folk tradition, and the Spanish gypsies have fashioned the *flamenco* style out of elements already present in Spain.

One type of *flamenco* music is the *cante hondo,* which means "deep" or "profound song." The words are frequently tragic, sometimes verses of complaint against injustices. The range of these songs rarely exceeds a sixth, and the structure is not strophic but consists of irregular repetitions and alternations of two or more phrases with variations. The singing is highly ornamented, non-metric, and contains occasional microtones. It is often accompanied by the guitar, which performs simple repetitive chord sequences in rapid triple meter and dominated by figures such as

♪ ♫♫ . The words of *flamenco* proper are usually erotic, and the dance is performed by a soloist or a couple, with the audience participating with encouraging shouts of *olé.*

In order to give the reader a somewhat more intimate insight into one aspect of Spanish folk music culture, let us consider briefly the performers on the *dulzaina* (*dulzaineros*) in the province of Léon, in Northwestern Spain.[5] The *dulzaina* is an oboe-like instrument that has evidently been widely used in the area for centuries, but is not necessarily known in all of its villages. In earlier times, the *dulzaina* was used by shepherds in order to help pass the time. It was also played in various social situations—dances, serenades, and spontaneous gatherings, such as feasts held after a hunt. Furthermore, it was also used on semi-religious occasions, such as the dances performed on Epiphany or certain

[5] The material on the *dulzaina* is based on field research carried out by Martha E. Davis, graduate student in anthropology at the University of Illinois.

saints' days, and it was even used as part of the liturgy, playing processionals and recessionals in church, and even parts of the mass. The *dulzaineros* were evidently professionals who performed without pay in their own villages, but were paid when asked to perform elsewhere. The *dulzainero* was frequently accompanied by singing (sometimes his function was to stimulate people to join in and to sing), and by a drummer (who was the junior partner of a rather stable combination), and sometimes by tambourines and castanets. There was usually one *dulzainero* per village, and, clearly, he occupied an important role in village life. Today, the instrument is used far less. Most of the *dulzaineros* are elderly men, some of them reluctant to play because their music is regarded as backward by more modern-minded villagers, and restricting their music to their own homes and to the late evenings. One reaction to the dwindling of *dulzaina* playing and the modernizing trend has been the establishment of *dulzaina* competitions with prizes. Shepherds no longer play the instrument, and in social gatherings it has been replaced by accordion and saxophone. Priests have forbidden its use in certain churches. But the instrument has not disappeared, having been adapted to new repertories such as popular songs from the cities, and having been changed to resemble, in appearance and sound, the modern clarinet.

Throughout these discussions of European folk music, we have pointed out the close relationship of this body of music with musics elsewhere. Despite the fact that European folk music turns out to be a rather homogeneous unit, contrasting markedly with the musics of other cultures such as China, India, Africa, and aboriginal America, those parts of Europe which are near other continents exhibit influences, moving in both directions, which testify to the mobility of music. Spanish folk music is perhaps the best example of this kind of mobility. The music of Spain has received much of its character from Asia, by way of North Africa; and it has, in turn, passed on this material to the Americas, where it was in turn combined with elements of yet other cultures, to form new and characteristic styles. At the same time, Spain and Portugal partake of the general character of European folk music through their similarity to the musics of France and Italy, the nations to whom they are historically and linguistically most closely related.

BIBLIOGRAPHY AND DISCOGRAPHY

An interesting collection of French folk song is Émile Barbillat and Laurian Touraine, *Chansons Populaires dans le Bas-Berri* (Paris: Gargaillou, 1930–1931, 5 vols.). The best discussion in English of French folk music is in the fifth edition of Grove's *Dictionary of Music and Musicians*, under "Folk Music" in the subdivision on France (by C. Marcel-Dubois). Rodney Gallop, "Basque Songs from Soule," *Musical Quarterly,* XXII (1936), 458–69, and Violet Alford, "Dance and Songs in Two Pyrenean Valleys," *Musical Quarterly,* XVII (1931), 248–58, are interesting readings on the area common to France and Spain. A large and comprehensive collection of Spanish and Portuguese music is Kurt Schindler, *Folk Music and Poetry of Spain and Portugal* (New York: Hispanic Institute, 1941). The best discussion, in English, of Italian folk music is in Grove's *Dictionary of Music and Musicians,* fifth edition, the supplement volume (1960)—not the section on Italian folk music in the body of the fifth edition. Alberto Favara, *Corpus di Musiche Popolari Siciliane* (Palermo: Accademia di scienze, lettere e arti, 1957, 2 vols.) is a comprehensive collection from Sicily. Discussion of one song type appears in Wolfgang Laade, "The Corsican Tribbiera, a Kind of Work Song," *Ethnomusicology,* VI (1962), 181–85.

For selections of French, Hispanic, and Italian folk music, the appropriate disks from the *Columbia World Library of Folk and Primitive Music* are especially useful. Also to be recommended are *Folk Music of France,* Folkways P 414; *Folk Music from Italy,* Folkways F 4220; *Songs and Dances of Spain,* Westminster WF 12001–5, with notes by Alan Lomax; *Flamenco Music of Andalusia,* Folkways 4437; and *Music of Portugal,* Folkways 4538 (2 disks).

SEVEN

MUSIC OF BLACK AFRICA

The music of Black Africa has been regarded as an essentially homogeneous mass, despite the many inhabitants and the large number of distinct cultures, and despite the many contacts that Africa has had, over the centuries, with peoples of other continents. It is true that hearing a few records of African music will probably give the listener a fairly good overview of the mainstream of the African styles. But it has become increasingly clear that the total picture of African music is a very complex one, that there is a large variety of sub-styles, that cultures vary greatly in the nature of their music, in its quantity and significance, and in the attitudes that people hold towards music. As in other chapters, we must here confine ourselves to a few examples of the kinds of things that are found, realizing that the world of African music is still largely unknown to scholars, and that generalizations can be made only with great caution.

We are considering the music of Africa, south of the Sahara only, in this volume. The area north of the Sahara and the Sahara itself have music which is very closely related to that of the Middle East and is thus discussed in another volume in this series, William P. Malm's *Music Cultures of the Pacific, the Near East, and Asia*. But there has, of course, been a great deal of exchange between the North Africans and the inhabitants of Black Africa. Instruments, such as harps and drums, have evidently been carried from one area to the other; similar formal types and certain techniques, such as responsorial singing, are held in common. There are some peoples, at the boundary between the two areas, who have music in both the distinctly Black African and the North African styles. On the other hand, while North African music has ties with the Middle East, the music of Black Africa has had, in the past two or three centuries, an enormous impact on the musical development of Europe and the Americas.

The part of Africa discussed here—and, for the sake of brevity, we will call it simply "Africa" from now on—is composed of (or was, before parts of it became thoroughly modernized) four culture areas, each of which has considerable homogeneity, and each of which contrasts in some rather specific ways with its neighbors. The western part of the very tip of Southern Africa is called the Khoi-San area; it is inhabited by the Bushmen and Hottentots. The Bushmen are a somewhat different group, racially, from Negroes, shorter and lighter skinned; the Hottentots are evidently the result of a racial mixture between Bushmen and Negroes. The Khoi-San area has a simple culture dependent mainly on nomadic gathering of food.

The eastern part of our Africa, from Ethiopia southward, is called the Eastern Cattle Area. Its cultures are complex and revolve about cattle, one of the main sustaining forces of life and also the symbol of wealth. Some of the tribes are warlike; some, such as the Masai and Watusi, are very tall and rule over neighboring tribes of smaller stature, living near them and maintaining a caste-like relationship.

The southern coast of the western extension of the continent, which includes Ghana, Nigeria, Ivory Coast, and Liberia, is known as the Guinea Coast. This area lacks cattle and is characterized by elaborate political organization which, before the imposition of European rule, gave rise to powerful kingdoms. Carved masks of great beauty are also typical here. The Congo area, north of the Khoi-San area and centered in the Congo republics, has to some extent a combination of Eastern Cattle and Guinea Coast traits. It includes a number of Pygmy and Negrito tribes who live in relative isolation in the jungle. The Congo area probably has the most highly developed visual art tradition in Africa.

A fifth area that properly belongs to sub-Saharan Africa consists of a strip immediately north of the Guinea Coast, and includes the northern sections of such nations as Ghana and Nigeria. Its cultures are related to those of the Guinea Coast and the Congo, but many of the peoples who inhabit it are Muslims.

There are several characteristics, found in a majority of African musical cultures, that give African music its distinctiveness. Several of them are discussed in some detail further on, but here is a brief listing: (1) Instruments are numerous; they are used individually, as accompaniment to singing, and in small ensembles. (2) There is a tendency to have at least two things going on at a time. Thus polyphony is widespread; polyrhythms performed by percussion ensembles are common; and even the players of simple instruments, such as the musical bow or the flute, may find ways, by manipulating the overtones produced by the bow, or by humming along with blowing, for example, to have two musical entities produced simultaneously. (3) The percussive sound is evidently an ideal; percussion instruments such as drums, xylophones, rattles, etc., are important, but even in the use of wind instruments that are played in groups, with each producing only one tone, the percussive principle seems to be present, and plucked string instruments greatly outnumber those played with a bow. (4) Variation of and improvisation upon short melodic motifs dominate melodic structure. (5) There is a close relationship between language and music. (6) Melodies are built of major seconds and minor thirds. (7) Even more than elsewhere, music is associated with dance. (8) Perhaps most significant, there is a tendency toward dualism: thus melodies often consist of two phrases; performance is often by a leader and a chorus; polyphony is usually structured so that there are two parts or two groups of vocalists or instruments; and in various other obvious or subtle ways, one can detect the essentially binary nature of this music.

However, almost the opposite of these characteristics is found in the northernmost part of sub-Saharan Africa, where Middle Eastern influences are strong. Thus solo performances, monophony, nonpercussive instruments, such as fiddles and oboes, and smaller intervals, such as minor seconds, are more prominent. Some peoples, such as the Hausa of northern Nigeria, have music in both the typical African and the Middle East-influenced styles.

THE USES OF MUSIC IN AFRICA

In Africa, music has many uses. It functions as accompaniment to all sorts of activities, but also for entertainment. Some of the general characteristics usually given for music in nonliterate societies do not appear strongly in Africa. For example, the idea that participation in music in a primitive society is quite general and that all persons participate equally cannot be accepted. In contrast to many tribes elsewhere, there are professional musicians who actually make their living from music, or who are regarded as trained specialists. There are so many instruments that it would be ridiculous to think that all members of a tribe could perform on all of them and know all of the tribe's music. But it cannot be denied that Africans, on the whole, do participate in musical life much more—and more actively, in singing, playing, composing, dancing—than do members of Western civilization.

In at least some of the African cultures, elaborate classification of types of musicians exists. According to Merriam,[1] the Basongye of the Congo have five classes of male musicians: (1) the *ngomba*, the professional instrumentalist; (2) the performer of slit drums; (3) the player of rattles and double-bells; (4) the song leader; and (5) the member of a singing group. These are listed here in the order of their prestige; only the first is a full-time musician, the second and third also receive some pay, while the lowest two classes are never paid. Despite this evidence of concern with the relative status of various kinds of musicians, the Basongye generally do not regard musicians highly; and in this they reflect a tendency found in the majority of the world's cultures. Rather, they regard musicians as being of low status. Musicians are said to be heavy drinkers, debtors, unreliable, impotent, adulterers, poor marriage risks, and they are the butt of many jokes. People do not want their children to become musicians, but the musicians are nevertheless tolerated because they are essential to the life of the whole group. The picture presented by Merriam appears to be roughly similar to that of some other African cultures.

Obviously, also, Africans think about music a good deal. For example, some tribes recognize many different types of songs and have elaborate terms for them. Thus, according to Merriam, the Bahutu of Ruanda-Burundi have at least twenty-four different types of social songs, including "those played by professional musicians for entertainment, songs for beer drinking, war homage to a chief, hunting, harvesting, and general work; songs sung at the birth of a child or to admonish erring members of the society, to recount a successful elephant hunt, to deride Europeans; songs of death, vulgar songs, and others."[2] These categories are separate from the other large group of ceremonial or religious songs. Some of these types are again sub-divided by the Bahutu, who, for example, distinguish among different kinds of songs associated with

---

[1] Alan P. Merriam, *The Anthropology of Music* (Evanston, Ill.: Northwestern University Press, 1969), pp. 129–30.

[2] Merriam, "African Music," in *Continuity and Change in African Cultures*, ed. William Bascom and Melville J. Herskovits (Chicago: University of Chicago Press, 1959), p. 50.

canoes: different songs are used when paddling against a strong current, when paddling with the current, and so forth.

Also of Ruanda-Burundi, the Watusi, whose lives center about their cattle, have many song types involving them: "songs in praise of cows, songs to indicate the importance of having cows, songs for taking cattle home in the evening . . . for drawing water for the cattle,"[3] and the like. There are special children's cattle songs, songs to praise the royal cattle, and songs that recount historical events in which cattle have played a part. There are two points to remember here: This classification of songs is one developed by the Africans themselves; and the music is a part of those activities which are most fundamental in the culture. In this sense, perhaps, music in African life can be said to have a greater or more important role than it does in Western civilization.

It would be useless to attempt to catalogue all the uses of music in Black African music. In many ways they parallel those of European folk music. Religious and ceremonial music is an ever-present category whose importance evidently increases as we move from complex to simpler cultures. The large amount of music for entertainment, such as the playing of xylophones at markets, is remarkable. Social songs, such as those mentioned above, are a larger category than in most folk and nonliterate societies. The use of music for political purposes of various sorts should be noted. Examples of the association of music with political strata and with the ruling individuals or classes abound. Among the Hausa of Nigeria, elaborate fanfares are played for ruling chiefs. The "royal drums" of the Watusi signal the appearance of the ruler in public. And among the Venda of South Africa we find an elaborate system (by no means unique in its general character but similar to systems found elsewhere in Africa) of classifying musical types in accordance with the level of political leadership permitted to sponsor it. Evidently in some of the African cultures it is easier to indicate discontent with employers or with the government if the discontent is sung than if it is spoken. We therefore find many songs expressing criticism of authority, but also songs composed especially to praise chiefs and wealthy men. Songs are used also to spread information on current events of interest and gossip, and to perpetuate knowledge, much in the way that broadside ballads functioned as newspapers in eighteenth-century England and America. Work songs—songs not only dealing with labor but also accompanying rhythmic work by groups and making it easier—are prominent in Africa. In the Western Congo, song-like passages appear in the litigations of clans and individuals who may argue about ownership of territory, wives, or honorific titles.

[3] Merriam, "African Music," p. 53.

INSTRUMENTS OF AFRICA

One of the characteristics of Negro Africa is its enormous variety of musical instruments. Far from being a land only of drums, as it is pictured by some early sources, it is an area in which varied instruments and instrumental music play a role equal to that of the voice and vocal music. There is in all areas a great deal of music for solo instruments, and there are instrumental ensemble groups consisting of unrelated instruments, or of several instruments of the same type. Also, accompanied singing is widespread.

The importance of rhythm in African music can be seen in the percussive quality of much of the instrumental sound. As we have noted, percussion instruments—drums, rattles, and melodic percussion instruments such as the xylophone—occupy a major role. Among the wind instruments, those in which each pipe performs only one note (panpipes or *hocket*-type performance on flutes or horns) are important. Among string instruments, those that are plucked are more prominent than the bowed ones. The percussive nature of much of the instrumental sound as well as the absence of the possibility of *legato* in the playing of most of the instruments is probably caused by the desire for strong rhythmic articulation.

It is impossible to describe or even to name all African instruments; but some of the most important ones are discussed briefly in the next few paragraphs. Among the idiophones (instruments whose bodies vibrate in order to produce sound), the xylophone is one of the most widespread. Consisting of anywhere from seven to twenty-five slabs of wood, it varies greatly in size. The largest ones lie on the ground, supported by small tree trunks; the smallest hang around the player's neck. In Central Africa, xylophones are frequently built with calabashes, gourds, or other hollow bodies attached to the slabs in order to add to the resonance. They are frequently played in groups; in parts of Central Africa, three players will entertain at a market together. In the Eastern part of Southern Africa, among the Chopi, orchestras of six and more xylophones of various sizes are used. This point is of great interest, since there is some evidence for the belief that xylophones were brought to Africa from Indonesia, perhaps a thousand years ago. The people of Madagascar speak Malayo-Polynesian languages which must have originated near Indonesia. And for centuries the Indonesians have had a very complex musical culture with instruments made of metal, of the xylophone type. It seems possible that the xylophone was brought to

Africa, or that the musical culture of Indonesia influenced the particular direction in which xylophones and xylophone playing developed in Africa. Xylophones of the simplest type—one or two slabs of wood which are struck—are found throughout the world, including indigenous Latin America; this has evidently given rise to an erroneous belief that the xylophone (or rather, its form with resonators, the marimba) came from Central America and was brought thence to Africa.

One instrument that apparently originated in Africa, and which is related to the xylophone, is the *sansa* or *mbira,* which is sometimes also called the "thumb piano" or "kaffir harp." Its provenience is largely East and Central Africa, and, except for some Negro cultures in the Americas, it is not found outside Africa. It consists of a small board or wooden box on which is nailed a bridge. Tied to this bridge are a number of "keys," made usually of iron pieces pounded flat, but occasionally of reeds. These are gently plucked by the thumb or the fingers to produce a soft, tinkling sound. The number of keys varies from eight to about thirty. Frequently a calabash resonator is attached to the instrument; sometimes beads, which produce a rattling percussive accompaniment, are also attached. The *sansa* is played as a solo instrument or in groups. It is frequently used to accompany singing, and in some African music of recent origin it is used to play an ostinato accompaniment not too different from the piano accompaniments of certain Western popular songs. The tuning of both xylophone and *sansa* varies greatly. The keys of the *sansa* may be tuned by moving them forward or backward in relationship to the bridge, or by adding some pitch or tar to them in order to increase their weight.

Other idiophones include rattles, bells, and the misnamed log drums. There are many types of rattles—pebbles enclosed in small woven containers (West Africa) and in antelope ears (the Hottentots); rattles made of fruits, nuts, reeds, or cocoons strung together (South Africa); and so on. Sometimes they are tied to the ankles of dancers. One characteristic of these idiophones is the importance evidently placed on distinctions in pitch. Rattles and bells (there are both metal and wooden bells) often appear in pairs, with one smaller than the other so that two pitches can be distinguished. This is also characteristic in the playing of the log drum idiophone, a hollowed log with one or two slits, which is most frequently used for signaling. Thus, while the rhythmic element seems to be pronounced in the melodic aspects of music and its instruments, we may also say that the melodic aspects of music are developed in that music and those instruments whose main function is rhythm.

There are several types of true drums, that is, drums with skin heads. The most common kinds have one head and are relatively tall; they are usually closed at the bottom. Two-headed drums and drums

West African xylophone with gourd resonators.

Sansa or mbira.

with an open end are also found. The drums are beaten with sticks, or with the hands, or both. Hand beating is characteristic, however, and the complex rhythms are often the results of intricate manipulation and alternation of fingers, thumb, and heel of the hand. Techniques somewhat similar to those of Africa are found in India, and there is a possibility that the rhythmic intricacies of India and Africa have a common origin. Typically drums are played in groups of three or more. They may stand on the ground, hang from a strap around the player's shoulder, be held in the player's arm or between his legs, or be sat upon when they are played.

The types of drums and of drumming may be intimately associated with different activities. Among the Yoruba of Nigeria, different types of drums are used for the various cults associated with the numerous gods in the Yoruba pantheon. For example, the *igbin* drums are upright drums with a single head, open-ended, with small wooden legs; *dundun* are kettle-drums with the skin stretched across a small bowl; *bata* drums are long truncated cones with two heads, one head being appreciably smaller than the other and producing a higher pitch; and there are several other types. Each type is used for one or several deities, and each deity has its distinctive rhythms, a practice carried over into parts of the Americas such as Haiti. Thus, as Bascom notes,[4] the *igbin* drums are sacred to *Orishanla* ("the great deity") and are played by members of his cult, among whom are albinos, hunchbacks, and cripples. *Bata* and *dundun* drums are played by professional drummers. *Dundun* are used for signaling—they are the "talking drums"—they are also used by the cult of *Egungun*, younger brother of the powerful *Shango* (the thunder god). *Bata* are sacred to the god *Shango* and his wife *Oya*, but may be played for other deities as well.

Several types of aerophones (wind instruments) are of great interest. Horns are common in various parts of Negro Africa. They are made of natural horn, wood, or ivory, and are used for music as well as signaling. They usually have no finger holes or valve mechanism, and only the open or natural tones can be played. In recent times, however, finger holes seem to have been introduced. One characteristic of African horns is the position of the mouthpiece or hole used for blowing, which is frequently on the side of the instrument rather than at the small end as is common in European horns. One use of horns that produce only one pitch is in the *hocket* technique, in which each horn plays only when its note is supposed to appear in the melody.

---

[4] William Bascom, notes accompanying the record, *Drums of the Yoruba of Nigeria*, Folkways P441.

West African ivory horn.

Flutes are also frequently without finger holes; they are some-times used for performance in the *hocket* technique in a fashion similar to horns. This is done particularly by Negro tribes of South Africa. En-sembles of flutes with finger holes are also found, as among the Mambuti pygmies of the Congo, who use as many as six flutes, each of which varies its own short ostinato figure. The flutes are most commonly true flutes rather than the plugged flutes like the recorder. Both end-blown and transverse flutes are found, the former being held vertically. Pan-pipes are also present in most of Black Africa, but little is known of the music that they produce.

Many instruments have very specific and restricted uses. Thus the *epudi*, a kind of ocarina used by the Basongye of Kasai, is associated with hunting. It accompanies hunters' songs before and after the hunt, and it is used as a signaling device during the hunt. It has one finger hole and produces two tones, about a major second apart. Its major use in sig-naling is for reproduction of the tones of the language in ways similar to drum and horn signaling techniques.[5]

Africa has developed a large number of chordophones, or string instruments. The simplest is the musical bow, which normally has only one string but sometimes produces fairly complex music. It is found through Black Africa, but evidently has more forms in Southeast Africa than elsewhere. It is shaped essentially like a hunting bow whose string is plucked or struck with a stick, and its sound is soft. Thus a resonator is almost always required. It may be attached to the end of the bow or to its middle. In the latter case, the string is usually stopped at the point at which the resonator is attached, so that in effect two strings, with con-trasting pitch, are used. If the resonator is not attached, the bow may be held against an inverted pot. A third way of producing resonance is for the player to hold the end of the bow in his mouth, which then acts as the resonator. If he changes the configuration of his mouth, different over-tones can be heard. The bow is used as a solo instrument as well as an accompaniment to song.

There has evidently been a development from the musical bow, through single-string fiddles and lutes, to more complex stringed instru-ments; the most important ones among African Negroes are zithers (with several strings stretched across a board of hollowed block), harps (usually with four to eight strings), and fiddles (with one to five strings). The shapes, arrangements, and tunings of these are almost innumerable. For example, the Ganda of Uganda tune their harps into five roughly equal intervals, each of about 240 cents (100 cents equal a tempered semitone)

---

[5] Alan P. Merriam, "The Epudi, a Basongye Ocarina," *Ethnomusicology* VI (1962), 175–77.

or five quarter tones. The *lulanga* of the Bashi (Congo), a trough zither in which eight strings are stretched along a concave block of wood between two and three feet long, has a tuning using mainly major and minor seconds. Frequently the tunings and thus the music produced seem to have little relationship to the intervals and scales of vocal music. The harps of East Africa bear a close resemblance to those of ancient Egypt.

Instrumental ensembles in Africa exhibit enormous variety. Ensemble playing on a single instrument is found, as in the zither-playing of the Bashi, in which one man plays the strings and another, opposite him, raps rhythmically on the instrument with his knuckles, or in the playing of large xylophones by two men next to each other or opposite each other, in West Africa and the Congo. At the other extreme are the xylophone orchestras of the Chopi of South Africa; these consist of some thirty men who play in a heterophonic style, with a conductor. Between these extremes there are ensembles of many sorts. Some consist of several instruments of the same type, such as xylophones, *mbiras,* or drums. Others are heterogeneous, consisting, for example, of drums, rattles, and bells (West Africa) or *mbira,* zither, and rattle (Congo), and a great many other combinations.

The distribution of instrument types in Africa is broad. Many instruments are found in almost all parts of the continent south of the Sahara. Drums, xylophones, the *mbira,* are practically universal. Musical bows are widespread. Nevertheless, there seems to be a great variation in the specific instruments, and in their number, used in individual tribal groups, and even neighboring peoples sometimes exhibit substantial differences. Thus the Ganda of Buganada have an enormous store of instruments: many kinds of idiophones, from the simple percussion beam to rattles, bells, and xylophones; several types of musical bows, lyres, a tube fiddle and a harp; flutes, animal horns, gourd trumpets; and many kinds of drums. On the other hand, the Bashi of the Congo area have only a few instruments: two types of zithers, two types of *mbiras* or *sansas,* a flute, and one kind of drum.

MUSIC AND LANGUAGE IN AFRICA

All over the world, music and language interact; but in Africa, this interaction appears to be more intense than elsewhere. In addition to music in the proper sense of the word, the use of musical sounds for signaling purposes is common in Africa. The relaying of drum signals over a long distance is legendary; horns are also used for this purpose, and also, for more conversational ends over short distances. In some tribes, signaling takes on the character of Morse code, that is, arbitrary signals are used to indicate words or concepts. More frequently, however, the system of signaling is tied to the pitch structure of the language.

The languages spoken in Black Africa belong mainly to three families: Khoi-San, characterized by clicks in the throat and mouth, which is spoken by the Bushmen and Hottentots; Niger-Congo (including the Bantu group), which occupies most of the area through the Congo region and the Guinea Coast, and which is a closely knit group of languages clearly related to each other; and Sudanic, which is spoken in the northeastern region of Black Africa. Most of the Bantu and many of the Sudanic languages are tone languages; that is, the relative pitch at which a syllable is spoken helps determine the meaning of the word. Thus, in Jabo, a language spoken in Liberia, there are four "tones"; that is, four different relative pitch levels of speech are distinguished for purposes of meaning, which we can number from 1 to 4, highest to lowest. In Jabo, the word *ba* may mean four different things, depending on the pitch. *Ba* (1) means namesake, *ba* (2) means "to be broad," *ba* (3) means "tail," and *ba* (4) is a particle expressing command.[6] In signaling, the pitches of the words—or rather their internal relationship, for of course the language tones are not fixed pitches but are relative to the pitch of the surrounding syllables and the speaker's voice range—are transferred to the drum. Jabo signaling is done with two drums made of hollowed logs with slits, one large, the other smaller. They are not true drums, of course, but idiophones. The pitch on each drum varies according to the place at which it is struck. And, interestingly, the two lower tones of the language are combined into one tone on the large drum. The fact that many words or sentences have the same sequence of tones, and that in the drum language tones 3 and 4 are indistinguishable, would seem to make deciphering of messages difficult. Only a few men are qualified to signal, and only certain things may be said in signal language. Understanding must come from knowledge of the kinds of things likely to be signaled, and evidently the Jabo restrict themselves to expressing thoughts, such as, "Our neighbors are on the warpath," or, more appropriately in this period of modernization, "Hide! The tax collector approaches!"

Just what happens when words in a tone language are set to music for the purpose of creating song? Does the melody slavishly follow the pitch movement of the words? Or is there free melodic movement which violates and to some extent obscures the meaning of the words by ignoring the linguistic tones? Not too much is known about this intricate relationship between music and speech, but it is obvious that no simple

[6] George Herzog, "Speech-Melody and Primitive Music," *Musical Quarterly,* XX (1934), 453.

rule describes it. And it may well be that each tribal culture has evolved its own accommodation between language and music in song. It is evident, however, that melody does not slavishly follow speech, but that the tones of the words do have an influence on shaping the melody.

The Ibo in Nigeria, according to one kind of analysis, use two tones, high and low. If it were possible to formulate a rule for Ibo on the basis of a small sampling of songs, we would have to say that the musical pitch sometimes moves up and down in the same direction as the pitch in speech, and that it sometimes remains the same while the speech tones change, but that pitch movement in the music is hardly ever contrary to that of the language. On the other hand, an example from the Chewa in Central East Africa, where the language also has two tones (marked in Example 7-1 by acute and grave accents, respectively), indicates very

EXAMPLE 7-1. Chewa song, from George Herzog, "Speech-melody and Primitive Music," *Musical Quarterly* XX (1934), 457.

close correspondence. These samples are intended only to show some of the kinds of things that may be found; they should not be used to draw conclusions regarding the way tone languages are set to music throughout Africa.

Another example of the close relationship among music, language, and other activities appears in some of the xylophone music of the Jabo in Liberia. According to Herzog, one form of evening entertainment is the repeated playing of short phrases on large xylophones which consist of big slabs laid across banana tree trunks.[7] These phrases are ordinary music to most listeners, but to a few who have inside knowledge they are musical versions of the tone patterns of sentences commenting on current events or mocking a member of the tribe. The person being mocked may not realize it, and the audience may burst into laughter when a piece that makes fun of an oblivious bystander is played. Sometimes this music is performed by two players sitting on opposite sides of the xylophone. They may perform a single melody together, they may play a canon, or they may repeat a tiny contrapuntal piece based on the speech tones of two sentences or phrases.

[7] George Herzog, "Canon in West African Xylophone Melodies," *Journal of the American Musicological Society,* II (1949), 196–97.

GENERAL CHARACTERISTICS OF AFRICAN FORMS

The most striking thing about the forms of African music is their dependence on short units, and in many cases on antiphonal or responsorial techniques. Most African compositions do not have units as long as the stanzas of typical European folk songs. They consist of short phrases that are repeated systematically, or alternated, or on which are based longer melodies in which a motif reappears repeatedly in different forms. Typical of the brevity of the phrases is Example 7-1, which in actual performance was probably repeated many times.

In instrumental music, short forms of this type are also found distributed over a large part of Africa. Example 7-2, recorded in Johannesburg and performed on the musical bow, consists of a systematic repetition of a rhythmic phrase that uses only two fundamental pitches. The upper voice in Example 7-2 is produced by overtones, and it, of course, is varied; but the piece consists of the manifold repetitions of this phrase.

EXAMPLE 7-2. South African musical bow melody, from Charles M. Camp and Bruno Nettl, "The Musical Bow in South Africa," *Anthropos* L (1955), 75.

Solo performance is common enough in Africa, but the most characteristic African music is performed by groups with alternating performance techniques of various kinds. We say "characteristic" because this kind of performance is more developed in Africa than elsewhere, and because it is this element which, more perhaps than any other, has been retained in the Negro cultures of the New World. The simplest of these alternating techniques is responsorial singing, the alternation between a leader and a group which is sometimes also called the "call-and-response" technique. Example 7-3, from the Republic of the Congo (Brazzaville), shows what may frequently happen in such a form. Drums and an iron bell provide a constant rhythmic background whose general outline and meter remain the same, but whose accent patterns and specific note values vary somewhat. A female soloist sings a two-measure phrase alternating with a two-measure monophonic phrase sung by a group of women. The two phrases are different in content, but are similar at the cadence.

Improvisation is an important feature in many African styles. Evidently there is some real improvisation—that is, the creation of music without the use of pre-existing models as the basis—but this seems to be rare. More common is improvisation in which a tune is varied as it is being performed. The forms, consisting of short phrases that are repeated many times, lend themselves especially well to this kind of improvisation, since it is possible for a singer to begin with the standard version of a tune and then to improvise variations that depart increasingly from the standard. This is what happens in the successive repetitions of the soloist's phrase in Example 7-3. The members of the chorus also improvise variations, but they do not depart as much from the original.

A further result of improvisation, presumably, is the creation of polyphonic forms. One of the characteristics of African music is har-

EXAMPLE 7-3. Kuyu (Congo) women's dance, from Rose Brandel, *The Music of Central Africa* (The Hague: M. Nijhoff, 1962), p. 197.

mony and polyphony, which are discussed below. Here it is relevant to point out that improvisation in choral and ensemble performance adds to the number of pitches heard at one time. Thus the fact that improvisation and variation are encouraged in some African cultures seems to have influenced the degree to which polyphony is accepted. Actually, variation by improvisation seems to be considered the mark of good musicianship in some African cultures. We should mention also a feature found in some African music that involves both form and polyphony, namely the tendency, in some pieces, for a number of apparently unrelated things to be going on at the same time. Some of this is due to the development of complex rhythmic polyphony, the simultaneous presentation of several rhythms which seem, to the Western listener, to have little in common. It is hard to say whether the African listener feels all of these rhythms to be part of one overall rhythmic structure (as a Westerner can conceive all of the voices in a Bach fugue to be independent yet united), or whether the African conceives of music as consisting of the simultaneous presentation of unrelated phenomena. At any rate, it is possible, in such a piece, to have phrases and other units of varying lengths appearing in different voices or instruments.

The performances are at least in some cases intricately structured, despite the fact that they may consist only of repetitions and variations upon a short theme. In the music performed on the *mbira*, or *sansa*, in Southern Africa (as illustrated and described in detail on the recording, *Mbira Music of Rhodesia*) the repetitions and variations on a basic theme are grouped into nine steps or stages. The *mbira* player begins by playing the basic chords of the underlying harmony; then, in the second section, he varies them slightly; and in the third step, he takes the basic chords and creates an accompanying melody out of them, playing their tones in alternation rather than together. This third step is considered the basic pattern which dominates the piece. In the fourth step, we find more and faster separation of the notes, rhythmic changes, and the addition of the singing voice. There is a climax at the end of this section, which is followed by variations on the vocal melody in the fifth and sixth steps. In the fifth, the singer introduces a yodel-like technique. Steps 7, 8, and 9 are more or less identical with the first three steps, presented in reverse order. Each of these stages has a name. The details of the sections, their length and specific content, may be improvised, but the form of the performance is essentially set.

Thus forms rivaling in sophistication those of European art music and the Far East are found in Africa, and they are built upon the basic formal principles of brevity, repetition and variation, binary structure, and improvisation. The amount of repetition and variation may be determined by the performer's interaction with his audience or by the needs of the activity which the music accompanies. Composite forms, consisting of series of pieces, are particularly common in ceremonial situations, where a large group of pieces, which may take a day or longer, must be performed in correct order. Perhaps the most complex forms are the suites performed by the xylophone orchestras of the Chopi, for here we find structures of six to eight related movements, each of which is cast in a mold similar to that of the *mbira* pieces described above.

MELODY

So far as the melodic elements of music are concerned, African music seems generally rather intelligible to the Western listener; it does not really have the exotic sound that some Oriental and some American Indian music has at first hearing. The conclusion we may tentatively draw from this fact is that African music, on the whole, fits more or less into the diatonic scheme that is also the basis of most Western art and folk music.

There have been attempts to identify a truly "African" scale. Ballanta-Taylor, an early West African scholar, believed that the basic scale of West African music has sixteen tones per octave, and statements regarding the importance of pentatonic scales in Africa have been made. But the consensus of scholars is that there is no single system, that exact measurement of intervals would produce—at least in vocal music—a clustering about the intervals found also in diatonic scales, and that in many ways the kind of melodic structure in Africa corresponds to that of European folk music. As in Europe, so in Africa, we find songs with few tones (ditonic and tritonic scales). There are pentatonic tunes with minor thirds and major seconds, and there are pentachordal ones as well. There are heptatonic songs, and there are occasional chromatic pieces. There are, moreover, intervals that do not fit into the diatonic scheme, such as neutral thirds (as are found also in Europe). There is, finally, a reported tendency in the heptatonic songs to use the intervals of minor third and minor seventh above the tonic. Our interest in this feature stems from certain phenomena of jazz (the lowered seventh is one "blue note"), but it seems doubtful that these intervals constitute a special feature common to all African music. The fact that glides and ornaments are common in some African singing techniques also adds to the difficulty of defining a specific scale structure. Thus we must content ourselves with the generalization that African scales are varied but that as a group they seem to be closely related to those of Europe.

Types of melodic movement also exhibit great variety. In one area, Central Africa, we find the following kinds described by Brandel:[8] melodies clustering around a nucleus of one or two tones; melodies based on the perfect fourth, either descending directly from one tone to another a fourth below it, or making use also of the intervening tones; melodies built on the tones of the triad, and others using a whole string of thirds with only occasional use of intervening tones; melodies built on the triad with an added sixth (♪); melodies with the augmented fourth predominating, sometimes made up of three major seconds in a row (♪); and melodies with the range of an octave or more, in which the lowest tone and its upper octave are the most important.

The melodic contours also have various types. Rather large ranges seem to be characteristic of Africa. Europe has many songs with a range of less than a fifth, relatively few (except for what appears to be recent material) with a range much larger than an octave. In African Negro music the number of pieces with a large range seems to be somewhat greater. Melodies move predominantly in three ways: (1) in a mildly undulating fashion, beginning on a low tone, rising gradually to a somewhat higher level, and returning to the low tone; (2) beginning on a high tone and descending; and (3) tracing a pendulum-like movement, swinging rapidly back and forth between high and low tones. Example 7-4 illustrates this pendulum-like movement; it also exemplifies the melodies made up largely of strings of thirds, discussed above.

EXAMPLE 7-4. Batwa Pygmy song (Ruanda), from Rose Brandel, *The Music of Central Africa* (The Hague: M. Nijhoff, 1962), p. 70.

Tone systems in African music are sometimes very restricted. The music of the Xhosa, a large group of people living at the tip of South Africa, lies almost entirely within the framework of a pentatonic scale, with minor thirds and major seconds. The melodies are almost always rather sharply descending. The tunes very frequently consist of two phrases, which are similar, identical, or analogous, the second phrase centering about a tone a major second below the tonal center of the first phrase.

[8] Rose Brandel, *The Music of Central Africa* (The Hague: Martinus Nijhoff, 1962).

The music of the Mbuti Pygmies of the Congo is largely built on a pentatonic scale consisting again of major seconds and minor thirds, but with the two thirds adjacent (e.g.,). On the other hand, in some other African cultures there appears to be a wide variety of scale types and a rather complex tone system. In instrumental music, of course, melodic movement is more specialized, for each instrument invites certain kinds of movement, range, and interval. Thus melodies played on the musical bow are likely to have a small range and use a melodic type clustering about one or two notes that are close together; horn music is likely to use larger intervals, while pendulum-like melody is more easily suited to the xylophone. We should also mention in this connection the great variety of tone colors achieved by the human voice. Yodeling, growling, raucous tones, and tense as well as relaxed singing are found. The imitation of animal cries and sounds of nature are also a part of vocal music in Africa. In general, Black African singing is relaxed, openthroated, and full-bodied, very much in contrast to the tense and tighter sounding Middle Eastern singing style found in the North. It is also usually unornamented and straightforward.

RHYTHM

The feature of African music that has been most widely discussed is rhythm, and obviously it has indeed been more highly developed in Africa than have some other features or elements of music, such as melody and form. To some extent we may say that African rhythm is also more highly developed than the rhythm of other cultures. The latter statement must be made with caution, of course, for certainly it would be possible for a composer of Western music to put together a piece with a rhythmic structure much more complex than that of any African piece. He could do this because he can use notation. It is, however, very difficult for a Western musician to reproduce or even to comprehend the more complex African rhythmic structures with the use of his ear alone. The level at which African music seems to be rhythmically more developed is that of listener and performer perception. It is doubtful whether a Western listener could, without special training, perceive and reproduce the most complex structures in Western music, especially without a score, simply from sound. With training he might, of course, learn to match the performance and perception of African musicians. But this sort of training is not present in our culture, while it is—though not always formally—a part of African Negro musical training, for both the listener and the performer.

The rhythm of African music must be approached from two points of view. First, we are interested in the rhythmic structure (and its complexity) in a single melodic line. Here the rhythm and meter are usually not too difficult to understand. Metric structure with regular beats appears to be the rule. Once beats are established it is possible to identify that widely discussed element, syncopation, which results from the regular articulation of notes at points other than the beginnings of beats. A distinctive feature of West African music that seems to have been carried over in Negro music of the New World is the ability of musicians to keep the same tempo for minutes and hours. Waterman refers to this ability (which no doubt is learned, not inherited) as the "metronome sense." We will never know, of course, whether such strict adherence to tempo has ever been practiced in Western music. Certainly in Western cultivated music in the twentieth century it is not found, something one can easily prove by playing a symphony recording and keeping time with a metronome. Rigid adherence to tempo may have made possible the considerable variety of rhythmic motifs and patterns in African music, for the musician who has a steady beat in his mind, and who does not deviate from it, can perhaps more easily elaborate the details of the rhythm. The compelling nature of rhythm is recognized in West African terminology, where the term "hot," applied to rhythmic drumming, evidently originated.[9] "Hot" rhythm in West Africa is particularly important in ceremonial music, and the more exciting the rhythm, the "hotter" the music is said to be.

The more spectacular rhythmic complexity of African Negro music appears, however, in the rhythmic polyphony, the superimposition of several rhythmic structures. Its most obvious manifestation is found in drumming, but of course it is also present in the combination of several voices or, more frequently, of instruments with voices. There is a great deal of drumming, but in other ways also, the music seems to be dominated by a percussive quality. Individual tones in singing are attacked strongly without a semblance of *legato*. There are few instruments on which one can slur notes together, and generally the music is vigorously accented. Thus the importance of drumming can perhaps be traced to the need for strong rhythmic articulation.

The perception of various simultaneous meters seems to be widespread among Africans. Rhythmic polyphony of a rather complex type

[9] Richard A. Waterman, " 'Hot' Rhythm in Negro Music," *Journal of the American Musicological Society*, I (1948), 25f.

can be performed by a single person who may sing in one meter and drum in another. The superimposition of duple and triple meters, one type of hemiola rhythm, is evidently a basic ingredient of much West and Central African rhythmic polyphony.

In music using three or more drums, the rhythmic polyphony is developed to its most complex level. While such music can be mechanically notated in a single meter, the various drummers are actually performing with independent metrical schemes; one drum may use duple, one triple, a third quintuple meter. Moreover, if the several drums or other instruments use the same basic metric scheme (such as 3/8), the beginning of the unit or measure may not come at the same time in all of the drums; thus we may have the following combination: 3/8, 5/8, 7/8, as in Example 7-5, which is a sample of Yoruba drumming with the pitch variations of the individual drums omitted.

EXAMPLE 7-5. Yoruba drumming in honor of Ogun (god of war). The top part is the smallest and highest drum, the lowest part, the largest and lowest drum. From Anthony King, "Employment of the 'standard pattern' in Yoruba Music," *African Music II*, no. 3 (1960), 53.

Percussion ensembles of various types are important in the Guinea Coast area of Africa. Typically, they consist of drums, rattles, and bells. Let us examine, as an example, the Abadja rhythm, used in social songs of the Ewe people of Ghana. Three drums of various pitches (each with one skin), several large gourd rattles, and two double-bells are used. The instruments enter in order, each playing its own rhythmic pattern without change, beginning with the bells, followed by the rattle, and finally by the drums. The last to enter is the master drum, which improvises against the consistent rhythmic background produced by the others, using motifs from their patterns, combining and rearranging them. The first bell is regarded as having the fundamental rhythm. The rhythms could be reduced to a common 12/8 meter, but the Ghanaian listener is more interested in the interaction of the various rhythms and hears them as individual entities rather than as "rhythmic chords." Thus the various instruments begin their patterns at various points, not simultaneously, and there is tension between those which are essentially in 6/8 and those that appear to be in 3/4 meter. Example 7-6 gives the patterns of all but the master drum (which does not play only a single pattern in its performance).

The melodic element in drumming, as illustrated by the "royal drums" of the Watusi, which accompany the supreme chief whenever he emerges from his tent, is also important; drums used together always contrast in size and thus in pitch, and it is possible to follow each drum individually. In music using several melodic instruments, or voices and instruments, the structure of the rhythm is as complex as it is in the drumming, and the various voices often perform in different meters. To what extent the performers are listening to each other cannot always be ascertained, and to what degree an African listener perceives the total rhythmic structure is also unknown. An important feature of West African rhythmic polyphony, and perhaps a major key to its understanding, is the hemiola concept. The juxtaposition of three beats against two, and of more complex rhythms composed of these units, both simultaneously and in alternation, is the basis of a great deal of this music; it can be found, for instance, in Example 7-6, in which the *kidi* drum performs a rhythm that can be reduced to 3/4, and the *kagan* drum another in 6/8, while the rattle alternates these two meters in its short repeated phrase.

EXAMPLE 7-6. Abadja rhythm, used in Ghana. After William K. Amoakn.

POLYPHONY

Closely related to rhythmic polyphony and to the problem of perception of a group of individual rhythmic lines as a unit is the field of polyphony at large, and the question is whether in Africa several voices are perceived independently or as a single vertical harmonic structure.

Whether it is polyphony or really harmony, it is very well developed in African Negro music. And it appears in many media. There is choral singing, usually in the responsorial form. There is instrumental music of an orchestral nature, with a number of instruments of the same type playing together. And there is something similar to chamber music —instruments of different types playing together, alone or along with singing. Drumming and other percussion may of course act as accompaniment. Finally, there is also the concept of accompaniment for singing. There is polyphony of many types, and it seems to be present throughout the African Negro area, although concentrated in the Eastern cattle area and the Congo or Central Africa.

The fact that many kinds of polyphony are present in Africa, and that this also seems to be the case elsewhere in the world where polyphony is found, strengthens our belief that polyphony is a unified concept. When a culture discovers or learns to perform polyphony it seems to learn several different kinds. There are cultures with no polyphony at all, but there are few, if any, that use, for example, only parallel fifths and nothing else.

Most African polyphony belongs to two types: that in which all of the voices use the same melodic material, and that which comes about through the peculiarities of the instruments. In the former category we find, of course, parallelism. There are parallel thirds, fourths, fifths, and occasionally sixths, but other intervals seem to be rare. In the case of parallel thirds, alternation between major and minor thirds is usual, made necessary by the diatonic seven-tone scales which, as we have said, are common in Africa. Parallel fourths and fifths seem to be more common in East Africa, while thirds and sixths seem to dominate in the Congo and Guinea Coast areas. Parallelism is rarely completely exact, for the tendency to improvise seems to militate against slavish following of one voice by another.

Example 7-7 illustrates parallelism among the Thonga of South Africa. A chorus of men and women is led by a female soloist and accompanied by a musical bow, which also plays interludes between the stanzas. The player of the musical bow, which is evidently limited to the

EXAMPLE 7-7. South African choral song with musical bow, from Charles
M. Camp and Bruno Nettl, "The Musical Bow in Southern Africa," *Anthropos*
L (1955), 80.

tones D, E, and F, plays the melody along with the soloist and with the
second part of the chorus, but switches to an approximation of the highest part of the chorus when his range permits it.

African music also possesses rounds, which often seem to have
come about through antiphonal or responsorial singing. For example, if
leader and chorus use the same tune, the chorus may become overanxious
and fail to wait for the leader to finish his turn, and a round of sorts is
born. The fact that many African rounds do have the entrance of the
second voice near the end of the first voice's rendition of a tune points to
this matter of origin; so also does the fact that most known African
rounds have only two voices. Also resulting from the antiphonal technique
is the kind of polyphony in which one voice sustains a tone, perhaps the
final tone of its phrase, while the other voice performs a more rapidly
moving melody, at the end of which it, in turn, holds a long note while

the first voice performs a moving part. This gives rise to a sort of drone relationship between the voices.

In Southern Africa, where polyphony appears to be most widespread, we find a type of relationship among the voices that appears to be similar to the Western harmonic system in its eighteenth- and nineteenth-century manifestations. The compositions are, as one might expect, in two sections, each consisting of a melody, sometimes accompaniment as well, and sometimes of several intertwined melodies. In most cases, however, the material in each section revolves about one triad, and the relationship of the two triads is analogous to the relationship between a dominant and a tonic chord, although the roots of the two African chords are separated not by a fourth or a fifth but by a major second. The consistent harmonic movement, however, justifies the hypothesis that here we have a harmonic system that dominates the music much as harmony dominates Western music.

There is also a relationship between the voices that could be called real counterpoint, but this seems to appear most frequently in instrumental music, where the structure of the instrument may in itself be conducive to certain melodic patterns and devices. Thus the accompaniment of singers on a harp, a xylophone, or a *mbira* (see page 131) may have nothing to do melodically with the tune of the singers. In the case of accompaniment, an "ostinato" relationship between voices and instruments is frequent. A short bit, perhaps a two-measure phrase, is repeated (with variations) by the instruments, while the singer or singers perform a longer melody which, however, is also repeated with improvised variations. This sort of structure is similar, of course, to that of much Western music, especially of popular or folk provenience; and Africans in the cities, who have come under the influence of Western popular music, have composed songs in which the African sort of accompaniment by an ostinato figure, with a very short stanza by the singer, is used. We will have occasion to discuss the results of combining Western and African elements in the New World; but here is an example of the same sort of things in modern Africa. In both places, those features in African music which are highly developed but which have a European counterpart seem to be preserved in the acculturated music of Africans and Afro-Americans.

REGIONAL VARIATION IN BLACK AFRICAN MUSIC

We have noted the fact that each African tribe has its own songs and music, and that each tribe may differ in its musical style from its

neighbors. On the other hand, we have also cited a number of characteristics present in Black African music as a whole. These characteristics are
not equally pronounced in each tribe or each area. Just as there are culture areas in Africa, there are also music areas, regions in which the
musical style is more or less homogeneous, and which contrast with their
neighboring areas in some specific way. The music areas coincide, on the
whole, with the culture areas, and this is not surprising when we consider
the essential roles of music in the culture as a whole. Thus Merriam[10]
recognizes the following music areas: the Khoi-San area (Bushmen and
Hottentots), East Africa, Central Africa (mainly the Congo region), and
the West Coast (plus several areas in the northern part of the continent
that are largely under the influence of Islamic musical culture). The four
areas we have mentioned comprise the main body of Black African music.
To them should be added the music of the Pygmies, who live in various
isolated parts of central Africa surrounded by Negro groups but whose
music is a distinctive unit. The differences among these groups are expressed not in clear-cut dichotomies but rather in statistical terms. What
may be found in one area is also present in another, but with a markedly
different degree of frequency or complexity.

The main characteristics of the West Coast are the metronome
sense and the accompanying concept of "hot" rhythm, the simultaneous
use of several meters, and the responsorial form of singing with overlap
between leader and chorus. The Central African area is distinguished by
its great variety of instruments and musical styles and by the emphasis,
in its polyphony, on the interval of the third. East Africa has, for centuries,
been somewhat under Islamic influence, though by no means to as great
an extent as the northern half of Africa. Vertical fifths are more prominent here, and rhythmic structure is not so complex, nor are percussion
instruments so prominent. The development of a sense of harmony seems
likely. The Khoi-San music area is evidently similar in style to East
Africa, but has simpler forms and instruments. It contains a good deal of
music performed with the *hocket* technique, as does the Pygmy sub-area
of Central Africa, which is also characterized by the presence of a vocal
technique similar to yodeling.

We have been describing those aspects of African Negro music
which seem to have developed without influence from other cultures, or
of which Africans have made a specialty. But outside influence is not
just a recent phenomenon in African music. Thus it shares some traits
with European folk music, indicating perhaps a period of contact many
centuries ago. Also, contact with Indonesian music seems likely, and the
influence of the Near East and possibly of India is ancient and has in-

[10] Alan P. Merriam, "African Music," p. 77.

Central African musical, bow, played with mouth of resonator.

creased greatly in the last few centuries. Western culture has also played
a part for centuries and has grown especially in the last hundred years.
Thus we find African music now—and it has probably always been this
way to a degree—in a state of change, and it is both difficult and perhaps
useless to try to single out unchanged elements. On the contrary, it behooves us to observe the changes as they take place, for this is the way to
study music as a living phenomenon. We find that some tribes have almost completely changed to music in a Near Eastern style. We find that
others have retained, in part, a repertory of "pure" African music but
have added to it songs in an Arabic style; this is true of the Watusi,
who have solo drumming of a kind unknown in the Near East but
also songs strongly reminiscent of Arabic music, and of the Hausa.
We find North and Latin American popular songs known in tribes that
otherwise perform aboriginal songs. And we find that because of the
improvement of communication and transportation as well as through the
growth of unified African nations on a supratribal level, African tribal
groups are learning more from each other, musically and otherwise, than
they did before.

Like music everywhere, African music has changed rapidly in the
twentieth century, particularly because of the increased contact with
Western music and musical thought, and with Western technology such
as is exhibited in the mass media. Africans hear much of their music on
records and on the radio, and the degree of general participation in
musical activities appears to be declining. They hear the music of different tribal groups, and they have created popular musical styles by combining their resources and mixing them with Western elements. The
very popular high-life style of West Africa is such a combination, and
throughout Africa one can find music which is essentially Western, but
which retains those elements of African music that are most developed
and most prominent. There have also been attempts, sometimes resulting
from the increasing nationalism of the various new nations of the continent and sometimes from an antiquarian attitude, to preserve old forms,
and the interest in African music has been stimulated by institutions of
recent origin, such as contests among xylophone orchestras among the
Chopi of South Africa. Thus African music continues as a lively and ever-
changing art; but its most important features seem to remain relatively
constant even in the face of the onslaught of Westernization.

We should not leave a discussion of African music without mentioning its enormous impact on much of the world's music in the last
hundred years. Its chief characteristics have been brought to the Americas and form the basic elements of all types of Afro-American performance practice. It is less well known that Africans who were brought to

various parts of the Old World over the past several hundred years also brought with them much musical material. Thus, for example, the folk music of the Persian Gulf area has many African characteristics, and their origin is attested to by the presence of many individuals of African racial type. Most important, however, the main distinguishing features of the popular musics of the Western world, and of jazz, are ultimately of African origin.

BIBLIOGRAPHY AND DISCOGRAPHY

Several publications by Alan P. Merriam discuss sub-Saharan African music as a unit: "African Music" in *Continuity and Change in African Cultures*, edited by William J. Bascom and Melville J. Herskovits (Chicago: University of Chicago Press, 1958); "Characteristics of African Music," *J-IFMC*, XI (1959), 13–19; and 'The African Idiom in Music," *Journal of American Folklore*, LXXV (1962), 120–30. George Herzog, "Speech-Melody and Primitive Music," *Musical Quarterly*, XX (1934), 452–66, is an excellent discussion of tone languages and their relationship to music. Regional studies of African music are not numerous. As samples we might mention J. H. Kwabena Nketia, *African Music in Ghana* (Evanston, Ill.: Northwestern University Press, 1963), for West Africa; and Rose Brandel, *The Music of Central Africa* (The Hague: M. Nijhoff, 1962), for Central Africa. Sir Percival Kirby, *The Musical Instruments of the Native Races of South Africa* (London: Oxford University Press, 1934) is a classic on the instruments and their musical styles in one area. A book profusely illustrated, dealing with instruments, in Bertil Söderberg, *Les Instruments de Musique au Bas-Congo et dans les Régions Avoisinantes* (Stockholm: Ethnographic Museum of Sweden, 1956).

Many excellent records of African music are available. A survey is presented on *Africa South of the Sahara*, edited by Harold Courlander, Folkways FE 4503 (2 disks). South and East Africa are represented on a constantly growing set of records, now already over 200 disks in number, published by the International Library of African Music, Johannesburg: *The Sound of Africa*. It is accompanied by detailed notes on a large set of catalog cards. The Central African area is well represented on *Voice of the Congo*, edited by Alan P. Merriam, Riverside RLP 4002; *Music of Equatorial Africa*, Folkways P 402; *Folk Music of the Western Congo*, Folkways P 427. West African drumming in its many varieties is illustrated in *Drums of the Yoruba of Nigeria*, Folkways P 441. The music of Madagascar is illustrated on *Valiha, Madagascar*, Ocora OCR 18. *Mbira* music of South Africa is found in *Mbira Music of Rhodesia*, performed by Abraham Dumisani Maraire, University of Washington Press 1001. The area which combines Black and North African elements is exemplified on *Ethiopia,* Anthology Records AST 6000, and *Nigeria-Hausa Music I,* Unesco Records BM 30 L 2306. *Voice of the Congo* also includes examples of modern African music that combine traditional and Western elements.

EIGHT

THE AMERICAN INDIANS

This and the following chapters discuss the folk and traditional musics of the Americas. The American continents possess a great wealth of traditional music. That of the American Indians has been in existence for a long time, though no doubt in constantly changing forms. Other repertories have been brought from other continents, mainly Europe, and preserved more or less intact. Still other musics of the Americas began as offshoots from these imported traditions, then developed into independent styles with their own character and internal dynamics; this is true particularly of the various Afro-American traditions. Some musical repertories in the Americas came about through interaction and fusion of older musics which were found here or brought from elsewhere. And finally, although it would be difficult to state unequivocally that there are traditions in the Americas that grew up entirely without influence from older, Indian, African, or European musics, there are some styles that can be said to be in real essence American.

It seems logical to discuss the music of the Americas in three categories; (1) the music of the Indians, which is a tradition relatively undisturbed by the influx of other music; (2) the Afro-American musics, whose main characteristic is the combination of styles which were originally widely separated and highly distinctive; and (3) the folk music of peoples of European origin—Spanish and Portuguese, English, French, German, and Eastern European—which is characterized by the retention of archaic forms no longer known in their original home as well as by the development of distinctive offshoots of the European models.

There is little doubt any more that the American Indians came from Asia, across the Bering Straits, in several or many separate waves, beginning some 50,000 years ago; that they are Mongoloid in race; and that the simplest tribes were pushed to the edges of the area (Tierra del Fuego, for example) and into relatively undesirable spots such as the jungles of Brazil and Bolivia, the Great Basin area of Nevada and Utah, and the tundra of North Canada and the icy wastes of the Polar area. While we realize that in 50,000 years there must have occurred a great deal of change in the styles and uses of Indian music, and while we know practically nothing about the music of East Asia of thousands of years ago, it is still possible to discover certain similarities between Indian and Oriental music, and especially between the musics of the Eskimos and of the Paleo-Siberian tribes living in easternmost Siberia. These similarities involve emphasis on melody rather than on polyphony, some use of relatively large intervals (thirds and fourths) in the melodies, and, possibly, a rather strained, tense-sounding vocal production. On the other hand, there are many different styles and style areas in North and South America, and music of the simplest sort as well as musical cultures of great complexity are found. The latter had largely disappeared by the time ethnomusicologists became competent to deal with them and they can be studied only by archeological techniques; but some of the simplest styles are still with us. The size of the Indian population seems always to have been small; north of Mexico there were probably never more than one or two million, while South and Middle American Indians apparently never exceeded about five million. That such a small number of people developed so varied and intensive a musical culture is a fact that should inspire in the modern reader a good deal of respect. Except for the similarity among the simplest tribes in both continents, there is today a great difference between South and North American Indians as a whole: The South American tribes, for the most part, have been absorbed into the Hispanic-American cultures, to which they have contributed greatly, and whose music they have to a large degree adopted; thus, for knowledge of their aboriginal music, we must depend on a few isolated tribes. The North American tribes have generally remained more separate from their white and Negro compatriots and seem to have preserved earlier musical styles to a much greater degree. For this reason, and because South American Indian music is not yet well known, our emphasis in this chapter must be on the North American Indians.

THE SIMPLEST STYLES:
EXAMPLES FROM BOLIVIA AND CALIFORNIA

Among some Indian tribes we find music as simple as any in the world. Melodies with only two or three tones, and with a single phrase which is repeated imprecisely many times, can be found in several areas. The Sirionó of Bolivia are an interesting example,[1] for they contradict one of the truisms often repeated about the "earliest" music: rather than fulfilling ritual functions, it seems to be used mainly for entertainment. The Sirionó have no instruments and only a few simple tunes. They sing in the evening after dark, and in the morning, in their hammocks, before beginning the day's activities. The words of the songs are evidently improvised and deal with all kinds of events, past and present, assuming in a way the role of conversation. The songs usually have descending melodic contour and are sung with a "decrescendo" as the singer's breath runs out. Curiously, it seems that each member of the tribe has one tune that is the basis of all the songs he sings. He makes up different words but uses one and the same tune, possibly throughout his life. Even in such a simple musical culture there are some individuals who are said to be superior singers and who teach the young people to sing. Example 8-1 illustrates a Sirionó song.

Similarly simple styles are found in the music of some tribes of

EXAMPLE 8-1. Sirionó Indian song, from Mary Key, "Music of the Sirionó (Guaranian)," *Ethnomusicology,* VII (1963), 20.

repeats many times

[1] Mary Key, "Music of the Sirionó (Guaranian)," *Ethnomusicology* VII (1963), 17–21.

Northern California. Detailed analysis of the songs in such a repertory may reveal, however, that within the severe limitations that the composers in a tribe place upon themselves there is a great deal of variety and sophistication. The last "wild" Indian, Ishi, who was discovered alone in 1911, the last living member of the Yahi tribe, and who sang all of the songs that he knew for anthropologists at the University of California Museum of Anthropology before he died in 1916, provides an interesting example. The songs of Ishi are all extremely short—five to ten seconds of music, repeated many times—and they use two, three, or four tones (in very rare cases, five) within a range of a fourth or fifth. Most of the songs consist of two or three short phrases, related to each other in various ways. The second phrase may be a variation of the first, an inversion, an extension, a condensation. A large number of different kinds of relationship between two or three short bits of music are exhibited; the composers had done everything possible, as it were, to provide musical variety and interest within the strict limitations that tradition had placed on them. Example 8-2 illustrates two of the songs of Ishi.

EXAMPLE 8-2. Two Yahi Indian songs, sung by Ishi, from Bruno Nettl, "The Songs of Ishi," *The Musical Quarterly* LI (1965), 473, 474.

USES OF INDIAN MUSIC:
AN EXAMPLE FROM THE PLAINS

In their traditional culture, Indian tribes with more complex kinds of musical culture usually had several types of songs, each of which was associated with different activities. For example, the Arapaho Indians of the North American Plains had ceremonial and secular songs. Among the former, the most elaborate are the songs of the Sun Dance, a ceremony performed in the summer, when the various bands of the tribe came together after being separated all winter. The Sun Dance involves the search for a vision in which the individual warrior receives a guardian spirit. The vision is brought on by self-torture and by dancing around a pole while looking at the bright sun for hours. With the exception of the Ghost Dance and Peyote songs which are discussed below, all of the

Arapaho songs are very much alike; they consist of two sections, each descending in a terrace-like contour; they have a range greater than an octave and scales of four, five, or six tones; and they are sung with great tension on the vocal chords and with rhythmic pulsations on the long notes. Even though they sound much alike, the various types of songs have certain individual characteristics. Thus the Sun Dance songs are a bit longer than the rest; have a slightly larger average range (about a twelfth); and their final phrase, in the last repetition at a performance of a song, is sung by the women alone. Songs learned in visions are another type, and songs belonging to the various age-grade societies, a third. (Each man was a member of one of seven age-grade societies, with elaborate initiations and with particular duties in war; as he aged he was promoted from one society to the next.) Among the secular songs, we may mention various types of social dance songs—the snake dance, turtle dance, round dance, and rabbit dance. Each has minor characteristics distinguishing it: The round dance songs are usually in rollicking triple meter; the rabbit dance—danced by couples and evidently introduced after contact with the whites—has songs that ordinarily begin with descending fourths. There are war songs intended to inspire warriors, and others used to recount events in recent battles. There are also songs said to be taught by the guardian spirit, which the recipient is to sing only when he is near death. Also, there are children's songs, lullabies, and love songs.

Finally we must mention two types of songs recognized as separate genres by the Arapaho and by other Plains tribes, the Ghost Dance and Peyote songs. The Ghost Dance is a religion that was introduced in the 1880s by tribes further west, in the Great Basin of Nevada; it was a cult, outlawed by the United States in 1891, which preached war and annihilation to the encroaching whites, a last-ditch stand against the inevitable. The Ghost Dance movement brought with it, from the Great Basin, a musical style different from that of the older Plains songs. Typically its songs had a smaller range and a form in which each phrase is repeated once, for instance, AABB or AABBCC. Among the Plains Indians, such as the Arapaho, these songs came to be associated with the Ghost Dance religion, and when the dance was outlawed, the songs continued to be sung. Their style was also associated with hand games and gambling games.

Another musical style was brought to the Arapaho and to many other tribes throughout the United States and particularly to the Northern Plains, by the Peyote religion. Peyote, a cactus indigenous in Mexico, has buttons which when chewed have a mild narcotic effect, producing euphoria and eventually pleasant hallucinations. The Aztecs already had a cult built around Peyote, but a religion of a different sort, preaching conciliation with the whites and including some superficial elements of Christianity, was based on this drug in North America. Peyote reached some of the Apache tribes after 1700 and spread from them to the majority of tribes in the United States during the nineteenth and early twentieth centuries. The style of Peyote music is essentially the same among all of the North American tribes that use the Peyote ceremonies; and it differs uniformly from the older musical styles of those tribes. Its form is similar to that of the older Plains songs, but its rhythm is characterized by the fact that it is rapid and composed mainly of only two note values which can be notated by quarter and eighth notes; also it is accompanied by rapid playing of the drum and rattle. Special kinds of meaningless syllables and a particular closing or cadential formula are used. Peyote songs are definitely considered as a special type by the Arapaho.

The Arapaho culture did not have as many uses of music as did some other Indian tribes. For example, the Pueblo Indians had much more complex and numerous ceremonial songs. They also used music to accompany work, something unusual among Indians. The Navaho had elaborate curing rituals accompanied by several series of songs, and a large body of corn grinding songs. The Indians of the Southeastern United States had many kinds of social dances. Throughout, music was associated with religion, and no description of a ceremony would be complete without a discussion of the songs. In most tribes, the most significant musical creations were those in the ceremonies. Among the Eskimos, some songs were used to settle disputes and to relieve the resulting tension.

MUSIC IN INDIAN THOUGHT

We have only little knowledge regarding the musical aesthetics of Indian tribes. Ability to sing many songs, and to sing high, is the mark of a good singer on the Plains; the Pueblo Indians, on the other hand, prefer singers with low, growling voices. Songs are judged according to their "power" rather than their beauty. Various ideas regarding the origin of songs are found among the North American tribes. According to some, all songs were given to the tribe "in the beginning," and the idea that new songs can be made up is not accepted. Among the Yuman tribes of the extreme Southwest, songs are thought to be "dreamed," that is, made up or given to a person while he is asleep.[2] Curiously, Yuman persons who

[2] George Herzog, "Music in the Thinking of the American Indian," *Peabody Bulletin*, May, 1933, pp. 1–6.

are disturbed or emotionally maladjusted retire for a few weeks to a secluded hut, there to meditate and to "dream" songs, eventually to emerge much improved. Among the Pima of the Southwest, we find the idea that songs already exist, and that it is the job of the composer simply to "untangle" them. Among the Plains tribes, the idea that songs come in visions is prevalent; of course all songs do not come in this way, but those which are ceremonially most significant do. The possibility of learning songs from other tribes is accepted variously; Herzog found that the Pima, who sang songs with Yuma words, would not admit that these songs could have been imported. On the other hand, Plains tribes regularly label the songs borrowed from other tribes; thus the Cheyenne Indians have "Kiowa songs" and "Comanche songs."

The degree to which songs retain their form from year to year and from generation to generation also varies. Some tribes, such as those of the Northwest Coast, consider it important to keep a song intact. Change or error might invalidate its purpose in ritual or rob it of its power. Thus organized rehearsing was instituted and errors were punished. The attempt to retain the cultural heritage intact and the resistance to change in general is also felt, of course, in the musical culture. The Pueblo Indians, who have tended to resist change in all areas, have also kept their musical culture away from Western influence more than have some other tribes. The Plains Indians, who had a rather loose and informal political and ceremonial structure, evidently did not adhere to such standardized forms; one Arapaho informant, upon hearing a recording of one of his tribal songs, performed what he considered "the same song" by singing what seemed to the investigator a totally different melody.

MUSICAL INSTRUMENTS

The instruments of the North American Indians are relatively few in number, but the Middle and South American tribes had a considerable wealth of them. In North America, flutes and various sorts of percussion instruments constitute an overwhelming majority. Flutes are usually of the recorder type, with varying numbers of finger holes; the tunes they are used to perform are frequently those of songs that are also sung. True flutes, without the plug of the recorder, also appear. In some cases, ornamentation in the vocal line is faithfully reproduced on the flute; in others, the flute embellishes the tune. Flutes are most frequently used to play love songs, and they are played almost exclusively by men. Whistles of various sorts, made of bone, pottery, or wood, are used in conjunction

Ancient Mexican clay flute.

Plains Indian gourd rattle.

with songs and ceremonies. Drums and rattles are the main percussion instruments of North America. The drums are usually beaten with sticks rather than the hand, and they (as well as the rattles) are used only to accompany song. Most Indian drums have a single drumhead; some are so large that they can be played by several players simultaneously. Some are held in one hand, the player grasping the leather thongs that hold the skin against the rim. Kettledrums, sometimes filled with water, are also used. The Peyote ceremony requires such a drum, its drumhead moistened to attain appropriate pitch. Typically, each drum is associated with one or several specific ceremonies and is an object of importance beyond its musical service.

Rattles are also of various types and associated with specific ceremonies. Gourd rattles (with pebbles inside the gourd) are used for Peyote ceremonies. Also used in North America are rattles made of deer hooves strung together; rattles made on a base consisting of a turtle shell; notched sticks held against a basket resonator and rubbed with another stick; and wooden bells. The South American Indians also have a larger variety of rattles, but they are particularly distinguished from the North American tribes in their development of panpipes and of chordophones (string instruments). Panpipes made of fired clay and of wood seem to have been used in the highlands of Peru and Bolivia for centuries. Some have pipes up to five feet tall. The number and arrangement of pipes vary, but, interestingly enough, this type of instrument has been altered and its scale made to fit Western popular music, so that some of the present-day Indians of Peru, for example, use them to play tunes in the prevalent Hispanic style. While there is inconclusive evidence that some North American tribes used hunting bows to play simple tunes, the musical bow, played in much the same ways as in Africa, appears among several South American tribes, including the simple Araucanians of Patagonia. The high cultures of Peru, Colombia, and Mexico had rather elaborate instruments of various sorts, but we know little about the music produced on them.

STYLES BY AREA IN NORTH AMERICA

The distribution of musical styles among the North American Indians coincides more or less with that of the culture areas. There appears to be, however, a somewhat smaller degree of correspondence here than there is in Africa. South American Indian music is not yet sufficiently well known for us to construct musical areas. In North America (north of Mexico) there are six main areas; in some cases these cannot be distinguished on the basis of single pieces of music, and the distinctions among them are statistical, that is, they depend on the frequency of a given trait rather than its simple presence or absence.

1. The Northwest Coast-Eskimo area contains, besides the areas mentioned, the Salish Indians in the interior of British Columbia and in the state of Washington. While these groups have little in common culturally, they seem to be among the most recent immigrants from Asia. Their music is characterized by nonstrophic forms, by complex and sometimes nonmetrical rhythmic organization, by the prominence of small intervals such as minor seconds, and by a relatively small range in the melodies. The melodic contours in Eskimo music tend to be undulating, while they are more frequently of a pendulum type in Northwest Coast and Salish music. One important characteristic is the use of rhythmic motifs in the percussive accompaniment. Generally, in Indian music, drums and rattles follow a simple pulse. But in the Northwest Coast-Eskimo area, designs such as ♪♪♪↝ or ♪♪ ♪ are found. In spite of unity, however, the Eskimo music is generally simple while that of the Northwest is complex and, in its relative wealth of instruments, indicates some relationship to the culture of the Mexican civilizations.

2. The California-Yuman area, consisting of tribes in Central California and of the Yuman-speaking tribes of the extreme Southwestern United States, is characterized by singing in a relatively relaxed manner. Most Indian tribes use a tense, harsh vocal technique, but here the singing is more in the style of Western or Central European folk singing. The songs are not in strophic form; rather, they consist of two or more separate sections or phrases which are repeated, alternated, and interwoven without a predetermined pattern. The most characteristic feature of this area is the so-called rise, a form discovered and labeled by George Herzog.[3] The rise itself is a section of a song that is slightly higher in pitch than the rest of the song if not very obviously so. The Yuman Indians recognize this feature and use a word roughly translated as "rise" to indicate it. The rise is found in most songs of the Yuman-California area, and also elsewhere, mainly along the coasts of North America. Thus, it is found in some twenty or thirty percent of the songs of some Northwest Coast tribes, and in those of the Southeastern Choctaw; in ten to twenty percent of the songs of the Northeastern Penobscot and the Northwestern Nootka, and in less than ten percent of the repertory of the Southeastern Creek, Yuchi, and Tutelo.

3. A third area is centered in the Great Basin of Nevada, Utah,

[3] George Herzog, "The Yuman Musical Style," *Journal of American Folklore,* LXI (1928), 183–231.

and northern interior Canada, basically a desert area with simple hunting and gathering cultures. The style of the music here became the style of the Ghost Dance songs further to the East. Singing is in a relatively relaxed manner, melodic range is small, and the typical form is that of paired phrases, with each phrase repeated once. In the northwestern part of the area, some tribes with even a simpler style—the Modoc and Klamath, for example—have many songs consisting of a single repeated phrase. This kind of form is found, of course, in traditional musics throughout the world, and there are a few Indian tribes such as the previously mentioned Sirionó of Bolivia whose entire repertories don't go beyond this level of simplicity. But it seems possible that the simple repetitive forms of the Modoc and Klamath are historically related to the somewhat more complex but still essentially repetitive forms of the Great Basin proper. Because of long-standing contacts with the Plains Indians, the Great Basin tribes also have songs in the Plains style. And an interesting exception to the tendency of Indian songs to be short and to eschew narration is the existence, among the Ute, of some songs that serve as vehicles for reciting tales. These narrative songs do not have strophic forms (as do European ballads), but continue in unstructured fashion, liberally repeating and varying a few basic musical motifs. Example 8-3 illustrates the Great Basin style.

EXAMPLE 8-3. Paiute Indian song, transcribed by the author from the recording, *Great Basin. Paiute Washo, Ute, Bannock, Shoshone* (Library of Congress AAFS L38), recorded and edited by Willard Rhodes.

4. A fourth area, the Athabascan, seems to coincide with a language family by the same name. It consists of the Navaho and Apache tribes and, possibly, of another group of tribes, the Northern Athabascans in Western Canada. Though these northern tribes have for centuries been separated from the Navaho and Apache by a thousand miles, there is evidence that the musical styles of the two areas are related. The music of the Navaho is the most complex of this area, perhaps because it has been greatly influenced by the neighboring Pueblo tribes. Its melodies have a large range, a pendulum-like melodic movement, large intervals, and liberal use of falsetto. The Apache songs tend to have smaller range and tenser singing. What relates them is the form—usually nonstrophic and resembling that of the California-Yuman tribes

—and the rhythmic structure, in which meter is rather well established but changes frequently and suddenly. The note values in each song are few, usually just two, quarters and eights, and it seems likely that the style of Peyote music, as described for the Arapaho above, is in this respect based on the music of the Apache, from whom the use of Peyote for ceremonies had spread to the other tribes. Example 8-4 is a Navaho song.

EXAMPLE 8-4. Navaho Indian Enemy Way ceremony song, from David P. McAllester, *Enemy Way Music* (Cambridge, Mass.: Peabody Museum Papers 49, no. 3, 1954), song no. 35.

5. The Plains-Pueblo area takes in two of the most important cultural groups, the Plains Indians (Blackfoot, Crow, Dakota, Comanche, Kiowa, etc.) and the Pueblo Indians. The most recent aboriginal form of living of the Plains Indians was nomadic; their economy was based on the buffalo. Their loose political and ceremonial structure contrasts with the elaborate organization of life and religion among the Pueblo Indians (Hopi, Zuni, Taos, etc.), and in recent centuries there has been only slight contact among these two groups. Yet their music shares some im-

portant characteristics, particularly the great amount of tension in the singing and the two-part song form, which was described above for the Arapaho. The use of terrace-like melodic contour, gradually descending and leveling off on a long, low tone, is also typical (although the Pueblo songs often precede this form with a low-pitched introduction). The area directly east of the Plains, including such tribes as the Pawnee and the Eastern Woodland tribes such as the Menomini, Chippewa, and Winnebago, shares the main traits of the Plains but adds some characteristic ones of its own. Typically the Plains songs do not have strongly pronounced metric units, nor are repeated rhythmic patterns or motifs usually evident. Among the tribes to the east, however, repeated rhythmic motifs can be identified, and a good many songs have elements of isorhythmic form—a rhythmic pattern repeated several times, with different melodic content each time. Of course, this practice is also found here and there among the typical Plains tribes. Example 8-5 presents an Arapaho song.

EXAMPLE 8-5. Arapaho Sun Dance song, from Bruno Nettl, *Musical Culture of the Arapaho* (M. A. thesis, Indiana University, 1951), p. 100.

Song is repeated four times. Drum begins before the singers.
* Women enter here in repeat.
⊕ During last rendition, women finish alone, without drum.

6. The eastern portion of the United States and Southern Canada may be considered as one musical area, although it is only sporadically known. Perhaps the most distinctive feature is the development of responsorial singing—shouts thrown back and forth between leader and chorus, probably as a result of rudimentary rounds. Forms are frequently elaborate and composed of several phrases, some of which recur. Thus the Eagle Dance ceremony of the Iroquois has many songs with the form of AABAB, in which section A is always accompanied by quick shaking of a rattle, while B has slower percussive accompaniment. Similarly,

some of the southeastern tribes have social dances accompanied by groups of songs strung together in series that are repeated and interwoven in intricate sequences. Vocal technique is tense, and melodic contour usually descending, though not in the predictable terrace patterns of the Plains. The tribes living in the Gulf of Mexico area seem to have had, before the advent of the whites, a very complex culture related to that of the Aztecs, but it is possible that their music was similarly more complex. But little of this remains. Example 8-6 is an Iroquois song, an example of music from the eastern area.

EXAMPLE 8-6. Iroquois thanksgiving ritual song, from Wallace Chafe, *Seneca Thanksgiving Rituals* (Washington, D.C.: Bureau of American Ethnology, Bulletin 183, 1961), p. 66.

The level of musical complexity among these areas varies. Pueblo, eastern, and Northwest Coast are the most complex and developed, while the Great Basin is, on the whole, the simplest. Although the musical areas do not correspond precisely to the culture areas, they do coincide at various major points. Such easily defined culture areas as the Plains and the Northwest Coast have a unified musical style. The greatest cultural diversity as well as the greatest musical variety is found in the western part of the continent. On the other hand, the large number of language families found in North America do not coincide in their geographic distribution with either the musical or the culture areas.

INDIAN MUSIC OF LATIN AMERICA

It is interesting to find some of the North American stylistic traits paralleled in South America. This is true of the terrace-shaped melodic contours of the Plains tribes, which are found also among tribes in Northern Argentina. But in contrast to North America, the South American Indians seem to have developed some polyphony to the level of definite intention; thus the tribes of Tierra del Fuego occasionally sing in parallel fifths.

The Latin America area produced several Indian cultures whose technology and whose social and political organization were considerably higher than those of most nonliterate tribes, and which were comparable perhaps to some of the ancient civilizations of Europe and Asia. We are speaking, of course, of the Mayas of the Yucatan peninsula (who developed a kind of written communication), the Aztecs, and some of their predecessors, the Inca of Peru, and the Chibcha of Colombia. Little of their musical culture has remained, but there is archeological evidence to support the belief that they had rather elaborate musical practices and styles. Their instruments were larger in number,. though not much more complex, than those of other tribes. Pictorial representations of groups of instrumentalists indicate that playing in ensembles was a common practice. The Mexican cultures, though together they span hundreds of years, seem to have used essentially the same instruments: Prominent were the *teponatzli*, a log drum with a slit similar to some of the West African signal drums; the *tlapitzalli* (our names here are the Nahuatl forms—this is the language of the Aztecs), a true flute with four finger holes, made of clay, reed, or bone, with major seconds and minor thirds as the main intervals; the *huehuetl*, a kettle drum which was produced in several distinct sizes and pitches; a conch-shell trumpet; rattles; and rasps. The Incas added to these types a large number of ocarinas, flutes with varying numbers of finger holes (three to eight), and panpipes. The identity of tuning of some Peruvian panpipes with some of Oceania has been a factor in the debate about the possibility and nature of contact between native South America and Oceania.

According to early Spanish accounts[4] of the remnants of Aztec culture, the Aztecs recognized only religious music, and musical life was

---

[4] See Robert Stevenson, *Music in Mexico* (New York: Thomas Y. Crowell Company, 1952), pp. 14–19.

largely in the hands of a professional religious caste. Some instruments themselves had divine power. Music was normally performed by groups in concert, and responsorial singing was heard. Musicians were trained rigidly, and performances had to be completely accurate in order to please the deities; performers who made errors, such as missed drumbeats, were punished.

Before their discovery by the Spaniards, the Inca evidently had an even more elaborate musical culture than the Aztecs. The ruler had specially trained musicians for entertainment at his court. A school of music was instituted at Cuzco by the Inca Roca about 1350,[5] and in the fifteenth century the Inca Pachacuti ordered the collection of narrative songs about the deeds of the earlier Inca rulers; these were organized in song cycles.

THE WORDS OF INDIAN SONGS

The words of Indian songs are of considerable interest, for they frequently fit into the musical structure in unexpected and interesting ways. For example, the Plains Indians, with their two-part song structure, have developed a rather dramatic but simultaneously utilitarian way of setting words to music. Most of the song is taken up with meaningless syllables, such as "he-he" or "ho-ho," but meaningful text appears at the beginning of the second section, which starts again (as does the first) on a high note and works its way downward. The text's structure does not have the characteristics, such as rime or meter, of European poetry; it is rather like prose, although meaningless syllables sometimes appear between words and even between the syllables of one word, presumably in order to keep the stressed syllables on stressed musical beats. The text does not fill the whole second part of the song; when it is finished, meaningless syllables are again used to fill in the rest of the melody. This kind of structure gives considerable flexibility to the composer or poet, for it enables him to substitute new words for old in the same tune, or to make slight changes in the words in order to keep up with the times. Thus warriors of the Plains would report on their exploits in such songs, and the same tune could be used for various exploits. After World War I in which many Indians served as soldiers, old tunes with new words recounting stories of the war began to appear. Such words as "Germany" and an Arapaho word for submarine began to appear in the songs. Frequently these songs used texts from the tribal wars, but simply substi-

[5] Robert Stevenson, *The Music of Peru: Aboriginal and Viceroyal Epochs* (Washington: Pan American Union, 1959), p. 39.

tuted German soldiers for Indian tribes; for example, "The German officer ran and dragged his blanket along." The following are song texts of the Arapaho:[6]

Woman, don't worry about me; I'm coming back home to eat berries.
I am the crow; watch me.
The bird has come; it makes yellow the sky.
Young man, be brave; you're going to a dangerous place; your chieftainship
    will become famous.
Really it is good to be young, for old age is not far off.
The Ute Indian, while he was still looking around for me, I scalped him alive.
Young man, it is good that you are going to war.

Elsewhere among the North American Indians, however, meaningless syllables are not so prevalent, and entire tunes are accompanied by words; the subjects range from serious thoughts about the gods to lyrical complaints about the weather, to frivolous love songs. But the meaningless syllable songs occupy an important role, analogous perhaps to instrumental music. Thus there are entire bodies of song that use meaningless syllables. The famous night chant of the Navaho, the "yeibetchai," includes a group of songs sung by masked dancers in falsetto with only syllables. Many of the Peyote songs use only meaningless words, but, interestingly enough, they use special patterns such as "yowitsini," "heyowitsi," and "heyowitsinayo," which can easily be identified as belonging to the Peyote. Some of the Indian texts are long and elaborate; the Navaho songs may enumerate holy people, places, or things in great numbers. More commonly, however, a short sentence or phrase is repeated several times.

INDIAN MUSIC IN MODERN AMERICA

Considering the small number of Indians and the tremendous impact of Western culture on their lives, it would be surprising if their music had remained uninfluenced by that of the West, and particularly by Western thought and ideas about music. The effect of Westernization can be seen in many, sometimes contradictory, ways. It is important, first, to note that there is an important difference between North and Latin American Indian cultures. The Indians of Latin America, who in several countries now make up the bulk of the Spanish-speaking popula-

[6] Collected by Bruno Nettl.

tion, have learned the folk music styles of Spain and have also developed styles that are to a considerable extent mixtures of European and Indian materials. For example, in the Andes of Peru, tunes in an essentially Hispanic style are played on the aboriginal Indian panpipes; many similar illustrations could be cited. On the other hand, in North America —probably because the Indians have largely been segregated—such a mixture of styles did not take place. But there is a great deal of evidence that principles of musical thought, aesthetics, and social organization from the white Americans have made their mark in contemporary North American musical culture. To be sure, many American Indians now participate in purely Western musical practices; but they do not have, as a major part of their repertory, music that sounds both Indian and Western, although their way of singing the strictly Indian music may be influenced subtly by Western ideas of making music.

The fact that North American Indian and European musical styles have not merged is probably in part due to the great difference between them, a difference verging on incompatibility (in contrast, for instance, to the greater compatibility between European and African musics). But despite the points made in the previous paragraph, there are some changes in style that have come about through Western music. More recent Indian songs appear to have an interval and intonation structure more like that of Western music than do older songs. Accompaniment of piano or guitar is occasionally found.

Even so, the influence of Western civilization on Indian music is most commonly felt in less direct ways, and this is true of both the historical and the contemporary Indian cultures. In Mexico and Peru, the relatively high developments of music were reduced to simpler levels and styles through the annihilation of the aboriginal ruling classes, and through the introduction of Christianity. In Central America, the presence of simple xylophone-like instruments facilitated the introduction of the African *marimba*. In North America, tribes with radically different cultures became neighbors and learned from each other. One example is the Shawnee tribe, which at the time of first white contact was located in the southeastern United States, but had probably come from the Northeast a few centuries before. The Shawnee tribe participated in the music of the eastern musical area but was forced to migrate repeatedly and was finally located largely in Oklahoma, near the Plains Indians. Its repertory today contains songs in both the Eastern and Plains styles, simple songs of an older layer which the Shawnee may have brought with them from the Northeast, and songs in the Peyote style.

The spreading of the Peyote and Ghost Dance styles to tribes with other kinds of music, such as the Plains Indians, was also a result, though somewhat indirect, of the impact of Western culture, which caused the rapid spreading of new religions that were needed to cope with the drastically changed condition of the Indians, and which brought about the equally rapid distribution of musical styles. These kinds of indirect influences of Western civilization that we can trace in the period of American history before 1950 continue into the present.

Among the Indians of the United States, and of the Northern Plains in particular, music is developing and flourishing. Its role now is primarily that of a symbol of Indian identity, because it is one of the few aspects of Indian life into which the white man has not penetrated, and which he is usually unwilling to take the trouble to imitate. While Indians can hardly avoid trying to enter the Western economic and political systems, and while they have been converted religiously as a result of centuries of missionizing, there is little reason why they should not continue to sing in distinctively Indian musical styles. But many of the activities to which music was essential in the past are now gone—religion, war, the buffalo. On the other hand, the fact that Indians of various tribes have been thrown together on some of the reservations, and also their relatively greater mobility (along with other Americans), has added to a desire on their part to ,retain single, Indian identity, rather than separate tribal identity, and has facilitated musical contact and exchange of materials among Indian tribes. All of this has led to a pan-Indian culture and musical style, based essentially on the culture of the Plains, as far as music is concerned, but distributed throughout a large part of the United States and Canada. In this culture, the older, largely ceremonial musics live on only as relics, to be occasionally dusted off and brought out for the sake of tradition, and living vividly only in the memory of older persons who remember earlier times. (But there is evidence that each generation, as it grows older, begins to take an interest in this older material, so that it does not completely die out.)

Flourishing, however, is the music accompanying social dances. Here we find many songs being composed each year, and we see the development of a class of singers and drummers who are semi-professional, admired not for the power which their knowledge of songs brings them but for their knowledge of a repertory, and for the excellence with which they perform it—a way of thinking about music typical of Western culture. We see Indians recognizing musical composition as a human rather than a supernatural act. We find older practices, such as the Sun Dance, translated into the modern powwow, which has the social functions of the old Sun Dance—bringing the tribe together and permitting social interchange, gambling, and athletic contests—but which no longer has the religious function. We find a higher degree of standardization of musical forms, due perhaps to the greater standardization in the forms of Western music known to the Indians, hymns and country and Western music, but also perhaps due to the need for learning songs from other tribes as quickly as possible. Large intertribal festivals in such places as Anadarko, Oklahoma, and Gallup, New Mexico, accelerate the inter-tribal contacts and provide a Western-style forum for star Indian musicians and dancers. Because Indian languages are no longer spoken by all Indians, and because speakers of various languages will sing a song together, there is an acceleration of the old Plains practice of singing songs without words, with meaningless syllables only, or, occasionally, of singing Indian songs with English words. And Indian music has become, like Western music, something which expert musicians perform for an audience (both Indian and white), rather than as an integral part of many everyday activities. Record companies now issue disks primarily for an Indian market. All of this shows that Indian musical culture in North America is still very much alive, but that its functions and uses have changed as the life-style of the Indians has changed, in the direction of Western culture. Thus the role of music in Indian life is today very much like the role of folk music in the life of other minorities in North American culture.

BIBLIOGRAPHY AND DISCOGRAPHY

Since this chapter introduces the music of the Americas generally, besides covering American Indian music, some publications on the entire subject may be cited here. Charles Haywood, *A Bibliography of North American Folklore and Folksong,* rev. ed. (New York: Dover, 1961, 2 vols.) and Gilbert Chase, *A Guide to the Music of Latin America,* 2nd ed. (Washington: Pan American Union, 1962) are indispensable bibliographies. Bruno Nettl, *An Introduction to Folk Music in the United States* (Detroit: Wayne State University Press, 1960) is a brief survey.

Two attempts to show the various styles in North American Indian music are Helen H. Roberts, *Musical Areas in Aboriginal North America* (New Haven: Yale University Press, 1936) and Bruno Nettl, *North American Indian Musical Styles* (Philadelphia: American Folklore Society, 1954). The most prolific author on North American Indian music was Frances Densmore, and all of her publications, many of them published by the Bureau of American Ethnology, Smithsonian Institution, Washington, D.C., are worth examination. Recent developments in this field are discussed by Willard Rhodes, "Acculturation in North American Indian Music," in *Acculturation in the Americas,* ed. Sol Tax (Chicago: University of Chicago Press, 1952).

The best overall study of the music and musical culture of an American Indian tribe is Alan P. Merriam, *Ethnomusicology of the Flathead In-*

dians (Chicago: Aldine Press, 1967). Special problems and styles are discussed in David P. McAllester, *Peyote Music* (New York: Viking Fund Publications in Anthropology, 13, 1949) and *Enemy Way Music* (Cambridge, Mass.: Peabody Museum of Harvard University, 1954), and Bruno Nettl, "Studies in Blackfoot Indian Musical Culture," *Ethnomusicology*, 11–12, 1967–68.

Among the important publications on Indian music in Latin America are Robert Stevenson, *Music in Aztec and Inca Territory* (Berkeley: University of California Press, 1968), Marguerite and Raoul d'Harcourt, "La musique des Aymara sur les hauts plateaux boliviens," *Journal de la Société des Américanistes*, 48, (1959), 5–133, and Karl G. Izikowitz, *Musical and Other Sound Instruments of the South American Indians* (Goteborg: Elanders, 1935).

The Library of Congress has issued a number of recordings made from Frances Densmore's and Willard Rhodes's collections in its series, *Folk Music of the United States*. North American Soundchief Enterprises has issued a number of records, primarily of Plains Indian music, and mainly illustrative of recent developments, in a series, *Songs of the Red Man*. This series, and the records issued by Indian House, Taos, N.M., are for use by scholars as well as American Indians interested in hearing songs of their own heritage. Other recordings of North American Indian music of interest are *Indian Music of the Canadian Plains*, Folkways P 464; *American Indians of the Southwest*, Folkways FW8850, and *Music of the Sioux and Navaho*, Folkways P 401. Indian music of Latin America is presented on *Indian Music of Mexico*, Folkways P 413; *Music from the Mato Grosso*, Folkways P 446; *Indian Music of the Upper Amazon*, Folkways P 458; *Instruments and Music of Bolivia*, Folkways FM4012; and *Mountain Music of Peru*, Folkways FE4539.

NINE

LATIN AMERICAN FOLK MUSIC

by Gérard Béhague

The Latin American continent presents, on the whole, cultural traits obviously inherited from the Iberian Peninsula, but its folk music traditions have generally preserved less of that old heritage than North American folk music has kept of British lore. Many parts of what (for the sake of convenience) is called "Latin America" are virtually devoid of any Latin cultural elements. Many tropical-forest Amerindian cultures, for example, and some Indian groups of the Bolivian *altiplano* are still relatively untouched by European traditions. Moreover, in many cases the prevailing cultural influences are Afro-American and not Latin American. The study of folk music in individual countries or territories is bound to be somewhat artificial, although common cultural traits do exist in very large geographical areas, such as the areas, formerly occupied by the Inca Empire, that extend from Western Argentina to the highlands of Northern Ecuador, or in the areas of Afro-American populations, found in Brazil, Trinidad, Cuba, and Western Colombia, Ecuador, and Venezuela with their analogous developments. In such areas a geographical approach to the study of folk music could be justified.

The degree to which a single culture predominates—Hispanic, Amerindian, or African—varies greatly among the nations; and, within nations, among regions. For example, Bolivia, whose people of Indian descent represent about seventy percent of the total population, has essentially traditional music (Aymara, Quechua) in the *altiplano* area but, in the valleys and the eastern provinces, has typical mestizo (a term indicating culturally and racially mixed groups in Latin America) folk music, characterized by Spanish tunes and words but using Indian instruments and accompanying dances of Indian origin. Conversely, it is not uncommon to find rather isolated highland Indian groups using string instruments clearly of Spanish descent, such as the ubiquitous *charango* (an instrument with five double strings, made in its most rustic form out of an armadillo shell) and the harp. As opposed to Indian music of tropical forest cultures (Mato Grosso, Upper Amazon), Indian music of the Andean countries represents, as a whole, a dominant ingredient of the folk music traditions of the area. In the transfer of Hispanic or African material to the Americas, syncretism accounts for the creation of certain forms and the preservation or rejection of others. It is, therefore, accurate to assume that genuine Latin American folk music traditions are the result of mestizo cultures.

In addition, the actual history and ethnohistory of a given country or area should be considered in accounting for specific stylistic traits. A case in point would be a comparative historical study of such Caribbean islands as Haiti, Jamaica, and Trinidad. While all three countries have a large majority of population of African descent, they were at various periods of their history under the political and cultural domination of Spain, France, and Great Britain. In the case of Trinidad, although France actually never dominated her, French influences (e.g., Trinidadian *créole*) have been considerable. In addition, the Western African cultures transferred to those areas have quite diverse origins: Ewe (Dahomey) in the case of Haiti, mostly Yoruba (Nigeria) and Ashanti (Ghana) in Jamaica and Trinidad. The problem becomes exceedingly intricate when one considers the immigration of East Indians to Trinidad, Guiana, and Surinam, or more recently, that of Germans and Italians to Brazil, Uruguay, and Argentina.

The Latin American folk music arena is, then, a very complex one, and a macroscopic exposition alone will be presented here, resorting to a few illustrations of what is found rather than a survey of the entire wealth of song, dance, and instrument types. For the sake of clarity, though somewhat arbitrarily, we should distinguish between the Hispanic related folk music genres, on the one hand, and Mestizo folk genres, subdivided into Indian-Hispanic and Afro-Hispanic, on the other. Afro-American music in Latin America is discussed in Chapter Ten.

SOUTH AMERICA

Folk Songs

Examples of autonomous folk song genres are relatively few in South American folk music, since, in a very high proportion of the repertory, song functions as an accompaniment to dancing. Throughout the continent we find a multitude of song types derived from the old Spanish *romance*, a narrative song form dating back to the early Renaissance, typically based on eight-syllable lines and four-line stanzas. Under different local names, *romances* have been preserved sometimes in their original form (e.g., in Colombia) and sometimes with significant variations which reveal the characteristic thought and feeling of the creole of a given region. The *copla*, a ballad type derived from the *romance*, is common throughout Colombia, the Andean countries, and Argentina. Typically, *romances* and *coplas* describe, in an epic lyrical manner, famous historical events of a region or episodes of everyday life. Apart from their poetic and musical value, they often provide significant sociological data. Other folk songs, such as the Argentine and Chilean *tonadas* and *tonos*, have maintained old Spanish literary forms besides that of the *romance*. The *glosa* and the *décima* are forms consisting of two parts, the first a quatrain which sets the basic subject, the second a development of it in a stanza of ten octosyllabic lines. This structure is found in Chilean, Peruvian, Ecuadorian, and Colombian *décimas*, Argentine *estilos* and *cifras*, and in many other genres, such as the *guabina* of Colombia or the *romances* and *xácaras* of Brazil. The classical rhyme scheme of the Spanish *décima*, ABBAACCDDC, prevails in most of the folk song types mentioned. Example 9-1 shows two versions of a traditional *romance* known in Lima, Peru. Entitled *La esposa difunta o la Aparición*, its origin has been traced to sixteenth century Spain. The regular two- and four-bar phrases and their isometric structure are characteristic of Spanish folk song. Literary versions of the same *romance* have been collected in New Mexico, California, Mexico, Nicaragua, Cuba, the Dominican Republic, Puerto Rico, Venezuela, Ecuador, and several provinces of Argentina, which attests to the wide diffusion of the *romance* tradition in Latin America.

But actual Iberian folk melodies still extant in Spain and Portugal today are very rare in Latin America. Children's songs seem to be the

EXAMPLE 9-1. Two versions of the romance *La esposa difunta o la Aparición*. From Emilia Romero, *El Romance Tradicional en el Perú* (Mexico: El Colegio de México, 1952), p. 89.

notable exceptions, for many of them remain basically the same in both areas. The problem of the origin of Hispanic tunes in Latin American folk music is generally unsolved. But we can say with some certainty that the tunes sung in Latin America are for the most part not simply imports from Spain and Portugal (the texts more frequently are). They are more usually songs either composed in Latin America in the styles brought from Europe, or they are indeed songs brought from Europe centuries ago but so changed by the process of oral tradition that the tunes in Europe that are related to them can no longer be recognized as relatives; or perhaps it is the European tunes that have undergone change. This situation is not completely paralleled by the traditions of minority groups living in South America—Germans, East Europeans, Italians—for these have preserved many of the songs that they brought from Europe, but they have not to a large extent created new material in the traditional styles.

A recent study of the Chilean *verso*,[1] a traditional type of sung poetry, has conclusively shown stylistic similarities with Spanish Medieval and Renaissance genres (*cantigas, villancicos*), especially as to modality and cadential practices. Such archaic elements are also found in

[1] María Ester Grebe, *The Chilean Verso: A Study in Musical Archaism* (Los Angeles: Latin American Center, University of California, 1967).

Brazil in some folk melody types associated with the *desafio* (literally "challenge"), with texts consisting of questions and answers, that are performed by two singers, often presenting antiphonal musical structure with instrumental interludes (guitar) between the vocal sections. The most common literary form of *desafio* in Brazil is the six-line heptasyllabic stanza, common in Portuguese popular poetry. One of the most popular song types, closely related to the *desafio,* is the *embolada,* found throughout Brazil's hinterland. Mostly improvised, it presents a characteristic refrain in addition to the six-line stanza. As in many Brazilian songs, the refrain makes use of alliteration, assonance, and onomatopoeia in a syncopated melodic line and an unusually fast tempo. The text of the *embolada,* based on stereotyped models, comments on local customs and criticizes figures and events of the community in a very provocative manner. The *embolada* has actually penetrated the urban areas in the last few decades; there it is used mostly as a chronicle of current events. But, as a whole, *desafios* and *emboladas,* together with songs of praises (*louvações*) constitute the main bulk of the folk song repertory of Northeastern Brazil. This particular folk music tradition is referred to in Brazil as the "caboclo" tradition, i.e., showing traits inherited from the Portuguese and some local Amerindian cultures. In this tradition, we generally find modal melodies, with frequent occurrences of the Lydian and Mixolydian modes. In addition, an artificial mode consisting of a major diatonic scale with the fourth degree sharpened and the seventh flattened often appears in the *caboclo* repertory.

Song genres similar to the *desafio* are widely used elsewhere in South America, variously called *contrapunto* and *cifra* in Argentina, *payas* in Chile, or *porfias* in Venezuela.

Folk songs of lyrical character whose subject matter is associated with love abound in South American folk music. Generically known as *tonadas* in the Spanish-speaking countries, and *toadas* in Brazil, they appear, typically, in four-, five-, or ten-line stanzas, sometimes incorporating a refrain. The Argentine *estilo* will serve as an example. According to Isabel Aretz, the *estilo* is a well defined lyrical song genre; made up of two melodic ideas, the "theme," properly speaking, and a somewhat faster strain known as *alegre.*[2] The overall formal aspect of the song is ternary, ABA. The text of the *estilo* is generally set in quatrains or *décimas.* In the Cuyo province of Argentina as well as in Chile, the *estilo* is known as *tonada,* and in the northern provinces it is called *verso* or *décima.* The *estilo* is also common in Uruguay. Example 9-2 illustrates

---

[2] Isabel Aretz, *El folklore musical argentino* (Buenos Aires: Ricordi Americana, 1952), p. 144.

the characteristics of this folk song species: guitar accompaniment (both picked and strummed styles), vocal duet, and the "theme" and "alegre" sections.

EXAMPLE 9-2. *Estilo.* From Isabel Aretz, *El Folklore Musical Argentino* (Buenos Aires: Ricordi Americana, 1952), p. 147.

An interesting example of folk song in South America is the Brazilian *modinha*, for its origin has been traced to cultivated musical circles in Portugal and Brazil of the eighteenth century. It is a love song type whose actual printed examples from the nineteenth century reveal a strongly melodramatic character, fairly similar to salon music of the period. *Moda* is a generic term applied vaguely to a song, or any melody. The *Moda-de-viola*, however, is a lyrical folk song type known especially in the rural areas of the central and southern states. Its Portuguese antecedents are most obviously seen in the singing in parallel thirds and the ·guitar accompaniment. The text assumes very often a narrative, satirical, or sentimental character, with strong reminiscences of the Iberian *romance*. *Modinha*, the diminutive of *moda*, actually became part of Brazilian folk music only in the latter part of the nineteenth century, when it lost gradually its original Italian operatic flavor and became a simple sentimental song. In the course of its popularization it acquired simpler structures, such as ABACA, or a refrain and a stanza. With its cultivated origin, the *modinha* clearly illustrates the transplanting of European musical culture into the popular music of Brazil.

A fairly important body of folk songs in South America comes from popular religious customs accompanying the liturgical calendar of the Catholic church. Here again, the repertory exhibits close relationship with the Iberian Peninsula. Brought to the New World by Spanish missionaries, hymns and songs of praise are still found today and are known as *alabados* and *alabanzas*. Most of them are prevailingly modal and follow the traditional pattern of folk-hymn singing, i.e., alternation of refrain (*estribillo*—chorus) and stanza (*copla*—solo). In the Chocó province of Colombia, the *alabado* is also used at wakes to pay tribute to the dead person; the text represents the autobiography of that person and is improvised. Most religious folk songs are associated with the Christmas season. Thus the traditional Spanish *villancico* has developed into numerous folk song genres, known as *aguinaldo, adoración, coplas de Navidad, esquinazo,* and others in the various countries of Latin America. While most of this body of songs obviously relates to its Spanish counterpart, it also displays many mestizo or *criollo* characteristics. For example, the Venezuelan *villancicos* and *aguinaldos* present a regular meter in 2/4, 6/8, or 3/4, regular phrases of two- and four-bar lengths, major and minor mode or bimodality, melodies in parallel thirds with a range not exceeding a sixth, almost total absence of modulation and chromaticism, and syllabic setting of the text.[3] All of these features are part of the Hispanic Christmas *cancionero*. But most *aguinaldos* differ from the

[3] Isabel Aretz, *Cantos navideños en el folklore venezolano* (Caracas: Casa de la Cultura Popular, 1962), pp. 40–42.

Spanish *villancico* in rhythmic structure. In addition to the indispensable *cuatro* (a small four-string guitar), they are accompanied by various percussion instruments, such as a double-headed drum (*tambora criolla*), a friction drum (*furruco*), a shaker-rattle (*chineco*), a *güiro*-type rattle (*charrasca*), and maracas. This accompaniment typically is based on the alternation of binary and ternary rhythmic figures, so common in mestizo dances such as the *merengue* and the *guasa*.[4] The melodies of the Venezuelan *aguinaldos* tend also to be more syncopated than the Spanish *villancico*. Example 9-3 shows some of the features of the Venezuelan *aguinaldo*.

EXAMPLE 9-3. Venezuelan Aguinaldo. From Isabel Aretz, *Cantos navideños en el folklore Venezolano* (Caracas: Casa de la cultura popular, 1962), p. 111.

[4] *Ibid.*, p. 92.

Autos and Dramatic Dances

Many of the Latin American Christmas songs are associated with popular dramatizations of the Nativity and the journey of the Three Kings, as well as with processions of various kinds. Such festivities are known throughout the continent and are variously called *posadas, auto sacramental, pastoris,* etc. Dance forms an integral part of such revelries.

True rituals associated with the Roman Catholic feasts of the Lord and the commemoration of saints' days, offering examples of cycles of syncretic feasts, are quite common in Latin America. Among these, the carnival is the most popular one. Many folk dances and songs function within the summer and winter cycles of feasts, such as St. John's day or feasts to the Virgin, in which syncretism with African deities is often present. In Brazil, for example, there exist many dramatic dances whose central subject is always religious. Conversion is the main theme of such dramatic dances as *congada, marujada,* and *moçambique,* while *quilombo caiapó, cabocolinhos,* and *lambe-sujo,* among others, are concerned with resurrection. Most of these dances appeared during the colonial period as a result of the Hispanic catechization. In Brazil, specifically, the Jesuits were responsible for diffusing many of them and for giving them unity and uniformity. Indeed, the *congada,* for example, is known all over Brazil. It combines elements of the popular religious theatre of the Peninsula and Afro-Brazilian traditions and customs, such as the coronation of Black Kings during the slave period. But in spite of its name and the fact that Blacks participate in it in large numbers, the history of the dance suggests that it is not of African origin but simply "a remembrance of the *Chanson de Roland* (the medieval French *chanson de geste*) wisely turned to the advantage of the catechist."[5] A consideration of the musical components of this dramatic play points to the absence of any particularly evident African element, although call and response pattern is often found, and drums frequently accompany the chorus. The songs accompanying the cortege, which is led by the main characters, show typical traits of Portuguese folk songs. The text of the play always appears in verse rather than prose, resulting in the adoption and transformation of the main incidents of the medieval epic poem.

---

[5] Alceu Maynard Araújo, *Folclore Nacional,* Vol. I (São Paulo: Edições Melhoramentos, 1964), p. 216.

Folk Dances

In the category of "secular" folk and popular dances the Latin American continent enjoys a well-known distinction. Many such dances originated in the Iberian peninsula, and while they have undergone considerable changes in the New World, choreographic traits specific to much Spanish folk dancing, such as shoe-tapping or finger snapping, remain significant in many dances. This is the case of the Argentine *chacarera* whose actual origins remain to be uncovered. The name of the dance is apparently derived from *chacra* meaning "farm" (from the Quechua *chagra*—"corn field"); thus it is believed that the *chacarera* was probably created by the farmers of the plains in the province of Buenos Aires, although it is used in almost all Argentine provinces. The choreography includes stamping of the feet and snapping of the fingers. Musically, Spanish ancestry appears, among other elements, in the hemiola rhythm (alternation of 6/8 and 3/4 meters) of the instrumental introduction, generally six or eight measures long. The rhythmic pattern of that introduction is 𝄞 , and that of the vocal part which follows is 𝄞 ; both are very common in Spanish folk music.[6] The vocal part is generally sung by one soloist, although trios have gained much popularity in the last few decades. The text, of good-humored, satirical, or comic character, consists of four quatrains of octosyllabic lines, coinciding with the six figures of the dance. The *chacarera* also appears in exclusively instrumental versions; the instruments used are harp, guitar (*punteada*), violin, or accordion, with a drum accompaniment.

One of the most important *criolla* dances (i.e., native, indigenous) of the Argentine countryside is the *gato*. Not only is it widespread, but other dances derive from it. Here also the Spanish heritage comes to light. Dance figures include shoe-tapping steps performed by women. Much like *flamenco* female dancers, the women lift their long skirts to show the agility of the foot movements. Another familiar choreographic figure is the so-called *escobillado* (or *escobilleo*), a very fast foot movement performed by men, consisting of swinging one foot after the other with scraping of the ground. Rhythmically and formally, the *gato* presents singular features. The text of the sung *gato* follows the form of the *seguidilla*, a four-line verse pattern in which the second line is assonant with the fourth. But the lines of the *gato* are of seven and

[6] Cf. Isabel Aretz, *El folklore musical*, pp. 202–205.

five syllables, in alternation. This textual irregularity creates, in a strict syllabic setting, a rather uneven melodic phrasing. In actual performance, however, the difficulty is surmounted by anticipating the last accent of the seven-syllable line and by augmenting the note values in the melodic phrase corresponding to the five-syllable line. The *gato* is accompanied by a guitarist who also sings. The specific Spanish guitar technique known as *guitarra rasgueada* (strumming) is used here consistently, in a 6/8 meter. Picked guitar is used only in the prelude and interludes. Characteristically, the rhythmic formula of the *gato* alternates between 6/8 and 3/4 meters (the hemiola rhythm again). Generally, the sung *gato* is made up of four melodic phrases, repeated with some minor variants in the following order: prelude, AABB, interlude, AB, interlude, CD, in which prelude and interludes are strictly instrumental. Whenever it is sung in duet, parallel thirds prevail, a characteristic of Iberian folk polyphony.

Among the many Argentine folk dances for couples, the *zamba* should be mentioned. Together with such dances as the *aires* and the *lorencita*, it is a "scarf dance" (*danza de pañuelo*). According to Carlos Vega and Isabel Aretz, there exists in Argentina (and in Chile, Peru, and Ecuador for that matter) a true code involving the use and function of the scarf. The *zamba* has a rather obscure history. An old colonial Peruvian dance known as *Zamacueca* or *Zambacueca* (today *marinera*) was introduced into Argentina during the first half of the nineteenth century. Out of this dance emerged the *zamba* on the one hand, and the *cueca* on the other. The latter became one of the most familiar dances of Chile and Bolivia. In the Western provinces of Argentina the name *chilena* was used to designate the Chilean *cueca*. Thus the three names *zamba*, *cueca*, and *chilena* have survived and have, nowadays, specific meanings. Choreographically, *zamba* and *cueca* differ considerably. While the basic figures are similar, the overall development of the dances depart from each other. The *cueca* allows extemporized shoe-tapping, whereas the *zamba* adheres more strictly to less vivid and traditional figures. Musically, both dances are indistinguishable as to general form but present different melodic types. Both show preference for four musical phrases, the last two of which are repeated. They both start with an eight-measure introduction and end with a coda in which new melodic material is presented. The prevailing meter is 6/8, with subdivisions of ternary and binary figures. For the *zamba* the basic rhythmic formula for both accompaniment and melody is $\frac{6}{8}$ ♫♫♩ ♪♩ , although a $\frac{3}{4}$ ♩ ♩ ♩ accompaniment figure occurs rather frequently.

The *zamba* is essentially instrumental, although vocal versions also exist.

Traditionally, the performing ensemble includes the violin for the melody, the guitar for harmonic support, and the drum (*bombo*) for accompaniment. In recent times, the accordion tends to substitute for the violin. Older *zamba* melodies tend to exhibit a modal ambiguity, due to the alternation of major and minor thirds, or that of B natural and B flat in the dorian mode; the melodic minor scale also appears. More recent melodies adhere strictly to the major mode; so do *cueca* melodies, which tend, however, to end on the fifth degree of the scale. But it is in their rhythmic cast that *cuecas* differ intrinsically from the *zamba*. *Cuecas* are essentially vocal and their texts follow the *seguidilla* form, resulting in the same metric irregularity observed previously with the *gato*. Only the guitar accompanies the *cueca*, with the occasional addition in the Western provinces of the *charango*, under the influence of the Chilean and Bolivian *cueca*. The accompaniment consists typically of a regular strumming in 6/8 (♩ ♫ ♫ ♪ ♪ ♪), creating cross-rhythmic effects with the vocal line.

Many Brazilian folk songs and dances also exhibit considerable European retentions. For example, many of the round dance types used in the *fandangos* in southern Brazil are of Portuguese derivation. These *fandangos* are popular rural revelries in which regional dances, such as the *tirana, tatu, balaio, recortado*, and many others, are performed. One of the most frequent components of these dances is shoe-tapping; another, in the state of Rio Grande do Sul, is the use of castanets. Thus *fandango* was transformed in Brazil into a generic term, which suggests that the Spanish dance of the same name was once popular there, as it was in Portugal. The numerous designations of these dances derive from the song texts. Typically, the singing, which alternates stanza and refrain and is always in fauxbourdon style, is the responsibility of the guitar players.

The Andean Area

Bolivia, Peru, and Ecuador are good examples of nations in which the Spanish culture was greatly influenced by that of the Indians. The combination of stylistic elements from the Indian and Spanish populations in the whole area formerly occupied by the Inca Empire—a combination which did not occur with the English and Indian styles in North America—was probably due to the greater musical sophistication of the Andean populations as compared to the relatively simpler musical cultures of the North American Indians. In his study of instruments used by the Incas and their predecessors, Robert Stevenson (see bibliography for this chapter) has conclusively shown that the Andean peoples had, at the time of the conquest, the most refined musical culture of the whole American continent. Not only did they know five- and six-hole flutes with unequal finger-holes, fourteen- and fifteen-tube *antaras* (panpipes made of clay), double-row panpipes with unequal pipe-growth, and cross flutes, but their instrument making proves their intent to use predetermined pitches. Today, in the Andean area there is hardly any village or town (even in the Spanish-speaking villages) that does not have a kind of traditional music with elements of Indian musical culture. The widespread use of pre-Colombian instruments, such as the panpipe (called *sicu* by the Aymaras and *antara* by the Quechuas) and vertical flute (*pincollo, pincullo*), attests to that influence. The ubiquitous end-blown flute known as *quena* is used along with European types of drums in processions for Catholic saints, and in social dances, along with post-Colombian indigenous instruments such as the *charango*. It is very difficult in Bolivia, Peru, and Ecuador to separate the musical elements of Indian origin from those of the European tradition. Acculturation began in the sixteenth century; it was consciously fostered by the Catholic missionaries, who realized that the survival of Christianity depended in part on its absorption of native elements. The elements of the two cultures combined to form inseparable units. Essentially, the tunes are European in style, but a very large number show a great deal of repetition and make use of tetratonic and pentatonic scales. The introduction of diatonic scales in modern times has required adjustments in instrument making. Thus, today, six- and seven-hole *quenas* are more common than the three- or four-hole models. In addition, European string instruments (violin, guitar, lute, harp) have, to a great extent, modified the essential character of highland Indian music. For example, European harmonic patterns have been added to a music that was probably essentially monodic. These patterns form today the basic support for melodies of clearly non-European character. In their study (see bibliography), the d'Harcourts have analyzed the various modes used in Quechua music. Out of some two hundred melodies collected in the highlands, the majority show a descending progression and are built on the pentatonic scale without semitone, G-E-D-C-A, where the highest tone tends to act as a dominant. Literally hundreds of songs in the highland Andean area present this melody type. Obviously mestizo melodies abound, many of them based in part on the European diatonic scale. But all tunes maintain a modal flavor, a prevailingly descending tendency, large intervals, and few modulations. Rhythmically, Indian traits also prevail. Duple meters, with binary and ternary divisions, are the most frequent, especially a dactylic formula for percussion accompaniment. Syncopated melodic lines are also very common in pure song genres, such as the *yaravi*, and in dance types, such as the *huayno*. Particularly important is the syncopation of ♪♪ ♩ together with ♩. ♩. While the same syncopation occurs in most Afro-American music in Latin America, the resulting effect (here) is quite different, partly because the first note of each beat tends to be strongly accented. Another rhythmic peculiarity of much Andean melodic material is an emphasis of shorter note values when they occur at the beginning of a beat. Example 9-4, taken from the d'Harcourts' study, illustrates these peculiarities. 6/8 meters are also very common

EXAMPLE 9-4. Rhythmic formulas of Andean music. From Raoul and Marguerite d'Harcourt, *La Musique des Incas et ses survivances* (Paris: P. Geuthner, 1925), p. 156.

and frequently used in alternation with 3/4 (again the hemiola we noted in Argentine dances). Triple meters are found in mestizo music in which Spanish elements appear more clearly, but tunes of song types of Indian descent, such as the *yaravi*, are also often cast in triple meter. Finally, many Indian and mestizo song melodies are of a non-mensural nature. Typical accompanimental rhythmic figures of the Andean area represent the unmistakably Indian percussion style. This style consists, for the most part, in a straightforward, systematic repetition of the simplest figures. In addition to the dactylic rhythm in 2/4 already mentioned, the percussion presents the following figures: ¾ ♩ ♫ ♩ and ⅜ ♩ ♪♪♩. . In some instances, such as the *cachua*

(or *kashua*) dance of the Aymaras of Bolivia, the percussion accompaniment consists of a simple continuous rolling of the drum. String accompaniment, whether with harp, *charango*, or guitar, also presents distinct features. Among these, one particularly favored pattern which can be considered as a true trademark of the Andes is a series of arpeggios based on two fifths, with roots a minor third apart, presented in a rhythmic figure of an eighth followed by two sixteenths (Example 9-5). This pattern represents the basic accompaniment of many dances, such as the *wayno* (*huayno*), *carnaval, pandilla, and pampeña*, to name a few.

Formally, strophic form dominates much of Quechua and Aymara music. The simplest types of variation are fairly common as well. Improvisation does exist but does not have a major role. Mestizo songs or tunes tend to be in binary or ternary structures, with parallelism

EXAMPLE 9-5. Accompanimental patterns of Andean dance music. From Raoul and Marguerite d'Harcourt, *La Musique des Incas et ses survivances* (Paris: P. Geuthner, 1925), p. 162.

in thirds. Aymara instrumental ensembles, on the other hand, very often present the melody doubled at the fourth and the octave, especially in the *sicus* ensembles.

Many indigenous dances of the Aymara and Quechua Indians, including pantomime dances, have become traditional for celebrating Catholic religious feasts as well as their own rituals. For example, the dance of *Kena-Kena* (or *Uturunku*) is used for the feast of the Holy Cross; that of the *Wipfala* is associated with the agrarian rituals (to the deity of the earth, Pachamama) and is preferably performed during the harvest season and on August 15 (Assumption day). The Quechua and Aymara peoples also have dances like the numerous dramatic dances of Latin America involving Christians and Moors, but reminiscent of events from the conquest period, or of the glory of the past. For example, the *Chunchus and Collas* dance of Peru involves two sides representing Spanish soldiers and Indians, and the well-known *Baile del Inca* of the Quechuas and Aymaras reminds one of Atahualpa's cruel death.

Among the principal social dances of the Andes is the *huayno*, popular from Northern Argentina to Ecuador where it is known as *sanjuanito* (this term could be derived from "huainito" rather than San Juan). Although an Indian dance, it has been adopted by mestizos of the highlands as their own. The Aymara and Quechua *huaynos* still exhibit an aboriginal character, but with an increasing degree of Spanish flavor in both music and texts. Indian *huaynos* are generally sung in the native languages, although lyrics in both Spanish and Quechua, for example, are not uncommon. In lively tempo, the *huayno* appears most of the time in duple meter and in binary form, consisting of two phrases (AB) of equal length (generally four measures each) repeated *ad libitum*. Versions alternating triple and duple meter (or compound duple), or simply alternating binary and ternary divisions in a single meter, are fairly frequent. Most tunes associated with the dance take the pentatonic mode (G-E-D-C-A) as their basis. Example 9-6 shows one of the most typical versions of the *huayno*.

EXAMPLE 9-6. The typical *huayno kaypipas,* from Cuzco, Peru. From *Cancionero Andino Sur,* ed. by Consuelo Pagaza Galdo (Lima: Casa Mozart, 1967), p. 13. Collected by Consuelo Pagaza Galdo and transcribed by Rodolfo Holzmann.

Afro-Hispanic Folk Music

The last major South American folk musical tradition to which we shall turn our attention derives from the complete fusion of African and Hispanic styles. This Afro-American tradition is particularly important in Brazil, Venezuela, and Colombia, and to a lesser extent in Uruguay, Argentina, and the lower coastal regions of Peru and Ecuador.

The special character of Brazilian folk music is largely due to the importance of the Black population in much of the national culture as a whole. Not only do the Black communities have their own traditions, which often revolve around styles that are still very close to Africa, as we indicate in Chapter Ten; the folk music of the Brazilian mestizos and whites, in many instances, can hardly be distinguished from that of the Afro-Brazilians, since they both result from basically identical syntheses. The Afro-Brazilian components are especially recognized in the driving rhythms, the particular performance practices, and the explicit importance of percussion instruments. The emphasis on dancing can also be interpreted as a result of the same syntheses. The number of Brazilian distinct folk dance forms of Luso-African derivation is genuinely striking. Among these, the best known are *batuque, samba, jongo, côco, lundu, baiano,* and some purely urban types, such as the *samba de morro, maracatu, maxixe, chôro,* among others. All Afro-Brazilian folk dances include specific choreographic traits, such as tapping, marked movement of the hips and the shoulders, and *umbigada. Umbigada* (from the Portuguese *umbigo* meaning navel) is the most characteristic choreographic elements of these dances, a sort of "invitation to the dance" manifested by the touching of the couple's navels. When there is no *umbigada* in a given dance, the dance generally belongs to the *caboclo* folklore or has an Hispanic origin. The *umbigada* is therefore a diagnostic trait defining the different origins of these dances.

Samba is a generic term designating, along with *batuque,* the choreography of certain round dances imported from Angola and the Congo area. We should distinguish between the various rural versions of the folk *samba* and the popular urban dance which developed only after World War I. The rural versions have different musical characteristics from most urban dances, although the responsorial singing and the use of syncopations are elements of both. The vocal line of the rural expression (as studied by the Brazilian musicologist, Mário de Andrade) tends to be divided into irregular patterns: three to five units for the stanzas, four to seven for the refrain, with variants. The melodies rarely go beyond the range of a sixth. Syncopations do occur in the folk *samba* but not as frequently as, and without the numerous variants found in, the urban expression. The exclusively percussive accompaniment of both versions is based on the following rhythmic figures: $\frac{2}{4}$ ♪. ♪♪♪ , ♪♪♪♪♪♪ , and the superimposition of the dotted figure on four regular sixteenths. A peculiar variety of *samba* which developed mostly in the city of Rio de Janeiro and has become the carnival dance par excellence is the *samba de morro.* This type, cultivated among the poor people inhabiting the hillside slums of the city (*morro* means "hill" in Portuguese), preserves some aspects of the rural *samba:* responsorial pattern, with solo part often improvised; mostly two-part form; and accompaniment exclusively by percussion instruments. Example 9-7 is a typical *samba de morro*, transcribed from a field collection made in the late 1930s. It shows most of the rhythmic-melodic patterns of the rural *samba*, i.e., repeated notes, intervallic skips within a melodic progression up to the sixth, offbeat phrasing of accents (represented notationally by ties across beats), frequent descending melodic movement, and the contrasting regularity of the solo part. Many varieties of *samba* are found through-

EXAMPLE 9-7. Brazilian *samba de morro.* From Egydio de Castro e Silva, "O samba carioca," *Revista Brasileira de Música,* VI (1939), 49–50. (*Surdo* is a low-pitched drum, *cuíca* a friction drum, *pandeiro* a tambourine, and *tamborim* a tabor-like instrument.)

Solo (without accompaniment)

out the country. Some, such as the *samba de roda*, maintain the typical Afro-Brazilian accompanimental formulas, but the melodic material tends to show Hispanic influences (regular phrasing, parallelism).

Afro-American musical traits are quite prominent in some aspects of Venezuelan and Colombian folk music. Marked Black musical influence in these countries is to be found above all in the coastal regions which properly belong to the Caribbean area. The most authentically African drumming and dancing in Venezuela comes from the states of Zulia and Trujillo, along Lake Maracaibo. Among the various percussion instruments, three types of drum should be mentioned: the *mina* drum (or *tambor grande*), more than six feet tall, with a single head fastened by ropes and wedges; the *curbata* drum, of the same family but smaller; and the *tambor redondo* ("round drum"), double-headed and always played in a battery of three (these round drums are also called *culepuyas*). Stamping bamboo tubes, called *quitiplás*, are also part of the African heritage of Venezuela. Most of the percussion instruments have an almost exclusively accompanimental function. The fact that a significant body of Afro-Venezuelan folk music is used in connection with Catholic feasts (e.g., feasts of St. John, St. Benedict) is again indicative of the strong local cultural blending.

One of the most typical dances and songs of Venezuela today is the *joropo*. The term itself has a generic sense of music for dancing. According to the Venezuelan ethnomusicologist Ramón y Rivera,[7] there are four main categories representing the music used to sing and dance the *joropo;* the *corrido, galerón, pasaje,* and *golpe.* As a result, the melody of this dance presents greatly diversified aspects. But the urban *joropo*, which is generally composed and has significantly penetrated the rural regions as well, is a fast dance in triple time, with a strongly syncopated accompaniment and frequent hemiola effect. Its choreography (for solo couple) seems to be analogous to that of the Colombian *pasillo* and *bambuco.* The latter is one of the most representative dances of the Colombian mestizo. It also alternates 3/4 and 6/8 meters. Its text, Spanish-derived, consists of four octosyllabic lines with an occasional refrain, and its accompaniment calls for Spanish folk instruments, such as the *tiple* and the *bandola* (respectively, a small guitar and a mandolin). In the Pacific Lowlands the *bambuco* is related to the *currulao.* (See Chapter Ten).

CENTRAL AMERICA: MEXICO AND THE CARIBBEAN

Mexican folk music is largely in the Spanish tradition, and while the Mexican Indians retain to some extent their native musical styles, there seems to have been less influence of the Indian styles on the Spanish-derived folk music here than in the Andean countries. Therefore, the basic difference between the Inca and the Aztec areas seems to be that the former could be considered as "the product of Hispanic influence upon an indigenous foundation," while the latter appears to reveal "an indigenous influence upon a Hispanic foundation," as Rodney Gallop has characterized Mexican art. This Hispanic foundation is manifested in Mexico mainly in the melody types of mestizo folk songs, the Spanish-derived choreography in numerous mestizo folk dances, and the widespread adoption of Hispanic instruments, even among rather isolated Indian groups. But one important difference between Spanish and Central American folk music in general is the importance of instruments in the

[7] Cf. Luis Felipe Ramón y Rivera, *El joropo: baile nacional de Venezuela* (Caracas: Ministerio de Educación, Dirección de cultura y bellas artes, 1952).

latter. In Mexico, the Spaniards at the time of the conquest found highly sophisticated instruments (mainly percussion instruments, flutes, ocarinas, and the famous multiple flutes) and a refined melodic system, if we can accept as evidence the testimony of early Spanish missionaries and the conclusions that have been drawn from the study of archaeological instruments.

The early missionaries in Mexico evidently tried hard to suppress the native Indian musical culture. They did not succeed entirely, but as a result of their work much of the folk music of the Hispanic tradition has found its way into the culture of some Mexican Indian groups. Vicente Mendoza,[8] a well-known authority on Mexican music, presents songs of the Otomí Indians of Northern Mexico which show the characteristic triplets of Spanish folk song and have elements of major tonality emphasizing tonic and third. Other Otomí songs give even greater evidence of European influence in their parallel thirds and sixths, which are hardly to be found in aboriginal Indian music. This is not to say that these songs are simply Spanish songs sung by Indians; their style is simpler than the Spanish, for they typically have short melodies, few tones, and small range. More likely they are songs composed by Indians who were still steeped in the Indian tradition but who had had contact with Hispanic folk music in Mexico. Likewise, the most typical mestizo musical forms are a result of the local adoption and gradual adaptation of both Spanish and Indian material throughout post-conquest Mexican history. Almost never has a Spanish folk song form or dance been adopted *in toto*. For example, the Spanish *romance* was transformed in Mexico and some Caribbean countries into the *corrido*, although its general character remained closely identifiable with that of its generator. The *corrido* continued to be essentially a narrative song type, with a four-line stanza or a *décima* form but with repetitive melodic structure, with many regional sub-types. *Corridos* often dealt with current events, crimes, and love stories, much as the English broadside ballads tell of sensational happenings; new ones are still coming into existence. Art songs are also sometimes reshaped into the form of the *corrido* by the folk tradition.

Among the numerous kinds of mestizo songs and dances, the *jarabe, jarana, huapango, son, canción,* and *valona* should be mentioned. The *jarabe* is one of the oldest and most popular folk dances of Mexico. Indians, rural and urban mestizos, and white people dance to it. It shows preference for triple meter, occasionally alternating with 6/8, and follows a binary form. The name *jarabe tapatio* is given to that form of

---

[8] Vicente Mendoza, "Música indígena Otomí," *Revista de Estudios Musicales* II, No. 5–6 (1950–1951), 527.

the dance which developed in Jalisco. The name "hat dance" by which the *jarabe* is called in the United States, is derived from a choreographic section in which the man puts his sombrero on the ground and his partner dances around in the wide brim. The urban *jarabe* has become a conventionalized and abbreviated version of the old dance still performed in many villages. Each section has its own melody, called a *son,* of sixteen or twenty-four measures. In the sixteen-measure *son,* the first half is instrumental and the last half vocal with accompaniment. The twenty-four-measure *son* has an eight-measure addition of an instrumental ending.

Similar to the *jarabe* is the *jarana,* the most popular dance in Yucatan. The music has the same lively character as that of the *jarabe,* but the dance proper is generally not accompanied by singing. The word *jarana* is said to be derived from the small stringed instrument of the same name, belonging to the *vihuela* family. The dance is accompanied by an ensemble composed of *jaranas,* drums, cornets, and sometimes *güiro*-type rattles.

The *huapango* is a well-known folk dance from the Gulf coast province of Veracruz and the central region of Huasteca. According to Paul Bowles, the Huasteco and Veracruzano types have in common "an extremely successful exploitation of contretemps: voices go along seemingly unaware of each other or of the rhythmical variations in the accompanying bass. The Huasteco is the simpler of the two, the disparity in rhythm between the melody and accompaniment is less, and the melodies themselves are less involved and less soaring."[9] Other musical characteristics, noted by Stevenson, are (1) the rapid shift from 3/4 to 6/8; (2) the rapid gait of the beats and alternation of accents; (3) a frequent sharp accent on the last eighth note in a measure; and (4) the frequent harmonic use of interior tonic pedals. In modern *huapangos,* such as the well-known *La Bamba,* the typical instrumental accompaniment includes a violin, two *guitarrones* (large five-string bass instrument, with a convex-shaped body), and a *jarana,* although the *huapango* ensembles also use harps and *jabalinas* (similar to the *guitarrón*).

Considerable confusion accompanies the use of the word *son* in Mexican music. As has been mentioned previously, the word sometimes refers to individual sections of *jarabes* and *huapangos,* sometimes to any song or portion of a song. It is also used to designate a separate choreographic genre. But the precise meaning of *son* also depends on association with a particular region or state: *son huasteco, son veracruzano, son jaliciense,* etc.

Vicente Mendoza depicts the *son* as one of the most genuinely

9 Paul Bowles, "On Mexico's Popular Music," *Modern Music,* XVIII, 4 (May–June, 1941), 225–226.

Mexican of all folk genres. It is associated with an instrumental group comprising violins, guitars, *jaranas*, and *guitarrón*, and sometimes harp. To this combination the *mariachi* bands add trumpets, trombone, or clarinets. The development of the *mariachi* orchestras—groups of three to a dozen players of string instruments—is an interesting manifestation of the instrument culture in Mexico. In recent decades, brass instruments have been added to the traditional ensemble. The *son* constitutes an integral part of the *mariachi* band repertory. Rhythmic vigor characterizes the *son,* and alternating or simultaneous use of 3/4 and 6/8 meter are again standard. Often a unit of three notes and one of two notes is combined with a resultant 5/8. Example 9-8 shows six characteristic rhythmic patterns for *sones* from the Jalisco region.

EXAMPLE 9-8. Characteristic rhythmic patterns of Mexican *sones.* From Paul Bowles, "On Mexico's Popular Music," *Modern Music,* XVIII, 4 (May–June, 1941), 227.

The song associated with the *son* intersperses short vocal verses with ritornello-like instrumental sections. Sequences abound, and parallel thirds, sixths, and triads accompany the melodic line.

The *canción* is a Mexican song of lyric expression which has assimilated many characteristics of nineteenth century Italian opera. It is not confined within any given meter or rhythm, but its form generally is a binary structure consisting of the song itself and an instrumental ritornello. The variety within the boundaries of the genre is abundant. Mendoza classifies the *canción* according to the following criteria: the meter of the versification, the musical structure, geographical features which it describes, area of the country in which it is sung, the time of day or the circumstances in which it is sung, the character of the tune, age or occupation of the users, and the rhythm of the accompaniment expressed in terms of European dance forms.

The *valona* (or *balona*) is a declamatory genre whose poetic form follows the *décima* model. The themes of this genre run the gamut of human sentiment, from dramatic to humorous and satirical. The vocal part is in parlando-rubato style, while the instrumental part (known as *sinfonía*) is strictly metrical. The instrumental ensemble in Jalisco includes usually two guitars, two violins, harp, and possibly *jaranas*.

The most typical performance characteristics of Mexican folk music comprise a high tension of the voice, producing an extremely vigorous incisive effect; a slight continuous nasalizing of the voice and a preference for high pitch, frequently passing into falsetto; instrumental pieces often beginning in a slower tempo than is used in the main body of the piece, with a gradual acceleration to the desired tempo, which is then maintained rigorously until the final cadence. Improvisation is not emphasized in Mexican music, and melismatic ornamentation, of the Andalusian *cante hondo* type, is largely absent, as it is in all of Latin America.

The states of Central America, from Guatemala to Panama, have greatly varied musical traditions. In addition to the same Hispanic foundation of Mexican folk music, the area has a number of aboriginal Indians with traditional music and a marked Black influence. For example, in spite of the fact that the most popular dance of Guatemala, the *son chapín*, exhibits clear European traits, the national instrument of the country is the marimba. Likewise, the *sique*, the most characteristic folk dance of Honduras, is closely related to the Spanish *jota*. But it is also in Honduras and Nicaragua that Black Carib settlements are to be found. The Black Caribs are descendants of Arawak and Carib Indian tribes and former African slaves. But in spite of their Afro-Indian past, their culture and their music are derivative of West Africa, combined with ceremonial dancing of tropical forest Indian cultural derivation.

Panama is a good example of a country whose musical traditions clearly reflect its ethnohistory. Traditional music is found among Indian groups, such as the *Cunas* and the *Guaymíes;* Hispanic music is represented by various folk song genres and dances, above all the *mejorana* or *socavón;* and African-derived music is represented mostly by dances of the *tamborito* type.

The *mejorana* is a ballad type, although purely instrumental pieces accompany a dance of the same name. The sung version, exclusively for male voice, is commonly referred to as *socavón* and shows the following traits: a descending tendency of the melodic phrase, progressing by disjunct rather than conjunct motion, and a text based on the *décima* preceded by a quatrain with the typical rhyme scheme ABBA. Although many *mejorana* melodies are cast in the major and minor modes, the mixolydian mode also occurs frequently. Typically the accompanying instrument is a modern guitar or the native *mejoranera* whose tunings are either e, b, a, a, d, or e, c sharp, a, a, d. Hemiola rhythm between the voice and the accompaniment is quite common. The singing style involves a penetrating harsh voice (without tremolo), with frequent alternation of falsetto and normal voice, extending the range to more than two octaves. As a dance, the *mejorana* presents traditional Spanish choreography divided into two parts: the *zapateo* (foot figures) and the *paseo* (promenade as in the square dance).

The most typical example of Afro-Panamanian singing and dancing is to be found in the *tamborito,* danced by mixed couples but sung exclusively by women (both solo and chorus). Generally a short phrase is sung alternately by soloist and chorus, although other forms may occur, such as two different phrases of equal or varying length; in the latter case, the longer phrase is that of the soloist. Typically the dance is in duple meter and is accompanied by hand clapping and drums. The drums are played in a battery of three, in complex rhythmic combinations.[10]

In general terms, two folk traditions form the basis of the music in such "Latin" Caribbean islands as Cuba, Puerto Rico, and the Dominican Republic: the Hispanic tradition and the African tradition. Among the Cuban peasants (the *guajiros*) of the Eastern province and the interior of the country there survive two song types, the *punto* and the *guajira,* showing the same stylistic peculiarities as most Spanish-related folk music of Latin America. The *punto* is spread throughout the Caribbean; it is found in Puerto Rico, the Dominican Republic, Colombia, Venezuela, and Panama.

[10] Fourteen notated examples of *tamborito* are given in *Boletín del Instituto de Investigaciones Folklóricas,* Vol. I, no. 1 (Panamá: Universidad Inter-Americana, 1944).

    Afro-Cuban music, in addition to the cult-related music examined in Chapter Ten, is represented by such important dance forms as the *conga*, the *rumba*, and other well-known hybrid forms, such as the *son*, the *danzón*, the *guaracha*, the *habanera*, and the *bolero*. Together with the various drum types associated with cult music, the typical Afro-Cuban instrumental ensembles include *maracas*, *güiros*, *claves*, and bongo drums. The *tres* and *cuatro* (small three- and four-string guitars) are commonly added to the percussion. Example 9-9 illustrates the fundamental rhythmic figures of Afro-Cuban music. The first figure, called *tresillo* in Cuba, is often notated as a simple triplet (A), but in actual performance appears as in (B) or (C). In other words, by taking the sixteenth note as the unit, the duple meter is actually subdivided as 3-3-2. The second figure, notated as (D) but performed as (E), is further complicated in the basic *conga* rhythm by tying together the first two notes of that rhythmic cell (F). The third figure (G) is perhaps the most characteristic formula of Cuban folk and popular music. It is known as *cinquillo* and results possibly from a contraction of the rhythm (H), quite African in its symmetry. It also forms the basis of much ritual drumming of the Haitian *vodoun*, as well as the Caribbean dance known as *merengue* (Haiti, Dominican Republic). It sometimes appears as (I), and it generates the basic rhythm of the Cuban *danzón* (J). The last two models show the typical figures, in duple and triple meters, associated with the *claves* in almost all Afro-Caribbean dances. The first measure of the duple meter

EXAMPLE 9-9. Rhythmic figures of Afro-Cuban music. From Gaspar Agüero y Barreras, "El Aporte Africano a la Música Popular Cubana," *Estudios Afrocubanos*, (1946), p. 77.

example is the *habanera* rhythmic formula, the epitome of Latin American dance music.

BIBLIOGRAPHY AND DISCOGRAPHY

The best and most comprehensive bibliographical discussion of Latin American folk and primitive music is found in Gilbert Chase, *A Guide to the Music of Latin America* (Washington, D.C.: Pan American Union, 1962). An updated account of the literature appears in the music section of the *Handbook of Latin American Studies,* published annually by the Hispanic Foundation of the Library of Congress.

A very useful study of Aztec and Inca musics and their development is Robert Stevenson, *Music in Aztec & Inca Territory* (Berkeley and Los Angeles: University of California Press, 1968). Mexican folk music is also studied, with many musical examples, in Stevenson, *Music in Mexico: A Historical Survey* (New York: Thomas Y. Crowell Co., 1952); in Vicente T. Mendoza, *Panorama de la Música Tradicional de México* (México: Imprenta Universitaria, 1956); and in Mendoza, *La Canción Mexicana* (México: Universidad Nacional, 1961). Gertrude P. Kurath and Samuel Martí, *Dances of Anahuac* (Chicago: Aldine Publishing Company, 1964), discusses the Maya and Aztec traditional dances and music and the extent of their preservation in present-day Middle America.

Studies of Latin American folk and popular musical instruments abound. For Central America, Vida Chenoweth, *The Marimbas of Guatemala* (Lexington: The University of Kentucky Press, 1964), Samuel Martí, *Instrumentos musicales precortesianos,* 2nd ed. rev. (Mexico City: Instituto Nacional de Antropología e Historia, 1968), and Charles L. Boilès, "The Pipe and Tabor in Mesoamerica," *Yearbook* of the Inter-American Institute for Musical Research, Tulane University, Vol. II (1966), should be consulted. For South America, the most useful single-volume items are: Isabel Aretz, *Instrumentos musicales de Venezuela* (Cumaná, Venezuela: Universidad de Oriente, 1967), and Carlos Vega, *Los instrumentos musicales aborígenes y criollos de Argentina* (Buenos Aires: Ediciones Centurión, 1946). Works mentioned below also contain sections on instruments.

Most studies of South American folk, primitive, and popular music are in Spanish or Portuguese. Items in English appear in specialized journals, such as the Latin American issue of *Ethnomusicology,* Vol. X, no. 1 (January, 1966). For the Andean area, Raoul and Marguerite d'Harcourt, *La Musique des Incas et ses survivances* (Paris: P. Geuthner, 1925) is still valuable. A more recent study is Marguerite and Raoul d'Harcourt, *La Musique des Aymara sur les Hauts Plateaux Boliviens* (Paris: Société des

Américanistes, 1959). Important collections of folk music for the same Andean area are: *Cancionero Andino Sur* (Lima: Casa Mozart, 1967) and *Panorama de la Música Tradicional del Perú* (Lima: Casa Mozart, 1966). A good survey of Argentine folk music is the study of Isabel Aretz mentioned in the text, p. 185. Oneyda Alvarenga, *Música Popular Brasileira* (Rio de Janeiro: Editôra Globo, 1950) is the best introduction to its subject. Rossini Tavares de Lima, *Melodia e rítmo no folclore de São Paulo* (São Paulo: Ricordi, 1954) presents numerous musical notations and excellent photographs of musical instruments. Aspects of Colombian folk music are discussed in José Ignacio Perdomo Escobar, *Historia de la Música en Colombia*, 3rd ed. (Bogotá: Academia Colombiana de Historia, 1963).

Among the many recordings of Latin American folk music available commercially, the following items are recommended. Folkways Records catalogs contain some of the most useful recordings. Mexican and Central American material appears on *Songs of Mexico*, Folkways FP 15; *Mexican Folk Songs*, Vol. 2, Folkways FP 815/2; *Folk Music of Honduras*, Folkways FP 834; *Black Caribs of Honduras*, Folkways P 435; and *Mexican Corridos*, Folkways FW 6913. Caribbean collections include *Caribbean Dances*, Folkways FP 840; *Calypso, Meringues*, Folkways FP 8; *Songs & Dances of Puerto Rico*, Folkways FP 80/2; *Música del Pueblo Puertorriqueño*, Troutman Press, UB-137; and the recent *The Music of Trinidad*, National Geographic Society, 3297.

South American materials are found in *Folk Music of Colombia*, Folkways FW 6804; *Folk Music of Venezuela*, Library of Congress, Archive of Folk Song, AFS L15; *Venezuelan Folk and Aboriginal Music*, The Columbia World Library of Folk and Primitive Music, Columbia KL-212; *Music of Peru*, Folkways P 415; *Traditional Music of Peru*, Folkways FE 4456; and *Kingdom of the Sun*, Nonesuch H-72029. The music of Bolivia is well represented in *Instruments and Music of Bolivia*, Folkways FM 4012; and *Songs and Dances of Bolivia*, Folkways FW 6871. An excellent collection of Argentine music is *Argentine Dances*, Folkways FW 8841 and 8842. The album *Argentine Folk Songs*, Folkways FW 6810, presents selections of songs accompanying such dances as the *gato* and the *chacarera*. The music of Brazil is not well represented on the United States record market; however, the album *Songs and Dances of Brazil*, Folkways FW 6953, includes good examples of *emboladas*.

TEN

AFRO-AMERICAN FOLK MUSIC IN NORTH AND LATIN AMERICA

by Bruno Nettl and Gérard Béhague

One of the truly important developments in the recent history of world music was initiated by the forced migration of great numbers of Africans, as slaves, to various parts of the Americas. Coming mostly from West Africa but also from other regions, such as Angola, they brought with them their music and other elements of their cultures, which served to provide a common context for the continuation, at least in part, of the African traditions. The Africans in the New World came into contact with a large variety of European musics, and the nature of the contact was different in North and South America, in the Caribbean, on plantations, and in towns. Their reactions to these European—and sometimes American Indian—musics called into being a whole group of musical sub-cultures that have had an impact on all strata of twentieth-century music in the West and elsewhere.

Not only are the folk musics of the various Black populations and communities in the New World intrinsically interesting and alive, they

207

have also influenced the folk music of the whites to the extent of having played a major role in the development of some typical North and Latin American forms. They are responsible for the development of a great deal of Western popular music; their role in the development of ragtime and jazz cannot be overestimated; their urban outgrowths, such as gospel, rock, and soul music, are major forces in everyday musical life; and their effect on composers of art music in the United States and Latin America as well as on such Europeans as Antonin Dvořák and Igor Stravinsky has been considerable.

The origin of the styles of Black music in the New World has been the subject of much debate. Extreme and opposing views have been advanced: the music is actually African, unchanged by migration; the music is simply a copy of Western form and style; the Black American is a superlatively creative individual; he is capable of creating nothing but the simplest spontaneous musical utterances. The definition of "Black" music has been argued as well: is all music composed or performed by Afro-Americans Black music? Or is it only that part of the repertory of Afro-American musicians that shows a distinctly African-derived character? Much as the latter view seems more reasonable, the former one corresponds to a great deal of ethnomusicological practice, since scholars, in assessing the musical style of a culture, tend to base their findings on a sample of that culture's complete repertory, whatever its origins.

A more moderate view of the origins of Afro-American styles is now widely accepted. There is no doubt, of course, that the slaves from Africa did bring with them their music. In areas in which they greatly outnumbered their white neighbors and masters, and where they were isolated from the whites, they retained this African heritage with relatively little change. It is even conceivable that they now retain some practices that have changed more rapidly in Africa than in the New World. Some of their songs and rhythms can still be found in Africa, but their repertory appears to be largely material actually composed in the Americas, although using styles and patterns very largely derived from Africa. In areas in which Afro-Americans associated more closely with whites, and lived in less self-contained communities, they appear to have taken over a great deal of folk, church, and popular music from the whites (while probably also holding on to aspects of the African tradition), gradually absorbing it. Everywhere, in any event, they were influenced by the music of the whites (and in some cases by that of the Indians), and accordingly they modified their own way of singing to some extent. Thus their musical acculturation could take three forms: they may have learned the songs of the whites together with white performance practices; they may have learned the performance practices of the whites and superimposed these on their own songs; or they may have learned the songs of the whites and superimposed on them African performance practices.

All of these things happened to some degree. The Blacks of the United States learned songs from their white masters, from missionaries, and from neighbors in the towns. Some songs they sang in styles indistinguishable from those of the whites, but on most of them the Blacks imposed some stylistic traits derived from Africa. They presumably also continued to sing African songs and to compose new songs in the African styles; this appears to have been true more in Brazil and the Caribbean than in the United States to which slaves were not brought directly from Africa but rather from the Caribbean, where linguistic and tribal ties were broken down. The African elements that were retained were among those also found, at least to some extent, in European folk and popular music, a fact that stimulated anthropologists to develop a theory of culture change symbolized by the word "syncretism." According to Waterman,[1] when one culture is, as it were, absorbed by another, those traits of the two cultures which have similarity or compatibility tend to syncretize, or grow into a new combined form. Thus, for example, since both Africa and Europe have harmony, Afro-American music also has it, and its character is derived from both African and European models. In contrast, since North American Indian and European music have little in common, a form of music having features of both did not arise.

What actually are the African features that were carried into the New World? One that comes to mind immediately is the emphasis on rhythm; it appears in many different forms, including the importance of drums and other percussion instruments in the Black cultures of the Americas, the use of syncopation and complicated rhythmic figures in North America (and of complex rhythmic ensemble music in Latin America), and an emphasis on the beat, and a tendency to adhere very strictly to meter and tempo (the "metronome sense" of West Africa). Another feature is the tendency to use call-and-response patterns, so important in Africa, that is manifested not only in ordinary antiphonal or responsory techniques but also in more complex alternating devices, such as the rotation of the solo part in jazz. The love of instruments and instrumental music is also one of these African features, although only some Afro-American instruments are derived from Africa, others being ordinary Western instruments, such as guitar and harmonica, or adaptations of them, such as the gutbucket. Extremely important among African features is the use of improvisation and a tendency to vary a short theme. Polyphony, although not really typical of West African music or, for that

---

[1] Richard A. Waterman, "African Influence on American Negro Music," in *Acculturation in the Americas*, ed. Sol Tax (Chicago: University of Chicago Press, 1952), p. 212.

matter, of much Black music in the Americas, may perhaps, where it is found, be traceable to African roots. Most important, the manner of singing, the way in which the voice is used and the typical vocal tone color in the Black musics, appears to be closely related to Africa.

These are the features of music that appear to have been brought from Africa. They are techniques of making music, and the actual musical sounds that Afro-Americans produce when using such techniques may actually not seem very much like African music. It is frequently difficult to decide whether something that we notice about a piece of Black music results from the African heritage or not. As has been pointed out, African musical techniques have maintained themselves in a hostile cultural environment largely because their counterparts in Western folk and popular music are somewhat similar. But it is interesting to find that, on the whole, those features of music that were most strongly developed in Africa have to some extent also been retained in Afro-American music; and, conversely, those which were not developed to any great degree of complexity or distinctiveness (such as scale) seem to have given way to traits bearing the European trademark.

Students of the relationship between African and Afro-American cultures have often remarked on the extent to which African characteristics have remained in the Afro-American musical repertories, in contrast to the lower degree of retention in most other aspects of culture. At times this fact has been ascribed to the presumably special native musical talent of Blacks, and it has even been supposed that certain elements of music (rhythm, call-and-response, etc.) are part of the Black's biological heredity. The question of musical talent is unsolved, but until concrete evidence to the contrary is presented, it must be presumed that no racial group differs from others in the inheritance of such a complex group of behavioral patterns. And it has never been possible to prove the biological inheritance of specific aspects of musical behavior. The explanation is probably much closer at hand. Music plays an important role in African life, especially in ritual; as such, it is of major cultural value. It is not surprising that Africans cherished their musical heritage when they were brought to the New World. (Similarly, we find that European immigrant groups also tended to lay greater stress on their musical traditions in the strange environment of America than they did in the old country.) Furthermore, music was in various ways more complex and more highly developed in Africa than in the Western folk cultures with which the Blacks came into contact in the Americas.

It is possible to rank the various Afro-American communities by the degree to which their musical styles adhere to African models. Among the musics that are reasonably well known, those of Haiti, the Guianas, and Northeastern Brazil (particularly the state of Bahia) are closest to the African. Jamaica, Trinidad, and Cuba are next, followed by the Southern United States and, finally, the United States North. Generally speaking, religious music tends to be closer to African styles than does secular. In general, also, Africanisms are more readily found in rural than in urban situations, for the culture of the cities lends itself more to Westernization and acculturation, and a resulting modernization. This is particularly true of the United States, but there appear to be exceptions, as in the city of Salvador, Brazil, West African religious cults remain an important force, and are accompanied by extremely African-sounding music.

The kind of ranking produced here is complicated by the fact that each Afro-American community has a variety of styles. For example, the island of Jamaica provides a characteristic microcosm of this variety. Inhabited almost entirely by Blacks, it contains a number of distinct musics related in various ways to Africa. In the rural areas there are remnants of cult music with African-sounding melodies and drum patterns; there are also the songs of revival cults, based on Protestant fundamentalism, with songs that are European in character but sung with African modes of performance. In the port of Kingston, dock workers sing work songs in a style closely related to the music of Haiti and Cuba. The popular music of Kingston, however, is distinctively Jamaican, having developed, in the last two decades, three types of style, the Ska, the Rock-steady, and Reggae, all based essentially on North American models but with prominent African and Latin American elements. Jamaica participated, of course, along with Trinidad, in the development of a distinctive song type, the calypso. Thus, while we may rank Jamaica at a particular point in the scale denoting degrees of Africanism or African retention in music, we must realize that this ranking is not based on a homogeneous musical culture. The same sort of statement could be made about each of the communities mentioned here.

AFRO-AMERICAN INSTRUMENTS

A great many instruments that are at least partly of African origin are used by the Afro-American communities of Latin America. For example, in Haiti certain drums are made of hollow logs. Normally they have single heads and are cylindrical in shape. Their height varies from six feet to eighteen inches. Among the idiophones, the *ogan*, a kind of iron bell struck with an external clapper, is prominent, as are gourd rattles. Double-headed drums are also used, and so are shallow, single-headed, open drums similar to a tambourine. Various kinds of sticks are used to beat the drums, each cult having its own type of drum sticks and combination of drums. The mosquito drum, a type of musical bow, of which one end is attached to the ground while from the other extends a string attached to a piece of skin covering a hole in the ground, is used as an accompaniment to singing. In this instrument, the hole in the ground functions as a resonance chamber, much as the calabash or the player's mouth adds resonance to the sound of musical bows in Southern and Central Africa.

Stamping tubes, hollow tubes struck on the ground or on a board, provide another kind of rhythmic accompaniment. A rather large and deep-sounding version of the African *sansa* or *mbira* (called *marimba* in Haiti and *marimbula* in Puerto Rico) is also found in the Caribbean. Horns and trumpets made of bamboo, each capable of playing only one pitch, are used, as are cows' horns, conch-shell trumpets, and horns improvised from various objects, such as phonograph loudspeaker horns. The *claves*, short sticks made of hardwood that are struck together by hand, are important in the Caribbean. The xylophone, common in Africa, is not as widespread in the Afro-American cultures but does seem to have become one of the important instruments of Central America. In Guatemala, the marimba (xylophone with gourd resonators) has become a national instrument. A form of musical bow with gourd resonator, called *berimbau*, is used in Brazil and played in an essentially Central and South African manner. Throughout the area under discussion, the Negro community has brought instruments directly from Africa, has adapted Western materials and technology to the needs of African instruments, and has exerted an African cultural influence by its interest in instruments and instrumental music and its creation of many musical types, also by the prestige and ritual significance that it has placed on the instruments themselves and on the instrumentalists.

The steel drum, an instrument invented in Trinidad during or after World War II, is a fascinating example of the results of the acculturation of African practices in modern Western civilization. Steel oil containers, abandoned and available, their tops hammered into shapes producing the desired scales, were combined into groups of three or four different sizes and accompanied rhythmically by idiophones—rattles, *claves,* or bells. The bottom sections of the containers were cut off later, and the steel drums were placed on special stands. Each "drum" is capable of playing simple melodic material. The result is music of a strongly rhythmic character, with polyphony of an ostinato nature, and with each "drum" (or "pan," as they are called by the players) having a particular musical function, as in a jazz band.

Aside from African-derived and invented instruments, Western instruments such as the guitar and the banjo (which may itself have been

Drum type common in West Africa and the Caribbean.

developed under African influences) are widely used in the Negro communities of Latin America and the Caribbean.

In the Black folk music of the United States, instruments play a larger role than in the Anglo-American tradition, although the Blacks' interest in instruments appears to have infected the white communities to a certain extent in the course of the twentieth century. Many of the Afro-American instruments in the United States are European-derived (mouth organ, banjo, fiddle, brass instruments), while others are actually derived from African models or fashioned so as to produce sounds similar to those produced by African instruments. In the former category are several that are hardly found today but are reported to have been present in the United States in the nineteenth century and earlier: the *sansa* or *mbira*, hollowed log drums, and gourd rattles. In the latter category we find the gutbucket or washtub, related to the musical bow and to the Haitian mosquito drum; washboards used as scrapers and placed on baskets for resonance; and frying pans, cowbells, bottles, wood or bone clappers to replace the bells and rattles of the West African percussion ensembles. These instruments are not themselves descendants of African forms, but they seem to have been invented or improvised to fulfill the functions once performed by African instruments.

AFRO-AMERICAN MUSIC IN LATIN AMERICA

In the Latin American context, the definition of "Black" music, as discussed above, becomes extremely complex. First of all, the general acceptance of what constitutes, culturally and ethnically, an Afro-American is not as unequivocal as in North America. There are several examples in Central and South America of Black groups whose African cultural identity is virtually non-existent, such as the Caribs of Honduras and Nicaragua who are Black representatives of an Indian culture. Conversely, important non-Black segments of certain communities have perfectly definable African-related cultural traits, such as, for example, some East Indian groups of Trinidad, or the Cayapa Indians of Western Ecuador. In many areas of Latin America, Negro acculturation has been considerable and has affected other ethnic groups or the wide range of mixed groups. In such cases we are confronted with ethnically diverse groups with a remarkably homogeneous "Black" culture. Race alone cannot, then, be considered a valid criterion in discussing Afro-American musical styles in Latin America. Although we are stressing Africanisms in our discussion here, it should always be borne in mind that Afro-American music cuts across ethnic lines.

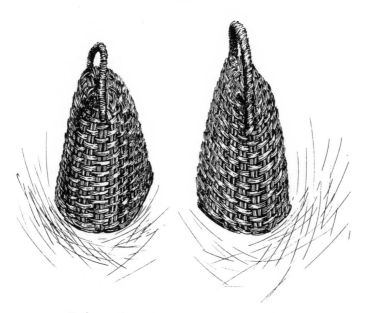

Basket rattles, as found in Haiti or West Africa.

Black music in Latin America functions in both sacred and secular contexts, but generally it is in the sacred context that African musical elements are most strongly preserved. Various cults involving deities (called *orishás, vodouns,* saints, etc.) that have been transferred from the West African homeland but whose character has often changed in the process are found conspicuously in Cuba, Haiti, Jamaica, Trinidad, and Brazil. Among the Afro-American communities of Latin America a cult implies the recognition of African deities and a belief system essentially African. Syncretism, however, has taken place almost everywhere, in varying degrees. Most cults show features of Christian belief systems, although not necessarily a recognition of a Christian God or saint. Often, as a result of socio-historical accommodation, a Catholic saint has been assimilated into the personality of an African deity, but the equivalence of saints and deities is by no means uniform throughout the continent. West African religions as developed in the Americas are monotheistic, animistic in nature, and involve a pantheon of major and lesser deities, each of which is worshipped with characteristic ceremonies, songs, and drum rhythms. The most obvious African features prevailing in such ceremonies include the ritual use of blood (animal sacrifices), initiatory rites, ritual dancing with a highly symbolic choreography, personification of the *orishás* through spirit possession, and offering of food to the gods. The most outstanding Christian or reinterpreted Christian elements include the use of the Bible, Catholic prayers, cross and crucifixes, candle burning, and lithographs of saints. Misconceptions about Afro-American belief systems, epitomized by the term "Black magic," arise from the fact that most cult leaders practice some aspect of folk medicine.

The most important Afro-Cuban cults include the *Lucumi* (derived from the Yoruba of Nigeria), the *Kimbisa* or *Mayombé* (from the Congo area), and the *Abakuá* (combining beliefs and practices of the other cults; its members are referred to as *ñáñigos*). In Brazil, the cult groups are called the *candomblé* in Bahia, *xangô* (shango) in Pernambuco, and *macumba* in the central and southern states. The Bahian groups include the *Ketu* (or *Nago*) and *Jesha* (Yoruba), the *Gêgê* (Dahomey), the *Congo-Angola,* and the *Caboclos* (derived from some Amerindian beliefs combined with those from the other cults). Most important among the Haitian cult groups are the *Vodoun* or *Rada* cult (*Arada-Nago* family) and the *Pétro* group (*Congo-Guinée* family). According to Courlander (see bibliography) other lesser family groups include the *Ibo-Kanga,* the *Congo,* and the *Juba-Martinique,* each with a distinct set of dances and accompanying songs. In Jamaica and Trinidad the groups include respectively the *Kumina* and the *Shango* cults, in addition to Afro-Christian groups under Protestant denominations' influence, such as the Pukkumina, Revival and

Revival Zion of Jamaica, and the Spiritual Baptists (or Shouters) of Trinidad. Revivalist cult music in these areas is quite similar to much Black Protestant music of the Southern United States. It is basically a mixture of various types of traditional Protestant hymnody, with an important body of Gospel hymns of the type composed by Ira Sankey and disseminated throughout the area by various evangelical crusaders during the nineteenth century. In both Jamaica and Trinidad the word "Sankey" has actually become a generic term for "hymn." A basic difference of Revival cult music from that of the other cults is the constant presence of harmonized choruses, much like congregational hymn singing in southern United States Black churches, and the nature of the accompanying rhythmic patterns, substantially less African than in the Cuban, Haitian, or Brazilian cults. The type of call and response practice in Jamaican revivalist music could be considered a retention of an African feature, although it is not unlike that of the commercial gospel music that one can hear in all large American cities.

Protestant-related cults excepted, the most obvious stylistic trait common to the musics of cult-groups in Latin America is the predominant use of call and response patterns. The leader or solo singer may be either a woman or a man, but the chorus is usually composed of women. The chorus sings in monophonic fashion, but occasionally individual singers deviate from the main melodic line. Among the most acculturated groups (*Abakuá* in Cuba, *Caboclo* and *Umbanda* in Brazil), heterophony is not uncommon. Sometimes soloist and chorus overlap. The scales are most commonly pentatonic without semitones, although diatonic scales are found in many songs. Tempo varies considerably from one cult group to another and, within the same cult, in accordance with a particular song cycle. Gradual acceleration in many songs or in drum music is fairly frequent, depending on their particular ritual function. The ranges of the melodies are not uniform; for example, the *Gêgê* cult of Bahia has songs with wide range (most with more than an octave), while those of the *Jesha* cult in the same area average less than an octave. The melodic contours are generally descending, but frequent pendulum-like movements are also characteristic, as in the series of songs to the deity *Exú* in the Bahian *Ketu* cult. Melodic intervals are frequently quite large. Whenever there is leader-chorus alternation, the melodic phrases tend to be short, but with solo songs or duets the melodic line becomes longer and more complex. The form, within the framework of the solo-chorus alternation, is frequently based on the repetition of a single phrase, with some variations through ornamentation. The soloist is likely to present a theme with variations as the basis of his tune. Leader and chorus often use the same tune, sometimes related tunes, and sometimes completely unrelated materials. Occasionally the chorus uses material from the last portion of the soloist's line. The large majority of songs follow the strophic form. Examples 10-1 and 10-2 illustrate some of these characteristics of the Afro-Bahian cult songs. In Example 10-2, the *rumpi* and *lê* figures, taken together, form the following pattern:

EXAMPLE 10-1. Brazilian Gêgê cult song (text omitted), from Alan P. Merriam, "Songs of the Gêgê and Jesha Cults," *Jahrbuch für musikalische Volks- und Völkerkunde* I, ed. Fritz Bose (Berlin: Walter de Gruyter & Co., 1963), 122.

EXAMPLE 10-2. Brazilian Ketu cult song (Field collection of G. Béhague). Transcribed by Robert E. Witmer and G. Béhague. Text omitted.

The singing styles of most Afro-American cults are essentially like the relaxed, open manner of singing common in Africa. Female voices present a characteristically hard, metallic quality, with a preference for the upper range of the voice. Falsetto is often used by both soloist and chorus.

The song repertories of Afro-American religions have never been fully codified, but we know that a multitude of songs attributed to a given deity form the bulk of the repertories. Cycles of songs are performed in a ritual order, according to a well established tradition. Song texts appear in various languages, from Yoruba (Nago), Fon, various Congo dialects, to Spanish and Portuguese, Haitian *créole*, or a combination of all of these. Typically, song texts are simple praise or imprecation directed to the gods; sometimes they refer to specific events in the lives of the deities or to their remarkable feats, following West African mythology as reinterpreted in the New World through the influence of popular Christianism.

Although the large majority of song repertories are traditional, evidence has been gathered recently pointing to stylistic changes and to the elaboration of a more recent repertoire. According to the testimony of cult leaders in Salvador, Bahia, many songs attributed to specific deities have disappeared from the repertory, and new songs are being incorporated. These are not, in general, songs composed by the priest or priestess of a cult house; they are spontaneously created when an initiating member, in a state of possession, sings his or her song to his or her *orixá*. Such songs are apparently remembered afterwards. Especially among the Congo-Angola and the Caboclo cults, these "new" songs frequently include elements from folk music or urban musical culture (such as carnival street music) foreign to the tradition but familiar to the songmakers.

The single most important ritual and musical element in Afro-American cults is the drumming. Drums are considered sacred instruments. They undergo ritual baptism by means of animal sacrifices and food offering. In the case of the Cuban *Abakuá*, some have an exclusively symbolic function and are never played. Such complex ritual involving drums is essential since they alone are thought to have the power to communicate with the deities. In most cult groups, drums are played in a battery of three, in conjunction with an iron gong or a rattle. They vary in size and shape among the various cults, but the trio always comes in three different sizes. The largest drum (called *rum* in the *Ketu* of Bahia, *iyá* among the *Lucumis* of Cuba, *maman* in the *Vodoun* cult, *mama* or *bemba* in the *Shango* of Trinidad) is played by the master drummer. The medium size drum (known as *rumpí, itótele, seconde,* and *congo*, in the same order) and the smallest one (respectively *lê, okónkolo, bébé, oumalay*) usually repeat a single steady rhythm. In contrast, the largest and lowest drum varies its beats, producing some of the complex and intensely exciting rhythms typical of the Afro-American styles. The gong (variously called *agogó, gan, ogan,* or *ekon* in Brazil and Cuba) or the rattle generally sets the fundamental beat; the drums join in a few seconds later. As Herskovits has pointed out, the melody of the song is but the accompaniment to the rhythm of the drums. This emphasis on rhythm is an obvious African heritage. Each cult, dance, ceremony, or deity has its characteristic rhythms, on the basis of which the master drummer improvises. Drum music per se, that is, separate from an accompanimental function, also exists in large quantity. Its major function is to "call" the gods and to bring on "possessions," also to provide materials for the many ritual dances. Cross rhythms and polyrhythms form the major substance of the music. Examples 10-3 and 10-4 show several rhythmic patterns, with their respective names, of the Bahian *Ketu* cult, and the Afro-Cuban *Lucumi*. The *rum* part of the *avaninha* pattern often presents a subtle duple-triple ambivalence. For example, it sometimes sounds like ♪ ɤ ɤ ♪ ɤ ɤ ♪ ɤ ɤ ♪ ♪ ɤ ɤ. Likewise, in the *toque de Iansa*, the 4/4 gong pattern often approaches a triple feeling, as for example ♪ ɤ ♪ ɤ ♪ ɤ ɤ ♪ ɤ ♪ ɤ ɤ. In the same pattern, the *rum* also expresses a duple feeling, like the gong: 𝄴 ♪ ♪♪ ♪ ɤ ♪ ♪ ɤ.

In general, the meters of this cult music are most commonly duple but often also triple, and the hemiola rhythm—African par excellence—finds its way into much of the drum music repertory. While there is no definite evidence of the retention in Latin America today of the African talking drum techniques, it is believed that the various ritual drum patterns (attributed to each deity) were, originally, rhythmic renditions of the melodic shape of certain phrases of the Yoruba language which is a tone language. Such renditions would have been learned, memorized, and transmitted by use of onomatopoeias.

EXAMPLE 10-3. Abstract of some basic patterns in Afro-Bahian drumming.

"Avaninha"

(1) The duple triple ambivalence is subtle,

e. g.,

sometimes sounds like :

"Toque de Ianas"

The $\frac{4}{4}$ gong pattern often approaches the triple feel, as for example :

The *rum* also gets into a duple feel, like the gong :

"Bravum"

"Apanijé, Opanijé"

EXAMPLE 10-4. Lucumi Bata drum pattern to the deity Obba. From Fernando Ortiz, *La Africanía de la Música Folklórica de Cuba* (Habana: Ediciones Cardenas y Cia., 1950), pp. 417–18.

Within the social structure of the Afro-American cults, women have a particularly important position. In the Afro-Bahian cults, while many leaders are men, the great majority are women; so are most of the initiates. The leaders, referred to in Bahia as "Pai" or "Mãe-do-santo," in Cuba as "Padrino" or "Madrina," represent the maximum spiritual and temporal authority of the cult house, and determine the degree of orthodoxy in it. They are, for the most part, leading singers themselves, responsible for transmitting the knowledge of their vast repertory and for the supervision of instruction in music and dancing in the house. Drummers have a very exalted position. They are musicians par excellence. According to Herskovits, the master drummer "moves about the scene, confident, respected. . . . Relaxed, the drum between his legs, he allows the complex rhythm to flow from his sure, agile fingers. It is he who brings on possession through his manipulation of these rhythmic intricacies, yet he himself never becomes possessed."[2] Drummers go through a series of tests before they are allowed to perform in ritual ceremonies. Their acceptance into the cult is publicly signified by means of a "confirmation" ceremony. A drummer may become a master drummer only after many years of experience, and only under certain circumstances, for it is considered as a very special privilege.

There also exist, in Latin American Black culture, instances of what might be termed "secular rituals" in which, once more, music appears as a cultural focus. The *currulao*, or marimba dance, of Southwestern Colombia and Northwestern Ecuador is such a ritual, i.e., a socializing occasion at which a highly symbolic behavior takes place. According to Whitten, the *currulao* gives us an excellent example of the function of music not only in social integration but also in the "development of personal networks." One of the important conclusions of Whitten's study is that "the currulao provides an expressive context which permits household and marital structure to be realigned when necessity demands it. . . ."[3] The music itself of this marimba dance preserves many African patterns. It requires an ensemble of six to seven male musicians, two of whom play the marimba and the others drums. The marimba may have from twenty to twenty-eight hardwood keys (each with bamboo resonators), and it functions both melodically and harmonically. The player called *bordonero* is in charge of the melody on the lower half of the instru-

[2] Merville J. Herskovits, "Drums and Drummers in Afro-Brazilian Cult Life," *Musical Quarterly*, XXX (1944), 477–80.

[3] Norman E. Whitten, Jr., "Personal Networks and Musical Contexts in the Pacific Lowlands of Colombia and Ecuador," in *Afro-American Anthropology, Contemporary Perspectives*, ed. Norman E. Whitten, Jr., and John Szwed (New York: The Free Press, 1970), p. 214. See also by the same author the essay "Ritual Enactment of Sex Roles in the Pacific Lowlands of Ecuador-Colombia," in *Afro-Hispanic Culture* (Cambridge, Mass.: Shankmann Press, 1972).

ment; the *tiplero*, on the upper half, of the counterpoint and harmony. The tuning of the marimba is by no means uniform. Solo-chorus alternation predominates in the *currulao*. Many female singers, called *respondedoras*, participate in the chorus. The leading male musician is the *glosador;* his function is to lead the singing, to give the shouts, and to indicate to the women what part of the repertory should be sung at a given time. Accompanimental drumming is produced by two *bombos* (large double-headed drums), two *cununos* (single-headed cone-shaped drums played with the hands), and rattles (maracas and *guasás*, the latter being bamboo tubes filled with seeds and into which hardwood nails are driven).

The relationship of the religious material to social dance and song is, in Latin American Black culture, always a close one, and one for which explanations vary from area to area. Some of the Haitian and Afro-Bahian ceremonial material has lost its religious significance and has become part of the social side of musical life. This is also true of the *Candombe,*[4] an Afro-Uruguayan ritual dance performed at the time of the Mardi Gras carnival in Montevideo. Here are found certain stock characters—the *gramillero* (an agile young dancer representing a tottering old man), an old Negro woman, a broom-maker, a drummer, and a trophy-bearer. These characters dance in the parade, but it is likely that they represent figures from the earlier time of slavery and the period after emancipation, when African cults and tribal rivalries dominated the life of the urban Negro community.

Among the Afro-Bahians, a particular secular form of singing and dancing, although not entirely dissociated from the sacred context, is the sort of athletic game known as *Capoeira Angola*. In spite of its name, this game seems to have been invented in Brazil by former slaves, and must have been, in its original form, a simple offensive and defensive type of fight.[5] Today it is reduced to a simulated fight, with the preservation of stylized steps (strokes). Only the legs and feet are involved in this dance-like game. The *capoeira* makes use of a small instrumental ensemble, including the *berimbau* (musical bow, also called *urucungo*), the tambourine (called *pandeiro*), a cone-shaped drum (*atabaque*), and a little basket rattle (*caxixi*) of the type illustrated in this chapter. Sometimes, though infrequently nowadays, a *ganzá* or *reco-reco* (*giiiro*-type of rattle) and an *agogó* (iron gong) may participate in the ensemble. Specific rhythmic patterns (each with a special name, such as *São Bento Grande*,

---

[4] Paulo de Carvalho Neto, "The Candombe," *Ethnomusicology* VIII (1963), 164–74. See also Nestor Ortiz Oderigo, *Calunga, Croquis del Candombe* (Buenos Aires: Editorial Universitaria de Buenos Aires, 1969), pp. 29–41.

[5] Cf. Waldeloir Rego, *Capoeira Angola, Ensaio Sócio-Etnográfico* (Salvador, Bahia: Editora Itapuã, 1969), pp. 30–46.

Benguela, and *Angola*) accompany the dancing and the singing. *Capoeira* songs are among the oldest in Brazil; very often they originate in repertories of the music of other folk dances and from songs such as the children's round songs or *samba de roda* described in the previous chapter. One of the most significant characteristics of the *capoeira* song is its dialogue form, between the *capoeira* singer himself and some abstract, imagined character. Fernando Ortiz[6] has observed the same characteristic, under its multiple aspects, not only in Cuba but in various other Afro-American areas of Latin America. Strikingly similar genres still exist in distant areas of the continent. For example, the well-known stick-fight game of Trinidad associated with the *kalinda* and accompanied by drum music has its equivalent in Bahia: the *maculelê.*

While the ceremonial music (sacred and secular) of the Black communities of Latin America and the Caribbean is its most prominent—and stylistically most African—musical expression, we must not forget that other kinds of music are also produced. There are work songs, social dance songs, narrative songs of various sorts, love songs. The calypso, which presumably originated in Trinidad and spread rapidly throughout the Caribbean (but there are satirical songs in Africa), is a unique kind of satirical song that grew out of the racial tensions present in the island; musically, it is a combination of African, North American Negro, and Spanish popular styles. Jamaican Negroes sing spirituals and sea shanties whose words are of English and North American origin but also preserve the call-and-response pattern of the African tradition (which may have been reinforced by the existence of similar forms in the English sea shanties). Likewise, Afro-Cuban, Afro-Brazilian, Afro-Colombian, and Afro-Venezuelan urban popular musical species exhibit various patterns that can be related to several stylistic origins. Some of these are mentioned in Chapter Nine.

BLACK FOLK MUSIC IN THE UNITED STATES

The musical development of North American Black communities has proceeded rather differently from that of other Afro-American groups. Rather than living in relatively closed communities in which African tribal groups could still function, the Blacks were brought to the

---

[6] Fernando Ortiz, *Los Bailes y el Teatro de los Negros en el Folklore de Cuba* (Havana: Ediciones Cárdenas, 1951), pp. 6–36.

United States from the West Indies, where elements of African culture had already begun to change and to disappear; and, once on the continent, they tended to live in close contact with their white masters. While the survival of the West African religious cults was to some extent assured in Latin America because of their similarity to some aspects of Roman Catholicism, the impact of the Protestant denominations in the United States was of such a nature as to annihilate many, if not most, of the West African religious practices. Nevertheless, much of the value structure of the African heritage was retained, and while most of the Black folk music in the United States does not sound like African music in the way that the cult music of Haiti and Bahia does, it contains some African stylistic features. More important, the independent developments that took place in Afro-American music were frequently the result of African musical values. For example, call-and-response patterns, in pure form, are not found too frequently in Black folk song of the United States. But the original importance of this kind of practice—essentially alternation, dividing up of a tune between leader and chorus, and the encouragement of improvisatory variations—seems to have led to other practices involving alternation and improvisation, for instance, the sophisticated dividing up of a performance among different soloists in jazz and the principle of improvisatory variation that is the essence of jazz. Similarly, the importance of rhythm in West African music became part of the American Black tradition, even though the rhythmic structure of North American Black folk songs is very distant from that of Africa. When it comes to singing style, of course, Black Americans share the qualities of other Afro-American groups and exhibit a really close tie to West Africa.

There are reports of the southern scene by nineteenth-century American observers which mention the existence of musical practices, such as African-derived cults and cult music, similar to those that can be observed in twentieth-century Brazil and the Caribbean. The songs of the southern slaves were numerous and were associated with a large number of uses. There were work songs, many of them rhythmic to accompany the hard labor performed by groups but some, such as the field blues, slow and languid. The work songs with driving rhythms were related to similar songs used in Africa to accompany rowing and other group activities, but they also derived in part from British work songs, such as the sea shanties. Dance and play songs, related to the playparty songs of the whites, were used when time for recreation was available. A few narrative songs, similar to the Anglo-American broadside ballads, or derived from the African practice of singing while telling stories about animals (like the stories of Uncle Remus, with heroes like Br'er Rabbit or Anansi, the spider), are still used and were probably once much more numerous. Short field and street cries or hollers, consisting of a single, repeated, and varied musical line, are also an important ingredient of the Black folk music repertory. Most important, perhaps, is the spiritual, the religious musical expression of the slaves, which exists in many different forms and styles, from the slow, lyrical, and devotional spirituals sung at services, to the quick, driving, and ecstatic "shout spirituals" of the revival meetings.

The spiritual, in its basic content, is closely associated with the "white spirituals" sung in the South, particularly in the Appalachians. Many of the Negro spirituals use words and tunes also found in the "white spirituals" sung in the South, particularly in the Appalachians. more percussion accompaniment, the use of antiphonal techniques, and improvised variation. (Parenthetically, we should point out that the question of the origin and development of the Negro spiritual's style has not been answered in a satisfactory way, for the white spirituals are also frequently sung in a very vigorous and rhythmically un-hymn-like way, whether through Black influence or not, we don't know.

George Pullen Jackson (1874–1953)[7] found, in tunes he took largely from nineteenth-century published collections, a great number of parallels between Negro and white spirituals. However, although he presents the tunes of the songs, the early notation gives us no information about the style(s) of singing used. Nevertheless, obviously some tunes were used as both white and Negro spirituals, like the one shown in Example 10-5: it is the famous "Swing Low, Sweet Chariot," which is similar in melodic content to a white American hymn tune entitled "Gaines."

Many songs of the Black Americans have simply been taken over from the heritage of the whites, and others, although composed by Blacks, are patterned after the music of the Anglo-American community. The Black tradition has always been influenced by the whites, and much of the basic material in it is essentially of European origin; it is in the style of performance that we can detect definitely African roots.

But there are exceptions to the tendency of Blacks to take over the forms of white songs. One such exception is the blues, a term actually referring to a number of different types of forms. The so-called "field blues" are simply short calls and wails, frequently with indefinite pitch, repeated several times, which perhaps originated as communication by field hands in the cotton fields; sometimes they are sung alternately by two persons. This type of song gradually developed into the "rural blues,"

[7] George Pullen Jackson, *White and Negro Spirituals* (New York: J. J. Augustin, 1943); also his *White Spirituals in the Southern Uplands* (New York: J. J. Augustin, 1933).

EXAMPLE 10-5. Negro spiritual, "Swing Low, Sweet Chariot," and analogous white spiritual, from George Pullen Jackson, *White and Negro Spirituals* (New York: J. J. Augustin, 1943), pp. 182–83.

accompanied most frequently by guitar, and, eventually, to the "urban blues" style, which is based on a specific harmonic pattern and has a definite though flexible musical and textual form.

The Afro-American community in the United States has produced a great number of prominent musicians who have become widely known outside the folk culture and, indeed, have gone on to become nationally famous. A typical example is Leadbelly, whose real name was Huddie Ledbetter, a Texas convict who was discovered by the pioneer folk song collector, John Lomax. Leadbelly sang many songs, but perhaps his main contribution was a number of blues songs. Typically the form of these was also adopted by the early jazz bands that played blues. It consists of three parts, the first two similar in content (both musically and textually), while the third contrasts. This form can be observed in such well-known pieces as "St. Louis Blues" and also in some of Leadbelly's songs, such as "Shorty George" and "Fort Worth and Dallas Blues." Many songs in the rural blues category have different forms, some of them based essentially on one musical phrase. Thus "Now your man done gone" (Example 10-6), collected in Alabama, is essentially a descending set of variations on the first phrase. Typically, Afro-American folk songs tend to be based on a smaller number of different melodic phrases than are most of the songs of the American whites—another possible survival of African music.

A frequently mentioned characteristic of Afro-American music is the so-called "blue note," the flatted or sometimes just slightly lowered third and seventh degrees in a major scale. The origin of this phenomenon is not known, but it cannot with certainty be traced to Africa. If indeed it is African in origin, it must have been selected from a considerable number of deviations from Western scales (or, rather, differences between African and Western scales) that African musics exhibit. Its survival must have a special reason, such as compatibility with Western

EXAMPLE 10-6. U.S. Negro folk song, "Now your man done gone," collected in Alabama, from Harold Courlander, *Negro Folk Music, U.S.A.* (New York: Columbia University Press, 1963), p. 108.

musical patterns. Possibly it originated among urban Afro-American musicians and moved from them into the folk music repertory.

Another group of Black songs in North America that is rather distinct from its counterpart in white culture consists of counting-out rimes and other children's game songs and rimes. These, again, are performed in a style perhaps derived from Africa, with strict adherence to metric patterns, some rhythmic complexity such as syncopation, and the undeviating tempo typical also of much West African music and perhaps resulting from the "metronome sense" described in Chapter Seven. These rimes, among the most popular of which are "I asked my mother for fifty cents" and "Head-shoulder baby," are sometimes sung, sometimes spoken. Call-and-response techniques are very common. The melodic materials are part of a world-wide pattern of children's songs with few tones, intervals of the minor third and major second, and repetitive structure. These children's songs are found not only in the South, but also in the Black ghettoes of the Northern cities, and they are frequently disseminated from Black to white children.

In the work songs of Afro-Americans, African patterns also appear. Work songs that are actually sung to accompany rhythmic labor are not common in the white American tradition, with the exception of sea shanties. But they are widespread in West and Central Africa, and their existence may have contributed to their prominence in the Afro-American folk tradition, as may the fact that rhythmic labor was very much a part of the slaves' way of life. The style of these songs is a mixture of Anglo-American and African elements. Some of the songs, such as "Pick a bale of cotton," actually deal with the work. Others, such as Leadbelly's "Elnora," are simply a group of words, euphonious but hardly related to the job, which supply a pleasant rhythmic accompaniment to work.

The use of the voice by Afro-American folk singers is often traceable to African singing styles. The much more relaxed, open way of singing, sometimes varied by the use of purposely raucous and harsh tones, is rather similar to African singing and certainly quite different from the rather tense and restrained manner of singing common among southern whites. It is important to repeat that there is no evidence to support the idea that the difference is due to heredity; much more likely, it is due to the persistence of African musical ideals in the Afro-American community, and possibly it is related to the difference between the culture patterns of the Anglo-Americans and the Afro-Americans, a difference due both to the African heritage of the latter and to the life-style developed from slavery and gradual, though partial, emancipation.

BIBLIOGRAPHY AND DISCOGRAPHY

Among the numerous publications on Black folk music in the United States, the following older ones are most useful: Harold Courlander, *Negro Folk Music U.S.A.* (New York: Columbia University Press, 1963); John and Alan Lomax, *Negro Folk Songs as Sung by Lead Belly* (New York: Macmillan, 1936); and, for its study of the relationship between Black and white spirituals, George Pullen Jackson, *White and Negro Spirituals* (New York: J. J. Augustin, 1943). A more modern view is presented in Charles Keil, *Urban Blues* (University of Chicago Press, 1966) and the very important survey by Eileen Southern, *The Music of Black Americans* (New York: Norton, 1971). Among the many publications in jazz, we mention only Marshall Stearns, *The Story of Jazz* (New York: Oxford University Press, 1958; also Mentor Books); Andre Hodeir, *Jazz, its Evolution and Essence* (New York: Grove Press, 1956); and Neil Leonard, *Jazz and the White Americans* (University of Chicago Press, 1962).

Two publications by Richard A. Waterman provide theoretical background for the study of New World Negro music: " 'Hot' Rhythm in Negro Music," *Journal of the American Musicological Society*, I (1948), 24–37, and "African Influence on American Negro Music," in *Acculturation in the Americas*, ed. Sol Tax (Chicago: University of Chicago Press, 1952). Several studies of South American Black music are important reading: Alan P. Merriam, "Songs of the Ketu Cult of Bahia, Brazil," *African Music*, I (1956), 53–82; Melville J. Herskovits, "Drums and Drummers in Afro-Brazilian Cult Life," *Musical Quarterly*, XXX (1944), 447–92; Luis Felipe Ramon y Rivera, "Rhythmic and Melodic Elements in Negro Music of Venezuela," *J-IFMC*, XIV (1962), 56–60; and Mieczyslaw Kolinski, "Part III, Music" in *Suriname Folklore* by M. J. and Frances Herskovits (New York: J. J. Augustin, 1936). Black music in the Caribbean is discussed, with musical transcriptions, in Harold Courlander, *The Drum and the Hoe* (Berkeley: University of California Press, 1960), a study of Haitian voodoo culture. Peter Seeger, "The Steel Drum: A New Folk Instrument," *Journal of American Folklore*, LXXI (1958), 52–57, presents a recent development.

The most important studies on Afro-Cuban music are those of Fernando Ortiz. In addition to the two references in the text, see his *Los instrumentos de la música afro-cubana* (Havana: Ministério de Educación . . . , 1952–55), 5 vols. For Jamaican music, see the introductory study by Olive Lewin, "Jamaican Folk Music," *Caribbean Quarterly*, XIV

(1969), 49–59. A systematic study of cults in Jamaica is George E. Simpson, "Jamaican Revivalist Cults," *Social and Economic Studies* V, i–ix (1956), 321–42.

Important recordings of Black music in Latin America are: *Music of Haiti* collected by Harold Courlander, Folkways P 403, 407, 432 (3 disks); *Cult Music of Trinidad*, Folkways 4478; *Afro-Bahian Religious Songs of Brazil*, Library of Congress AAFS 61–65; *Cult Music of Cuba*, Folkways 4410; *Afro-Hispanic Music from Western Colombia and Ecuador*, Folkways 4376; *Jamaican Cult Music*, Folkways FE 4461; and *From the Grass Roots of Jamaica*, Dynamic (Kingston, Jamaica) 3305.

Among the numerous recordings of North American Black music, we recommend two large sets of records, *Music from the South*, recorded by Frederic Ramsey, Folkways FP 650–58 (9 disks), and *Southern Folk Heritage Series*, edited by Alan Lomax, Atlantic 1346–52 (7 disks, including white and Negro music). Also worth mentioning are *Leadbelly's Last Sessions*, Folkways FP 241–42 (4 disks) and *The Rural Blues*, edited by Samuel B. Charters, RFB Records RF 202 (2 disks).

ELEVEN

FOLK MUSIC IN
MODERN NORTH AMERICA

The culture of modern North America is essentially a European one; its most prominent ingredients have come from Great Britain and, to a somewhat smaller extent, other Western European countries. But there have been other major influences, such as Hispanic culture, although this is largely confined to certain areas of the continent, principally the Southwestern United States. Eastern and Southern European elements are also important. And among the most important distinguishing features is the influence of two originally non-Western cultures: the African, which has had an enormous impact, and the American Indian, whose thrust has been less noticeable but is nevertheless pervasive. At certain levels of activity and thought, North American culture is a rather homogeneous blend of all these ingredients. At other levels, however, it is a conglomeration of enclaves—Scotch-Irish in the Appalachians, Mexican-American in Arizona, French-Canadian in the province of Quebec and in northern New England, Polish-American in Chicago and De-

troit, Afro-American in the ghettos of large cities and in parts of the rural
South, with small pockets of separation, such as the Indian tribes on
reservations and various communities of religious groups (the Amish in
the Midwest or the Doukhobors in the western United States and Canada). Each of these enclaves has kept a distinctive way of life; thus, in
certain respects, there is enormous variety in the panorama of North
American culture. In some ways, then, this continent is in the vanguard
of what appears to be a gradually developing universal culture; in
other respects, it functions as a museum, preserving in isolated and
archaic forms the otherwise rapidly changing cultures of other lands.

The profile of folk music in modern North American is similar.
The songs of peoples from everywhere have been brought here, sometimes sung for generations, sometimes rapidly forgotten; sometimes
developed into new, more distinctly American phenomena, sometimes preserved in old forms; sometimes combined with the music of other groups
from elsewhere, and with strange styles, but sometimes held in isolation.
We find that the enclaves of European, African, and American Indian
cultures have retained their old songs and styles; but we also find that
new styles, resulting from combinations, have come about. We are forced
to conclude that the homogeneity of modern American life, and particularly the prominence of radio, television, and the record industry has also
homogenized musical life to the extent that the old tri-partite view of
music (art, popular, and folk) has lost much of its meaning, and that all
elements of the population share in a musical culture dominated by what
we have for some time called popular music, based on rock, with elements of jazz, blues, country and western, folk, and even to some extent
art music—a musical culture with a certain amount of stylistic unity based
on aesthetic as well as technological criteria.

Our task here is to describe the role of the surviving traditional
folk music in this complex situation; to a smaller extent, it is to point out
those elements in the homogeneous culture that come from folk music.

ETHNIC MINORITIES IN RURAL AMERICA

We have mentioned the existence of isolated groups which retain
their traditional culture essentially outside the framework of modern
American civilization. Among them are the English-descended New
England farmers and the Scotch-Irish of the Appalachians, we have already (in Chapter Four) examined their retention of older British songs
and singing styles. Although their place in American history and the
character of their culture is different, the American Indians occupy
something of a similar role. In both cases, distinctiveness of musical cul-

ture helps to provide a feeling of cultural and, to some extent, racial identity. The most dramatic examples of such conservatism in both life-style and music is found in some of the religiously-based enclaves.

In many cultures, religious and ceremonial life tends to reveal the most conservative elements, and the most archaic aspects of a tradition are usually to be found in its religious manifestations. Thus, perhaps the oldest European folk music preserved in the Americas is that which is associated with religion. The Spanish liturgical dramas are one example; another is the tradition of German spiritual folk song which is found especially in Pennsylvania and also among the Amish of the mid-western United States.

The Amish are a religious community related to the Mennonites. Of Swiss and German origin, they began leaving Germany in the seventeenth century, some migrating first to Russia and then, in the early nineteenth century, to the United States, others coming directly to America. Their austere manner of living and their conservative traditions have kept them essentially out of contact with other German-Americans. Devoting themselves exclusively to farming, they use music only for worship. Their hymns are of two types, an older one that is possibly a survival of a medieval hymn-singing tradition, and a newer one evidently part of the German-American spiritual tradition of Pennsylvania.

To most listeners, the older hymns of the Amish scarcely sound like a product of Western musical culture. They are monophonic and sung without accompaniment, without perceptible meter, with syllables drawn out over many tones, and with slowly executed ornaments. Only when one becomes acquainted with the style does one see in it any resemblance to the hymn tunes of the German reformed churches. This can be done by connecting the first notes of the textual syllables to each other, even when they are short and seemingly insignificant. Since this style of singing is not found in Europe today, how did it come about? Possibly the Amish, after arriving in Russia or the United States, began to slow down the hymns they had sung in Germany, to add ornaments, and to draw out the metric structure until it was not to be recognized. On the other hand, possibly their way of singing was once widely used in the German-speaking rural areas of Europe, and has simply been retained by the Amish in America although undergoing complete change in Europe under the impact of the all-pervading musical influence of the cities and courts. At any rate, the Amish hymns are an example of the marginal survival that characterizes some of the musical culture of the Americas to the extent that it is derived from Europe.[1]

The newer hymns of the Amish correspond to the spiritual tradi-

[1] Bruno Nettl, "The Hymns of the Amish, An Example of Marginal Survival," *Journal of American Folklore*, LXX (1957), 327–28.

tion of the Pennsylvania German culture. This culture represents an interesting mixture of German—particularly South German—and British elements, including a special dialect of German that includes certain elements of American English phonology. The songs of the Pennsylvania Germans are in part simply those of the German tradition, in part based on tunes from the Anglo-American heritage. Thus the so-called Pennsylvania spirituals, folk hymns with German words, are really products of the spiritual revival of the early 1800s, which involved Methodists and Baptists in the English-speaking community, and the influence of Negro music and of Negro spirituals, all converging on the Pennsylvania German community. As a result, the tunes are of various origins. Some are those of secular German folk songs; a few are derived from early German hymns; some come from the white spiritual tradition ("The Battle Hymn of the Republic" appears with several sets of words). The Pennsylvania German spiritual is not, of course, a purely folkloric type of music. Hymn books were printed and professional hymn writers contributed to them. But much of the musical material was and is identical to that which lives in the authentic folk culture; and most of the tunes, in contrast to the words, were actually passed on by oral tradition, performed at camp meetings without the use of books, and lived by means of variation and communal re-creation.

Just as the German folk culture lives on in the small towns of Eastern Pennsylvania, other Western European traditions can be found thriving in other rural areas of North America. Northern Michigan and Minnesota are repositories of Scandinavian and Finnish folklore. The southern Midwest and Louisiana are the homes of people who still sing, or at any rate can occasionally remember for a collector, the folk songs of France. Of course the eastern part of Canada, especially the province of Quebec, is rich in the folklore of French-Canadians. Much as the United States yields a repertory of English songs at least as large as that of England herself, the French-Canadians sing essentially all of the older French folk songs; and Marius Barbeau, veteran collector of songs in this tradition, records that for song upon song more variants have been found in America than in France. One group of individuals who particularly carried the French tradition was the *voyageurs*, French Canadians who paddled canoes through the Great Lakes in the fur trade, and who sang for amusement and in order to provide rhythmic accompaniment to paddling. On the whole, the French-Canadian folk song heritage does not seem to differ appreciably from that of France, and in its wealth it parallels the Anglo-American folk song tradition. The penetration of French melodies to other repertories can be seen in some of the tunes of the Haitian voodoo cults, whose musical style is generally Caribbean and closely related to African music but among whose songs are tunes and fragments of melodies highly reminiscent of French music. A similar situation obtains among the Cajuns of Southern Louisiana, descendants of the Acadians whose deportation from Canada to Bayou Teche, Louisiana, in 1755 was chronicled by Henry Wadsworth Longfellow in "Evangeline." The Cajuns continue to speak French and to sing French songs, but their music has also absorbed elements of Anglo-American and Afro-American styles, paticularly in the repertories of their string bands.

THE ROLE OF FOLK MUSIC
IN URBAN AMERICAN CULTURE

The early settlers in America who came from the British Isles, Scandinavia, France, and Spain developed a largely rural culture, and their folk music is preserved mainly in small towns, in villages, and on farms. On the whole, the peoples who came to North America from Italy, the Balkan peninsula, and Eastern Europe arrived later, when cities had already developed into centers of industry; they emigrated at the end of the nineteenth century and the beginning of the twentieth, to work in these cities. Thus their folk music, to the extent that it is preserved, is found in an urban milieu. These same cities also draw upon the rural population, and thus many of the Western European immigrants also found their way into them as did members of non-European minorities— the Blacks, Mexican-Americans, Chinese, Japanese, and even some American Indians. The rapidly expanding North American city—different from the typical European city, which took centuries to grow to its present size—tended to become a complex of sections, neighborhoods, villages almost, that served as focal points for various ethnic groups. These tended to try to maintain in some respects the culture and tradition of their countries and places of origin, as a way of preserving identity and of easing the dislocations of Americanization, Westernization, and modernization. They could obviously not retain their rural work habits, economic systems, transportation, and so on, but they could attempt to retain their folklore, art, and music.

At the same time, the North American cities, in the twentieth century, have been wellsprings of technical innovation and social change. It is difficult to imagine that music could have escaped the impact of the kinds of development that resulted from the turmoil caused by the throwing together of many disparate cultural groups, and of the constant pressure to change the approach to all of life's problems. Thus the folk music of the American city also reflects the most important social attitudes that developed, and we find song associated with various movements of social and political forces, particularly with movements whose function was to protest.

Preservation and response to the pressures of modernization are both evident in the music of Eastern European groups in those cities, particularly in the Midwest, which grew primarily as industrial centers. By no means have the folk song repertories of all groups been collected and studied, but a generous sampling is already available. Thus large collections of Hungarian and Slovak songs have been made in Cleveland;[2] Yiddish and Puerto Rican folk music has been studied in New York, and the songs of Poles, Syrians, and many other groups have been recorded in Detroit. In some cases, old songs can be found relatively undisturbed, and the American city acts as the agent of marginal survival. At other times, the European traditions are changed because of the pressures of urban American culture. Thus there seems to be a tendency to favor dance and instrumental music over other types; perhaps this is due to the fact that young Americans of foreign descent have less interest in the words of the songs, which they may not even understand, than in the tunes. Organized teaching of folk songs, even from song books, by members of the ethnic group who are noted for their knowledge may be one way of preserving the material. Group singing is more prominent than in the European parent traditions. Singing clubs and dance groups are formed in order to keep the tradition alive, for music and dance play an important part in keeping an ethnic group in a city from losing its identity.

Furthermore, the musical style of Eastern European folk songs sung in the American cities may change, for those songs which come closest to being acceptable in terms of the American popular tune tradition are those which are preserved by the ethnic groups. The younger individuals in these communities, who by the middle of the twentieth century were no longer able to speak the languages of their grandparents, have been stimulated by the appearance in concerts of professional dance and instrumental groups from Europe. The original functions of the folk songs on the whole have disappeared in the American city, and the music must serve mainly as entertainment, as an expression of sentimental feeling, and as accompaniment to dancing. Occasionally, new songs in Polish, Hungarian, Slovak, and other languages are created, though in such cases it is usually only the words, dealing with American life, that are new and that serve as a setting for an old tune. On the whole, the ethnic groups in the United States perform the music of the old country,

[2] Stephen Erdely, "Folksinging of the American Hungarians in Cleveland," *Ethnomusicology*, VIII (1964), 14–27.

sometimes preserving tunes already forgotten in Europe, but more frequently singing the old tunes in less ornamented, shorter, and frequently impoverished style, and often tending to change modal tunes to major or minor, heterometric structure to isometric, and unaccompanied tunes to songs with chordal accompaniment or singing in parallel thirds. Example 11-1 illustrates a Polish folk song (possibly unchanged in transit) collected in Detroit.

EXAMPLE 11-1. Polish folk song, "Czterty Mile za Warszawa" ("It was four miles out of Warsaw"), collected in Detroit. Reprinted from *Merrily We Sing, 105 Polish Folksongs* by Harriet M. Pawlowska by permission of the Wayne State University Press. Copyright 1961.

To a smaller extent than the non-English-speaking groups, the Anglo-American and Black communities in the cities also have a folk music tradition, largely because many members of these two groups are recent immigrants from the countryside. The older, traditional sort of Anglo-American folk song, when known to urban individuals or families, tends to live essentially in the memories of singers rather than functioning in social situations. In the music of urban Afro-Americans, on the other hand, folk music has functioned as an inspiration for the creation of various popular styles and musical forms, like jazz, blues, and gospel song.

Throughout Western history, music has been used as a symbol of political actions and positions. Songs of political and social protest are known even from the late Middle Ages; nations and political parties developed solemn anthems for inspiration and rousing songs to stimulate rallying to a cause. It is not surprising that folk music, the music most closely associated with the poor, the minorities, and the disestablished, has provided the natural stylistic symbol, even in the mainstream of society, for social criticism and for protesting intolerable conditions, while music associated with the established order was more likely to hew closely to a stylistic line derived from art music. Folk songs voicing protest have been composed in many corners of the world; it appears that thoughts that would not be acceptable in speech are frequently permitted in song.

Of great interest in this connection is the body of songs revolving about, and in some cases integrally a part of, the labor movement. These are songs of relatively recent origin, their poets and composers are normally known, and they are usually learned first from song books and taught by trained organizers. Stylistically they are part of the broadside ballad tradition, and they use original tunes composed in the broadside idiom, or tunes from other folk songs, hymns, and popular music. One of the best known is the ballad of "Joe Hill," a martyred leader of the IWW, whose ghost returns to exhort laborers to organize. Some of these songs have passed into oral tradition and are also sung outside the labor movement. Many of them have words protesting the bad treatment of factory workers, miners, migrant farmers, and minority groups. Others sing the praises of labor organizations. Usually, tunes of older folk songs, hymns, music hall ditties, and minstrel songs are used. Often the words parody songs already in the folk tradition. For example, a song sung during a New York State milk strike in 1939 is a parody of "Pretty Polly," a version of the British ballad of the "Cruel Ship's Carpenter":

Mister farmer, mister farmer, come go along with me (twice)
Come hitch up with the milk trust and we'll keep the system free.
So they followed the milk trust stooges and what did they find? (twice)
Nothing in their pockets and a knife from behind.[3]

The use of folk songs as protest has deep roots in Afro-American culture and is an essential ingredient of the texts of entire genres such as blues and spirituals. It was not adopted as rapidly by the white mainstream of American society. But beginning in the 1930s, the idea of protesting through folk song began to spread to segments of the white population. One of the characteristics of this movement was the development, especially in the 1950s and '60s, of star folk singers who performed songs with important elements of Anglo-American folk song styles (e.g., characteristic melodic devices and contours, text patterns with the basic structure of folk poems, accompaniment by folk instruments, such as the guitar, dulcimer, banjo, etc.). But although traditional folk songs

[3] John Greenway, *American Folksongs of Protest* (Philadelphia: University of Pennsylvania Press, 1953), p. 215.

are occasionally used, it is more typical of these singers to perform original songs only reminiscent of the rural tradition. Many of these songs
—and indeed, the most famous—are songs of protest. The Vietnam War in
particular produced a large number of such protest songs; many of the
performances of singers, Bob Dylan, Joan Baez, and others fall in this
category. While some of these performers, including Dylan and Baez
are very close to the traditional folk styles, others, such as Simon and Garfunkel, have adopted styles intermediate between folk music and the
mainstream of urban popular music; still others (such as the Byrds)
exhibit a style essentially in the realm of popular music but influenced by
folk song. Precursors of this movement, Pete Seeger, Burl Ives, and
others, tended to adhere more closely to the folk tradition; thus the urban
folk singing movement in the middle of the twentieth century follows a
course of gradual assimilation into popular music, and simultaneously
an increasing popularity and acceptance among many segments of the
population.

Those who believe in authenticity as a major criterion may decide
that the phenomenon described above is not really folk music. But the
role of folk music in contemporary popular culture is a musical and cultural phenomenon worthy of detailed study. This kind of folk music differs from the authentic folk tradition mainly because the songs are
learned not from friends and family but from books, records (field recordings and professional performances), and trained musicians; because
many of the songs are composed especially for city consumption (but
this may also have been true of many "real" folk songs when they were
first composed); because the performer consciously tries to develop certain idiosyncracies and to repeat them in an identical way each time; and
because the style of singing—polyphonic, sometimes with virtuoso accompaniment on banjo, guitar, piano, etc.—may be completely different
from the style in which the same songs are sung in the countryside. And
an urban folk singer may use several traditions and many languages.

As was pointed out in Chapter One, it may be possible for a song
to be a folk song and not a folk song at the same time. And thus we may
insist that folk songs sung by musicians in the popular music tradition,
by professionals who make use primarily of the mass media, in styles
which may have little to do with any rural folk tradition, are no longer
really folk songs. It may be simply a semantic problem. But perhaps a
good solution to this definitional dilemma is to regard the music that
consists of actual folk songs, and of songs composed in a style derived
from folk music by urban song writers and performed by professional en-
tertainers, as the true folk music of urban culture.

The relationship of this kind of music to the broadside ballad traditions of the eighteenth and nineteenth centuries cannot be overlooked.

Both kinds of music made use of a variety of musical sources; both depended on the current interest of their subject matter for rapid dissemination; both dealt with content close to the interests of many segments
and classes of society; and both depended upon rural and perhaps ancient
singing traditions for important elements of their performance practice.
Thus there is at least some justice in calling this urban material folk
music, and in considering it the logical result, in a rapidly urbanizing
and modernizing society, of the rural folk music tradition.

The use of folk music by urban musicians in the twentieth century
is, of course, not unique to the United States. Folk songs have been used
as a way of representing political and social views, and also as a method
of music education, in Europe and elsewhere as well. In the Soviet
Union, songs praising the communist way of life and Joseph Stalin were
introduced and passed into oral tradition in city and countryside long
before the 1950s. In Nazi Germany, the singing of German folk songs was
obligatory in patriotic organizations. In Hungary, authentic folk music
has become the mainstay of elementary music education. Even in Vietnam, a folk singing movement using traditional tunes with new words
treating matters of war and liberation, and with American-style guitar
accompaniment, has become widespread, largely due to the efforts of the
famous singer, Pham Dui. Thus the kind of urban folk singing that is now
so prominent in the United States has precedents and analogues in many
parts of the world.

THE RURAL ANGLO-AMERICAN TRADITION

In the United States, the development of urban folk song culture
is partly a result of the maintenance of a strong folk music tradition in
the rural Anglo-American community. We have pointed out the importance of this tradition to the survival of British folk music, and we have
noted that British material is often better preserved in the New World
than in the Old. Of course, the British folk song tradition has undergone
changes in America, influenced by the peculiar course of American history and the development of American culture.

The music of Anglo-American folk songs is partly composed of
British and Irish tunes that are not easily distinguished, individually, from
their forms as they are found in the British Isles. Some come from popular
song and from broadside ballad tunes. The differences between American
and British song are greater in the words than in the music, for the
words are much more frequently of American origin (often they are
parodies of British songs), embodying specific events of American history

or reflecting particular features of American culture—the frontier, the religious revival of the 1880s, the love of humor and exaggeration, the presence of various ethnic minorities, and the particular occupations (cowboys, miners, Indian fighters, etc.) in which Americans engaged while building a new country.

Taken as a whole, the style of American folk music in English has more melodies in major, fewer pentatonic tunes, more songs in duple meter, less use of accompaniment (but more use of the drone principle in instrumental accompaniment) than the style of Britain. Like the British tradition, but unlike the Afro-American and some of the ethnic group styles, it is essentially one of solo singing. Melodies that are obviously of nineteenth-century origin, with a definite implied harmony, are common. The words of the English songs in America have also been changed, and Americans have made a special selection of material from the British repertory. Thus there are more humorous folk songs in the American repertory than in the British. Tall tales and other humorous exaggerations are typical. Folk heroes, such as the Black superman John Henry, the bad-man Jesse James, and the Slavic steel worker Joe Magarac, abound. Broadside ballads telling of the murders and railroad wrecks of a locality are particularly popular, and songs telling of shipwrecks are a specialty of the populations of Newfoundland, Labrador, and New England. Besides preserving British broadsides, Americans have composed a body of broadsides of their own, especially during the nineteenth and early twentieth centuries. These are more apt to deal with violence and romantic love and less with the supernatural and with battles than are their British counterparts.

Regional differences do, of course, appear in folk singing of the United States. According to Alan Lomax,[4] northern folk singers produce a rather relaxed, open-voiced tone, while southern ones are tenser and "pinched-voiced," and those of the West are a blend of the two. Lomax attributes these differences to deep-seated cultural differences involving the relationship between the sexes, the hardships of frontier life, and the presence of the Negro minority in the South.

The fact that dancing was prohibited or at least frowned upon by many religious leaders of early America tended to drive dance music from the British Isles into the background, but it produced a distinctly American type of song, the "play-party song," which accompanies marching and dance-like movements similar to those of some children's group games. Dancing has, however, played a part in the British-American folk culture, as may be seen from the prominence of the square dance, which

---

[4] Alan Lomax, *The Folksongs of North America in the English Language* (New York: Doubleday & Company, Inc., 1960), p. 1.

is derived from the eighteenth- and nineteenth-century quadrilles of European high society. A distinctive American feature is the presence of a "caller," who speaks or sings verses instructing the dancers in the routine required in the execution of the dance.

There is also in the American tradition a large body of instrumental music that is used for dancing, some of which was at one time also used for marching. As a matter of fact, the earliest jazz bands in New Orleans were brass bands that played marching music for funerals and other processions. At the same time, in the white North, fiddle and fife players played ornamented versions of song tunes as well as tunes of popular and art music origin. The main instruments of the American folk tradition are the guitar, the banjo, the mandolin, the dulcimer, the violin, and the mouth organ. The dulcimer appears in various forms, some of them similar to those of the Swedish dulcimer described in Chapter Four. As in Europe, the American string instruments are frequently used for music in which the drone principle somehow appears.

Just as many of the instrumental tunes came from the vocal repertory, many tunes originally played were eventually sung. Again, this is a tendency found also in some European cultures. Example 11-2 is a fiddle tune with words; its large range suggests that it may have originated as an instrumental piece which only later began to be used vocally.

Finally, the Afro-American impact on the white American folk song tradition has been enormous. It can be felt in the occasional "hot

EXAMPLE 11-2. Fiddle tune and song, "Prettiest Little Gal in the County, O," collected in Florida, from Alton C. Morris, *Folksongs of Florida* (Gainesville: University of Florida Press, 1950), p. 226.

rhythm" of singing and accompaniment, in the development of the so-called hillbilly style, in the tendency to stick to one meter (although many white singers do not do this but sing in the parlando-rubato style), in the use of rhythmic handclapping by white folk audiences, and, of course, in the many Negro songs that have become part of the white repertory.

If the singing of Joan Baez, Pete Seeger, Bob Dylan, and Simon and Garfunkel is the consequence of the impact of urbanization on folk music, then the result of modernization and the use of the mass media on rural America must be the large body of country and Western music. Beginning with music growing directly out of the traditional folk songs of the Appalachians, taking with it musical elements of the broadside ballad and a large repertory of folk hymnody that goes back to colonial times, and constantly interacting with the developments in urban culture, this highly distinctive musical style remains exceedingly prominent in contemporary American culture despite the shrinking of rural America and the all-pervading influence of television, to which it has readily adapted. And while country and Western music has traveled far from traditional folk song in its style, its origins nevertheless remain obvious. The relationship to the old Appalachian folk music is most evident in the structure of the melodies and the physical stance of the singers and particularly in the singing style, that least changeable aspect of musical performance.

CONCLUSION

The American folk music scene is a fitting one for closing a survey of folk and traditional music in the Western continents, for it shows us many of the things that are typical and interesting in folk music everywhere—the preservation of archaic forms, the creation of new styles under the impact of acculturation, special developments due to particular trends in cultural values, and the growth of a special kind of folk music culture in the modern city.

One of the things that our consideration of folk music in the Americas and, indeed, of folk and traditional music everywhere, has shown in the condition of flux in which the material is constantly found. Change, brought about through intercultural contact and through the creative elements within each society, has evidently been present in even the simplest cultures, and it has increased in rapidity as the world's traditions are thrown into contact and conflict with each other as a result of the accelerating Westernization of the entire planet. Will it be possible for traditional musics to survive and to retain some measure of the distinctiveness that has characterized them in the past? Prognostication is not our task here. But if we consider folk music as merely the product of the rural, unlettered classes, and if we consider "primitive" music as nothing but the product of backward peoples, we are bound to find that the traditions in which we are interested are receding and will eventually disappear. On the other hand, if we can retain an interest in the musical cultures of nations and peoples rather than only that of a musically professional elite, and if we are willing to bend our definitions of folk and traditional music to include such things as popular music, jazz, and urban folk song, we may be in a position to investigate the kind of music which is rapidly replacing, in its social function, the folk and traditional music of the past and present.

While we must perhaps concede the eventual disappearance of traditional musics in the present sense of the concept, we should not assume that this demise is imminent. For many decades, some collectors have pursued their material with the attitude of a last-minute rescue operation, proclaiming the doom of authentic folklore. And indeed, since traditional music is always changing, something of it must always be disappearing. Nevertheless, each year brings new discoveries of unknown styles, unexplored musical cultures, unexpected instruments, and new distributions of musical types, always requiring changes in theory and reorientation of scholarly thought. As long as this is the state of traditional music, one can hardly claim that it is a dying art.

BIBLIOGRAPHY AND DISCOGRAPHY

The developments in collecting and studying American folk song are discussed in D. K. Wilgus, *Anglo-American Folksong Scholarship Since 1898* (New Brunswick, N.J.: Rutgers University Press, 1959). A bibliographic survey of ballads originating in America is Malcolm G. Laws, *Native American Balladry* (Philadelphia: American Folklore Society, 1950). The classic collection of British song in the United States is Cecil J. Sharp, *English Folk Songs from the Southern Appalachians* (London: Oxford University Press, 1952, 2 vols.). A modern collection covering all types of song is Alan Lomax, *The Folk Songs of North America in the English Language* (New York: Doubleday & Company, Inc., 1961). Samuel P. Bayard, *Hill Country Tunes* (Philadelphia: American Folklore Society, 1944), is a collection of instrumental folk music. Charles Seeger, "The Appalachian Dulcimer," *Journal of American Folklore,* LXXI (1958), 40–52, discusses one important American folk instrument.

The role of folk music in entertainment and education is discussed in Sven Eric Molin, "Lead Belly, Burl Ives, and Sam Hinton," *Journal of American Folklore*, LXXI (1958), 58–78; and Charles Seeger, "Folk Music in the Schools of a Highly Industrialized Society," *J-IFMC*, V (1953), 40–44.

The music of other ethnic groups in America is presented in Marius Barbeau, *Jongleur Songs of Old Quebec* (New Brunswick, N.J.: Rutgers University Press, 1962); Harriet Pawlowska, *Merrily We Sing, 105 Polish Folk Songs* (Detroit: Wayne State University Press, 1961); Bruno Nettl, "The Hymns of the Amish: An Example of Marginal Survival," *Journal of American Folklore*, LXX (1957), 323–28; Stephen Erdely, "Folksinging of the American Hungarians in Cleveland," *Ethnomusicology*, VIII (1964), 14–27; and Jacob A. Evanson, "Folk Songs of an Industrial City" in *Pennsylvania Songs and Legends*, ed. George Korson (Philadelphia: University of Pennsylvania Press, 1949), which deals with Slovak songs in Pittsburgh.

It is difficult to select a group of recommended records from the multitude available for the European-American folk traditions. For the United States, the series *Folk Music of the United States* issued by the Library of Congress is excellent. Especially to be mentioned among these recordings are *Folk Music from Wisconsin*, AAFS L55; *Songs of the Michigan Lumberjacks*, AAFS L56; *Anglo-American Songs and Ballads*, AAFS L12, 14; *Songs and Ballads of the Anthracite Miners*, AAFS L16; and *Sacred Harp Singing*, AAFS L11. Lectures on collecting by John Lomax appear on *The Ballad Hunter*, AAFS L49–53 (5 disks). Fine Canadian collections are *Maritime Folk Songs from the Collection of Helen Creighton*, Folkways FE 4307; *Folk Music from Nova Scotia*, Folkways P 1006 (also edited by Helen Creighton); and *Songs of French Canada*, Folkways FE 4482. An excellent collection of non-English language songs from the United States, with detailed notes, is *Lithuanian Folk Songs in the United States*, Folkways P 1009.

INDEX

251